Handbook of
Organizational Change and Innovation

Handbook of

Organizational Change and Innovation

Edited by

Marshall Scott Poole

Andrew H. Van de Ven

OXFORD
UNIVERSITY PRESS

2004

OXFORD
UNIVERSITY PRESS

Oxford   New York
Auckland   Bangkok   Buenos Aires   Cape Town   Chennai
Dar es Salaam   Delhi   Hong Kong   Istanbul   Karachi   Kolkata
Kuala Lumpur   Madrid   Melbourne   Mexico City   Mumbai   Nairobi
São Paulo   Shanghai   Taipei   Tokyo   Toronto

Library of Congress Cataloging-in-Publication Data
Handbook of organizational change and innovation /
edited by Marshall Scott Poole, Andrew H. Van de Ven.
    p. cm.
Includes bibliographical references and index.
  ISBN 978-0-19-513500-8
 1. Organizational change—Handbooks, manuals, etc.
I. Poole, Marshall Scott, 1951- II. Van de Ven, Andrew H.
  HD58.8 .H3614 2004
   658.4'063—dc22   2003022780

Preface

This handbook had its beginnings in the 1980s and 1990s, a time of ferment in research on organizational change and innovation. Breaking the mold of traditional stage theories, researchers posited theories of change and development incorporating new explanations based on evolutionary processes, dialectics, institutional economics, structuration theory, and complexity theory, among others. This blossoming of theory was stimulated in large part by concurrent major social changes. Organizations were growing larger in vertical and virtual connections, merging and acquiring others with colliding cultures, reducing employment and relying on more temporary workers, hiring more technical/professional workers, interfacing in more competitive international and global economies, and adopting highly distributed and flexible work and information technologies. The net result was that organizations were becoming more pluralistic and interdependent. These changes reverberated throughout nested hierarchies of organizations. They both affected and were affected by changes in the identities, jobs, and careers of individuals; the use and development of work and project teams; organizational innovation, transformation, and restructurings; and evolution of industries, populations, and more encompassing systems.

This multiplicity of theories and issues offered new chords for researchers to strike, but could also descend into cacophony due to the sheer variety and complexity of ideas. The objective of this handbook is to harmonize new trends in organizational change and innovation research. The various chapters organize and integrate theories and research on organizational change and innovation at different levels of analysis. The handbook presents a "state of the art" view of theory that we hope will serve as a springboard for further advances in this area.

The idea for this handbook can be traced to our experiences in the Minnesota Innovation Research Program (MIRP). This project began in 1983 with the objective of developing a process theory of innovation in organizations and society. Fourteen research teams, involving more than 30 faculty and doctoral students at the University of Minnesota, conducted longitudinal studies that tracked a variety of new technologies, products, services, and programs as they developed from concept to implementation in their natural field settings. Initial findings were published in *Research on the Management of Innovation: The Minnesota Studies*, edited by Andrew Van de Ven, Harold Angle, and Marshall Scott Poole (1989; and reissued by Oxford University Press, 2000).

By documenting the historical and real-time events in the development of a wide variety of innovations, this volume provided a broad comparative look at how innovations emerged and developed over time. A second study, *The Innovation Journey* by Andrew H. Van de Ven, Douglas E. Polley, Raghu Garud, and Sankaran Venkatraman (Oxford, 1999), developed an in-depth analysis of three new product innovations from the original set.

The MIRP studies highlighted the need for theories of change processes and for methodologies specifically adapted to developing and testing process theories of organizational change and innovation. Workshops to address these needs eventuated in the publication of *Organizational Change and Innovation Processes: Theory and Methods for Research* by Marshall Scott Poole, Andrew H. Van de Ven, Kevin Dooley, and Michael E. Holmes (Oxford University Press, 2000).

As we worked on these projects, we were struck by the variety of theory and research on organizational change and innovation. The literature was vast and spread across a number of disciplines. A number of useful and powerful theories had evolved, but they had often developed in relative isolation. It was difficult to see the bigger picture that showed relationships among theories and possibilities for integration. We identified leading scholars who had worked in developing theoretical traditions and charged them to develop broad, theoretically driven reviews that encompass the best of previous research and break new ground on their subject. Several presented their initial thoughts at the 1999 Academy of Management Conference in Chicago as part of an all-Academy symposium on the conference theme, "Change and Development Journeys into a Pluralistic World." We continued to work with author teams for the next several years, and the result was this handbook.

Each chapter of this handbook sums up and assesses the state of knowledge in its area and builds on this foundation to advance a new view. The chapters advance our thinking by developing integrative theories, by establishing connections among theories from different fields and research traditions, and by introducing new lines of inquiry. In our work with these authors we have been constantly impressed by their ability to combine careful scholarship with creativity. We thank them for undertaking the difficult task of bringing order to the extensive range of theory and research they synthesized.

The result is a book that we hope will serve as a springboard for another two decades of research on organizational change and innovation. The great Elizabethan Francis Bacon wrote, "Some books are to be tasted, others to be swallowed, and some few to be chewed and digested." We think that this handbook offers something for those who just wish to taste and swallow. But we believe and hope that it proves to be a book that is chewed and digested by many students of organizational change and development.

We are indebted to a number of people and organizations who supported this work. The Office of Naval Research supported the Minnesota Innovation Research Project with a grant from 1983 to 1986. The Decision, Risk and Management Science program of the National Science Foundation, and in particular its director Arie Lewin, provided encouragement and support for the first conference that introduced these methods. The second and third conferences were sponsored by the Consortium of Centers for Organizational Research and the Strategic Management Research Center of the University of Minnesota.

Herbert Addison of Oxford University Press helped us envision this handbook and provided valuable guidance in the early years of this project. In his distinguished career as Oxford's executive editor of business books, Herb has made major contributions to management and organization science. His able successor, Martha Cooley, was a source of encouragement and faith in the project, and though she moved on to other pursuits, her imprint on this book is lasting. Frank Fusco and John Rauschenberg of Oxford University Press steered this project through its final stages, and we are grateful for their steady hand. Thanks also to Lisa Stallings for her help in managing the manuscript through to production. Julie Trupke of the University of Minnesota contributed to the editing of several chapters, adding considerably to their readability, and performed yeoperson's work in obtaining permissions. We also thank Clarissa Martinez of Texas A&M University, who checked and rechecked references with precision and patience.

We dedicate this book to our parents Edward and Helen Poole, and Arnold and Josephine Van de Ven.

Contents

Contributors

Joel A. C. Baum
University of Toronto
Toronto, ON

Jean M. Bartunek
Department of Organization Studies
Boston College
Chestnut Hill, MA

Todd Dewett
Department of Management
Texas A & M University
College Station, TX

Kevin Dooley
Department of Management
Arizona State University
Tempe, AZ

Robert Drazin
Goizueta Business School
Emory University
Atlanta, GA

James D. Emery
Duke University
Fuqua School of Business
Durham, NC

Mary Ann Glynn
Goizueta Business School
Emory University
Atlanta, GA

Royston Greenwood
Department of Strategic Management and
 Organization
Carlson School of Management
University of Minnesota
Minneapolis, MN

Timothy J. Hargrave
Department of Strategic Management and
 Organization
School of Business
University of Alberta
Edmonton, AB

Mary Jo Hatch
McIntire School of Commerce
University of Virginia
Charlottesville, VA

C. R. (Bob) Hinings
Department of Strategic Management and
    Organization
Carlson School of Management
University of Minnesota
Minneapolis, MN

Robert Kazanjian
Goizueta Business School
Emory University
Atlanta, GA

Jisung Kim
Duke University
Fuqua School of Business
Durham, NC

Arie Y. Lewin
Duke University
Fuqua School of Business
Durham, NC

Joseph McGrath
117 W. Pennsylvania
Urbana, IL

Linda L. Putnam
Department of Speech Communication
Texas A & M University
College Station, TX

Hayagreeva Rao
Goizueta Business School
Emory University
Atlanta, GA

Trish Reay
Department of Strategic Management and
    Organization
School of Business
University of Alberta
Edmonton, AB

Myeong-Gu Seo
Management and Organization Department
Robert H. Smith School of Business
University of Maryland
College Park, MD

Roy Suddaby
Department of Management and
    Organizations
Henry B. Tippie College of Business
University of Iowa
Iowa City, IA

Franziska Tschan
Marienstrasse 9
Bern, Switzerland

Andrew Van de Ven
Department of Strategic Management and
    Organization
Carlson School of Management
University of Minnesota
Minneapolis, MN

Carmen Weigelt
Jones Graduate School of Management
Rice University
Houston, TX

Richard W. Woodman
Department of Management
Texas A & M University
College Station, TX

Introduction

Marshall Scott Poole & Andrew H. Van de Ven

Many scholars in many disciplines have sought to explain how and why organizations change and innovate. Change is at the heart of such important organizational phenomena as individual careers, teamwork, organizational strategy making, and the growth and decline of industries. Even apparently stable and fixed phenomena—individual traits, organizational structure, economic institutions—take on a different aspect when considered in terms of the processes that constitute them. William James (1909/1996, p. 263) wrote, "What really exists is not things made but things in the making." To understand organizational change is to understand organizations as we experience them, and to explain organizational change is to articulate what makes organizations what they are and to suggest how we may shape and reshape them.

Innovation is an important partner to change. It is the wellspring of social and economic progress, and both a product and a facilitator of the free exchange of ideas that is the lifeblood of progress. It is reflected in new products and production processes, advances in communications technology, and novel organizations and services in the public and nonprofit sectors. Contemporary intellectual currents in organizational studies increasingly focus on change and innovation,

echoing Heraclitus's maxim that "Nothing is permanent save change."

We define organizational change as a difference in form, quality, or state over time in an organizational entity. The entity may be an individual's job, a work group, an organizational subunit, the overall organization, or larger communities of organizations, such as industries. Change in any of these entities can be determined by measuring the same entity at two or more points in time on a set of dimensions, and then comparing the differences over time in these dimensions. If the difference is greater than zero (assuming no measurement error), we can say that the organizational entity has changed. Much of the voluminous literature on organizational change focuses on the nature of this difference, what produced it, and its consequences.

Change can take many forms; it can be planned or unplanned, incremental or radical, and recurrent or unprecedented. Trends in the process or sequence of changes can be observed over time. These trends can be accelerating or decelerating in time, and they can move toward equilibrium, oscillation, chaos, or randomness in the behavior of the organizational entity being examined. Thus, the basic concept of organization change involves three ideas: (1) difference,

(2) at different temporal moments, (3) between states of an organizational unit or system.

Organizational change and innovation have fostered a wide variety of research across many levels of organizations. Thousands of studies have been conducted on change processes in individuals and groups (typically by psychologists, social psychologists, and communication scholars) and in organizations and populations or communities of organizations (by sociologists, political scientists, and scholars in professional schools such as business management, public policy, urban planning, medical care, and other fields). Though impressive, the sheer volume of research is also daunting. It is difficult to get the big picture. There has been a tendency for research in different fields to develop in independent "silos." Scholarship in one area often does not cite much research from others. Even within a single field, different lines of research often develop along parallel paths. There is a need for integration across fields and for cross-fertilization of theories.

This handbook advances the integration of social scientific knowledge about change and innovation within and across different levels of organizations and across a range of disciplines. Authors were charged to develop broad, theoretically driven reviews that incorporate the best of previous research and break new ground on their subject. Each chapter sums up and assesses the state of knowledge in its area and builds on this foundation to advance a new view. The chapters advance thinking by developing integrative theories, by establishing connections among theories from different fields and research traditions, and by introducing new lines of inquiry.

The handbook explores the most popular current theories of change and innovation, including evolutionary perspectives, institutional theories, life-cycle models, and models of planned change. It also includes emerging theoretical perspectives including coevolutionary theory, dialectical theory, and complexity theory. A broad range of theories and perspectives are included: all of the generative mechanisms described in Van de Ven and Poole's (1995) typology of change theories—life-cycle, teleological, dialectical, and evolutionary—are featured in one chapter or another.

The contributions to this handbook focus on theories of change and innovation rather than on specific types of changes or innovations, such as new product innovation or change in human resource

systems. To generate the broadest possible theoretical statements, authors focused on change in the key constituents of organizations—individual members, groups, organizational systems, and organizational and institutional fields—without consideration of the specific "content" of the change or innovation. However, throughout this handbook chapter authors provide useful summary statements and examples of the major types of changes and innovations typically examined at each organizational level.

The book is organized roughly according to levels of analysis. We use the term "roughly" because most authors adopted a multilevel approach, and therefore most chapters span several levels. Together the chapters of this book cover the entire spectrum of organizational levels from the individual to the nation-state.

Chapter 1 explores issues that bridge the theories and perspectives in this book. It starts with some key distinctions concerning theories of change and innovation and positions many of the theories covered in this book in terms of these concepts. The chapter then outlines the two major approaches in the study of change and innovation—the variance and process approaches—and considers how they might be integrated. Following this, it focuses on three key parameters of change and innovation theories—agency, levels of analysis, and time, evaluates how they have been dealt with in existing research, and offers suggestions for future development. The focus of this chapter is to define possibilities for theory and research as well as to consider current trends. It provides a comparative perspective on the theories and models in this handbook.

In chapter 2 Woodman and Dewitt focus on the important problem of how organizations change individuals. They observe that most attention has been directed to the obverse problem—how individuals change organizations (see, e.g., chaps. 4 and 7). Woodman and Dewitt take an interactionist approach that focuses on three dimensions underlying individual change: the changeability of individual characteristics and behaviors, the depth of change required, and the length of time the change process takes. These dimensions influence the extent to which individuals change and the rate at which the changes come about through four key processes: socialization, training, programmed change, and interpersonal interactions with managers and coworkers. Woodman and Dewitt's model provides an important synthesis of numerous studies in search of the key factors that govern processes of individual changes in organizations.

McGrath and Tschan advance a dynamic model of change in groups and work units in chapter 3. The key problem they address is the tendency to treat groups as single-level phenomena and to focus on only a single aspect of group activity, such as work, conflict, or member relationships. Their model combines Arrow, McGrath, and Berdahl's (2000) complex systems model of groups with action theory to advance a multilevel model of operational, developmental, and adaptive processes in groups. McGrath and Tschan conceptualize development and change as a process of coevolution of these processes across multiple levels of group activity. Their analysis adds much-needed subtlety to the study of change and development in groups.

The next four chapters move up a level to the organization as a whole. Seo, Putnam, and Bartunek deal with planned change in chapter 4. They divide thinking on planned change into three generations that differ in terms of the target of change and characteristics of the change process they posit. Seo et al. identify a number of tensions and dualities in thinking about planned change and differentiate the three generations by how they deal with these tensions. This chapter produces important insights into planned change and also provides a unique dialectical perspective on planned change and innovation in organizations.

In chapter 5, Lewin, Weigelt, and Emery conduct a sweeping review of theories of organizational adaptation and selection. They start with firm-level theories such as organizational learning, punctuated equilibrium, and the resource-based view of the firm. Next, they explore mesolevel theories that link the organization to the environment or institutions, such as contingency theory, transaction cost economics, and evolutionary economics. Then, they discuss macro level theories that link the firm to its environment, such as institutional theory and population ecology theory. They identify several ways of making the connection across multiple levels of analysis and discuss trends in recent research. Looking at the array of theories covered in chapter 5, it is striking to see the potential for integrating theories of adaptation and selection across multiple levels of organizations.

Drazin, Glynn, and Kazanjian provide a novel examination of organizational change and innovation in terms of their underlying organizational logics in chapter 6. An organizational logic is the cognitive and practice-based set of core principles and processes that constitute the structural design of an organization. In this sense, the structure of an organization at any moment in time represents a "time capsule" of the logics and design knowledge embedded in the structure at the time of its construction. An organizational logic lends purpose and meaning to an organization's structure and provides members with norms and interpretive schemes. Drazin et al. discuss three modes of change involving organizational logics: change through the establishment and elaboration of logics, change through the breakdown and replacement of current logics, and change via logics that incorporate change as a basic premise. The first and third types of change tend to be continuous and the second discontinuous. Chapter 6 offers a broad view of organizational logic that pulls together work from a variety of areas and goes beyond views of logics as stable deep structures to consider how they reflect design changes in organizations.

In chapter 7 Hatch addresses change in organizational cultures, a neglected topic in organizational culture research. Hatch provides an intriguing review of theories of culture change in anthropology and sociology, divulging a rich array of theoretical thinking that can inform research on organizational culture. Hatch considers three theories of organizational culture change in depth: Schein's (1992) theory of leadership and culture, Gagliardi's elaboration of Schein's model, and her own theory of cultural dynamics. Similar to Drazin et al.'s approach, theories of organizational culture change posit deeper structures in organizations that interact with surface behavior and change according to somewhat different processes. Hatch's chapter construes culture as a process that constitutes organizations rather than a stable characteristic of organizations, a perspective that fulfills the early promise of culture research to conceptualize culture as something the organization is, rather than as something the organization has.

The next three chapters move up another level of analysis and view the organization as part of an interorganizational community, industry, or population. In chapter 8 Baum and Rao present a dual-hierarchy model of organizational evolution that unifies the population ecology and community ecology perspectives. They develop a theory of coevolution of populations and communities in a nested hierarchy that extends from groups within organizations to community and population levels. Their model builds a case for particular types of influence across levels and between populations and communities, advancing specific hypotheses that can guide future research in this area. This chapter provides an important synthesis of efforts to integration the population and community perspectives that have been emerging in recent years.

Van de Ven and Hargrave present a comprehensive review of concepts of change and innovation in institutional theory in chapter 9. They delineate four schools of thought on institutional change and innovation: institutional design, institutional adaptation, institutional diffusion, and collective action. Each school, they argue, advances a different generative mechanism for change and incorporates a different view of the role of agency in change and innovation. They discern trends in the development of institutional theory that point to a greater emphasis on agency and greater articulation of the individual responses of organizations to institutional environments. This chapter contributes by mapping the field of institutional theory in a concise and insightful way and highlighting often underemphasized change and innovation processes in institutions.

Hinings, Greenwood, Reay, and Suddaby present a theory of institutional change in organizational fields in chapter 10. They build on previous work to develop a full-blown theory of how institutions develop through structuration processes. The model posits five stages of institutional change and explicates the structuring processes that occur in each stage. Just as the surface institutional structure changes, so do the nature and impact of the underlying structuring processes. This model is an important addition to institutional theories of organizational change because it conceptualizes the change process at several levels and admits human agency into the field of change.

In chapter 11, Lewin and Kim raise the focus yet another level, considering the role of the nation-state in organizational change and innovation. They develop a comparative analysis of three major states—the United States, Japan, and Germany—that differ fundamentally in the environments they provide for organizational change and innovation. By relating the organizational level to the level of the national economy and culture, Lewin and Kim transcend the field and population level. To our knowledge, this is the first review of its type in the scholarship of organizational change and innovation.

The last two chapters are concerned with meta-level analyses of change and innovation theory. In chapter 12, Dooley discusses complexity models and their application to change and innovation research. Complexity theory has received much attention in recent years and has been hailed as a major breakthrough in change and innovation research (e.g., McKelvey, 2003). The complex systems field, however, often seems as confusing and chaotic as the processes that it studies. Dooley distinguishes four approaches to modeling complex systems, discussing the conditions under which each is appropriate and outlining possible applications. This chapter performs an important service by sorting out the different modeling strategies and tracing their implications for research on change and innovation.

In chapter 13, Poole and Van de Ven expand the typology of change and innovation theories presented in their 1995 article (Van de Ven et al., 1995). They enlarge this scheme to include variants of the four basic generative mechanisms (motors) introduced in their article and discuss how simpler models might be combined systematically into more complex theories. This chapter represents a significant expansion of the original typology and specifies in more detail the types of relationships that motors may have in theories that incorporate more than one generative mechanism. Several of the theories in this volume are analyzed in terms of this typology.

The contributions to this handbook review a broad range of literature on change and innovation from the fields of anthropology, communication, education, information systems, management, psychology, public administration, sociology, and urban planning. The theories, concepts, ideas, and ways of thinking are also enriched by contributions from other fields including the biosciences, chemistry, computer science, engineering, and physics. The breadth of this handbook provides a representative sample of past and current thinking on change and innovation.

Several general observations can be made about theories of change and innovation based on these contributions. First, it is clear that there has been a maturation of institutional theory and evolutionary perspectives, the two theories of organizational change that have dominated the past twenty years. Scholars in these areas have embarked on a second wave of development. Evolutionary models based on direct analogies to biology are being replaced by coevolutionary theories that posit mutual influence of organization and environment and more complex schemes for variation, selection, and retention (see, e.g., Baum and Rao, chap. 8). Institutional theories that treated institutions as unitary, supraorganizational entities are being supplemented by models that recognize the changes and diversity that characterize institutional environments and organizational responses to them (see Van de Ven and Hargrave, chap. 9, and Hinings et al., chap. 10). These developments promise significant advances in both theories in the near future.

Second, an increasing number of theories of change and innovation posit deep, hidden structures underlying organizational processes. Marx's theory of social development is a classic exemplar of this approach. In current thought, deep structures have been elaborated as part of Gersick's (1991) expansion of punctuated equilibrium theory, the theory of structuration (e.g., Hinings et al., chap. 10), theories of organizational logics (Drazin et al., chap. 6), and theories of organizational culture change (Hatch, chap. 7). One advantage of these theories is that they explain how organizations that seem to change constantly on the surface maintain their coherence through more stable deep structures. The key to change and innovation lies in the dynamics of these deep structures and their interplay with the surface. One challenge these theories face is the difficulty of identifying deep structures, which by definition are hidden below layers of other activity. This makes research involving these hard-to-access structures challenging.

Third, there is a noticeable trend toward favoring multilevel theories of change and innovation. Most of the chapters in this book differentiate two or more levels of influence on change and innovation and attempt to specify the nature of interlevel effects: Baum and Rao's coevolutionary model (chap. 8) and McGrath and Tschan's theory of group systems (chap. 3) are two good examples. They concur with the judgment of Dansereau, Yammarino, and Kohles (1999, p. 346) that "an approach to viewing multiple levels of analysis over time should improve our ability to better choose our lenses, focus on phenomena, and capture the impacts of people shifting and organizing themselves dynamically over time." Recent advances in theory on multiple levels and multilevel research methods (Klein and Koslowski, 2000) should promote our ability to incorporate them into research on change and innovation.

Time continues to be a missing element in most research on change and innovation. The theories in this volume do not, for the most part, explicitly consider time. They treat time as a backdrop for change and a metric in research, but they do not incorporate it as a variable, nor do they consider the social construction of time and the impacts of different temporal perspectives. As Poole notes in chapter 1, there has been an upsurge of interest in time in organizational research, and the study of change and innovation could benefit from emerging frameworks.

A fifth trend is the ongoing romance between organizational research and complex systems theories such as complexity theory and chaos theory. The chapters of this volume display clearly the level of interest in these novel perspectives. Complex systems theories have great potential to provide rigorous models for critical aspects of change including emergence, interlevel relationships, critical incidents, and unintended consequences. McKelvey (2003) makes a compelling case that describes in some detail the contributions complexity theory can make to the study of change and innovation. While we do not wish to dull this enthusiasm too much, some cautions are in order. To date there have been few rigorous applications of complexity theory to organizational change and innovation. The applications that have been pursued are fairly limited and highlight the many difficult choices that must be made in modeling organizations in this perspective (for example, compare Cheng and Van de Ven [1996] with Dooley and Van de Ven's reanalysis of the same data [chap. 9 in Poole, Van de Ven, Dooley, and Holmes 2000]). There are also limitations in the extent to which these models can capture agency and complex interpretive processes (see chap. 1). It will be some time before complex systems theory is more meat than metaphor in organizational research, and its ultimate implications—though highly promising—are still unclear.

Finally, and perhaps most encouraging, is a growing sophistication in which scholars treat organizational change and innovation. As this handbook shows, tremendous advances in our understanding have been made in the past two decades.

However, changes in basic assumptions come more slowly. For the most part, there has been a bias toward stability in our thinking about change, a bias rooted in essentialistic philosophies that trace back to Aristotle and Plato. The most common approach is to conceptualize change in contrast to stability, which is taken as a reference point for gauging change. The definitions of change and innovation presented at the beginning of this chapter reflect this presumption and the chapters of this book, in large part, share this bias. Tsoukas and Chia (2002) observe that this way of thinking prevents us from giving change its due place in our theories, because it generates a tendency to treat stability as the given state and consider change as something unusual, a departure from stability. Instead, they argue, "Change must not be thought of as a property of organization. Rather organization must be understood as an emergent property of change" (2002, p. 570). Hernes (1976) offers a more balanced opinion, asserting that it is important that our theories provide a balance between stability and change by explaining them both as part of the same process. As we continue to deepen our understanding of organizational innovation and change, we trust that our ability to think in terms of change and our vocabulary for expressing these thoughts will grow.

References

Arrow, H., McGrath, J. M., & Berdahl, J. L. (2000). *Small groups as complex systems: Formation, coordination, development, and adaptation.* Thousand Oaks, CA: Sage.

Cheng, Y. & Van de Ven, A. H. (1996). Learning the innovation journey: Order out of chaos? *Organization Science, 7,* 593–614.

Dansereau, F., Yammarino, F. J., & Kohles, J. C. (1999). Multiple levels of analysis from a longitudinal perspective: Some implications for theory building. *Academy of Management Review, 24,* 346–357.

Gersick, C. J. (1991). Revolutionary change theories: A multilevel exploration of the punctuated equilibrium paradigm. *Academy of Management Review, 16*(1), 10–36.

Hernes, G. (1976). Structural change in social processes. *American Journal of Sociology, 82,* 513–545.

James, W. (1909/1996). *A pluralistic universe.* Lincoln, NE: University of Nebraska Press.

Klein, K. J. & Koslowski, S. W. J. (2000). *Multilevel theory, research, and methods in organizations: Foundations, extensions, and new directions.* San Francisco: Jossey-Bass.

McKelvey, B. (2003, October 3). Sending evolutionary entrepreneurial research the way of the dodo bird by replacing Darwin with Schumpeter and Benard. Paper presented at the Journal of Business Venturing.

Poole, M. S., Van de Ven, A. H., Dooley, K., & Holmes, M. E. (2000). *Organizational change and innovation processes: Theory and methods for research.* New York: Oxford University Press.

Schein, E. (1992). *Organizational culture and leadership* (2nd ed.). San Francisco: Jossey-Bass.

Tsoukas, H. & Chia, R. (2002). On organizational becoming. *Organization Science, 13,* 567–582.

Van de Ven, A. H. & Poole, M. S. (1995). Explaining development and change in organizations. *Academy of Management Review, 20,* 510–540.

Handbook of
Organizational Change and Innovation

1

Central Issues in the Study of Change and Innovation

Marshall Scott Poole

This handbook is a rich tapestry of theories, its warp the levels of analysis from individual to nation-state and its weft the time through which change and innovation processes unfold. As with many tapestries, what first strikes the eye is the amazing diversity of ideas and subject matter. But as we step back and look a little longer, patterns and central themes emerge. These patterns are the subject of this chapter.

Across the diverse and wide-ranging contributions to this handbook three basic questions consistently present themselves:

What is the nature of change?

How should we study change and innovation?

What are the key concepts a theory of change and innovation should incorporate?

This chapter will explore various answers to these questions and consider their implications for future research on organizational change and innovation. It will also attempt to illuminate various theories in this book and their relationship to one another by identifying their positions on these questions.

The chapter is organized around the three questions. The next section discusses three viewpoints on the nature of change and innovation and considers how some of the theories discussed in this handbook fit with them. Each of the three perspectives focuses on different aspects of change and innovation and suggests different ways of distinguishing among theories of these phenomena. We then turn to paradigms for the study of change and innovation. Three approaches—variance research, process research, and modeling—are distinguished in terms of what they can tell us about change and innovation, the type of explanation they offer, and the general research methodology they employ. In the third section we consider key facets of organizational change and innovation theories—agency, levels of analysis, and time. These three terms are common touchstones for theory development in this area. We delineate recent trends and advances with respect to the three facets and suggest some possible trajectories for future development. The chapter concludes with a discussion of worthwhile directions suggested by some theoretical voices not heard in this volume.

What Is the Nature of Change?

How one answers this question defines how one divides the field of organizational change and innovation theories. Taking a position on the nature of change requires the theorist to focus on some aspects of change and innovation and to divert attention from others. Change is such a multifaceted phenomenon that every attempt is necessarily limited, but by piecing together partial views, a broader understanding may emerge. In this section we will consider three answers to the question "What is the nature of change?" each of which focuses on particular aspects of change and innovation. While none is complete in itself, together they suggest some of the dimensions that ought to be addressed in theories of change and innovation.

Theories of Change Versus Theories of Changing

Crucial to defining change and innovation is delineating the role of people in these processes. To this end Bennis's (1966) distinction between theories of change, which focus on how organizations change and factors that produce change, and theories of changing, which focus on how change can be brought about and managed in organizations, is useful. This distinction highlights the role of human agency in organizational change and innovation in terms of the contrast between planned and unplanned change discussed by Seo et al. in chapter 4. Planned change is consciously conceived and implemented by knowledgeable actors, and how planned change may be effectively accomplished is explained in theories of changing. There is a normative cast to planned change; planned change attempts to improve the situation and has as its reference point a desired end state. By contrast, unplanned change may or may not be driven by human choice. It is not purposefully conceived and may move the organization in either desirable or undesirable directions. The contrast between planned and unplanned change focuses our attention on the degree to which change and innovation can be choreographed, scripted, or controlled. Theories of planned change specify ways to manage and control change processes. Theories of unplanned change, on the other hand, imply that change is to some degree a force in its own right, susceptible to channeling, but not necessarily to control or management.

While planned and unplanned change may be viewed as opposite ends of a continuum, it is also useful to consider them together. All planned change occurs in the context of the ambient change processes that occur naturally in organizations. For example, a strategic planning process occurs in an organization that is going through its own life cycle and also evolving as part of a population of other organizations. The intersection of these three change processes, one planned and the other two unplanned, will shape the organization, and knowledge of the ambient change processes can enable the managers to conduct strategic planning more effectively. Conversely, unplanned change processes can be "domesticated" through interventions and driven in useful directions. In order to do this, the planner makes a virtue of necessity. Drawing on his or her knowledge of how natural change processes unfold, the planner uses the processes' momentum to push through needed measures.

Most theories discussed in this book are best classified as theories of change, including McGrath and Tschan's complex adaptive group theory (chapter 3), Baum and Rao's coevolutionary theory (chapter 8), the various institutional theories discussed by Van de Ven and Hargrave (chapter 9), Lewin et al. (chapter 5), and Hinings et al. (chapter 10), the theories of culture change discussed by Hatch (chapter 7), and Dooley's typology of complexity models (chapter 12). While they suggest some prescriptions for changing organizations, the theories themselves are not explicitly designed to advise change agents. The chapters primarily focused on changing are those by Woodman and Dewett on individual change (chapter 2) and Seo et al. on planned organizational change (chapter 4). Drazin et al.'s logics of organization (chapter 6) occupy an intermediate position, because the theories of logics are theories of change, but managers and change agents also utilize logics as targets or stimuli for the purpose of changing organizations.

Theories of organizational change focus on change and innovation in their own right, seeking to understand them as objects of scientific study, rather than in practical terms. This approach has an advantage in that researchers are likely to cast a wider net if they seek to understand change and development per se than if they are focused on what works or doesn't work or on management issues. The resulting theories and research are more likely to identify the most important factors and processes that shape change and innovation and to avoid the blinders that some-times accompany research primarily concerned with factors that can be managed or manipulated. As Pfeffer (1982, p. 37) put it, "adopting managerial def-initions of what are important problems, what are the important variables, and sometimes even how to mea-sure the variables may lead to neglect of important explanatory factors and to the phrasing of issues in ways that make them scientifically useless." On this view a pure scholarly approach is most likely to generate useful insights.

However, such wide-open inquiry may generate theories that have little direct connection with prac-tice. The processes described in population ecology and institutional theories of change, for instance, would be difficult to control or manage. In population-level and institutional theories individual organiza-tions and their members are, with few exceptions, portrayed as objects tossed about on an ocean with currents too powerful for them to resist. There are some lessons in this literature for reshaping and re-acting to these currents, but for the most part they are more relevant to government policy makers and long-term strategists than to day-to-day managers. The pri-mary advice is that managers and change agents should realize how difficult change and innovation are to script and manage, as these processes constantly move in unexpected directions and are driven by dy-namics that are either too powerful to control or too subtle to understand. A valuable insight, perhaps, but hardly helpful to managers wondering how to manage organizational change and innovation.

There is a pressing need to work out the im-plications of theories for the practice of organiza-tional change and innovation. The lack of theories that translate into practical terms may be due, in part, to the emphasis of much recent research on macro level societal processes that occur in organizational fields and populations. This tends to direct attention away from human agency and factors that can be managed or engineered. The theories of active change in individuals (chapter 2), groups (chapter 3), and organizations (chapters 4, 6, and 9) may provide insights more easily turned to practice.

Episodic Versus Continuous Change

Weick and Quinn (1999) characterize change in terms of its tempo, defined as "characteristic rate, rhythm, or pattern of work or activity" (Random House Dictionary, cited in Weick and Quinn 1999, p. 365). Based on tempo, they differentiate episodic and continuous change. Episodic change is conceived to be "infrequent, discontinuous and intentional" (p. 365), while continuous change is conceived as "ongoing, evolving and cumulative" (p. 375). The two forms of change are associated with different meta-phors of the organization, analytical frameworks, the-ories of intervention, and roles attributed to change agents, as shown in table 1.1. The distinction between episodic and continuous change is correlated with several others, including incremental versus radical change (e.g., Tushman et al. and Romanelli, 1985) continuous versus discontinuous change (e.g., Meyer, Goes, and Brooks, 1993), first-order versus second-order change (Meyer et al., 1993) and competence-enhancing versus competence-destroying change (Abernathy and Clark, 1985).

Theories in this volume that are episodic include:

- Training and programmed change approaches to individual change discussed by Woodman and Dewett (chapter 2)
- Punctuated equilibrium theory (discussed in several chapters)
- Theories of organizational logics (chapter 6)
- Most of the first and second generation theories of planned change discussed by Seo et al. (chapter 4)
- Strategic choice theory (Lewin et al., chapter 5)
- Evolutionary economics (chapter 5)
- Schein's theory of culture change (chapter 7)
- Most of the institutional adaptation and col-lective action perspectives discussed by Van de Ven and Hargrave (chapter 9)
- Greenwood et al.'s theory of institutional change in organizational fields (chapter 10)

Theories that are continuous include:

- The socialization and interpersonal interaction approaches to individual change (Woodman and Dewett, chapter 2)
- The theory of learning organizations discussed by Seo et al. (chapter 4) and Lewin et al. (chapter 5)
- Contingency theory (chapter 5)
- Population and community ecology theories (Baum and Rao, chapter 8)
- Hatch's theory of culture change (chapter 7)
- The institutional design and diffusion per-spectives discussed by Van de Ven and Har-grave (chapter 9)

Table 1.1 Comparison of episodic and continuous change

Characteristic	Episodic Change	Continuous Change
Metaphor of organization	Organizations are inertia-prone and change is infrequent, discontinuous, and intentional.	Organizations are emergent and self-organizing and change is constant, evolving, and cumulative.
Analytic framework	Change is an occasional interruption or divergence from equilibrium. It is externally driven. It is seen as a failure of the organization to adapt to a changing environment.	Change is a pattern of endless modifications in work processes and social practice. It is driven by organizational instability and alert reactions to daily contingencies. Numerous small accomodations cumulate and multiply.
	Perspective: Macro, distant, global Emphasis: Short-run adaptation Key concepts: Inertia, deep structure, or interrelated parts, triggering, replacement and substitution, discontinuity, revolution	Perspective: Micro, close, local Emphasis: Long-run adaptability Key concepts: recurrent interactions, response repertoires, emergent patterns, improvisation, translation, learning
Intervention theory	Intentional change: Unfreeze, change, refreeze. Change is inertial, linear, progressive, and requires outside intervention.	Redirection of existing tendencies. Change is cyclical, processual, without an end state, equilibrium-seeking, eternal.
Role of change agent	Prime mover who creates change by finding points of leverage in organization. Change agent changes meaning systems, schema, and punctuation.	Sense maker who redirects and shapes change. Change agent recognizes, makes salient, and reframes current patterns. Change agent unblocks improvisation, translation, and learning.

Source: Adapted from table 1 in Weick and Quinn (1999).

Some theories incorporate elements of both continuous and episodic change. The various stage theories of development described throughout the book generally emphasize continuous change at the micro level of system behavior, but stage changes are often conceptualized as episodic. McGrath and Tschan's complex adaptive systems theory of groups also is built around both continuous and episodic elements. Moreover, some of the theories listed above, such as Greenwood et al.'s theory of institutional change, incorporate continuous change at the level of concrete action that moves the process through (episodic) stages. While the theory focuses on episodic, stagewise changes, it presumes an underlying continuous process of activity as a means for constructing the stages.

That some theories fall somewhere in between the two types suggests that the distinction is not necessarily clear-cut. Since episodic change is best understood from a macro or global analysis, while continuous change is better discerned through micro level or local analysis, it has been suggested that they are not incompatible and that which perspective is applicable is

a matter of perspective (see chapter 13). However, the fact that some changes appear to us to be gradual and almost indiscernible, whereas others are attended by major breaks and disruptions, continues to give the episodic-continuous distinction traction.

Four Basic Motors of Change

A third approach defines change in terms of the mechanisms that bring it about. Van de Ven and Poole (1995) defined four relatively simple theories that serve as ideal types for the explanation of change and innovation processes. Figure 1.1 shows that each theory views the process of development as unfolding in a fundamentally different progression of change events, and as governed by a different generative mechanism or motor.

- A life-cycle model depicts the process of change in an entity as progressing through a necessary sequence of stages or phases. The specific content of these stages or phases is

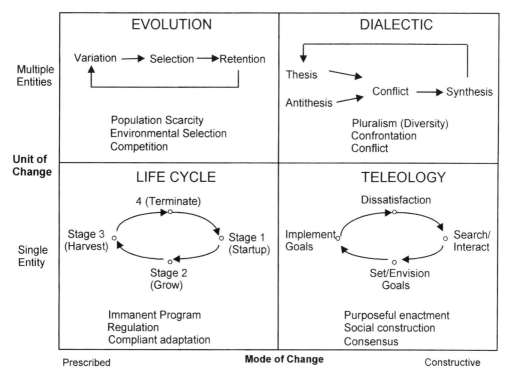

Figure 1.1 Typology of theories of change and innovation. Note: Arrows on lines represent likely sequences among events, not causation between events. *Source*: Van de Ven and Poole (1995).

prescribed and regulated by an institutional, natural, or logical program prefigured at the beginning of the cycle.

- A teleological model views development as a cycle of goal formulation, implementation, evaluation, and modification of actions or goals based on what was learned or intended by the entity. This sequence emerges through the purposeful enactment or social construction of an envisioned end state among individuals within the entity.

- In dialectical models of development conflicts emerge between entities espousing an opposing thesis and antithesis that collide to produce a synthesis, which in time becomes the thesis for the next cycle of a dialectical progression. Confrontation and conflict between opposing entities generate this dialectical cycle.

- An evolutionary model of development consists of a repetitive sequence of variation, selection, and retention events among entities in a designated population. This evolutionary cycle is generated by competition for scarce environmental resources between entities inhabiting a population.

The four theories can be distinguished along two dimensions. The unit of change dimension indexes whether the change in question is premised on the actions of a single entity or multiple entities. Evolutionary and dialectical theories operate on multiple entities. Evolutionary forces are defined in terms of their impacts on populations and have no meaning at the level of the individual entity. Dialectical theories require at least two entities to fill the roles of thesis and antithesis. On the other hand, life cycle and teleological theories operate on a single entity. In the case of a life-cycle model, development is explained as a function of potentials immanent within the entity. While environment and other entities may shape how this immanence manifests itself, they are strictly secondary to the immanent potentials. The real push to development comes from within the single, whole developing entity. Teleological theories, too, require only a single entity's goals, social construction, or envisioned end state to explain development. A teleological theory can operate among many members of an organization or a set of organizations when there is sufficient consensus among the members to permit them to act as a single organizational entity.

The generative mechanisms of the four process theories also differ in terms of a second dimension regarding whether the sequence of change events is prescribed a priori or whether the progression is constructed and emerges as the change process unfolds. A prescribed mode of change channels the development of entities in a prespecified direction, typically of maintaining and incrementally adapting their forms in a definite, calculable way. A constructive mode of change generates unprecedented, novel forms that, in retrospect, are often discontinuous and unpredictable departures from the past. A prescribed motor evokes a sequence of change events in accord with a pre-established program or action routine. A constructive motor, on the other hand, produces new action routines that may (or may not) create an original (re)formulation of the entity. Life cycle and evolutionary theories operate in a prescribed modality, while teleological and dialectical theories operate in the constructive modality.

The two dimensions of unit and mode of change define generative mechanisms in terms of their action and process. They differ from other dimensions such as incremental and radical change and competence-enhancing and competence-destroying change which classify organizational changes based on their consequences or outcomes, rather than by their starting or process conditions. One advantage of the typology is that it is possible to identify the motor(s) of a change process before it has concluded.

The most common theoretical frame for the study of change and innovation in this book is the life-cycle model, which reflects the emphasis on stage models in development in the thinking on development and change. Examples of life-cycle models include theories of group development (chapter 3), stage models of collective action (chapter 9), and stages of socialization (chapter 2). Teleological models, which emphasize the role of leaders and change agents as well as the construction of change by organizational members, are also quite common. Examples in this volume include Schein's theory of culture change (chapter 7), theories of institutional design (chapter 9), and self-organizing systems theory (chapters 6 and 12). Increasingly popular over the past two decades have been evolutionary theories. The community and population ecology models (chapter 8) are illustrative. The dialectical model has not been used as

much. In this volume Seo et al. base chapter 4 on a dialectical analysis and dialectical models figure in the collective action theories and institutionalization theories discussed in chapter 9 and in Hatch's theory of culture change (see chapters 7 and 13). Other studies employing dialectical frameworks include Farjoun (2002) and Smith and Berg (1987).

However, theories of change are not always built around just one motor. Van de Ven and Poole (1995) also argued that combinations of these motors create composite change theories capable of capturing the complexity of change and innovation processes more completely than single motor theories are capable of. If we consider that one, two, three, or four motors might operate in a given theory, it is evident that sixteen explanations of organizational change and development are logically possible. This array, shown in table 1.2, is analogous to examining the simple main and interaction effects of each of the four motors on alternative applied theories in the management literature.

The first four alternatives represent the "main effects" of the generating mechanisms underlying our four ideal-type theories: the regulated program of life cycle theory, purposeful enactment of teleological theory, conflict and confrontation of dialectical theory, and competitive selection of evolutionary theory. These "single-motor theories" apply to cases when only one of the four generating mechanisms or change motors is in operation.

The remaining twelve alternatives represent "interaction effects" of the interdependent operation of two or more of the four generative mechanisms. Alternatives 5 through 10 are called "dual-motor theories" because they represent cases when only two of the four change motors are in operation in a given organizational change process. Alternatives 11 through 14 represent "tri-motor theories," when three of the four change motors operate interdependently. Alternative 15 is the "quad-motor theory," which represents the most complex situations when all of the four generating mechanisms operate interdependently in a given situation. Finally, alternative 16 represents the null set, when none of the motors identified in the typology are operating. Examples of several of these motors and examples are discussed in Van de Ven and Poole (1995) and Poole et al. (2000). In chapter 13, Poole and Van de Ven expand the framework to include variations on the basic motors.

A few theories in this book explicitly combine two or more basic motors. In Greenwood et al.'s theory of

Table 1.2 Logically possible theories of organizational change and development

	Interplays Among Generating Mechanisms			
	Prescribed Motor within Entity: Imminent Program	Constructive Motor Within Entity: Purposeful Enactment	Constructive Motor Between Entities: Conflict and Synthesis	Prescribed Motor Between Entities: Competitive Selection
1. Life-cycle (Cameron and Whetten, 1983)	yes	no	no	no
2. Teleology (March and Simon, 1958)	no	yes	no	no
3. Dialectics (Benson, 1977)	no	no	yes	no
4. Evolution (Hannan and Freeman, 1977)	no	no	no	yes
Dual-motor theories				
5. Design hierarchy theory (Clark, 1985)	yes	yes	no	no
6. Group conflict (Simmel, 1908; Coser, 1958)	no	yes	yes	no
7. Community ecology (Astley, 1985)	no	no	yes	yes
8. Adaptation-selection models (Aldrich, 1979)	yes	no	no	yes
9. Org. growth and crisis stages (Greiner, 1972)	yes	no	yes	no
10. Org. punctuated equilibrium (Tushman and Romanelli, 1985)	no	yes	no	yes
Tri-motor theories				
11. Partisan mutual adjustment (Lindblom, 1965)	yes	yes	yes	no
12. ?	no	yes	yes	yes
13. ?	yes	no	yes	yes
14. Social psychology of organizing (Weick, 1979)	yes	yes	no	yes
Quad-motor theories				
15. Human development progressions (Riegel, 1976)	yes	yes	yes	yes
16. ?—Garbage can (Cohen, March, and Olsen, 1972)	no	no	no	no

Source: Adapted from Van de Ven and Poole (1995).

institutional change (chapter 10), a life-cycle model describes the macro level progression of change, but change is driven by teleological action by individuals and organizations. Chapter 9 describes theories of institutional change through collective action that change institutions which are based on dialectical conflict, but also unfold through stages of a life-cycle model. Implicit within these theories at the micro level is a teleological theory of individual agency. As this last sentence implies, other models of change are often implicit in theories based on a single model. One way to surface assumptions underlying theories of change and innovation is to identify other motors that operate alongside those explicitly incorporated in a theory.

The three conceptualizations of change illuminate different aspects of the phenomenon and offer a useful way to map the basic assumptions of theories of change and innovation. Their answers to the question "What is the nature of change?" complement one another. Bennis's distinction focuses attention on the role of human choice and on the

management of change, Weick and Quinn's on the character of the change itself, and Van de Ven and Poole's on how the change comes about. Bennis's theories of change generally fit into the life cycle, evolutionary, and dialectical categories, whereas theories of changing tend to fall into the teleological quadrant. Most theories of change are continuous, whereas theories of changing tend to be episodic. Though the correspondence is less clear, evolutionary and life cycle motors tend to operate in continuous terms, whereas dialectical and teleological motors are more episodic.

Change and innovation may well fit into the category of "essentially contested concepts" for which no generally agreed upon definitions can be derived. The struggle to answer the question "What is the nature of change?" is worthwhile, however, because it encourages us to work out what is fundamental about change and clarify the "differences that make a difference" across the varied theatres in which change and innovation occur.

Much the same can be said about the second question, "What is the best approach for the study of change and innovation?"

Approaches to the Study of Change and Innovation

Mohr (1982; Poole et al., 2000) first distinguished variance and process approaches to social scientific research, and the distinction has been quite influential in organizational studies. In general terms, a variance theory explains change in terms of relationships among independent variables and dependent variables, while a process theory explains how a sequence of events leads to some outcome. The two approaches yield quite different conceptualizations of change and imply different standards for judging research on change and innovation. Figure 1.2 provides a pictorial comparison of the two approaches.

A variance theory focuses on variables that represent the important aspects or attributes of the subject under study. Explanations take the form of causal statements or models that incorporate these variables (e.g., X causes Y, which causes Z), and an implicit goal of variance research is to establish the conditions necessary and sufficient to bring about an outcome. Variance research employs experimental and survey research designs and is grounded in the general linear model that underlies most common statistical methods, including analysis of variance (ANOVA),

regression, factor analysis, and structural equation modeling. A key criterion for assessing variance theories is their generality, which refers to the range of cases, phenomena, or situations the causal explanation applies to.

Several different types of studies of organizational change and innovation follow the variance approach:

1. Probably the most common type of variance study treats change as a variable such as rate of innovation (Rogers, 1995), or depth of change (Harrison 1970, see also Woodman and Dewett, chapter 2). The goal of these studies is to explain and/or predict the occurrence and magnitude of change or the effects of change on other variables. The methodologies employed in these studies range from relatively straightforward laboratory (Mathieu et al., 2000) and survey (Morrison, 1993) designs to sophisticated time series and event history models (Mayer and Tuma, 1990).

2. Some studies treat change as the context for other causal processes. They do not study change per se, but instead take change as the frame in which other phenomena occur. The object of these studies is to develop and test cause-effect relationships within a changing context or to test theories of individual units' reactions to change in higher-level units. A study of how individual hospitals respond to changes in institutional practices in the medical field by Goodrich and Salancik (1996) is one example of this type of research.

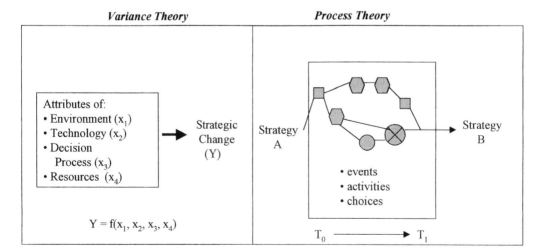

Figure 1.2 Two approaches to explaining strategic change. Based on Mohr (1982) and Langley (1999).

3. An increasingly popular approach is to study change at multiple levels of analysis (Dansereau et al., 1999). Some studies in this group focus on the effects of change in a variable at one level of analysis on variables at other levels—for example, how transformational leadership styles influence work units and create collectives in organizations over time (Avolio and Bass, 1995). Methods for conducting multilevel analysis include hierarchical linear modeling, within-and-between analysis, and interdependency analysis (Kashy et al. 1999; Klein and Koslowski, 2000).

The variance approach is useful in the study of change and innovation processes in two important respects. First, variance theories offer good pictures of the mechanisms that drive a process, and variance research methods are well suited for testing hypotheses related to mechanisms. Second, the variance approach is useful for the study of processes that run very rapidly on a human scale, as is the case for many individual or group level change processes (e.g., social identity formation or change in cognitive structures). While these may unfold as the process approach describes below, they operate so quickly that they can be studied quite effectively with variance methods that assume homogeneous, immediate causality.

The variance approach also has limitations (Poole et al., 2000). It is difficult to study the activities or steps in which change and innovation unfold using variance methods. While some methodologies for the study of processes have been applied in variance research (e.g., Davison et al. 1980; Davison et al. 1978; Poole and Roth 1989a; Poole and Roth 1989b), they require researchers to abstract variables from the process data, which forces them to study the process at one remove (at least). As a result, variance approaches make it difficult to study important aspects of how the change comes about. Behind most variance theories is a process-based "story" about the relationships among variables that give the theories coherence. However, it is difficult to test or study the narrative itself with variance approaches.

The statistical methods of variance research assume that causality in the system is "well behaved." This entails (a) that causes flow from larger units to smaller ones, but not vice versa (e.g., the organization can affect its members, but a single member's behavior cannot affect the organization) and (b) that causal factors operate homogeneously across cases and on approximately on the same time scale (Abbott, 1988).

These assumptions do not seem particularly restrictive within the variance framework, but they rule out the influence of some factors and influences that might figure in a process, including critical events, multiple causes operating unevenly in different parts of the organization and at different points in time, causes operating across greatly different time scales, and sequences of events that chain together in a contingent fashion to lead up to some outcome. Such are the subjects of history or biography, not structural equation models. Process theories attempt to incorporate these factors and influences.

The primary focus of a process theory is a series of events that unfold through time to bring about some outcome. Explanations in process theories tend to be more complex than variance explanations due to the complexity of events, the need to account for temporal connections among events, different time scales in the same process, and the dynamic nature of processes. Process explanations may include (a) an account of how one event leads to and influences subsequent events (e.g., events of type A have a .7 probability of being succeeded by events of type B and a .3 probability of being succeeded by events of type C); (b) an explication of the overall pattern that generates the series (e.g., the process develops in three stages, A, B, and C), or (c) both (in which case the micro level explanation and overall pattern should be linked). Process theories may incorporate several different types of effects into their explanations, including critical events and turning points, contextual influence, formative patterns that give overall direction to the change, and causal factors that influence the sequencing of events. Poole et al. (2000) argue that process explanations incorporate three of Aristotle's four causes, adding formal and final causation to the efficient causation that is the basis of causal explanation in variance research (see McKelvey [2002] for a related case for the inclusion of all four Aristotelean causes in organizational research).

Process research employs eclectic designs that identify or reconstruct the process through direct observation, archival analysis, or multiple case studies. Analysis of process data requires methods (a) that can identify and test temporal linkages between events and also overall temporal patterns (Poole et al., 2000) and (b) that can cope with the multiple time scales that often occur in processes (where some events extend for years, other events embedded in them run for shorter periods, and others embedded within these even shorter periods) (Langley, 1999). Whereas the great majority of variance research follows hypothetico-deductive procedures, process research employs a mixture of approaches. Most often, process studies derive theory from observation, but in some cases they test hypothesized models of the change process, and in others they use retroduction whereby theories are used to guide observation that further specifies the theories (Poole et al., 2000, pp. 115–117); indeed, in-depth studies of processes may employ two or even all three of these approaches (e.g., Van de Ven et al., 1999) As a result, both qualitative and quantitative approaches are used in process research (see Langley, 1999, and Poole et al., 2000 for description of process methods).

Like variance theories, process theories strive for generality, but for a process theory generalization depends on versatility, "the degree to which it can encompass a broad domain of developmental patterns without modification of its essential character" (Poole et al., 2000, p. 43). A versatile process explanation can "stretch" or "shrink" to fit specific cases that may differ in their tempo and time span. For instance, the punctuated equilibrium model of organizational change (Gersick, 1991; Tushman and Romanelli, 1985) is highly versatile because it can be applied to processes that take a week and those that take years and to a wide range of different processes, including organizational change, group development, and the evolution of technology. Table 1.3 summarizes some basic comparative points about variance and process approaches.

Langley (1999) and Poole et al. (2000) identify several different types of change and innovation studies that follow the process approach. They range along a rough continuum from highly interpretive to quantitative:

1. Some of the most influential work in organizational studies has taken the form of narrative histories that tell the story of a process in detail (e.g., Bartunek, 1984; Chandler, 1964; Pettigrew, 1985). These rich accounts have multiple interwoven themes and, as Langley (1999) notes, their very density may make deriving parsimonious theories something of a challenge.

2. A more focused approach is the multiple case study (Leonard-Barton, 1990). These studies are designed to compare and contrast a limited number of cases that "either (a) predict similar results (a literal replication) or (b) produce contrary results but for predictable reasons (a theoretical replication)" (Yin 1984, pp. 48–49) through intensive qualitative analysis. These studies often use various methods of summarization and display to draw meaning from their cases, such as visual mapping (Langley and Truax, 1994; Mintzberg, Raisinghani, and Theoret1976; Quinn, 1980; Van de Ven and Grazman 1999), matrix displays (Kuhn and Poole, 2000; Miles and Huberman, 1994), and comparison of extracts and digests of events (Leonard-Barton, 1990). The accounts yielded by multiple case studies are typically quite rich, though not as detailed as narrative histories, and they often have a more compact and explicit theoretical focus than do narrative histories.

Table 1.3 Variance and process approaches compared

Variance Approach	Process Approach
Focus: Fixed entities with variable attributes	Focus: Entities that participate in events and may change over time
Satisfactory explanations specify necessary and sufficient causality	Satisfactory explanations specify necessary causality
Satisfactory explanations are comprised of efficient causes	Satisfactory explanations may be comprised of final, formal, and/or efficient causes
Generality of explanation depends on uniform application across range of cases and contexts	Generality of explanation depends on its versatility
Monotonic, "well-behaved" causal relationships	Temporal ordering is critical to outcome
	Explanations include multiple causal factors operating at different levels and for different temporal spans
	Causal relationships are not monotonic or "well behaved"

3. A long-standing research tradition conceptualizes process in terms of a sequence of phases or stages (Bales and Strodtbeck, 1951; Barley, 1986; Fisher, 1970; Langley and Truax, 1994; Poole, 1981). Phasic analysis attempts to identify the coherent periods of activity through which a process unfolds. The most common type of explanation that employs phases is the life-cycle model (Cameron and Whetten, 1983; Greiner, 1972; Lacoursiere, 1980), but other types of theories also view processes in terms of phases (Poole, 1983; Saberwhal and Robey, 1993). Poole et al. (2000) discuss several methods, both qualitative and quantitative, for the identification of phases and the testing of phase sequence hypotheses. Phase theories attempt to encapsulate the essentials of rich process data in a simpler account of stepwise development or typical activities.

4. A final approach investigates processes through quantitative analysis of event series. This strategy (a) specifies indicators or variables that characterize attributes of events, (b) codes events to assign values to these variables, and (c) analyzes the resulting time series to test hypotheses about the sequence or identify patterns in the process. Van de Ven and Polley (1992) for example, segmented a multiyear product innovation process into months and counted the number of changes in the innovation idea, interventions by external resource controls, and feedback events per month in rich descriptions of events. They used time series regression to test a model of learning during innovation and also discovered a pattern in the time series that suggested that the innovation process was characterized by an initial phase of disorganization in the learning process that settled down into a phase of organized learning. Using a different type of data, Romanelli and Tushman (1994) coded variables from a documentary database comprised of newspaper articles, annual reports, and the like to study patterns of change in the microcomputer industry. Quantitative process analyses utilize a range of techniques, including Markov analysis, multivariate time series techniques, event history analysis, and nonlinear systems analysis, to uncover and test for properties of series of events and the mechanisms that drive the process. In some cases these studies draw substantial samples (e.g., Nutt, 1984; Poole and Roth, 1989a; Poole and Roth 1989b) but other studies focus on one or two cases with a large number of events and analyze the event series in detail (Van de Ven and Polley, 1992). Quantitative process analysis attempts to bring the rigor and system of variance research to the study of processes. Results of quantitative process studies may seem thin to those who favor narrative histories and multiple case studies.

As these examples show, process research is capable of tapping aspects of processes that variance research cannot. However, the process approach has its own limitations. Process studies are very labor-intensive to conduct and typically involve the collection of large amounts of multifaceted data, so that the researcher is in danger of what Pettigrew (1990) has termed "data asphyxiation." As described above, processes are often quite complex, so developing process explanations and discerning patterns in process data is a difficult undertaking. The depth of process data and complexity of processes tends to limit the number of cases that can be collected, thereby limiting confidence in the generalizability of the conclusions of process research.

The complexity of process research has motivated several heuristics and systems to aid the researcher in tackling process studies. Langley (1999) offers an insightful and readable guide to approaches to building theories of processes. Poole et al. (2000; Van de Ven and Poole, 1995) lay out four archetypal theories of change processes and describe how these can be identified in process data and how more complex process theories can be built from these simple motors (see chapter 13 for an expansion of this framework). Pentland (1999) describes how narrative analysis can be used to build process theories. A special issue of *Organization Science* (Huber and Van de Ven, 1990) is devoted to various methods of studying processes, and Poole et al. (2000) describe four methods for quantitative analysis uniquely adapted to process research.

The process approach is sometimes portrayed as opposed to the variance approach. However, it is more appropriate to view them as complementary. Variance studies can explore and test the mechanisms that drive process theories, while process studies can explore and test the narratives that ground variance theories. Rather than arguing that the two approaches are mutually exclusive, the relevant question is how to combine the two approaches.

One tack is to conduct both variance and process studies of the same data set and combine the results. Saberwhal and Robey (1995) conduct such a study and show how the results of variance and process analyses can be interleaved to illuminate the process (see Poole and Roth 1989a and Poole and Roth 1989b for another example of this approach). Even better, however, would be to find a way to combine elements of variance and process approaches in a single analysis.

Formal modeling using mathematical or simulation methodologies offers one way to bridge the gap between process and variance approaches. A discussion of several approaches to formal modeling is presented by Dooley in chapter 12. A model is a representation of a situated theory in some formal language, such as mathematics or a computer algorithm. The model draws on verbal theory and observation to derive a precise theory of a process in some specific context that can be used to project how the process would unfold and compared to process data gathered in that context. The relationship between theory, data, and model is depicted in figure 1.3, which is based on a discussion in Leik and Meeker (1975). As the figure indicates, models abstract (a) and formalize (e) theory using mathematics or computer based modeling tools. The model can be "run" to generate a trajectory through time of the variables or objects incorporated in the model, and this can then be used to get insights into the implications of the theory (b) and derive hypotheses implied by the theory (f). Information from observations can be used to specify the model (c) and the predictions of the model can be compared to observations to test it (g).

In a good example of the modeling process, Lomi and Larson (1996) developed a model of organizational population dynamics that draws on theories of density dependence. They incorporated the assumptions that "individual organizations craft their competitive strategies in reaction to—or in anticipation of—the behavior of a small number of other, clearly identified organizations," but that "organizational populations evolve according to global processes of legitimation and competition" (p. 1293). In moving from theory to model, Lomi and Larson abstracted a general model from theoretical assumptions (arrow a) using cellular automata modeling that formalized theoretical relationships currently expressed in looser verbal terminology (arrow e). The model was run for different numbers of competitors (8, 24, and 48) and evolutionary conditions. One insight from the modeling process was that organizations with more local

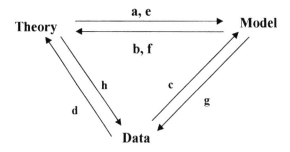

Inductive Modes
    a - Mathematical generalization of the theory
    b - Substantive interpretation of mathematical patterns
    c - Mathematical generalization of empirical patterns
    d - Substantive interpretation of data
Deductive Modes:
    e - Formalization of theory
    f - Derivation of substantive hypotheses from mathematical patterns
    g - Mathematical prediction or extrapolation
    h - Substantive prediction

Figure 1.3 The theory-model-data triangle. Adapted from Leik and Meeker (1975).

focus (e.g., smaller reference groups of competitors) "responded less strongly to population-level processes of legitimation and competition related to density" than those with larger reference groups (arrow b). This suggested the hypothesis that some density dependence may influence different organizations differently (arrow f). Lomi and Larson report that empirical findings on the impact of density dependence on foundings is consistent with this hypothesis (arrow g). Findings from organizational research were used to specify the model (arrow c), and Lomi and Larson discuss several ways in which the models can be extended so they more accurately reflect rational choice models of organizations.

Models are in some respects more specific than theories, because they are built around specific assumptions about key constructs in the theory (e.g., the type of variable they are, how they are measured, etc.) and the relationships the theory posits (e.g., the specific functional form of relationships among variables or software agents). However, models also abstract the theory by reformulating verbal statements into mathematics or computer modeling languages. Models are useful for deriving implications of theories that cannot be deduced from their verbal forms either because there are hidden complexities in the theory that verbal expressions cannot adequately represent or because the theory is so complex that it is impossible for the theorists to think through how constructs interact. Since innovation and change processes are inherently complex, formal modeling has great potential as a theory-building tool in this area. Much attention has been given in recent years to models of chaos and complexity theories as promising depictions of processes (McKelvey, 1999, 2002).

In chapter 12 Dooley distinguishes four different approaches to modeling change and innovation processes:

1. Dynamic models employ mathematical methods to represent systems of variables that represent key features of the process. These systems of equations are then used to derive a map of the trajectories of the values of these variables over time, giving a representation of the process generated by the mechanism built into the equations. Examples include Doreian and Hummon's (1976) use of linear differential equations to develop a control model of structural change in organizations and Guastello's

(1987, 1995) application of statistical techniques to fit catastrophe models of change in employee motivation. Doreian and Hummon used statistical estimation procedures to "solve" their model and generate predicted trajectories that the values of four interrelated structural variables—number of employees, number of divisions, number of supervisors, number of hierarchies—would follow over time. They then tested this model against longitudinal data. Guastello identified the variables that "controlled" the trajectory of motivation over time in a catastrophe model and used nonlinear regression to fit the model to a set of observations. The well-known system dynamics models developed by Forrester (1961) and others (Sterman, 2000) are also examples of dynamical models. Simulation software such as Stella and Vensim is available to support systems dynamics modeling.

The variables in these models need not be continuous. Event models that develop formal representations of the process in terms of discrete events utilize variance methods to explain the pattern. Poole et al. (2000) develop a Markov model that depicts the pattern of transitions among four types of discrete events during innovation development—expansion of the course of action, contraction of the course of action, modification of activities, and continuation of the same course of action. They compared the transition matrices for early and late periods of a product innovation process using an analog of analysis of variance and found the patterns to be different, suggesting different mechanisms drove the process in early and late stages.

2. Computational models simulate how a system or parts of a system evolve over time. These have been influential in organizational studies, especially Cyert and March's (1963) behavioral theory of the firm and Cohen, March, and Olsen's (1972) garbage can model. In chapter 12, Dooley discusses two promising types of models for complex systems. Cellular automata (Corman, 1996; Latane, 1996; Lomi and Larsen 1996, 1999) represent how interconnected units influence each other over time and can be used to model the spread of ideas, emotions, and behaviors through a system. Lomi and Larsen (1999) show how cellular automata can be used to model evolutionary change in organizational systems and Corman and Latane use them to model social influence in systems.

The rugged landscape model (Kauffman, 1993; 1995) has received much attention by theorists of organizational evolution and coevolution, as Baum and Rao illustrate in chapter 8.

3. Self-organizing system models depict how order is created by a system within itself. The system reorganizes under conditions that push it away from its equilibrium and the resulting processes of innovation, learning, and development enable the system to dissipate the energy that has created the disequilibrium. Contractor and Grant's (1996) model of the emergence of shared interpretations in groups and organizations adopts the self-organizing systems framework.

4. Complex adaptive system models, a newly developed approach, are simulations where agents pursue teleological ends. Agents embody sets of action rules that specify how they interact with each other and the environment. Over time, agents learn how to improve their fitness in the system. Axtell's (1999) computational model of the emergence of firms, described in chapter 12, is an example of this type of modeling. The insights from complex adaptive systems modeling come from showing how change and innovation processes at higher levels emerge from the interaction of autonomous agents.

Each of the four approaches offers a different way to integrate process and variance approaches. Dynamic models and computational models represent the mechanisms that generate a process (a variance theory) and "run" these to generate characteristics of the process. Systematically varying the parameters that govern these models or the structure of the models would enable variance methods to be applied in rigorous comparisons of the outputs. Qualitative features of the outputs, such as the shape of the trajectories of various variables over time, can be used to gather insights into the nature of the process. Self-organizing systems models represent processes in terms of the mechanisms by which the system responds to changes in its environment through reorganization. The impact of the environmental change can be studied using variance methods, and systematic variation of the rules governing the self-organizing process would enable variance-based comparison of different self-organizing schemes. Complex adaptive systems models are well suited for the study of teleologically oriented processes and can model the emergence of higher-level effects from the

action of multiple interacting agents. They are also suited for the study of evolutionary processes when interactions between agents can be specified. Variance approaches can be used to identify and study mechanisms through which the higher-level effects emerge, such as factors that constrain interactions among agents and factors that influence evolutionary processes, such as environmental change.

Like both variance and process approaches, modeling has its limitations. Models are generally much simpler than the actual processes they represent. Simplicity is one of the features that make models powerful, but simplification may also distort representations. Distortions include introducing restrictive assumptions and force-fitting theories into existing modeling techniques (McPhee and Poole, 1981). Verbal formulations of theories are more flexible and capable of capturing nuances of phenomena than are models, which are limited to the language and logic of their formalism. But while modeling does impose limitations on the form of theories, Dooley's review in chapter 12 shows that much progress has been made in developing diverse forms of models that can fit a wider variety of phenomena. Modeling is still in its infancy. Models will become more complex. They will be able to incorporate key junctures, critical events, and causes operating at different rates and strengths, and on different levels and at different times. If something can be described in words, it can be modeled.

The variance, process, and modeling approaches offer a rich array of possibilities for the study of change and innovation. Which is best for a particular study depends on the type of questions addressed, the researchers' assumptions about change and innovation, and the data they have access to. In the long run, a thorough understanding of a particular change or innovation probably requires all three approaches.

What Are the Key Concepts in Theories of Change and Innovation?

Whatever assumptions about change a theory may adopt, whatever approach it may take, several fundamental issues face all theorists of organizational change and innovation. Three terms run through the chapters in this book—*people*, *space*, and *time*—the "least common denominators" of change and innovation theory. These three terms are fundamental to any human science: before all else, social life is comprised of people who exist through space and time.

The key issue indexed by *people* is the role of human agency in change and innovation. Because organizational change and innovation often occur on a very large scale, involve multiple actors and units, and extend over a considerable period of time, the role of agency in these processes is easily obscured. Theories differ in the attention they accord to the role of agency in change and innovation, but every theory makes some assumptions about the nature of human action and how it connects to broader changes and innovations. The term *space* references the issue of levels of analysis in organizational change and innovation. It is becoming accepted that organizational theory in general and theories of change and innovation in particular must incorporate multiple levels of analysis. However, there are several responses to this realization, because it is far less clear how to build levels into theories of change and innovation. *Time* is the least explored of the three terms, but it may be the most important. To understand innovation and change it is critical to understand how they unfold over time and how time and timing affects them. Perhaps because it is the backdrop of life's events and therefore taken for granted, or perhaps because of the difficulty of the subject, time has been largely neglected in organizational scholarship. Recent work, however, has made some advances.

Time, space, and people are not always acknowledged explicitly in theories of innovation and change. However, because they are ubiquitous in change and innovation processes, theories make implicit assumptions about time, space, and people, albeit sometimes highly simplifying ones. This section will consider conceptual schemes for these terms that may clarify their role in change and innovation theories.

The Role of Human Agency

What role should theories of organizational change and innovation grant to agency? While there may well be an "invisible hand" that guides organizations, the role of human intention and human intervention is all too visible, and scholars of change and innovation must come to terms with them in one way or another. As the chapters of this book show, there are a variety of responses to this issue that vary in the assumptions they make about how agency works,

their focus on human versus organizational agency, and the complexity they accord to agents.

One approach focuses on the individuals who take control, create, and remake organizations. These "great individuals"—executives, entrepreneurs, organizational statespersons, transformational leaders, strategic decision makers, planners, designers, change agents—represent a potent expression of the human will as maker of the organization. Several theories and research traditions discussed in this volume embody this focus. In punctuated equilibrium theory the executive transforms the organization so that it can respond to a crisis or environmental jolt, shepherding the organization through the revolutionary period that sets the stage for the succeeding evolutionary period. Theories of organizational logics (chapter 6) posit that the entrepreneur elaborates the logic of the organization and the executive helps to break down the existing logic and manages the transformation to a new logic. In Schein's (1992) theory of organizational culture and cultural change (chapter 7) the transformational leader establishes and brings about changes in the deep structure of the culture. Perhaps the most influential of these positions is Child's (1972) classic statement of contingency theory as strategic choice. These and other compelling statements highlight the important role an individual can play in organizational change. They portray agency in the traditional sense of the active individual who shapes the world according to his or her intentions and actively monitors the course and effects of his or her activities (Anscombe, 1957; Giddens 1979, chapter 3; von Wright, 1971). They also help managers and other practitioners envision what can be done by the right person in the right place at the right time.

However, this concept of agency is subject to several qualifications. For one thing, external conditions limit the agent's power and capacity to control events and manage organizational change. Environmental factors can be so powerful that even the best leader can make little difference. In the face of a recession, for example, there may be little an executive can do to alter the economic circumstances of a firm or the services a government agency can offer. Second, there may be multiple agents, and it has been observed that the great individual is sometimes a figurehead, a stand-in for the team. While this is an important role (Mintzberg, 1973), agency is more complex when multiple interacting agents are involved. For example, it is possible that a less powerful agent may well take the crucial action that determines the success or failure of a change. Should the great individual be credited with agency for this act? Multiple agency is difficult to deal with, because it is difficult to know whose intention counts in such cases.

Finally, it is often difficult to trace the impacts of actions, which makes it difficult to ascertain the ultimate impact of a great individual. As has been observed, we tend to attribute results to human agency without asking whether other factors in the situation might have been more important. Outcomes such as economic improvement are attributed to presidential policies, regardless of the role of the economic cycle, and corresponding improvements in a firm's bottom line are attributed to adept management rather than to a rising tide that raises all boats. The same can be said of failures: often there is a search for a scapegoat, a responsible agent, who is the locus for the defeat. In both cases, we face the notorious problem of linking action to outcome when they are mediated by an extremely complex system of people, technology, organizational structure, and contextual factors, among others. Does agency even make sense in such a welter of other causes?

One way of dealing with this problem is to locate agency in the organization, group, work unit, or even industry. This is, in effect, an inversion of the position just discussed and grants characteristics of human agency to collectives or suprahuman entities. This move makes agency manageable—thus sidestepping some of the problems with the previous position—by rolling up the actions of multiple agents and the complexities of the organizational system into a single entity that embodies and contains them, the organization.

Several theories and research traditions take this approach to agency, and they differ mainly in the level of complexity attributed to the agent. One group of perspectives conceives of the organizational agent in fairly simple terms. The adaptive learning approach (chapter 7) models the agent as a simple learning system similar to those in learning theory in psychology: the agent explores its environment, acting and learning in response to positive or negative outcomes. Population ecology and community ecology research (chapters 5 and 8) take organizations as the members of populations or communities and treat each member as operating according to a simple

logic, such as survival or maximizing utility. Resource dependency theory (chapter 5) construes organizational agency as a function of resources possessed and needed.

Other perspectives treat organizational agents in more complex terms, analogous to the human agents highlighted in the great individual approach. In this case, the processes by which the agent operates are not described in explicit terms, but instead the agent is presumed to be so complex that it cannot be fully described in terms of a learning cycle or the rational model. The theories of groups as complex action systems discussed in chapter 3 take this approach. While the nature of group processes can be described, how these processes unfold and the particular set of processes that will occur when a group acts are assumed to be indeterminate, subject to the response of the group to the exigencies of its situation. The institutional theories discussed in chapters 5, 9, and 10 also adopt this approach. Institutions are taken to be complex entities whose histories shape their responses in complex ways. Though regularities in responses to institutional pressures and phases of institutionalization can be identified, these are assumed to be general patterns and each organizational agent is assumed to craft its own response, much like a human agent would construct its own course of action. Theories of cultural change in response to external events (chapter 7) also adopt a complex view of how organizations adapt to events.

Many of these theorists have probably adopted the language of agency for the sake of convenience rather than to posit suprahuman agents. While this may be their intent, rhetorical strategy does contribute to the construction of the theoretical object. The resulting theories construct groups, organizations, and industries as though they were entities making choices and monitoring the outcomes of their activities. There has been a long tradition of debate over whether agency is meaningful at levels other than the human individual (Pfeffer, 1982). Methodological individualists argue that action is not meaningful unless linked to individual human agents. On the other hand, action can be defined in terms of its attributes. Any system that consciously formulates intentions when engaging in new courses of actions, monitors the outcomes of action and adjusts its course accordingly, embeds intentions in routines to minimize the need for deliberation in repetitive everyday activities, and can problematize routines when there is evidence they do not work is by definition doing the same things human agents do. Though they may not have souls, organizations can be agents. This debate began long before this writing and no doubt it will continue long into the future. It is worth noting that those adopting the assumption that groups and organizations are agents may face fundamental questions on the foundations of their theories.

One way to address these questions is to build theory on how collective agency can arise from the activities of human agents. Several theoretical perspectives in this volume tackle this issue. They, too, differ in the degree of complexity they accord the human agents whose actions transform into collective agency. They also differ in whether human agents are treated as the background of collective agency or given prominent status along with collective agents.

Theories based in economics rest on a foundation of rational choice theory that has been developed over the past 150 years. This foundation treats the choice processes of all individual agents as though they were the same, greatly simplifying agency. This is a powerful move that enables whole societies of agents to be aggregated into higher-level economic effects. Theories such as transaction cost economics, industrial economics, and evolutionary economics (chapter 5) are grounded in this form of reasoning, which uses the rational agent as background for theory development. The same can be said for the complex coevolutionary theory of organizational change described in chapter 8 by Baum and Rao. In dealing with populations of groups and organizations, Baum and Rao posit that they all operate according to a similar logic that emphasizes survival and growth.

Other perspectives feature the organization but incorporate a more complex view of human agency as part of the underpinning of organizations. The learning-organizations perspective that builds on the work of Argyris, Schon, and Senge (chapters 4 and 7) focuses primarily on the organization as whole, but it also acknowledges the important role of individual members' analytical, creative, and learning processes in enabling the learning organization to break out of current frames and "learn to learn." This theory still features the organization, and it is not clear exactly how these individual actions and initiatives congregate to the organizational level. Hatch's theory of organizational culture change (chapter 7) conceptu-alizes organizational culture change in terms of processes of manifestation, symbolization, realization, and interpretation—organizational level processes that clearly must be driven by individual agents and articulated in the organizational system.

There are also theories that try to give individuals and organizations equal status. Collective action theories, discussed in chapter 9, address how change initiated by individual agents in the aggregate or critical mass can create organizational change. Interactionism, discussed in chapter 2, also provides a balanced account of how the individual and organization interact as they change. Theories of structuration (chapters 4, 9 and 10) also incorporate both the individual agent and collective agents in their explanations. Finally, one of the best developed current theories that links individual and organizational action is Coleman's (1990) theory of social action, which will be discussed briefly in the subsequent section on levels of analysis.

Several authors in this volume have observed that recent theories of organizational change and innovation are placing increasing emphasis on agency and allowing for greater heterogeneity of action. As this development proceeds, there is a need to clarify further the nature of collective agency and how it relates to human agency. The tendency to treat collective agents as though they were simply human agents writ large should be questioned. It is possible that collective agency operates according to different principles and processes than does human agency. Certainly the work on collective action has some important insights to offer.

It is also important to consider the interaction of different sorts of agents in the production of change. Agents differ in power, in scope of activity, and in whether they are human or collective. How do these disparate agents interact and what are the consequences for change processes? One promising tool to address both issues is agent-based modeling, discussed in chapter 11 (see also McKelvey, 2002). It supports theoretical models of communities of agents, which could be used to explore how individual and collective agents relate and also how agents with different capacities interact. However, agent-based modeling has its limitations, too, when it comes to depicting strong forms of agency. While agent-based models can address issues concerning how system-level consequences emerge from the interaction of multiple agents, they do not capture the meaning of action or its consequences for agents. Interpretive and critical theories such as the theory of structuration or symbolic interactionism are better suited for the study of interpretive processes. Current agent-based modeling systems will need considerable development to deal with meaning and interpretive processes, if they can do so at all (for an optimistic view, see Leveque and Poole, 1998; Poole, 1997).

The past decade has witnessed increasing sophistication in our concepts of agency and the role agency plays in organizational change and innovation, and no doubt this will continue. The multiple levels of agency in contemporary research on change and innovation suggest it is also important to consider the more general issue of levels of analysis, the "space" component of change and innovation.

Levels of Analysis

There is general consensus that organizations are multilevel phenomena. A growing body of scholars holds that adequate theories of organizational phenomena should incorporate concepts from multiple levels and explain the relationships among levels. A small group of scholars has conducted studies incorporating multilevel analysis and some, as this book shows, have developed multilevel theories of organizational change and innovation (e.g., Klein and Koslowski, 2000). Only a few scholars have tackled the problem of how to develop multilevel theories, and fewer still the issues involved in developing multilevel theories of change and innovation.

A splendid analysis by Dansereau, Yammarino, and Kohles (1999) has some important implications for developing multilevel theories of change. They take as their starting point groups of units (individuals, groups, organizations) on a single level of analysis and distinguish three types of groupings:

- A homogenous group is present when all members are merged into a single higher-level unit and act "as one." When we speak of an organization or work unit as a single entity, we are referring to this level of analysis.
- A heterogeneous group is composed of members that are interdependent, but not merged into a single unit. Heterogenous groups may be composed of subgroups or of individuals who are interdependent, yet different and separable from one another.

- A group of independent units consists of independent units who act on their own without reference to the group as a whole.

Dansereau et al. argue that one important type of cross-level change is when one type of group changes into another. For example, a group of independent individuals may be melded into a homogeneous group by a transformational leader. In this case the developing set of units is moving from one level to another as part of the change process. Dansereau et al. differentiate several types of transforming change that can be grouped into two general categories:

- Upward changes occur when lower-level independent units are transformed into heterogeneous or homogenous groups. For example, a leader may create heterogeneous groups of favored and nonfavored members through the LMX process. Upward change also occurs when a heterogeneous group is changed into a homogeneous group, as might occur when a transformational leader unifies divided factions into a cohesive organization.
- Downward changes occur when higher-level homogeneous units are transformed into heterogeneous groups or independent units. For example, a strong culture can be broken into several factions by organizational crises that cause members to assign blame to some parts of the organization and not others. Downward change also happens when a heterogeneous group dissolves into individuals. One commonly observed example of this is the dissolution of an organization or group.

Note that in this case change is occurring in the relationships of units to one another as well as to the units themselves. In moving from a collection of individuals to a cohesive team, for example, the relationships among individuals change, and the individuals themselves may change as well.

Transforming change can be distinguished from cases in which a unit remains at the same level over time and changes within that level. For instance, lifecycle models of the organization are often cast at the same level of analysis, mapping the change over time in the organization. State changes can also be distinguished from cases in which units at one level influence those at another level without a change in state. For example, the organization can change its individual members and both the organizational and individual levels remain "intact."

This suggests that in conceptualizing change across levels, then, we must distinguish state changes (when change occurs through units changing from one type to another) from cross-level influence (when units at one level influence change in units at another level without a state change). State changes involve alterations in the entity undergoing change and have multiple-level implications through bridging or moving through levels. Change through cross-level influence is somewhat more straightforward because the levels remain stable and influence runs from one to the other.

In McGrath and Tschan's theory of groups as complex adaptive systems, levels are kept clearly separate and only cross-level influences are posited. For example, a group's long term project influences its shorter term tasks in a higher- to lower-level relationship. Baum and Rao's theory of coevolution mingles cross-level influence and state change: units at different levels of populations and communities influence each other across levels. In addition, communities may change state over time, as the populations that comprise them enter into relationships with different levels of complementarity and symbiosis. Communities with little symbiosis among populations are more akin to a group of independent units (and hence are weaker communities), whereas those with tighter linkages are more like heterogeneous or homogeneous groups (and hence stronger communities).

The fact that both types of changes may occur in the same change process presents a challenge for theory and research on change and innovation processes. It increases the complexity of theories and the problems that empirical research must cope with. This is highlighted even more when we consider the role of time.

Time

Time is the "ether" of change. We judge that change has occurred against the background of time. We use metrics on this background for assessing when changes occur, the rate of change, and the extent of change, and also to establish the opposite of change, stability. As important as time is to the study of change and innovation, until recently it has remained as obscure as the ether of classical physics.

Time is a profound and daunting subject, but it is important to engage it. While we are far from understanding the full import of time in research on change and innovation, several frameworks and studies of time and its role in organizations have been advanced (Ancona, Okhuysen, and Perlow 2001; Barkema, Baum, and Mannix, 2002; Goodman, Ancona, Lawrence, and Tushman 2001; McGrath and Kelly, 1986; McGrath and Rotchford, 1983). These highlight several key issues: What is the nature of time? What is its role in theories of change and innovation? How do we best capture time as a metric and construct in our theories?

The nature of time is a problem as old as philosophy and certainly will not be resolved here. However, it is possible to identify several relevant perspectives on the nature of time based on an influential analysis by McGrath and Kelly (1986).

Newtonian time is the time of classical physics. This perspective assumes time is a linear continuum that is divisible into uniform units that are all equivalent to each other. Time is independent of the objects and people who experience it. Time can be measured objectively, and it is reversible in that it is simply an abstract dimension. A researcher adopting the Newtonian view of time would regard time as a neutral, abstract medium that is external to subjects and organizations and measure it with a clock.

Transaction time is the time of significant events. This perspective regards time as "divisible, but differentiated, with certain points serving as 'critical values' (e.g. birth, metamorphosis, cell division, etc.)" (McGrath and Kelly, 1986, p. 33). The observer is critical in determining these key points, and therefore time is dependent on the observers operating within it. Significant events are determined not by a uniform measure with respect to a background that can be unitized mathematically, but by what the observer notices or believes is significant. The flow of time is irreversible and temporal succession is seen as a developmental process. A researcher adopting the transactional view of time would measure it by identifying events critical or significant to subjects. In some cases this is done "from the outside" by the researcher who defines the critical events, which may be major turning points (e.g., an organizational crisis or a performance evaluation) or more commonplace events (e.g., each interaction the employee has with her manager or each statement made by an group member during a decision-making discussion). In other cases this is done "from the inside" by having subjects indicate which events are significant to them, as Van de Ven, Polley, Garud and Venkatraman (1999) did when they interviewed members of innovation teams, asking them to identify significant events. Each occurrence of the critical or significant event demarcates a time unit in the transactional view.

Dominant cultural time is similar to the Newtonian conception of time, but the flow of time is regarded as unidirectional rather than bidirectional. Whereas the Newtonian conception of time is suited to a physical world independent of human concerns, the dominant cultural time perspective adds the human dimension to the Newtonian view. Humans, living irreversible lives, use precise metrics to divide up and measure time but also see time as a progression that goes through regular cycles. A researcher working with this perspective on time would use socially meaningful metrics, such as the calendar, which measures time in equal units that are socially meaningful such as the day or the week. This approach has been adopted by most social scientific research that regards time as an objective medium. For example, in longitudinal analysis it is common to adopt the day, week, or month as a basic unit of analysis.

Organizational time combines Newtonian and transactional views. A precise metric is needed to co-ordinate activity, but significant events are scattered along the continuum and give it meaning. Time is unidirectional, but also developmental, in that people work to accomplish tasks that take time to unfold and develop as they are carried out. This perspective assumes that people and organizations orient themselves to common externally defined time scales such as calendars, but also experience critical and significant events that interact with the objective temporal scale. Much of the research that focuses on life cycle or stage models employs this view of time. The development of people, groups, organizations, and industries is measured using both external metrics such as days, weeks, months, or years and the stages that indicate meaningful periods of activity.

Each of these perspectives has important implications for theories of organizational change and innovation. The Newtonian conception of time is most likely to be associated with theories that regard time as a background or medium for processes rather than an active part of the theory itself. On the transactional and organizational concepts, time is re-garded as meaningful and therefore becomes part of the theory itself. Both the dominant cultural and organizational views of time seem to capture the nature of organizational change and development better than either the Newtonian or transactional views. The key players in these processes, human beings, have con-structed precise systems for the measurement of time but use them in a social worlds composed of sig-nificant junctures, goals, and milestones. However, natural affinities aside, all four perspectives on time can be found in this volume.

Implicit within each perspective on time are no-tions on how time can be incorporated into theories of change and innovation. We can distinguish four roles that time may play in organizational theory and research. Most commonly, time figures as a medium in theories of change and innovation processes. On this view—most commonly associated with the Newtonian perspective but implicit in the transac-tional perspective as well—time is treated as a trans-parent background for other phenomena that are the primary focus of the investigation. Temporal metrics imposed on this medium are used to generate units for longitudinal analysis and scales for establishing duration and change versus stability. Such metrics vary in precision, from the fine, evenly spaced units required for time series analysis to the more granular and approximate units of case studies and ethno-graphies. While metrics may seem more pertinent to measurement, the multiple types of metrics im-plicated in the study of change and innovation makes this a theoretical issue (Zaheer, Albert, and Zaheer, 1999). We will consider the complexity of metrics later in this section.

Time may also serve as a variable in theories of change and innovation. The role of time as medium is directly related to its role as variable, because the

Table 1.4 Key distinctions related to time in theories of change and innovation

Perspectives on Time	Time's Role in Theory	Time Scales
Newtonian	medium	existence interval
transactional	variable	validity interval
dominant-cultural	predisposition	observation interval
organizational	social construction	recording interval
		aggression interval

same metrics applied in the study of other phenomena can be used to transform time into an independent, dependent, or moderating variable. When time is an independent variable, the duration or passage of time is a factor in change. For example, Gersick's well-known study (1989) found that project teams often experience a midpoint transition in which they reorganize and rethink their task strategies. Theories of how time changes individuals (Woodman and Dewett, chapter 2), group development (McGrath and Tschan, chapter 3), evolutionary economics (Lewin et al., chapter 5), and institutional change (Hinings et al., chapter 10) employ time as an independent variable. When time is a dependent variable, the duration or passage of time is used as an indicator of key events. Event history analyses of organizational failure rates (see Baum and Rao, chapter 8), for example, predict length of time to failure with various factors that explain organizational demise. When time is a moderating variable, the causal effects of other independent variables are assumed to change as a function of time. For example, Agarwal, Sarkar, and Echambadi (2002) report evidence that as an industry matures, the relationships between order of entry and density and firm survival change. In some theories of institutions (Van de Ven and Hargrave, chapter 9; Lewin et al., chapter 5), different factors are important depending on the age of the institutional field.

A third way in which time may enter into theories is in terms of temporal predispositions of people, organizations, and cultures. Time is a fundamental medium of social life and a key variable in the social world, and individuals, groups, organizations, and cultures develop predispositions in their perceptions of, reactions to, and use of time. Several types of predispositions have been incorporated into theories of change and innovation. Individual-level predispositions include time urgency (Waller, Conte, Gibson, and Carpenter, 2001), temporal orientation (past, present, future) (Waller et al. 2001; Zimbardo and Boyd, 1999), and interaction tempo (Warner, 1988). Organizational predispositions include temporal orientation (Lawrence and Lorsch, 1967) and pace (Perlow, Okhuysen, and Repenning 2002). Cultural predispositions include monochronic versus polychronic time (Hall, 1983), present versus future time orientations (Jones, 1988), and pace (Levine, 1988). Different logics of organization (Drazin et al., chapter 6) incorporate different temporal perspec-

tives, as do different national systems (Lewin and Kim, chapter 11).

Finally, time may be socially constructed as part of a change or innovation process. When time is treated as a variable or in terms of temporal predispositions, it is a "free-standing" construct that can be separated from other constructs in the change or innovation process. However, time is so intimately bound up with change and innovation that it is also useful to consider how it might be constructed over the course of the process. Orlikowski and Yates (2002) present a useful perspective on how structuring processes in organizations can be used to construct "a variety of temporal structures which in turn shape the temporal rhythm and form of their ongoing practices" (p. 684). Such structures include schedules, project plans, deadlines, and temporal closures (see also Yakura 2002). While temporal construction is not considered much in this volume, it is implicit in theories of the social construction of institutions (Van de Ven and Hargrave, chapter 9) and groups as activity systems (McGrath and Tschan, chapter 3).

The four roles are not mutually exclusive. Time's role as metric is the foundation for the other three roles, and a theory may incorporate several temporal elements. For instance, the important role of rhythms—recurrent cycles of behavior—in individual, group, and social processes (Warner, 1988) can be studied employing rhythm as independent, dependent, or moderating variable, as a predispositional construct, or as a social construction, and sometimes more than one of these. And this does not mention the essential role of temporal metrics in assessing properties of rhythm. There are also relationships among different temporal constructs. For example, individual and cultural predispositions toward time will influence this social construction process, and they are most likely shaped by it.

Just as with levels of analysis, multiple temporal elements are involved in most change and innovation processes. This is true not just because of the substantive role that time plays in theories of change and innovation, but also because of the complex way in which time enters into human activity. As particularly interesting human activities, building theories and conducting research involve multiple temporal elements as well. Zaheer et al. (1999) develop an insightful analysis of how time scales figure in organizational theory and research. They distinguish five different types of time scales:

1. The existence interval refers to "the length of time needed for one instance of the process, pattern, phenomenon, or event to occur or unfold" (p. 730). This interval may be objectively set—as in the case of the 24-hour period for circadian rhythms—or socially constructed—as in the case of the time a law firm sets for junior associates to make partner.

2. The validity interval refers to the time scale over which a theory holds. For example, circadian rhythms are assumed to hold for all days of the year or life of the organism in question.

3. The observation interval refers to the amount of time the researcher devotes to studying the process, pattern, phenomenon, or event. Typically this must be longer than the existence interval.

4. The recording interval is the length of time each record of the process, pattern, phenomenon, or event spans. Choice of recording interval influences the conclusions researchers can draw about the object of study: a recording interval of 1 minute will produce a very different depiction of the group decision-making process than will one of 6 hours.

5. The aggregation interval represents the choice regarding "over what time scale the recorded information is to be aggregated for theorizing or testing theory about" the process, pattern, phenomenon, or event (p. 731). In many cases aggregating and recording intervals are the same, but if records are combined, then the aggregation interval is longer. As with recording interval, the length of the aggregation interval affects the view of the phenomenon researchers derive.

For example, a study of organizational evolution may posit that the existence interval for one VSR cycle in an industry is the length of one of Kondratieff's long economic waves, while the validity interval is, for all intents and purposes, infinity (i.e., evolutionary theory will be valid for the foreseeable future). Due to the fact that the researcher will utilize economic records for the industry in question, the observation interval is not relevant in this case, but because records are available only for quarters, the recording interval is 3 months. Due to a need to balance questions about the reliability of the records with having enough data to conduct time series analysis, the researcher decides to set the aggregation interval at 6 months.

The first two of Zaheer et al.'s time scales pertain to the conceptualization of the phenomenon or process itself, whereas the last three refer to the researcher's frame of reference. Zaheer et al. argue that the existence interval constrains the other intervals, while the aggregation and recording intervals are typically also constrained by the observation interval.

The existence and validity intervals are boundary conditions for theories of change and innovation in two respects. First, different theories may be required to explain change and innovation over different time scales. For example, organizational evolution theories have been advanced to explain the long-term implications of individual organizational activity; the individual actions of the organizations that comprise the population, which unfold in much shorter time scales, are often explained with rational choice theory (or a nonrational alternative [March 1994]). Second, "the choice of time scale determines not simply which phenomena are observed, but their meaning as well" (Zaheer et al., 1999, pp. 734–735). To continue our example, the meaning of action within the evolutionary and rational choice frames is quite different: Rational choice theory regards each action as an individualized, reflective decision that responds to the exigencies of the situation, whereas evolutionary theory views the same acts as contributing to the organization's survival (or demise) as part of a long-term selection process.

Different studies of the same phenomenon may utilize quite different sets of time scales. Returning to our previous example of evolutionary theory, a different type of study might focus on industries that evolve quite quickly, such as computer chip makers. A researcher might posit that two cycles of Moore's law is the existence interval for a VSR cycle and project the validity of the theory as indefinite. She might devote ten years to direct study of firms as the observation interval and interview each of ten firms bimonthly for a 2-month recording interval. She might then analyze data over three recording periods for a 6-month aggregation interval. The differences between this and the archival study described previously in terms of temporal scale are highlighted by Zaheer et al.'s classifications, as are the different types of insights the researcher are likely to draw.

Zaheer et al.'s framework highlights the complex set of choices researchers make in developing theories and designing studies. When we consider it in light of other ideas discussed in this chapter, further complexities are evident. First, consider the possibility that multiple theories (motors) may operate in any change or innovation process. The two motors (VSR and rational choice) at work within an evolutionary theory are a good example of this. This implies that more than one set of time scales may need to be considered for some theories. Second, Zaheer et al.'s description of temporal scales says nothing about the perspective on time in the theory. Most of their examples refer to clock time and they do not devote much discussion to other perspectives. If we cross the temporal scales with the perspectives on time—e.g., each interval could be expressed in terms of Newtonian, transactional, dominant cultural, or organizational temporal units—the range of temporal possibilities multiplies considerably. Clearly, working out the temporal implications of change and innovation theories is both important and complicated.

Concluding Thoughts

The assumptions that a theory of change and innovation makes about agency, levels of analysis, and time are not always well articulated. Often they are part of the baggage that comes with adoption of certain perspectives and terms. However, there are benefits to explicitly considering these fundamental decision points in developing and testing theories. Deliberate consideration of the conception of levels, agency, and time in a theory encourages both theorists and readers to probe the theory for consistency and to ask what it has omitted. It invites readers to ask whether the theory may be oversimplifying things or, on the other hand, whether it is too complex. It also facilitates comparison and contrast of theoretical positions. While it may difficult to compare a theory of career development to a theory of individual decision making in terms of their respective content, agency, levels, and time represent common denominators for all theories of change, development, and innovation. Comparative analysis of these aspects will show the degree to which the two theories are similar or incompatible in their basic workings. This, in turn, may facilitate the development of integrative positions or the delineation of basic differences among theories of change and innovation. The more conscious of our assumptions and the need to justify them we are, the stronger our theories will be.

Can the time and space elements of change and innovation theories be combined in a single manifold, as is the case in physics? Agents would then operate in a more homogeneous time-space con-

tinuum. While this is an appealing notion, it will not be straightforward to do so. Levels of analysis are not just dimensions of space, but social constructions with unique and sometimes complex structures of their own. For example, rather than just having a "group" level in an organization, there may be various types of groups—work units, informal cliques, cross-functional teams—that are related in complex ways. As this example shows, level is far from a homogeneous construct. As the preceding discussion indicates, the same is true for time. While time and space are as fundamental to the human sciences as they are to the natural sciences, they are more variegated, lumpy, and idiosyncratic in the social world than in the physical world.

Voices Not Heard in This Volume

In developing the contents for this volume, we consulted widely and selected lines of research that had produced a substantial body of work on change and innovation. In so doing, we decided not to include a few research traditions that appeared to have great promise but had not generated much substantive theory on change and innovation. This section will briefly mention two of these areas and acknowledge some relevant work.

Critical and Postcritical Theory

Critical and postcritical (postmodern, feminist, cultural-studies-based) theories have been a rich source of new insights about organizations (e.g., Alvesson and Willmott, 1992; Benson, 1977; Calas and Smircich, 1999; Deetz, 1992; Deetz, 1995; Edwards, 1979; Martin, 1990; Mumby, 1988; Sztompka, 1993). They have directed our attention to the deeper dynamics of power and ideology within and between organizations and to the processes by which voices different from the prevailing power holders are marginalized or silenced. They have offered alternative views of organizations and life in organizations that promise greater fulfillment of human needs and capitalize on the creativity inherent in diversity. It would seem likely that critical and postcritical studies would offer insights into organizational change and innovation.

Marx's classic account of the evolution of society and technology and its subsequent developments

(Sztompka, 1993) remains an important theory of change and innovation at the societal level. Several anthropological theories of culture change with critical elements are reviewed by Hatch in chapter 7. However, the attention of most contemporary critical and postcritical research has seemingly been directed more at explaining why things are and contrasting them with what they could be than with theorizing the change process itself.

The critical enterprise consists, ideally, of three aspects: (1) explanation and critique of current systems and the historical currents that have given rise to them, (2) an alternative vision of organizations and society that resolves the problems and oppressions in the current systems, and (3) an account of how one moves from the current system to the envisioned one, either naturally or through planned change. Critical research on organizations has generally been weakest in terms of this third aspect. No doubt this is due, in large part, to the Sisyphean tasks of explaining the subtle and often hidden means of control that preserve current systems and going beyond them to envision alternatives that are exceptionally difficult to distill and express in terms that make them plausible to most readers. Living in a world dominated by current ideologies and disciplinary practices, many people experience difficulty understanding that there are alternatives, much less accepting them as plausible and attainable. Having devoted extensive labor to developing these two aspects, critical scholars have tended to pay less attention to explaining how one transforms the organization or the process by which transformation takes place. In some cases, there seems to be a presumption that raising subjects' awareness of control processes will be sufficient to effect change. In others, opening up the organization to increase participation is advocated. Models of open discursive processes such as those advanced by Habermas are used to provide models for a truly participative system (Deetz, 1992). But for the most part critical and postcritical work has provided good portraits of what the end point of change should be, but much less insight on change or changing themselves.

An exception to this is the work by Deetz (1992, 1995) on transformation of business organizations into "responsive and responsible workplaces." Like many critical theorists Deetz provides a thorough diagnosis of the problems underlying what he terms "the corporate colonization" of contemporary Western society, along with an excellent historical ac-

count of these problems and why they are resistant to traditional remedies such as unionization and participatory management. Deetz argues that the change process to overcome existing distortions and power structures occurs not through changing structures per se, but by changing how the organization decides what its structures should be and how work should be managed. Deetz, drawing on both critical and postcritical sources, describes an open deliberative process based on a conception of "strong democracy" that is both the ideal end state that change aims for and the means of changing the organization through empowered participation by all members of the organization. Deetz (1995) describes a negotiative organization in which all assumptions are open to challenge, one constantly renewing itself through critical analysis of existing relationships and reorganization so that the organization can meet the unique, locally situated set of goals set by its members and key stakeholders. Such goals are not limited to profit, efficiency, and survival and may include environmental, community building, and personal elements, whatever combination members and key stakeholders arrive at through an open deliberative process.

Postcritical scholarship has followed much the same trajectory as critical studies. Postcritical scholars have problematized the ideal visions of the critical scholars, often substituting multiple perspectives for the idealized vantage point of critical theory and attempting to establish stances in which no position is privileged over any other. Like critical research, these studies have been concerned mostly with analysis of existing organizational phenomena in order to surface silenced or marginalized voices and with articulating alternatives to the taken-for-granted, dominant views. Such analysis is perhaps even more difficult for postcritical scholars than for the critical scholar, because they do not enjoy the benefit of the guiding light that the ideal situation gives the critical scholar. As a result, there has not been much attention to the process of change or of changing organizations.

Postcritical scholars have, however, engaged in much reflection on the grounds of social theory, and this holds insights for the study of change and innovation. One of these, the importance of nostalgia as a reaction to change, will be discussed in the next section. Another insight comes from reflections on the role of time and space in postcritical analysis.

Grossberg (1993) argues that time has, for the most part, been privileged over space in cultural studies. Much cultural studies scholarship focuses on unpacking historical roots of cultural phenomena, and Grossberg argues that this had led to a neglect of the role of space in human existence. He makes the case that spatial separation and proximity are critical to the exercise of power, a fundamental aspect of organizations, and distinguishes three interacting mechanisms that organize power via space: (1) hidden but pervasive processes that foster and maintain value systems and privilege some ways of life and social roles over others, (2) processes by which social identity is created and differentiated, and (3) processes by which resources are unequally distributed among socially constructed groups. All three processes rely on spatial separation and segregation of different social classes who live, work, and play in different places. Without spatial distribution it would be impossible to sustain such differentiations without considerable tension, so space is as fundamental to the development of social structures as time. While Grossberg's analysis is couched in the difficult concepts and language of cultural studies, his contention that modern societies—and the theories that emerge within them—tend to be oriented more toward time than space is worth serious consideration. To take one example, the increasingly popular process approach encourages researchers to explicitly think about time but is largely silent on space.

Though critical and postcritical scholarship has not provided much in the way of theories of organizational change per se, both are premised on the assumption that the social world is comprised of processes, not static entities. Hence, there are many insights for scholars of change and innovation in this body of work. This section has mentioned only a few, and readers are encouraged to explore this literature.

Symbolic and Affective Aspects of Change

In the past decade there has been an upsurge of interest in "noncognitive" aspects of organizations, such as emotions and symbolism (Ashkanasy, Hartel, and Zerbe, 2000; Staw, Sutton, and Pelled, 1994; Whetten and Godfrey, 1998). This interest has also shaped scholarship on organizational innovation or change (e.g., Fiol and O'Connor, 2002; Gioia and Thomas, 1996; Huy, 1999). Current theoretical thinking on organizational change and innovation is dominated by rational, instrumental viewpoints, which tend to neglect or downplay the nonrational side of human experience. This has not always been the case. Early work on organizational change and development by Lewin and the human relations school emphasized affective processes (see chapter 4). It now appears that these concerns are resurfacing in current thinking.

Change and innovation are passionate processes. Successful planned change requires a commitment grounded in an engaging vision and deep emotional involvement with the program. Visions have a cognitive component, but their appeal does not lie in reason. Rather it stems from their connection to participants' desires and identities, connections made through symbolic appeals that index fundamental values. When change occurs, it has an important emotional component because it involves giving up arrangements in which considerable energy and time has been invested. Fiol and O'Connor's (2002) study of community change offers an excellent illustration of the ways in which change affects and is affected by participant's identities and attendant emotional dynamics. They develop a model in which "hot emotional interpretations and relatively colder cognitive interpretations interact to initiate, mobilize, and sustain radical change" (p. 532).

Symbolic and emotional aspects of resistance to change are also in need of study. One example is the concept of nostalgia. Nostalgia, as discussed by postmodernists, is a common reaction to change. It involves an imaginary projection of good characteristics onto the past to recreate a past much better than the present situation. This past is constructed by inversion: undesirable characteristics of the present are mirrored with desirable characteristics of the past, which is then regarded as something to recapture and recreate in the present. Disregarding that "the good old days" were never as good as they are recalled, nostalgia can be a powerful emotional stimulus for resistance and reaction to change and innovation. Exploring the complex web of meaning and interpretation attached to concepts like nostalgia would illuminate aspects of resistance in ways that current rationality-based theories do not.

Greater attention to affect, identity, symbolism, aesthetics, and related subjects would provide a useful balance to change and innovation research. It is important to acknowledge the many sides of human beings and consider how they may figure in starting, sustaining, and resisting change.

Conclusion

This chapter suggests a number of new patterns that could be woven into the tapestry. Doing so will require some unraveling, but as the tapestry is rewoven and grows, it will become even more vibrant and illuminating.

References

Abbott, A. (1988). Transcending general linear reality. *Sociological Theory*, 6, 169–186.

Abernathy, W. J. & Clark, K. B. (1985). Innovation: Mapping the winds of creative destruction. *Research Policy*, 14, 3–22.

Agarwal, R., Sarkar, M. B., & Echambadi, R. (2002). The conditioning effect of time on firm survival: An industry life cycle approach. *Academy of Management Journal*, 45, 971–994.

Alvesson, M. & Willmott, H. (1992). *Critical management studies*. Newbury Park, CA: Sage.

Ancona, D., Okhuysen, G. A., & Perlow, L. A. (2001). Taking time to integrate temporal research. *Academy of Management Review*, 26, 512–529.

Anscombe, G. E. M. (1957). *Intention*. Oxford, UK: Basil Blackwell.

Ashkanasy, N., Hartel, C., & Zerbe, W. (Eds.) (2000). *Emotions in organizational life*. New York: Quorum.

Avolio, B. J. & Bass, B. M. (1995). Individualized consideration viewed at multiple levels of analysis: A multi-level framework for examining the influence of transformational leadership. *Leadership Quarterly*, 6, 199–218.

Axtell, R. (1999). *The emergence of firms in a population of agents*. Santa Fe Institute, paper no. 99-03-019.

Bales, R. F. & Strodtbeck, F. L. (1951). Phases in group problem solving. *Journal of Abnormal and Social Psychology*, 46, 485–495.

Barkema, H. G., Baum, J. A. C., & Mannix, E. A. (2002). Special Research Forum: A New Time. *Academy of Management Journal*, 45, 916–930.

Barley, S. R. (1986). Technology as an occasion for structuring: Evidence from observations of CT scanners and the social order of radiology departments. *Administrative Science Quarterly*, 31, 78–108.

Bartunek, J. (1984). Changing interpretive schemes and organizational restructuring: The example of a re-

ligious order. *Administrative Science Quarterly*, 29, 355–372.

Bennis, W. G. (1966). *Changing organizations*. New York: McGraw-Hill.

Benson, J. K. (1977). Organizations: A dialectical view. *Administrative Science Quarterly*, 22, 1–21.

Calas, M. B. & Smircich, L. (1999). Past postmodernism? Reflections and tentative directions. *Academy of Management Review*, 24, 649–671.

Cameron, K. & Whetten, D. (1983). Models of the organizational life cycle: Applications to higher education. *Review of Higher Education*, 6, 269–299.

Chandler, A. D. (1964). *Strategy and structure*. Cambridge, MA: MIT Press.

Child, J. (1972). Organizational structure, environment, and performance: The role of strategic choice. *Sociology*, 6, 2–22.

Cohen, M. D., March, J. G., & Olsen, J. (1972). A garbage can model of organizational choice. *Administrative Science Quarterly*, 17, 1–25.

Coleman, J. S. (1990). *Foundations of social theory*. Cambridge, MA: The Belknap Press.

Contractor, N. & Grant, S. E. (1996). The emergence of shared interpretations in organizations: A self-organizing systems perspective. In J. H. Watt & C. A. VanLear (Eds.), *Dynamic patterns in communication processes* (pp. 215–230). Thousand Oaks, CA: Sage.

Corman, S. (1996). Cellular automata as models of unintended consequences in organizational communication. In J. H. Watt & C. A. VanLear (Eds.), *Dynamics patterns in communication processes* (pp. 191–212). Thousand Oaks, CA: Sage.

Cyert, R. & March, J. G. (1963). *A behavioral theory of the firm*. Englewood Cliffs, NJ: Prentice-Hall.

Dansereau, F., Yammarino, F. J., & Kohles, J. C. (1999). Multiple levels of analysis from a longitudinal perspective: Some implications for theory building. *Academy of Management Review*, 24, 346–357.

Davison, M. L., King, P. M., Kitchener, K. S., & Parker, C. A. (1980). The stage sequence concept in cognitive and social development. *Developmental Psychology*, 6, 121–131.

Davison, M. L., Robbins, S., & Swanson, D. B. (1978). Stage structure in objective moral judgments. *Developmental Psychology*, 14, 137–146.

Deetz, S. (1992). *Democracy in an age of corporate colonization: Developments in communication and the politics of everyday life*. Albany: State University of New York Press.

Deetz, S. (1995). *Transforming communication, transforming business: Building responsive and responsible workplaces*. Creskill, NJ: Hampton.

Dorcian, P. & Hummon, N. P. (1976). *Modeling social processes*. New York: Elsevier.

Edwards, R. (1979). *Contested terrain: The transformation of the workplace in the twentieth century*. New York: Basic Books.

Farjoun, M. (2002). The dialectics of institutional development in emerging and turbulent fields: The history of pricing conventions in the on-line database industry. *Academy of Management Journal, 45,* 848–874.

Fiol, C. M. & O'Connor, E. J. (2002). When hot and cold collide in radical change processes: Lessons from community development. *Organization Science, 13,* 532–546.

Fisher, B. A. (1970). Decision emergence: Phases in group decision making. *Speech Monographs, 37,* 53–66.

Forrester, J. W. (1961). *Industrial dynamics*. Cambridge, MA: Productivity Press.

Gersick, C. J. (1989). Marking time: Predictable transitions in task groups. *Academy of Management Journal, 32,* 9–41.

Gersick, C. J. (1991). Revolutionary change theories: A multilevel exploration of the punctuated equilibrium paradigm. *Academy of Management Review, 16*(1), 10–36.

Giddens, A. (1979). *Central problems in social theory: Action, structure, and contradiction in social analysis*. Berkeley, CA: University of California Press.

Gioia, D. A. & Thomas, J. B. (1996). Identity, image and issue reinterpretation: Sensemaking during strategic change in academia. *Administrative Science Quarterly, 41,* 370–403.

Goodman, P. S., Lawrence, B. S., Ancona, D., & Tushman, M. (2001). Special topic forum on time and organizational research. *Academy of Management Review, 26,* 507–511.

Goodrich, E. & Salancik, G. (1996). Organizational discretion in responding to institutional practices: Hospitals and caesarean births. *Administrative Science Quarterly, 41,* 1–28.

Greiner, L. (1972). Evolution and revolution as organizations grow. *Harvard Business Review,* 165–174.

Grossberg, L. (1993). Cultural studies and/in New Worlds. *Critical Studies in Mass Communication, 10,* 1–22.

Guastello, S. J. (1987). A butterfly catastrophe model of motivation in organizations. *Journal of Applied Psychology, 72,* 165–182.

Guastello, S. J. (1995). *Chaos, catastrophe, and human affairs: Applications of nonlinear dynamics to work, organizations, and social evolution*. Mahwah, NJ: Erlbaum.

Hall, E. T. (1983). *The dance of life: The other dimension of time*. Garden City, NY: Anchor Press/Doubleday.

Harrison, R. (1970). Choosing the depth of organizational intervention. *Journal of Applied Behavioral Science, 6,* 182–202.

Huber, G. P. & Van de Ven, A. H. (1990). Longitudinal field research methods for studying processes of organizational change. *Organization Science, 1,* 213–335.

Huy, Q. N. (1999). Emotional capability, emotional intelligence, and radical change. *Academy of Management Review, 24,* 325–345.

Jones, J. M. (1988). Cultural differences in temporal perspectives: Instrumental and expressive behaviors in time. In J. M. McGrath (Ed.), *The social psychology of time* (pp. 21–38). Newbury Park, CA: Sage.

Kashy, D. A. & Kenny, D. A. (1999). The analysis of data from dyads and groups. In H. T. Reis & C. M. Judd (Eds.), *Handbook of research methods in social psychology* (pp. 451–477). London: Cambridge University Press.

Kauffman, S. (1993). *The origins of order: Self-organization and selection in evolution*. New York: Oxford University Press.

Kauffman, S. (1995). *At home in the universe*. New York: Oxford University Press.

Klein, K. J. & Koslowski, S. W. J. (2000). *Multilevel theory, research, and methods in organizations: Foundations, extensions, and new directions*. San Francisco: Jossey-Bass.

Kuhn, T. & Poole, M. S. (2000). Do conflict management styles affect group decision-making? Evidence from a longitudinal field study. *Human Communication Research, 26,* 558–590.

Lacoursiere, R. B. (1980). *The life cycle of groups: Group developmental stage theory*. New York: Human Sciences Press.

Langley, A. (1999). Strategies for theorizing from process data. *Academy of Management Review, 24,* 691–710.

Langley, A. & Truax, J. (1994). A process study of new technology adoption in smaller manufacturing firms. *Journal of Management Studies, 31,* 619–652.

Latane, B. (1996). Dynamic social impact: The creation of culture by communication. *Journal of Communication, 46,* 13–25.

Lawrence, P. W. & Lorsch, J. W. (1967). *Organization and environment*. Boston: Harvard University Press.

Leik, R. K. & Meeker, B. F. (1975). *Mathematical sociology*. Englewood Cliffs, NJ: Prentice-Hall.

Leonard-Barton, D. (1990). A dual methodology for case studies: Synergistic use of a longitudinal single site with replicated multiple sites. *Organization Science, 1,* 248–266.

Leveque, C. & Poole, M. S. (1998). Systems thinking in organizational communication inquiry. In P. Salem (Ed.), *New directions in organizational communication research* (pp. 79–98). Creskill, NJ: Hampton.

Levine, R. V. (1988). The pace of life across cultures. In J. M. McGrath (Ed.), *The social psychology of time* (pp. 39–60). Newbury Park, CA: Sage.

Lomi, A. & Larsen, E. R. (1996). Interacting locally and evolving globally: A computational approach to the dynamics of organizational populations. *Academy of Management Journal*, 39, 1287–1321.

Lomi, A. & Larsen, E. R. (1999). Evolutionary models of local interaction: A computational perspective. In J. A. C. Baum & B. McKelvey (Eds.), *Variations in organization science: In honor of Donald T. Campbell* (pp. 255–278). Thousand Oaks, CA: Sage.

March, J. G. (1994). *A primer on decision making.* New York: Free Press.

Martin, J. (1990). Deconstructing organizational taboos: The suppression of gender conflict in organizations. *Organization Science*, 1, 339–359.

Mathieu, J. G., Heffner, T. S., Goodwin, G. F., Salas, E., & Cannon-Bowers, J. (2000). The influence of shared mental models on team process and performance. *Journal of Applied Psychology*, 85, 273–283.

Mayer, K. U. & Tuma, N. B. (1990). *Event history analysis in life course research.* Madison, WI: University of Wisconsin Press.

McGrath, J. M. & Kelly, J. R. (1986). *Time and human interaction: Toward a social psychology of time.* New York: Guilford.

McGrath, J. M. & Rotchford, N. (1983). Time and behavior in organizations. In L. Cummings, & B. Staw (Eds.), *Research in organizational behavior* (Vol. 5, pp. 57–101). Greenwich, CT: JAI Press.

McKelvey, B. (1999). Self-organization, complexity, catastrophe and microstate models at the edge of chaos. In J. A. C. Baum & B. McKelvey (Eds.), *Variations in organization science: In honor of Donald T. Campbell* (pp. 279–307). Thousand Oaks, CA: Sage.

McKelvey, B. (2002, October 3). Sending evolutionary entrepreneurial research the way of the dodo bird by replacing Darwin with Schumpeter and Benard. Paper presented at the Journal of Business Venturing Conference: Evolutionary Approaches in Honor of Howard Aldrich.

McPhee, R. D. & Poole, M. S. (1981). Mathematical models in communication research. In M. Burgoon (Ed.), *Communication yearbook* (Vol. 5). New Brunswick, NJ: Transaction Books.

Meyer, A. G., Goes, J. B., & Brooks, G. G. (1993). Organizational reacting to hyperturbulence. In G. P.

Huber & W. Glick (Eds.), *Organizational change and redesign.* New York: Oxford University Press.

Miles, M. & Huberman, A. M. (1994). *Qualitative data analysis.* Newbury Park, CA: Sage.

Mintzberg, H. (1973). *The nature of managerial work.* New York: Harper & Row.

Mintzberg, H., Raisinghani, D., & Theoret, A. (1976). The structure of "unstructured" decision processes. *Administrative Science Quarterly*, 21, 246–275.

Mohr, L. (1982). *Explaining organizational behavior.* San Francisco: Jossey-Bass.

Morrison, E. W. (1993). Longitudinal study of the effects of information seeking on newcomer socialization. *Journal of Applied Psychology*, 78, 173–183.

Mumby, D. (1988). *Communication and power in organizations: Discourse, ideology, and domination.* Norwood, NJ: Ablex.

Nutt, P. C. (1984). Types of organizational decision processes. *Administrative Science Quarterly*, 29, 414–450.

Orlikowski, W. J. & Yates, J. (2002). It's about time: Temporal structuring in organizations. *Organization Science*, 13, 684–700.

Pentland, B. (1999). Building process theory with narrative: From description to explanation. *Academy of Management Review*, 24, 711–724.

Perlow, L. A., Okhuysen, G. A., & Repenning, N. P. (2002). The speed trap: Exploring the relationship between decision making and temporal context. *Academy of Management Journal*, 45, 931–955.

Pettigrew, A. (1985). *The awakening giant: Continuity and change at ICI.* Oxford, UK: Basil Blackwell.

Pettigrew, A. (1990). Longitudinal field research on change: Theory and practice. *Organization Science*, 1, 267–292.

Pfeffer, J. (1982). *Organizations and organization theory.* Cambridge, MA: Ballinger.

Poole, M. S. (1981). Decision development in small groups I: A test of two models. *Communication Monographs*, 48, 1–24.

Poole, M. S. (1983). Decision development in small groups, III: A multiple sequence model of group decision development. *Communication Monographs*, 50, 321–341.

Poole, M. S. (1997). A turn of the wheel: The case for a renewal of systems inquiry in organizational communication research. In G. Barnett & L. Thayer (Eds.), *Organization-communication: Emerging Perspectives V, the renaissance in systems thinking* (pp. 47–64). Norwood, NJ: Ablex.

Poole, M. S. & Roth, J. (1989a). Decision development in small groups IV: A typology of decision paths. *Human Communication Research*, 15, 323–356.

Poole, M. S. & Roth, J. (1989b). Decision development in small groups V: Test of a contingency model. *Human Communication Research, 15,* 549–589.

Poole, M. S., Van de Ven, A. H., Dooley, K., & Holmes, M. E. (2000). *Organizational change and innovation processes: Theory and methods for research.* New York: Oxford University Press.

Quinn, J. B. (1980). *Strategies for change: Logical incrementalism.* Homewood, IL: Irwin.

Rogers, E. (1995). *Diffusion of innovations.* New York: Free Press.

Romanelli, E. & Tushman, M. (1994). Organizational transformation as punctuated equilibrium: An empirical test. *Academy of Management Journal, 37,* 1141–1166.

Saberwhal, R. & Robey, D. (1993). An empirical taxonomy of implementation processes based on sequences of events in information system development. *Organization Science, 4,* 548–576.

Saberwhal, R. & Robey, D. (1995). Reconciling variance and process strategies for studying information system development. *Information Systems Research, 6,* 303–327.

Schein, E. (1992). *Organizational culture and leadership* (2nd ed.). San Francisco: Jossey-Bass.

Smith, K. K. & Berg, D. N. (1987). *Paradoxes of group life.* San Francisco: Jossey-Bass.

Staw, B., Sutton, R. I., & Pelled, L. H. (1994). Employee positive emotion and favorable outcomes at the workplace. *Organization Science, 5,* 51–71.

Sterman, J. (2000). *Business dynamics: Systems thinking and modeling for a complex world.* New York: Irwin.

Sztompka, P. (1993). *The sociology of social change.* Oxford, UK: Blackwell.

Tushman, M. & Romanelli, E. (1985). Organizational evolution: A metamorphosis model of convergence and reorientation. In B. Staw & L. Cummings (Eds.), *Research in organizational behavior* (Vol. 7, pp. 171–222). Greenwich, CT: JAI Press.

Van de Ven, A. H. & Grazman, D. N. (1999). Evolution in a nested hierarchy: A genealogy of Twin Cities health care organizations, 1853–1995. In J. A. C. Baum, & B. McKelvey (Eds.), *Variations in organizational science: In honor of Donald T. Campbell* (pp. 185–212). Thousand Oaks, CA: Sage.

Van de Ven, A. H. & Polley, D. (1992). Learning while innovating. *Organization Science, 3,* 92–116.

Van de Ven, A. H., Polley, D., Garud, R., & Venkatraman, S. (1999). *The innovation journey.* New York: Oxford University Press.

Van de Ven, A. H. & Poole, M. S. (1995). Explaining development and change in organizations. *Academy of Management Review, 20,* 510–540.

Von Wright, G. H. (1971). *Explanation and understanding.* Ithaca, NY: Cornell University Press.

Waller, M. J., Conte, J. M., Gibson, C. B., & Carpenter, M. A. (2001). The effect of individual perceptions of deadlines on team performance. *Academy of Management Review, 26,* 586–600.

Warner, R. (1988). Rhythm in social interaction. In J. E. McGrath (Ed.), *The social psychology of time* (pp. 63–88). Newbury Park, CA: Sage.

Weick, K. & Quinn, R. E. (1999). Organizational change and development. *Annual Review of Psychology, 50,* 361–386.

Whetten, D. & Godfrey, P. C. (Eds.). (1998). *Identity in organizations: Building theory through conversations.* London: Sage.

Yakura, E. (2002). Charting time: Timelines as temporal boundary objects. *Academy of Management Journal, 45,* 956–970.

Yin, R. (1984). *Case Study Research.* Beverly Hills, CA: Sage.

Zaheer, S., Albert, S., & Zaheer, A. (1999). Time scales and organizational theory. *Academy of Management Review, 24,* 725–741.

Zimbardo, P. G. & Boyd, J. N. (1999). Putting time in perspective: A valid, reliable, individual-differences metric. *Journal of Personality and Social Psychology, 77,* 1271–1288.

2

Organizationally Relevant Journeys in Individual Change

Richard W. Woodman & Todd Dewett

It is axiomatic that changing individual knowledge, attitudes, and behavior is key to effective organizational change. That is, it is not possible for the organization to change in meaningful ways unless employees change—people must believe differently, they must think differently, and they must behave differently. Thus, the role of the individual actor in group and organizational change has been explored at length through a variety of theoretical models or lenses (e.g., Van de Ven and Poole, 1995; Weick and Quinn, 1999; Woodman, 1989). What is much less explored, however, is the reverse of the individuals-change-organizations perspective. Organizations change the people who reside in them. These changes occur in many ways, both subtle and not so subtle. The purpose of our chapter is to develop a theoretical lens through which to explore the effects that organizations have on individuals—the ways that organizations change their employees.

Our perspective on behavior—both individual behavior and organizational behavior—is an interactionist one. The behavior of a person at any point in time is a complex mixture of person and situation.

Elsewhere, we described this interactionist perspective as follows:

Imagine a bird in a cage. This situation contains both the idea of "bird" and an easily definable current reality within which the bird finds itself. In this instance, the environmental press explains most, if not all, of the bird's behavior. Having accounted for 100% of the variance with the situation, is there anything left to say regarding the bird and its behavior? Indeed, there is; in fact, perhaps everything of importance remains to be explained. In other words, a careful description of the situation and the bird's responses to its environment does not begin to explain the behavior of all birds, all of the time. What other things might the bird do if the situation changed? Why might the bird do these things? For starters, we could imagine (armed as we are with other information) that the bird may well fly if the environmental constraint of "cage" is removed. From an interactionist position, there is always something more to understanding behavior than just describing the observed behavior per se. This "something more" has to do with the essence of the organism and its behavioral potentiality. (Woodman and Schoenfeldt, 1989, p. 79–80)

An interactionist perspective on organizational behavior and organizational change suggests the importance of understanding reciprocal influences in the change process. Further, the interactionist lens suggests the importance of behavioral potentiality—the developmental journeys both individuals and organizations undertake. As individuals act on their environment to effect change, so too does the organizational environment change those working within it.

As we said, organizations change people in many ways. We will explore some of the major sources or antecedents of this change in this chapter: socialization processes, training, supervisory and managerial influences of subordinates, and effects of the organizational change process itself on participants in the change journey. First, we will define what we mean by "individual change." Individual change includes changes in behavior and changes in both cognitive and noncognitive individual difference characteristics. Then we will develop a model that identifies and explains the role of the organization in creating individual change. Finally, we will explore the implications of and use of our model in change management and research on organizational change.

Individual Change in Organizational Settings

Deeply embedded in organizational folklore is the notion that employees do not really change in meaningful ways. Indeed, this belief mirrors some commonsense notions in society regarding change. "You can't teach an old dog new tricks" and similar sentiments suggest that individuals never really change much. Despite the stability in personality and other individual differences across time, conventional wisdom with regard to individual change is actually somewhat wide of the mark. People do change, and they do so in fairly predictable ways during the entire course of their lives (Hellervik, Hazucha, and Schneider, 1992). Work experiences are an important part of the complex mosaic of influences that shape and move individual cognitions, motivations, beliefs, attitudes, some aspects of personality, and so on over time. We need to understand more about such influences within the wider context of organizational change.

We define individual change within organizations as changes in behavior (e.g., job performance), and changes in individual characteristics (e.g., job knowledge, job attitudes, job motivation) that are relevant to organizational functioning and effectiveness. As such, we intend to limit our discussion of individual change to the work setting, recognizing that such changes are only a portion of those experienced by people during their lives.

There are three dimensions of individual change in particular that we want to explore: the changeability of individual characteristics and behaviors, the depth of the changes, and the time involved in the changes. By *changeability* we refer to the degree to which or the ease by which some characteristic might be changed. By *depth*, we refer to the magnitude of changes—how far the new behavior or changed characteristic is from its original value. By focusing on *time*, we attempt to capture the process of change and recognize that different changes take differing amounts of time. Every behavior and every individual characteristic (a personality trait, an attitude, and so on) can be examined in terms of its degree of changeability. Also, every change in these variables could be evaluated in terms of its depth and the amount of time that unfolds during the process of changing.

The three dimensions are interrelated, however an important difference in them should be noted. Changeability is an aspect or feature of the individual characteristic or behavior being addressed. Depth and time, in contrast, can be considered as an aspect of the change process that the individual characteristic or behavior is undergoing. Despite this difference, we posit that all three dimensions act similarly as modifiers of the effects of organizational influences on individual change.

Changeability

Characteristics of individuals may vary markedly with regard to their changeability. For example, the relative stability versus changeability of various aspects of personality has been the subject of extensive research focus for some time (cf. Caspi and Roberts, 1999). Personality theories often distinguish between peripheral and core personality traits with peripheral traits being the most changeable during the course of an individual's life (Funder, 2001; Pervin and John, 1999). It is well established that strong attitudes are more resistant to change than weaker ones (Ajzen,

Table 2.1 Example of a hypothetical, partial hierarchy of changeability

Individual Change	Changeability	
	Higher	Lower
behavior	task-specific behavior	norm-regulated behavior
cognitive	knowledge about a specific task	knowledge about the organization's culture
affective	job satisfaction	job commitment
conative	extrinsic motivation	intrinsic motivation

2001; Wood, 2000). Some cognitive aspects of the mind are very stable (e.g., general intelligence), while others, such as some task-specific knowledge, are more readily changed (Lubinski, 2000; Markman and Gentner, 2001). Hellervik et al. (1992) argued strongly that the changeability of individual characteristics is a key notion in terms of understanding behavior change in organizational settings. They advocated the establishment of and research into a "hierarchy of changeability" in order to advance our knowledge of behavioral change stemming from organizational training among other issues. We are not going to develop such a hierarchy in detail in this chapter, although table 2.1 provides an example of the insights that might be developed by such an approach.

In table 2.1, we list four varieties of individual change (behavioral change, cognitive change, affective change, and conative change, to be discussed shortly) and contrast higher degrees of changeability with lower degrees of changeability on each of these factors. For example, changes in some task-specific behavior are easier, and perhaps more likely, than are changes in some norm-regulated behavior. The social dimension of the latter behavior makes it more resistant to change. In the same sense, knowledge that an employee has about a specific task in her job is more changeable than knowledge about some complex aspect of organizational life such as organizational culture. The attitude of job satisfaction is generally considered to be more changeable than the attitude of job commitment. Commitment is typically more stable than satisfaction and less likely to vary with day-to-day events (Hellriegel, Slocum, and Woodman, 2001, p. 54). From an interactionist perspective, an argument can be made that extrinsic motivation, as a

function of the rewards available in a given situation, has a higher degree of changeability than does intrinsic motivation, which is more strongly related to core personality dimensions and values of the person. We will have more to say about changeability throughout the chapter. At this point we simply suggest that changeability is important in our model in the following fashion:

> Proposition 1: The changeability of individual characteristics and behaviors moderates the influence of the organization on individual change.

Depth of Change

Over thirty years ago, Roger Harrison (1970) popularized the notion of "depth of change" in an attempt to better understand the effects of planned change interventions on organizations. While Harrison was, in a sense, treating depth as a contextual variable descriptive of certain aspects of change programs, we employ a similar term in an attempt to further our understanding of the effects of organizations on individual change. As with the changeability construct, changes in behaviors and characteristics of employees can vary with regard to their magnitude. For example, it is one thing to slightly alter some procedural aspect of job behavior; it is something else again to completely change the behaviors that must be employed in order to complete a task. Similarly, we can imagine how an organizational socialization program might slightly alter one attitude of an employee while dramatically altering another attitude while leaving other attitudes totally unaffected. Further, an influence that might create deep change in some characteristic of a particular individual may have less influence on the same characteristic of other employees. It makes sense that we need a way to talk about the richness, complexity, and magnitude of individual change—its depth. We posit that:

> Proposition 2: The depth of individual change "required" by a specific organizational influence (e.g., a socialization attempt, a training program) moderates the impact of the organization on individual change.

Time

Pettigrew, Woodman, and Cameron (2001) have argued that notions of time are sorely needed in theory and research about organizational change processes. Indeed, to adequately investigate processes of change means that we must include sequences of individual and collective activities, actions, and events as they unfold over time. The same argument holds, logically, for individual change processes. Thus, we need to incorporate the dimension of time into our understanding of individual change.

Further, from an interactionist perspective, we are particularly interested in the reciprocal influences between person and situation as behavior unfolds over time. Including the time dimension provides an opportunity to focus on change processes, both individual and organizational, consistent with our interactional framework. A good example of the importance of investigating both individual and organizational change across time is provided by the work of Engleman and Van de Ven (2002). Using both quantitative and qualitative methodology, they explored individual (physicians', nurses', and staff) responses to organizational change within a health care environment. Engleman and Van de Ven uncovered virtuous, vicious, and ambivalent cycles in participants' interactions during the change journey, as some employees became empowered, some disenfranchised, while yet others withdrew from the change process. Only longitudinal work would have any hope of teasing out such rich behavioral patterns.

In sum, how long change processes take to unfold is a key variable in our model. We posit:

Proposition 3: The time "required" by a specific organizational influence—the length of the change process—moderates the impact of the organization on individual change.

The Role of the Organization in Creating Individual Change

Some of the ways that organizations change their employees are intentional and programmatic (e.g., a change intervention designed to improve job performance), and some of them are accidental (e.g., unintended consequences of a supervisor's behavior toward a subordinate). In figure 2.1, we suggest that individual change is created by the organization's socialization processes, by training programs utilized in the organization, by a variety of planned programmatic efforts to improve organizational functioning (change interventions), and by the myriad of day-to-day influences stemming from interpersonal interactions with managers and supervisors. These influences can alter the individual behavior and individual difference characteristics of employees. It is these alterations that we are defining as individual change. These four sources of individual change

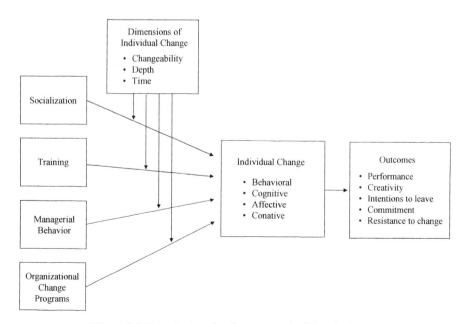

Figure 2.1 Organizational influences on individual change.

do not exhaust the possibilities, but we posit that they capture a significant portion of the variation in changed behaviors and characteristics.

A fundamental property of the model is worth noting at this point. The congruency or incongruity among these organizational sources of influences could have a big impact on individual responses to them. For example, organizational socialization processes and training programs could induce congruent changes in individual characteristics or behaviors. The interaction of congruent forces could strengthen their effects. Similarly, such influences could work at cross-purposes, reducing their potential for change. In addition, incongruent forces could create situations of felt conflict in employees, thus leading to a variety of negative outcomes including heightened stress, lowered job satisfaction, and the like. Individual responses to incongruent situations seem particularly important to understand. We will have more to say about the potential congruency/incongruity among these influence categories later, when we discuss implications for organizational research and change management practice.

In figure 2.1 we adopt the schema advanced by Ackerman and Humphreys (1990) with regard to categorizing individual differences as cognitive (e.g., mental abilities, knowledge), affective (e.g., personality, attitudes), and conative (e.g., motivation). Finally, as stated in propositions 1, 2, and 3, we posit that the dimensions of changeability, depth, and time moderate the effects of the organizational antecedents on individual change.

We will address each of the four major categories of organizational sources of individual change in turn in the following sections of the chapter.

Organizational Socialization

Socialization may be characterized as a change process (Fisher, 1986). This process is said to occur in different stages (Feldman, 1976; Louis, 1980; Van Maanen, 1975) utilizing an array of tactics (Van Maanen and Schein, 1979) to address different content needs (Chao, O'Leary-Kelly, Wolf, Klein, and Gardner, 1994). Among the outcomes of individual change affected by socialization are changes in job satisfaction, commitment, turnover, role innovation, learning, job performance, role clarity, role stress, and so on (Bauer, Morrison, and Callister, 1998). Thus, socialization is seen to be a very complex and important phenomenon.

It is often the case that socialization research has addressed newcomers to an organization in terms of how newcomers perform their role. However, Ashforth and Saks (1996) provided a key insight into understanding the role of socialization in actually creating change in the individual. They state that the literature on socialization has neglected to move past addressing the changes in the way a newcomer performs a role to examine changes in the newcomer as a person. They define person change in the context of work adjustment as alterations in the new employee's values, attitudes, personality, and career plans. Given that core aspects of the self, such as values and personality, are fairly resistant to change, they suggest that socialization primarily influences the more labile self.

Bauer et al. (1998) concur and suggest that socialization has a strong and potentially enduring impact on the behaviors of employees who remain with the organization. Behaviorally, socialization has the potential to instruct newcomers how to approach their job tasks. What methods are used? Which resources? Undoubtedly, one of the key aspects of any socialization process is the indoctrination of a new employee into a new set of skills. Affectively, socialization has the potential to influence new employees as well. For example, Louis, Posner, and Powell (1983) found that interactions with peers, supervisors, and senior coworkers were among the most important socialization practices and were positively related to various newcomer job attitudes. Beyond these important attitudes lies a cognitive aspect of socialization: the way new employees form a mental understanding of their new roles and their new organization. To the extent that tangible elements (e.g., goals) and intangible elements (e.g., cultural symbols and stories) of the workplace are communicated, the employees will begin to form a personal understanding of their jobs, their coworkers, and their organization (Louis, 1980). In terms of motivation, conative change may be vital given that socialization processes tend to be finite in duration. The amount of motivation the employees experience during socialization will serve as a foundation for their moving forward. For example, during socialization, employees first learn about the types of goals that will guide their work as well as the nature of effort-outcome relationships in the organization.

When one considers socialization from the perspective of the moderators shown in figure 2.1, it becomes apparent that socialization as a source of individual change may offer several advantages over other potential agents of change. As noted earlier, some individual characteristics are more readily changeable than others (e.g., Caspi and Roberts, 1999). Among those characteristics that are changeable, socialization offers a unique opportunity to mold the individual in a way that aids both the newcomer as well as the organization. Consider the case of the employees' mental framework for understanding their jobs and the organization. At no time will the organization be more able to affect these cognitions than during the socialization process, given that as employees develop within their roles, mental sets become more concrete and potentially resistant to change.

In terms of depth of change, it would seem that during socialization the opportunity to make deeper and more meaningful impressions is higher than at any other time. This logically follows from the premise that as employees develop a foundation of experiences and thoughts, the degree to which a given organizational effort can change their perception (or attitude, behavior, and so on) will decrease. Thus when employees are new, and have not yet developed their own repository of organizational experiences, the socialization process affords the opportunity to create a deeper level of change.

Using similar logic, it is likely that the time dimension is important also in terms of the effects of socialization processes. Processes of individual change that require only short amounts of time would seem to be those most likely affected by, at least, early socialization experiences in the organization. While socialization might set in motion, so to speak, longer change processes, it is more problematic that these individual changes are most effectively made by socialization influences. To the extent that depth and time are strongly related (i.e., deeper changes take longer) for some individual change, then the effects of socialization would seem somewhat unpredictable. On balance, however, by definition socialization is something that happens before an individual becomes part of the organizational culture; thus individual change requiring longer amounts of time would be less amenable to processes of socialization than would change requiring shorter amounts of time.

It is well established that newcomers engage in proactive behaviors to learn about their work environments (e.g., Ashford and Black, 1996; Morrison, 1993a, 1993b). During proactive socialization, newcomers may seek out role—or referent—information, feedback information, social information (Miller and Jablin, 1991), and organizational information (Ostroff and Kozlowski 1992). However, Bauer and Green (1998) point out that research on the most typical proactive behavior, information seeking, has tended to study this process without examining other socialization mechanisms. In addition, socialization researchers have long contended that organizational incumbents, especially the managers of newcomers, seek to provide guidance and information to the new entrants (e.g., Ashford and Black, 1996). Building on Jones's (1983) and Reicher's (1987) interactionist view of socialization, Bauer and Green (1998) moved a step further to assess managers as proactive partners in newcomer socialization and found that while information seeking is important, certain managerial behaviors also have a strong influence on newcomers.

From an individual change perspective, this work brings into focus the long-term efficacy of socialization. It must be noted that over time newcomers may become less receptive to institutionalized socialization practices and more receptive to a variety of other stimuli in the workplace (Ashforth and Saks, 1996). After socialization practices have provided whatever amount of acculturation they can achieve, more specific skills and needs, in terms of individual change initiated by the organization, will often be facilitated by other means including training, organizational change programs, and managerial behaviors.

In short, socialization is significantly related to a number of key individual outcomes (Bauer et al., 1998). This process can affect several vital facets of the employee's work experience, including job performance, professional relationships, and the employee's understanding of the organization's culture (Chao et al., 1994). As such, following figure 2.1, we provide the general proposition that:

Proposition 4: Socialization processes in organizations are an important source of influences for individual change.

Training in Organizations

Training is a form of systematic and structured learning. Aside from copious scholarship that examines the efficacy of training, its popularity is seen in industry as well, with companies spending in the billions each year for everything from teaching new employees to read to the development of executive skills (Eurich, 1985). Some authors suggest that the general trend is toward employees spending even more time in training situations in the future due to the rapid pace of technological developments in the world economy and the additional skills these developments require of workers (Goldstein, 1991).

The training process can be defined as the systematic acquisition of attitudes, concepts, knowledge, rules, or skills that result in improved performance at work (Goldstein, 1991, 1997). From the perspective presented in figure 2.1, this implies behavioral, cognitive, and affective individual change. In addition, motivation is also considered an integral aspect of training (Goldstein, 1991), here referred to as conative change. Given this definition, one might suggest that training bears much in common with socialization, the important difference being that socialization is associated with a particular time in the employee's relationship with the organization and is intended to serve the broad goal of assimilation or acculturation of the employee into the organization. Training, on the other hand, typically refers to more specific learning goals that often have a more applied intent relative to socialization. Nonetheless training, like socialization, is often applied when employees are first transitioning into an organization or into a new role within the organization. Organizations have many forms of training at their disposal, including management training and development, various forms of behavioral role modeling, simulations, and so on.

One approach to conceptualizing how an organization can enact change in individuals through training is offered by Goldstein (1986). The process begins with a needs assessment, which is required to establish both the training program and the evaluation model used to assess the program. The needs assessment phase of the training process highlights the issue of how organizations can enact change in individuals (cf. Salas and Cannon-Bowers, 2001). Managers responsible for training must complete a needs assessment at the organizational level, the task level, and the person level (McGehee and Thayer, 1961). Person analysis asks two questions (Goldstein, 1991): Who within the organization needs training, and what kind of instruction do they need? Clearly, there will be a close tie between the appraisal system and the person-needs assessment, which can be conducted as part of the larger performance appraisal process or separately.

Beyond the task of assessing individual needs as an antecedent to individual change through training, the organization faces another challenge—constructing a training environment conducive to learning. One might suggest that to apply traditional learning principles to modern training would be effective, yet this is often not the case. The clear gap between learning theory and application has led many scholars to call for a new theoretical link between the laboratory and the applied setting (Goldstein, 1991). To this end Howell and Cooke (1989) have suggested that identifying types of tasks and skills might only be a first step and that needs assessments may require the further step of determining the types of cognitive processing and learning that are required to perform the task in question. Hence, subsequent work has advanced a cognitive perspective. For example, Mathieu, Heffner, Goodwin, Salas, and Cannon-Bowers (2000) found that task- and team-based mental models positively predicted team processes and performance and suggested that training interventions were among the most important tools for enhancing shared cognitions in work groups.

In fact, the training-related literature as a whole has grown significantly in recent years (Salas and Cannon-Bowers, 2001). Several new theoretical approaches and empirical findings have emerged. For example, Ford, Kozlowski, Kraiger, Salas, and Teachout (1997) have developed "the opportunity to perform" concept as a means of understanding the transfer of training process. Colquitt, LePine, and Noe (2000) provided an integrated model of training motivation. Cannon-Bowers and Salas (1997) provided a framework for understanding performance measurement in training.

In terms of figure 2.1, Howell and Cooke's (1989) comments draw attention to the different forms of individual change noted above. However, regardless of the form of individual change addressed, a more fundamental concern is the need to consider the dimensions of individual change. In terms of changeability, the key aspect of training is the needs assessment. Stated simply, effective training requires extensive analysis of training needs at the organizational level, task level, and person level (McGehee and Thayer, 1961). Key to the success of any needs assessment will be the recognition of which needs are changeable and to what degree. Earlier we noted that some individual characteristics are not readily changeable (e.g., general intelligence), while others are more easily changed (e.g., task-specific knowledge). Thus, managers would be well served to consider the changeability of the various task-specific skills, weighing the importance of each against the likelihood of positive change resulting from training.

In terms of depth of change and the time needed for the change process to unfold, training faces unique challenges compared to the other organizational sources of individual change noted here, given the removed nature of most training environments. That is, aside from on-the-job training, most training programs take place outside of an employee's actual job. Thus, when a training period has ended, the ultimate depth and time required for individual change is yet to be determined. How deep or rich a training-initiated change will be and how long it will require can be addressed from the perspective of the training transfer climate. Goldstein (1991) notes several elements of a successful transfer climate that will aid in achieving increased depth and decreased time. For example, existing managers can endeavor to make sure that newly trained employees have an opportunity to use their training immediately, they can provide training aids on the job to support the employee's training, and they can have newly trained employees share their learning with coworkers. Research in this area has even begun to look backward in the process to consider in-training conditions that enhance transfer (Thayer and Teachout, 1995).

In summary, this area of inquiry has moved from early definitions of needs analysis (McGehee and Thayer, 1961) to more recent theoretical advances (e.g., Thayer and Teachout, 1995) and empirical examinations (e.g., Colquitt et al., 2000). The recent review provided by Salas and Cannon-Bowers (2001) makes it clear that while we have a great deal to learn about training, we have made significant progress toward understanding how training produces change in individuals. Thus, following figure 2.1, we offer the following general proposition:

Proposition 5: Training programs in organizations are an important source of influences for individual change.

Organization Change Programs

Organizational change programs often include changes in individual behaviors and characteristics among their change targets (see also chapter 4). As we stated in the opening paragraph of this chapter, it is not really possible to change organizations in any truly meaningful sense unless organizational participants perform their jobs differently, change their thinking or attitudes in ways that support the needed changes, and so on. Indeed, changes in individual behavior have traditionally been viewed as the central focus of change efforts by many in the field of organizational change and development. For example, Porras and Robertson stated: "Change in the individual organizational member's behavior is at the core of organizational change and, therefore, any successful change will persist over the long term only if, in response to changes in organizational characteristics, members alter their on-the-job behavior in appropriate ways" (1992, p. 724). However, it is quite important to note that the planned changes in individual behaviors and characteristics that may be part of an organizational improvement effort are only a portion of the effects of interventions into organizations. Other changes, both unintentional and perhaps unknown, can occur. Further, it is meaningful to conceptualize the intentional changes as both direct and indirect. That is, an intervention focused directly on changing a specific behavior or individual characteristic may also, indirectly, change other individual differences or behaviors. For example, a conflict-resolution workshop that successfully changed a participant's conflict-handling styles and skills might also alter the person's communication behaviors. We would argue that the changed communication skills and behaviors were not a direct target of the change program, but neither was it really unintentional; hence we describe the changed communications as an intentional, indirect change. The point of this discussion is that we need to think deeply about the complexity of the individual changes engendered by organizational change programs. Often such changes are treated in a rather simplistic manner, even in relatively sophisticated research studies.

There are many interventions specifically designed to create change in organizational members (cf. Cummings and Worley, 2001; French and Bell, 1999). It is not our purpose to catalogue these here, but we would like to relate some broad categories of interventions to the individual change that we are examining. McMahan and Woodman (1992), building on the work of Friedlander and Brown (1974), categorized change interventions in U.S. firms as falling into four basic types: human processual, technostructural, strategic planning, and systemwide change programs. Human processual interventions are those that emphasize interpersonal working relationships, team building, work-team dynamics, process consulting, and conflict resolution. Technostructural interventions are focused on sociotechnical systems, task and technology work designs, and group and organization structure. Strategic planning interventions are those involving strategic planning processes, strategic change or visioning, and typically emphasize top management involvement. Systemwide change programs are characterized by an emphasis on leadership, culture, quality improvement, and organizational transformation.

Of these four categories of interventions, the human processual interventions are the most likely to have individual characteristics, such as job attitudes or motivation levels, as direct targets of change. Changes in individual behavior are perhaps more likely to be indirect, albeit still intentional, change goals. Technostructural interventions are very likely to have targeted individual behavior while changes in characteristics of employees may be more likely to be indirect change targets in this family of interventions. Systemwide change programs, as defined here, include a rather wide array of both micro and macro foci suggesting that both behavior and individual characteristics are often change goals. Cultural change programs, for example, frequently directly target both behaviors and individual characteristics (job attitudes in particular). Of these categories, strategic planning interventions seem the furthest removed from a focus on individual change. While we certainly would expect some focus on employee characteristics and behavior, individual changes may be more often indirect rather than direct targets of the change effort. Of course, these are very broad generalizations and it would not be surprising if an intervention in any category was not particularly consistent with this broad-brush analysis.

In terms of the changeability dimension, organizational change programs may follow the same logic already discussed for training programs. That is, targeting change efforts at behaviors and characteristics with a reasonable prospect of success makes sense. There are some complications, however, that keep organizations from focusing exclusively on changeability. For one, there are potential ethical issues confounded with the changeability criterion (cf. Stephens, D'Intino, and Victor, 1995). Just because a

characteristic is attractive in terms of easy changeability does not mean that it is ethical or wise to attempt to change it. For example, due to limited education about such matters, an employee might hold relatively unsophisticated attitudes about the importance of protecting the environment. An organization intent on inappropriately exploiting the environment might attempt to change employee attitudes that are perceived as standing in the way of this strategy. Many individual characteristics (e.g., core personality traits) are outside the realm of what organizations should be doing in change programs.

Harrison (1970), writing about organizational change programs, offered the notion that one should intervene at a level no deeper than that needed to achieve success. The same suggestion would seem sensible to follow in terms of targeting individual change. On the other hand, an organization cannot select individual behaviors and characteristics to target simply because they are highly changeable, not too deep, and don't require much time. To approach things this way would be to ignore the effectiveness criterion. Change programs are designed to improve organizational functioning and effectiveness. Thus, behaviors and characteristics of employees that will result in needed improvement are going to become change targets even when they are not highly changeable and may require deeper and more time-consuming efforts.

The effects at the individual level stemming from formal change programs have been extensively documented. Not surprisingly, the unintended effects stemming from planned organizational change are less well known. However, a full accounting of the effects of the organization on individual change would need to recognize and explain such unintended consequences as well. We expect that formal change programs, though operating primarily in the service of organizational development rather than individual development goals, nevertheless provide a significant amount of the impetus for individual change.

Thus, both developed theory regarding the importance of creating sustained organizational change through changes in individual attitudes and behavior (e.g., Porras and Robertson, 1992; Woodman, 1989) and a significant body of published research showing the extent of individual change associated with planned organizational change efforts (e.g., Cummings and Worley, 2001; Porras and Hargis,

1982; Robertson, Roberts, and Porras, 1993; Woodman and Sherwood, 1980) support the logic of figure 2.1. This can be summarized as:

Proposition 6: Interventions designed to improve organizational functioning and effectiveness are an important source of influences for individual change.

Managerial Behavior

Aside from the formally established vehicles of change an organization might employ, there is another, more subtle, stimulus to individual change: ongoing managerial behavior directed toward subordinates. Every employee has some amount of interaction each day, some level of professional relations, with one or more relevant supervisors. These relationships hold the potential to spur individual change. Specifically, we are referring to overt behaviors directed from a superior to a subordinate within the scope of their professional relationship. To illustrate, below we will briefly consider three common managerial behaviors: feedback, granting autonomy, and support/encouragement.

Copious research has established performance feedback as a valuable resource that influences motivation and behavior for both individuals and groups (e.g., Annett, 1969; Fedor, 1991; Ilgen, Fisher, and Taylor, 1979). Feedback is most valuable for improving performance when it provides information useful for choosing specific performance-enhancing behaviors (Ashford and Cummings, 1983). The exact nature of the effect of feedback depends on the nature of the task's quality and quantity interdependence as well as whether feedback functions to direct behavior or to motivate it (Locke, Cartledge, and Koeppel, 1968). When serving to direct behavior, feedback aids in learning the correct response, as compared to its motivation function, which serves to stimulate action (Ilgen and Moore, 1987).

Thus, within the boundaries of figure 2.1, it is clear that feedback serves to influence both behavioral and conative individual change. Behaviorally, to the degree that feedback is constructive and prescriptive, specific data will be accumulated by employees over time that direct their behavior toward increased performance. Conatively, to the degree that feedback provides knowledge of results, feedback offers motivation to the individual that is necessary to engender continued and/or increased effort. For example, work requiring creative outcomes often requires great persistence (Amabile, 1996), highlighting the importance of the motivational aspect of feedback. This is not to say that these are the only forms of individual change associated with the use of feedback. For example, it stands to reason that affective change in the form of changed attitudes may result. When we consider feedback from the perspective of being supportive or not supportive it becomes clear that one's attitude toward several objects (e.g., the task, one's supervisor, the organization) may be influenced.

A manager's use of autonomy presents another common managerial behavior that we believe may influence individual change. In the most general sense, autonomy refers to the degree to which a task provides substantial freedom, independence, and discretion to individuals in determining the procedures to be used in carrying out a task (Hackman and Oldham, 1980). Hackman and Oldham's (1976) job characteristics model suggests that autonomy supports one's experienced responsibility for the outcomes of the work. It has been suggested that the use of autonomy not only leads to feelings of ownership or responsibility, but that it leads to valued outcomes such as creativity (e.g., Amabile, 1996; Zhou, 1998). In the context of creativity, such an effect is thought to occur by causing conative change in the individual, specifically, that autonomy positively relates to intrinsic motivation—one's inherent enjoyment of the task predicated on feelings of competence and self-determination (Deci and Ryan, 1985). Behaviorally, this motivation often takes the form of increased experimentation and exploration of alternative methods for completing one's work (Amabile and Gryskiewicz, 1987).

As an example of how ongoing managerial behaviors lead to affective individual change, consider the notion of supervisory support and encouragement. Staying with the example of creativity as an outcome, encouragement and supportive communication are among the most frequently mentioned facilitating factors for creativity (Amabile, Conti, Coon, Lazenby, and Herron, 1996). In general, encouragement and enthusiasm for risk taking and idea generation at all levels of the organization has been a recurring theme (e.g., Abbey and Dickson, 1983; Amabile, 1988). Why is this so? While it may be true that communication of this sort may produce conative change over time such that individuals experience increased motivation, a more proximal explanation may be the influence of support and encouragement on affective individual change. Simply stated, when a positive environment is fostered, employees are less likely to experience the fear of negative criticism that can undermine the intrinsic motivation necessary for creativity (Amabile et al., 1996).

Returning to figure 2.1, it is interesting to consider how each of these types of managerial behaviors may be affected by the dimensions of individual change: changeability, depth, and time. For example, the most pronounced effects of these moderators may be manifest in the case of feedback. Behaviorally, specific task-related actions would be most changeable due to the prescriptive nature of feedback. However, in terms of depth of change and the required time for change, a decidedly interactionist perspective is required. One can imagine that the degree to which feedback is effective in producing change in individuals is somewhat dependent on individual differences such as ability as well as task characteristics such as complexity.

In the case of autonomy and support/encouragement, the role of these three moderators is less immediate. Although we are not aware of research that examines these issues from the perspective of changeability, depth, and time, we can speculate as to their role. The challenge of understanding the role of these moderators in this context is that the potential of autonomy or support/encouragement to effect individual change evolves over some period of time. Thus, significant changeability and depth are likely possible only over longer durations as relationships develop, suggesting that the length of the change process may be key. Nonetheless, these managerial behaviors clearly deserve attention as antecedents to individual change given their long-term availability, unlike, say, socialization, which tends to exist over more finite periods of time.

Maintaining a focus on an interactionist perspective, it is clear that several individual differences will influence the relationships between these antecedents and the different forms of individual change. For example, research suggests that employees vary in the degree to which they actively seek information (e.g., Callister, Kramer, and Turban, 1999). This suggests that in the case of one who actively seeks feedback, any changes associated with this information may occur quicker as compared to more passive recipients of supervisor feedback. Or consider the case of autonomy, which is thought to support conative individual change in the form of intrinsic motivation. Given that initial levels of intrinsic motivation will vary from employee to employee during the early stages of their relationship with their supervisor, it stands to reason that when one's initial level of intrinsic motivation is low, changeability may be higher, depth deeper, and time shorter.

In short, three key ideas highlight the importance of managerial behaviors as a source of change in individuals. First, there are scores of managerial behaviors that may influence individual employees. Above, we briefly considered three—feedback, autonomy, and support/encouragement. In addition, one might examine work monitoring (George and Zhou, 2001), efforts made to include employees in decision making (Wagner, 1994), and the use of rewards and recognition (Livingstone, Nelson, and Barr, 1997), just to name a few. Next, it is interesting to note that many of these managerial behaviors have not been considered from the perspective of change in individuals. Instead, each is shown to be related to one or more valued employee outcomes (e.g., work attitudes, work behaviors, and so on). While this general approach clearly has strong merit, our understanding of individuals in organizations may advance further by considering the broader influence of these behaviors on individuals (e.g., a more careful consideration of the change dimensions of changeability, depth, and time). Finally, it bears mentioning that as compared to the other organizational sources of individual change explored earlier, managerial behaviors represent the most enduring source. That is, while socialization, training, and change programs are all basically finite in duration, managerial behaviors are better characterized as a constant. Thus, in summary, figure 2.1 suggests:

> Proposition 7: The behavior of managers and supervisors is an important source of influences for individual employee change in organizational settings.

Implications for Research on Organizational Change

We heartily endorse the call by Hellervik et al. (1992) for research on a "hierarchy of changeability." Hellervik et al. were particularly interested in measuring the relative changeability of individual characteristics because of the implications for organizational training. As they argued, individuals could benefit by targeting their own development efforts at characteristics with a reasonable chance of success, and organizations could design training programs such that the probability of accomplishing its training goals was enhanced. There would be implications for personnel selection as well. By the same logic, developing a hierarchy of changeability of the individual characteristics included in figure 2.1 would have important implications for the organizational change arena. As discussed previously, change programs typically have both direct and indirect effects on individual behavior and characteristics. Valid information concerning the changeability of individual differences and behavioral patterns would be of immense value when designing change programs. One is struck by how parallel this argument is to the justification for using force field analysis (Lewin, 1951). That is, an established strength of force field analysis, when used in organizational diagnosis, is its potential for identifying aspects of the situation (whether resistances or pressures for change) that can be changed and aspects that cannot. At the risk of stating the obvious, conventional wisdom has long seen the advantages of change agents and work groups focusing their efforts on aspects of the situation amenable to change.

The development of reliable and valid information concerning a hierarchy of changeability of individual characteristics could be furthered by meta-analyses of the existing literature. We have a wealth of (admittedly somewhat fragmented) knowledge about outcomes of interventions into organizations. Many of the documented outcomes of organizational change efforts could be framed within the parameters of figure 2.1. Changes in various attitudes and work behaviors have frequently been assessed, for example. Less common are measured changes in motivation levels, personality traits, and so on. In addition, there is a tradition of research within the psychological sciences devoted to the assessment of the consistency or stability of human characteristics over time (e.g., Conley, 1984). Meta-analytic work could conceivably combine results from these two literatures to develop a valid hierarchy of changeability. Of course, additional research could be designed to fill in the inevitable gaps that will be discovered in the extant literature.

A valid hierarchy of changeability would need, of course, to go far beyond the simple observations

of table 2.1. For example, considerable evidence exists with regard to the changeability of various attitudes including those most salient for performance in organizational settings. A developed hierarchy of changeability, then, might include an array of affective characteristics with supporting evidence for their relative rankings in terms of changeability. The same could be true of various cognitive characteristics, various "types" of work behavior, and so on.

Earlier we stated that an important property of the model shown in figure 2.1 is the attention called to the possibility of congruency and/or incongruity among the organizational sources of influences on individual change. The advantages of socialization processes, organizational training programs, and planned change efforts being harnessed in a congruent manner in the service of desired employee change are obvious. In addition, it is easy to imagine the potential problems and reduced effectiveness created by incongruent efforts in any of these domains. Having made these obvious observations, it also appears that there is a considerable amount that we don't know about both how to create the desired congruency and how to avoid incongruence that reduces the probability of desired changes. While good management practice is often commonsense—and such would seem to be the case here, in part—nevertheless investigation of the conditions for and effects of congruency and incongruity would seem to be a fruitful avenue of inquiry for organizational researchers. In particular, the impact on individual change stemming from conflicting "signals" and how organizational participants perceive and adapt to this incongruity would seem to define a promising research agenda.

Learning theory represents a theoretical framing that seems particularly relevant to the ideas explored here, as we mentioned earlier in the discussion of organizational training. By extension, theory and writing concerning concepts of learning organizations also represents a potentially useful line of inquiry that could contribute to a deeper understanding of individual change within complex social systems. Learning organizations, by definition, have the capacity for effective change and also possess the ability to develop the people working within them (Burgoyne, 1998). The learning organization construct provides a rich tapestry or theoretical frame that could serve to integrate the developing knowledge about individual and organizational change. Further, the learning organization as a conceptual device or organizational metaphor is already well integrated into the literature of organizational change (e.g., Lundberg, 1989; Mohrman and Mohrman, 1997; Purser and Pasmore, 1992). Linking the learning organization with notions of individual change journeys within such organizational environments seems a promising arena for further work.

Finally, we advocate that research and writing focused on investigations of individual change stemming from organizational influences can profitably be framed by an interactionist perspective that allows for theorizing and research across levels of analysis. As mentioned earlier, Engleman and Van de Ven (2002) provide a good example of the value of examining both individual and organizational change, and their reciprocal influences, within the same study. In our model (figure 2.1), we posit that organizational socialization processes and planned organizational change processes, among other influences, impact individual characteristics and behaviors. An examination of such cross-level influences requires a multilevel, interactionist approach. Further, we argue that cross-level influences, such as those shown in figure 2.1, often provide much of the explanatory power in an interactionist context (cf. Woodman, Sawyer, and Griffin, 1993). Certainly, most of the organizational sciences have matured to such an extent that crossing levels of analysis in theorizing and research is no longer considered invalid. However, our point is not just that it is acceptable to do this; rather, we maintain that it is essential to do this.

Implications for Change Management

Pettigrew et al. (2001) argued for a renewed commitment to bridging the gap between the theory and practice of organizational change. They espoused a deeper "engagement" between scholars and practitioners in the change arena by, among other things, recognizing that researchers and management practitioners are—or need to be—cofunders, coproducers, and codisseminators of knowledge gained from and about organizations. Woodman (1993) has argued that the schism between the science of organizational change and the practice of changing organizations is the single biggest impediment to progress in effective change management. So, how do we bridge the gap? How do we get beyond slogans and high-minded ideals and actually bring scientific

inquiry and change management practice into a constructive symbiosis? There is no easy answer to this question, nor is there a single answer. A partial answer obviously lies in the application of knowledge generated by organizational research to real problems of change management. Change management experience, in turn, can be used to generate questions worthy of investigation. Quality research is often largely a function of asking the right questions. Yet another partial answer is to think seriously about the implications of our theory for designing and managing complex organizational changes. Toward these ends, we have some specific suggestions and observations for change management that stem from the ideas explored here.

The notion that effective change must be systemwide is well established in the change and development arena. While this notion is so widely accepted as to become almost reified, it is interesting to note that recent, careful systematic empirical work has supported its validity. For example, the Innovative Forms of Organizing (INNFORM) program of research conducted in Europe concluded that there was a strong association between whole system change and firm performance. (Whole system change was defined as changing structures, work processes, and boundaries among parts of the firm.) Firms that typically made partial changes (for example, changing organizational structure, but not processes or boundaries) revealed a negative association between change efforts and performance (Pettigrew and Fenton, 2000; Pettigrew, Massini, and Numagami, 2000). This finding is bolstered by meta-analytic work in North America that found that significant improvement following change programs requires congruent changes in a wide array of organizational variables (Robertson, Roberts, and Porras, 1993) and typically utilizes multiple change levers (Macy and Izumi, 1993). There are really two related implications from these and other related research studies: (1) Effective organizational change requires systemwide efforts, not piecemeal approaches, and (2) the changes in various aspects (or subsystems) of the system must be congruent. This latter implication is certainly consistent with our earlier discussion of the importance of congruency among the organizational influences on individual change highlighted in figure 2.1. In terms of our model, if change managers wanted to optimize the positive aspects of organizational influences on individual changes, then they would pay particular attention to the congruency issue by insuring (to the extent possible) that socialization processes, management and supervisor coaching and teaching, formal organizational training programs, and the like were reinforcing the needed behavioral and characteristics (e.g., job attitudes) changes and not working at cross-purposes. This is obviously easier said than done. But recognizing the importance of congruency is, at least, a beginning. Further, the systemwide aspect of figure 2.1 suggests that more powerful positive change may well stem from the use of many programs, processes, and change levers. Research and theory would strongly suggest that to rely too extensively on a single influence program (for example, organizational training) is unlikely to be as effective as more coordinated, programmatic efforts in multiple areas.

As a related point, training in organizations is most effective when tightly coupled with needed changes in individual (and group) behavior and characteristics. While this is hardly a new or earth-shattering observation, conducting organizational training programs that are, in fact, relatively disassociated from many important aspects of organizational functioning continues to be a pervasive problem (Woodman and Pasmore, 2002). The model shown in figure 2.1 and the ideas explored here provide further argument for tightly tying organizational training into needed individual and organizational change efforts.

Resistance to change is a phenomenon of more than passing interest to change management. The dimensions of individual change that we have explored here (changeability, depth, and time) could provide a meaningful approach to further understanding of resistances in organizations. For example, Piderit (2000) reconceptualizes resistance to change as attitudinal and argues that resistance to change can be considered as negative emotional, cognitive, and intentional responses to change. In terms of figure 2.1, resistance might be highest when dealing with individual characteristics and behaviors that are the least changeable, and the required change processes that are deepest and take the greatest amounts of time. In general, a richer understanding of resistance to change could be fostered by theory and research on organizational influences on individual change. And in terms of the practice of change management, a better understanding of resistance can facilitate effective change at both the individual and organizational level. Perhaps the constructs of changeability, depth,

and time provide change managers and researchers with additional "vocabulary" to utilize when exploring resistance to change.

Yet another critical dynamic for change management is captured by the construct of commitment. Commitment in the organization can be meaningfully conceptualized as a generalized job attitude related to the strength of organizational attachment, the desire to continue association with the organization, and the willingness to invest energy in pursuing organizational goals (Guest, 1998). An individual's commitment is one of the characteristics that can be affected by the antecedent conditions identified in figure 2.1. We see commitment as a crucial "change lever" in organizational improvement. Further, Armenakis, Harris, and Feild (1999) identified commitment as a key factor in institutionalizing organizational changes. An organization can develop an effective new strategy. It can acquire cutting-edge technology. It can fine-tune its production processes, decision processes, information gathering processes, and so on. It can redesign its jobs in the most clever manner possible, but all of this will fail without committed human actors to make things happen. Individuals must be committed to make the task design, the structure, the strategy, and the technology work. Absent this commitment, nothing happens. The ideas explored here, when investigated further, may shed additional light on the crucial commitment variable and how commitment might be developed in employees, thus improving both our ability to manage change and the ability of organizational participants to lead valuable, productive work lives.

Finally, it is not possible to address either individual or organizational change without confronting ethical issues. Just as the field needs to understand the change journeys undertaken by organizational employees, so too might individuals benefit from having a keener appreciation of the potential impact that organizations might have on their behavior, and cognitive and noncognitive characteristics. Can organizations have influence that is detrimental to individual health and well-being? To what extent do individuals understand and agree to the changes they undergo, either as part of organized improvement efforts or simply in the course of day-to-day interactions with the organization? Do people really appreciate what they are "signing up" for when spending a significant portion of their life in the organization? Not only should we be concerned with which changes matter the most in terms of organizational performance and effectiveness, we need to worry about which changes matter the most in terms of individual psychological health, job satisfaction, stress, and so on. These questions represent important issues that must be addressed in any comprehensive attempt to fully understand organizationally relevant journeys in individual change.

Concluding Comments

In sum, figure 2.1 represents the ideas presented about organizational influences on individual change at work. We posit that many of the important organizational antecedents of individual change can be captured by the categories of organizational socialization processes, organizational training, organizational change programs, and various managerial behaviors that contribute to employee change both intentionally and unintentionally. The effects of these influences are moderated by three dimensions of individual change that we also have discussed at length: changeability, depth, and time. Individual change encompasses both changes in behavior and changes in cognitive, affective, and conative characteristics of the person.

We suggest that understanding the change journey in complex organizations requires a duality of theorizing and research that extends across the organizational and individual levels of analysis. At the end of the day, to grasp the totality of organizational change involves understanding the changes that individual participants in the organization are undergoing during their time in the system. Just as individuals change organizations, and no meaningful organizational change is possible unless individuals change their behaviors, their attitudes, their thinking, and so on to effect and sustain the change, so too do organizations change those who reside in them. Until we understand these individual change journeys, we will only understand organizational change in incomplete and partial ways.

Note

We would like to thank the coeditors of this volume, Scott Poole and Andy Van de Ven, as well as our colleagues Adrienne Colella and Bill Pasmore, for comments and suggestions on earlier drafts of this chapter.

References

Abbey, A. & Dickson, J. W. (1983). R&D work climate and innovation in semiconductors. *Academy of Management Journal*, 26, 362–368.

Ackerman, P. L. & Humphreys, L. G. (1990). Individual differences theory in industrial and organizational psychology. In M. D. Dunnette & L. M. Hough (Eds.), *Handbook of industrial and organizational psychology* (2nd ed.) (Vol. 1, pp. 223–282). Palo Alto, CA: Consulting Psychologists Press.

Ajzen, I. (2001). Nature and operation of attitudes. In S. T. Fiske, D. L. Schacter, & C. Zahn-Waxler (Eds.), *Annual review of psychology* (Vol. 52, pp. 27–58). Palo Alto, CA: Annual Reviews.

Amabile, T. M. (1988). A model of creativity and innovation in organizations. In B. Staw & L. L. Cummings (Eds.), *Research in organizational behavior* (Vol. 10, pp. 123–167). Greenwich, CT: JAI Press.

Amabile, T. M. (1996). *Creativity in context*. Westview Press.

Amabile, T. M., Conti, R., Coon, H., Lazenby, J., & Herron, M. (1996). Assessing the work environment for creativity. *Academy of Management Journal*, 39, 1154–1184.

Amabile, T. M. & Gryskiewicz, S. S. (1987). *Creativity in the R & D laboratory*. (Technical Report no. 30). Greensboro, NC: Center for Creative Leadership.

Annett, J. (1969). *Feedback and human behavior: The effects of knowledge of results, incentives, and reinforcement on learning and performance*. Baltimore, MD: Penguin Books.

Armenakis, A. A., Harris, S. G., & Feild, H. S. (1999). Making change permanent: A model for institutionalizing change interventions. In W. A. Pasmore & R. W. Woodman (Eds.), *Research in organizational change and development* (Vol. 12, pp. 97–128). Stamford, CT: JAI Press.

Ashford, S. J. & Black, J. S. (1996). Proactivity during organizational entry: A role of desire for control. *Journal of Applied Psychology*, 81, 199–214.

Ashford, S. J. & Cummings, L. L. (1983). Feedback as an individual resource: Personal strategies for creating information. *Organizational Behavior and Human Performance*, 32, 370–398.

Ashforth, B. E. & Saks, A. M. (1996). Socialization tactics: Longitudinal effects on newcomer adjustment. *Academy of Management Journal*, 39, 149–178.

Bauer, T. N. & Green, S. G. (1998). Testing the combined effects of newcomer information seeking and manager behavior on socialization. *Journal of Applied Psychology*, 83, 72–83.

Bauer, T. N., Morrison, E. W., & Callister, R. R. (1998). Organizational socialization: a review and directions for future research. In G. R. Ferris (Ed.), *Research in personnel and human resource management* (Vol. 16, 149–214). Greenwich, CT: JAI Press.

Burgoyne, J. (1998). Learning organization. In C. L. Cooper & C. Argyris (Eds.), *The concise Blackwell encyclopedia of management* (p. 359). Oxford, UK: Blackwell Publishers.

Callister, R. R., Kramer, M. W., & Turban, D. B. (1999). Feedback seeking following career transitions. *Academy of Management Journal, 42,* 429–438.

Cannon-Bowers, J. A. & Salas, E. (1997). Teamwork competencies: The interaction of team member knowledge, skills, and attitudes. In H. F. O'Niel (Ed.), *Workforce readiness: Competencies and assessment* (pp. 151–174). Mahwah, NJ: Erlbaum.

Caspi, A. & Roberts, B. W. (1999). Personality continuity and change across the life course. In L. W. Pervin & O. P. John (Eds.), *Handbook of personality: Theory and research* (2nd ed.) (pp. 300–326). New York: Guilford Press.

Chao, G. T., O'Leary-Kelly, A. M., Wolf, S., Klein, H. J., & Gardner, P. (1994). Organizational socialization: Its content and consequences. *Journal of Applied Psychology, 79,* 730–743.

Colquitt, J. A., LePine, J. A., & Noe, R. A. (2000). Toward an integrative theory of training motivation: A meta-analytic path analysis of 20 years of research. *Journal of Applied Psychology, 85,* 687–707.

Conley, J. J. (1984). The hierarchy of consistency: A review and model of longitudinal findings on adult individual differences in intelligence, personality and self-opinion. *Personality and Individual Differences, 5,* 11–25.

Cummings, T. G. & Worley, C. G. (2001). *Organization development and change* (7th ed.) Cincinnati, OH: South-Western College Publishing.

Deci, E. L. & Ryan, R. M. (1985). *Intrinsic motivation and self-determination in human behavior.* New York: Plenum.

Engleman, R. & Van de Ven, A. (2002). Individual responses to organizational change: virtuous, vicious, and ambivalent transition cycles. Paper presented at the national meeting of the Academy of Management, Denver, Colorado.

Eurich, N. P. (1985). *Corporate classrooms.* Princeton, NJ: Carnegie Foundation.

Fedor, D. B. (1991). Recipient responses to performance feedback: A proposed model and its implications. In G. R. Ferris & K. M. Rowland (Eds.), *Research in personnel and human resources management* (Vol. 9, pp. 73–120). Greenwich, CT: JAI Press.

Feldman, D. C. (1976). A contingency theory of socialization. *Administrative Science Quarterly, 21,* 433–452.

Fisher, C. D. (1986). Organizational socialization: An integrative review. In K. M. Rowland & G. R. Ferris (Eds.), *Research in personnel and human resources management* (Vol. 4, pp. 101–145). Greenwich, CT: JAI Press.

Ford, J. K., Kozlowski, S., Kraiger, K., Salas, E., & Teachout, M. (Eds.) (1997). *Improving training effectiveness in work organizations.* Mahwah, NJ: Erlbaum.

French, W. L. & Bell, C. H. (1999). *Organization development: Behavioral science interventions for organization improvement* (6th ed). Upper Saddle River, NJ: PrenticeHall.

Friedlander, F. & Brown, L. D. (1974). Organization development. In M. R. Rosenzweig & L. W. Porter (Eds.), *Annual review of psychology* (Vol. 25, pp. 313–342). Palo Alto, CA: Annual Reviews.

Funder, D. C. (2001). Personality. In S. T. Fiske, D. L. Schacter, & C. Zahn-Waxler (Eds.), *Annual review of psychology,* Vol. 52 (pp. 197–221). Palo Alto, CA: Annual Reviews.

George, J. M. & Zhou, J. (2001). When openness to experience and conscientiousness are related to creative behavior: An interactional approach. *Journal of Applied Psychology, 86,* 513–524.

Goldstein, I. L. (1997). Training. In L. H. Peters, C. R. Greer, & S. A. Youngblood (Eds.), *The Blackwell encyclopedic dictionary of human resource management* (pp. 352–359). Oxford, UK: Blackwell Publishers.

Goldstein, I. L. (1986). *Training in organizations: Needs assessment, development and evaluation* (2nd ed.). Monterey, CA: Brooks/Cole.

Goldstein, I. L. (1991). Training in work organizations. In M. D. Dunnette & L. M. Hough (Eds.), *Handbook of industrial and organizational psychology,* (2nd ed.) (Vol. 2, pp. 507–619). Palo Alto, CA: Consulting Psychologists Press.

Guest, D. (1998). Commitment. In C. L. Cooper & C. Argyris (Eds.), *The concise Blackwell encyclopedia of management* (pp. 84–85). Oxford, UK: Blackwell Publishers.

Hackman, J. R. & Oldham, G. R. (1976). Motivation through the design of work: Test of a theory. *Organizational Behavior and Human Performance, 16,* 250–279.

Hackman, J. R. & Oldham, G. R. (1980). *Work redesign.* Reading, MA: Addison-Wesley.

Harrison, R. (1970). Choosing the depth of organizational intervention. *Journal of Applied Behavioral Science, 6,* 182–202.

Hellervick, L. W., Hazucha, J. F., & Schneider, R. J. (1992). Behavior change: Models, methods, and a review of evidence. In M. D. Dunnette & L. M. Hough (Eds.), *Handbook of industrial and organizational psychology* (2nd ed.) (Vol. 3, pp. 823–895). Palo Alto, CA: Consulting Psychologists Press.

Hellriegel, D., Slocum, J. W., Jr., & Woodman, R. W. (2001). *Organizational behavior* (9th ed). Cincinnati, OH: South-Western.

Howell, P. M. & Cooke, N. J. (1989). Training the human information processor: A review of cognitive models. In I. L. Goldstein (Ed.), *Training and development in work organizations: Frontiers of industrial and organizational psychology* (pp. 121–182). San Francisco: Jossey-Bass.

Ilgen, D. R., Fisher, C. D., & Taylor, M. S. (1979). Consequences of individual feedback on behavior in organizations. *Journal of Applied Psychology, 64,* 349–371.

Ilgen, D. R. & Moore, C. F. (1987). Types and choices of performance feedback. *Journal of Applied Psychology, 72,* 401–406.

Jones, G. R. (1983). Psychological orientation and the process of organizational socialization: An interactionist perspective. *Academy of Management Review, 8,* 464–474.

Lewin, K. (1951). *Field theory in social science.* New York: Harper & Brothers.

Livingstone, L. P., Nelson, D. L., & Barr, S. H. (1997). Person-environment fit and creativity: An examination of supply-value and demand-ability versions of fit. *Journal of Management, 23,* 119–146.

Locke, E. A., Cartledge, N., & Koeppel, J. (1968). Motivational effects of knowledge of results: A goal-setting phenomenon. *Psychological Bulletin, 74,* 474–485.

Louis, M. R. (1980). Surprise and sense making: What newcomers experience in entering unfamiliar organizational settings. *Administrative Science Quarterly, 25,* 226–251.

Louis, M. R., Posner, B. Z., & Powell, G. N. (1983). The availability and helpfulness of socialization practices. *Personnel Psychology, 36,* 857–866.

Lubinski, D. (2000). Scientific and social significance of assessing individual differences: "Sinking shafts at a few critical points." In S. T. Fiske, D. L. Schacter, & C. Zahn-Waxler (Eds.), *Annual review of psychology* (Vol. 51, pp. 405–444). Palo Alto, CA: Annual Reviews.

Lundberg, C. C. (1989). On organizational learning: Implications and opportunities for expanding organizational development. In R. W. Woodman & W. A. Pasmore (Eds.), *Research in organizational change and development* (Vol. 3, pp. 61–82). Greenwich, CT: JAI Press.

Macy, B. A. & Izumi, H. (1993). Organizational change, design, and work innovation: A meta-analysis of 131 North American field studies—1961–1991. In R. W. Woodman & W. A. Pasmore (Eds.), *Research in organizational change and development* (Vol. 7, pp. 235–313). Greenwich, CT: JAI Press.

Markman, A. B. & Gentner, D. (2001). Thinking. In S. T. Fiske, D. L. Schacter, & C. Zahn-Waxler (Eds.), *Annual review of psychology* (Vol. 52, pp. 223–247). Palo Alto, CA: Annual Reviews.

Mathieu, J. E., Heffner, T. S., Goodwin, G. F., Salas, E., & Cannon-Bowers, J. (2000). The influence of shared mental models on team process and performance. *Journal of Applied Psychology, 85,* 273–283.

McGehee, W. & Thayer, P. W. (1961). *Training in business and industry.* New York: Wiley.

McMahan, G. C. & Woodman, R. W. (1992). The current practice of organization development within the firm: A survey of large industrial corporations. *Group and Organization Management, 17,* 117–134.

Miller, V. D. & Jablin, F. M. (1991). Information seeking during organizational entry: Influences, tactics, and a model of the process. *Academy of Management Review, 16,* 92–120.

Mohrman, S. A. & Mohrman, A. M., Jr. (1997). Fundamental organizational change as organizational learning: Creating team-based organizations. In W. A. Pasmore & R. W. Woodman (Eds.), *Research in organizational change and development* (Vol. 10, pp. 197–228). Greenwich, CT: JAI Press.

Morrison, E. W. (1993a). Longitudinal study of the effects of information seeking on newcomer socialization. *Journal of Applied Psychology, 78,* 173–183.

Morrison, E. W. (1993b). Newcomer information seeking: Exploring types, modes, sources, and outcomes. *Academy of Management Journal, 36,* 557–589.

Ostroff, C. & Kozlowski, S. W. J. (1992). Organizational socialization as a learning process: The role of information acquisition. *Personnel Psychology, 45,* 849–874.

Pervin, L. A. & John, O. P. (Eds.) (1999). *Handbook of personality: Theory and Research* (2nd ed.). New York: Guilford Press.

Pettigrew, A. M. & Fenton, E. M. (Eds.) (2000). *The innovating organisation.* London: Sage.

Pettigrew, A. M., Massini, S., & Numagami, T. (2000). Innovative forms of organizing in Europe and Japan. *European Management Journal, 18*(3), 259–273.

Pettigrew, A. M., Woodman, R. W., & Cameron, K. (2001). Studying organizational change and development: Challenges for future research. *Academy of Management Journal, 44,* 697–713.

Piderit, S. K. (2000). Rethinking resistance and re-cognizing ambivalence: A multidimensional view of attitudes toward an organizational change. *Academy of Management Review, 25*, 783–794.

Porras, J. I. & Hargis, K. (1982). Precursors of individual change: Responses to a social learning theory based on organizational intervention. *Human Relations, 35*(11), 973–990.

Porras, J. I. & Robertson, P. J. (1992). Organizational development: Theory, practice, and research. In M. D. Dunnette & L. M. Hough (Eds.), *Handbook of industrial and organizational psychology* (2nd ed.) (Vol. 3, pp. 719–822). Palo Alto, CA: Consulting Psychologists Press.

Purser, R. E. & Pasmore, W. A. (1992). Organizing for learning. In W. A. Pasmore & R. W. Woodman (Eds.), *Research in organizational change and development* (Vol. 6, pp. 37–114). Greenwich, CT: JAI Press.

Reicher, A. E. (1987). An interactionist perspective on newcomer socialization rates. *Academy of Management Review, 12*, 278–287.

Robertson, P. J., Roberts, D. R., & Porras, J. I. (1993). An evaluation of a model of planned organizational change: Evidence from a meta-analysis. In R. W. Woodman & W. A. Pasmore (Eds.), *Research in organizational change and development* (Vol. 7, pp. 1–39). Greenwich, CT: JAI Press.

Salas, E. & Cannon-Bowers, J. A. (2001). The science of training: A decade of progress. In S. T. Fiske, D. L. Schacter, & C. Zahn-Waxler (Eds.), *Annual review of psychology* (Vol. 52, pp. 471–499). Palo Alto, CA: Annual Reviews.

Stephens, C. U., D'Intino, R. S., & Victor, B. (1995). The moral quandary of transformational leadership: Change for whom? In W. A. Pasmore & R. W. Woodman (Eds.), *Research in organizational change and development* (Vol. 8, pp. 123–143). Greenwich, CT: JAI Press.

Thayer, P. W. & Teachout, M. S. (1995). A climate for transfer model (Rep. AL/HR-TP-1995-0035). Air Force Material Command, Brooks Air Force Base, Texas.

Van de Ven, A. H. & Poole, M. S. (1995). Explaining development and change in organizations. *Academy of Management Review, 20*, 510–540.

Van Maanen, J. (1975). Police socialization: A longitudinal examination of job attitudes in an urban police department. *Administrative Science Quarterly, 20*, 207–228.

Van Maanen, J. & Schein, E. H. (1979). Toward a theory of organizational socialization. In B. M. Staw (Ed.), *Research in organizational behavior* (Vol. 1, pp. 209–264). Greenwich, CT: JAI Press.

Wagner, J. A., III. (1994). Participation effect on performance and satisfaction: A reconsideration of research evidence. *Academy of Management Review, 19*, 312–330.

Weick, K. E. & Quinn, R. E. (1999). Organizational change and development. In J. T. Spence, J. M. Darley, & D. J. Foss (Eds.), *Annual review of psychology* (Vol. 50, pp. 361–386). Palo Alto, CA: Annual Reviews.

Wood, W. (2000). Attitude change: Persuasion and social influence. In S. T. Fiske, D. L. Schacter, & C. Zahn-Waxler (Eds.), *Annual review of psychology* (Vol. 51, pp. 539–570). Palo Alto, CA: Annual Reviews.

Woodman, R. W. (1993). Observations on the field of organizational change and development from the lunatic fringe. *Organization Development Journal, 11*(2), 71–75.

Woodman, R. W. (1989). Organizational change and development: New arenas for inquiry and action. *Journal of Management, 15*, 205–228.

Woodman, R. W. & Pasmore, W. A. (2002). The heart of it all: Group and team-based interventions in organization development. In A. H. Church & J. Waclawski (Eds.), *Organization development: A data driven approach to organizational change* (pp. 164–176). San Francisco: Jossey-Bass.

Woodman, R. W., Sawyer, J. E., & Griffin, R. W. (1993). Toward a theory of organizational creativity. *Academy of Management Review, 18*, 293–321.

Woodman, R. W. & Schoenfeldt, L. F. (1989). Individual differences in creativity: An interactionist perspective. In J. A. Glover, R. R. Ronning, & C. R. Reynolds (Eds.), *Handbook of creativity* (pp. 77–91). New York: Plenum.

Woodman, R. W. & Sherwood, J. J. (1980). The role of team development in organizational effectiveness: A critical review. *Psychological Bulletin, 88*, 166–186.

Zhou, J. (1998). Feedback valence, feedback style, task autonomy, and achievement orientation: interactive effects on creative performance. *Journal of Applied Psychology, 83*, 261–276.

3

Dynamics in Groups and Teams

Groups as Complex Action Systems

Joseph E. McGrath & Franziska Tschan

This chapter examines recent and current theoretical and empirical research information about dynamics, development, and change in groups within organizations. Its central purpose is to integrate theoretical views and empirical information about dynamic processes in groups. A secondary aim is to take a step toward integrating ideas about groups across both disciplinary and geographic/cultural boundaries.

Introduction

In this introductory section, we begin by distinguishing three domains of temporal processes that we mean to include in the concept of dynamic processes in groups, namely operational, developmental, and adaptive processes. Despite considerable rhetoric in the small group research field about "group dynamics," over the 100-year history of research on groups the importance of all of those dynamic processes have been "honored more in the breech than in the observance." In contrast to that pattern, we note a number of recent theoretical formulations that

have begun to take dynamic processes in groups more adequately into account. We identify two of them in particular—one, action theory, and the other, complex systems theory—that we will draw heavily upon in this chapter. Then, we outline the overall organization of the chapter.

Three Domains of Temporal Processes in Work Groups: Operational, Developmental, and Adaptive

Groups are characterized by the continuous and simultaneous operation of at least three distinct though related sets of temporal processes:

1. *Operational processes* describe how the group does its work. As groups carry out their main intrinsic functions, group action consists of the simultaneous "flow" of multiple processes over time. Each of those processes may have its own temporal cadence. Some of the processes are results of the group's intentional and deliberate structuring of its action. Subsets of those processes tend to become "entrained" to one

another, and/or entrained to certain signal events (zeitgebers), internal or external to the system. This is analogous to how various bodily rhythms of individual humans become entrained, in subsets, to various internal and external conditions (e.g., how the so-called circadian rhythms become entrained to the day-night cycle). Some of those processes reflect responses of the group to externally imposed operational or task requirements.

2. *Developmental processes* describe how the group as an entity changes over time. Each group has a history that consists of the evolution over time of patterns of relations involved in its formation and operation, and perhaps its metamorphosis or transformation. Each group also has an anticipated or potential future, both in the perceptions of group members and in the eyes of persons external to that group. Both the group's past history and its potential future impinge upon its status and actions in the present. This developmental path, in turn, is affected by the particulars of membership, projects, technology, context, and their interactions. These developmental processes entail effects of practice/experience, learning, and change.

3. *Adaptive processes* describe how the group reacts to events. The continual mutual interchanges between the group and its embedding systems constitutes a pattern of adaptation. These adaptation processes entail not only changes that arise in the group's environment, but also the reactions (and anticipations) of the group-as-a-system to those events. In the case of groups in organizations, those embedding systems consist of other groups and entities (at the same "level" of the organization), entities at various nested higher levels of the organization, and entities outside of the organization with which the group or its members may have to deal.

All three sets of processes operate continually and simultaneously in groups. They are mutually intertwined and interdependent but are worth distinguishing for analytic purposes. The first of these temporal domains, operational processes, has often been talked about in terms of "phases of group problem solving" (or, more generally, as phases of group task or project performance). The second domain, developmental processes, has often been talked about as "stages of group development." Moreover, in past theory and research on groups, those two domains have often been inextricably confounded with one

another. The third domain, adaptive processes, has often been ignored.

An Integration of Theory

In recent years, a number of theoretical treatments of small work groups have begun to take one or more of these levels of dynamics seriously—that is, to be concerned with an array of temporal factors in groups. These include, for example: Moreland and Levine's socialization model (1982); work on group processes by Hackman and colleagues (e.g., Hackman, 1986, 1992; Hackman and Morris, 1975); work by West (1996); by Walther and colleagues (Walther, 1994; Walther and Burgoon, 1992); Worchel's developmental theory (Worchel, 1996; Worchel, Coutant-Sassic, and Grossman 1992); Mantovani's (1996) work; work by Poole and colleagues (Poole, 1981, 1983; Poole and DeSanctis, 1989, 1990; Poole and Roth 1989a and 1989b) on adaptive structuration in groups; the functional treatment of group interaction by Hirokawa (1983, 1985, 1988); and work by Ancona and Chong (1996) and by Kelly and McGrath (Kelly and McGrath, 1985; McGrath and Kelly, 1986) on entrainment processes in groups. Of particular interest for this chapter are two recent theoretical formulations that focus strongly on the dynamic nature of groups. One is action theory as applied to groups by von Cranach, Tschan, and others (Tschan, 1995; Tschan and von Cranach, 1996; von Cranach, 1996; von Cranach, Ochsenbein, and Vallach, 1986). The other is a recently formulated theory of groups as complex systems by Arrow, McGrath, and Berdahl (Arrow, McGrath, and Berdahl, 2000; McGrath, Arrow, and Berdahl, 2000).

The former, action theory (AT), is a set of ideas that has guided work by many European social psychologists (Frese and Sabini, 1985; Frese and Zapf, 1994; Hacker, 1985; Semmer and Frese, 1985). While most of that work has been done at the level of individuals, action theory has been applied to small groups as well. It has been articulated clearly at the group level by von Cranach, Tschan, and colleagues (Tschan, 1995; Tschan and von Cranach, 1996; von Cranach, 1996; von Cranach et al. 1986; von Cranach, Ochsenbein and Tschan, 1987).

At the same time, recent critiques of social psychology within the U.S. community have led to a push for consideration of concepts from dynamical systems theory and complexity theory. That viewpoint has been articulated for social psychology in general by Vallacher and Nowak (1994), and for small groups in particular by Baron and colleagues (Baron, Amazeen, and Beek, 1994), Latané and collaborators (Latané and Nowak, 1994), and most recently by Arrow, McGrath, and Berdahl (Arrow et al. 2000; McGrath et al., 2000).

We are struck by the similarities between action theory and complex systems theory, as applied to the small group area in the publications cited above. We think there are many points of possible connection between the work of von Cranach and Tschan, on the one hand, and of Arrow, McGrath, and Berdahl, on the other. Furthermore, we also find some crucial differences between them, so an integration of them can extend both theories as well. We believe that future advances in our understanding of the nature and processes of small groups, in work organizations and elsewhere, and in particular our understanding of the operation of dynamic temporal processes in those groups, can be facilitated by a fruitful blending of those two perspectives.

Organization of the Chapter

The next section of the chapter presents brief summaries of key ideas from the von Cranach and Tschan application of action theory to groups, and from the Arrow, McGrath, and Berdahl formulation of groups as complex, adaptive, dynamic systems, followed by a brief reprise of major similarities and differences between the two. We then use that integrated formulation to discuss, in successive sections, each of the three domains of temporal processes noted earlier. Those three sections, respectively, focus in particular on: (a) the hierarchical, sequential, and cyclical nature of the operational processes by which groups carry out projects or tasks that require coordination of action and of communication; (b) the developmental patterns by which groups form and change over time as they learn from their experience; and (c) the adaptation patterns by which groups engage in two-way interchanges with their embedding contexts or environments. In terms of the Arrow, McGrath, and Berdahl formulation, these three (coordination, development, and adaptation) reflect the local, global, and contextual dynamics, respectively, of groups as complex dynamic systems.

In these sections, we will also being in ideas and findings from other theoretical conceptualizations,

both European and North American, that take dynamic processes seriously. Many of them were noted above (e.g., Mantovani, 1996; Moreland and Levine, 1982; Poole and DeSanctis, 1989, 1990; West 1996; Worchel, 1996). However, we are selective rather than exhaustive in our coverage of all of these theories.

We conclude the chapter with a brief summary of its major themes, and some comments on key issues for future research in this domain.

Toward an Integrated Theory of Groups as Complex Action Systems

A Brief Summary of Action Theory (AT)

To summarize Action Theory, as applied to groups, we draw heavily upon von Cranach's (1996) treatment. In that chapter, he lays out four underlying assumptions and formulates three principles, which serve as the conceptual underpinnings of action theory as a "frame theory" for understanding groups. The underlying assumptions are: (a) that human groups are highly developed living systems, (b) that they exist in the context of other social systems and of environments, (c) that they exist largely through their own actions, and (d) that they are involved in constant development so that their present state must be explained from their history.

Von Cranach's three principles are: (1) the principle of multilevel organization, which states that human affairs are organized on many levels—the individual and several social levels; (2) the principle of self-activity, which says that human individuals and social systems act on their own, on the basis of internal energy and internally stored information, in interaction with their environments; and (3) the principle of historicity, which states that important human affairs, including individual and social structures, processes, and future development, can be understood only in the context of their historical embeddedness—the present and future are understood from the past.

With these assumptions and principles as a basis, von Cranach then proceeds to explicate action theory for groups in the form of 28 theses. We will paraphrase those theses below, in related sets.

The first seven theses have to do with definitional issues and the nature of groups. The term *group* refers to a particular class of small social systems with specific properties. There are various types of groups that exemplify sets of those properties. Groups are usually embedded in larger social systems and embed smaller social systems within themselves. They are in continual interaction with both embedding and embedded systems.

Groups are acting units and cease to exist when they cease to act. Group processes occur on group and individual levels, and often in the group's interaction with embedding and embedded systems. The multilevel history of groups is essential to understanding group function, structures, and processes. Groups develop in a process of multilevel coevolution.

The next five theses have to do with general characteristics and types of group action. A group serves four functions: (a) to achieve effects in its environment and suprasystems; (b) to create, maintain, and adapt its own processes and structures; (c) to fulfill the needs of its suprasystems; and (d) to fulfill the needs of its subsystems and members.

Actions on different levels show both similarities (homologies and analogies) and differences. Long-term activities consist of (a) recurrent themes and (b) long-term projects. Short- and midrange group activities that have an identifiable object are group actions; and those that are socially well-defined situations may be called acts. Six types of group actions are: (a) primary goal-directed; (b) routine goal-directed; (c) trial-and-error goal-directed; (d) meaning-oriented; (e) process-oriented; and (f) agitated group actions.

The next set of nine theses has to do with goal-directed actions of groups. Goal-directed action is based on tasks, which may be given by an external system or posed by the group itself. Steering functions give an action its direction; energizing functions provide the action with energy.

Group action is sequentially and hierarchically organized via a projection of the task structure onto group structure. Group action encompasses two processes—information-elaboration and execution—and each of them operates on at least two levels. For information-elaboration, those levels are individual cognition and emotion, and intragroup communication. Knowledge is processed on individual and group levels, and its primary function is the organization of action. Communication is information elaboration at the group level. For execution those two levels are individual actions and their coordination in cooperative action.

It is assumed that the components of group action, at various levels, serve different steering functions: situation orientation, goal determination, choice of plans, starting the execution, controlling the execution, stopping the action, and evaluation and consumption of results. In extended actions, these run off as recurrent loops.

Group communication varies in openness, as a function of the perceived difficulty of the task, the need to transfer task-relevant information between members, and the extent to which there are conflicting individual action-related cognitions and emotions. Groups create and maintain taboos regarding the transmission of information that seems to endanger the group's structure or features important to it. Groups elicit, maintain, or inhibit individual energizing processes through the exertion of social influence or power, both direct and indirect.

The final set of seven themes has to do with the relation of group action to group structure and processes. Group structure results from the interaction of tasks, supersystem factors, member characteristics, existing traditions and history of the group, and constraints of the environment. Roles are part of the group action structure; they form the basis of the work division in group action and depend on the task structure.

Hierarchy and status derive from the whole set of long-term group activities and influence the distribution of roles. Leadership is a function of group action, and power is an indispensable function of leadership. Personal relationships and group action structure mutually determine one another. Conventions, rules, and norms, the prescriptive knowledge systems of the group and their social supersystems, influence and control the actions of groups and their members and can be changed by group actions.

As will be apparent, most of these principles and theses are very similar to the basic propositions and conceptions of a theory of groups as complex systems recently formulated by Arrow, McGrath, and Berdahl (2000; McGrath et al., 2000), which is presented in similarly brief form below. The several places at which the two theoretical perspectives depart from each other are also instructive.

A Brief Summary of a Theory of Groups as Complex Systems (CST)

Arrow, McGrath, and Berdahl (2000) recently presented a theoretical formulation that draws on concepts from dynamical systems and complexity theory.

It, too, offers a "frame theory" of groups, rather than a specific set of theoretical hypotheses. That formulation regards groups as open and complex systems that interact with the smaller systems (i.e., the members) embedded within them and the larger systems (e.g., organizations) within which they are embedded. Groups have fuzzy boundaries that both distinguish them from and connect them to their members and their embedding contexts.

Arrow, McGrath, and Berdahl (2000) propose a causal formulation about groups that differs dramatically from the one characteristic of work done in the dominant methodological paradigm. They argue that, throughout a group's life, three levels of causal dynamics continually shape the group: Local dynamics involve the activity of a group's constituent elements. Local dynamics give rise to group-level or global dynamics. Global dynamics involve the behavior of system-level variables that emerge from and subsequently shape and constrain local dynamics. Contextual dynamics involve those aspects of a group's elements, operating conditions, and actions that are shaped by actions and events in the group's embedding contexts, and by the group's responses to them. Contextual dynamics shape and constrain the local and global dynamics of a group.

All groups act in the service of two generic functions: (a) to complete group projects and (b) to fulfill member needs. A group's success in pursuing these two functions affects and depends on the viability and integrity of the group as a system. Thus (c) maintaining system integrity becomes a third generic group function, instrumental to the other two. A group's system integrity in turn affects its ability to complete group projects and fulfill member needs.

Groups include three types of elements: (a) people who become a group's members; (b) intentions that are embodied in group projects; and (c) resources that get transformed into the group's technologies. Group members vary in what they can offer the group in terms of interpersonal, task, and process skills; values, beliefs, and attitudes; and personality, cognitive, and behavioral styles. Group members also differ in demographic attributes, such as sex, race, and age, and in the needs they seek to fulfill via group membership. Group projects vary in the opportunities they offer and the requirements they place on members to engage in interpersonal, task, and procedural activity. Projects also differ in their requirements for instrumental functions such as information

processing, managing conflict and consensus, and coordinating behavior. Technologies differ in how much they facilitate or constrain interpersonal activity, task activity, and procedural activity, and in how effectively they support different instrumental functions (i.e., processing of information, managing of conflict and consensus, and motivation, regulation, and coordination of member behaviors).

A group pursues its functions by creating and enacting a coordinated pattern of member-task-tool relations, its coordination network. The full coordination network includes six component networks: (a) the member network, or pattern of member-member relations (such as friendship or status relations); (b) the task network, or pattern of task-task relations (e.g., the required sequence for completion of a set of tasks); (c) the tool network, or pattern of tool-tool relations (e.g. the procedure by which a given piece of equipment can be used most efficiently); (d) the labor network, or pattern of member-task relations (i.e., who is supposed to do what); (e) the role network, or pattern of member-tool relations (i.e., how members do their tasks); and (f) the job network, or pattern of task-tool relations (e.g., what piece of equipment must be used for a given task).

The life course of a group can be characterized by three logically ordered modes that are conceptually distinct but have fuzzy temporal boundaries: formation, operation, and metamorphosis. As a group forms, people, intentions, and resources become organized into an initial coordination network of relations among members, projects, and technology that demarcates that group as a bounded social entity. As a group operates over time in the service of group projects and member needs, its members elaborate, enact, monitor, and modify the coordination network established during formation. Groups both learn from their own experience and adapt to events occurring in their embedding contexts. If and when a group undergoes metamorphosis, it dissolves or is transformed into a different social entity.

Combining the Two Theories into a Theory of Groups as Complex Action Systems (CAST)

These two theoretical formulations are strikingly similar in many aspects. Although there are some important differences, many of those differences are matters of emphasis, and/or matters of scope, rather than fundamental disagreements. Hence, the integrated version is, in a sense, the union of the two.

The cores of the two theories are in substantial agreement. Both specify the nature of groups as complex systems that embed and are embedded in other systems. Both deal with groups as systems and give emphasis to the interchanges between group and embedding and embedded systems. They are also similar in the functions they purport for groups. While action theory lists four functions and complex systems theory lists three, the actual content of the two sets of functions is quite compatible. Both theories stress the idea of intentionality, and both stress the importance of history. Both give a key role to communication, viewed as information processing at the group level.

At the same time, the two theories differ in a number of places where one of the theories addresses a topic that is relatively ignored by the other. For instance, action theory has much more to say about levels and complexity of group task performance. (Some of this will be discussed in a later section of this chapter.) On the other hand, complex systems theory has much more to say about membership characteristics, and about technology. Complex systems theory also talks about formation of the group separately from its operations, whereas action theory is mainly concerned with the operations mode of the group's life. One key difference in scope is that action theory stresses groups in action, whereas complex systems theory also deals with "states"—that is, it deals with "standing groups" as well as "acting groups." Action theory stresses the self-activating facet of groups and specifically treats steering and energizing functions. Complex systems theory stresses intentionality of the group, its members, and its embedding systems.

Complex systems theory deals with an elaborated coordination network, whereas action theory deals with hierarchically and sequentially organized task activities. In the next section, we will interweave those two. In its consideration of group structure, action theory merges role and labor networks because it does not distinguish between task and technology as major constituent elements of groups. In considering the establishment and enactment of a group's coordination network, complex systems theory distinguishes between role and labor networks and also distinguishes a job network (or task-tool relations). Complex systems theory has a more explicit treatment of development and of adaptation than does action theory. Action theory distinguishes information and

action, but doesn't explicitly deal with multiple levels of causal processes, which is at the heart of complex systems theory. Finally, complex systems theory gives more attention to members and their attributes.

So we can consider the union of the two theories, with minor adjustments, as a single integrated theory of larger scope—covering all the ground dealt with by either theory, with emphasis on the central ground covered by both of them. We will refer to this as a theory of Groups as Complex Action Systems (CAST).

We will now use this theoretical framework as a template for discussing each of the three domains of temporal processes listed earlier in this chapter. In doing so, we will try to connect ideas and findings from the work of other researchers with our central theoretical formulation.

Operational Processes: The Dynamics of Coordination and Task Performance

Complex action theory proposes that there are three levels of hierarchy at which the group's action takes place. The levels will here be called Purpose, Planning, and Performance. (See figure 3.1.)

The topmost or macro level is the Purpose or Project level. It consists of the selection/acceptance/modification of the group's project(s), and the allocation of resources, including a general period of time and a complement of members and tools, that will be devoted to accomplishment of the project(s). This purpose level is knowledge- and intention-based.

The second or mesolevel is the level of Planning. It is the structuring of the group's work processes. In complex systems theory terms, it consists of the establishment of an articulated network of member-task-technology relations. In action theory terms it consists of the middle level of a hierarchically and sequentially organized set of actions. For both theories, it is *a structuring of the process by which the group will carry out its project(s)*. It involves a hierarchical, sequential, referential, and technical structuring. That is, it specifies what will be done, when, by whom, and how (that is, with what tools). Action theory calls this level "rule-based," but we will expand that notion to say that it is "lore- and logic-" based. It involves the establishment of a member-task-tool-time network of relations.

The third level is the level of Performance, or Action. This consists of a series of interrelated "orient-enact-monitor-modify" cycles (see figure 3.1). This

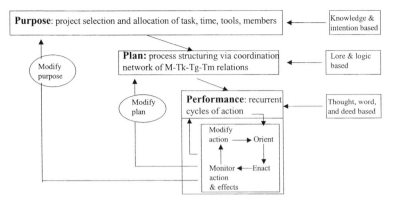

Figure 3.1 Hierarchical-sequential activity cycles.

third, micro level is "action"-based, but it must be remembered that in this context action refers not only to motoric action but to cognitive and verbal action as well. If the monitoring shows the results of the action to be "on target," then no modification is needed. If monitoring shows it to be off target, then a modification is called for in the enactment part of that recurrent cycle. The modification part of each cycle is addressed in the first instance to the "action" itself—that is, at the lowest level of the hierarchy. If that modification is insufficient to bring the effect of the action into line with the intended effect, then the modification process is directed at the plan level—a change in the structuring of the process. If that is also insufficient to deliver the intended results, then the modification process may be directed at the project or purpose level. Thus, these recurrent orient-enact-monitor-modify cycles at the micro or action level potentially can cascade upward to the higher levels of this hierarchical array (i.e., to Planning or Purpose levels).

While all of this sounds stylized and static, that is so mainly because we need to describe it in print as though it were a fixed sequence. In practice, these are all processes that take place fluidly, sometimes with and sometimes without much overt or manifest attention by the group. Indeed, some groups do the same project, or same kind of project, over and over again. In those cases, there is little need for activity at the Project or Purpose level; and unless something has changed, little effort needs to go into the Plan level as well. On the other hand, some groups have to deal with brand new projects, requiring attention at the plan level. Moreover, many groups have multiple

projects active at the same time, or in overlapping time frames. Hence, they have multiple plan/structuring at the same time, and they may have multiple, interwoven, sets of action cycles.

We will discuss each of those three levels of operational action in this section. We will also discuss the related question of whether or not there are fixed sequences of phases of group task activity that are advantageous for effective performance.

Purpose or Project Level: Goal Choice and Resource Allocation

The topmost or macro level of the hierarchy is the purpose or project level.

Here, the group translates its intentions into the formulation of a group project, and an overall allocation of its resources (tools, time, and effort) to carry out that project. In effect, the group selects, accepts, generates, and/or modifies one or more potential projects that it intends to undertake within a given time frame.

In complex systems theory terms, group types can be distinguished by the pattern of forces that leads to the group's formation. Some groups form based primarily on "top-down" or directive forces, either internal to or external to that group (for concocted and founded groups, respectively). Other groups form based mainly on internal emergent forces (self-organizing groups) or external conditions (circumstantial groups). For the most part, work groups in organizations are of the former types: concocted or founded groups, deliberately formed by someone sufficiently powerful to reallocate people, time, and other resources to form the new group (Argote and McGrath, 1993). Such groups are formed for specific purposes, and those purposes get translated into projects as part of the rationale for that group's formation and existence. The group itself thus may have its major projects imposed upon it, either by its own founding leaders or by people outside the group who were responsible for its creation. In such cases, a given group is likely to spend little or no time "choosing" a project. It may still need to give attention to acquiring the resources it will need to carry out any given project, as well as to the coordination needed for interweaving the execution of multiple projects that are to be pursued simultaneously.

Groups formed as self-organizing groups, on the other hand, face a wide array of potential purposes and projects that they might pursue. Their purposes, and projects, emerge during the course of group formation, and selection/modification of those projects will likely command a lot of explicit attention.

Whether group projects are assigned or emergent, the allocation, and often the very acquisition, of appropriate resources for project fulfillment is almost always a crucial problem that requires time and attention by the group. Acquiring resources, in this context, refers to acquiring an appropriate number of group members with appropriate attributes (knowledge, skills, and abilities; values, beliefs, and attitudes; and personality, cognitive, and behavioral styles); along with acquiring an appropriate set of tools (both hardware and software) that are adequate for project accomplishment, and that are within the capabilities of members; and allocating an appropriate period of time sufficient for effective completion of the project during which those people and tools will be committed to work on the given project.

The group's attention to its projects (including allowable variations), as well as its efforts toward acquisition of appropriate resources, often involve interactions between the group and various agents in the group's embedding systems. There is little research available on these issues. Past research in social and organizational psychology, even when dealing with extant work groups in organizational settings, has generally neglected the investigation of transactions across that group-organizational boundary, including those involving resource acquisition. A notable exception is the work of Ancona and Caldwell (Ancona and Caldwell, 1988, 1990). Moreover, laboratory-experimental research on groups has, for the most part, tacitly assumed that available resources, as well as assigned projects, are inherently "givens" for any particular group. Consequently, the processes by which groups "choose" or "refine" projects—when they do—and the processes by which they acquire or allocate resources of various kinds, are areas requiring focused research attention.

Planning Level: Structuring of the Work Process

When the group has fixed upon a project and a general allocation of resources for its accomplishment, it then needs to integrate available information into a plan, or shared strategy. That plan must adapt the coordination network thus far established (during group formation, or in pursuit of earlier projects) into one organized for execution of this particular project. The group must somehow distribute tasks, tools, and other resources among group members, pool expert information, plan timing and sequencing of actions, and so forth. This includes discussion of procedures concerning the group's operation (Fisher and Stutman, 1987; Putnam, 1981) as well as strategic planning concerning the content of the group's task products.

Ideally, such planning would take place at the start of a group's work on a given project. In practice, however, the group may or may not engage in an explicit discussion about how to proceed, how to establish (or modify) the role, labor, and job networks for a given project. Empirical research shows that groups often fail to discuss their strategies of task performance spontaneously (Hackman and Morris, 1975) and certainly do not often engage in such strategy discussions at the beginning of their work. Hackman, Brousseau, and Weiss (1977) showed that groups did not plan ahead and organize their work unless they were told to do so. Weingart's (1992) research shows that preplanning (that is, strategy discussion before the group engages in task fulfillment) rather seldom occurs. However, if groups are forced to plan at the outset, their task performance improves (Larson and Schaumann, 1993; Shure, Rogers, Larson, and Tassone, 1962), at least if the task is sufficiently complex to require preplanning (Hackman, Brousseau, and Weiss, 1977).

Whether or not groups engage in project planning or organization may be influenced by task characteristics, by the existing member, role, and labor networks, and by the experience the group has with the project. Projects that are more complex and that consist of tasks with greater interdependence requirements should elicit more planning behavior than simpler and less interdependent projects (Poole, 1983; Fisher and Stutman, 1987). Lord and Rowzee (1979) showed that interdependence requirements of tasks led to an increase in problem definition, planning, and coordinating/directing behavior by group members. However, groups may not realize that investments in planning, which are costly in the short term, will in the long run pay off. In experimental groups, Weingart (1992) found a decrease in preplanning activities for a complex versus a simple task; she interprets this as an urge on the part of the group members not to lose time with planning but rather to immediately start work.

The existing role-network, division of labor, and other aspects of the group's structure also influence the occurrence of planning behavior. For example, whether or not there is a clear formal leader should make a difference in whether the group engages in planning behavior, since a leader's role is in part to be responsible for strategic or planning level aspects of the group's work. Even when leaders are randomly assigned, as in Tschan's computer-supported groups, they did indeed assume responsibility for most of the planning discussion of the group (Tschan, Semmer, Nägele, and Gurtner, 2000). Boos and Meier (1993) compared differently organized groups working on a similar, very complex decision making task and found that groups with assigned leaders showed a higher density of procedural acts aimed at organizing the group, compared to groups with less hierarchic organization. The latter groups, however, showed more overall procedural remarks across the whole project, due to a much longer discussion time that they needed for task completion.

Planning is also affected by the existence and pattern of any previously established coordination network, both those established through early adoption of routines and those modified through experience. Explicit planning is most important in early phases of a group's life, and at the beginning of a new and different project. Groups quickly adopt common task patterns (Gersick, 1988; Bettenhausen and Murnighan, 1985), often tacitly (Wittenbaum and Stasser, 1996). Once a task plan is adopted, there is less need for explicit planning, thus freeing the group's time and efforts for direct task action. This can enhance

group efficiency in the short run. However, Gersick and Hackman (1990) also note some potentially dysfunctional consequences of rapid development of such habitual routines, especially if they are not revised or adapted when appropriate—for example, under conditions of major changes in the task environment, of ineffectiveness in progress on the task, or of dysfunctions of the group as an intact system. Gersick's project teams, both in and outside of the laboratory, took approximately half of their project "lifetime" before they reviewed and revised their initial work process (Gersick, 1988, 1989).

Not all planning statements (sometimes referred to as routing statements) lead to a change in the trajectory of the group. Their effectiveness depends on several factors, among them a proper timing (premature planning or shortcuts are often ignored by the other group members) and issue relevance (Fisher and Stutman, 1987).

Research on how experts work suggests that they revise their strategies periodically, that they pay attention to and adapt to new knowledge, and that they undertake deliberate practice efforts (Ericsson and Lehmann, 1996). West's work on reflexivity suggests that the same should hold for groups (West, 1996).

Some organizations impose similar task plans on all their groups and train members to carry out those plans, even for complex tasks. For example, all pilots of an airline are trained to function in a very similar way, so pilots can minimize the time it takes for mutual adjustment in new crews (Hackman, 1993). However, even these groups seem to profit from explicit planning discussions. More successful cockpit crews, studied in simulators by Orasanu (1993, 1994), used low-workload periods for strategic discussion. For example, they planned alternate routes or studied landing procedures for alternate airports. In emergency situations, successful crews explicitly discussed plans and strategies for problem solution, as well as issues regarding team coordination.

Performance Level: Executing the Group's Project(s)

On the micro level, groups or group members carry out acts that are hierarchically related to the project's goal, or subgoals, or sub-sub-goals, and thereby are instrumentally related to the overall project goal. On this level, an act consists of a (subordinate) goal, and regulation and execution activities associated with attaining it. At this action level, groups and group members plan or orient with regard to the intended action, enact it, monitor that action with regard to its effects, and if needed, modify the action, the plan, or the goal.

There has not been very much research to investigate cycles, or ordered sequences of communication and motoric action, at this micro level. Much more attention has been devoted to more macro levels of group task performance, such as questions about problem-solving phase sequences (which will be discussed later in this section).

However, besides his work on phase sequences, Bales also carried out some sequential analysis regarding his problem-solving groups (Bales, 1950). He found two distinct patterns. One pattern was a tendency for sequences to involve "more of the same"; that is, for an act of a certain kind (e.g., a task solution proposal) to trigger more acts of the same type. The other pattern was a conversational tendency—for example, for a question to elicit an answer.

Other researchers have postulated different expected structures of sequences. For example, Stech (1975) proposes a "generalized sequence of the discussion process." It starts with (1) a question or problem statement, that is followed by (2) an answer, a proposal, or a clarification of substance, and this step is followed by (3) either a positive or negative evaluation. Although the empirical evidence supporting these suppositions is relatively weak, Stech claims that between 41 and 50% of sequences of interacts of different categories fit this structure.

In a sequential analysis of group communication for groups solving the tower of Hanoi problem, Gundlach and Schultz (1987) distinguished between proposals for the next move and evaluations of proposals, relating the complexity of proposal-evaluation cycles to problem-solving performance. They found that better-performing groups showed longer sequences of discussion before making a move, and that the structure of the sequences showed not only proposals for moves, but also multiple evaluations of those proposals.

This leads to the hypothesis that group productivity should be higher if the communication process follows an "ideal" micro structure. Stech's (1975) analysis suggests that groups whose communication patterns follow the proposed sequential structure tended to perform better. Tschan (1995) identified a micro level sequence for motoric actions: plan/orient, execute, evaluate. She found that high-performing groups had a larger percentage of their cycles as "ideal" cycles that included all three elements in an ideal sequential order (i.e., starting with orientation and ending with evaluation).

This research, in turn, suggests that a well-ordered sequential structure not only reflects a better understanding of the requirements of the task (in that all the necessary acts are done), but also represents a relatively efficient task performance process (hence less "process losses"), since it minimizes redundant and fragmented activities.

But sequence is not all there is to temporal aspects of operational processes. Activities within the group's operational processes also are subject to complex patterning in terms of pace and timing. It has long been recognized that a number of human physiological processes tend to become entrained—that is, matched in frequency, phase, and sometimes amplitude—to one another and to outside "signals." For example, there are a number of biochemical and physiological processes that tend to become entrained to one another and to the day/night cycle of the planet (hence the name circadian rhythms). A number of researchers (e.g., Ancona and Caldwell, 1988; Kelly and McGrath, 1985; McGrath and Kelly, 1986) have shown that various aspects of individual task performance and communication activities tend to become "entrained" both to the activities of other individuals with whom they are interacting and to the occurrence of pacing signals (zeitgebers) external to the group. Such entrainment both facilitates within-group coordination of overt action and potentially affects the group's adaptation to features of its environment (see below). Thus, not only do member and group activity at the micro level yield complex patterns of member-task-tool relations; they are also likely to involve complex temporal patterning as well.

Is There an Ideal Sequence of Problem-Solving Phases?

The previous discussion of group operations points to a set of issues that has been given a lot of research attention in the past. First is the question of whether groups, confronted with a project (for example, a decision to make or a problem to solve), characteristically follow a particular sequence of phases of task fulfillment. If there is such a predictable sequence of different types of task activity, is that sequence instrumentally related to task accomplishment? Assuming that there is such a most-effective phase sequence, some researchers have pursued a further question of whether various potential interventions regarding process could be used to improve group performance. We will examine research on those questions historically, and in the light of our theoretical framework.

A fixed sequence of well-defined phases of group activity has been proposed mainly in the domain of problem solving tasks. Some of that work has built on Dewey's (1933) propositions about "how we think" (Fisher, 1970). Several normative models have been proposed (e.g., Bales and Strodtbeck, 1951; Fisher, 1970; Hirokawa, 1983), the best known of which is Bales and Strodtbeck's three-phase sequence: orientation, evaluation, control. They proposed that sequence, and found evidence for it, in laboratory groups engaged in what they referred to as "full-fledged problems." That phrase meant that for the sequence to apply, the group had to deal with the whole problem from beginning to end—from problem analysis, to proposing criteria and solutions, to evaluating alternatives and implementing solutions. Talland (1955) and Psathas (1960) found mixed support for this phase sequence in some kinds of extant groups (e.g., therapy groups).

The normative or "fixed-sequence" model of problem solving has been questioned by a number of researchers, who argue that in problem solving, even if phases can be distinguished, there is a recycling of different phases, especially for difficult problems (e.g., Burnstein and Berbaum, 1983; McGrath, 1991). Hirokawa (1983) tested a sequence model of problem solving phases and did not find the theoretically proposed sequence, nor any other specific sequence, as being superior for group productivity. However, he did find that successful groups engaged in problem analysis early on, whereas less successful groups tended to skip problem analysis altogether. This is in line with research on more and less successful individual problem solvers (Janis and Mann, 1977). Hirokawa then proposed a task-contingent model, namely that there is not a single fixed sequence of phases that leads to high performance, but rather that groups do show certain phases contingent upon task requirements, but not necessarily in a fixed order. Poole and colleagues (1981, 1983; Poole and Roth 1989a and 1989b), working within an adaptive structuration model, arrived at even more complex results. They

distinguished task content, task process, and relational activity. For task content, they observed that as the group progresses on the task, different phases recycle several times. They did not find support for a single best phase sequence. How many phases can be distinguished, and how often a phase is recycled, are the result of an interaction between task process activities, relational activities, and task content activities. (These distinctions are related to the role and labor networks considered in complex systems theory). Poole and Roth observed, for example, that the level of conflict combined with the power structure of the group predicts the amount of solution searching activity that will occur (Poole and Roth 1989a and 1989b).

There has also been a failure to find single sequences of decision making phases in organizational psychology. Instead, iterative processes and recurrent cycles of different sets of phases seem to be the prevalent finding (Mintzberg, Raisinghani, and Théorêt, 1976) and seem to be influenced by problem type and problem complexity (Nutt, 1984).

Some other conceptualizations about this issue fit within our hierarchical, sequential perspective (e.g. McGrath, 1991; Gollwitzer 1990). For example, McGrath (1991) postulated four modes of activity in groups. The first, goal choice or the acceptance of a project, and the last, execution of project or goal attainment, are a necessary part of each completed group project. They will most likely occur in this temporal sequence; that is, goal choice before goal attainment. The other modes—means choice and policy choice—will occur or not depending on task requirements, past experience of the group, group member characteristics, group context conditions, and the like. Duration and sequence of the four modes will also be variable and depend on requirements of the actual coordination network. Moreover, these two, three, or four mode cycles may recur. The two essential modes of this classification—goal choice and execution—are akin to the macro and micro levels of the hierarchical schema used here. The middle two—means choice and policy choice—are related to the meso- or planning level.

A somewhat different kind of phase sequence is proposed by Gollwitzer (1990). The model was developed and tested with regard to individual actors, but seems applicable to groups as well. It distinguishes four different phases of an action, or task fulfillment, that relate to the three hierarchical levels dealt with here. It starts with a predecisional phase of an action, in which preferences are created. Here, action tendencies (wishes) are considered in a rather unstructured, open-minded fashion that the author calls deliberative mind set. Conclusion of this phase leads to the building of an intention, a decision to pursue a specific goal. (This is like our macro or purpose level.) After having adopted the goal, the actor makes a transition to a much more focused "implemental" mind set and prepares for implementation of the actions required to attain this goal. That is, he or she plans the "when, where, how, and how long" (Gollwitzer 1990, p. 290) of task fulfillment. Because nothing has been achieved so far, the phase between the decision on the goal and the initiation of the action is named the "preactional phase." (This is like our meso- or planning level.) Only after this phase is the action initiated. The actor is determined to and does pursue completion of the goal in a persistent way. He or she normally stays in the implemental mind set, focusing on the goal and the necessary steps to fulfill it. After goal completion, the actor enters the postactional phase, where he or she evaluates whether further goal attainment actions are worthwhile. Here, the mind returns to the more open and less structured deliberative mode. (These last two phases reflect the orient-enact-monitor-modify cycles of the micro or performance level.)

In groups these different phases may be reflected in different communication patterns—less focused and structured communication before concrete implementation plans have been worked out, and more focused communication once the action is initiated. Some data of Gersick's study (1989) seem to fit this theory quite well. Gersick states that, after the transition phase, which occurred in most of her groups at about the temporal midpoint, the groups showed a "shift of attention" (1989, p. 291). She describes this transition as "when a system . . . turns from confusion towards clarity." The action-phase model also fits some of the propositions by Silver, Cohen, and Rainwater (1988). And, as suggested above, it also fits the hierarchical, sequential model proposed here.

The structure of the group's task process thus seems to be flexible, and it is influenced by the state of all of the coordination network—members, tasks, tools, and their interrelations. Groups show fixed sequences of phases only if the projects being carried out have clear sequential requirements. The different hierarchical levels of project activity influence each other.

Research on process interventions seems to suggest that any given (reasonable) deliberate intervention that forces or induces groups to adopt a fixed structuring of their task process may or may not lead to better group performance, compared to any (reasonable) alternative intervention. But such a process intervention is likely to lead to better performance than no intervention at all (Brilhart and Jochem, 1964; Hirokawa 1985, Jarboe, 1988, 1996; Sambamurthy, Poole, and Kelly, 1993).

The conception offered here—complex action system theory (CAST)—would suggest that group task performance is highly patterned, but not in a form reflecting a single fixed sequence of phases, or even different sequences of phases for tasks of different types. In this conception, group task performance reflects a hierarchical, sequential patterning of project, tasks, subtasks, and so on. At the highest or purpose level, project choice must get done initially, albeit sometimes tacitly, and need not be addressed again unless the group encounters major difficulties or unusual circumstances. At the middle or planning level, the process can be structured once (a "planning" phase, early in the period of group work), and that too does not need to be addressed again unless its implementation proves to be unfeasible. At the micro or action level, work unfolds in recurrent cycles (orienting-enacting-monitoring-modifying) whose sequence reflects the mesolevel plan.

Such a complex patterning—hierarchical, sequential, and differentiated with respect to technology and enactors—is not likely to be "discovered" by a simple slicing of a group's work session (or lifetime) into a certain number of equal temporal segments. Work at the micro level involves recurrent cycles, which, when the monitor part of the cycle indicates that a correction is needed, and the modify part of the cycle indicates that a change in action will not suffice, leads to a cascading modification of the higher-order plan, or even of the goal choice. Thus, although it is intricately patterned, group task performance does not reflect a single sequence of task performance phases. Our conception is a good fit with the empirical evidence on the issue of phase sequences.

Developmental Processes: The Dynamics of Development and Learning

Classically, the topic of group development has been approached by attempting to identify a series of regular and predictable stages through which a group must (or usually does, or is best off if it does) go through, in a prespecified order and within a reasonably specific time period. These stages are seen as relatively independent of the nature of the group or its tasks, and of the basic characteristics of its members. Some of the theories mentioned in the previous section (e.g., Bales and Strodtbeck, 1951; Fisher, 1970; Poole and Roth 1989a and 1989b) have often been labeled as theories of group development. However, that work concentrates on the group's performance of a certain type of task, rather than on the longer-run development of the group-as-a-system. Hence, their generalizability to groups doing other tasks, or even to the same groups on the same tasks but over a longer "life course," is unclear. Here, we concentrate on conceptions that are meant to apply to a wide variety of groups, independent of specific tasks, and that have reference to the development of the group itself, rather than just its performance of a task.

Theories of Group Development

The most widely and solidly established such set of stages is by Tuckman (1965; see also the later Tuckman and Jenson 1977 revision). It is based on empirical studies, mostly of therapy and training groups. It is summarized as forming, storming, norming, performing, and adjourning. In the forming stage, the group members engage in "orienting and testing" each other, the situation, and the task requirements. They then move on to a stage with more emotional potential (storming), where the group members negotiate the group structure and the acceptance and definition of the task. The next stage (norming) includes the development of group cohesion, which allows the group to approach the task in a coherent but open manner. Then the group moves to the performing stage, where members cooperate and focus on the task, without much emotion. The last stage (adjourning) describes the dissolution or the ending of the group. This model is very widely known, but its empirical basis is rather limited.

Some theorists (e.g. Hill and Gruner, 1973; Poole and Baldwin, 1996) have argued against an order of stages of group development that is both strictly sequential and normative, in that it sees deviations as the inability of a group to progress toward greater maturity and sees change to the next stage as progress. They propose cyclical or multistage models and suggest that groups indeed show different, distinguishable phases of behavior patterns, but may recycle through similar phases several times or may show the phases in a nonpredictable sequence, depending on multiple contingency factors (Poole and Baldwin, 1996).

Other authors see group development as a result of critical events or milestones that are turning points in the group's process. These can occur at a specific time period: Gersick (1988, 1989) found that both laboratory and extant groups went through a transition phase at the midpoint of their lifetime that changed their behavior patterns in a profound way. Fisher and Stutman (1987) analyzed the impact of routing statements as breakpoints of group phases. They found that phases are typically introduced by prospective routing statements and typically are brought to a close by retrospective routing statements.

Earlier, Bion and colleagues (Bion, 1961; Thelan, 1956; Thelan, Stock, and Others 1954) offered a "work and emotionality" theory based on psychoanalytic traditions, which can be viewed either as a conceptualization of the "phases of group work" or of the "stages of group development." They describe different phases in groups in terms of emotional preoccupations or emotional cultures of the groups. The dependency stage is characterized by group members being dependent either on the leader or on some external standard. In the fight-flight stage, the group members behave as if they were fighting some enemy or fleeing from some threat or danger. Pairing describes a phase of increased intimacy of group members, and the expression of warmth and supportiveness.

Currently, Wheelan and colleagues (Verdi and Wheelan, 1992; Wheelan and McKeage, 1993) are doing work that draws upon the Bion theoretical perspective, but expands it by incorporating other developmental perspectives as well. Wheelan (1994) describes group development as a process of groups achieving maturity rather than as a strictly sequential process. Her five stages are: (1) dependency and inclusion, when group members like to please, get integrated, and explore the norms; (2) counterdependency and fight, characterized by conflict but also by establishing role clarity; (3) if the conflict at stage two can be resolved, the group members develop trust, and more mature interaction is possible; (4) work, when the group is optimally prepared for effective task performance, because norms, roles, and rules are developed; (5) termination, which marks the ending of that group as a distinct social entity. Although Wheelan's stages include some sequential patterning, they are seen as "stages of group maturity": A group can attain a certain stage but then fall back to another stage.

Wheelan and colleagues have obtained some empirical evidence supporting their theory. In an analysis of ten faculty groups, Wheelan and Tilin (1999) found a more mature stage of group development to be associated with higher school academic rank, higher parent involvement, and higher staff perception of productivity. Buzaglo and Wheelan (1999) describe a method to increase the developmental level and the effectiveness of groups, based on their group development theory.

So far, we have discussed theories that treat group development mainly on the group level. Recently, Worchel (1996; Worchel et al., 1992) has offered a developmental-stages schema that considers the importance of the group for its members' needs and interests, but also predicts intragroup behavior and intergroup perceptions. Groups may repeatedly recycle through six different stages:

1. Discontent, characterized by an alienation of the individual from the group due to the low importance the group has for that individual. At the group level, groups may suffer from low and irregular attendance or group member departures.
2. A precipitating event may "wake up" the group and lead to identification of the members who want to remain in the group and comply with the group goals.
3. Groups then begin to establish identity and independence. In this stage, group position, boundaries, and group membership are defined, and group members develop a sense of cohesiveness and belonging, but also exert pressure to conform on deviants. The in-group is perceived as homogenous and superior to outgroups, and group members may even wish conflict and competition with the outgroups.
4. After identification is established, the group can now turn its attention to group productivity, set and achieve goals, and seek out and make use of relevant individual skills to reach the common goal. Because goal achievement is so important, some cautious cooperation and alliances may be sought with relevant outgroups, as long as this cooperation does not threaten group identity.
5. A well-functioning group needs less attention, and the members can turn their concerns to individual needs and be preoccupied with the

individual's relations with the group, such as personal recognition or equity. The relationship to out-groups becomes more cooperative as group members evaluate the individual benefits that can be achieved from out-groups.
6. Decay is the stage at which the individual's needs are predominant and the group becomes less salient, which can lead to more open conflict. Failures are attributed to the in-group rather than to the out-group, which can become an attractive alternative for a group member.

Using this conception of development, Worchel et al. (1992) predicted and found that many group phenomena, such as groupthink, stereotyping, and social loafing, are more likely to occur in some stages of group development than in others.

Moreland and Levine (Moreland and Levine, 1982; Levine and Moreland, 1981) have addressed the socialization process, which is one aspect of development that is even more concentrated on the relationship between the group and the individual level. The underlying model states that groups and their members evaluate the instrumentality and attractiveness of each other for fulfilling their needs. Depending on the "fit" between group and member needs, adjustment processes or role transitions may take place that alter the relation between member and group. One such transition is group entry, another is the acceptance of a person as a full member, and a third is group exit. Such role transitions are a result of this basic two-way evaluation process between member and group, both initially and in subsequent negotiations between the member and the group to maximize mutual gains. Depending on the outcome of those negotiation processes, a group member goes through different stages, from a prospective member before acceptance into the group, to a new member, to a full member, if the person has negotiated his or her role in the group. If the role negotiation fails, or if needs or circumstances change, the group member may become marginal and a resocialization process begins. Resocialization has two possible outcomes: either the member regains status as a full member or group membership terminates, which makes the person an ex-member.

The transition between different statuses of group membership depends on meeting the respective evaluation criteria of both parties. For group entrance, the entry criteria have to be met, and the transition between the status of new to full members is done if the acceptance criteria are met. If the mutual commitment falls below the divergence criteria, transition from full to marginal member occurs.

There is a logical sequence of the different socialization steps, but there can be recycling between full and marginal member status. The pace of role transitions, however, is dependent on many factors, and may occur at different paces for different members. Moreland and Levine see a mutual influence of group member socialization and group development. Acceptance of new members, socialization and resocialization, and even the remembrance of ex-members may affect group development. Depending on the developmental stage of the group, the different socialization stages may be omitted, or altered. The Moreland and Levine model puts emphasis on the interplay between the individual group members and group development.

The theories about group development and group socialization cited above assume that groups change over time. Most of them are also based on the underlying assumptions that groups, much like individuals, tend to achieve greater maturity or need to resolve different prototypical problems at different phases (such as finding a common way to proceed in the norming stage or developing mutual trust in the pairing stage). But even if we accept these assumptions, the process of group development seems to be dependent on too many factors (for example individual member socialization) to be similar for and generalizable to all types of groups.

Group Development in Complex Action System Theory

Our complex action system theory (CAST) perspective offers an entirely different approach to the idea of group development. In CAST, developmental history of a group is to be reckoned in terms of a matrix of three modes of a group's life course and three levels of causal dynamics. The three time-ordered modes of a group's life course are formation, operations, and metamorphosis. This says nothing more than that (a) groups form, (b) they do what they do, and (c) at some point they may cease to exist or get transformed into a recognizably different system.

All three of these modes of a group's life course are infused with the continual and simultaneous operation of three levels of causal dynamics: local, global,

and contextual. Local dynamics refer to the complex interdependencies among members, tasks, tools, and features of the embedding contexts, as they play out over time. Global dynamics refer to system-level processes that emerge from, and subsequently shape and constrain, the operation of local dynamics. Contextual dynamics refer to the complex interplay between events in the group's embedding contexts and the system's responses to those events. The three levels of causal dynamics, local, global, and contextual, map more or less to the three kinds of temporal processes discussed earlier: operational, developmental, and adaptive.

Formation of groups entails some mix of four sets of forces: external versus internal forces on the one hand, and planned versus emergent forces on the other. Those in combination lead to four prototypical kinds of groups: (a) concocted groups, formed when external top-down (i.e., planned) forces predominate (as when a manager creates a group and assigns them projects and personnel); (b) founded groups, when top-down (planned) but internal forces predominate (as when someone creates a designed group of which he or she will be a key member); (c) self-organized groups, where bottom-up (emergent) but internal forces predominate; (d) circumstantial groups, where external but emergent forces set up circumstances that lead a set of people to engage in concerted action.

For work organizations, concocted groups are most numerous, though members at management levels often create founded groups as well. Self-organized groups often emerge informally. A good example would be the production-level-maintaining informal groups that plagued management in the classic Western Electric studies (Roethlisberger and Dickson 1936/1964). Such informal groups are often countervailing to the intentions of management.

Within any of these kinds, we can think about groups that are composed with more or less emphasis on the different constituent parts—members, projects, technology. One type of group that is very prevalent in organizations, and in studies of groups in organizations, is what complex systems theory calls task forces. Here, the main emphasis is on the project, and on the member-task relations or labor network. Another type of group is one that complex systems theory calls teams. Here the emphasis is on membership, and on the member-tool relations (or role network). A third type is a crew. Here, the technology and the task-tool relations or job network are most important. All three types are very prevalent in work organization, although many groupings that are called teams are actually task forces or crews. Because of their different developmental histories (i.e., which constituent elements and subnetworks are developed earliest and given most emphasis), these different types of work groups are differentially vulnerable to different kinds of change. Task forces are most vulnerable to a change in project. Teams are most vulnerable to a change in membership. Crews are most vulnerable to a change in technology.

Formation brings about the development of a rudimentary member-task-tool pattern, for the general class of projects that that group may undertake. This pattern becomes more richly articulated in the operations mode when the group selects a particular project and undertakes its execution. They become specified as a member-task-tool-time process structure. That structure gets modified as action unfolds.

So from the point of view of complex action system theory, the structure of the group's action process subsumes the group structures that consist of the member, task, tool, labor, role, and job subnetworks. These emerge from group action itself. So a group's structure is a complex set of relations that derives from, or emerges out of, its action. These structures subsequently guide and constrain subsequent action.

In this view, group development—both potential and actual—depends on what kinds of projects that group is going to do, as well as on what members are a part of it, and what technologies are in use. From the point of view of CAST, there is no such thing as a generic and ordered set of developmental stages, except for the quite abstract three modes of formation, operations, and metamorphosis.

Adaptive Processes

The relation between developmental patterns and patterns of adaptation is like the relation between inside and outside forces for change. Group development, as commonly conceived, is driven by intrinsic or internal forces that derive from the particular group's constituent parts and their patterning (i.e., their local dynamics). Development results in, and is the result of, the group's own structure and processes. In contrast, adaptation is driven by actions and events in the group's various embedding contexts. Adapta-

tion refers to (reciprocal) changes in the group as a system, and in parts of its embedding contexts, that arise in response to various (actual and anticipated) actions and events in the embedding systems that have implications for the group. Adaptation carries the implication of "response to change." It does not carry the implication of "effective response."

Though most social and organizational psychologists would probably accept the assertion that groups carry on continuous, multifaceted interchanges with aspects of their embedding contexts, there is nevertheless relatively little theory or empirical research that explores how embedding environments affect groups as systems and how those groups respond. Notable exceptions include work by Ancona and colleagues (e.g., Ancona and Caldwell, 1988, 1990) and by Hackman and colleagues (e.g., Allmendinger and Hackman, 1996). There is an extensive theoretical treatment of these issues in Arrow, McGrath, and Berdahl (2000) and in McGrath and Argote (2000), both reflecting the complex systems theory orientation. We will draw heavily upon those presentations here.

Complex systems theory proposes that groups operate in a "fitness landscape"; some "locations" (i.e., states) of the group in relation to its external contexts are better for the group than others—they have better payoffs for the group and its members, and/or lower costs. (This concept of "fitness landscape" is complex and requires considerable elaboration to be fully explicated. It is presented in some detail in other chapters of this book, notably Baum and Rao's, and will not be elaborated further here.) Changes in the group's relation to its external contexts are sometimes advantageous to the group and sometimes detrimental.

Types of Change Events

Change events come in various forms. First of all, changes may come in the form of intrusive or nonintrusive changes. Some changes simply change the environment with no direct impact on the group—they change the "fitness landscape" that the group is operating in (e.g., a competing product may be developed). Others changes directly impinge on the group itself (e.g., a manager may remove a key member). Change events also differ in magnitude, and in valence; some changes pose threats, some offer potential opportunities to the group, and some do both.

Embedding contexts vary in richness (potential resources) and volatility (rate and temporal patterning of change). Change events have a number of temporal properties. They vary in abruptness of onset, in rate and frequency, and in temporal patterning of various kinds. A series of changes all of the same kind and in the same direction is a trend, and its course is relatively predictable. Alternatively, a set of changes, collectively, can constitute a cycle. Or, a set of changes can vary in an apparently random way, constituting "fluctuation" in no apparent pattern.

Change events also vary in predictability, and controllability. If both predictable and controllable, they can be prevented, or if favorable they can be induced to occur at the time and circumstances of the group's choosing. If changes are unpredictable, and/or uncontrollable, they pose potential problems for the group.

Types of Adaptation to Change Events

Relations between external events and the system's responses to them can be very complex. There is a range of potential patterns of response to external events/actions, including accommodation to them, attempts to assimilate the changes or attenuate their effects, and "doing nothing," which is sometimes both a deliberate and a wise strategy. Changes often lead to unintended consequences. Moreover, there is often a nonproportional relation between amount and type of change event and the size and direction of change in the group. Sometimes big events yield small changes or none at all; sometimes small events yield big changes.

Adaptation may be *directed* or *undirected*. Undirected adaptation is like species evolution; it is a cycle of variation (in system structure, in system behavior, and/or in conditions in the environment), selection, and stabilization (retention). Directed adaptation is intentional action on the part of the system; it is a cycle of information processing (about the system, its environment, and their relations), planning, choice, and self-regulation.

There are some barriers to both kinds of adaptation, and other barriers to one kind or the other. Barriers to both direct and indirect adaptation include conditions in which there is a fluctuating and unpredictable environment. They also include situations involving conflicting motives, in which what is good for individuals or parts of a system does not correspond with what is good for the system as a whole.

There are some additional barriers for undirected adaptation. For example, conditions in which there is too little variation in the environment, or a too for-

giving environment, do not provide much force for variation. Moreover, undirected adaptation will not be very successful in the long run when selection is based on false association (superstitions, or spurious correlation). Finally, undirected adaptations may fail to take hold under conditions in which it is difficult to maintain or stabilize the new "form."

There are also some additional barriers for directed adaptation. A notable one is when there is a misunderstanding or erroneous prediction of the state of the environment (that is, errors in the group's "mental model" of the fitness landscape). Another is when there is a lack of consensus in the group regarding strategy or tactics (i.e., failure to achieve a coordination of interest or of understandings), or a lack of coordination of actions needed for execution of the intended changes. Finally, there may be an inability to keep the group on track after setbacks; and there may be explicit or tacit resistance to the changes by entrenched routines or factions.

The latter several examples suggest that internal factors also affect ability to adapt. Such internal factors include the state of the system at the time of the event (i.e., the group's current structure and functioning), the "legacy of the past" (its history, including its entrenched routines and its record of past actions and effects), and the type of group it is. As noted earlier in this chapter, different types of groups (teams, task forces, crews) are especially vulnerable to different types of changes.

Different forms of group may show different "change models." For example, crews may fit a "crisis adaptation" model in which one pattern holds for all normal operations, and a different structure and process "kicks in" when there is an emergency (e.g., the crew staffing a hospital emergency room when a major disaster occurs nearby). Task forces often may fit a "punctuated equilibrium" model, as did Gersick's (1988, 1989) groups. Only certain types of teams, which are organized with the expectation of persisting for considerable time and of carrying out multiple projects, may fit the kind of "developmental stage" model that is the most prevalent one used in research on group development (see prior section).

Time-Shifting of Responses to Change

Groups often "time shift" their response to a given change event. Such time shifts may place the response either before or after the change event. For events with negative implications for the group, McGrath and Beehr (1990) identified five "temporal zones" for coping responses:

1. Preventive coping: actions taken long before the change event.
2. Anticipatory coping: actions taken just before the event.
3. Dynamic coping: actions taken while the event is ongoing.
4. Reactive coping: actions taken immediately after the event.
5. Residual coping: actions taken long after the event.

While for negative events these are reasonably called "forms of coping," for positive events they reflect different timing in the pursuit of opportunities.

Preventive and anticipatory coping may try to prevent the event, but more often they are attempts to mitigate its consequences. The building of a levee along a riverbank does not prevent some later rise in the level of the water in the river, but rather prevents or attenuates the negative consequences of that high water for land beside the river. Reactive and residual coping are likely to occur in reaction to multiple occurrences of a given kind of change, or to occurrences of multiple changes; hence it is often difficult to "assign" antecedent conditions to them with precision.

Forms of Response to Change Events

From a systems-process point of view, there are three general forms of responses to such external system actions or events:

1. Negative feedback loops. These are system responses that attempt to attenuate or eliminate the impact of the change on the system.
2. Positive feedback loops. These are system responses that magnify the impact of the change on the system. This can be in the form of (a) switching (before, during, or after the event) to alternative structures or functions, (b) increased disorder beyond what is directly produced by the change event itself and, if the increased disorder is extreme enough, (c) either "creative innovation" or "collapse."
3. No response. The system may give no apparent response to a given event: This may occur because (a) the group failed to note the event, or assumed it would not alter the group's "fitness

landscape," or (b) some feature of the group's history, its self-regulatory processes, and/or its routines prevented or impeded response. Alternatively, an apparent "no response" may be an artifact of the observation process. It may be imputed to a system by an observer erroneously, because the system's response to the event was time-shifted. If the change event is already anticipated, or if response to it is delayed, the response occurs before or long after the observer "looks" at the group and concludes "no response."

Negative feedback dampens the impact of events. Positive feedback magnifies the impact. Time shifting obscures the impact. Hence, we should not expect to find the impact of events on the system to be isomorphic, in either valence or magnitude, with the valence and magnitude of the event.

This discussion implies several "principles" of adaptation worth noting:

• There is no reason to expect strong proportionality between magnitude of change events and responses to them.
• Responses to change events often have unintended consequences, both desirable and undesirable.
• Temporal displacement can obscure the fact of, and the nature of, adaptive changes.
• All changes are not adaptations; some are spontaneous innovations. That is, new patterns of group action may occur that are not traceable to any particular event in the system's embedding contexts. Such changes are sometimes attributable to the intentionality of the system or its embedded members.

Concluding Comments

This chapter offers a "frame theory" that combines action theory as applied to groups (AT) with a theory of small groups as complex systems (CST). We use that blended theory—a complex action systems theory (CAST) for groups—as an organizing framework for a detailed analysis of three crucial sets of temporal processes that operate continuously, and interdependently in groups: *operational processes* by which the group does what it does; *developmental processes* by which the group forms, develops, and changes as a system; and *adaptive processes* by which the group responds to, and/or anticipates, events and actions in its embedding systems that have impact on the operation and well-being of the group. Processes in all three of these temporal domains have been seriously neglected in past research and theory in social and organizational psychology and many related fields. Perhaps the frame theory offered here, and our discussion of these temporal issues, will encourage more frequent and serious attention to them in future theory and research on work groups in organizations.

Our theory, however, carries with it not only an implied "research program" that could greatly enlighten our understanding of groups and how they behave, but also some vexing methodological issues that must be surmounted to carry out that research program. The conceptual and substantive possibilities and the methodological issues are closely intertwined.

Thus, for example, our theoretical perspective implies a need for more emphasis in future research on studies of extant groups, over substantial periods of their life course, while they are interacting in natural contexts and under circumstances in which important costs and benefits are at stake—rather than continuing to compile studies of ad hoc groups in artificial circumstances and in isolation from embedding systems. It also implies a need for research that takes into account multiple attributes of membership, of projects/tasks, of technology, of embedding contexts, and of their combinations—rather than continuing to execute studies focusing on one or a very small number of these attributes.

In addition, CAST emphasizes (a) the importance of initial conditions, (b) the relatively greater predictability of system-level (global) variables rather than the micro level (local) variables on which so much past work has been focused, (c) the need to track the evolution of system level (global) variables over time and pay attention to the shape of that function, rather than to compare average quantitative levels of either local or global variables at some specific point in time, (d) the important role played by intentionality in human systems, and (e) the need to pay attention to dynamic operational processes, to developmental patterns, and to adaptive changes in response to changing external conditions.

But the same features of CAST that point to these prescriptions for future research in this domain also challenge many of the most basic assumptions of our major methodological perspectives. CAST presents a different logic of inquiry than the one to which we have become accustomed. In CAST, the emphasis is on tracking the evolution over time of global variables descriptive of the system, rather than on comparing average levels of local or global variables at some particular point in time. Our theory also raises some profound questions about issues of internal validity of study designs. For example, are we to regard effects traceable to "history" and "maturation" as artifacts threatening internal validity (the stance of current mainstream methodology), or are we to regard them as inherent features of the operation of the system, hence worthy of study in themselves? Our theory also raises questions about the roles of between-group and within-group designs, about the interplay of nomothetic and ideographic approaches, and about whether we should regard prediction and control or description and understanding as the central goals of the scientific enterprise. Finally, our theory raises immense questions about the nature of causality. Specifically, it challenges us to give a more prominent role in our studies of groups as complex systems to causal processes that reflect Aristotle's formal causality (e.g., unfolding developmental patterns), final causality (e.g., recognizing the important role of intentionality in human systems), and material causality (e.g., the key role of compositional issues), along with the strong emphasis that has always been given to so-called efficient or mechanical causality in the paradigm of positivistic science.

All of these issues are discussed in some detail in Arrow, McGrath, and Berdahl (2000). Those authors also discuss a general three-legged strategy for carrying out research compatible with their CST perspective. That triadic strategy involves the close intertwining of three major research approaches: formulation of comprehensive (verbal) theory, about the entire system or major parts of it; careful compilation of empirical evidence, both from prior research and from theoretically relevant subsequent research (especially studies using comparative field study and experimental simulation strategies); and development of computational models of the system or subsystems of interest. Using those three strategies interdependently in both mutually challenging and mutually supportive ways can at least let us move forward in our search for an improved understanding of operational, developmental, and adaptive dynamic processes in groups.

References

Allmendinger, J. & Hackman, J. R. (1996). Organizations in changing environments: The case of East German symphony orchestras. *Administrative Science Quarterly, 41*, 337–369.

Ancona, D. G. & Caldwell, D. F. (1988). Beyond task and maintenance: External roles in groups. *Group and Organization Studies, 13*, 468–494.

Ancona, D. G. & Caldwell, D. F. (1990). Information technology and new product teams. In J. Galegher, R. Kraut, & C. Egido (Eds.). *Intellectual teamwork: Social and technological foundations of cooperative work* (pp. 173–190). Hillsdale, NJ: Lawrence Erlbaum.

Ancona, D. G. & Chong, C. (1996). Entrainment: Pace, cycle, and rhythm in organizational behavior. In B. Staw & L. L. Cummings (Eds.), *Research in Organizational Behavior* (Vol. 18, pp. 251–284). New York: JAI Press.

Argote, L. & McGrath, J. E. (1993). Group processes in organizations: Continuity and change. *International Review of Industrial and Organizational Psychology, 8*, 333–389.

Arrow, H., McGrath, J. E., & Berdahl, J. L. (2000). *Small groups as complex systems: Formation, coordination, development, and adaptation.* Thousand Oaks, CA: Sage Publications.

Bales, R. F. (1950). *Interaction process analysis: A method for the study of small groups.* Cambridge, MA: Addison-Wesley.

Bales, R. F. & Strodtbeck, F. L. (1951). Phases in group problem solving. *Journal of Abnormal and Social Psychology, 46*, 485–495.

Baron, R. M., Amazeen, P. G., & Beck, P. J. (1994). Local and global dynamics in social relations. In R. R. Vallacher & A. Nowak (Eds.), *Dynamical systems in social psychology* (pp. 111–138). New York: Academic Press.

Bettenhausen, K. L. & Murnighan, J. K. (1985). The emergence of norms in competitive decision-making groups. *Administrative Science Quarterly, 30*, 350–372.

Bion, W. R. (1961). *Experience in groups and other papers.* New York: Basic Books.

Boos, M. & Meier, F. (1993). Die Regulation des Gruppenprozesses bei der Ensheidungsfindung [The regulation of group processes in decision making]. *Zeitschrift fuer Sozialpsychologie, 24*, 3–14.

Brilhart, J. K. & Jochem, L. M. (1964). Effects of different patterns on outcomes of problem-solving discussion. *Journal of Applied Psychology, 48*, 175–179.

Burnstein, E. & Berbaum, M. L. (1983). Stages in group decision making: The decompensation of historical narratives. *Political Psychology, 4*, 531–561.

Buzaglo, G. & Wheelan, S. A. (1999). Facilitating work team effectiveness: Case studies from Central America. *Small Group Research, 30*, 108–129.

Dewey, J. (1933). *How we think.* Boston: D. C. Heath & Co.

Ericsson, K. A. & Lehmann, A. C. (1996). Expert and exceptional performance: Evidence of maximal adaptation to task constraints. *Annual Review of Psychology, 47*, 273–305.

Fisher, B. A. (1970). Decision emergence: Phases in group decision making. *Speech Monographs, 37*, 53–66.

Fisher, B. A. & Stutman, R. K. (1987). An assessment of group trajectories: analyzing developmental breakpoints. *Communication Quarterly, 35*, 105–124.

Frese, M. & Sabini, J. (Eds.) (1985). *Goal directed behavior.* Hillsdale, NJ: Erlbaum.

Frese, M. & Zapf, D. (1994). Action as the core of work psychology: A German approach. In H. C. Triandis, M. D. Dunnette, & L. D. Hough (Eds.), *Handbook of organizational and industrial psychology* (2nd ed.) (Vol. 3, pp. 271–340). Palo Alto, CA: Consulting Psychologists Press.

Gersick, C. A. G. (1988). Time and transition in work teams: Toward a new model of group development. *Academy of Management Journal, 31*, 9–41.

Gersick, C. A. G. (1989). Marking time: Predictable transitions in task groups. *Academy of Management Journal, 32*, 274–309.

Gersick, C. A. G. & Hackman, J. R. (1990). Habitual routines in task performing groups. *Organizational Behavior and Human Decision Processes, 47*, 65–97.

Gollwitzer, P. M. (1990). Action phases and mind-sets. In E. T. Higgins & R. M. Sorrentino (Eds.). *Handbook of motivation and cognition: Foundations of social behavior* (Vol. 2, pp. 53–93). New York: Guilford Press.

Gundlach, W. & Schultz, G. (1987). Ist die Effektivitaet von Problemloesungen aus Diskussionen voraussagbar? [Can problem solving effectiveness be predicted from discussions?]. *Psychologie fuer die Praxis, 4*, 350–368.

Hacker, W. (1985). Activity: a fruitful concept in industrial psychology. In M. Frese & J. Sabini (Eds.). *Goal directed behavior* (pp. 262–285). Hillsdale, NJ: Erlbaum.

Hackman, J. R. (1986). The psychology of self-management in organizations. In M. S. Pallak & R. O. Perloff (Eds.), *Psychology and work: Productivity, change, and employment.* Washington, DC: American Psychological Association.

Hackman, J. R. (1992). Group influence on individuals in organizations. In M. D. Dunnette & L. M. Hough (Eds.), *Handbook of industrial and organizational psychology* (2nd ed.) (Vol. 3, pp. 199–268). Palo Alto, CA: Consulting Psychologists Press.

Hackman, J. R. (1993). Teams, leaders, and organizations: New directions for crew-oriented flight training. In E. L. Wiener, B. G. Kanki, & R. L. Helmreich (Eds.), *Cockpit resource management* (pp. 47–69). San Diego, CA: Academic Press.

Hackman, J. R., Brousseau, K. R., & Weiss, J. A. (1977). The interaction of task design and group performance strategies in determining group effectiveness. *Organizational Behavior and Human Performance*, 16, 350–365.

Hackman, J. R. & Morris, C. H. (1975). Group tasks, group interaction process, and group effectiveness: A review and proposed integration. In L. Berkowitz (Ed.), *Advances in Experimental Social Psychology* (Vol. 8, pp. 45–99). New York: Academic Press.

Hill, W. F. & Gruner, L. (1973). A study of development in open and closed groups. *Small Group Behavior*, 4, 355–381.

Hirokawa, R. Y. (1983). Group communication and problem solving effectiveness: An investigation of group phases. *Human Communication Research*, 9, 231–305.

Hirokawa, R. Y. (1985). Discussion procedures and decision-making performance: A test of a functional perspective. *Human Communications Research*, 12, 203–224.

Hirokawa, R. Y. (1988). Group communication and decision-making performance: A continued test of the functional perspective. *Human Communication Research*, 14, 487–525.

Janis, I. L. & Mann, L. (1977). *Decision making.* New York: Free Press.

Jarboe, S. (1988). A comparison of input-output, process-output, and input-process-output models of small group problem solving effectiveness. *Communication Monographs*, 55, 121–142.

Jarboe, S. (1996). Procedures for enhancing group decision making. In R. Y. Hirokawa & M. S. Poole (Eds.), *Communication and group decision making* (2nd ed.) (pp. 345–383). Thousand Oaks, CA: Sage Publishing.

Kelly, J. R. & McGrath, J. E. (1985). Effects of time limits and task types on task performance and interaction of four-person groups. *Journal of Personality and Social Psychology*, 49, 395–407.

Larson, J. R. & Schaumann, L. J. (1993). Group goals, group coordination, and group member motivation. *Human Performance*, 6, 49–69.

Latané, B. & Nowak, A. (1994). Attitudes as catastrophes: From dimensions to categories with increasing involvement. In R. R. Vallacher & A. Nowak (Eds.), *Dynamical systems in social psychology* (pp. 219–249). New York: Academic Press.

Levine, J. M. & Moreland, R. L. (1991). Culture and socialization in work groups. In L. B. Resnick, J. M. Levine, & S. D. Teasly (Eds.), *Perspectives on socially shared cognition* (pp. 257–279). Washington, DC: American Psychological Association.

Lord, R. G. & Rowzee, M. (1979). Task interdependence, temporal phase, and cognitive heterogeneity as determinants of leadership behavior and behavior-performance relations. *Organizational Behavior and Human Performance*, 23, 182–200.

Mantovani, G. (1996). *New communication environments: From everyday to virtual.* London: Taylor & Francis.

McGrath, J. E. (1991). Time, interaction, and performance (TIP). A theory of groups. *Small Group Research*, 22, 147–174.

McGrath, J. E. & Argote, L. (2000). Group processes in organizational contexts. In R. S. Tindale & M. Hogg (Eds.), *Handbook of Social Psychology: Vol. 3. Group processes.* London: Blackwell Publishers.

McGrath, J. E., Arrow, H., & Berdahl, J. L. (2000). The study of groups, past, present, and future. *Personality and Social Psychology Review*, 4, 95–105.

McGrath, J. E. & Beehr, T. A. (1990). Time and the stress process: Some temporal issues in the conceptualization and measurement of stress. *Stress Medicine*, 6, 95–104.

McGrath, J. E. & Kelly, J. R. (1986). *Time and human interaction: Toward a social psychology of time.* New York: Guilford Press.

Mintzberg, H., Raisinghani, D., & Théorêt, A. (1976). The structure of "unstructured" decision processes. *Administrative Science Quarterly*, 21, 246–275.

Moreland, R. L. & Levine, J. M. (1982). Socialization in small groups: Temporal changes in individual-group relations. In L. Berkowitz (Ed.), *Advances in experimental social psychology* (Vol. 15, pp. 137–192). New York: Academic Press.

Nutt, P. C. (1984). Types of organizational decision processes. *Administrative Science Quarterly*, 29, 414–450.

Orasanu, J. M. (1993). Decision-making in the cockpit. In E. L. Wiener, B. G. Kanki, & R. L. Helmreich (Eds.), *Cockpit resource management* (pp. 137–172). San Diego, CA: Academic Press.

Orasanu, J. M. (1994). Shared problem models and flight crew performance. In N. Johnston, N. McDonald, & R. Fuller (Eds.), *Aviation psychology in practice* (pp. 255–285). Hants: Avebury Technical.

Poole, M. S. (1981). Decision development in small groups I: A test of two models. *Communication Monographs, 48,* 1–24.

Poole, M. S. (1983). Decision development in small groups III: A multiple sequence model of group decision making. *Communication Monographs, 50,* 321–344.

Poole, M. S. & Baldwin, C. L. (1996). Developmental processes in group decision making. In R. Y. Hirokawa & M. S. Poole (Eds.), *Communication and group decision making* (2nd ed.) (pp. 215–268). Thousand Oaks, CA: Sage Publishing.

Poole, M. S. & DeSanctis, G. (1989). Use of group decision support systems as an appropriation process. *Proceedings of the 22nd Annual Hawaii International Conference on System Sciences* (Vol. 4, pp. 149–157). New York: ACM Press.

Poole, M. S. & DeSanctis, G. (1990). Understanding the use of decision support systems: The theory of adaptive structuration. In J. Fulk & C. Steinfield (Eds.), *Organizations and communication technology* (pp. 175–195). Newbury Park, CA: Sage Publications.

Poole, M. S. & Roth, J. (1989a). Decision development in small groups IV: A typology of decision paths. *Human Communication Research, 15,* 323–356.

Poole, M. S. & Roth, J. (1989b). Decision development in small groups V: Test of a contingency model. *Human Communication Research, 15,* 549–589.

Psathas, G. (1960). Phase movement and equilibrium tendencies in interaction process in psychotherapy groups. *Sociometry, 23,* 177–194.

Putnam, L. L. (1981). Procedural messages and small group work climates: A lag sequential analysis. In M. Burgoon (Ed.), *Communication yearbook* (pp. 331–350). New Brunswick, NY: Transaction Books.

Roethlisberger, F. J. & Dickson, W. J. (1936/1964). *Management and the worker.* Cambridge, MA: Harvard University Press.

Sambamurthy, V., Poole, M. S., & Kelly, J. (1993). The effects of variations in GDSS capabilities on decision-making processes in groups. *Small Group Research, 24,* 523–546.

Semmer, N. & Frese, M. (1985). Action theory in clinical psychology. In M. Frese & J. Sabini (Eds.), *Goal directed behavior: The concept of action in psychology* (pp. 296–310). Hillsdale, NJ: Lawrence Erlbaum.

Shure, G. H., Rogers, M. S., Larsen, I. M., & Tassone, J. (1962). Group planning and task effectiveness. *Sociometry, 25,* 263–282.

Silver, S. D., Cohen, B. P., & Rainwater, J. (1988). Group Structure and information exchange in innovative problem solving. *Advances in Group Processes, 5,* 169–194.

Stech, E. L. (1975). An analysis of interaction structure in the discussion of a ranking task. *Speech Monographs, 37,* 249–256.

Talland, G. A. (1955). Tasks and interaction process. Some characteristics of therapeutic group discussions. *Journal of Abnormal and Social Psychology, 50,* 105–189.

Thelen, H. A. (1956). Emotionality of work in groups. In L. D. White (Ed.), *The state of the social sciences.* Chicago: University of Chicago Press.

Thelen, H. A., Stock, D., & Others. (1954). *Methods for studying work and emotionality in group operation.* Chicago: University of Chicago Human Dynamics Laboratory.

Tschan, F. (1995). Communication enhances small group performance if it conforms to task requirements: The concept of ideal communication cycles. *Basic and Applied Social Psychology, 17,* 371–393.

Tschan, F., Semmer, N. K., Nagele, C., & Gurtner, A. (2000). Task adaptive behavior and performance in groups. *Group Processes and Interpersonal Relations, 3,* 367–386.

Tschan, F. & von Cranach, M. (1996). Group task structure, processes, and outcome. In M. A. West (Ed.), *Handbook of work group psychology* (pp. 92–121). Chichester, England: John Wiley.

Tuckman, B. W. (1965). Developmental sequences in small groups. *Psychological Bulletin, 65,* 384–399.

Tuckman, B. W. & Jenson, M. A. C. (1977). Stages of small group development revisited. *Group and Organizational Studies, 2,* 419–427.

Vallacher, R. R. & Nowak, A. (Eds.) (1994). *Dynamical systems in social psychology.* New York: Academic Press.

Verdi, A. F. & Wheelan, S. A. (1992). Developmental patterns in same sex and mixed sex groups. *Small Group Research, 23,* 356–378.

von Cranach, M. (1996). Toward a theory of the acting group. In E. Witte & J. H. Davis (Eds.), *Understanding group behavior: Small group processes and interpersonal relations* (pp. 147–187). Hillsdale, NJ: Lawrence Erlbaum.

von Cranach, M., Ochsenbein, G., & Tschan, F. (1987). Actions of social systems: Theoretical and empirical investigations. In G. R. Semin & B. Krahé (Eds.), *Issues in contemporary German social psychology—History, theories, and applications* (pp. 119–155). London: Sage Publications.

von Cranach, M., Ochsenbein, G., & Vallach, L. (1986). The group as a self-acting system: Outline of a theory of group action. *European Journal of Social Psychology, 16,* 193–229.

Walther, J. B. (1994). Anticipated ongoing interaction vs. channel effects on relational communication in computer-mediated interaction. *Human Communication Research, 20,* 473–501.

Walther, J. B. & Burgoon, J. K. (1992). Relational communication in computer-mediated interaction. *Human Communication Research, 19,* 50–88.

Weingart, L. (1992). Impact of group goals, task component complexity, effort, and planning on group performance. *Journal of Applied Psychology, 77,* 682–693.

West, M. A. (1996). Reflexivity and work group effectiveness: A conceptual integration. In M. A. West (Eds.), *Handbook of work group psychology* (pp. 555–579). Chichester: Wiley.

Wheelan, S. A. (1994). *Group processes: A developmental perspective.* Sydney: Allyn & Bacon.

Wheelan, S. A. & McKeage, R. L. (1993). Developmental patterns in small and large groups. *Small Group Research, 24,* 60–83.

Whellan, S. A. & Tilin, F. The relationship between faculty group development and school productivity. *Small Group Research, 30,* 59–81.

Wittenbaum, G. M. & Stasser, G. (1996). Management of information in small groups. In J. L. Nye & A. M. Brower (Eds.). *What's social about social cognition? Social cognition in small groups* (pp. 3–28). Thousand Oaks, CA: Sage Publications.

Worchel, S. (1996). Emphasizing the social nature of groups in a developmental framework. In J. L. Nye & A. M. Brower (Eds.). *What's social about social cognition? Social cognition in small groups* (pp. 3–28). Thousand Oaks, CA: Sage Publishing.

Worchel, S., Coutant-Sassic, D., & Grossman, M. (1992). A developmental approach to group dynamics: A model and illustrative research. In S. Worchel, W. Wood, & J. Simpson (Eds.), *Group Process and Productivity.* Newbury Park, CA: Sage Publishing.

4

Dualities and Tensions of Planned Organizational Change

Myeong-Gu Seo, Linda L. Putnam, & Jean M. Bartunek

Our purpose in this chapter is twofold. First we describe a variety of types of capacity-building planned change efforts in organizations (cf. Beer and Nohria, 2000) as these emerged and developed from the mid–twentieth century through the turn of the twenty-first century. Second, we explore underlying dualities and tensions and their implications within each of these change efforts. We do so to highlight some hidden dynamics of these approaches and to open up possibilities for their wider and deeper development. Thus, we examine both theories and practices linked with planned change to uncover dichotomies, or dualities, in approaches and tensions among underlying assumptions of these perspectives.

We discuss several approaches to planned organizational change that have been prominent for substantial periods of time, emphasizing the types of behavioral practices and assumptions associated with each of them. These include action research, sensitivity training, team building, sociotechnical systems and quality of work life, organizational transformation, large group interventions, learning organizations, and appreciative inquiry. We review these approaches both conceptually and practically, noting

how they have been implemented, their underlying dimensions, and what tensions characterize their change processes. In doing this, we hope to enhance scholarly understanding and appreciation of the underlying processes and dualities typically associated with planned organizational change. (Although practitioner understandings of planned change are not an explicit focus here, they are addressed by Austin and Bartunek, 2003.)

We focus on a common set of dualities and oppositional tensions that become evident in reviewing the vast literature on planned organizational change. These dualities are implicit in the theories of planned change and in the observed practices reported in the literature. Thus, the dualities arise from comparisons across literatures and unpacking assumptions embedded in particular approaches. Regardless of whether these dualities are privileged as figure or disguised as background, they affect how the various change processes are conceptualized and implemented. Through exploring the dualities in this literature, we set forth a framework for research on planned change that embraces the tensions that underlie change efforts rather than privileging one form over the other.

We begin this chapter by discussing the role of dualities in theory building and by explaining our approach to deconstructing the tensions implicit in this literature. First we describe briefly our findings on the dichotomies that surfaced in our review of planned change. Then we review and summarize the literature on the different approaches to planned change in three different sections, concluding each with an analysis and critique of the way tensions among these dualities are managed in the literature. This discussion is summarized in table 4.1, which presents the dualities underlying planned organizational change and the ways the different approaches conceptualize and manage them.

We group the approaches to planned change into three "generations" of planned change (cf. French and Bell, 1995), based primarily on when particular planned change approaches began to be implemented widely and on the more or less common assumptions that underlay these approaches. These are (1) first-generation planned change, including action research, sensitivity training, team building, sociotechnical systems, and quality of work life; (2) second-generation planned change, including organizational transformation and large group interventions; and (3) third-generation planned change, including learning organizations and appreciative inquiry. The great majority of these approaches to planned change have been subsumed under the rubric of organization development (OD), and we use this term to refer to them. Approaches associated with each of these generations continue to be implemented in organizations. Some of the dualities and tensions present in the first-generation approaches are similar to those of the second-generation approaches and some differ. Third-generation approaches represent in some ways an interesting blend of first-generation and second-generation assumptions, although they also embody different alternatives to managing the tensions that arise from these dualities.

Dualities and Tensions

Dualities and tensions play an important role in organizational change and in theory building about organizations (Cameron, 1986; Cameron and Quinn, 1988; Eisenhardt and Westcott, 1988; Frey, 1995; Ford and Backoff, 1988; Howard and Geist, 1995; Isaacs, 1993; O'Connor, 1995; Smith and Berg, 1987;

Stohl and Cheney, 2001). Dualities refer to polar opposites that often work against one another; thus, they represent oppositional pulls that vary in degrees. These dualities are not necessarily contradictions that are mutually exclusive. For example, organizations could clearly implement planned change at both the individual and organizational levels. However, because it is difficult to direct planned change programs at both levels simultaneously, this dichotomy surfaces as a tension in deciding the most appropriate entry level for a planned change effort. What is targeted and privileged often drives out or subjugates the polar opposite that resides in the background of the process. Thus, these dualities are not simply alternatives, e.g., invoking technical approaches or choosing humanistic perspectives. The choice to focus on one of the poles creates a tension and difficulty to enact both ends of the continuum simultaneously.

Moreover, dualities exist in bipolar relationships that imply multiple interrelated tensions. For example, certainty-uncertainty is tightly linked with bipolar relationships between predictable-unpredictable, expected-unexpected, and routine—non-routine. Hence, any one duality exists in larger systems of bipolar pairs that impinge on the ways that planned change approaches are understood and managed. In this chapter, we use dualities to reflect on and critique theories of planned change.

Similar to Poole and Van de Ven (1989, p. 562), this chapter operates from the presumption that "social science loses an important resource for theory development" by ignoring the incompatible or inconsistent elements associated with particular approaches to planned change. Incompatibilities contribute to theory building by signaling "implicitly stated assumptions and explanations" that determine the operative scope for an approach (p. 562). Thus, a major opportunity in theory building is to unpack these implicit assumptions, focus on theoretical tensions, and "use them to stimulate the development of more encompassing theories" (p. 563). This chapter, then, extends prior work on organizational contradictions, oppositional tensions, and social paradoxes into theories of planned change. It differs from previous work not only by unpacking the dichotomies across different approaches, but also by focusing on new dimensions of planned change that surface in this analysis. Thus, our goal in this chapter is to use dualities and tensions to extract the underlying dynamics of planned change and to posit new perspectives for work in this

Table 4.1 Types of and ways to handle dualities in planned organizational change

	First-Generation OD Approaches	Second-Generation OD Approaches	Third-Generation OD Approaches	
			Learning Organization	Appreciative Inquiry
Targets and Impetus of Change				
Individual/group vs. organization-wide	*Selection/denial*: focus on groups and individuals, ignoring the potential tension with organization-wide focus	*Integration/forced-merger*: privilege organization-wide focus over individual/group focus	*Transcendence/reframing*: incorporate both focuses by creating new terms and methods	*Integration/neutralization*: focus on both processes, not recognizing potential tensions
Internal *vs.* external	*Selection/denial*: focus on internal drivers, ignoring external forces	*Separation/temporal process*: both drivers work at different times	*Transcendence/synthesis*: build internal capacity to address external challenges	*Selection/overt choice*: decidedly focus on internal drivers and capacity for change
Human system vs. technical system	*Selection/coexistence*: human system is privileged over technical system	*Integration/forced-merger*: greater focus on strategic issues	*Transcendence/synthesis*: develop a human system that enables adaptation to strategic and technical challenges	*Selection/overt choice*: decidedly focus on the human system as both the means and the ends for change
First order vs. second order	*Selection/denial*: foster first-order change more than second-order change	*Separation/temporal process*: both types occur in different timing but focus on initiating second-order change	*Transcendence/reframing*: focus on learning that makes both possible	*Selection/coexistence*: with a preference for second-order change
Characteristics of Change Processes				
Negative focus vs. positive focus	*Selection/denial*: focus on negative sides, ignoring positive sides	*Integration/forced-merger*: privilege either positive or negative sides	*Transcendence/reframing*: learning encompasses both aspects	*Selection/overt choice*: decidedly focus on positive aspects
Continuous vs. episodic	*Selection/denial*: dominant emphasis on episodic processes	*Selection/denial*: dominant emphasis on episodic processes	*Integration/forced merger*: focus on continuous renewals to be ready for episodic processes	*Selection/denial*: dominant emphasis on episodic processes
Proactive vs. reactive	*Separation/topical dominance*: separate proactive and reactive processes	*Separation/temporal process*: both processes are emphasized in different timing	*Integration/neutralization*: being proactive in helping organization respond to changing environment	*Selection/coexistence*: with a strong preference for proactive processes
Open vs. closed	*Selection/overt choice*: strong emphasis on open processes	*Separation/topical dominance*: both processes used for different aspects or topics of change	*Selection/overt choice*: decidedly open	*Selection/overt choice*: decidedly open

area. We review the different ways that organizations manage dualities and then describe the eight dichotomies that surfaced in our analysis of the various approaches to planned organizational change.

Ways of Managing Dualities

Literature on paradoxes and contradictions suggests four different categories for managing dualities. These include selection, separation, integration, and transcendence. Selection entails denial in which parties ignore the opposite pole and, thereby, inadvertently select one side of the dichotomy over the other. "Just as both hands are necessary for clapping, two oppositional poles are essential" for understanding the dichotomies implicit in theory and research (Baxter and Montgomery, 1996, p. 61). Selection is the most typical way that theorists manage contradictions; however, it may "produce specialized versions of theories"—ones that may disregard key elements and their interrelationships or that may ignore the dynamic patterns of contradictory systems (Poole and Van de Ven, 1989). Reluctant coexistence is a variation of the selection approach. In this option, theorists acknowledge the existence of dualities, but place them in a "cold war" relationship that typically favors one side over the other. For example, many theorists recognize that change can be both proactive and reactive. But rather than explore the relationships between these tensions, theorists may treat them as discrete and threatening to each other and privilege either the reactive or the proactive processes. Coexistence then is a way of privileging one horn of the dilemma as correct and preferred.

Separation, the second approach, differs from selection in recognizing both poles of the dichotomy, but separating them through levels of analysis, topical domains, or temporal processes (Pearson, 2001; Poole and Van de Ven, 1989). For example, some theorists manage the tensions between individual/group and organization-wide change through appropriating them to different levels of analysis. A particular change intervention might be described as operating one way at the individual level and an opposing way at the organizational or institutional level. As another example, organizations might be described as handling tensions between open and closed change processes by adopting a closed process (not allowing employees' participation) in making decisions about change policies and relying on an open employee participation process to implement the designated change.

In like manner, theorists separate bipolar tensions by linking them to different topics. Thus, theorists might manage tensions between internal and external change by aligning particular issues such as quality of work life to internal drivers and assigning other topics such as productivity to the external arena. In actuality, quality of work life and productivity may be as inseparable as internal and external environments. Separation can also occur on a temporal level. In this way dualities exert similar influences but at different times. For example, planned change might be closed and exclusionary in early phases of change and then be open and participatory later. In each of these approaches, theorists treat the dichotomies as independent rather than tightly connected. The separation approach incorporates both poles of the duality but in ways that ignore the tensions, critical interdependence and mutual influence of these bipolar pairs. Thus, the ends of this bipolar continuum are treated as self-contained and fundamentally appropriate in isolation. Moreover, the separation approach does not effectively deal with conceptual limitations in the theory (Poole and Van de Ven, 1989). That is, managing tensions in planned change through shifting levels of analysis, topical domains, and time periods does not aid in addressing the shortcomings or limitations in developing theory or practice.

The third approach, integration, combines the dualities in one of two different ways—neutralization and forced merger. Neutralization is similar to compromise or splitting the difference in managing contradictions (Pearson, 2001). It refers to a balance in that both ends of the continuum are legitimate at once but remain unfulfilled in their totality. For example, in a neutralized, "middle of the road" approach to planned change, an intervention might be viewed as marginally proactive and somewhat reactive but neither characteristic is fully realized in the perspective. Since the bipolar pairs are compromised and diluted, this approach is an unstable response to the tensions between these pairs (Baxter and Montgomery, 1996). The forced-merger perspective parallels the selection approach in that theorists recognize both binary positions but force or bridge them in confounding ways. For example, certain approaches to triangulation of quantitative and qualitative methods, such as combining ethnographic analysis with quantifiable survey data, represent a forced merger in that the integration violates the epistemological assumptions of opposing perspectives. Moreover, the outcome of many forced mergers replicates the selection approach to managing contradictions in that one side of the pole typically ends up privileged in the final choice.

Transcendence, also known as synthesis and reframing, refers to managing dualities through transforming dichotomies into a new perspective or a reformulated whole. Drawn from dialectics and rooted in assumptions of thesis, antithesis, and synthesis, transcendence results from change that occurs when dualities are transcended so that the original tension among them no longer exists. In reframing, new conceptual definitions arise. For example in conflict situations, the tensions between cooperation and competition become reframed when parties transcend their differences and uncover a new definition of the dispute. What the parties may originally label as a relational problem can be transformed into differences in personal styles. Even though transcendence recognizes and embodies both sides of the pole, it does so by working toward a synthesis or a new definition. Hence, the way to manage dualities becomes channeling the tensions and energy between dichotomies into a new form. The transcendence approach then abandons the original poles through a redefinition or unique synthesis.

Dimensions and Dualities of Planned Organizational Change

To understand how dualities are managed in planned organizational change, we identified dualities, generated dimensions, and selected particular dichotomies from the appropriate literature. First, we developed a list of multiple dualities that surfaced or were implicit in the planned change literature. In developing this list, we looked at both the underlying theories and the associated practices of various approaches to planned organizational change. The criteria we used for identifying these dualities were both conceptual and historical; we focus on how conceptually different perspectives to planned organizational change have emerged over time. We also addressed whether those perspectives have created real or potential incompatibilities and/or tensions in a given historical moment.

The resulting list included two dimensions that characterized general concerns about planned change—the targets and impetus of change (what to change and when) and characteristics of the change process (how to change). Within these general dimensions we found eight bipolar pairs that recurred in the literature and subsumed other dichotomies (as indicated in table 4.1). Hence, both the dimensions and the dualities of planned change surfaced inductively from our survey of the literature. They provided a lens to explore underlying dynamics, hidden assumptions, and the management of tensions in planned change. We briefly introduce them here. We will use these bipolar pairs to analyze and critique various types of planned change later.

Targets and Impetus of Change

The first dimension, targets and impetus of change, centers on who should receive the change, the organizational level at which the change is aimed, and the driver for making changes. Four dualities characterize the tensions that arise in determining the targets and impetus of change: individual/group versus organizational, internal versus external, human system versus technical system, and first order versus second order. The individual/group level encompasses interventions aimed at teams, supervisor-subordinate relationships, and subsets of organizational members, while the organizational level focuses on systemwide interventions aimed at organization as a whole. One of the critical issues in this tension is the degree to which change at the individual/group level reverberates throughout the organizational system or, in contrast, change at the system level infuses the processes of individuals and teams.

The internal versus external distinction addresses whether change initiatives focus on responding to externally driven forces that demand organizational alterations or on addressing issues and factors arising from inside organizations, such as desires to increase employees' satisfaction or improve the quality of their work life. First-generation OD work focuses on internal drivers to move employees to higher order needs while second-generation approaches center more on external drivers of change (Mirvis, 1988).

The third duality, human system versus technical system, addresses the type of system that receives the impact of the change. Human systems refer to the unique needs, motives, and interaction patterns of organizational members while technical systems entail the information and materials that become transformed into economic, strategic, and technical outcomes. Issues that stem from either system can trigger organizational change, but once triggered, change is likely to affect both systems, although in ways that are often not anticipated. The two systems are not necessarily in harmony, because the issues and requirements of one system often counter those of the other, causing unexpected problems and obstacles to change.

Finally, first-order versus second-order change addresses the depth of organizational change, that is, how radical or fundamental the planned changes are. One similar distinction is between single- and double-loop learning (Argyris and Schön 1978). First-order change refers to changes aimed at increasing skill or solving problems in an already agreed-upon arena, while second-order connotes efforts aimed at changing organizational members' frames of reference or the ways that they understand key components and functions of organizing. On the whole, OD interventions claim to aim at second-order change. In many cases, however, their initiatives are not frame breaking, in that they culminate in improvements present in already existing functions (Bartunek and Louis, 1988).

Characteristics of Change Processes

Characteristics of the change processes depict the way change occurs. This dimension centers on the temporal dynamics of change and the way change is implemented within organizations. There are four pertinent dualities of change processes, negative versus positive focus, continuous versus episodic, proactive versus reactive, and open versus closed. First, negative focus versus positive focus highlights where to center attention on driving and mobilizing organizational energy to evoke change. Negative focus draws attention to approaches that stress negative aspects of organizations, such as various problems at hand, whereas positive focus emphasizes the positive reasons for organizational change, such as building a unique organizational history, creating opportunities in the environment, or developing a positive future vision.

The second dualism, continuous versus episodic processes, as articulated by Weick and Quinn (1999), represents two different temporal patterns of change initiatives. In the episodic approach, change is understood and implemented as an occasional inter-

ruption or a divergence from equilibrium. In contrast, the continuous approach assumes that change is a pattern of ongoing modification in work processes and social practice. Although changes may look as if they occur episodically, in fact, multiple small changes are always present. Thus, although some scholars (e.g., Tushman and Romanelli, 1985) see organizational changes as revolutionary and happening quickly and cleanly, others (e.g., Greenwood and Hinings, 1988) suggest that these changes evolve from many activities that happen quickly but occur over extended periods of time.

The third bipolar pair is proactive versus reactive change. *Proactive* refers to change processes that occur in advance of problems as preparation for these eventualities. In contrast, reactive changes occur in response to unanticipated events or crises. This distinction also addresses whether an organization needs a crisis in order to change successfully. In a similar vein, Nadler and Tushman (1989) focus on the relationship between anticipatory and reactive changes, arguing that incremental and revolutionary changes could be either anticipatory or reactive.

Finally, the open versus closed dichotomy focuses on how open and participatory change processes are, for example, how much the change initiative stems from the top as opposed to the grassroots level and how much of it is secret with limited information shared. Some change efforts adhere to a bottom-up, participatory approach, consistent with Likert's (1967) recommendation for participation. However, interventionists also question whether managers abdicate too much authority when they promote high levels of participatory decision-making (O'Connor, 1995).

The next section presents a description of the first-generation organization development approaches. We pay particular attention to the kinds of interventions and their underlying assumptions. This section culminates with a discussion of the salient dualities in this perspective and the way first-generation OD approaches managed tensions among these dualities.

First-Generation Approaches to Organization Development (OD)

Roots and Characteristics

It was during the late 1950s and early 1960s that the term *organization development* (or OD) first appeared and then began to be widely used (Beckhard, 1969; Burke, 1992). Among the many definitions of OD that emerged during the 1960s, one of the most influential was Beckhard's (1969). He described OD as an organization-wide planned effort managed from the top to increase organization effectiveness and health through interventions in the organization's "processes" using behavioral science knowledge. As the definition suggests, OD included several components: (1) focus on system-wide change, (2) process-oriented interventions, and (3) reliance on behavioral science knowledge as the basis for intervention (French and Bell, 1995). First-generation OD, and many of its successors as types of interventions, emerged from and incorporated advances in behavioral science knowledge that appeared during the 1940s and 1950s, including action research, sensitivity training, sociotechnical systems, and survey feedback. We will briefly summarize how these have been implemented and have evolved.

Types of First-Generation Approaches

Action Research

John Collier (1945), a commissioner of U.S. Indian Affairs from 1933 to 1945, first defined action research and advocated joint efforts of researchers and clients to effectively resolve ethnic relations. Kurt Lewin, a social psychologist, established this type of approach for various types of social change, such as race relations, leadership, eating habits, and intergroup conflict (Burke, 1992; French and Bell, 1995). Soon action research was adopted by researchers and practitioners in a variety of social science fields. Pioneering action research projects include Coch and French's study of workers' resistance to change in a pajama factory (1948) and Whyte and Hamilton's study of Chicago's Tremont Hotel (1964).

The core idea of action research within work organizations and elsewhere is that research needs to be closely linked to action if organization members are to use it to implement change. To do so, collaborative efforts should be initiated between organization members and researchers in collecting, analyzing, and using research data about organizational functioning in order to develop and implement solutions to organizational problems (Pasmore and Friedlander, 1982). The phases of action research interventions include (1) systematically collecting research data about an ongoing system relative to some objective, need, or goal of the system followed by (2) feeding the data back to the system (i.e., survey feedback), (3) taking action based on the diagnosis, and (4) evaluating the results of the action (French and Bell, 1995). Several authors have proposed additional steps based on this model (e.g., French, 1969; Frohman, Sashkin, and Kavanagh, 1976; Schein, 1980).

The goal of action research as originally formulated was twofold. Action research consultants or researchers work collaboratively with organizational members to solve immediate, practical problems and also to make a scholarly contribution based on the outcome (Rapoport, 1970). In practice, as action research was increasingly implemented in OD efforts, the focus was centered much more on practice (implementing change) than on scholarship (Bartunek, 1983). Over time, however, variations of the original approach have arisen that have maintained a scholarly emphasis more than earlier action research did. For example, Argyris and his colleagues created "action science" by suggesting a more scientific approach in action research, which aims to allow true inquiry and experiments (removing organizational defenses), generating valid information, and thus fostering profound (double-loop) learning and organizational change (e.g., Argyris, 1983; Argyris, Putnam, and Smith, 1985; Argyris, 1989). Whyte and his colleagues created "participatory action research," an approach that emphasizes the participation of organization members as full partners and coresearchers in the entire action research process (e.g., Greenwood, Whyte, and Harkavy, 1993; Whyte, 1991). Additional variations include participatory research (e.g., Brown and Tandon, 1983), cooperative inquiry (Reason, 1988; Reason and Heron, 1995), and action inquiry (Torbert, 1991; Fisher and Torbert, 1995).

Sensitivity Training

Sensitivity training, known for its use of t-groups, began in the summer of 1946 in New Britain, Connecticut, when Kurt Lewin was asked by the director of the Connecticut State Inter-racial Commission to conduct a training workshop to improve community leadership in general and interracial relationships in particular (Bradford, 1967; Marrow, 1967). He brought together a group of colleagues to serve as trainers and researchers for the workshop. The training consisted of lectures, role playing, and general group discussion.

In the evenings most researchers and trainers met to evaluate the training by discussing participant behavior. Soon a few participants asked if they could observe the evening staff discussions. Reluctant at first, the researchers and trainers finally agreed. Participants attended the evening sessions and had a chance to respond to feedback about them. The results were influential and far reaching; the staff and participants realized that the feedback the participants were receiving about their daytime behavior was teaching them as much or more as the daytime activities. As more participants were invited to observe the staff discussions, gradually there emerged three-way discussions among the researchers, trainers, and participants. These conversations evolved into unstructured small group discussions in which the primary source of information for learning is the behavior and feedback of the group members themselves (Bradford, 1967; Burke, 1992; Marrow, 1967); feedback became the learning source for personal insight and development.

During the 1950s sensitivity training gravitated to organizational life as an intervention for organizational change (Burke, 1992; French and Bell, 1995). Members of the t-groups were organizational cousins—from the same overall organization but not the same vertical chain of the organization's hierarchy—or members of the same organizational team. Sensitivity training was considered the most "in-depth" type of organizational change (Harrison, 1970). The first organizational uses of sensitivity training, led by Herbert Shepard and Robert Blake, took place with managers at some of the major refiners of Esso (now Exxon) in an attempt to move management in a more participative direction (French and Bell, 1995). At about the same time McGregor and his colleagues conducted similar training sessions at Union Carbide (Burck, 1965; McGregor, 1967).

Team Building

As experiences in sensitivity training accumulated, researchers began to learn that the lack of structure that characterized sensitivity training was not optimal for organizational work groups (French and Bell, 1995). A wide range of interpersonal issues might surface during sensitivity training, but these might have little to do with the work itself. Moreover, hierarchical relationships were not present during t-group sessions, but after a t-group had been ended, organizational participants returned to their established hierarchical roles and relationships, often with problems resulting from the kind of discussion they had had during their t-group. Team building, a more structured approach that is designed for foster work teams' capacity to work together, and that focused directly on work issues and maintained hierarchical relationships, emerged as a more effective way of dealing with work-related issues (e.g., Dyer, 1977; Lundberg, 1985).

Team building incorporates a wide variety of methods in order to improve processes and relationships in organizational groups and is sometimes considered the type of intervention by which OD is best known. Team building was used initially for work with intact work teams and included a large number of types of interventions, including process consultation, consensus building, intragroup conflict resolution strategies, role analysis techniques, role negotiation strategies, and grid team development, to name just a few (e.g., Lundberg, 1985). All of these approaches are aimed at improving the ways team members work together. Over the course of the years, the types of issues and groups for which team building techniques have been used have expanded considerably. Dyer (1995) noted, for example, that it is now being used with self-directed work teams, with TQM strategies, after downsizing events, in building up international teams and cross-functional teams, and after mergers and acquisitions, when members of newly merged organizations need to learn to work together. One of the frequent occasions in which team building is used is with newly forming organizational groups, and it often includes some type of outdoor "survival" experience, in which group members learn to rely on each other to do well (e.g., Mirvis, 1990).

Sociotechnical Systems

At the same time sensitivity training was beginning in the United States, Eric Trist of the Tavistock Institute in the United Kingdom was consulting with a coal mining company. The company was suffering problems of decreased productivity and increased absenteeism, mainly due to the introduction of new equipment that fundamentally changed the way work was conducted from group-based labor to individual-based, specialized labor. Trist, working with Bamforth, a foreman at the coal mining company, designed a new approach to the work that combined the essential social elements of the previous mode of work—team as opposed to individual effort—yet retained the new technology. This approach, which came to be labeled sociotechnical systems (STS), increased productivity to previous levels, if not higher, and significantly decreased absenteeism (Trist and Bamforth, 1951). Rice (1958) conducted similar interventions in two textile mills in Ahmedabad, India.

STS is based on a premise that an organization is simultaneously a social and technical system, both of which must be considered and optimized as a goal of any organizational change (Burke, 1992; Pasmore, 1988; Trist, 1989). These two aspects are independent, but necessarily related. The important issue is how to design the parts so that both outcomes are positive. Like the evolution of t-groups to team building, the insights from STS have continued to evolve. A primary place was in quality of work life programs.

Quality of Work Life

Quality of work life (QWL) programs emerged in northern Europe in the 1960s and moved to the United States in the late 1960s and early 1970s (Mirvis, 1988; Moch and Bartunek, 1990). Philosophically rooted in the sociotechnical systems tradition, early QWL practitioners in Great Britain, Ireland, Norway, and Sweden developed QWL programs that generally involved joint participation by unions and management in the design of work and resulted in work designs giving employees high levels of discretion, task variety, and feedback about the results (Moch and Bartunek, 1990).

The QWL movement was adopted in the United States in the early 1970s (Work in America Institute, 1973). The Ford Foundation sponsored a QWL conference that led to the formation of an international quality of work life council and then the National Commission on Productivity (NCOP). NCOP assisted with the initiation of several joint labor-management collaborative programs, and got other organizations, such as Rushton Coal Mine, the Tennessee Valley Authority, Mount Sinai Hospital, and Weyerhuaser involved in demonstration experiments (Camman, Lawler, Ledford, and Seashore, 1984). The QWL programs in the United States all

included joint union-management teams that led the efforts. The purpose of these committees was to work together outside the framework of the collective bargaining agreement to solve problems that labor and management experienced jointly (Moch and Bartunek, 1990). These labor-management committees, assisted by consultants, incorporated several types of strategies aimed at improving employee productivity and satisfaction. Examples of the types of initiatives implemented at one or more of the organizations included autonomous work groups, career development, reward systems, management styles and practices, group and intergroup relations, and physical and social work environments (Cummings and Worley, 1997; Suttle, 1977). QWL programs also focused on issues such as adequate and fair compensation, a safe and healthy working environment, personal growth and development, satisfaction of social needs in the workplace, personal rights, compatibility between work and nonwork activities, and the social relevance of work life (Walton, 1974).

Mirvis (1988, 1990) suggested that the QWL movement affected OD practice in three ways. First, with the increasing awareness of structural barriers and power relations in organizations (e.g., between management and labor), it helped OD embrace more power-based forms of change and conflict management, particularly a cooperative approach to union-management relations. Second, it contributed to the adoption and utilization of various collateral structures, such as autonomous work groups and quality circles, to address ill-structured problems in organizations. Third, it promoted more collective involvement (both management and labor) in the management of change in organizations and reinforced the OD ideal of human development and fulfillment (high quality of work life) as a means of increasing organizational effectiveness.

Quality of work life programs in their original guise are no longer widely used. However, they have helped give birth to a number of types of organizational interventions, especially what are called "high involvement" organizations (e.g., Lawler, 1986). As a primary manifestation of high involvement, self-managed work teams emerged and have been widely adopted (e.g., Manz and Sims, 1993; Stewart and Manz, 1995). In simplest terms, self-managed work teams are groups of employees organized into teams who are given increased autonomy in and control over their jobs. Many responsibilities traditionally reserved for managers and supervisors, such as the selection of work methods and schedules, the assignment of within-team job tasks, the solution of quality and interpersonal problems, and the authority to conduct team meetings, are delegated to the team. Self-managed work teams are increasingly prominent (Stewart and Manz, 1995).

Survey Feedback

The early development of OD was also influenced by survey feedback (Burke, 1992), a methodology developed in the 1940s at the Institute for Social Research (ISR) at the University of Michigan. Psychologists at ISR were using questionnaire surveys as a basis for systematic diagnosis of employee morale and attitudes (Burke, 1992). One of these psychologists, Floyd Mann, experimented with ways of giving results of these surveys to participating companies. He discovered in a study at Detroit Edison (Mann, 1962) that when a manager was given the survey results, any resulting improvement depended on what the manager did with the information. Little change occurred when managers failed to discuss the results with subordinates and plan with them what to do to bring about improvement. Instead, the joint effort of supervisors and their immediate subordinates discussing the survey data and developing action plans together on the basis of the data was critical to bring about substantial favorable changes (French and Bell, 1995; Mann, 1962). Therefore, survey feedback was developed in a way that included two steps. The first is a survey, collecting data to determine employees' perceptions of a variety of factors, particularly concerning management of their organization. The second is the feedback, reporting the results of the survey systematically in a summary form, down the hierarchy in an "interlocking chain of conferences"[1] (Mann, 1962, p. 609). This feedback is followed by a joint discussion by supervisors and their immediate subordinates regarding the meaning of the survey results for their particular groups and the action steps needed for improvement (Burke, 1992). There was a time in the 1970s when survey feedback was thought to be the most effective of the intervention strategies in use in OD (Bowers, 1973). Survey feedback in some form continues to be used as an integral part of most OD consultation; some data are collected, generally from a questionnaire, interviews, or small group exercises,

and are fed back to participants (Goode and Bartunek, 1990; Ramirez and Bartunek, 1989). Then the groups plan on the basis of the data.

Conceptual Basis of First-Generation OD Approaches

Early in the development of OD, Bennis (1966) distinguished between a theory of change (why and how change occurs) and a theory of changing (what must be done to induce change and how to best ensure the success of a change attempt). First-generation OD exhibited considerable diversity with regard to theories of changing. OD researchers and scholars proposed several types of strategies, intervention models, and techniques for implementing diverse types of organizational change (Burke, 1992; Porras and Robertson, 1987). As a result, there was substantial variety among OD researchers and practitioners on concrete action steps to be undertaken, key variables that should be analyzed for an effective diagnosis, key intervention targets, the conditions necessary for effective change, and characteristics of change agents (Beer and Walton, 1987; Porras and Robertson, 1987). Change agents with a sensitivity training background relied on group approaches, focusing on personal and interpersonal development through team building. Other change agents addressed individual jobs, for example, job design and improving work conditions for individual employees (e.g., Hackman and Oldham, 1980). Still others targeted the entire system. For example, Likert (1967) described four types of organizational systems—exploitive autocratic, benevolent autocratic, consultative, and participative—and focused on developing the last type of system (participative—System 4) through utilizing survey feedback.

However, there was a highly influential and commonly adopted theory of changing, one consistent with action research, that provided first-generation OD researchers and practitioners with an overarching framework that bound the diverse approaches together into a relatively unified direction. This is Lewin's (1951, 1958) three-step procedure of organizational change (unfreeze, movement, refreeze). Based on his early conceptualization of organization, in which organization is viewed as being at an equilibrium state of many opposing forces (driving and resisting), OD researchers need to first identify driving forces toward and resisting forces against the planned change, and then implement change by the following three steps: (1) unfreezing, providing disconfirming information that shows the discrepancies between the organization's desired state and the current state in order to reduce the possible resisting forces and to create desires (driving forces) for change (which builds on collecting data about a goal or problem); (2) moving, developing new behaviors, values, and attitudes through training sessions or changes in structures and procedures (which includes feeding back data, developing an action plan, and implementing new actions); and (3) refreezing, stabilizing the organization at a new state of equilibrium by means of various supporting mechanisms. This framework has been widely adopted by OD researchers and practitioners and further elaborated and expanded by other scholars (e.g., Lippitt, Watson, and Westley, 1958; Schein, 1987). Based on extensive analyses of OD-related literature, Porras and Robertson (1987) and Weick and Quinn (1999) found that in spite of the substantial disagreement on many other aspects (effective actions and key intervention variables), there is considerable consensus among OD practitioners on the use of an action research approach and on Lewin's three-stage model as a conceptual basis for this approach.

Just as there is some underlying agreement about theories of changing among OD practitioners, there is also underlying agreement about theories of change. The type of organizational change that most first-generation OD approaches implicitly adopt is teleological, one of the four basic types of organizational change elaborated in Van de Ven and Poole's (1995) typology. According to Van de Ven and Poole, teleological change has four distinctive characteristics: (1) goal enactment or purposeful social construction as the motor of change, (2) a cycle of goal formulation, implementation, evaluation, and goal modification as the change process, (3) a single organization as the unit of change, and (4) an emergent and constructive modality as the mode of change.

First, most of the first-generation OD approaches implicitly (if not explicitly) assume that the desired end state collaboratively envisioned by the organizational members is the fundamental driving force of organizational change. Collaborative identification of the undesirable present state (problem), followed by envisioning the desired state (action planning), is depicted as the core element for change in both Lewin's three-step model and the action research model. Employee participation and collaboration between researchers and organization members are emphasized and embraced by all the first-generation OD approaches. Moreover, organization members are considered as the primary change agents in most of the first-generation OD literature, while OD consultants act as facilitators and advisers. Second, as Porras and Robertson (1987) note, most procedural models of OD clearly incorporate the basic elements of teleological change processes, a cycle of goal formulation (diagnosis and action planning), implementation (intervention), and goal evaluation (evaluation). Third, most conceptualization in first-generation OD seems to assume that a group or organization acts as a singular, discrete entity that is the primary source and focus of change. Many of the first-generation OD approaches focus narrowly on various problems inside a system (individual, group, or organization). Although not completely ignored, the role of external environments is somewhat in the background (Beer and Walton, 1987). Fourth, therefore, both the content and process of organizational change conceptualized in the first-generation OD approaches are open-ended, constructive, and emerging, depending largely on how participants make sense (defining problems and finding solutions) of given situations.

Another theory of change that rather implicitly underlies the first-generation OD approaches is the presumed relationship between realizing humanistic ideals and initiating an effective organizational change. The primary value orientation for most first-generation OD researchers and practitioners was the implementation of humanistic ideals at work. These values included personal development, interpersonal competency, participation, commitment, satisfaction, work democracy, and quality of life (French and Bell, 1995; Gottlieb, 1998; Mirvis, 1988). The underlying assumption is that various OD approaches which aim to facilitate human development and participation will ultimately help organizations reach their desired end state—problem solving or enhanced system effectiveness. This assumption has been increasingly challenged since the 1980s, driving the second-generation OD in a radically different direction.

Dualities and Tensions in First-Generation OD Approaches

Close examination of first-generation OD work reveals two tensions that demonstrate the push and pull among bipolar pairs. In many of these cases one side of the dichotomy is partially privileged to the exclusion of the other. Thus, selection is a typical pattern for managing tensions in first-generation OD work.

The first duality that emerges is between individual/group and organization-wide interventions. Although first-generation organizational development efforts purport a systemic program of change, most interventions target the individual, group, or intergroup level. Rooted in social psychology, first-generation OD interventionists focused on team building, intergroup relations, job design, and participative managerial styles. Even survey feedback, which focuses on changes at multiple organizational levels, aggregates data through using individuals as the fundamental unit of analysis. Hence, although first-generation OD aims at organization-wide changes, the methodologies of change target the individual and group levels. In doing so, first-generation OD fails to recognize the tensions implicit in this duality and the inconsistency that may result from emphasizing one pole and purporting to achieve the other. One explanation for this discrepancy is that first-generation OD proponents implicitly believed that change at one level would reverberate to the entire organization. In effect, selection through denial typifies the management of individual/group versus organizational target of inventions.

A second dichotomy that surfaces in this work is the tension between the human system and the technical system in organizational change. This tension was first recognized in the Socio-Technical Systems (STS) approach, which purports that organizations consist of both human and technical systems, and thus both systems must be optimized simultaneously to conduct an effective intervention. However, most first-generation OD approaches focus almost exclusively on developing and improving the human side of organizations and presume that changes in the human system would automatically and fundamentally resolve the problems in the technical system. This pattern exemplifies another type of selection, coexistence, in which both pairs are deemed essential, but one pole surfaces as privileged. The potential tensions in managing the dichotomy this way resulted in subtle and indirect controversies among the first-generation OD scholars and practitioners on the issues of humanistic versus scientific approaches and emphasizing people versus structure. In the 1970s, for example, many scholars noted early

OD interventions, which had relied overly on humanistic ideals and approaches (e.g., t-groups), failed to incorporate scientific knowledge as the basis of OD or to take seriously various technical aspects of organizations, such as structure, technology, and work design, that could inhibit the potential for both human development and organizational change (cf. Argyris, 1970; Hackman and Lawler, 1971; Mirvis and Berg, 1977; Mirvis, 1988).

Dualities also surface between proactive and reactive poles in first-generation OD literature. While these approaches espoused a philosophy of human improvement and proactive desires for change, several interventions, such as action research, survey feedback, and STS, grew out of organizations with immediate and practical problems such as low productivity and/or high absenteeism as they attempted to address those problems reactively. Other types of first-generation OD, such as team building and sensitivity training, work proactively to prepare organizational members for handling future difficulties. This pattern for managing tensions exemplifies separation by topical domain; proactivity is dominant for some interventions, while alternative methodologies are employed for reactive changes. Thus, the split in the types of interventions segments first-generation OD efforts between the poles of being proactive and reactive.

There are additional ways that first-generation OD approaches emphasized one side of the bipolar pair and ignored the other. Specifically, internal organizational members' needs drove OD interventions more than external market factors. Moreover, virtually all first-generation OD approaches were negative focused or problem driven, paying little attention to positive aspects of organizations as drivers of organizational change (Cooperrider and Srivastva, 1987). Although first-generation OD approaches frequently used intervention methods that foster ongoing, continuous change processes, such as sensitivity training and team building, organizational change processes were predominantly understood as episodic processes, evident with Lewin's (1951, 1958) three-stage model being adopted as the standard approach to organizational change. Moreover, few even questioned whether continuous processes can potentially contradict episodic processes.

In addition, first-generation OD approaches typically set forth open processes, probably as a response to the prevalence of bureaucratic organizations during this period (Mirvis, 1990). Such an emphasis was evident in collaborative labor management teams, coresearch between organizational members and action researchers, and shared action steps in STS. Yet, openness was masked in some interventions through specifying clearly defined arenas and rules for participation, as in sensitivity training and team building. For example, sensitivity training allowed talk only in the "here and now." In like manner, first-generation OD interventions aimed to improve the existing organization (first-order change), rather than make fundamental changes in frames of reference or organizational direction (second-order change). Within first-generation OD work, interventions that aimed at deeper levels of transformation, such as changing members' deeply held attitudes and beliefs, were limited to only a few approaches, such as sensitivity training.

In summary, first-generation OD approaches emphasized the target and impetus of change more than the other dimensions of the change process. Moreover, tensions between dualities in this work were typically managed through selection by privileging one side of the pole as opposed to the other. Other patterns for managing dichotomies that surface in this work were coexistence in which human and technical systems worked together for the good of human development and separation of type of interventions into proactive and reactive categories. We turn now to a discussion of new emphases associated with second-generation approaches to planned change.

Second-Generation Organizational Development Approaches (1980s–)

Since the 1980s organizations have faced unprecedented changes in their environments. Business environments have been increasingly global, competitive, and turbulent, forcing many companies fundamentally to rethink their purposes and directions (Kilmann and Colvin, 1988). American industries have witnessed the decline of manufacturing industries and the growth of the service industry and the high-tech industry. Changes in the technological environment have been even greater, shaking up traditional approaches to work and creating whole new business opportunities. As a result, the scale and occurrence of organizational change have increased considerably (Nadler, Shaw, and Walton, 1995).

These environmental changes have fundamentally altered the way planned organizational change is understood, approached and handled. Shifts in approaches to accomplishing planned change to respond to these changes include the development of large-scale interventions (e.g., Bunker and Alban, 1996; Schmidt and Manning, 1998) and organizational transformation (e.g., Kilmann and Colvin, 1988).

Roots and Characteristics

A primary distinguishing characteristic of second-generation OD approaches is their explicit attention to the organizational environment and the organization's alignment with it (Bunker and Alban, 1997; Mirvis, 1988, 1990; Woodman, 1989). Conceptual frameworks that embrace and emphasize the organization's environment as a vital factor for organization development and change were developed and adopted earlier. For example, Katz and Kahn (1966) applied open system theory, which emphasizes effective exchange and alignment between the organization and its environment in a comprehensive way. Lawrence and Lorsch (1969) suggested a contingency approach in organizational development in the late 1960s, arguing that optimal work and organizational structure were contingent upon characteristics of organizational environments. Nadler and Tushman (1977) proposed a congruence model that focused on the fit between environment, strategy, and organizational components in the late 1970s. However, it was in the 1980s that these ideas and prescriptions became widely adopted among OD researchers and practitioners (Mirvis, 1988). Since then, OD practitioners have increasingly reframed their work within a strategic framework and adopted relevant techniques, such as environmental scanning, competitive analysis, stakeholder analysis, and business planning (Mirvis, 1988; Tichy, 1983; Woodman, 1989). This emphasis has led to change initiatives focused broadly on organizational transformation (Kilmann and Colvin, 1988; Mirvis, 1990; Woodman, 1989), although the terms used to describe the emphasis have varied.

By focusing on individual and group development, the organizational change envisioned and initiated by first-generation OD practitioners tends to be incremental and sequential, implicitly assuming that individual and group development will gradually and ultimately lead to system effectiveness (Bartunek and Louis, 1988). In the turbulent environments of the 1980s and 1990s, however, individual and group development became less important to organizational effectiveness unless the organization as a whole continued to be attuned to its rapidly changing environment. Instead, rapid, systemwide adaptation toward fast changing environments has become prerequisite for continual survival and growth, which often entails radical departure from the organization's past (Nadler et al., 1995). Many current OD researchers and practitioners focus their work on initiating and implementing organizational transformation (e.g., Kilmann and Colvin, 1988; Nadler et al. 1995; Quinn and Cameron, 1988; Tichy and Devanna, 1986; Torbert, 1989), or, as it is sometimes referred to, radical organizational culture change (e.g., Cameron and Quinn, 1999), or organizational frame bending or discontinuous change (Nadler and Tushman, 1989; Nadler et al., 1995).

Types of Second-Generation Approaches

Organizational Transformation

There are multiple approaches to and examples of transformation (e.g., Hansen, 1995; Nutt and Backoff 1997a, 1977b; Schwinn and Schwinn, 1996; Trahant, Burke, and Koonce, 1997; and Whyte, 1992); these describe different ways that transformation might be accomplished. However, there is substantial agreement that transformation depends considerably on the leadership of the CEO (e.g., Whyte [1992] emphasized the leadership of British Petroleum's CEO in a transformational change effort). There is also an agreement that transformation requires a new vision for the future to which the CEO subscribes, as well as ways of dealing with disagreements among organization members and groups in order to accomplish this vision (e.g., Nutt and Backhoff 1997a).

Nadler and his associates (1995) distinguish between two dimensions of organizational change, incremental or strategic and anticipatory or reactive. From these dimensions they derive four types of change: tuning (incremental change made in anticipation of future events), adaptation (incremental change made in response to external events), reorientation (strategic change in anticipation of external events that are expected to require it), and re-creation

(strategic change necessitated by external events, often events that require a radical departure from the past). The last two types of change, reorientation and, in particular, re-creation, are transformational. They are often extremely difficult for organizational members, who have to both "unlearn" old habits and learn radically new ones. Transformational change involves fundamentally altering the organization's vision, mission, strategy, and operating philosophy.

Miles (1997a, 1997b) presented an example of a successful CEO-led and consultant-assisted transformation process that took place at National Semiconductor. From this experience, he described four major tasks a CEO must accomplish to achieve organizational transformation. First, the CEO must generate energy for transformation among organizational members. This includes enabling them to confront their current situation and surface problems with it, to create and allocate resources to help the transformation, to "raise the bar" regarding the level of performance expectations, and to model desired behaviors. Second, the CEO must develop a clear and compelling vision of a desirable future state for the company that helps unveil what needs to be transformed there. In particular, major gaps between current practice and the desired end state must be identified. Third, the internal organizational context needs to be aligned in ways that reduce the gap between the current and ideal states. Tools for doing this include restructuring, implementing appropriate infrastructures, reshaping the culture, and building new or improved core competencies. Finally, a transformation "architecture" must be created. This includes education, involvement, communication, coordination and feedback mechanisms implemented at all levels in order to accomplish and continually refine transformation initiatives.

As is evident from this description, transformation is a very complex task. It typically requires substantial investments of time and resources from the organization.

Large-Scale Interventions

A new intervention that plays an important role in accomplishing transformation or similar change is large-scale interventions (Bunker and Alban, 1996). Large-scale interventions are based on a somewhat different premise than that of action research. As noted earlier, action research customarily starts by focusing on problems to be addressed. However, even early on, some concerns were raised about this focus. Bunker and Alban (1996) recount that in the 1970s Ronald Lippitt felt that starting with problems caused organization members to lose energy, to feel drained and tired. He began to think that problem solving was past-oriented. He wondered what would happen if people were asked to think of their preferred future instead, about what future state they would like for their organization (Lippitt, 1980).

Since the 1980s multiple interventions have been designed that shift the primary focus of OD from individual or group interventions to changing the entire system in a way that helps achieve a desired future (Bunker and Alban, 1997; Mirvis, 1988; Weber and Manning, 1998; Woodman, 1989). A large number of systemwide, large group intervention approaches have been developed and adopted by OD researchers and practitioners (Bunker and Alban, 1997; Schmidt and Manning, 1998; Weber and Manning, 1998). Examples include the search conference, the ICA strategic planning process, fast cycle full-participation work design, simu-real, and work-out. To give a more concrete sense of the large group interventions, we briefly describe a few of them that are currently in practice. These are open space, future search, and real-time strategic change.

Open space technology, the least structured of the large-scale methods, was developed by Harrison Owen (1991, 1992). It has been used all over the world in a large variety of groupings. A group of 5 to 1000 people assemble in a room that has enough chairs for all participants, arranged in circles, with only one facilitator. First, the facilitator states the theme of the meeting, the reason participants are gathered. Second, after briefly describing the process, rules, and norms, the facilitator asks participants to identify some issue or opportunity related to the theme for which they have genuine passion, and for which they will take real responsibility. They are asked to come out into the center of the circle, take a piece of paper and a magic marker, and write down a short title and their name. Then, they stand in front of the group, announce their topic and name, and post the piece of paper on a wall labeled "Community Bulletin Board." The next step is to invite the participants to approach the board and sign up for any and all discussions that they are interested in

attending. Based on the sign-up, people form small groups, discuss the issues, and construct a written report. As the final step, the reports are collected from all groups, summarized, and fed back to the entire assembly. Several norms and principles guide the group discussion. The "law of the two feet" encourages people to use their two feet and go to some more productive place if during the course of the gathering they find themselves neither learning nor contributing. Second, four principles increase flexibility and creativity: (1) whoever comes is the right people (free composition), (2) whatever happens is the only thing that could have happened (free content), (3) whenever it starts is the right time (little time constraint), (4) when it is over it is over (free closure). Open space gatherings are expected to result in "a powerful, effective connecting and strengthening of what's already happening in the organization: planning and action, learning and doing, passion and responsibility, participation and performance" (Hermon n.d.)

Future search is a future-oriented conference, developed by Weisbord and his colleagues (1995), aiming to explore possible agreements between people with divergent views and interests and to do consensus planning with them. Future search conferences are highly participative, involving those who can contribute to an issue or have a stake in it, either from within or beyond the organization. (The "ideal" size is about 70–80 people.) Six major tasks take place during the three-day conference. The first task is to focus on the past both in the local and global context. Participants are invited to make personal notes on what has happened to the global environments, their organization, and themselves during the past decades, and write their recollections on newsprint that will be posted on the walls. Heterogeneous small-group discussion follows in which participants interpret the wall charts and look for patterns and insights. The second task is to focus on the present, identifying the key external trends affecting the organization or the issue. A giant map is created on the wall with the organization or issue in the middle. The participants call out the trends that they believe are currently affecting this organization or issue, and the facilitators write these trends on the chart, creating a giant "mind map." Participants are then asked to highlight what they see as the most important factors affecting the issue or organization.

In step three the participants form stakeholder groups. Each stakeholder group makes up its own version of a mind map, discussing relationships among the trends they consider most important to them. They discuss how they feel about what they're doing now about the issue, in particular, what they feel "proud of" and "sorry" about it, shifting the focus from themselves to the good of the whole, from analysis to owning and responsibility. The fourth step focuses on the future. Returning to the heterogeneous groups, participants are asked to brainstorm their ideal future and then develop and present scenarios of that future in any way they choose (e.g., drama, skit, play, or news show). In the fifth step, participants identify common themes across all the scenarios and integrate them into one list, placing any item for which conflicts or disagreement emerges on a "disagree" list. The final step is action planning, which involves people deciding next steps, dividing up the work, setting goals, figuring out who else to involve, and making public their commitments and timetable.

This change strategy has been used in a number of organizations with good success. For example, Boeing used a version of it in the design of its 777 aircraft (Bunker and Alban, 1996).

Real-time strategic change (RTSC) has been described in most detail by Robert Jacobs (1994). The change objectives in RTSC can range from a new strategic direction or a new organizational design to planning for mergers. RTSC interventions are typically the largest of the large group change initiatives; with proper logistics they can enable several thousand people participating at once.

RTSC conferences normally last two to three days. In a fairly typical use of this approach, top management comes to the conference with a draft statement of their vision, values, and strategy with respect to some aspect of the company. Meeting in (many) small groups in a (very) large room, employees discuss and critique the managers' draft statement and present their proposed revisions in a public forum. Managers then take what they heard from the discussion and revise the document, integrating the feedback received. If they do not accept a suggestion, they must explain why during the conference.

Bunker and Alban suggest that most employees attending a meeting like this initially assume that it will be a waste of time and that there will not be a real change based on their input. However, over the course of the meeting, when management clearly responds to them, they begin to feel a sense of empowerment.

Conceptual Bases of Second-Generation OD Approaches

Tushman and Romanelli's (1985) punctuated equilibrium model has been the most commonly used conceptual approach to transformation, and it is certainly the approach that most undergirds the work of Nadler and his associates. Punctuated equilibrium depicts organizations as evolving through relatively long periods of stability—equilibrium or convergent periods—in their basic patterns of activity that are punctuated by relatively short periods of fundamental change—revolutionary periods. During equilibrium periods, organizations develop a coherent system around a set of fundamental choices, called deep structures—core value, strategy, power distribution, basic structure, and control system (Gersick, 1991; Tushman and Romanelli, 1985). Organizational change during this period is likely to be incremental and adaptive, aimed at achieving a greater consistency of internal activities with the organization's deep structures or strategic orientation (Tushman and Romanelli, 1985). Small and incremental changes are unlikely to lead to radical and revolutionary changes in this period because of the growing cognitive, motivational, and relational inertia as the system increases its structural and social complexity and interdependency to meet internal coordination requirements and external requirements for accountability and predictability (Gersick, 1991; Tushman and Romanelli, 1985).

Based on punctuated equilibrium models, radical and revolutionary change—a reorientation or recreation—is possible only through directly altering the core of a system's deep structure, and this can occur only under certain conditions. First, revolutionary organizational change is likely to be triggered by external forces, such as major changes in technological, market, or institutional environments, and/or by important internal forces, such as major declines in organizational performance or major shifts in the distribution of power. These forces must create an emerging sense of crisis that is strong enough to overpower the existing inertial forces (Romanelli and Tushman, 1994; Tushman and Romanelli, 1985). Second, direct executive leadership is required to initiate revolutionary organizational change, because top management has the power to directly and fundamentally modify a system's deep structure or strategic orientation and to overcome internal inertial forces (Nadler and Tushman, 1995; Romanelli and Tushman, 1994; Tushman and Romanelli, 1985). The likelihood of revolutionary organizational change is increased by installation of a new CEO from outside the organization who might be less committed to the previous strategies and policies, and who might also have fundamentally different views on effective ways of organizing (Romanelli and Tushman, 1994; Tushman and Romanelli, 1985).

As Van de Ven and Poole (1995) suggest, the punctuated equilibrium model of organizational transformation can be viewed as a combination of evolutionary and teleological change theories. During the convergent period, an evolutionary process of environmental selection works to incrementally change the subsystems of organizations toward increased interdependence and alignment with their strategic orientation and environment. Organizational transformation occurs when environmental shifts trigger the purposive actions of executive leaders to fundamentally transform an organization's deep structure toward realignment with its environmental change. The future direction can be freely constructed by top managers, but it may be significantly constrained by organizations' environmental and internal conditions (Gersick, 1991). Executive leadership is emphasized as a key determinant of successful organizational transformation (e.g., Romanelli and Tushman, 1994; Tushman and Romanelli, 1985).

Teleological assumptions that characterized first-generation OD continued to characterize second-generation approaches. Processes of purposeful social construction are commonly depicted as one of the most fundamental driving forces and methods for organizational change, including radical organizational change. Participation and collaboration are not only emphasized, but also extended to the entire system in second-generation OD (Bunker and Alban, 1996). Unlike first-generation OD, however, second-generation OD explicitly linked OD with environmental changes. Logics of strategic management that seek to improve the relationship between an organization and its environment have been extensively embraced by the second-generation OD models (Mirvis, 1988).

Participation in second-generation OD is not like the participation in one of the t-group sessions in first-generation OD, in which little agenda is set except the goal of open-ended exploration of human potential. Instead, the participation in second-generation OD approaches is directed and focused toward a specific strategic goal of an organization within a given time frame and space. The role of consultants in organizational change processes has also changed from a supporting and facilitating role (data collection, interpreting, and giving feedback to the system) to a more central role, helping plan intervention sessions, directing people, and driving their energy in certain directions (Miles 1997a, 1997b; Mirvis, 1988). Organizational changes envisioned and initiated by second-generation OD approaches are wider in scope, more rapid, and more radical in their change potential than were first-generation OD interventions. Several distinctive differences in the conceptual basis between first-generation and second-generation OD are compared in table 4.2.

Dualities and Tensions in Second-Generation OD Approaches

Most of the dualities in second-generation OD approaches are similar to those of first-generation OD approaches. However, they are manifested and handled in different ways. In general, the ways to manage dualities shifted from a form of selection in which only one side of the pole was emphasized while the other side was generally ignored, to a form of separation in which the other side is explicitly acknowledged but is handled in a separate manner—at different levels or at different points in time. Transformational approaches exemplify this shift. In punctuated equilibrium, which forms the basis of transformational models, the organization privileges stability for a long period and then shifts to revolutionary changes. Periods of stability highlight the individual/group-based, first-order, proactive ends of these poles through fine-tuning internal activities toward the pre-accepted strategic direction while periods of strategic action shift the pendulum to organization-wide, second-order, reactive change necessitated by external events. This pattern of working through tensions centers on separation through oscillation between temporal states as a means to obviate the dualities. Through vacillating between the bipolar pairs, tensions reduced through one pole influence or create conditions for the other (Van de Ven and Poole, 1988; Poole and Van de Ven, 1989).

Table 4.2 Underlying theories of change in first-generation OD and second-generation OD compared

	First-Generation OD	Second-Generation OD
Type of Change	Teleology	Teleology and Evolutionary
Motor of change	Purposeful social construction	Purposive and adaptive enactment
Primary change agent	Organizational members	Organizational members and consultants
Means of change	Participation and collaboration	Wide and directed participation
Role of consultant	Facilitating and developing	Planning, directing, and channeling
Focus of change	Problems inside a system	Possibilities in the environments
Mode of change	Emerging and open-ended	Open-ended but conditioned
Scope of change	Individual and group-centered	Systemwide/large-scale
Speed of change	Slow and thorough	Rapid
Tempo of change	Episodic	Episodic
Change potential	Incremental and sequential	Fundamental and simultaneous

A close examination of transformation approaches indicates that the organization-wide, radical-change pole exerts a privileged role. This end of the continuum moves to center stage through accentuating second-order changes rather than first-order ones, particularly ones initiated by top management. Transformation works through bending organizational frames and altering the architecture and infrastructure of the organization. Such a change is not incremental; rather it involves reorientation and recreation to alter an organization's fundamental vision, mission, philosophy, and operating strategy. Hence, change is not simply a separation and balance between two dichotomous temporal processes but grows out of a radical and episodic departure from the status quo. An organization-wide focus is also privileged over an individual/group focus. This privileging recognizes that leaders play an essential role in transformational models through having a clear and compelling vision.

In a similar way, large-scale interventions emphasize both proactive and reactive characteristics, recognize both internal and external impetuses for change, and open up both first-order and second-order possibilities, while centering primarily on externally driven, reactive, organization-wide, and second-order types of change. In particular, large-scale interventions shift the focus of change from the individual/group level to the entire organization. Although still acknowledging the essential role of key leaders, most organization members assume a secondary role by functioning primarily as recipients or

participants, as is evident in real-time strategic change interventions. Hence, this dichotomy is handled through an integration or forced merger between the two poles, but one that privileges organization-wide perspectives over the individual/group level of change.

One central difference between transformation and large-scale changes is the way they handle the open-versus-closed dichotomy. Participation is very limited in organizational transformation approaches; the focus is on strategic issues that top management sets forth. Large-scale interventions, in contrast, rely on participative processes in setting the strategic direction. This observation suggests that the open-versus-closed dichotomy is generally handled in a type of separation manner, topical dominance, in second-generation OD. Transformation approaches adopt one side of the pole (closed) while large-scale interventions rely on the other side of the pole (open). Although large-scale interventions emphasize open and participative processes in initiating organizational change, those processes indicate a different kind of participation compared to first-generation OD approaches such as t-groups and team building, one that is more structured, directed toward a limited range of issues, and occurring within a limited period of time. Large-scale interventions manage the tensions between open and closed processes through separation. Closed systems are applied to certain aspects of change and open processes are employed for others.

Second-generation OD approaches also make remarkable shifts in both recognizing and handling the tensions between negative focus and positive focus. Departing from viewing only the negative side of the pole, they explicitly acknowledge and actively utilize the opposite side of the pole in their intervention efforts. For example, while still driven by negative forces in environments, transformation approaches depict a strong, positive vision articulated by the CEO as a necessary ingredient for successful organizational change. Large-scale interventions such as open space technology and future search emphasize working from the strengths of the current system and extending them through planning, action, and future scenarios. External threats and organizational problems enter into the process only through assessment of local/global initiatives. In both approaches, however, handling the negative/positive dichotomy assumes a form of integration through a forced merger. The role of positive vision in transformation approaches is engulfed in an overly negative frame developed as a reactive response to the problems caused by environment. In large-scale interventions, in contrast, various external and internal problems are discussed primarily within the frame of leveraging an organization's positive past and exploring its optimistic future.

Another radical shift arises in the degree to which tensions between human and technical systems are recognized and handled. In second-generation OD approaches, the coexistence between the human system and technical system disappears, as organizations learn that developing a good human system does not guarantee its continued survival and growth in turbulent business environments. Second-generation OD approaches address this tension by moving to the other end of the pole and emphasizing change as a resolution to urgent strategic, economic, and technological issues. Although both human and technical systems are acknowledged and emphasized, the human system, which receives a privileged place in first-generation OD approaches, becomes integrated into the broader technical system in the process of strategic planning in large-scale interventions.

Managing the dichotomy of continuous versus episodic processes remains unchanged in second-generation OD approaches. They continue to conceptualize organizational change primarily as episodic events, taking an apparent form of selection and denial. Overall, second-generation OD interventionists acknowledge the tensions inherent in dualities of change, but they manage these tensions through oscillating in time or across domains between polar opposites or they attempt to merge them in ways that privilege one end of the pole over the other.

Third-Generation Organizational Development Approaches (Late 1980s–)

Next we focus on a third generation of planned change interventions that are particularly embodied in learning organizations and appreciative inquiry. Our grouping of these approaches as "third generation" does not mean that they constitute a completely new, coherent, and finite set of approaches to planned organizational change. Instead, we use this section to open up and explore new possibilities for planned organizational change by introducing and highlighting two change approaches which have not only been influential in many recent capacity-building planned change efforts but have also embraced very different assumptions or conceptualizations than first- and second-generation OD approaches.

To state the case simplistically, first-generation approaches to OD aimed to help organizations do better, typically (implicitly) within an already accepted framework for action and void of any explicit attention to an organization's past. Second-generation approaches focused more on transformational change, which has meant movement away from a particular framework or set of behaviors and toward a very different framework or set of behaviors. This approach has been based on the implicit and sometimes explicit assumption that the past has to be discarded for future success. Third-generation OD approaches are also concerned about major change and transformation. In contrast to second-generation approaches, however, they are also based on the assumption that the past can play an important role in the organization's ongoing life and change effort; it should not be discarded. We will describe how this basic set of assumptions holds for learning organizations and appreciative inquiry. Although these two types of intervention frameworks have a few characteristics in common, they are different in many more ways. Thus, we will examine each approach individually.

Learning Organizations

Scholars have noted for decades that organizations and/or their members learn. Organizational learning was originally viewed as an adaptive change in behavioral response to a stimulus, particularly the learning of routines (e.g., Cyert and March, 1963). Some scholars later challenged the stimulus and response paradigm and argued that organizational learning must include both behavioral and cognitive elements, as well as the capacity to challenge routines, not simply enact them (e.g., Argyris and Schön, 1978; Fiol and Lyles, 1985). It is this latter emphasis, informed also by systems dynamics, that has led to learning organizations.

In recent years the term *learning organization* has become one of the most popular concepts in the business lexicon (Jackson, 2000). Communities of researchers and practitioners that study and practice learning organizations have emerged and grown rapidly (Easterby-Smith, 1997; Tsang, 1997).

Core Processes and Practices of Learning Organizations

Although there are a number of academics, consultants, and managers developing and promoting the learning organization concept, Peter Senge's bestselling book *The Fifth Discipline* has been the most responsible for bringing the learning organization into the mainstream of business thinking (Jackson, 2000; Pedler, Burgovne, and Boydell, 1997). For Senge (1990), a learning organization is "an organization that is continually expanding its capacity to create its future" (p. 14), for which "adaptive learning must be joined by generative learning, learning that enhances our capacity to create" (p. 14). Senge described five different "disciplines" as the cornerstone of learning organization: (1) *systems thinking*, learning to better understand the interdependencies and integrated patterns of our world that ultimately influence the consequences of our action; (2) *personal mastery*, developing commitment to lifelong learning and continually challenging and clarifying personal visions; (3) *mental models*, developing reflection and inquiry skills to be aware, surface, and test the deeply rooted assumptions and generalizations that we hold about the world and that govern our action; (4) *building shared vision*, processes of developing shared images of the future we seek to create and the principles and guiding practices by which to get there; and (5) *team learning*, a discipline of group interaction that maximizes the insights of individuals through dialogue and skillful discussion or through

recognizing the patterns of interaction in teams that undermine learning.

In 1991 Senge and his colleagues created a community of research and practice at MIT, "The Center for Organizational Learning," to foster the development of learning organizations among a group of corporations. As membership grew and became diverse, they fundamentally changed the infrastructure of the former organization in 1995 and created a new self-organizing organization, "The Society for Organizational Learning." The accumulation of research and consulting experiences from both organizations has given birth to several books, especially *The Fifth Discipline Fieldbook* (Senge, Kleiner, Roberts, Ross, and Smith, 1994) and *The Dance of Change* (Senge et al., 1999). The former introduces practical strategies and tools useful to support and facilitate each of the five disciplines. The latter identifies challenges and obstacles involved in initiating and implementing the concepts and principles of learning organizations and introduces ways to overcome them.

The learning organization envisioned and promoted by Senge and his colleagues is only one of the many versions of learning organization currently available, although most other authors owe at least some of their approach to Senge's work (e.g., Garratt, 1990; Garvin, 1993; Lessem, 1991; Lipshitz, Popper, and Oz, 1996; Nevis, DiBella, and Gould, 1995; Pedler, et al. 1997; Watkins and Marsick, 1994; Wick and Leon, 1995; Wishart, Elam, and Robey, 1996). For example, Nevis et al. (1995) define a learning organization as one that is effective at acquiring, sharing, and utilizing knowledge. Garvin (1993) views systematic problem solving and ongoing experimentation as the core of learning organization, and suggests practical and measurable ways to develop learning organizations.

Although definitions of and prescriptions for learning organizations vary, several elements are generally shared. These indicate how the learning organization approach to planned change is distinct from other approaches. First, adapting to an uncertain and fast changing environment is typically the goal of or impetus for learning organizations. Second, developing a learning organization is primarily portrayed as organizational capacity building, increasing the capacity to learn, that is, to acquire, share, and utilize knowledge rather than immediate problem solving. Third, a powerful, shared vision or collective commitment to learning is regarded as the core energy for organizational change. Fourth, organizational learning capacity is enhanced through members developing their ability to continually and critically examine their own thought processes and action patterns, and/or through fostering group processes in which participants openly share, discuss, and experiment with diverse insights and ideas.

As noted above, there are several intervention tools aimed at facilitating the development of learning organizations. One of these tools, learning histories, is of primary importance. Learning histories are book-length descriptions of major changes that take place in organizations. These descriptions are written in a way that helps organizations reflect on and learn from their previous experiences (Kleiner and Roth 1997, 2000; Roth and Kleiner, 2000). Kleiner and Roth (1997, pp. 173, 176) describe a learning history as a story about a recent critical episode of a company, such as "a corporate change event, a new initiative ... or even a traumatic event like a downsizing." The document, which is extensive, is presented in two columns. In the right-hand column, the people involved in particular changes describe the relevant events involved in them. The left-hand column, in comparison, using an approach developed by Argyris (Senge et al., 1994), "contains analysis and commentary by the 'learning historians.'" The left-hand column identifies recurring themes, poses questions about the assumptions of the narrative, and raises "undiscussable" issues.

Conceptual Basis of Learning Organizations

Organizational change envisioned and described in the learning organization literature shares some characteristics with action research and sensitivity training, two types of first-generation OD interventions (Easterby-Smith, 1997). Assuming a close link between learning and changing, the action research model, a cycle of data collection, feedback, evaluation, and action, was originally a collective learning device, although the model was increasingly used to solve immediate organizational problems rather than creating knowledge (Hendry, 1996). Learning organizations create a significant extension of action research by their commitment to learning and by a vision that collective learning occurs continuously, at all levels, and by organizational members themselves,

not by consultants or behavioral scientists. Similar to the sensitivity training tradition in the first-generation OD, the learning organization approach focuses on building individual and/or group capacity to learn rather than on immediate business problems or opportunities, assuming that the former will naturally address the latter. To meet this goal, it also relies heavily on various group methods. For example, Senge and his colleagues (1990, 1994) not only suggest team learning as one of the core elements of the learning organization but also provide group-related methods (e.g., left-hand column and the ladder of reference) that have been used for OD interventions to facilitate learning. Moreover, various humanistic ideals emphasized throughout the OD literature, such as participation, commitment, and collaboration, also frequently appear as necessary means to build learning organizations in the learning organization literature.

The rhetoric and methods of the learning organization also share several components with second-generation OD approaches. Many authors have stressed adaptation to or alignment with the organizational environment as the core impetus or rationale for building learning organizations. In addition, in spite of its emphasis on developing individual and group learning capacity, the ultimate focus of the learning organization approach is at the system level, making the entire organization capable of continuous learning. Various system-level elements for building learning organizations, such as strategy, executive leadership, culture, structure, and governance, are discussed in conjunction with individual- and group-level issues (e.g., Senge et al. 1999; Wishart et al., 1996). Third, many authors emphasize the importance of developing a strong shared vision to create learning organizations and suggest various processes or methods to do so, assuming that processes for developing learning organizations are basically vision-driven rather than problem/adaptation-driven. This suggests that the learning organization approach is basically grounded on a teleological theory of organizational change.

On the other hand, organizational learning can be contrasted with organizational transformation, especially punctuated equilibrium approaches to transformation. Organizational histories and past experiences are regarded as valuable resources for both incremental (single-loop) and fundamental (double- or triple-loop) learning (Argyris and Schön, 1978;

Miner and Mezias, 1996) in learning organizations. However, punctuated equilibrium approaches depict history and past experiences as obstacles to radical and episodic organizational transformation.

Learning organizations are distinguished from prior-generation approaches to planned organizational change on another dimension as well. According to Weick and Quinn's (1999) typology based on the tempo of change, the organizational change envisioned or described by the previous approaches is episodic, occurring infrequently, discontinuously, and intentionally. It usually follows Lewin's unfreeze-transition-refreeze sequence and is understood primarily as a transition from one state of equilibrium to another. In contrast, the change envisioned by the learning organization approach is continuous, that is ongoing, evolving, cumulative, and resulting in ongoing states of disequilibria. Thus, the development of individual and collective skills and organizational processes to continuously and spontaneously reflect, reinterpret, reframe, and redirect the patterns of thoughts, actions, and organizational practices is the main focus of the learning organization approach.

Dualities and Tensions in Learning Organizations

A central feature that characterizes how learning organizations handle dualities and tensions is transcendence. For example, the primary dichotomy that surfaces in learning organizations is the target of the change dimension—individual/group versus organization-wide changes. Learning organizations, in comparison with first- and second-generation OD approaches, transcend the tensions in this dichotomy through creating new terms, correcting apparent logical flaws, and building an approach based on synthesis rather than on a forced merger. Terms such as "shared vision," "organizational capacity building," and "mastery models" are ways that learning theorists reframe and transcend the individual/ organizational dichotomy of change. Other aspects of learning organizations address logical flaws between bipolar pairs. For example, the reflection necessary for effective individual mental models requires systems thinking and attention to the interconnected patterns that influence organizational actions.

Learning permeates individual/group levels through personal mastery, lifelong understanding, and team dialogue. In like manner, learning infuses the system level through using strategy, culture, and structure to increase an organization's capacity to acquire and utilize system-level knowledge. By synthesizing dichotomous views, learning theorists develop a unique perspective that eliminates tensions, but only by losing some of the uniqueness and energy embodied in these dualities.

Transcendence at the individual-organizational level also spills into synthesizing first- and second-order changes, internal and external drivers, human and technical systems, and positive and negative focuses. Learning organizations engage in first-order change through adapting to and aligning with their environments. But they also focus on second-order changes in frames of reference, fundamental values, and basic structures through fostering double- and triple-loop learning. In addition, although this approach stresses internal processes of human development and formation of shared visions, learning organizations also center on the various strategic, economic, and technological issues linked to the external environment, ones that form an impetus for internal capacity-building experiences. Learning also encompasses both positive and negative experiences. Once learning occurs, it becomes a positive resource to address various negative and positive challenges from the environment. Thus, on the dimensions of target and type of change, learning organizations transcend dichotomies through synthesis and reframing.

In responding to the dualities of proactive versus reactive and continuous versus episodic, learning approaches shift from transcendence to integration. More specifically, this perspective neutralizes or creates a forced merger through compromising both reactive and episodic types of change with proactive and continuous ones. For example, learning organizations emphasize continual renewal and ongoing experimentation to be ready (proactive) for radical, episodic moments. By enhancing the capacity to create, learning organizations are only marginally proactive in helping members react to some fast-changing environments and organizational problems. In addition, learning organizations exist in an ongoing state of disequilibria; that is, organizational change occurs simultaneously and continuously. Change, then, cannot be fully episodic because it is merged with an ongoing process that is incremental and cumulative. For each of these dimensions, the opposite concept is acknowledged and neutralized into the other pole, which represents a particular type of change—one characterized by incremental, proactive learning to prepare for episodic, reactive changes that are discontinuous and revolutionary.

On the dimension of open versus closed, learning organizations ignore the opposite pole. For example, learning histories are decidedly humanistic and open, characterized by generating and critiquing organizational narratives through participation and collaboration. Thus, selection is the way that learning organizations handle the dualities of open versus closed.

Appreciative Inquiry

Basic ideas behind appreciative inquiry approaches began to arise in the mid-1980s. They were first expressed in a chapter by Cooperrider and Srivastva (1987). Since then, the philosophy behind appreciative inquiry (e.g., Cooperrider, 1990), and ways of implementing it (e.g., Watkins and Mohr, 2001) have been described more fully in a number of sources. The great majority of these sources are practitioner based (cf. Austin and Bartunek, 2003), something for which they have been criticized (Golembiewski, 1998). While academics have been slow to learn about and study appreciative inquiry, it has become one of the most widely used OD interventions in the world (see illustrations in Watkins and Mohr, 2001). Moreover, while there is a growing body of literature on appreciative inquiry, most of this literature focuses on its multiple uses; there is comparatively clear agreement (at least in comparison to other planned change approaches) about its philosophy and implementation.

Core Processes and Practices of Appreciative Inquiry

Appreciative inquiry is based on three important assumptions (cf. Cooperrider, 1990; Watkins and Mohr, 2001). First, the approach assumes that social systems are socially constructed, that people create their own reality through dialogue and enactment. Cooperrider (1990, p. 115) argues, for example, that "organizations as made and imagined are artifacts of the affirmative mind," and that "organizations create their own realities to a far greater extent than is normally assumed" (p. 117). In other words, the type of organization, and

the positive or negative image of it that organization members socially construct, is very important. Organization members have the capacity to create wide ranges of organizational realities.

Second, appreciative inquiry assumes that every social system has multiple positive elements, but that members of a system draw energy for change much more by focusing on positive aspects of the system than by focusing on its negative, problematic aspects. Cooperrider (1990) has argued forcefully that it is crucial to emphasize the positive in what exists now, and by doing so to create a positive "anticipatory reality." He has stressed that self-initiated mental imagery has strong consequences on people's affective experience and on their actions taken. Positive imagery and positive affect are much more likely to generate action than are negative imagery and affect, which tend to lead to more defensive behavior.

Third, appreciative inquiry assumes that it is quite possible for organizations to build consensus around positive elements. The more organization members experiment with positive imagery, the more competent they will be at affirming their organization, and this is very important; organizations need constant affirmation. It is such constant affirmation that maintains organization members' momentum and energy toward increasing the positives there.

Based on this philosophy, appreciative inquiry includes five generic processes. These are, briefly, (1) choose the positive as the focus for inquiry, (2) inquire into stories of life-giving forces, (3) locate themes that appear in the stories and select topics for further inquiry, (4) create shared images for a preferred future, and (5) find innovative ways to create that future. These processes are, in action, the "essence" of appreciative inquiry (Watkins and Mohr, 2001).

Watkins and Mohr (2001) discuss these processes of appreciative inquiry in depth. Briefly, "choose the positive as the focus for inquiry" means that, at the beginning of a change process, rather than begin by focusing on problems regarding a particular issue, organizations seek out the positive history of that issue and consider moments when that issue has given life to their organization. "Inquiring into stories of life-giving forces" means conducting initial exploratory interviews in a way that is a mutual learning process for interviewer and interviewee. This involves telling stories that bring to life the positive stories of the organization and that generate thinking about positive possibilities for the future. "Locate themes that appear in the stories" means exploring the interviews by looking for themes of life-giving forces in the interview data and by expanding positive dialogue about these themes to organization members. "Create shared images for a preferred future" means, briefly, engaging as many organization members as possible in developing a shared image or vision of a preferred future in a way similar to this dimension of future search processes. Organization members articulate their dream for the organization and generate an organization structure that is aimed at helping this dream become a reality. Finally, "find innovative ways to create that preferred future" refers to bringing to life in practice the new images of the future developed in the previous stage. This is often done by creating new organization designs.

There are many examples of the use of appreciative inquiry, for purposes ranging from becoming a better employer to strategic redesign, to transformation, to more sensitivity to others' perspectives (Watkins and Mohr, 2001). It is increasingly being used for change efforts in global settings in which participants are operating out of very different perspectives on the world (Tenkasi, 2000).

Conceptual Basis of Appreciative Inquiry

Appreciative inquiry departs radically from previous generation approaches to change in two conceptual areas. First, it presents one of the purest forms of teleological conceptualization of organizational change. Although most of the previous approaches are based, at least to a certain degree, on a teleological assumption that organizational change is driven by participants' purposeful social construction, they are not committed to this assumption as entirely as appreciative inquiry is. In appreciative inquiry, the social construction process for change can occur at any time in any circumstance—even without such previously emphasized driving forces as internal crises, shifts in external environments, or visionary leaders—because it relies on a strong belief that organizational members have the capacity to create their own future.

A more striking difference is in its theory of changing. The strong belief in social construction that characterizes appreciative inquiry explicitly rejects the intervention patterns of many other approaches to organizational change. First, appreciative inquiry theorists point out that previous approaches, action

research in particular, depend heavily on scientific, positivist methods that foster linear, cause-and-effect types of thinking but restrict human imagination for future possibilities and thus limit people's change potential (e.g., Cooperrider and Srivastva, 1987). Instead, appreciative inquiry depends on methods such as stories, narratives, dreams, and visions that stimulate human imagination and meaning systems and thus expand the possibilities for new social constructions. Second, it assumes that past interventions have overly focused on solving various organizational problems, which may also limit the possibilities for social construction by intimidating participants and inducing defensiveness. Instead, appreciative inquiry relies on intervention methods that decisively "appreciate" only the positive aspects of organizations both in the past and in the future. The assumption is that this should better motivate people for participation and facilitate more free generation of human imagination.

In addition, similar to learning organization approaches but dissimilar to the other approaches, appreciative inquiry views the past experiences of individuals and organizations as a viable resource for organizational change, in particular for generating imagination for future possibilities. However, appreciative inquiry differs from learning organizations in that the former appreciates only the positive aspects of the past while the latter values both its positive and negative aspects.

As noted above, there is almost no academic research on appreciative inquiry. Virtually all practitioner writing about it is very positive. Golembiewski (1998) challenges it on several grounds. He argues, among other things, that appreciative inquiry is not linked as much as would be appropriate with other relevant theory and practice, and that its supporters treat it somewhat like a conceptual island, although it is not totally separate from other approaches to change. For example, Golembiewski notes that the growth of cohesiveness (a positive aspect) is also emphasized in sensitivity training to address and solve more fundamental issues. Golembiewski also suggests that appreciative inquiry's overdependence on interactionist methods, such as dialogue and interview, can make its implementation potentially ambiguous, problematic, and even chaotic, by distancing itself from other intervention processes, such as organizational structures and politics. He believes that it also discourages inquiry about itself or constructive criticism, in part because of the positive focus of the approach.

Dualities and Tensions in Appreciative Inquiry

In handling dualities and tensions in organizational change, appreciative inquiry shows an interesting tendency of going to extreme positions, namely selection of one pole and intentional rejection of the other pole that has been traditionally selected and/or emphasized in most of the first- or second-generation OD approaches. This exclusive choice is most obvious in the duality of positive-focus versus negative-focus, where appreciative inquiry decidedly focuses on the positive aspects but intentionally avoids the negative sides. This emphasis is very different from most approaches to planned change. First-generation OD approaches assumed the necessity of beginning with a problem; otherwise there would not be enough of a "crisis" to get the organization to change. Second-generation approaches were more likely to stress some positive future, even while implicitly assuming that the present was problematic. However, in general (with the exception of a few of the large group interventions, such as future search), neither first- nor second-generation approaches emphasized positive features in what currently existed in the organization.

A similar overt choice of one pole over the other pole is apparent in the duality between the human system and the technical system. This tension grew out of first-generation OD approaches as issues of scientific versus humanistic and/or people versus structure. However, the relative emphasis shifted from the human system to the technical system in second-generation OD approaches as they placed primary concern on various strategic issues and scientific methods. This emphasis goes to the other extreme in appreciative inquiry as it decidedly focuses on the human system, in particular its capacity to create its own future. This emphasis is also apparent in the overt choice of various humanistic means and processes in initiating organizational change, such as stories, narratives, and visions (e.g., Watkins and Mohr, 2001), while explicitly rejecting traditional, positivistic means of change (e.g., Cooperrider and Srivastva, 1987; Golembiewski, 1998).

Tensions between external and internal and between open and closed poles are two other areas where appreciative inquiry makes an explicit choice

of one pole over the other pole. Based on its strong emphasis on social construction and human imagination, appreciative inquiry almost exclusively limits its focus within what is inside a certain organization— the good that was in the past and that might be in the future. This strong internal focus is similar to first-generation OD approaches (although they differ in how intentional their choice was) but dissimilar from second-generation OD approaches, which placed a primary emphasis on various external forces as core drivers of organizational change. In addition, like most of the first-generation OD approaches, appreciative inquiry places a strong emphasis on open and participative processes throughout the intervention— both for generating a future vision and for implementing this vision. Its total commitment to these open, relationship-based processes raises a concern that it may be "risking chaos and conceptualizing in unbounded space" (Golembiewski, 1998, p. 3). However, in spite of its determination to remain open and participative, this openness is limited by, even contrary to, its exclusive choices in other areas such as intervention methods (no use of scientific diagnosis) and discussion topics (not allowing negative stories).

For three other dichotomies, namely, first-order versus second-order, proactive versus reactive, and continuous versus episodic, appreciative inquiry does not make an explicit choice of one pole and ignore the other. However, it implicitly favors one side over the other using forms of selection (denial and coexistence). First, although researchers and practitioners of appreciative inquiry suggest that both first-order and second-order organizational change is possible, they fail to specify the relationship between the two or distinguish among interventions particularly designed for each type of change (selection coexistence). Instead, they suggest that second-order change is more likely with the use of appreciative inquiry because it appeals to the power of human imagination, which is a viable source of transformational, second-order type of organizational change (Cooperrider, 1990; Watkins and Mohr, 2001). This logic suggests that appreciative inquiry favors second-order change over first-order change (Golembiewski, 1998). Such a logic stands in contrast to the second-generation transformation approaches that see revolutionary organizational change evolving from negative forces in the environment that break the equilibrium of the current organizational state. Similarly, although appreciative inquiry can be used for reactive purposes (e.g., Watkins and Mohr, 2001), these types of interventions are rare both conceptually and practically. In effect, the core theories and practices of appreciative inquiry represent proactive processes, which can take place at any time for any purpose (Golembiewski, 1998). This preference reveals another selection/coexistence strategy that aligns with the proactive side of the pole.

In addition, appreciative inquiry is very similar to both first- and second-generation OD approaches in that it depicts organizational change processes as episodic, representing a pattern of selection and denial. Although ongoing, continuous dialogues among organizational members are central to its intervention, both its theory and its practice assume discrete starting and ending points and adopt distinctive action steps and phases for intervention (e.g., Barrett and Cooperrider, 1990; Watkins and Mohr, 2001).

Finally, the duality between the individual versus organization-wide focus is where appreciative inquiry moves beyond its general tendency of selection toward integration. At least conceptually, appreciative inquiry seems to balance an individual focus and organization-wide focus, as it starts by exploring life-giving individual experiences and then moves to developing organization-wide consensus over core themes to envision the possible future, and then moves back to the issue of individual-focused implementation of the shared vision. However, as Golembiewski (1998) argues, appreciative inquiry is based on a vulnerable assumption that individual-based dialogues will naturally grow larger and larger and reach some consensus at an organization-wide level. Researchers and practitioners of appreciative inquiry have not anticipated possible divisions or conflicts among organizational members, nor have they developed concrete ways to address these schisms. Thus, appreciative inquiry has not fully recognized possible tensions between individual and organization-wide processes. Consequently, its conceptual integration appears to neutralize or potentially limit both processes.

Discussion and Implications

Planned organizational change often appears as neat packages or sets of intervention tools brought into an organization to achieve a variety of goals. Planned efforts, however, are rooted historically, as is evident in the way change efforts have occurred concomitantly with the development of the behavioral and social sciences, the concern for collaboration between interventionists and organizational members, the aim to resolve quality and productivity problems, the desire to adapt organizations to their environments, and the goal for continuous renewal in response to a rapidly changing economy.

These historical developments fall into three general approaches—first-generation OD, second-generation OD, and third-generation OD. Conceptual developments in first-generation OD approaches exemplify a three-step framework of unfreezing, moving, and refreezing. Organizational change occurs through identification of undesirable present states followed by action that leads to a desired end state. By attending to humanistic ideals, organizations aim to reach this desired state of effectiveness. In contrast, second-generation OD approaches center on alignment between organizations and their environments. Arising within the open systems period, interventionists focus on transformation of deep structures and on large-scale changes that help organizations develop and attain future visions. Finally, third-generation OD approaches attempt a radical departure from earlier work in both understanding and implementing organizational change. Learning organizations move away from change as a state of equilibrium to envisioning learning as a continuous, ongoing, and cumulative process. It targets change at the organizational level, but by reconfiguring individuals and groups into learning systems united through shared visions. Appreciative inquiry also departs from viewing organizational problems as the driver and core process of organizational change, and instead identifies and envisions the positive aspects of organizations as ways to drive and implement organizational change.

Within each of these approaches, fundamental dualities of planned change spawn tensions among and between concepts and practices. In some instances, these tensions surface openly and explicitly as in struggles between incremental versus strategic and anticipatory versus reactive change in the transformation model (Nadler and Tushman, 1989). In most perspectives, the tensions are implicit in beliefs about planned change and the ways it should and should not be managed. The three generations of change differ markedly in the ways they manage the tensions that emerge from the eight dichotomies.

As table 4.1 shows, for targets of change at the individual/group versus organizational levels, first-generation OD approaches handled the duality through selecting one pole and denying the primacy of the opposing one. Thus, interventionists ignored the tensions that surfaced from targeting the organizational level and intervening at the group and individual levels. Second-generation OD approaches forced mergers between individual and organizational levels by recognizing the key role that leaders play in transformation, but by inadvertently privileging the organization over the individual. Forced mergers are unstable ways to manage contradictions because they often slip into favoring one end of the pole over the other end. Third-generation OD approaches create a synthesis between individual/group and organization—one that transcends targets and directed interventions in both levels. For example, learning in the organizational learning approach permeates the individual and group level as it infuses the organizational system with effective mental models, shared visions, and organizational capacity. Hence, planned change approaches manage tensions among targets of change through using selection, integration, and synthesis.

Another factor within the targets of change was the tension between internal versus external drivers. First-generation OD approaches managed this tension through selection, relying on internal organizational needs and denying the existence of external drivers. Second-generation approaches recognized the tensions and separated them through oscillating between internal and external foci. This oscillation occurred in a temporal pattern in that the organization fluctuated between internal fine-tuning in periods of stability and radical alignment with external environment in periods of strategic action. Third-generation OD approaches exhibit polarization in managing this duality. In learning organizations, a synthesis approach has emerged through focusing on the internal capacity to learn so that the organization can effectively address external challenges. In contrast, appreciative inquiry explicitly selects internal drivers and minimizes external factors.

Management of the tensions between the human and the technical systems revealed different patterns. First-generation OD approaches adopted coexistence as a means of coping with these tensions in a way that led to disconfirming the technical system when overt controversies arose. Second-generation OD approaches shifted the pendulum to strategic, economic, and technical systems, downplaying the role of the human system. Hence, this tension was managed through overt selection of one pole as privileged and rejection of the other pole as incidental. Third-generation OD approaches differed from the others in how they handle this duality. Learning organizations address these tensions through synthesizing human capacity building with strategic and technical issues into a new learning system, while appreciative inquiry decisively focuses only on the human system.

For the dichotomy of first-order versus second-order change, the three approaches differ in the way that dualities are acknowledged. For instance, first-generation OD approaches adopted interventions that emphasized first-order change while second-generation transformational approaches emphasized second-order change. Both used selection to manage contradictions through denying or underscoring the existence of the opposite pole. Third-generation OD approaches address this duality in transcending ways as both learning organization and appreciative inquiry approaches focus on radical, second-order organizational transformation, while emphasizing ongoing, incremental conversation and learning as a vital means to achieve organizational transformation.

Four types of tensions—negative-focus versus positive-focus, continuous versus episodic, proactive versus reactive, and open versus closed—exemplify characteristics of the change process and the three generations differ in how they managed the tensions among these dualities. For the duality of negative focus versus positive focus, selection has been the predominant form of handling dichotomies across the three generations of OD approaches. Most of the first- and second-generation OD approaches took one side of the pole, focusing on various negative problems within organizations or with external environments. In contrast, appreciative inquiry and some large-scale interventions emphasize the importance of identifying and leveraging the positive aspects of organization. A possible synthesis was evident in learning organization approaches where both positive and negative events were incorporated into the change processes under the overarching framework of organizational learning.

Selection, in the form of denial, has also been prevalent across the three generations of OD approaches in managing tensions between continuous and episodic change processes. Most first-

and second-generation approaches emphasized episodic processes of planned change through advocating stages of change and transformational episodes and ignoring the links between continuous change and change episodes. In contrast, learning organizations merge bipolar positions into a force fit by making episodic changes part of a continuous state of learning. Thus, the effects of episodic changes are reduced and folded into continuous renewal and ongoing experimentation.

Proactive versus reactive is one duality in which all three approaches acknowledge and manage both sides of the continuum. First- and second-generation OD work addressed the tensions between these poles through separation. First-generation OD perspectives appropriated some interventions to proactive use and employed others reactively to address immediate problems. Second-generation OD approaches separated these poles through temporal processes that aligned proactive and reactive responses with different stages of transformation and large-scale change. Third-generation OD approaches shifted from separation to integration in managing tensions between these poles. For example, learning organizations relied on neutralization, in which organizations found a middle ground through being partly proactive and somewhat reactive.

The one duality in which all three approaches have favored the same pole is open versus closed processes of change. All three approaches have leaned toward open, participatory, and employee-involvement models of change. Specifically, first-generation OD reacted to the closed forms of change evident at the time with a strong and overt recommendation for collaboration. A similar preference for open processes is evident in third-generation OD approaches. For example, learning organizations favor technologies and methods rooted in open systems, and thus parallel first-generation OD efforts in privileging openness and in managing tensions through selecting one side of the polar opposite. Tensions between open versus closed processes emerged in second-generation OD approaches through the belief that participation alone was not sufficient to evoke a radical departure from the past. Openness was allocated to topical categories, for example, aligning innovation and design with closed systems and implementation processes with employee participation. Second-generation OD work, then, adopted

a separation approach and moved between openness and closeness depending on topical categories in processing change.

In sum, the three approaches to change vary in the degree to which they recognize, process, and manage dualities that underlie the dimension of planned change. A dominant way of managing dualities surfaces for each approach, with first-generation OD relying on selection of one pole and denial of the dichotomous one, second-generation OD employing separation either through temporal or topical balance, and third-generation OD preferring to use synthesis to transcend tensions between the poles or to select the pole that was traditionally ignored.

We believe that dualities of change are inevitable; they will frequently surface in the gap between developing a perspective and implementing it in planned change programs. Exploration of these dualities offers a means to move below the surface of planned change activities and to see the tensions that inevitably arise there and that also affect the development of planned change programs.

Some of the ways of handling the dualities have more shortcomings than others, influencing the later development of change programs that emerged to address concerns about prior ineffectiveness. Selection, through denial, overt choice, and coexistence, culminates in problems when the opposite pole surfaces in managing and implementing planned change. Separation is also problematic in that oscillation between poles may result in one pole becoming dominant and shaping the conditions for the opposite one. Moreover, by ignoring or segmenting dualities, separation and selection lose the energy and creativity essential for enacting complex change processes. Thus, learning organizations have the potential to manage dualities in a creative manner through transcending opposites, reframing situations, and integrating dualities. Synthesis, however, embraces a resolution model for managing dualities, one in which scholars mitigate rather than enhance complexity.

Overall, our review suggests that planned change has been evolving in a way that enables more and more complex and effective methods of managing dualities and their related tensions. Here, we would like to recommend another alternative for managing dualities—one called connection, that can fruitfully inform and continue the development of the next stage of planned change efforts. A connection approach seeks ways to embrace, to draw energy from, and to give equal voice to bipolar positions (Bakhtin, 1981; Baxter and Montgomery, 1996). Connection legitimates dualities through demonstrating respect, empathy, and curiosity for differences. Rather than oscillating between them, unifying them, or merging and transcending dichotomies, connection seeks to embrace differences. When dualities are treated as mutually reinforcing, they remain connected, use each other to generate insights, and are open to multiple and evolving interpretations. Thus, connection as a way of managing tensions rejects overly teleological change in favor of indeterminacy. To return to the cooperative-competitive example presented at the beginning of the chapter, connection would cast cooperation as essential for competitively producing optimal solutions and it would simultaneously treat competition as essential to cooperation by counteracting groupthink. Hence, both cooperation and competition are respected, valued, and connected in this unique perspective. Through this approach, dichotomies surface as mutually beneficial and mutually privileged. They are not mutually privileged in merging, segmenting, diluting, or abandoning bipolar concepts—only through seeking ways to connect, to engage, and to appreciate the diversity evident in treating change as the nexus of these dualities.

This approach to managing dualities of planned change yields several advantages for both theorists and practitioners. First, it enables us to draw a realistic picture of planned organizational change, particularly its complex and dynamic nature. The underlying dynamics of planned organizational change are usually far from the neat and harmonious processes that often appear in descriptions of change interventions. Instead, conflicts, dilemmas, and tensions are better descriptors of the reality of these changes. Therefore, we should be skeptical of interventions that oversimplify the change process, ignore possible tensions, or take extreme responses to handling the tensions among them. In fact, the history of planned organizational change itself reveals that failure to attend to these tensions and dualities early in the process will likely lead to unexpected consequences later in implementation. This insight also explains why some planned change interventions have a short life span. For example, many of the human system interventions championed by the first-generation OD efforts are obsolete today, in part because the neglected

technical system returned in force to dominate the landscape of organizational practices.

Second, focusing on links between dualities provides a framework for making tacit processes of change explicit and available for examination. In particular, we contend that managing various dualities and tensions inherent in the process is a core element of organizational change and can serve as essential criteria for evaluating approaches to planned change. Using the framework presented in this chapter, for example, we can explain why a popular intervention such as reengineering (e.g., Hammer and Champy, 1993; Davenport, 1993) cannot endure over time. Reengineering represents an organization-wide, externally driven, episodic change that focuses heavily on the organization's technical system and mostly relies on closed, top-down processes. Due to its overt privileging of one pole over the other, our framework would predict that certain problems would occur and that has been the case. For example, numerous studies document the unexpected problems of implementing reengineering programs that stem, in part, from ignoring the human system (e.g., Knights and McCabe, 1998).

As suggested above, these implicit processes hold keys to the next developments on the planned change horizon. As appreciative inquiry exemplifies, identifying a previously hidden and critical duality in the change process (in this case a negative focus versus positive focus) can lead to developing a new approach to organizational change. Hence, understanding the dualities of planned change has the potential to facilitate ongoing theory building in this area. Even when particular interventions fail, they may uncover new dualities and open up ideas for understanding this complex process.

Third, this approach offers important practical implications. Namely, the dualities and tensions identified in this paper reflect the choice points that people make, either implicitly or explicitly, as they initiate and/or implement a planned change program. Our framework may increase practitioners' awareness of various hidden but essential dynamics associated with organizational change and its consequences. More importantly, this framework emphasizes the importance of acknowledging and valuing dualities and tensions in planned change rather than (perhaps implicitly) assuming that change efforts should privilege one pole. Moreover, this framework suggests that the emergence of a new approach does not necessarily nullify previous ones, but may add other dimensions that have not been addressed adequately by the previous approaches. The issue is to identify and acknowledge the core dualities and manage their underlying dynamics through balance and connection.

However, the connection approach to managing tensions is not simple. It may also yield disadvantages that, potentially, will lead to even newer and more effective ways of managing dualities. First of all, connecting dualities is complex to handle. Managing organizational change is an inherently complex process, even in its simplest form. Managing connection while maintaining the requisite balance among multiple dualities can be extremely difficult and may delay the change process substantially. Moreover, connection leads to a great deal of ambiguity in a given situation as practitioners work through embracing and respecting dualities. Ambiguity, in this sense, needs to be a valued asset to be preserved rather than eliminated. But organizations are not generally equipped to cope with fragmentation and high ambiguity. As our review attests, knowledge of the ways to adequately address the dualities and tensions in organizational change is still limited.

Both the advantages and disadvantages of connection lead us to several directions for future research. First, the dualities listed in this chapter are not the finite set of all possible bipolar tensions in planned organizational change. No doubt, dualities and ways to manage them will continue to evolve as organizational environments change and knowledge of organizational interventions increases. Thus, one promising research direction is to uncover other dualities in planned change efforts. Second, our analysis suggests that past approaches to planned organizational change often privilege one side of the pole and ignore the other side. As a result, our knowledge of ways to manage dualities effectively is far more limited than our knowledge of the kinds of dualities present in planned organizational change. Therefore, future studies should investigate innovative and effective ways to manage the push and pull of competing forces in planned change. Finally, the effectiveness of the connection approach compared with other ways of managing the dualities and tensions in planned organizational change is an empirical question. For example, an alternative to the connection approach is a contingency perspective, a type of separation, which suggests that different approaches to planned change are effective in different situations (for handling different dualities) and that no single approach (e.g., connection) is better than others. Hence, future research needs to articulate alternative ways to embrace and/or privilege dualities and test the relative effectiveness of these approaches in different situations. Operating from a presumption that an intervention is by definition effective has often limited both the theories and the practices of planned organizational change. Empirical studies that examine the relative effectiveness of different approaches to managing dualities of planned organizational change would be a valuable research program.

Using dualities to understand organizational theories is not new to the field (Poole and Van de Ven, 1989). In fact, organizational change often occurs through the dynamics of paradox and contradiction. In this chapter, however, we have centered on the dualities implicit in planned change to ascertain the dimensions and key elements of this process. Moreover, we posit that the relationships among and the management of these bipolar pairs are the keys to grasping the complexities and dynamics of planned change. Such understandings can help researchers and practitioners alike view planned change in ways that transcend its surface characteristics and address the dualities and tensions that give it life.

Note

1. However, Burke (1992) argues that current OD approaches using survey feedback do not always follow this top-down process. It can start in the middle of the managerial hierarchy and move either or both.

References

Argyris, C. (1970). *Intervention theory and method: A behavioral science view*. Reading, MA: Addison-Wesley.

Argyris, C. (1983). Action science and intervention. *Journal of Applied Behavioral Science, 19,* 115–140.

Argyris, C. (1989). *Overcoming organizational defenses: Facilitating organizational learning*. Englewood Cliffs, NJ: Prentice Hall.

Argyris, C. & Schön, D. A. (1978). *Organizational learning: A theory in action perspective*. Reading, MA: Addison-Wesley.

Argyris, C., Putnam, R., & Smith, D. M. (1985). *Action science*. San Francisco: Jossey-Bass.

Austin, J. R. & Bartunek, J. M. (2003). Theories and practices of organizational development. In W. Borman, D. Ilgen, & R. Klimoski (Eds.), *Handbook of psychology:* Vol. 12, (pp. 302–332). New York: John Wiley & Sons.

Bakhtin, M. M. (1981). *The dialogic imagination: Four essays by M. M. Bakhtin* (C. Emerson & M. Holquist, Trans.). Austin: University of Texas Press.

Barrett, F. J. & Cooperrider, D. L. (1990). Generative metaphor intervention: A new approach for working with systems divided by conflict and caught in defensive perception. *Journal of Applied Behavioral Science, 26,* 219–239.

Bartunek, J. (1983). How organization development can develop organizational theory. *Group and Organization Studies, 8,* 303–318.

Bartunek, J. M. & Louis, M. R. (1988). The interplay of organization development and organizational transformation. In R. W. Woodman & W. A. Pasmore (Eds.), *Research in organizational change and development* (Vol. 2, pp. 97–134). Greenwich, CT: JAI Press.

Baxter, L. A. & Montgomery, B. M. (1996). *Relating: Dialogues and dialectics.* New York: Guilford.

Beckhard, R. (1969). *Organizational development: Strategies and models.* Reading, MA: Addison-Wesley.

Beer, M. & Nohria, N. (2000). Cracking the code of change. *Harvard Business Review, 78,* 133–141.

Beer, M. & Walton, A. E. (1987). Organizational change and development. *Annual Review of Psychology, 38,* 339–367.

Bennis, W. G. (1966). *Changing organizations.* New York: McGraw-Hill.

Bowers, D. G. (1973). OD techniques and theory in 23 organizations: The Michigan ICL study. *Journal of Applied Behavioral Science, 19,* 21–43.

Bradford, L. P. (1967). Biography of an institution. *Journal of Applied Behavioral Science, 3,* 127–143.

Brown, D. & Tandon, R. (1983). Ideology and political economy in inquiry: Action research and participatory research. *Journal of Applied Behavioral Science, 19,* 277–294.

Bunker, B. B. & Alban, B. T. (1997). *Large group interventions: Engaging the whole system for rapid change.* San Francisco: Jossey-Bass.

Burck, G. (1965, Dec.). Union Carbide's patient schemers. *Fortune,* 147–149.

Burke, W. W. (1992). *Organization development: A process of learning and changing.* Reading, MA: Addison-Wesley.

Cameron, K. S. (1986). Effectiveness as paradox: Consensus and conflict in conceptions of organizational effectiveness. *Management Science, 32,* 539–553.

Cameron, K. S. & Quinn, R. E. (1988). Organizational paradox and transformation. In R. E. Quinn & K. S. Cameron (Eds.), *Paradox and transformation: Toward a theory of change in organization and management* (pp. 1–18). Cambridge, MA: Ballinger.

Cameron, K. S. & Quinn, R. E. (1999). *Diagnosing and changing organizational culture.* Reading, MA: Addison-Wesley.

Camman, C., Lawler, E. E., III, Ledford, G. E., & Seashore, S. E. (1984). *Management-labor cooperation in quality of worklife experiments: Comparative analysis of eight cases.* Ann Arbor: University of Michigan.

Coch, L. & French, J. R. (1948). Overcoming resistance to change. *Human Relations, 1,* 512–532.

Collier, J. (1945). United States Indian administration as a laboratory of ethnic relations. *Social Research, 12,* 275–276.

Cooperrider, D. L. (1990). Positive image, positive action: The affirmative basis of organizing. In S. Srivastva & D. L. Cooperrider (Eds.), *Appreciative management and leadership: The power of positive thought and action in organizations* (pp. 91–125). San Francisco: Jossey-Bass.

Cooperrider, D. L. & Srivastva, S. (1987). Appreciative inquiry in organizational life. In W. A. Pasmore & R. W. Woodman (Eds.), *Research in organizational change and development* (pp. 129–169). Greenwich, CT: JAI.

Cummings, T. G. & Worley, C. G. (1997). *Organization development & change* (6th ed.). Cincinnati, OH: South-Western College.

Cyert, R. M. & March, J. G. (1963). *A behavioral theory of the firm.* Englewood Cliffs, NJ: Prentice-Hall.

Davenport, T. M. (1990). *Process innovation: Reengineering work through information technology.* Boston: Harvard Business School Press.

Dyer, W. G. (1977). *Team building.* Reading, MA: Addison-Wesley.

Dyer, W. G. (1995). *Team building: Current issues and new alternatives* (3rd ed.). Reading, MA: Addison-Wesley.

Eisenhardt, K. M. & Westcott, B. J. (1988). Paradoxical demands and the creation of excellence: The case of just-in-time manufacturing. In R. E. Quinn & K. S. Cameron (Eds.), *Paradox and transformation: Toward a theory of change in organization and management* (pp. 169–203). Cambridge, MA: Ballinger.

Easterby-Smith, M. (1997). Disciplines of organizational learning: Contributions and critiques. *Human Relations, 50,* 1085–1113.

Fiol, C. M. & Lyles, M. (1985). Organizational learning. *Academy of Management Review, 10,* 803–813.

Fisher, D. & Torbert, W. R. (1995). *Personal and organizational transformation*. London: McGraw-Hill.

Ford, J. D. & Backoff, R. H. (1988). Organizational change in and out of dualities and paradox. In R. E. Quinn & K. S. Cameron (Eds.), *Paradox and transformation: Toward a theory of change in organization and management* (pp. 81–121). Cambridge, MA: Ballinger.

French, W. L. (1969). Organization development: Objectives, assumptions, and strategies. *California Management Review, 12*, 23–34.

French, W. L. & Bell, C. H. (1995). *Organization development* (5th ed.). Englewood Cliffs, NJ: Prentice Hall.

Frey, L. R. (1995). Magical elixir or what the top tells the middle to do to the bottom? The promises and paradoxes of facilitating work teams for promoting organizational change and development. In R. Cesaria & P. Shockley-Zalabak (Eds.), *Organization means communication: Making the organizational communication concept relevant to practice* (pp. 173–188). Rome: Sipi Editore.

Frohman, M. A., Sashkin, M., & Kavanagh, M. J. (1976). Action research as applied to organization development. *Organization and Administrative Science, 7*, 129–142.

Garratt, B. (1990). *Creating a learning organization*. Cambridge: Simon & Schuster.

Garvin, D. A. (1993). Building a learning organization. *Harvard Business Review, 71*, 78–91.

Gersick, C. G. (1991). Revolutionary change theories: A multilevel exploration of the punctuated equilibrium paradigm. *Academy of Management Review, 16*, 10–36.

Golembiewski, R. T. (1998). Appreciating appreciative inquiry: Diagnosis and perspectives on how to do better. In R. W. Woodman & W. A. Pasmore (Eds.), *Research in organizational change and development* (Vol. 11, pp. 1–45). Greenwich, CT: JAI Press.

Goode, L. L. & Bartunek, J. (1990). Action research in underbounded settings: The example of an apartment complex. *Consultation, 9*, 209–228.

Gottlieb, J. Z. (1998). Understanding the role of organization development practitioners. In R. W. Woodman & W. A. Pasmore (Eds.), *Research in organizational change and development* (Vol. 11, pp. 117–158). Greenwich, CT: JAI Press.

Greenwood, D. J., Whyte, W. F., & Harkavy, I. (1993). Participatory action research as a process and as a goal. *Human Relations, 46*, 175–192.

Greenwood, R. & Hinings, C. R. (1988). Organization design types, tracks, and the dynamics of strategic change. *Organization Studies, 9*, 293–316.

Hackman, J. R. & Lawler, E. III. (1971). Employee reactions to job characteristics. *Journal of Applied Psychology, 55*, 259–286.

Hackman, J. R. & Oldham, G. R. (1980). *Work redesign*. Reading, MA: Addison-Wesley.

Hammer, M. & Champy, J. (1993). *Reengineering the corporation: A manifesto for business revolution*. London: Nicholas Brealy.

Hansen, C. D. (1995). Occupational cultures: Whose frame are we using? *Journal for Quality and Participation, 18*, 60–64.

Harrison, R. (1970). Choosing the depth of organizational intervention. *Journal of Applied Behavioral Science, 6*, 81–202.

Herman, M. (n.d.). Open space technology: What is it? [On-line]. Retrieved January 4, 2003, from http://www.openspaceworld.org/wiki/wiki/wiki.cgi?AboutOpenSpace

Hendry, C. (1996). Understanding and creating whole organizational change through learning theory. *Human Relations, 49*, 621–635.

Howard, L. A. & Geist, P. (1995). Ideological positioning in organizational change: The dialectic of control in a merging organization. *Communication Monographs, 62*, 110–131.

Isaacs, W. N. (1993, Autumn). Taking flight: Dialogue, collective thinking, and organizational learning. *Organizational Dynamics*, 24–39.

Jackson, B. G. (2000). A fantasy theme analysis of Peter Senge's learning organization. *Journal of Applied Behavioral Science, 36*, 193–209.

Jacobs, R. W. (1994). *Real time strategic change*. San Francisco: Berrett-Koehler.

Katz, D. & Kahn, R. L. (1966). *The social psychology of organizations*. New York: Wiley.

Kilmann, R. H. & Colvin, T. J. (1988). *Corporate transformation: Revitalizing organizations for a competitive world*. San Francisco: Jossey-Bass.

Kleiner, A. & Roth, G. (1997). How to make experience your company's best teacher. *Harvard Business Review, 75*, 172–177.

Kleiner, A. & Roth, G. (2000). *Oil change: Perspectives on corporate transformation*. New York: Oxford University Press.

Knights, D. & McCabe, D. (1998). "What happens when the phone goes wild?" Staff, stress, and spaces for escape in a BPR telephone banking work. *Journal of Management Studies, 35*, 163–194.

Lawler, E. E. III. (1986). *High-involvement management: Participative strategies for improving organizational performance*. San Francisco: Jossey-Bass.

Lawrence, P. R. & Lorsch, J. W. (1969). *Developing organizations: Diagnosis and action*. Reading, MA: Addison-Wesley.

Lessem, R. (1991). *Top quality learning: Building a learning organization*. London: Basil Blackwell.

Lewin, K. (1951). *Field theory in social science*. New York: Harper.

Lewin, K. (1958). Group decision and social change. In E. E. Maccoby, T. M. Newcomb, & E. L. Hartley (Eds.), *Readings in social psychology* (pp. 163–226). New York: Holt, Rinehart, and Winston.

Likert, R. (1967). *The human organization*. New York: McGraw Hill.

Lippitt, R. (1980). *Choosing the future you prefer*. Washington, DC: Development Publishers.

Lippitt, R., Watson, J., & Wesley, B. (1958). *Dynamics of planned change*. New York: Harcourt, Brace, and World.

Lipshitz, R., Popper, M., & Oz, S. (1996). Building learning organizations: The design and implementation of organizational learning mechanisms. *Journal of Applied Behavioral Science, 32*, 292–305.

Lundberg, C. C. (1985). Microinterventions for team development: Toward their application and use. In D. D. Warrick (Ed.), *Contemporary organization development: Current thinking and applications* (pp. 114–122). Glenview, IL: Scott Foresman.

Mann, F. (1962). Studying and creating change. In W. Bennis, K. Benne, & R. Chin (Eds.), *The planning of change: Readings in the applied behavioral sciences* (pp. 605–615). New York: Holt, Rinehart, and Winston.

Manz, C. C. & Sims, H. P. (1993). *Business without bosses: How self-managing teams are building high-performing companies*. New York: Wiley.

Marrow, A. J. (1967). Events leading to the establishment of the national training laboratories. *Journal of Applied Behavioral Science, 3*, 145–150.

McGregor, D. (1967). *The professional manager*. New York: McGraw-Hill.

Miles, R. H. (1997a). *Leading corporate transformation: A blueprint for business renewal*. San Francisco: Jossey-Bass.

Miles, R. H. (1997b). *Corporate comeback: The story of renewal and transformation at national semiconductor*. San Francisco: Jossey-Bass.

Miner, A. S. & Mezias, S. J. (1996). Ugly duckling no more: Organizational learning research. *Organization Science, 7*, 88–99.

Mirvis, P. H. & Berg, D. (1977). *Failures in organization development and change*. New York: Wiley Interscience.

Mirvis, P. H. (1988). Organizational development: Part I—An evolutionary perspective. In W. A. Pasmore & R. W. Woodman (Eds.), *Research in organizational change and development* (Vol. 2, pp. 1–57). Greenwich, CT: JAI Press.

Mirvis, P. H. (1990). Organizational development: Part II—A revolutionary perspective. In W. A. Pasmore & R. W. Woodman (Eds.), *Research in organizational change and development* (Vol. 4, pp. 1–66). Greenwich, CT: JAI Press.

Moch, M. K. & Bartunek, J. M. (1990). *Creating alternative realities at work: The quality of work life experiment at Food Com*. New York: Harper Business.

Nadler, D. A. & Tushman, M. L. (1977). A diagnostic model for organizational behavior. In J. Hackman, E. Lawler, & L. Porter (Eds.), *Perspectives on behavior in organizations* (pp. 85–100). New York: McGraw-Hill.

Nadler, D. A. & Tushman, M. L. (1989). Organizational frame bending: Principles for managing reorientation. *Academy of Management Executive, 3*, 194–204.

Nadler, D. A. & Tushman, M. L. (1995). Types of organizational change: From incremental improvement to discontinuous transformation. In D. A. Nadler, R. B. Show, & A. E. Walton (Eds.), *Discontinuous change: Leading organizational transformation* (pp. 15–34). San Francisco: Jossey-Bass.

Nadler, D. A., Shaw, R. B., & Walton, A. E. (1995). *Discontinuous change: Leading organizational transformation*. San Francisco: Jossey-Bass.

Nevis, E. C., DiBella, A. J., & Gould, J. M. (1995, Winter). Understanding organizations as learning systems. *Sloan Management Review*, 73–85.

Nutt, P. C. & Backoff, R. W. (1997a). Facilitating transformational change. *Journal of Applied Behavioral Science, 44*, 490–508.

Nutt, P. C. & Backoff, R. W. (1997b). Transforming organizations with second-order change. In W. A. Pasmore & R. W. Woodman (Eds.), *Research in organizational change and development* (Vol. 10, pp. 229–274). Greenwich, CT: JAI Press.

O'Connor, E. S. (1995). Paradoxes of participation: A textual analysis of case studies on organizational change. *Organizational Studies, 16*, 769–803.

Owen, H. (1991). *Riding the tiger: Doing business in a transforming world*. Potomac, MD: Abbott.

Owen, H. (1992). *Open space technology: A user's guide*. Potomac, MD: Abbott.

Pasmore, W. A. (1988). *Designing effective organizations: The sociotechnical systems perspective*. New York: Wiley.

Pasmore, W. A. & Friedlander, F. (1982). An action-research program for increasing employee involvement in problem solving. *Administrative Science Quarterly, 27*, 343–362.

Pearson, J. C. (2001). Conflict in our intimate relationships. In W. F. Eadie & P. E. Nelson (Eds.),

The language of conflict and resolution (pp. 47–56). Thousand Oaks, CA: Sage.

Pedler, M., Burgoyne, J., & Boydell, T. (1997). *The learning company.* New York: McGraw-Hill.

Poole, M. S. & Van de Ven, A. (1989). Using paradox to build management and organizational theories. *Academy of Management Review, 14,* 562–578.

Porras, J. I. & Robertson, P. J. (1987). Organizational development theory: A typology and evaluation. In W. A. Pasmore & R. W. Woodman (Eds.), *Research in organizational change and development* (pp. 1–57). Greenwich, CT: JAI Press.

Quinn, R. E. & Cameron, K. S. (1988). *Paradox and transformation: Toward a theory of change in organization and management.* Cambridge, MA: Ballinger.

Ramirez, I. L. & Bartunek, J. (1989). The multiple realities of organization development consultation in health care. *Journal of Organizational Change Management, 2,* 40–57.

Rapoport, R. N. (1970). Three dilemmas in action research. *Human Relations, 23,* 488–513.

Reason, P. (1988). Experience, action, and metaphor as dimensions of post-positivist inquiry. In W. A. Pasmore & R. W. Woodman (Eds.), *Research in organizational change and development* (Vol. 2, pp. 195–233). Greenwich, CT: JAI Press.

Reason, P. & Heron, J. (1995). Co-operative inquiry. In R. Harre, J. Smith, & L. Van Langenhove (Eds.), *Rethinking psychology* (Vol. 2, pp. 122–142). London: Sage.

Rice, A. K. (1958). *Productivity and social organization, the Ahmedabad Experiment.* London: Tavistock Publications.

Romanelli, E. & Tushman, M. L. (1994). Organizational transformation as punctuated equilibrium: An empirical test. *Academy of Management Journal, 37,* 1141–1166.

Roth, G. & Kleiner, A. (2000). *Car launch: The human side of managing change.* New York: Oxford University Press.

Schein, E. H. (1980). *Organizational psychology* (3rd ed.). Englewood Cliffs, NJ: Prentice Hall.

Schein, E. H. (1987). *Process consultation: Vol. 2. Lessons for managers and consultants.* Reading, MA: Addison-Wesley.

Schmidt, P. & Manning, M. R. (1998). A comparative framework for large group organizational change interventions. In W. A. Pasmore & R. W. Woodman (Eds.), *Research in organizational change and development* (Vol. 11, pp. 225–251). Greenwich, CT: JAI Press.

Schwinn, C. & Schwinn, D. (1996). Lessons for organizational transformation. *Journal for Quality and Participation, 19,* 6–10.

Senge, P. (1990). *The fifth discipline: The art and practice of the learning organization.* New York: Doubleday Currency.

Senge, P., Kleiner, A., Roberts, C., Ross, R. B., & Smith, B. J. (1994). *The fifth discipline fieldbook.* New York: Doubleday Currency.

Senge, P., Kleiner, A., Roberts, C., Ross, R. B., Roth, G., & Smith, B. J. (1999). *The dance of change: The challenge to sustaining momentum in learning organization.* New York: Doubleday Currency.

Smith, K. K. & Berg, D. N. (1987). *Paradoxes of group life.* San Francisco, CA: Jossey-Bass.

Stewart, G. L. & Manz, C. C. (1995). Leadership for self-managing work teams: A typology and integrative model. *Human Relations, 48,* 747–770.

Stohl, C. & Cheney, G. (2001). Participatory processes/paradoxical practices: Communication and the dilemmas of organizational democracy. *Management Communication Quarterly, 14,* 349–407.

Suttle, J. L. (1977). Improving life at work—Problems and prospects. In J. R. Hackman & J. L. Suttle (Eds.), *Improving life at work: Behavioral science approaches to organizational change* (pp. 1–29). Santa Monica, CA: Goodyear.

Tenkasi, R. (2000). The dynamics of cultural knowledge and learning in creating viable theories of global change and action. *Organizational Development Journal, 18,* 74–90.

Tichy, N. M. (1983). *Managing strategic change.* New York: Wiley-Interscience.

Tichy, N. M. & Devanna, M. A. (1986). *The transformational leader.* New York: Wiley.

Torbert, W. R. (1989). Leading organizational transformation. In W. A. Pasmore & R. W. Woodman (Eds.), *Research in organizational change and development* (Vol. 3, pp. 83–116). Greenwich, CT: JAI Press.

Torbert, W. R. (1991). *The power of balance: Transforming self, society, and scientific inquiry.* Newbury Park, CA: Sage.

Trahant, B., Burke, W. W., & Koonce, R. (1997). 12 principles of organizational transformation. *Management Review, 86,* 17–21.

Trist, E. (1989). Aspects of the professional facilitation of planned change. In R. McLennan (Eds.), *Managing organizational change* (pp. 42–45). Englewood Cliffs, NJ: Prentice Hall.

Trist, E. & Bamforth, K. (1951). Some social and psychological consequences of the Long Wall Methods of coal-getting. *Human Relations, 4,* 1–8.

Tsang, E. W. K. (1997). Organizational learning and learning organization: A dichotomy between descriptive and prescriptive research. *Human Relations, 50,* 73–89.

Tushman, M. L. & Romanelli, E. (1985). Organizational evolution: A metamorphosis model of convergence and reorientation. In L. L. Cummings & B. M. Staw (Eds.), *Research in organizational behavior* (Vol. 7, pp. 171–222). Greenwich, CT: JAI Press.

Van de Ven, A. H. & Poole, M. S. (1988). Paradoxical requirements for a theory of organizational change. In R. Quinn & K. Cameron (Eds.), *Paradox and transformation: Toward a theory of change in organization and management* (pp. 19–80). New York: Harper Collins.

Van de Ven, A. H. & Poole, M. S. (1995). Explaining development and change in organizations. *Academy of Management Review, 20,* 510–540.

Walton, R. E. (1974). Quality of working life: What is it? *Sloan Management Review, 15,* 11–21.

Watkins, J. M. & Mohr, B. J. (2001). *Appreciative inquiry: Change at the speed of imagination.* San Francisco: Jossey-Bass.

Watkins, K. E. & Marsick, V. J. (1994). *Sculpting the learning organization.* San Francisco: Jossey-Bass.

Weber, P. S. & Manning, M. R. (1998). A comparative framework for large group organizational change interventions. In R. W. Woodman & W. A. Pasmore (Eds.), *Research in organizational change and development* (Vol. 11, pp. 225–252). Greenwich, CT: JAI Press.

Weick, K. E. & Quinn, R. E. (1999). Organizational change and development. *Annual Review of Psychology, 50,* 361–386.

Weisbord, M. R. & Janoff, S. (1995). *Future search.* San Francisco: Berrett-Koehler.

Whyte, A. F. (1992). Organizational transformation at BP: An interview with the chair. *HR: Human Resource Planning, 15,* 3–14.

Whyte, W. F. (1991). *Participatory Action Research.* Newbury Park, CA: Sage.

Whyte, W. F. & Hamilton, E. (1964). *Action research for management.* Homewood, IL: Irwin-Dorsey.

Wick, C. W. & Leon, L. S. (1995). From ideas to action: Creating a learning organization. *Human Resource Management, 34,* 299–311.

Wishart, N. A., Elam, J. J., & Robey, D. (1996). Redrawing the portrait of a learning organization: Inside Knight-Ridder, Inc. *Academy of Management Executive, 10,* 7–20.

Woodman, R. W. (1989). Organizational change and development: New arenas for inquiry and action. *Journal of Management, 15,* 205–228.

Work in America Institute. (1973). *Work in America.* Cambridge, MA: MIT Press.

5

Adaptation and Selection in Strategy and Change

Perspectives on Strategic Change in Organizations

Arie Y. Lewin, Carmen B. Weigelt, & James D. Emery

The study of organizational change, as the many chapters in this handbook demonstrate, reflects extensive and diverse theoretical perspectives and empirical approaches. In this chapter we return to an examination of the adaptation-selection debate (Baum, 1996, Lewin and Volberda, 1999). Our purpose is to consider the implications of the different theories on adaptation and selection for strategy and change. In particular, we reconsider theories and empirical studies that inform organization-level adaptation as a direct outcome of strategic management and organizational change or have implications for organizational change but make no direct or explicit assumptions about managerial intentionality.

In this chapter we do not review theories and consequences of change where the unit of analysis is the individual or the group. We recognize that managers and individuals vary greatly in their information processing and decision making due to social cognition, selective perception, managerial construction of environment, individual traits, judgment and decision making biases, escalation of commitment, and

contextual interaction outcomes. Managers are largely self-taught; their knowledge structures and cognitive process are anchored in direct experience, and that experience shapes, to a large extent, what they know and what they do. It is also beyond the scope of this chapter to review the empirical evidence involving idiosyncratic contextual explanations of specific organizational adaptations (DeSanctis and Poole, 1994; Sydow and Windeler, 1998; Walsh, 1995).

In structuring this chapter we recognize that the empirical data supports the observation that most firms are selected out. However, the literature does not distinguish between the survival chances of firms that are managed for the long term relative to those managed for the short term. The empirical adaptation-selection literature is to a great extent handicapped by relying on the same outcome measure of survival as direct support for the specific adaptation or selection theory. Theories of strategic adaptation interpret survival as proof that the firm in question had unique resources and capabilities or superior regimes of routines or optimal resource allocation strategies that account for competitive advantage, and therefore for survival. Population ecology theories interpret survival as proof that new entrants are the surviving organization form and that incumbent firms have been selected out. Theoretically or empirically, however, the population ecology literature is not concerned with studying the adaptation of individual firms. Therefore, the theories or the empirical research offer no insights about individual firms that do successfully adapt and change as their original population coevolves into the new organizational forms represented by the new entrants.

One conclusion that emerges from this review is that selection and adaptation studies represent two levels of analyses that do not intersect. Thus, much of the adaptation selection debate is not a debate at all. Strategic adaptation theories are not concerned with macro- (population-)level adaptation and population level theories ignore microlevel adaptation. Moreover, the strategic adaptation literature itself is handicapped by a split, a disconnect between macro-organization and strategy theories of adaptation and change. Although the overall conclusion of population studies regarding survival is supported by the extant empirical literature (most firms are selected out) we offer, in the final section of this chapter, a reinterpretation for why few surviving firms are able to counteract structural inertia, coevolve, adapt, and reinvent themselves over time.

This chapter is organized into four major sections: (1) firm-level theories that link firm level capabilities and strategy to adaptation and survival, (2) mesolevel or boundary theories that link the firm to the macro or the institutional environment, (3) theories linking the firm to the macro environment, and (4) implications for adaptation and change and future research. Figure 5.1 depicts a coevolution view of the theories reviewed in this chapter, their position in the adaptation-selection debate, their causal direction, and levels of analysis. Specifically, we review theories that focus on internal firm strategies and change, mesolevel theories that focus on the boundary between the firm and its competitive environment, theories of the role of the institutional environment on industry and firm adaptation, and theories of population-level dynamics involving new entrants and macro forces of change such as technological advances and social movements. We review theories and empirical studies originating in sociology (population ecology, institu-

tional theory), economics (industrial organizations, evolutionary economics, transaction costs economics, behavioral theory of the firm), and strategic management (resource dependence, punctuated equilibrium, strategic choice, learning- and resource-based view) as they inform organizational adaptation.

The overall goal of this chapter is a unifying synthesis of what Pfeffer (1993) described as a "weed patch" literature of proliferating theories advancing seemingly competing and contradictory research paradigms, supported by their own measures, terms, and concepts. Although it may be comforting to subscribe to Pfeffer's conclusion that it is difficult to discern in what direction knowledge of organization science is progressing, we believe that collectively the theories and research reviewed in this chapter inform many dimensions of strategy and adaptation research. This body of research can be viewed as informing a multivariate, multilevel, coevolutionary view of adaptation. Moreover, we believe that multiple lenses within a coevolution framework are necessary for a more comprehensive understanding of organization adaptation and change as embedded within larger environmental and institutional context.

In section 4, we discuss the implications of our review for organization adaptation and change and specifically consider why few firms are successful in surviving, adapting, and coevolving over time with some implications for future research on adaptation and change.

Theories Focusing on the Firm

Resource-Based View

The description of the firm as "a bundle of resources" was initially articulated by Penrose (1959), who framed the idea of heterogeneity "of the productive services available or potentially available from its resources that gives each firm its unique character" (p. 75). In this framework, firm resources were defined as tangible and intangible assets (e.g. physical assets, human assets, as well as organizational resources such as firm attributes, capital, or organizational processes) that were embedded in the firm (Barney, 1991; Wernerfelt, 1984). Although resource-based theory concentrates on the conditions under which firm resources lead to sustainable competitive advantage,

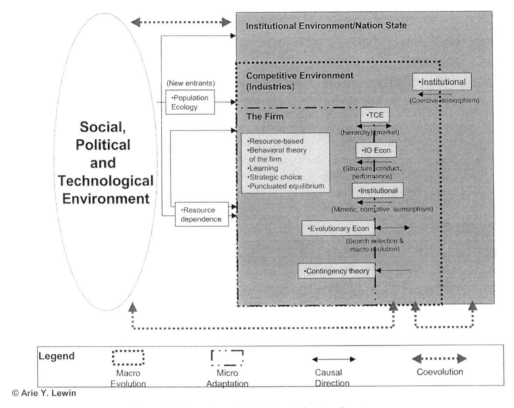

Figure 5.1 Framing of adaptation/selection literature.

it appropriately recognizes that not all resources are a source of sustainable advantage. Only those resources that are valuable, rare, imperfectly imitable, and strategically unique with no substitutes are believed to provide sustainable competitive advantage (Barney, 1991).

Central Focus and Assumptions

The resource-based view focuses on the firm as the level of analysis and on its resources as the unit of analysis. The central objective of the resource-based view is to address how individual firms leverage their resources to build sustainable competitive advantage. Resource-based theory is built on a number of key assumptions including resource heterogeneity, the existence of unique or inimitable resources, limits to resource mobility and competition, and the role of dynamic capabilities such as knowledge creation and integration. Resource-based theory has also tended to view change from an equilibrium-oriented perspective; this view has implications for future research initiatives including opportunities for integration with other theoretical perspectives. We explore each of these points below.

In contrast to the typical assumption in economic theory of homogeneity among firms within an industry, the resource-based view assumes resource heterogeneity among firms. Such heterogeneity in resource endowments among firms derives from differences in information gathering, luck, managerial ability, or technical know-how. These resource differences can present a source of rents and sustainable advantage (Barney, 1986, 1991; Mahoney and Pandian, 1992). In particular, the distinctive competence of a firm to make effective use of its unique resource capabilities can enable the firm to appropriate sustainable rents (Penrose, 1959; Hitt and Ireland, 1985). Thus, rather than focusing on the "representative firm" and its behavior, the resource-based view focuses on unique and firm-specific resources that significantly differentiate firms and firm performance within an industry (Mahoney and Pandian, 1992; Prahalad and Hamel, 1990).

In this view, resources are considered valuable if they enable a firm to increase its efficiency and effectiveness, and rare if they allow a firm to implement a strategy that cannot be simultaneously implemented by other firms (Barney, 1991). Furthermore, rare and valuable resources are a source of sustained competitive advantage only if they are simultaneously inimitable by competitors and immobile, thereby making it impossible for other firms to obtain them (Barney, 1991; Peteraf, 1993). Resources are generally considered to be inimitable if (a) they are embedded in firm history, (b) their relationship to performance outcomes is causally ambiguous (Lippman and Rumelt, 1982), or (c) they are socially complex (Dierickx and Cool, 1989). Limits to resource mobility may similarly arise from a number of factors.

A number of researchers have explored the concepts of barriers to entry at the firm level (Bain, 1956) and mobility barriers at the strategic group level (Caves and Porter, 1977). Some have discussed "isolating mechanisms" to describe the phenomena that shelter firm strategic resources from acquisition or imitation (Rumelt, 1984). Such isolating mechanisms can, for instance, be reflected in intellectual property rights as well as in information or learning asymmetries (Rumelt, 1987). Other researchers, such as Peteraf (1993), have emphasized ex post and ex ante limits to resource competition as important for sustainable competitive advantage based on resource differences among firms. Often unique, inimitable, and immobile resources are path-dependent; that is, these resources have developed within an organization over time and therefore are neither purchasable in the market nor imitable in the short term. Teece, Pisano, and Shuen (1997) suggest that dynamic capabilities, the mechanisms through which firms develop and dissipate new capabilities, form a primary source of competitive advantage. Thus, internally developed and accumulated resources that are dependent on learning processes and routines specific to the organization defy imitation and build strategic advantage, leading to the perspective that knowledge creation and integration are perhaps the most important strategic assets of the firm (Conner and Prahalad, 1996; Dierickx and Cool, 1989; Grant, 1996; Leonard-Barton, 1992).

Finally, resource-based theory considers the implications of environmental change on a firm's sources of competitive advantage. Environmental change and turbulence are believed to erode competitive advantage by rendering strategically unique resource endowments obsolete. Thus, to maintain competitive advantage over time, firms have to consistently regenerate and develop their resource base. Wernerfelt (1984) states that "the optimal growth of the firm involves a balance between exploitation [*maximizing utilization*][1] of existing resources and development of new ones" (p. 178), implying a dynamic change process. However, resource-based theory tends to be equilibrium-oriented. Dierickx and Cool (1989), for example, adopt a static perspective of resource-based theory by arguing that changing a firm's resource endowment takes considerably longer than altering its market strategy. Their key assumption is that fitness levels of organizations change at a slower rate than environmental, technological, regulatory, and social changes. Therefore, they suggest that resource-based theory could benefit from a more process-oriented model that, for example, involves a synthesis with evolutionary theory (Foss, Knudsen, and Montgomery, 1995).

Main Empirical Focus

The resource-based approach has influenced a number of streams of empirical research, including: (a) entry timing into new markets (Mahoney and Pandian, 1992) and first mover advantage (Lieberman and Montgomery, 1998), (b) diversification, and (c) mergers and acquisitions. We briefly examine each of these areas of research in this section.

The relationship of market entry timing to firm performance has long been of interest to both researchers and managers. Empirical studies on entry timing have shown firm resources, such as technological and marketing capabilities, to be significantly associated with entry timing (Mitchell, 1989; Schoenecker and Cooper, 1998). Robinson, Fornell, and Sullivan (1992) also found a positive relationship between a firm's strong finance skills and its pioneering market entry. First-mover advantages are often considered to be important as a source of entry barriers into a market. In the resource-based view, strategic, scarce and inimitable resources can result in first-mover advantages (Lieberman and Montgomery, 1988, 1998; Makadok, 1998). According to Barney (1991, p. 102) the sustainability of competitive advantage "depends upon the possibility of competitive duplication" rather than on the elapsed calendar time. Thus "a competitive advantage is sustained only if it continues to exist after efforts to duplicate that advantage have ceased." Studying the money market mutual funds industry, Makadok (1998) showed first-mover advantages in market share were only gradually and modestly eroded by new entrants. He also noted that it seemed to take a large number of new entrants for first-mover advantages to erode. He attributed the resistance of first-mover advantages to erosion to the first-movers' possession of inimitable resources.

The resource-based view asserts that firm resources can be drivers for diversification and acquisition, in addition to first-mover advantages and entry barriers (Barney, 1991; Conner, 1991; Penrose, 1959; Wernerfelt, 1984, 1989). A significant body of research on diversification has been influenced by resource-based theory. For example, the resource-based view has been used to explain limitations of growth through diversification, motivations for diversification, and different returns to different types of diversification. The resource-based view has also been used to provide a theoretical basis for predicting the direction of diversification (Ramanujam and Varadarajan, 1989). For instance, the resource-based view predicts that firms should benefit most from diversification into markets in which their current resource strength can be applied (Chang, 1996; Chatterjee and Wernerfelt, 1991; Montgomery and Hariharan, 1991). Many empirical studies on diversification and performance have supported this prediction by finding higher performance outcomes for related, rather than unrelated, diversification (Rumelt, 1974; Montgomery and Wernerfelt, 1988; Palepu, 1985; Singh and Montgomery, 1987; Varadarajan and Ramanujam, 1987). Chang (1996) has also shown that dissimilarity in human resource profiles between firm core business and a potential new market may reduce the likelihood of a firm entering that market. Further, he has demonstrated that firms are more likely to exit business lines that lack resource similarity with their core business (Chang and Singh, 1999). However,

some contradictory evidence exists, as a few studies have failed to find support for the hypothesized positive relationship between resource fit and post-entry performance (Sharma and Kesner, 1996).

Since strategic and rent-generating resources are assumed to be not tradable or mobile across firms, mergers and acquisitions are often the only way to obtain bundles of strategic resources (Wernerfelt, 1984). The resource-based perspective assumes that multibusiness firms gain sustainable advantage only if unique resources can be effectively shared across units (Robins and Wiersema, 1995) or that acquisitions create abnormal value only if acquirer and target resources can be uniquely and strategically combined (Barney, 1988). Given these caveats, it is perhaps not surprising that the stream of research on mergers and acquisitions has not found support for acquirers appropriating rents and above-normal returns from acquisitions (Agrawal, Jaffe, and Mandelker 1992; Malatesta, 1983). Building on resource-based theory, Barney (1986, 1988) argues that rents will accrue to acquirers only if the bidding firm possesses private information, luck, or specific synergies with the potential target that are not easily imitable by other potential acquirers. As a result, some researchers have suggested that such synergies are more likely in related acquisitions (Chatterjee, 1990). Hence, while resource-based theories have generated a wealth of empirical research, the occasionally equivocal findings of these studies have produced certain controversies for the resource-based view.

Controversies

Some key challenges directed at the empirical research associated with the resource-based view note that (a) certain key concepts such as resources or capabilities are difficult to observe or measure directly (Godfrey and Hill, 1995; Reed and DeFillippi, 1990; Robins and Wiersema, 1995) and (b) the theory does not clearly state whether it is a combination of resources or a single resource that provides the source of competitive advantage. These criticisms prove especially challenging in large, multi-industry, and cross-sectional studies that are typical of strategy research (Ramanujam and Varadarajan, 1989; Rouse and Daellenbach, 1999). As a result, empirical studies have often used proxy and more distant measures for firm resources such as R and D intensity, advertising intensity, and capital intensity to address these limitations.

Implications for Adaptation and Change

Because of its strong focus on firm-specific resources and competitive advantage at the organizational level, the resource-based view has a strong adaptive orientation. Sustained superior performance resulting from unique resource endowments is expected to increase firm survival and its ability to adapt to changing environments and realize new opportunities. From this perspective, management's task is to detect, accumulate, develop, and use strategically valuable resources to gain sustainable competitive advantage as well as to guard those resources and their streams of rents against competitors (Amit and Schoemaker, 1993; Peteraf, 1993).

Behavioral Theory of the Firm

A *Behavioral Theory of the Firm* (Cyert and March, 1963) challenges both profit maximization as the sole goal of organizations and perfect knowledge as basis of firm operation. Using the firm as unit of analysis, *A Behavioral Theory of the Firm* (BTOF) advances a process theory of organizational decision making and adaptation. A number of the more recent theories, such as evolutionary economics (Nelson and Winter, 1982) and organizational learning (Hedberg, 1981; Levinthal and March, 1981, 1993; March, 1991), build on the key constructs and ideas of BTOF.

Central Focus and Assumptions

The BTOF views the organization as a coalition whose members and stakeholders seek to maximize their personal goals while satisfying the demands of the organization. Thus rather than viewing the organization as a profit maximizing entity, as in the classical economic view of the firm, management is seen as balancing resources to satisfy competing claims of multiple stakeholder. Organizational goals are measured against aspiration levels that are based on manager experience, past performance and goals, performance of competitors, and on industry experience. The major assumptions underlying BTOF are "quasi resolution of conflict, uncertainty avoidance, problemistic search, and organizational learning" (Cyert and March, 1963, p. 116). Prior to addressing

these key assumptions, we first turn to a brief review of the concept of organizational slack, a pivotal and integrating construct in BTOF.

Organizational slack is defined as the "difference between total resources and total necessary payments" (Cyert and March, 1963, p. 36). It serves to buffer the organization from environmental uncertainty, stabilizing the organizational coalition by smoothing variability in performance levels and providing the source of resources for innovation. Through these mechanisms, organizational slack plays a central role to the key assumptions of BTOF.

Within BTOF, conflict can arise from a number of sources, including: (a) changing environmental conditions that create uncertainty for the firm, (b) differences between the individual goals of different managers within the firm, and (c) differences between individual manager objectives and the goals of the other various stakeholders of the organization. Because organizational slack provides the resources that enable the firm to respond to varying environmental conditions and differences among individual, firm, and stakeholder goals, organizational slack plays an important role in mediating conflict for the firm.

Another major assumption of BTOF involves the need to reduce environmental uncertainty described as uncertainty avoidance behavior. Organizations seek to reduce uncertainty by negotiating their environment and using organizational slack to buffer variability in performance. Rather than treating the environment as exogenous and deterministic (Hannan and Freeman, 1977), BTOF portrays organizations as seeking to control it. Organizations negotiate and influence their environment through plans, industry standards, contractual arrangements, and congruence with industry practices and institutional norms. BTOF uncertainty-reduction strategies are similar to those postulated in resource dependence theory (Pfeffer and Salancik, 1978). For instance, in resource dependence theory uncertainty-reduction strategies consist of forming industry associations, alliances, or interlocking directorates.

Problemistic search is the basic failure-driven process reflecting bounded rationality that explains when and how routines are improved and the nature of the solution process. Problemistic search is motivated by recognizing or identifying a specific problem associated with an operational practice (routine). The intensity of organizational search processes is dependent on disparity between organization goals and achievement. When performance exceeds the goals, search intensity declines and organizational slack grows. Organizational slack accumulates during periods when performance exceeds aspiration levels or, more generally, when the environment is munificent. During unfavorable environmental conditions, BTOF assumes that the firm rationalizes slack through some restructuring strategies as a means of achieving performance levels. Thus, organization slack represents a cushion for counteracting environmental uncertainty and performance failure.

Problemistic search and the implementation of adaptation heuristics are also key processes associated with organizational learning. Finally, because organizational slack provides the resource for problemistic search, it is again viewed as a necessary, but not sufficient, condition for innovation and adaptation.

Main Empirical Focus

Empirical research on BTOF has taken many forms, including simulation studies (March and Olsen, 1976). Much of the empirical research supporting BTOF assumptions and predictions derives from empirical studies applying evolutionary economics or organizational learning. Empirical research on organization slack has had mixed results (Bourgeois, 1981; Singh, 1986) and points to some of the challenges associated with BTOF.

Controversies

Similar to some of the criticisms directed at the resource-based view, BTOF suffers from the endemic problem of investigating concepts such as firm dynamic capabilities (Teece et al., 1997). While these concepts have explanatory power and are intuitively appealing, they have proven difficult to apply ex ante.

Implications for Adaptation and Change

Similar to many other theories focusing on the firm, BTOF views firms as possessing "considerable latitude in selecting their strategies for dealing with their environments" (Child, 1972, p. 244). A major assumption of BTOF is that organizations are capable of changing their goals, focus of attention, and search procedures as a consequence of organizational learning. Further, BTOF seems to go a step further than some theories with a strong adaptation view

by suggesting that firms can affect or even alter the external environment in which they operate. However, BTOF seems to put little emphasis on some of the inertial factors that create resistance to adaptation and change for organizations.

Organizational Learning

A *Behavioral Theory of the Firm* (Cyert and March, 1963) introduced organizational learning as a feature of organization adaptation by viewing organizations as "adaptive learning systems" in which behavior is driven by procedures, routines, and incremental learning. However, subsequent research in organizational learning has varied greatly in how learning is defined and what aspects are emphasized. For example, learning has been defined as new knowledge or insights (Argyris and Schoen, 1978), new structures (Chandler, 1962), or merely a change in actions (Cyert and March, 1963). March and Olsen (1975) focused on the cognitive limitations of learning and Huber (1991) framed organizational learning within an information-processing perspective. At other times, researchers have emphasized learning as routine-based, history-dependent, and target-oriented (Levitt and March, 1988). Despite the lack of convergence on a definition and the widely divergent conceptualizations for organizational learning (Huber, 1991), there appears to be strong conceptual agreement on a positive relationship between organizational learning and future performance (Fiol and Lyles, 1985; Levitt and March, 1988).

Central Focus and Assumptions

Organizational learning theories seek to explain how individuals and their organizations acquire, process, distribute, integrate, and dissipate information associated with the functions of the firm. Several assumptions are integral to the study of organizational learning, including (a) learning occurs on multiple levels, (b) learning occurs through multiple mechanisms, (c) learning contributes to organizational success through both adaptation and exploitation processes, and (d) the rate of learning can have both positive and negative consequences for organizations. We examine each of the assumptions in turn.

Organizational learning is a multilevel phenomenon that may occur at the level of the individual, the group, the organization, or the population (Fiol and

Lyles, 1985; Crossan, Lane, and White, 1999). At the individual level, learning has focused on the acquisition of new skills, knowledge, norms, and values (Argyris and Schoen, 1978), and on the process of learning by trial and error (Miner and Mezias, 1996). Learning at the group level has emphasized "performance feedback, shared understanding, and coordinated behavior" (Miner and Mezias, 1996, p. 91). At the organizational level, learning has usually addressed the interplay between aspiration levels, inter- and intraorganizational knowledge transfer, and information processing (Miner and Mezias, 1996). More recently, researchers have studied learning processes at the population level with groups of organizations acquiring new knowledge and routines through common experience or imitation (Barnett and Hansen, 1996; Darr, Argote, and Epple, 1995; Ingram and Baum, 1997a, 1997b; Mezias and Lant, 1994). The findings from this research have suggested that in processes of technological diffusion some organizations learn too early and others too late (Miner and Haunschild, 1995).

Just as learning occurs at multiple levels, many different mechanisms are believed to contribute to organizational learning. For instance, learning can result from socialization processes through reinforcement of routines and internalization of firm procedures. Learning can also occur as a result of activities intentionally directed at improving organizational performance and/or routines (Huber, 1991). Directed processes typically use explicitly defined search-and-evaluation procedures, although trial-and-error experimentation can also occur in which successful processes are retained and reinforced, while unsuccessful processes are abandoned (Cyert and March, 1963; Levitt and March, 1988; March and Olsen, 1976; March and Simon, 1958). Further, organizations learn from both their own experience and the experience of other firms through imitation of successful practices or through acquisition (Herriott, Levinthal, and March, 1985; Huber, 1991). Moreover, organizations may engage in competitive learning races with other firms, resulting in a "Red Queen" effect in which firms match one another as fast as possible, but no firm achieves a lasting advantage (Barnett and Hansen, 1996). However, for successful assimilation of new external knowledge, cumulative experience and the development of absorptive capacity are assumed to be necessary organization capabilities (Cohen and Levinthal, 1990; Lane and Lubatkin, 1998).

The impetus for organizational learning may come from within the organization or it may result from environmental change. Not surprisingly, changing organizational routines is more likely to be initiated in times when performance fails to achieve set goals than in times when performance exceeds goals. Often these performance decrements occur in times of environmental turbulence, when previously successful organizational routines have become outdated, leading the organization to fall into "competency traps" (Levitt and March, 1988; March, 1981).

To avoid competency traps, successful long-term organizational adaptation and renewal require organizations to exploit and refine existing routines and capabilities embedded in "old knowledge" and, simultaneously, to explore new approaches that can supplant obsolete practices, capabilities, and knowledge bases (March, 1991; Crossan et al., 1999). Thus, March (1991) stressed the importance of finding a balance between exploration and exploitation in organizational learning to promote organizational adaptation and survival. Moreover, learning and unlearning are both believed to be necessary for understanding organizational adaptation and change (Hedberg, 1981). Unlearning old routines opens possibilities for new learning to occur (Hedberg, 1981; Huber, 1991), while cumulative learning reinforces existing skills and improves organizational position on the learning curve (Dutton, Thomas, and Butler, 1984; Levitt and March, 1988). However, overvaluing current information at the expense of long-term prospects or overly emphasizing past success and local searches can lead to myopic learning, which can inhibit long-term adaptability (Levinthal and March, 1993). Avoiding competency traps and the myopia of learning in relentlessly shifting environments requires that organizations simultaneously stress exploration of new routines and exploitation of known expertise (Levinthal and March, 1993; Lewin, Long, and Carroll, 1999; March, 1991).

While the benefits of balancing exploitation and exploration in organizational learning have gained broad consensus, the advantage of speed in organizational learning has generated mixed support. Rapid learning has been hypothesized to affect organizational adaptability and survival with the consequence that often organizations select skill acquisition over internal skill development (Cohen and Levinthal, 1990). Results of simulation studies show that fast-learning organizations reached expertise and equilibrium in new routines earlier than slow-learning organizations (March, 1991). Hence, in stable environments fast learning is positively associated with performance. However, in rapidly changing environments, where routines become obsolete at varying rates and requirements shift quickly, fast learning is more vulnerable to the risk of competency traps and maladaptive specialization (Levinthal and March, 1993; Levitt and March, 1988).

Main Empirical Focus

Empirical research on organizational learning comprises simulation studies (Lant, 1992; March, 1991), case studies (Garud and Van de Ven, 1992; Kim, 1998), and a few quantitative studies (Barnett and Burgelman, 1996; Lant, Milliken, and Batra, 1992). This research has focused on a number of aspects of organizational learning, including (a) learning mechanisms, (b) the influence of prior experience and other contextual factors, (c) the rate of knowledge transfer and decay, and (d) overall industry-based learning versus learning from specific competitors.

Given the many mechanisms identified as important to organizational learning, it is not surprising that many empirical studies have been developed to examine these mechanisms. In a case study of technological transformation at Hyundai Motor Company from 1967 to 1995, Kim (1998) illustrated organizational learning through imitative processes and through the deliberate construction of crises. In this study, Kim showed that Hyundai gained prior knowledge experience through partnerships with Ford and that Hyundai proactively created crises involving a gap between actual and aspired-to performance to intensify search efforts for alternatives while inhibiting the accumulation of structural inertia that might inhibit future change. Garud and Van de Ven (1992) studied the trial-and-error learning process of corporate venturing covering the 12-year venture of cochlear implants. They demonstrated that causal ambiguity, uncertainty, and availability of slack resources highly influenced trial-and-error learning as an adaptive process. Specifically, they demonstrated that in the presence of high levels of slack resources and causal ambiguity, unsuccessful corporate ventures tended to persist longer than ventures developed in situations of no slack or ambiguity.

Using a sample of firms in the furniture and computer software industry, Lant et al. (1992) tested

the influence of past performance and management interpretation of past learning, including cause-and-effect relationships, on the likelihood of reorientation and strategic change. They found that the likelihood of organizational reorientation and change varied as a function of industry context, past performance, and management interpretation and characteristics. Simulating aspiration level adaptation at the group level, Lant (1992) found that groups reacted to performance feedback and adjusted their aspiration levels analogous to individual trial-and-error processes.

A number of other studies have examined the relationship of prior experience and knowledge on performance, organizational learning, and change. For example, in a study of the broadcasting industry Greve (1998) demonstrated the positive effect of aspiration levels on performance evaluation and future organizational change. Greve also demonstrated that current knowledge and perceived probability of successful performance were sensitive to past aspiration levels and experience. Similarly, Cohen and Levinthal (1990) modeled the absorptive capacity of an organization to imitate and assimilate external knowledge as a function of prior knowledge experience and intensity of effort. Finally, in studying the diversification history of 14 nonfinancial firms in the Netherlands over a 23-year time period, Pennings, Barkema, and Douma (1994) found cumulative and past learning to indicate future diversification moves. Firms were more likely to diversify into fields whose knowledge requirements were related to their past capabilities than into new fully unrelated areas—a finding compatible with results of Chang (1996) on diversification in U.S. firms.

Empirical research in organizational learning has also examined rates of knowledge transfer and decay. Studying the transfer of organizational learning across shipyards, Argote, Beckman, and Epple (1990) found support for knowledge transfer as well as for rapid knowledge depreciation. They also found organizations entering the production process at a later stage to be more productive. In their study of learning among 36 pizza stores in southwestern Pennsylvania, Darr et al. (1995) showed that learning was transferred among stores owned by the same franchise, but not across franchises. This study also supported Argote et al.'s (1990) findings on the rates of depreciation of learning over time.

Another line of organizational learning research has focused on whom organizations learn from. In their study of dyadic multimarket relationships among California commuter airlines, Korn and Baum (1999) reported that in addition to learning from their own experience, airlines imitated successful strategies of competitors. Studying the U.S. hotel industry from 1896 to 1985, Ingram and Baum (1997a) found that hotels experienced learning from both industry and organizational experience with learning from one's own organizational experience being weaker for generalists than for specialists. Furthermore, their findings imply that industry experience might be more beneficial to organizations in the long run due to its higher variance and lack of path dependence on any specific organization, thereby reducing the likelihood of learning myopia. In a related study involving survival of Manhattan hotel chain affiliations, Ingram and Baum (1997b) showed that learning within chain affiliations was positively related to improved organizational survival.

Finally, interorganizational learning within strategic alliances and mergers has been the focus of a number of recent empirical studies on the effect of learning on future alliance or merger performance (Hamel, 1991; Koza and Lewin, 1998; Makhija and Ganesh, 1997). Lane and Lubatkin (1998), for example, studied the role of firm absorptive capacity between firms in alliances. They found that the more similar the alliance partner's structures, knowledge bases, and dominant logics, the stronger was the effect of interorganizational learning. Empirical research on firm merger behavior over time showed that later firm acquisitions benefited from prior acquisitions, indicating the presence of learning (Haleblian and Finkelstein, 1999; Pennings et al., 1994). However, in their study of the merger behavior of 47 large U.S. banks from 1982 to 1998, Weigelt and Lewin (2000) found that bank learning effects were time dependent and that a strategy of repeated exploitation mergers (related to existing product-geography mix) did not result in increasing efficiency, suggesting that most organizations lack or do not apply specific routines such as reflection and refreshing as proposed by Winter and Szulanski (2001).

Controversies

Like other strategy and adaptation theories and frameworks, organizational learning faces challenges associated with its empirical analytics. For example, quantifying knowledge creation continues to be a major challenge (Grandori and Kogut, 2002). Furthermore, studying knowledge and learning processes within longitudinal coevolutionary inquiry systems involving path-dependent dynamic models and incorporation of multilevels of analysis remains more of a hope than a reality. Nevertheless, the importance of learning to organizational change and performance ensures that it will continue to be a vibrant research field for strategy research.

Implications for Adaptation and Change

Although a strong consensus exists in the literature on the positive relation between organization learning and adaptation, the relationship is not unidirectional or even contingently causal. In terms of strategic adaptation, learning frames strategy as an emergent process. It mediates and moderates adaptation and it is facilitated and impeded by experience. Learning is affected by preferences for assured proximate or less assured distant returns. It can be the cause of structural inertia, and it depreciates and decays with disuse and with repeated applications. Learning is driven by comparison with competitors but is contingent on firm absorptive capacity. The underlying premise of learning is the utilization of existing knowledge, as in the activation of existing routines, incremental adaptation of existing routines due to problemistic searches or directed improvement, and the creation of new knowledge through serendipitous discovery, directed investment in innovation, and/or imitation of another organization's best practice. Yet the fundamental theme of organizations as creating, applying, imitating, supplanting, and/or failing to utilize new knowledge and its relation to organization adaptation and selection remains largely unexplored.

Clearly, organization capacity for learning is necessary for interpreting and making sense of the environment and for designing strategies of adaptation (Daft and Weick, 1984). However, it can also result in superstitious learning (Levitt and March, 1988), which can occur when organizations infer the wrong causal relationships between their actions and successful outcomes followed by retention and replication (repeating and reinforcing) of this action (Levitt and March, 1988). Furthermore, skills and capabilities that organizations learn and internalize over time are more likely to endure if practiced repeatedly and refreshed. Thus for organizational experience to remain relevant and applicable, it has to be consistently applied and refined (Herriott et al., 1985).

Punctuated Equilibrium

Building on theoretical aspects from population ecology (Hannan and Freeman, 1977), adaptation (March and Simon, 1958), and transformational models of metamorphic change (Greiner, 1972), punctuated equilibrium views organizational evolution as alternating between long periods of convergence and incremental change and brief but intense periods of revolutionary disturbance (Abernathy and Utterback, 1978; Gersick, 1991; Miller and Friesen, 1980; Tushman and Romanelli, 1985). A central assumption of punctuated equilibrium distinguishing it from population ecology is that organizations can and do undergo transformational change (Tushman and Romanelli, 1985) and overcome inertia built up in their system. Stressing the idiosyncrasy of organizational evolution, Tushman and Romanelli stated that "organizations do not evolve through a standard set of stages. . . . [they] may reach their respective strategic orientations through systematically different patterns" (p. 208).

Punctuated equilibrium theorists have also proposed that a key linkage exists between the type of innovation (incremental or revolutionary) and stage of development for an organization or its products (Utterback and Abernathy, 1975). Technological progress as it proceeds through stages of incremental and radical change, plays a key role in the punctuated equilibrium process.

Central Focus and Assumptions

Punctuated equilibrium focuses on the organization as unit of analysis with an emphasis on understanding "patterns of fundamental organizational transformation" (Romanelli and Tushman, 1994, p. 1142). Organizational patterns of activity, established at the time of organizational founding (Boeker, 1988; Stinchcombe, 1965), are reinforced and institutionalized over time, resulting in a buildup of structural inertia throughout the organizational system (Hannan and Freeman, 1984). However, unlike population ecology, punctuated equilibrium theory argues that organizations can overcome inertia through radical and discontinuous change. The three main

elements of punctuated equilibrium include (a) deep structures, (b) equilibrium, and (c) revolutionary periods (Gersick, 1991). We examine each of these elements in turn.

Gersick (1991) defined deep structures as the set of fundamental "choices" involving basic structural elements for reconfiguring organizational units and basic activity patterns that sustain the organization existence (p. 14). Deep structures are seen as highly stable due to their path dependence and strong interrelationship with other organizational components and the environment. Deep structures comprise core values and beliefs, strategy, distribution of power, organizational structure, and control systems (Tushman and Romanelli, 1985).

Equilibrium tends to exist during periods of incremental change and convergence. During these equilibrium periods, organizations align their structures and activities to their strategies, thereby reinforcing their deep structures. During revolutionary periods of intense reconstruction, deep structures are dismantled and the strategies and structure of the organization are fundamentally transformed (Gersick, 1991; Tushman and Romanelli, 1985). For this transformation process to take place, structural inertia has to be released, but what are the forces that contribute to these periods of radical change? Punctuated equilibrium theory cites major environmental shifts such as regulatory changes, technological innovations, or internal organizational changes such as CEO succession, product life cycle maturation, or below-average performance as potentially strong stimuli for deconstructing inertial forces (Romanelli and Tushman, 1994).

Main Empirical Focus

Little empirical research has been done to test the validity of the assumptions and arguments underlying punctuated equilibrium theory. However, a few studies of these assumptions do exist. Using case history studies of AT&T, General Radio, Citibank, and Prime Computers, Tushman, Newman, and Romanelli (1986) were able to provide detailed accounts in support of long periods of equilibrium, involving structural and systems reinforcement, followed by punctuated short periods of radical change. Further support has been provided through a study of the life history of 25 U.S. minicomputer producers founded between 1967 and 1969 (Romanelli and Tushman, 1994). In this study, the researchers found revolutionary and rapid transformations to be the fundamental mode of change influenced by major environmental shifts and CEO succession.

In addition to these few studies examining the underlying structures of punctuated equilibrium, some research exists on the forces believed to contribute to incremental versus radical change. For example, Tushman and Anderson (1986) identified technological evolution as a process of long periods of incremental change and short periods punctuated by competence-destroying or competence-enhancing technological discontinuities. While competence-enhancing discontinuities build on the current skills of incumbents, competence-destroying discontinuities render such skills obsolete, thereby posing a threat to survival of established organizations (Tushman and Anderson, 1986; Tushman and Romanelli, 1985). In their longitudinal study of cement, glass, and minicomputer manufacturers, Anderson and Tushman (1990) traced the "emergence of a dominant design" (p. 606) during the era of ferment and incremental change following technological discontinuity. Similarly, in a study of environmental jolts in the health care industry, Meyer, Brooks, and Goes (1990) found that discontinuous environmental change that altered the competitive landscape triggered profound changes in organizations. Finally, Miller and Friesen (1982, 1984) and Virany, Tushman, and Romanelli (1992) concluded that performance of organizations undergoing radical and punctuated change of organizational structures and processes was superior to organizations changing gradually.

Controversies

Although empirical data is sparse, some controversy exists as to whether organizational transformation can be accomplished proactively or whether it is primarily a reactive process. For example, whereas Tushman et al. (1986) and Romanelli and Tushman (1994) viewed organizational reorientation as reactive, Gersick (1988, 1989) found transitions in her study of groups that were proactive and predictable. This contradictory finding might be due to the effect of deadlines experienced by groups that generally do not operate at the organization level of analysis (Eisenhardt, 1989). However, Gersick (1989) was able to

predict the timing of transformation within groups and why groups switched between momentum and transformation.

Implications for Adaptation and Change

Punctuated equilibrium theory assumes that adaptation holds during one time period and selection holds during another period. Between those forces of organizational convergence and radical transformation that make up organizational evolution, management becomes the agent initiating and implementing strategic change. "Executive strategic choice is, then, the primary mechanism through which strategic orientations get initiated and implemented" (Tushman and Romanelli, 1985, p. 210). In this paradigm, the central challenge for executives is how to manage the dichotomy between incrementally improving current routines while simultaneously supplanting those same activities (Lewin and Volberda, 1999). It should also be noted that none of the minicomputer firms that were studied by Romanelli and Tushman (1994) survived the emergence of personal computer and network industries, which suggests that punctuated equilibrium explanations of adaptation are at best incomplete.

Strategic Choice

The strategic-choice view argues that firms have the ability to reshape their environment rather than simply being powerless recipients of environmental forces (Child, 1972, 1977; Miles and Snow, 1978, 1994; Thompson, 1967). Although the degree of strategic choice that management can exercise depends on the nature of choice, limits to information processing capacities, potentially ambiguous information and decision processes, technology constraints, the size of the organization, and the environment it faces, Child (1972, 1997) makes the case that management is still left with the option, discretion, and opportunity both to choose its competitive environment and to partially shape it. While the environment might constrain some actions, it also provides opportunities and strategic alternatives. Strategic choice, therefore, presents an inherently dynamic process and perspective of adaptation associating superior managerial strategic decisions with positive performance effects (Child, 1972, 1997).

Central Focus and Assumptions

Strategic choice theories focus on the dynamic process of making strategic choices to effectively position an organization within its environment. The units of analysis in this paradigm include both the organization and management. Given this focus and the units of analysis, it is not surprising that a fair amount of the work around strategic choice has centered on developing an understanding of different environments and managerial emphasis. We examine some of the developments in each of these areas below.

A key assumption of strategic choice is that organizations are both influenced by and are able to take actions that shape their environment. As organizations have different capabilities and managers vary greatly in their interpretation of environmental changes, organizational adaptation is expected to be heterogeneous. To more clearly understand these phenomena, Hrebiniak and Joyce (1985) developed a typology that related the extent of strategic choice to the extent of environmental determinism. Four types of environment were proposed, including strategic choice, differentiation or focus, undifferentiated choice, and natural selection. Following the development of this classification system, a number of researchers undertook studies to test the applicability of the topology as a useful tool in understanding strategic choice. The findings of some of these studies are discussed in the next section below.

Another key assumption of strategic choice is that managers have a central role in determining the long run performance of the firm by, among other things, determining the organization's structure. Miles and Snow (1978) studied the role of management in processes of organizational adaptation and identified a typology of management approaches consisting of four types: prospectors, analyzers, defenders, and reactors. Categorizing the vast range of heterogeneous organizational adaptation strategies into four general classes resulted in this typology. In this classification scheme, reactors are viewed as lacking a coherent strategy of adaptation and are therefore least adaptive. While prospectors are seen as constantly searching for new opportunities, stressing innovations, and responding quickly, defenders are considered to remain within their domain and field of strength, striving for specialization and expertise. Finally, analyzers are believed to engage in formal planning as well as striving for efficiency improvement and stability (Miles and Snow, 1978).

Main Empirical Focus

Both the environmental and managerial classification systems have been widely applied in empirical research (Fox-Wolfgramm, Boal, and Hunt, 1998; Hambrick, 1983; Hrebiniak and Joyce, 1985; James and Hatten, 1995; Lawless and Finch, 1989; Snow and Hrebiniak, 1980; Zajac and Shortell, 1989). With respect to the environmental classification system, Lawless and Finch (1989) used data from 146 firms in 52 manufacturing industries to show that single-industry firms' strategies were contingent on the four types of environments classified by Hrebiniak and Joyce (1985). Furthermore, Lawless and Finch found that the relationship between strategy type and performance varied as a function of that environment. In their test of Hrebiniak and Joyce's theory, Marlin, Lamont, and Hoffman (1994) found, using data on 147 hospitals in Florida, that both organizational and environmental factors determined the range of strategic choice and determinism. Overall, both studies found Hrebiniak and Joyce's framework to be superior to the traditional view that considered strategic choice and determinism as endpoints on a continuum.

Similarly, Miles and Snow's managerial typology has been used in studies involving both self-typing and archival data to assign organizations to one of the four categories (Shortell and Zajac, 1990). Some of these studies have found that while prospectors, analyzers, and defenders have been found to outperform reactors in competitive environments, they seem to be inferior to reactors in regulated industries (Snow and Hrebiniak, 1980). Studies on the banking industry using Miles and Snow's typology found that banks used different strategic choices and adaptation patterns to adapt to environmental changes over time (Fox-Wolfgramm et al., 1998, James and Hatten, 1994). Furthermore, studying the health care industry, Zajac and Shortell (1989) found that prospectors and analyzers outperformed defenders.

Controversies

The use of these typologies, particularly the Miles and Snow classification system, is not without controversy in the strategic choice literature. For example, in their review of empirical studies using the Miles and Snow typology, Zahra and Pearce (1990) found the inferiority of reactors in performance outcomes to be questionable. Moreover, out of Miles and Snow's three typology dimensions—entrepreneurial, engineering, and administrative—the entrepreneurial is the one studied most. Studies testing Miles and Snow's (1978) four strategic types have placed different emphasis on the single categories (Zahra and Pearce, 1990), often focusing on only two of them (Fox-Wolfgramm et al. 1998; Hambrick, 1983). Furthermore, most research on the Miles and Snow typology has been cross-sectional (Zahra and Pearce, 1990), with few studies trying to cover longer periods of 4 to 7 years (Fox-Wolfgramm et al., 1998; James and Hatten, 1995). These controversies point to the need to continue to empirically test and refine the concepts used in strategic choice theory.

Implications for Adaptation and Change

In contrast to deterministic views of organizational adaptation and selection (Bain, 1968; DiMaggio and Powell, 1983; Hannan and Freeman, 1977; Lawrence and Lorsch, 1967; Mason, 1959; Meyer and Rowan, 1977) that downplay the role of human actors, strategic choice views managers as proactive and able to influence their environment (Child, 1972). The deterministic view holds that the "variables controlled by the organization are subordinated to the constraints and contingencies" (Thompson, 1967, p. 78) of the environment. According to contingency theory, organizations have to adapt their structures, conditions, strategies, and capabilities to the requirements of the external environment in order to achieve fit and organizational survival (Donaldson, 1996a Lawrence and Lorsch, 1967). The strategic choice view, however, emphasizes that organizational actors can enact their environment as well as make strategic choices that change the organization's adaptation-selection equation (Bourgeois, 1984; Child, 1972; Weick, 1969). Thus, the strategic choice of organizations extends to selecting the environment within which the firm competes, in addition to the more traditional choices involving the selection of goals and organizational structure (Bourgeois, 1984; Child, 1972, 1977).

This concludes the section on firm-level theories. In the next section we review theories that span the firm and its institutional and competitive boundaries.

Boundary Theories Linking Firm to Institutional or Competitive Environment

Industrial Organization Economics

Bain and Mason's market structure—conduct-performance framework represents the traditional paradigm of industrial organization economics (IO economics). In this perspective, market structure is seen as the exogenous context determining industry conduct and performance. Market structure is defined at the industry level and is comprised of the three elements of concentration (size and size distribution), entry barriers, and product differentiation. These elements vary across industries and influence a firm's performance within its industry (Bain, 1968; Grether, 1970; Mason, 1959). Conduct represents firm decisions regarding variables such as price, capacity, advertising and R&D expenses that are selected in direct response to market structure and in pursuit of profit maximization (Porter, 1981). Since IO economics views firm conduct and strategy as directly determined by and as an immediate consequence of market structure, research often represents market structure as a direct influence on firm performance without the mediating effect of conduct (Porter, 1981). Typically, firm performance itself is measured as profitability (allocative efficiency) and cost minimization (technical efficiency) (Porter, 1981).

Central Focus and Assumptions

The field of IO economics has seen at least two foci for analytical work. In the traditional view the industry is the unit of analysis, while a second view has emerged with more of a focus on the firm. In each "branch" of IO economics, market power and industry profits in a nonmonopolistic environment are associated with the key variables of industry concentration, competitive intensity, and barriers to entry. We briefly examine how each branch views the concepts below.

In the traditional IO economics paradigm, scale economies, market power, and product differentiation are regarded as properties of the industry rather than of the firm (Rumelt, 1984, 1987; Schmalensee, 1988). Further, firms are assumed to be generally homogeneous in an industry with respect to strategic preferences, efficiency, and performance outcomes. Hence, the primary difference among firms is assumed to be variation in firm size. In this framework, the key variables of industry concentration, competitive intensity, and barriers to entry are all seen as integrally related.

First, industry concentration and competition are inversely related; that is, the more concentrated the industry, the less rivalry occurs resulting in greater average industry profitability (Bain, 1951). Market power is viewed as the ability to maintain long-term abnormal profits; this power depends directly on the strength of industry barriers to entry. Effective barriers to entry were identified as a pre-condition for long-run market power (Bain, 1956). In Bain's view, economies of scale, cost advantages of incumbents, absolute capital costs, and product differentiation were industry sources of barriers to entry.

However, some challenges to the traditional IO economics focus and assumptions began to emerge within the field. For instance, it was noted that the traditional IO economics structure-conduct-performance paradigm assumed market structure to be exogenous. However, firm conduct and competitive behavior such as R&D investments or collusion among firms could lead to the erection of industry barriers that might actually shape market structure, thus turning market structure into an endogenous variable (Schmalensee, 1988). Further, researchers acknowledged that individual firms can also implement strategies to deter entry such as excess capacity, vertical integration, limit pricing, or strategies tying customers to products that create high switching costs (Bain, 1956; Baumol, Panzar, and Willig, 1982; Schmalensee, 1982, 1988).

In recognition of intraindustry differences that were often perceived to be larger than interindustry differences (Schmalensee, 1985), another branch within IO economics began to emerge with a greater focus on firms and away from industries (Demsetz, 1973). In this new IO economics approach, Caves and Porter (1977) introduced the concept of strategic groups and of mobility barriers. Further, these researchers assumed that firms within an industry differed along dimensions other than size. For example, firms were viewed as pursuing different strategies, including varying their degree of vertical integration, product differentiation, distribution channels, or diversification (Caves and Porter, 1977; Porter, 1979). Often several different firm strategies could lead to high performance within an industry (Oster, 1982). Thus, due to interfirm strategic differences within an industry, entry barriers came to be viewed as group- rather than industry-specific; this perspective was used to explain persistent performance differences among firms within the same industry.

Within this new IO economics perspective, mobility barriers protected a group of firms against new entrants to the industry, as well as against entry by firms from other groups in the same industry. Firms within a strategic group (Hunt, 1972) were believed to follow similar strategies and, due to their structural similarity, to respond in the same way to disturbances within their industry. Strategic group firms resembled each other more closely and experienced greater mutual dependence with each other than with non—group members in the same industry (Caves and Porter, 1977; Porter, 1979). Furthermore, strategic groups often formed on the basis of initial environmental and resource differences. In contrast to the traditional IO assumption of homogeneity in firm performance, the concept of strategic groups predicted that performance differences would exist between strategic groups due to mobility barriers. Such performance differences would depend on the degree of competition and scale differences of firms within the groups, the degree of mobility among groups, and the total number of strategic groups (Caves, 1984; Porter, 1979). Hence, the same basic assumptions of concentration, competitive intensity, and barriers to entry were recast in light of strategic groups to explain performance differences among firms within the same industry.

Main Empirical Focus

Because of the general assumption of firm homogeneity within an industry, empirical studies in traditional IO economics focused on interindustry differences rather than intraindustry variations in firm performance (Rumelt, 1987; Schmalensee, 1988). Bain (1951, 1956) introduced statistical interindustry cross-sectional studies to IO economics. However, many of the initial empirical studies consisted of book-length industry research that employed relatively little formal economic analysis or techniques. Case studies were usually conducted in a cross-sectional design reflecting the static perspective of the Bain/Mason paradigm. As a response to the repeated critique that cross-sectional studies were unable to capture structural relationships within the structure-conduct-performance paradigm, empirical research in IO economics eventually shifted to industry- and firm-level panel data studies (Bresnahan and Schmalensee, 1987; Geroski, 1988; Schmalensee, 1988).

Within the new IO economics, empirical research has focused largely on strategic groups. Initially, this research predominantly took a cross-sectional perspective at one point in time, thus mobility among strategic groups over time was not evaluated (Amel and Rhoades, 1988; Lewis and Thomas, 1990; Newman, 1978). Some researchers (e.g., Oster, 1982) argued that the difficulty of strategic change due to long-term commitments and investments required by some strategic moves might indicate the persistence of strategic groups over time. Furthermore, Oster stressed the importance of persistent strategic differences for groups even over their short-term existence. Eventually researchers suggested that whether and to what degree mobility barriers and strategic differences among groups exist and persist over time could be assessed only in longitudinal research (Day, Lewin, and Li, 1995). In their longitudinal study on strategic groups in the insurance industry from 1970 to 1984, Fiegenbaum and Thomas (1995) found that firms used strategic group behavior as a reference point and adjusted their strategies toward it over time. In another study of the insurance industry, both the number and composition of strategic groups were found to change over time (Fiegenbaum and Thomas, 1990). Similarly, Cool and Schendel (1987) found that strategic repositioning took place in the U.S. pharmaceutical industry between 1963 and 1982. Thus, strategic groups appear to be a rather unstable phenomenon when viewed across time. Further adding to the debate on the strategic group phenomena, some studies have found support for the theoretically hypothesized performance differences among strategic groups (Fiegenbaum and Thomas, 1990; Mascarenhas and Aaker, 1989), while others (Cool and Schendel, 1987; Lewis and Thomas, 1990) have not found such support. These inconsistent findings may result from several factors, including the use of multiple, rather than only one, performance measures

(Cyert and March, 1963); differences in key goals among organizations; or path dependence, which causes the same strategy to have different outcomes in different firms (Nelson and Winter, 1982).

More recently, in contrast to widely used parametric methods of analysis (e.g., cluster analysis) in strategic group research, Day et al. (1995) have used nonparametric frontier analysis methods (DEA) to identify strategic leaders and groups. Although their findings do not reject the concept of strategic groups, they have stressed the importance of redirecting the focus on strategic leaders as firm-specific barriers to imitation rather than allowing intergroup mobility to explain heterogeneity in performance among firms (Day et al., 1995). However, as Day et al. have noted, performance differences also arise due to firms choosing to maximize different objective functions (e.g., market share, cost minimization, rates of return on assets or equity, etc.). With these differences in theoretical assumptions and research methods, it is not surprising that certain controversies persist within the field of IO economics.

Controversies

The field of IO economics has witnessed an ongoing debate on whether firm or industry effects are more dominant in predicting performance. Traditional IO economics research following the Bain/Mason paradigm has ignored the existence of diversity and variation among firms within an industry due to "differing histories of strategic choice and performance" (Rumelt, 1984, p. 558) or due to different managerial decision making. Empirical studies testing the relative importance of industry and firm effects in predicting performance have found that industry effects explained 17 to 20 percent of the variance in financial performance (Schmalensee, 1985; Wernerfelt and Montgomery, 1988; Rumelt, 1991). For example, Schmalensee (1985) found significant industry effects explaining 20% of the variance in performance along with insignificant corporate effects, suggesting strong support for the traditional IO paradigm.

However, Rumelt (1991), distinguishing between stable and yearly fluctuating performance effects, found that stable industry effects explained only 8% of the variance in business performance, while 80% of the variance in business-unit performance was not related to either stable or fluctuating industry effects.

Using Schmalensee's (1985) sample data, Rumelt showed that business-specific effects explained 46% of the variance in performance—a finding inconsistent with the traditional IO paradigm. In another study, Wernerfelt and Montgomery (1988), using the Tobin q as performance variable, found strong industry effects. However, they also detected strong firm-specific effects that were roughly 13–21% larger than the industry effects. Consistent with Wernerfelt and Montgomery (1988), Hansen and Wernerfelt (1989) found that although industry effects explained 19% of the variance in returns, organizational factors were about twice as important. Similarly, using a sample of 217 large U.K. firms from 1951 to 1977, Cubbin and Geroski (1987) estimated the percentage of firm profitability that was related to firm uniqueness over time. They found strong heterogeneity within most industries, as well as a lack of common industry-wide response to change among almost half of the firms studied. More recently, both Mauri and Michaels (1998) and Brush, Bromiley, and Hendrickx (1999) found that firm effects outweighed industry effects in affecting firm performance. These inconsistent findings have led to the ongoing debate regarding the traditional IO economics assumptions of greater differences across industries than within industries and that firm performance is mainly a function of industry membership.

Implications for Adaptation and Change

Although IO economics did not develop to specifically deal with the issues of adaptation and selection, it is instructive to consider this theory through the lens of adaptation and selection. Because traditional IO economics largely ignores firm conduct as a driver of performance, the traditional IO economic perspective appears to favor selection arguments. For example, Porter (1981) describes the firm as "stuck with the structure of its industry" (p. 613) with "no latitude to alter the state of affairs" (p. 613). Even within new IO economics, firm performance is often linked to strategic groups, which, depending on one's beliefs about barriers to mobility between groups, can again be seen as an argument favoring selection.

However, theorists within IO economics have also published perspectives on strategy that, at the firm level, can certainly be viewed as permitting, if not promoting, adaptation. For example, two books by Porter (1980, 1985) are among the most cited and well known writings in industrial economics and strategy. Building on the Bain/Mason paradigm of structure-conduct-performance, Porter emphasizes strategy and fitness at the firm level. His framework of five competitive forces, aimed at explaining sustained competitive advantage, has been applied at the industry, strategic-group, and individual-firm levels. At the firm level, the five forces framework focuses on positioning the firm within its industry to gain sustainable competitive advantage through consideration of factors including competitive scope, product composition, geographic locations, and degree of vertical integration. Competitive advantage, in the Porter tradition, is believed to derive from some combination of three generic strategies—cost leadership, differentiation, and niche/focus strategy (Porter, 1980, 1991). To evaluate and determine firm strategic position, the firm value chain and systems have to be analyzed for disaggregation of costs, differentiation, and scope at the level of activities (Porter, 1985). This perspective portrays a firm as capable of successfully adapting to its environment. However, Porter's model appears to embody a static view of competition as it does not incorporate evolutionary changes over time. Once achieved, competitive advantages such as cost leadership are assumed to be sustainable in the long run.

Transaction Cost Economics (TCE)

The normative goal of TCE is to prescribe how organizations should align different types of transactions with governance structures entailing different costs and competencies of controlling opportunism in order to achieve maximum efficiency (Williamson, 1975, 1979; Shelanski and Klein, 1995). In this framework, transaction costs include negotiating, monitoring, and enforcing contracts. Similarly, the TCE perspective distinguishes between three broad types of governance structures: market, hierarchy, and hybrid. Depending on the characteristics of the transaction—its level of uncertainty, asset specificity, and frequency—the suitability of each of the three "generic" governance structures varies (Williamson, 1979).

Central Focus and Assumptions

The TCE approach uses the transaction as unit of economic analysis (Commons, 1934). TCE focuses on explaining firm choice of boundary decisions using the central elements of governance structure, threat of opportunism, asset-specificity, and uncertainty of transactions (Barney, 1999; Poppo and Zenger, 1998). We examine the key relationships between these elements in TCE.

In TCE the three governance structures identified above are seen as playing a key role in promoting transaction efficiency. The goal within TCE is to align the appropriate governance structure to the transaction type. Failures of alignment may cause higher "cheating" costs due to uncontrolled opportunism in market transactions or excessive "shirking" costs due to overbureaucratization (Hennart, 1993). Hence, the selection of the appropriate governance structure depends on the existing conditions of the other key elements.

Extant opportunistic behavior—self-interest seeking with guile—is a major concern in the TCE framework (Williamson, 1975, 1979, 1985). Threats of opportunism evolve because some transaction partners incur certain transaction-specific investments that reduce their flexibility of switching trading partners without costs (Walker, 1994; Williamson, 1975, 1981). Thus, contracting through markets is not without costs and, under conditions of high threats of opportunism, contracting can be achieved more efficiently within hierarchies (Coase, 1937). In this situation, transaction efficiency is improved due to the hierarchical governance structure's capacity to mitigate threat of opportunism (Barney, 1999); this benefit outweighs the costs of shirking involved in organizing through hierarchy (Masten, Meehan, and Snyder, 1991). Thus, arms-length transactions (market governance) outside the boundaries of the organization are viewed as the most efficient form of exchange in situations in which the number of trading partners is high and the specificity of the transaction is low. However, in the presence of high transaction specificity requiring transaction-specific investments in exchange relationships, hierarchical governance within the boundaries of the organization is the most efficient governance form. Empirical studies have supported these theoretical predictions, finding that transactions with high asset-specificity are more efficiently performed within organizations than markets, while efficiency does not markedly change between hierarchy and market for low asset-specific transactions (Masten et al. 1991; Walker and Poppo, 1991; Walker, 1994).

Transaction uncertainty, like threats of opportunism and asset specificity, plays an important role in TCE theory. Traditionally, the TCE perspective has argued that in the face of high transaction uncertainty (e.g., altering volume and transaction requirements), hierarchical governance structures are superior to market governance due to their ability to rely on fiat. In particular, suppliers with transaction-specific investments are assumed to face problems of transaction efficiency in the face of production volume uncertainty (Lieberman, 1991; Masten et al. 1991; Walker and Weber, 1984, 1987), and, thus, these organizations are assumed to benefit from more hierarchical governance. However, empirical research has found that in situations of environmental uncertainty and rapid technological obsolescence, organizations benefit from market transactions by maintaining their strategic flexibility (Balakrishnan and Wernerfelt, 1986; Barney, 1999; Teece, 1992). Thus, TCE theory has developed the perspective that the efficient management of transactions is a key source of firm competitiveness and the correct alignment of governance structures with transactions is essential to efficiency, survival, and adaptation (Alchian and Demsetz, 1972; Williamson, 1991).

Main Empirical Focus

Empirical studies using the TCE approach have primarily involved investigations of vertical integration, make-or-buy decisions, joint ventures, and strategic alliances (Shelanski and Klein, 1995). In this research, asset specificity has been found to be a main driver of vertical integration (Shelanski and Klein, 1995). Klein (1988), for instance, found that human asset specificity was the main determinant of GM corporation's vertical integration strategy, while Masten, Meehan, and Snyder (1989) found that human asset specificity determined vertical integration more strongly than physical or site specificity. Monteverde's (1995) study of vertical integration in the semiconductor industry further supports the contention that asset specificity drives integration. Clark (1989), finding that product time to market could be reduced by early supplier involvement, suggested that vertical integration might allow a more accurate and less costly assessment of in-house resources than in-market (Alchian and Demsetz, 1972). Further, Monteverde and Teece (1982), as well as Poppo (1995), found support for firm adaptation benefits arising from vertical integration in cases where internally developed, transaction-specific knowledge is not easily transferable. However, preferences for vertical integration have been found to differ across industries and to be positively related to firm size (Levy, 1985; Ohanian, 1994). For example, capital, advertising, or research-intensive industries have been found to be more prone to vertical integration (Levy, 1985; MacDonald, 1985).

TCE studies have also examined how cross-country specific factors such as degree of labor unionization, social acceptability, and government legislation restricting firm bargaining power may moderate firm decisions regarding organizational form and level of vertical integration (Argyres and Liebeskind, 1999). In a comparative study of U.S. and Japanese automotive companies, Dyer (1996a) found that U.S. automakers relied more strongly on markets and hierarchies than Japanese automakers, who predominantly governed exchange relationships through hybrid forms (alliances). While showing country-specific differences in governance structure tendencies, including a stronger trend toward vertical integration in the U.S., Dyer (1996a, 1996b) found differences in asset specificity to be stronger between Toyota and Nissan than between U.S. auto manufacturers. Thus, both firm-specific and country-specific factors seem to influence asset specificity in the auto industry (Dyer, 1996b). In reference to human asset specificity, Dyer (1996a) reported Japanese firms to experience higher asset specificity than their American counterparts. Moreover, counter to TCE expectations, Dyer (1997) showed that Japanese automakers had lower transaction costs, while their suppliers incurred a higher level of transaction-specific investment than the suppliers of U.S. carmakers, despite the greater level of vertical integration in the U.S. carmaker industry. Ironically, relatively few empirical studies using the TCE approach have focused on the effects of governance structure choice on firm performance (Shelanski and Klein, 1995).

Controversies

The TCE perspective has been repeatedly critiqued for its lack of social and institutional embeddedness (i.e., its decoupling of transaction cost and efficiency considerations from social influences), as well as for its strong focus on rationality (Granovetter, 1985; Martinez and Dacin, 1999; Roberts and Greenwood, 1997). Specifically, Granovetter (1985) has called for transactions to be seen as embedded and nested within the context of multiple transactions rather than as independent and isolated events. Furthermore, TCE's exclusive focus on transactions and their efficiency fails to consider the effect of transaction configurations on firm-level performance and survival (Masten et al., 1991). Yet transaction configurations affect not only efficiency of a single transaction but also the efficiency and competitiveness of the entire organization.

Another criticism of TCE has been that the major independent variables, including asset-specificity—physical, human, and financial—and uncertainty have been operationalized differently, making comparability of findings across TCE studies difficult. For instance, Lieberman (1991) measured asset specificity as sunk investment costs and percentage of upstream costs to total costs, whereas Walker and Poppo (1991) measured it as the extent to which the buyer required equipment and labor skills that were unique to the supply relationship. Finally, most research testing TCE has been static, using cross-sectional study designs. This static approach is also viewed by critics as neglecting the dynamic aspects of transactions over time. In particular TCE does not provide a basis for explaining reversals of governance choices to internalize capabilities at one point in time, then reverse this decision (i.e., externalizing same capability) at a later time.

Implications for Adaptation and Change

Similar to other boundary theories, TCE was not intended to specifically address arguments for adaptation and selection. Nevertheless, TCE principles can be examined through the lens of adaptation and change. Fundamentally, TCE presents a theory examining considerations for matching governance structure to transaction type. In this paradigm, bounded rationality and cognitive limits in decision-making processes (March and Simon, 1958) can cause "failures of alignment" to occur when actors match wrong governance structure and transaction type (Dyer, 1996a). Misalignments may result in loss of strategic focus due to too much integration or in loss of competitive advantage due to too little integration (Barney, 1999). In either case, inefficiency resulting from transaction-governance structure misalignment is expected to cause performance deterioration and to increase the likelihood of the organization to be selected out (Roberts and Greenwood, 1997). This may be seen both at the individual firm level and even at the industry level.

However, the ability of TCE to explain the evolution of organizational forms and adaptation is highly constrained due to its static, comparative-efficiency basis. That is, TCE does not account for how organizations should change their governance structures as circumstances alter (Roberts and Greenwood, 1997). For instance, Argyres and Porter-Liebeskind (1999) argue that past governance decisions influence a firm's future governance choices due to path dependence, thereby suggesting the need to study transactions as interconnected over time. Ohanian's (1994) finding that once firms chose a vertical integration governance structure they rarely change their form of contracting provides additional support for this contention. Thus, the decision of whether to contract within a hierarchy or market may be largely embedded in the organization environment and its past history and scope.

TCE also does not specifically or formally consider the effect of firm capabilities on governance decisions, further limiting its ability to explain adaptive phenomena. For example, the TCE perspective ignores firm-level idiosyncratic routines, as well as the creation of competitive advantage through the development and refinement of capabilities (Madhok, 1997; Barney, 1999). Interestingly, however, since unique organizational capabilities are usually not bought in the market, but evolve and develop within organizations (Dierickx and Cool, 1989; Lippman and Rumelt, 1982), these capabilities may offer an alternative explanation as to why hierarchies may be a better form of adaptation than market transactions under certain conditions. Arguments for examining the implications of TCE over time and considering firm-specific issues suggest that TCE may benefit from integration with other theoretical constructs, such as evolutionary economics or the resource-based view. In his study on corporate diversification, for example, Silverman (1999) integrates the resource-based view with transaction cost economics to examine the ability of firms to contract rent-generating resources that are often believed to be too asset-specific to be contracted. These types of theoretical integration may well provide more insight into adaptation and change than individual theories have contributed to date.

Contingency Theory

Contingency theory holds that organization efficiency and effectiveness depend on a fit between structure and organizational and environmental contingency factors. Contingency factors such as strategy, task uncertainty, technology, or size are firm-related; however, they are also seen as reflecting the environment. Environmental hostility (Khandwalla, 1977) and product life cycle (Donaldson, 1985), on the other hand, are seen as more environment-related contingency factors. In this framework, organizations whose structures deviate from the normatively specified contingent form are expected to experience performance deficiencies. Hence, organizations are viewed as adapting to their environment (Donaldson, 1995, 1996a).

Central Focus and Assumptions

Structural contingency theory focuses on understanding how organizations adapt their structures as a result of changes in environmental and organizational contingency factors. As such, contingency theory uses the organization as the unit of analysis, and the theory comprises three interrelated areas of research: strategy and structure, size and bureaucracy, and task uncertainty and structure (Donaldson, 1995). We briefly examine each of these areas and then consider the challenge of organizational response to multiple conflicting contingencies.

Studying the business history of large U.S. corporations, Chandler (1962) concluded that strategy determined structure. He argued that changes in strategy, such as the contingency of diversification, force organizations to adapt their structure toward multidivisional form (M-Form) in order to maintain their strategy-structure fit and sustain their performance. During the same period, Burns and Stalker (1961) argued that in stable environments organizations adopt a mechanistic structure, while changing environments require adoption of organic structures for maintaining efficiency. Later, Khandwalla (1977) found that increases in organizational size led to higher degrees in bureaucratization, specialization, and formalization. From these various sources several key assumptions of contingency theory were developed, including (a) that tasks with low uncertainty are most efficiently conducted in centralized structures, (b) that smaller organizations may also benefit from a centralized structure, and (c) that when task uncertainty and organizational size increase, decentralization becomes important for maintaining efficiency (Pugh et al., 1969). Hence, although contingency theory states that organizations adapt their structure to environmental contingencies implying a single contingency framework, there is no single structure and no single contingency framework that fits all organizations within the same environment equally well (Donaldson, 1996a).

The reality is that organizations face multiple, even conflicting, contingencies to which they have to adapt their structure (Drazin and Van de Ven, 1985; Gresov, 1989). Further, Lawrence and Lorsch (1967) argued that different parts of an organization—e.g., finance, R&D, manufacturing—face different levels of environmental uncertainty and therefore require different organizational structures at different times. Thus, rather than having one single structure, organizations may require different structures across organizational units, creating the need for coordination among them. The higher the rate of environmental change, the higher the level of differentiation, and the greater the need for coordination. Hence multiple conflicting contingencies act to increase the complexity of locating environmental-structure fit, as well as the probability of misfits (Gresov, 1989).

Ironically, the concept of multiple conflicting contingencies might allow for more than one single form of structure without jeopardizing performance outcomes, thereby providing organizations with discretion in structure. Such potential discretion or strategic choice, however, challenges traditional contingency theory and provides room for the argument of equifinality. Equifinality implies that the same state (performance outcome) can be achieved with different means and in different ways (different structural configurations) from initially different starting points (Gresov and Drazin, 1997; Pennings, 1987). Thus, equifinality accounts for the wide latitude and discretion within which organizations can design their structure and still achieve environmental fit and effectiveness (Pennings, 1987). Most contingency research, however, provides little insights

into who determines or what drives specific organizational designs.

Main Empirical Focus and Controversies

Empirical research on contingency theory has been primarily cross-sectional and static, investigating strategic fit at a single point in time by testing single bivariate relationship dimensions of environment-structure fit. Typical contingency theory research has differed in terms of the types of contingency factors being investigated, such as strategy (Chandler, 1962), technology (Woodward, 1965), or environmental change (Burns and Stalker, 1961). The common feature is the relationship of these contingency factors to organizational structure. Some representative studies of this type include (a) Woodward's (1958, 1965) study of 100 manufacturing firms, using quantitative measures of structure such as span of control and levels of hierarchy, which found technology to be the key determinant of organizational structure, (b) Gresov's (1989) study using data on 529 work units in 60 Californian and Wisconsin employment security offices, which showed that units confronting conflicting contingencies were more likely to create misfit and to experience lower performance than units facing uniform contingency requirements, and (c) Drazin and Van de Ven's (1985) study using the Gresov data set, which found that macro-organizational level contingencies constrained the structural options of work units.

Since the assumption of linearity and nonmonotonical symmetry of contingency relationships has guided empirical research, studies in contingency theory usually do not test for nonlinear relationships. Moreover, empirical research in contingency theory has focused primarily on comparing organizations to each other in terms of their structures and contingencies (Donaldson, 1996b; Ginsberg and Venkatraman, 1985; Venkatraman and Prescott, 1990; Zajac, Kraatz, and Bresser, 2000). However, contingencies change over time, affecting strategic fit and forcing organizations to adapt their structures. Thus, environment-structure fit and co-alignment is a dynamic process requiring longitudinal research design for investigating the theory. Using data on over 4,000 S&Ls over a 9-year period, Zajac et al. (2000) studied the consistency of strategic change with both internal and external contingencies. They found that changes in contingencies affected the "direction, magnitude, and timing of changes" (p. 442) of S&L strategies. Furthermore, they showed that organizations that fail to achieve a contingency fit experienced lower performance. Venkatraman and Prescott (1990) investigated a sample of strategic business units (SBU) drawn from the PIMS database over two 4-year periods. They found that environment-strategy fit had positive performance consequences. They also stressed the need for a stronger focus on longitudinal studies "modeling environment-strategy co-alignment" (Venkatraman and Prescott, 1990, p. 18). In addition to these empirical challenges, contingency theory is sometimes criticized for focusing almost exclusively on reactive adaptation, ignoring the opportunity that firms may have to influence their environment.

Implications for Adaptation and Change

The contingency theory view of organizational change and adaptation as largely driven by changes in contingency factors runs counter to population ecology assumptions that structural inertia is the cause of the inability of organizations to change and adapt (Hannan and Freeman, 1977). While contingency theory adopts a strong adaptation perspective, assigning a critical role to top management to successfully interpret contingency factors and implement appropriate changes in organizational form, selection arguments can be seen as relevant. That is, organizations that fail to adjust their forms appropriately will underperform and, ultimately, be selected out of the market. Hence, adaptation and selection each have their role within contingency theory; however, the mechanisms leading to success or failure are viewed as fundamentally linked with decisions made by the firm's actors in response to environmental changes.

Evolutionary Economics

Evolutionary economics (Nelson and Winter, 1982) builds on and extends the Behavioral Theory of the Firm (Cyert and March, 1963), and incorporates the ideas of evolutionary processes (Schumpeter, 1950). Schumpeter originally argued that "in dealing with capitalism we are dealing with an evolutionary process" (p. 82) in which industry structure is constantly evolving and firms adapt over time in a "process of creative destruction." Within the process of creative destruction, organizations try to outperform each

other through innovation and new inventions, thereby improving their fit with the changing environment. In this tradition, evolutionary economics provides a framework for understanding how economic changes in product demand, in factor supply conditions, or innovation influence the firm (Nelson and Winter, 1982).

Central Focus and Assumptions

Evolutionary economics develops different models that focus on different aspects of economic change using both the organization and the population as its units of analyses. In this regard the theory links micro evolutionary processes inside the firm with macro evolutionary process in the environment. The key elements of evolutionary economics include heterogeneity leading to path and rate differences in firm evolution, organizational capabilities as embedded in routines, and a variation selection and retention (VSR) process for evolving firm routines over time as it interacts with variation and selection processes in the environment. We examine each of these key elements in turn.

In contrast to neoclassical economic theory, evolutionary economics stresses the existence of differences in technology, productivity, and profitability among firms, and, in doing so, provides an explanatory foundation for the sources of firm heterogeneity (Nelson and Winter, 1974; Nelson, 1991, 1995). Whereas change and variation are suppressed in neoclassical aggregation, evolutionary economics focuses on firms as vehicles of innovation and drivers of change at the industry level (Nelson and Winter, 1973, 1974, 1982). Firm heterogeneity is central for explaining the observed differences in rates and paths of firm adaptation to environmental change.

Building on A Behavioral Theory of the Firm (Cyert and March, 1963) and consistent with organization learning theories, evolutionary economics holds that firms largely operate on the basis of executable decision rules that are reflected in routinized behavior and methods that adapt (e.g., in response to problemistic searches) and are maintained and reinforced over time. Hence, the organization's managerial, organizational, and technological capabilities are viewed as embedded in the firm's unique regime of routines. Evolutionary economics assumes firms that possess superior regimes of routines will have superior performance. Poorer performing firms are assumed to be selected out at increasing rates because they lack equally effective regimes of routines (Dosi, Nelson, and Winter, 2000). The theory substitutes the "maximization" assumptions of neoclassical economics with firm-specific "search and selection" processes which are assumed to be heterogeneous across firms. Search processes are partially institutionalized but are also subject to change in response to poor performance or obsolescence of existing routines (Nelson and Winter, 1973, 1974, 1982). Consistent with Cyert and March (1963), Nelson and Winter (1982) assume both a "local" search for new techniques taking place within the organization (e.g., R&D) and an imitation mechanism by which the organization adopts successful techniques and strategies of its competitors. In general, "local" search mechanisms are the primary source of incremental improvements in performance because they are limited by earlier search activities. Imitation mechanisms, however, can yield alternatives that significantly differ from current techniques (Nelson and Winter, 1973, 1982). These ever-changing firm processes lead to the continuous evolution of both organizations and industry structure itself.

Main Empirical Focus

"Taking an evolutionary perspective on strategy means developing dynamic, path-dependent models that allow for possibly random variation and selection within and among organizations" (Barnett and Burgelman, 1996, p. 7). Given this perspective, testing evolutionary models has favored longitudinal study designs for modeling the rates, paths, and patterns of firm and industry changes. Some empirical research findings are highlighted and summarized in this section.

Search behavior has been a key interest of many evolutionary economic studies. For instance, Stuart and Podolny (1996) studied the evolution of technological positions among 10 Japanese semiconductor firms over the period 1982 to 1992. The shift in firm technological position, measured in patent citations, was used as an indicator of firm technological search behavior. Stuart and Podolny found that Japanese firms engaged in search activities as a group rather than in isolation. Their findings imply that firm technological positioning is partly dependent on competitors' search trajectories. In a related study of Japanese semiconductor industry, Podolny and Stuart (1995) introduced the concept of the "technological

niche" (p. 1224) and showed that as technological innovations become more refined and persistent in their use over time, the more other firms focused their search activities on these innovations. Makadok and Walker (1996) also studied the effect of search behavior on organizational survival in the money market fund industry from 1975 to 1991. Applying a hazard-rate model, they found that too much search across product breadth increased the organizational failure rate. Further, they found that heightened search behavior for a better strategy did not lower the risk of failure in a growth industry.

Path dependence is another important element examined by evolutionary economics research, particularly as it relates to search behavior. In their study of 2,970 retail banks in Illinois from 1900 to 1993, Barnett and Hansen (1996) argued that organization fitness with its environment was simultaneously dependent on its own experience and search behavior, and the experiences and search behaviors of its competitors. The study emphasized the reciprocal recursive relationship between search and learning by an organization and its rivals in the population. Barnett and Hansen (1996) found support for the "Red Queen" effect among Illinois banks and concluded that evolutionary processes are adaptive for recent experience, but maladaptive for distant past experience. In a related study of acquisitions and performance among Illinois banks, Barnett, Greve, and Park (1994) found that the larger multiunit banks had gained competitive positions that sheltered them from selection forces, while single-unit banks were more exposed to competition. This study reported strong path dependence on organizational performance. In his study of exit and entry behavior of U.S. manufacturing firms from 1981 to 1989, Chang (1996) reported on the importance of path dependence in the form of past knowledge that serves to guide firm search activities. He showed that firms were more likely to enter businesses that required human resource capabilities similar to those of their core business. Hence, past firm experience was found to strongly affect and guide present search behavior for diversification.

Path dependence and search routines have also been examined in the context of strategic alliances and competitive imitation. For example, Doz (1996) analyzed the historical evolution of three strategic alliances and their sequences of search, learning, and reassessment. He illustrated that organizations are constrained in interorganizational learning by their own routines, particularly as the activation of those routines can cause the potential for misunderstanding. Similarly, Barnett and Burgelman (1996) demonstrated that prior experience and development of routines could create inertia and constrain organizational efforts of adaptation. Henderson and Clark (1990) showed that the destruction of old established procedures and routines brought about by architectural innovations presented challenges that can affect organizational survival. Szulanski's (1996) study of 122 internal transfers of best practices in eight organizations revealed major barriers to effective knowledge transfer. Firm internal replications of best practices and routines were often hampered by lack of absorptive capacity, causal ambiguity of the best practice, and the nature of the relationship between the transmitting and receiving unit. Zander and Kogut (1995) also studied the transfer of internal organizational capabilities as a function of knowledge codification and the ability of competitors to imitate those capabilities. They found that the easier it is to replicate technology and capabilities internally, the more likely it is that these technologies and capabilities can be easily imitated by competitors (Kogut and Zander, 1992). Thus, while rapid internal replication of best practices fosters organizational growth, it also exposes the organization to imitation threats from competitors that, if successful, erode the firm's market position (Kogut and Zander, 1992). Finally, in their analysis of replication of merger routines, Winter and Szulanski (2001) argue that successful replication requires routines for reflection upon the most recent merger experience, followed by renewal of the merger routine. They argue that the ability to reflect and refresh is at the heart of best practice routines.

Simulation studies have also been used to provide support for the theory. For example, Nelson and Winter (1974, 1982) describe simulation studies involving the interaction of heterogeneous firms over time that have reproduced estimates of aggregate production functions and macroeconomic growth models consistent with those proposed by Solow (1956, 1957).

Controversies

Although evolutionary economics has its origin in 1982, there are not many direct studies of the evo-

lution of firm-specific regimes of routines. With the exception of case studies (e.g., Burgelman, 2002), little empirical support exists describing the adaptation of routines, the nature of the hypothesized hierarchy of superior from less effective regimes of routines. Thus, for example, it is not clear what is the regime of routines that defines a firm's absorptive capacity or what is the nature of metaroutines that govern rate of change or degree of adaptive tension. Although evolutionary economics theory specifically describes internal processes and capabilities that subsume concepts and dynamics from resource-based and dynamic-capabilities theories, the empirical studies do not illuminate the inside of the proverbial "black box."

Implications for Adaptation and Change

Evolutionary economics provides several interesting implications for adaptation, selection, and change. Because evolutionary economics focuses on the intensity, direction, and strategy of organizational search activity, and on the factors influencing these search activities, the theory establishes a strong link between organizational search, dynamic changes, and selection in the environment. That is, changes in business strategies and search activities affect firm profitability and investments; these changes create the varying rates of expansion and contraction of individual firms leading to dynamic changes at the aggregate firm level (Nelson and Winter, 1974). Further, selection within the organization operates through adoption and rejection of routines for innovations leading to varying organizational investments. At the industry level, selection operates through expansion of profitable firms and contraction of unprofitable ones. Thus, "the phenomena of search and selection are simultaneous, interacting aspects of the evolutionary process. Firms evolve over time, with the condition of the industry on each day bearing the seeds of its condition on the day following" (Nelson and Winter 1974, pp. 893–894).

With respect to adaptation, evolutionary economics assumes that organizations have different strategies for adaptation with some organizations being pioneers (first-movers) and others being late adopters. In evolutionary economics, organization success and survival are determined ex post rather than ex ante, because organizations are assumed to have a low capacity for predicting which innovation strategies will succeed (Nelson, 1991). Thus, differences in strategic preferences are assumed to result in performance outcome variations. However, less successful firms will tend to imitate strategies of companies selected by the market, thereby reducing strategic diversity (Barnett and Burgelman, 1996; Nelson, 1991, 1995). Path dependence of organizational adaptation and cumulative learning of technologies generally favor innovative firms over followers (Nelson, 1995). This theoretical conclusion for the adaptive advantage of innovative organizations has it roots in Schumpeter (1934). From an evolutionary perspective, organizational differences are seen as grounded in the ability to generate and implement innovations, rather than in the possession of certain technologies (Nelson, 1991). Ultimately, successful firms are expected to have a coherent, path-dependent strategy that has evolved through cumulative learning and encompasses a bundle of routines that are difficult to imitate (Dosi, Teece, and Winter, 1992; Nelson, 1995). However, a micro understanding of what differentiates innovative from imitating firms in terms of specific descriptions of the regime of routines that distinguish VSR processes of the two classes of firms is still largely absent (Lewin and Massini, 2004).

Resource Dependence Theory

Resource dependency theory emphasizes organizational adaptation to environmental uncertainty through active organizational management of resource flows and interdependencies (Pfeffer and Salancik, 1978). Building on Cyert and March (1963), the environment is seen as "negotiated environment," in which the focal organization engages and negotiates exchange relationships with other organizations (Oliver, 1991; Pfeffer and Salancik, 1978; Thompson, 1967). Although resource dependency theory stresses organizational will and ability to respond to environmental pressures, uncertainty, and interdependence, it recognizes the effect of organizational constraints and dependence on other organizations that control critical resources. Thus, organizations are viewed as making strategic choices and decisions within constraints (Greening and Gray, 1994; Hrebiniak and Joyce, 1985; Pfeffer and Salancik, 1978). In contrast to unconstrained strategic choice as advocated by Child (1972) and Andrews (1971), strategic choice in resource dependence theory extends to an organization's discretion over how to structure its interrelationship with its environment (Oliver, 1991).

Central Focus and Assumptions

Resource dependency theory utilizes the organization within its environment as the unit of analysis. The theory emphasizes the organization's focus on uncertainty reduction and managing interfirm relationships and power differentials. These key elements are interrelated within resource dependency theory. We examine the key aspects and relationships between these key elements below.

A central theme in resource dependence theory is that organizations will attempt to reduce environmental uncertainty by negotiating their environment. Similar to transaction cost economics (TCE), in which uncertainty is reduced by moving market transactions into a hierarchy (Williamson, 1985), resource dependence theory asserts that organizations reduce uncertainty by devising interorganizational power relations, thereby removing them from markets (Pfeffer and Salancik, 1978; Podolny, 1994). Resource dependence theory defines environmental uncertainty as "the degree to which future states of the world cannot be anticipated and accurately predicted" (Pfeffer and Salancik, 1978, p. 67). Furthermore, environmental uncertainty faced by organizations increases with the multiplicity of conflicting demands that an organization confronts, requiring a simultaneous increase in the levels of discretion in organizational responses (Oliver, 1991; Pfeffer and Salancik, 1978).

Resource dependence theory proposes two fundamental strategies for reducing external pressures and uncertainty: (1) dependence reduction, and (2) dependence restructuring (Green and Welsh, 1988). These strategies involve either changes to organizational boundaries or interfirm coordination mechanisms based on the type of dependence encountered (Pfeffer and Salancik, 1978). Dependence reductions can be compared to an organization strategy of avoidance (Pfeffer and Salancik, 1978; Thompson, 1967), since it entails changing or redefining organizational goals to eliminate resource dependencies that are unmanageable or too costly to control. Thus, rather than actively managing power relationships, the organization may choose to abandon the relationship (Green and Welsh, 1988). Dependence restructuring occurs when the organization elects to exchange one type of dependence for another, a decision that neither changes organizational goals nor requires the firm to shift its resources (Green and Welsh, 1988; Pfeffer and Salancik, 1978). Dependence restructuring may involve vertical integration, mergers, diversification, joint ventures, interlocking directorates, or participation in trade associations (Finkelstein, 1997; Pfeffer, 1972a; Pfeffer and Salancik, 1978).

Resource dependence theory also predicts that organizational response to environmental pressures will be mediated by organizational characteristics such as size. The theory asserts that the greater the scale and scope of an organization, the greater the organization's capacity to actively influence its environment (Greening and Gray, 1994; Oliver, 1991). Further, resource dependence theory expects that the lower the organization's ability to resist and the higher its compliance to external pressures, the more dependent the organization will be on external sources of resources (Pfeffer and Salancik, 1978). Pfeffer and Salancik state "for the dependence between two organizations to provide one organization with power over the other, there must be asymmetry in the exchange relationship" (p. 53). Thus, organizations may strive to establish and maintain relationships of symmetrical interdependence that, no matter how strong, are seen as not providing either organization with power over the other.

Main Empirical Focus

Empirical studies have applied resource dependency theory to a number of business relationship management activities, including mergers and interlocking directorates and board composition. In a study of 854 large mergers in the U.S. between 1948 and 1969, Pfeffer (1972a) found that interindustry mergers were significantly related to the proportion of total economic transactions taking place between two industries. Pfeffer concluded that organizations try to reduce uncertainty and manage interdependencies through acquisition of their transaction partners, thereby restructuring their resource-dependence relationship. In a replication of the Pfeffer (1972a) study over a time period from 1948 to 1992, Finkelstein (1997) obtained similar results. In another related study, Palmer, Barber, and Zhou (1995) reported that firms that exercised constraints on

organizations in other industries were more likely to undertake predatory rather than friendly mergers. D'Aveni and Kesner (1993) demonstrated a relationship between target management response to a tender offer and the interrelationships and connections existing between the target and bidding organization prior to the takeover attempt. They found that the more the target and bidding firm are connected and dependent on each other for resources, the friendlier the response of the target firm's management to the tender offer.

Another stream of empirical research has applied the resource dependency theory to the analysis of interlocking directorates and board composition. Such research has viewed the board as a means for gaining access to critical resources, reducing uncertainty, and exercising power over other organizations (Johnson, Daily, and Ellstrand, 1996; Pfeffer, 1972b; Pfeffer and Salancik, 1978). Stearns and Mizruchi (1993), for example, showed that the type and amount of financing obtained by an organization was a direct function of the financial institutions represented on its board. Interlocking directorates have also been shown to be a means to influence and monitor other organizations, to reduce uncertainty, and to increase coordination between competitors (Kaplan and Minton, 1994; Lang and Lockhart, 1990). Lang and Lockhart showed that increasing uncertainty in the airline industry brought about by deregulation led firms to increasingly establish indirect interlocks to reduce competition among each other and restore the lost certainty. Studying *keiretsu* networks of 50 financial and 200 industrial corporations in Japan, Lincoln, Gerlach, and Takahashi (1992) showed that "in Japanese business networks organization for mutual reinforcement and protection coexists with organization for control and intervention" (p. 52). Finally, some studies of board size and composition have examined this characteristic as a determinant of firm performance (Pearce and Zahra, 1992). Interlocking board composition has been demonstrated to be effective in maintaining working exchange relationships and exercising influence on external constituencies, significantly affecting organizational survival in chapter 11 bankruptcy reorganization filings (Daily, 1995; Sutton and Callahan, 1987). Daily, for instance, demonstrated that a high proportion of outside directors positively correlated with successful emergence from chapter 11.

Controversies

Resource dependency theory has not been widely researched empirically. It has a conceptual overlap with the construct of uncertainty avoidance in the BTOF (Cyert and March, 1963) and the organizational routines associated with uncertainty avoidance, such as negotiating the environment. It is difficult to test the theory directly because it requires assessing power differentials in relationships, and power models are difficult to operationalize for empirical research purposes (March, 1966).

Implications for Adaptation and Change

In contrast to some organizational theories (e.g., population ecology, institutional theory) that assume organizations are unable to respond to environmental changes or to counteract isomorphic forces, resource dependence theory has a strong adaptation perspective, assuming that organizations have latitude for discretion, capacity for decision making, and the motivation and ability to influence power constellations in their favor, thereby making compliance less crucial (Pfeffer, 1982; Oliver, 1991). Whereas "self-interested behavior tend[s] to be smuggled into institutional arguments rather than theorized explicitly" (DiMaggio, 1988, p. 9), it is explicitly formalized in the range of strategic choice actions considered by resource dependence theory. Thus, the resource dependence perspective sees adaptation to environmental change as driven by the essential process of organizations actively managing their interdependencies in an effort to control their environment and to reduce uncertainty (Oliver, 1991).

Theories Linking Firms to the Macro Environment

Institutional Theory

Institutional theory has gone through a distinct evolution from its original grounding in the work of Selznick (1948, 1949, 1957; see also chap. 9 in this volume). In "old" institutional theory, individual organizations are viewed as constantly adapting and changing as they struggle with new values, interests, and emerging coalitions. Institutionalization is seen

as a process of infusing and instilling organizations with value (Selznick, 1957). However, DiMaggio and Powell's (1983) work moved institutional theory away from its original focus on the institutional environment and toward a focus on multiple institutional environments, including the state, professional associations, and other organizations (Scott, 1987). This "new" institutional theory (DiMaggio and Powell, 1983, 1991; Meyer and Rowan, 1977) distinguishes itself by focusing on organizational fields, rather than individual organizations, and by emphasizing institutional rather than technical environments. Modern institutional theory is usually associated more with the new rather than the old institutional view; this review focuses on the key elements, empirical research, controversies, and implications for adaptation and change within the framework of new institutional theory.

Central Focus and Assumptions

Using populations within the organizational field as the unit of analysis, new institutional theory focuses on trying to explain "why there is such a startling homogeneity of organizational forms and practices" (DiMaggio and Powell, 1983, p. 148). A central assumption within institutional theory is that organizational change is highly constrained (Tolbert, 1985; Tolbert and Zucker, 1983). In this paradigm, persistence and stability are emphasized, and organizations are seen as becoming homogeneous and isomorphic. Based on Hawley (1968), DiMaggio and Powell (1983) define isomorphism as "a constraining process that forces one unit in a population to resemble other units that face the same set of environmental conditions" (p. 149). Over time, interactions among organizations emerge, structures of dominant coalitions develop, and mutual awareness is created, leading original diversity and variation among organizations to be replaced by a process of institutionalization and homogenization (DiMaggio and Powell, 1983). Once an organizational field is established, isomorphic organizational change will bring about only greater conformity and homogeneity (DiMaggio and Powell, 1983; Meyer and Rowan, 1977; Scott, 1998). Further, institutional environments are seen as requiring conformity and convergence among organizations, causing homogeneity and legitimacy to become sources of inertia and stability that impede those forces of change that might lead to divergence in organizational forms (DiMaggio and Powell, 1983, 1991).

The diffusion of institutional isomorphism can occur through three different mechanisms—coercive, mimetic, and normative (DiMaggio and Powell, 1983). These mechanisms are each caused by different conditions (Mizruchi and Fein, 1999) and partially overlap with other theories. Coercive isomorphism results from political pressures for legitimacy and social expectations that are predominantly exercised by the firm's external institutional environment. Coercive isomorphism can result, for example, from laws and regulations imposed by the state or trade organizations (DiMaggio and Powell, 1983). However, coercive isomorphic pressures can also emerge from large organizations controlling significant resources or market share. Due to their size, these organizations may be able to set the basis for competition in their market, causing politics to "reproduce the position of the advantaged groups" (Fligstein, 1996, p. 663). Furthermore, the higher the firm's resource dependence on other organizations, the more likely it is to adopt a structure and strategy similar to that of the organizations on which it is dependent (Pfeffer and Salancik, 1978). In addressing resource dependency considerations, coercive isomorphism has points of overlap with resource dependence theory.

Facing environmental uncertainty or ambiguous goals, organizations often mimic the practices and strategies of organizations they perceive as successful and legitimate (DiMaggio and Powell, 1983). Hence, mimetic isomorphism leads organizations to imitate others, modeling themselves after successful competitors, or, in the case of new organizations, adopting the structures and practices of incumbents. Although organizations may innovate with a focus on improving their performance, institutional theory assumes that mimetic organizational change and innovation are driven solely by the desire of an organization to increase its legitimacy (DiMaggio and Powell, 1983).

Normative isomorphic pressures arise from "professionalization," such as formal education, professional socialization, and professional networks spanning organizations (DiMaggio and Powell, 1983). Studying the involvement of firms in work-family issues as a response to normative and social pressures, Goodstein (1994) reported that the larger and more visible the organization was, the more likely it was to positively respond to normative pressures. Moreover, the more legitimized and widespread the work-family practices, the more likely firms are to adopt them. By establishing connections to a broader network of relationships, normative isomorphism has points of overlap with network theory.

Although institutional theory emphasizes isomorphism and homogeneity among organizations within a field, theorists recognize that variations exist in organizational exposure to isomorphic pressures; some firms are able to effectively isolate themselves, while others are much more severely exposed to these pressures. These differences may be due to factors such as ambiguous and hard-to-communicate goals or due to an organization's inability to control its boundaries (Zucker, 1987). Furthermore, the theory acknowledges that organizations may be highly homogeneous on some dimensions but very heterogeneous on others.

Main Empirical Focus

Given the key role that isomorphism plays in the assumptions of new institutional theory, it is not surprising that much of the existing empirical research relates to either demonstrating or studying the effects of this phenomenon. In their review of empirical studies of institutional theory, Mizruchi and Fein (1999) found that mimetic isomorphism was more strongly emphasized than coercive or normative isomorphism, and they found that most studies focused on one single type of isomorphism rather than on all three forms simultaneously. For example, studies like Fligstein's (1985) adoption of the multidivisional form, Fennell and Alexander's (1987) boundary-spanning activities among hospitals, and Haveman's (1993a, 1993b) analysis of savings and loan firms entries into new markets have provided support for mimetic isomorphism. In their study of nonprofit organizations, Galaskiewicz and Wasserman (1989) demonstrated mimetic isomorphism occurring through networks. However, in many empirical studies the phenomenon analyzed could be explained as any one of the three types of isomorphism, supporting DiMaggio and Powell's (1983) statement that the three mechanisms of isomorphism are not necessarily empirically distinguishable.

Levitt and Nass (1989) and Palmer, Jennings, and Zhou (1993) simultaneously operationalized all three forms of isomorphism. Palmer et al. found that both coercive and normative isomorphism supported the diffusion of the multidivisional form (M-form) in the 1960s. In a related study, Fligstein's (1985) analysis of the spread of the multidivisional form among large organizations from 1919 to 1979 provided support for mimetic isomorphism. His results reported that the higher the number of firms having already adopted the M-form, the more likely are nonadopters to select the multidivisional form.

A few empirical studies have also explored relationships that can be seen as linkages to other organizational and strategy theories. For example, in their study of executive succession in the publishing industry from 1958 to 1990, Thornton and Ocasio (1999) combined aspects of institutional theory with resource dependence theory. They explored the dependence of various sources of organizational power on prevailing institutional logics and the shifts in these logics over time. Their findings suggested that shifts in institutional logics moderate the sources of executive power and succession, thus supporting their argument "that when, whether, and how executives deploy their power to affect succession in organizations is conditional on the prevailing institutional logic in an industry" (p. 834).

Controversies

In general little consensus exists among empirical research studies of institutional theory on the measurement of the central concept of isomorphism (Tolbert and Zucker, 1996), thus making comparability among studies difficult. Furthermore, few studies have investigated the limitations of institutional theory by examining the consequences of organizational deviation from conformity and isomorphism. For example, in studying 631 liberal-arts colleges over a 15-year period, Kraatz and Zajac (1996) found that schools became less homogeneous over time, did not mimic prestigious schools, and that "illegitimate" changes had no negative impact on performance. Neither has empirical research differentiated between different forms of organizational response to institutional pressures as proposed by Oliver (1991). Oliver theorized that, rather than responding to institutional pressures in a uniform way, organizations might choose from a continuum of possible responses, ranging from passive compliance with norms to active defiance. Similar to Oliver, Scott (1991) argued "organizations may be expected to exercise 'strategic choice' (Child, 1972) in relating to their institutional environments

and responding to institutional pressures" (Scott, 1991, p. 170).

Another challenge directed at institutional research has been the research methodology used in many of the studies associated with the theory. For example, although isomorphic processes reflect dynamism, empirical studies have mostly been cross-sectional, measuring and specifying isomorphic processes as outcomes (Mizruchi and Fein, 1999) while neglecting the process of institutionalization. Measuring isomorphism as a process in longitudinal studies has been the exception rather than the rule (Covaleski and Dirsmith, 1988; Haveman, 1993a,b; Greve, 1995; Strang and Meyer, 1993). Studies on diffusion of institutional practices have emphasized the channel along which practices flow, but paid much less attention to variations in levels of institutionalization. Further, most studies have focused on single industries rather than comparing different patterns and causal mechanisms of institutionalization across industries (Strang and Soule, 1998; Tolbert and Zucker, 1996). These concerns have led some researchers (Tolbert and Zucker, 1996) to suggest that more careful consideration should be placed on historical context and organizational scope and range as factors affecting the rate and pattern of institutionalization.

Implications for Adaptation and Change

New institutional theory departs from traditional adaptation-theoretical perspectives that view organizations as readily able to change their structures and strategies to maintain alignment with changing technical environments (e.g., customers, suppliers, competitors, and regulators) (Thompson, 1967; Tolbert and Zucker, 1983). At the same time, in contrast to ecological models that argue isomorphism results in inefficient forms being selected out (Hannan and Freeman, 1977), institutional isomorphism stresses legitimacy over efficiency, thereby allowing for the persistence of inefficient, but legitimate, organizations (DiMaggio and Powell, 1983; Meyer and Rowan, 1977; Meyer and Zucker, 1990). Thus, institutional theory stresses that organizational adaptation occurs due to institutional pressures for legitimacy rather than market pressures for efficiency (Greenwood and Hinings, 1996). That is, while institutional theory proposes that organizational compliance with widely institutionalized practices and forms increases firm legitimacy and, thus, its likelihood of survival (Meyer and Rowan, 1977; Zucker, 1987), the theory also acknowledges that compliance with institutionalized practices may also limit the organization's efficiency. However, the theory does not provide any guide as to organizational internal processes that favor behavior consistent with isomorphic pressures, such as seeking legitimacy for their adaptation strategies, or for firms who chose to be innovators and early adopters when the legitimacy that is associated with their efforts is not yet visible.

Population Ecology

Guided by the question "Why are there so many kinds of organizations?" (Hannan and Freeman, 1977, p. 936), population ecology theory relates environmental factors to the abundance of different organizational forms and their transformations over time. In this framework, populations are defined as "a set of organizations engaged in similar activities and with similar patterns of resource utilization" (Baum, 1996, p. 77). Population ecology focuses on the processes and rates of organizational founding, disbanding, and change at the population level, rather than at the individual firm level, to explain organizational diversity. Evolution (within populations) is seen as a process of variation, selection, and retention (Aldrich, 1979; Hannan and Freeman, 1977).

Central Focus and Assumptions

In contrast to the adaptation perspective that views organizations as responding strategically to environmental changes and achieving survival and performance improvements through adaptation (Child, 1972; Cyert and March, 1963; Lawrence and Lorsch, 1967), population ecology generally perceives organizations as unable to adapt (Hannan and Freeman, 1977; Singh, House, and Tucker, 1986). Instead, selection is the major driver of transformation and change in organizational forms. In essence, population ecology theorists hypothesize that organizational successes and failures generally cannot be systematically attributed to managerial decisions at a population level, and hence, typically occur through an evolutionary selection process.

To explain this process, population ecologists have introduced the concepts of internal and external structural inertia. Internal structural inertia arises

from routines and competencies that have been developed and reinforced in organizations over the course of their existence (Nelson and Winter, 1982), ensuring activity patterns of high reliability and accountability that are favored by selection mechanisms. External structural constraints result from organizational embeddedness in its technical and institutional environment (Amburgey, Kelly, and Barnett, 1993; Granovetter, 1985). Because organizational change usually involves the destruction of existing patterns (Biggart, 1977), loss of competency through structural transformation or personnel loss (Boeker, 1989), disruption of external relationships (Amburgey et al., 1993), and the jeopardy of legitimacy (Hannan and Freeman, 1989), organizational change increases the likelihood of failure due to the disruption of established routines, core, and peripheral features (Hannan and Freeman, 1977, 1989; Singh, House, and Tucker, 1986). Population ecologists have compared this risk of failure resulting from organizational change to the risk faced by organizations at their founding (Haveman, 1992; Singh et al., 1986) framing change as "resetting the liability-of-newness clock" (Amburgey et al., 1993, p. 53; Hannan and Freeman, 1984, p. 160).

To see this entire evolutionary selection process, consider an organizational form at the time of its founding that matches the requirements of its environment. Over time, environmental changes result in misalignment between an incumbent organizational form and its environment. In this situation, structural inertia at the organizational level creates barriers to change, inhibiting the incumbents' ability to gain a new fit with the environment, thus increasing the risk of failure over time (Hannan and Freeman, 1984, 1989). The inability of incumbents to change provides an opportunity for new organization forms with a better environment-fit structure to enter the population, thereby introducing variation, which sets off increased selection rates. Incumbents misaligned with the environment are selected out, while the organizational forms exhibiting the best fit with the environment are retained (Aldrich, 1979; Hannan and Freeman, 1977, 1989). Thus, population ecology emphasizes selection as the primary driver of change, denying the ability of organizations to successfully alter their fitness levels in face of environmental change. Organizations are seen as incapable of effectively influencing their destiny, and managerial intentionality seems not to matter for long-term organizational survival at the population level.

Two other key concepts used in population ecology research are organizational founding and disbanding. Several theoretical approaches try to explain organizational founding, including density dependence and population dynamics. Other approaches deal with disbanding, including density dependence, fitness set theory, resource partitioning, founding conditions, liability of newness, liability of smallness, and community ecology (Singh and Lumsden,1990). These theoretical constructs are briefly addressed below.

Density dependence and population dynamics are used to explain why the intrapopulation processes of founding and mortality follow a concave pattern of growth and decline. These constructs operate through the following mechanisms. Initially, growth in population density (number of organizations with a new form) increases the legitimacy of a new population. Legitimacy gained from greater population density leads to an increase in the founding rates and a decrease in the failure rates among new organizational forms. However, population density eventually reaches a level at which surplus resources begin to decline, leading to a situation in which population density exceeds environmental carrying capacity. In this situation, greater competition among organizations for the remaining resources increases failures and reduces founding rates, leading to a new equilibrium (Carroll and Hannan, 1989; Hannan and Freeman, 1989; Hannan and Carroll, 1992).

Building on prior work in bioecology (Levins, 1968), fitness set theory compares the evolutionary advantages of specialist versus generalist organizations (Hannan and Freeman, 1977). To develop this approach, researchers distinguish between different "levels of environmental variability and grain" (Singh and Lumsden, 1990, p. 165). Whereas fine-grained environments (small periodic variations) generally favor specialist organizations, coarse-grained environments (large periodic variations) favor specialists under predictable environmental conditions, and generalists under uncertain conditions.

Specialist and generalist organizations also tend to respond differently to their environment, including occupying different niches and relying on different resources. These response differences tend to reduce the competition between specialist and generalist organizations. For example, Carroll (1985) found that while large generalist organizations occupy the center of the market, small specialist organizations exploit peripheral niches. Further, the rate of resource exploitation is believed to be much stronger for specialist organizations, allowing specialists to reach a better fit with their environment, while at the same time increasing their risk of failure in face of environmental change. Hence, whether selection favors small specialist organizations over large generalist organizations is uncertain and appears to depend on environmental conditions.

At the time of organization founding, environmental conditions and social structure are imprinted on organizational processes (Stinchcombe, 1965), influencing later organizational behavior, increasing variation, and moderating the probability of an organization being selected in or out. Thus, an organization's ability to change and adapt is considered to be largely determined by its founding conditions and external events subsequent to founding (Boeker, 1989). Organizational founding rates are also affected by ecological dynamics, prior rates of founding and disbanding, and institutional changes (Tucker, Singh, Meinhard, and House, 1988; Tucker, Singh, and Meinhard, 1990). The literature on organizational founding also distinguishes between entrepreneurial founding and new business ventures resulting from the entrance of an established organization into a new business (Low and MacMillan, 1988).

Age and size are two other factors believed to moderate the selection mechanism. The view of the liability of newness (Stinchcombe, 1965, pp. 148–149) holds that young organizations are more likely to be selected out than older, more established organizations, due to the young organization's low level of routines, social network, and legitimacy resulting in a lack of reliability and accountability (Hannan and Freeman, 1984). The view of the liability of smallness states that large organizations are less likely to be selected out than small organizations, due to their size, as size increases inertial tendencies favored by selection (Hannan and Freeman, 1984).

Finally, community ecology holds that populations of organizations don't evolve in isolation, but rather their evolution involves interrelationships with other populations (Astley, 1985; Fombrun, 1986). Thus the fate of a population is also dependent on the fate and fit of other related populations and their pattern of interrelationships. The level of selection is raised from the single organization failing, to the entire network (Barnett and Carroll, 1987).

Main Empirical Focus

Among the various theories on organizational adaptation and selection, population ecology is perhaps the most developed and tested. A large volume of empirical work in population ecology covers numerous industries over extensive time periods of sometimes a hundred years and longer. Furthermore, the research benefits from a generally high degree of consensus among its empirical findings and a consistent methodology (event-history analysis) across studies. Several key areas of analysis include organizational change, density dependence theory, fitness set theory, and population failure rates.

Population ecology empirical research has found organizational change to be a function of such endogenous factors as age (Delacroix and Swaminathan, 1991; Kelly and Amburgey, 1991), size (Haveman, 1993a,b; Mitchell, 1994), and experience with change (Amburgey and Miner, 1992; Amburgey et al., 1993). Among exogenous forces that have been found to affect change are the level of environmental munificence (Carroll, 1985; Delacroix and Swaminathan, 1991) and conditions at organizational founding (Tucker et al. 1990; Hannan, Carroll, Dundon, & Torres, 1995). Haveman (1993b), for example, found that, although larger organizations are expected to exhibit greater inability to change than smaller organizations due to higher levels of structural complexity and bureaucratization, the size, political insulation, and abundant slack resources of larger organizations were shown to actually facilitate change. Indeed, organizational transformation and the introduction of new organizational forms at the population level usually do not occur through organizational change, but rather through founding of new organizations and mortality or disbanding of established organizations due to loss of fit with their environment (Hannan and Freeman, 1977, 1984).

Density dependence theory has been empirically tested and supported for a number of industries. For example, Hannan and Freeman's (1987) study of national labor unions in the U.S. from 1836 to 1985, Barnett and Carroll's (1987) study of local telephone companies in Iowa from 1900 to 1917, Carroll and Hannan's (1989) study of newspapers in three countries from 1800 to 1975, and Hannan, Carroll, Dundon, and Torres's (1995) analysis of the automobile industry in 5 European countries from 1886 to 1981 found support for the predictions of density

dependence theory. Ranger-Moore, Banaszak-Holl, and Hannan (1991) studied the Manhattan banking (1791–1980) and American life insurance companies (1759–1937), also finding support for the applicability of the density dependent model in regulated industries. However, Delacroix, Swaminathan, and Solt (1989) failed to find support for the density dependence effect in their study of the wine industry in California. To achieve a more fine-grained understanding of population level evolution and change, researchers have tried to disaggregate population density, using factors such as geographic proximity (Carroll and Wade, 1991), resource requirements (Baum and Mezias, 1992), or by similarity of customers served (Baum and Singh, 1994).

Fitness set theory has been explored by Delacroix et al. (1989) and Delacroix and Swaminathan (1991) in their study of the Californian wine industry. In this study, these researchers demonstrated that specialists and generalists respond differently to competition. Further, Tucker et al. (1990) showed differential founding patterns for specialist and generalist organizations. However, empirical studies on founding face the challenge of determining the exact time and operationalization of birth, as well as of choosing the right environmental unit of analysis (Delacroix and Carroll, 1983; Tucker et al., 1990). "Since there is no organization prior to founding, organizational attributes cannot be used as independent variables" (Delacroix and Carroll, 1983, p. 275), and therefore the population becomes the unit of analysis.

Population ecology has usually defined organizational mortality as either dissolution, absorption by merger, or radical transformation (Carroll, 1984). Empirical studies have found that failure rates decline with both age (Freeman, Carroll, and Hannan, 1983; Singh et al., 1986) and size (Haveman, 1993b; Mitchell, 1994). However, few studies have simultaneously controlled for both age and size (Aldrich and Auster, 1986; Mitchell, 1994). Hence, while a considerable amount of empirical evidence has been generated from population ecology theory, much work remains, including responding to some challenges and controversies.

Controversies

Population ecology has been criticized for its determinism (Bourgeois, 1984), denying managerial intentionality and free will (Astley and Van de Ven,

1983) and thereby leaving organizations with little, if any, influence on selection. Hence, population ecology appears to overemphasize selection mechanisms, while largely ignoring adaptation mechanisms. Further, by concentrating on populations as the unit of analysis, population ecology does little to account for heterogeneity among organizations, other than attempting to control for differences in size and age, only two variables among many potential interorganizational differences.

The population ecology empirical literature also ignores cases of incumbent firms that successfully did adapt in the face of new entrants and technological discontinuities. The empirical research has been anchored on a single method of event history analysis. Event history modeling has become very sophisticated in its application, and this single shared methodology probably accounts for the cumulative nature of population ecology research, as we outlined in this section. However, the research has not benefited from cross-validation using alternative longitudinal research approaches.

In her critique of the use of institutional theory in population ecology research, Zucker (1989) questioned the use of the legitimacy construct, without actually measuring it, to explain density dependence of populations. Zucker claimed that density estimates are proxies for underlying institutional processes advocating a density-as-process view that sees legitimacy as a process relating density to founding and failure, rather than as a variable to be measured. These differences led Zucker to call for an ongoing dialogue between the fields of population ecology and institutional theory, rather than one field borrowing concepts from the other.

However, despite certain theoretical differences, some researchers have viewed population ecology and institutional theory as converging and complementary concepts (Hannan and Carroll, 1992; Hannan and Freeman, 1989). A few researchers have even suggested a hierarchical relationship, believing that institutional environments form the basis for ecological processes (Tucker, Baum, and Singh, 1992). For example, in studying child-care service organizations in Toronto between 1971 and 1987, Baum and Oliver (1991, 1992) found that populations of organizations with institutional relationships experienced higher survival rates, supporting the significant effect of institutional factors on selection. In addition to links to institutional theory, researchers have also combined

population ecology with concepts from the learning perspective. In their study on the Manhattan hotel industry from 1898 to 1980, Baum and Ingram (1998) found that organizational experience had a U-shaped relationship to failure. Furthermore, chain affiliations among hotels, serving as a source of knowledge transfer and risk sharing, improved the survival of hotels within the chain (Ingram and Baum, 1997b). This dynamic debate and the opportunity to establish important theoretical linkages supports a vibrant future for research in population ecology.

Implications for Adaptation and Change

The primary implication of population ecology research for adaptation and change is that incumbent firms are unable to change in the face of new entrants that introduce new organizational forms into the population. The overwhelming empirical findings strongly support the conclusion that most firms are selected out. The dominant explanation is inability to overcome embedded structural inertia. However, this finding does not distinguish, for example, between firms whose strategies are oriented toward short-term adaptation and those whose strategies are oriented toward managing the firm in perpetuity, as reported in von Werder (2001) in a historical analysis of Siemens. Ecology research empirically recognizes that some incumbent firms might have adapted, but these firms have not been the subjects of in-depth research.

Implications for Adaptation and Change and Future Research

One obvious, but perhaps simplistic, conclusion to be drawn from our review of the adaptation selection literature is that Pfeffer (1993) could be correct. It is relatively easy to argue that the extensive adaptation selection research literature spanning more than 30 years mirrors Pfeffer's depiction of a "weed patch." Figure 5.1 represents our attempt at positioning the various theories in terms of their primary causal focus, unit of analysis, and relationship to industry dynamics and to the institutional and macro environments. However, figure 5.1 also displays opportunities for achieving a theoretical integration across these single theme silos.

Theories have largely differed in their approach and underlying assumptions to studying adaptations and selection. Population ecology, for instance, assumes that organizations are unable to adapt in the face of environmental jolts. Change within populations and the emergence of new organizational forms (industries) are driven by new entrants that introduce new variants, resulting in the selection of outdated organizational forms and retention of the new form—which, by definition, exhibits superior fit with the altered environment (Hannan and Freeman, 1977, 1984, 1989). In contrast, according to institutional theory, firm survival depends on gaining legitimacy with the environment by adopting widely used and accepted practices and forms (DiMaggio and Powell, 1983). Thus, over time, firm practices converge and become more homogeneous. Resource-based theory views firm survival and its ability to adapt to be embedded in its resource endowment. Different inimitable resource endowments and characteristics across firms lead to heterogeneous adaptations and organizational forms (Barney, 1991; Wernerfelt, 1984). The evolutionary economics perspective (Nelson and Winter, 1982) focuses on organizational adaptation as embedded in the organizational capability to develop and improve routines involving information processing, decision making, and search and selection processes within the organization.

The various views on adaptation and selection also have differed in their level of analysis. Both population ecology and institutional theory have focused on adaptation and selection processes at the population level. Firm adaptation is seen as homogeneous within a population driven either by variation, selection, and retention (Hannan and Freeman, 1977) or by mimetic, coercive, and normative isomorphism (DiMaggio and Powell, 1983). Similarly, industrial organization in economics has concentrated on change at the industry level, while strategic group research has focused on differences among groups of firms within an industry (Caves and Porter, 1977; Hunt, 1972; Porter, 1979). The resource-based view (Barney, 1991; Penrose, 1959; Wernerfelt, 1984), behavioral theory of the firm (Cyert and March, 1963), strategic choice (Child, 1972; Miles and Snow, 1978), punctuated equilibrium (Gersick, 1991; Tushman and Romanelli, 1985), and transaction cost theory (Coase, 1937; Williamson, 1975, 1979) all focus on differences of adaptation and selection at the organizational level.

The research on adaptation, selection, and change also varies greatly in the application of empirical methods. Empirical population ecology studies are longitudinal, often stretching over several decades, encompassing an entire industry history and its evolution from its inception, while most other empirical studies of adaptation and selection have been primarily cross-sectional or short-term–oriented. Cross-sectional studies cannot capture long-term processes and effects of environmental changes or of organizational adaptation (Barnett and Burgelman, 1996; Miller and Friesen, 1980).

Table 5.1 summarizes the theories that collectively encompass the body of adaptation selection research reviewed for this chapter. Each theory is encapsulated and classified according to its unit of analysis, central research focus, underlying assumptions, main empirical focus, and its implications for managerial intentionality.

Table 5.1 shows the proliferation of theories, research paradigms, constructs, empirical approaches, and incompatible levels of analysis in this area. It also suggests that the dominant discourse on adaptation-selection mostly still takes place within single-theme theoretical "silos." The proliferation of theories, relatively few "cross-silo" citations, lack of shared models and variable definitions (dependent or independent), and diverse units of analysis have all contributed to a low level of empirical comparability and little accumulation and integration of knowledge across silos. Indeed, this voluminous literature has more to say about selection, sources, and causes of structural inertia than about the evolution, mutation, and survival of organizations over time or about the role and contribution of managerial intentionality.

The table makes clear that the literature is inconclusive on the role of managerial intentionality in organizational adaptation. While some theoretical approaches focus on the role of managerial intentionality, other theoretical lenses highlight the limitations of managerial intentionality or conclude that intentionality matters little in explaining organizational adaptation and survival over time.

Perhaps the most obvious and important conclusion is that single-theme explanations of the adaptation-selection phenomenon have reached their limit. It may be time to abandon naive selection or naive adaptation research in favor of directing the attention of strategy and organization theory scholars to researching the joint outcomes of intentional adaptation and environmental selection pressures. With a few exceptions, researchers have not addressed the interrelationship between firm-level adaptation and

Table 5.1 Overview of theories and adaptation and selection

Theory	Unit of Analysis	Central Focus	Central Assumptions	Main Empirical Focus	Implications for Managerial Intentionality
Population ecology (Hannan and Freeman, 1977, 1984, 1989)	Population (e.g., hotel industry in Manhattan; wineries in California; S&Ls in California)	"Why are there so many kinds of organizations?" • process and rates of organizational founding, disbanding, change • evolution as variation, selection, retention • generalists vs. specialists	• environmental determinism • organizations are unable to adapt • structural inertia source of maladaptation • liability of newness • liability of smallness • density dependence	• longitudinal studies of populations • survival analyses and hazard-rate models	• management cannot influence selection • managerial intentionality and strategy irrelevant in the long run • specialize in niche until selected out
Institutional theory (Meyer and Rowan, 1977; DiMaggio and Powell, 1983)	Population (within an organizational field)	"Why there is such a startling homogeneity of organizational forms and practices?" • explain homogeneity, not variation • emphasis on institutional, not technical, environment	• organizations become homogeneous and isomorphic over time • isomorphic pressures— mimetic, coercive, and normative—emanate from environment • change is constrained • organizations are reactive, seeking legitimacy • legitimacy dominates efficiency	• diffusion of institutional practices (e.g., M-form) • focus on outcomes of isomorphism • single-industry studies	• align organizational structure and values with institutional norms and expectations • gain legitimacy with environment • mimic successful organizations that are perceived as legitimate • determine organizational strategy through exchange with environment
Industrial organization economics (Bain, 1968; Caves, 1980, 1984)	Industry	• structure-conduct-performance • market power and concentration • intensity of industry rivalry • barriers to entry	• market structure is exogenous, determines industry performance • industry membership determines firm performance • homogeneity of firms within an industry • equilibrium-oriented	• interindustry differences rather than intraindustry variation • cross-sectional • industry case studies • industry- and firm-level panel data studies	• implement industry barriers to entry • barrier to entry through excess capacity, vertical integration, limit pricing, product differentiation, etc. • reduce intraindustry rivalry by colluding • enter attractive industry • individual firm cannot affect industry dynamics

Theory	Level/Focus				
Resource-based view (Penrose, 1959; Wernerfelt, 1984; Barney, 1991)	Firm resources	• sustainable competitive advantage • unique, inimitable, firm-specific resources • performance differences • causal ambiguity • social complexity • ex-post and ex-ante limits to resource competition	• resource heterogeneity among firms • firm as bundle of resources • competitive advantage based on unique resources • isolating mechanisms • equilibrium oriented	• diversification • first-mover advantage • cross-sectional • problems in operationalizing resource concept • proxies for resources (e.g., R&D intensity)	• protect unique resources from acquisition and imitation • create "isolating mechanisms" around resources (e.g., property rights/patents, information or learning asymmetries) • leverage your core competency • differentiate your strategy (niching)
Resource-dependence theory (Pfeffer and Salancik, 1978)	Organization within its environment	• reduction of environmental uncertainty • interfirm relationships • power constellations and interorganizational power relationships	• negotiated/enacted environment to reduce uncertainty • organizations can affect environment within constraints • organizations have latitude for discretion • organizations pursue self-interest • asymmetric interdependence	• explicating enactment of environment • interlocking directorates • board compositions • most studies cross-sectional	• enact your environment • negotiate exchange relationships with the environment • control and shape resource access through relationships with the environment
Transaction-cost economics (Williamson, 1975, 1979)	Transactions within and between organizations	• structuring firm boundary • alignment of transactions and governance structures: (market, hybrid, and hierarchy) • asset specificity • transaction uncertainty • transaction costs of negotiating, monitoring, and enforcing contracts	• opportunism, self-interest seeking with guile • bounded rationality • efficient transacting as source of competitive advantage • static	• vertical integration • make-or-buy decisions • joint ventures and strategic alliances • cross-sectional	• maximize performance through minimizing transaction costs • match right governance structure with right type of transaction • choose vertical integration for high asset-specific and uncertain transactions • choose market structure for low asset-specific transactions • avoid self-interest seeking of others

Table 5.1 (continued)

Theory	Unit of Analysis	Central Focus	Central Assumptions	Main Empirical Focus	Implications for Managerial Intentionality
Behavioral theory of the firm (Cyert and March, 1963)	Organization	• behavioral alternative to classical theory of the firm • uncertainty avoidance • organizational slack • organizations as coalitions • stability seeking	• organizations satisfy multiple stakeholders • structural inertia due to satisficing, bounded rationality, slack, and aspiration-level goals • slack necessary for innovation • organizational learning • managers maximize personal goals	• various elements empirically investigated in organizational learning and evolutionary economics • simulation studies	• accumulate slack to avoid uncertainty • allocate slack resources to innovation • negotiate your environment to reduce uncertainty • adapt goals, shift attention and search procedures as consequence of organizational learning
Evolutionary economics (Nelson and Winter, 1982)	Organization and Population	• organizations as routines • intensity and direction of search and selection in evolution of routines • process of creative destruction • local search and incremental improvement in routines • imitation as strategy to improve routines • replication as strategy	• capabilities are embedded in routines • firms adapt and change their routines • industry structure and organizations continuously evolve • organizations are heterogeneous • organizations differ in their rates and paths of adaptation • problemistic search	• longitudinal case studies • intraindustry studies • simulation studies	• replicate and retain successful practices and routines • develop a coherent, path-dependent strategy • leverage past competencies • actively manage routines for innovation
Organizational learning perspective (Cyert and March, 1963; Levinthal and March, 1981, 1993; March, 1991; Cohen and Levinthal, 1990)	Organization	• organization as adaptive learning system • intra- and inter-organizational knowledge creation and transfer • absorptive capacity • trial and error learning • process, rules, search • competency traps	• search and learning are goal oriented • problem-driven search • explicit link between learning and adaptation • learning depreciates • learning is cumulative • unlearning and learning • tacit/explicit knowledge	• simulation studies • case studies of single firms	• avoid competency traps • avoid myopic learning by focusing on long-term adaptation • continuously renew knowledge base • continuously manage incremental and radical innovation • create absorptive capacity for assimilating internal and external new knowledge

Theory	Level	Themes	Assumptions	Methods	Implications for managers
Strategic choice (Child, 1972; Miles and Snow, 1978)	Organization/management	• strategic renewal and repositioning • strategic choices of organizations • strategic types (prospector, analyzer, defender, reactor)	• organizations enact and shape their environment • managers determine organizational structure • organizational adaptation is heterogeneous among firms	• applications of Miles and Snow's typology • cross-sectional • strategic choice vs. determinism	• choose your environment to compete in • actively shape and enact your environment • choose strategic actions that maximize organizational performance
Contingency theory (Burns and Stalker, 1961; Lawrence and Lorsch, 1967; Donaldson, 1996b)	Organization	• organizational structure–environmental contingency fit • strategy-structure fit • centralization vs. decentralization • differentiation of organizational structures and coordination among them	• organization can adapt structures and strategies to external requirements • equifinality of organizational structure fits • centralized structure most suited for low task uncertainty and vice versa	• cross-sectional • bivariate contingency constellations • case studies	• design organization structure for maximum fit with environmental contingencies • monitor organization-environment fit • continuously differentiate and integrate structures to match changing environmental contingencies
Punctuated equilibrium (Tushman and Romanelli, 1985; Gersick, 1991)	Organization/Top Management Team (TMT)	• radical and discontinuous organizational evolution and transformation • growth, maturation, rejuvenation	• organizations can reinvent themselves and overcome inertia • long periods of incremental change build up inertia • short periods of radical change • reactive organizational transformation • management initiates change	• case studies of organizations • few population studies	• manage organizational transformation as punctuated change • be responsive to discontinuous changes in the environment • overcome inertia through radical and discontinuous change

population-level selection (Lewin and Volberda, 1999; McKelvey, 1998). Coevolutionary models (see chap. 8) have the potential of integrating complementary theories of adaptation and selection. Such models incorporate the premise that adaptation and selection are not orthogonal forces but are fundamentally interrelated, and that organizational change and mutation must be studied longitudinally. In coevolutionary models, change is not an outcome of managerial adaptation or environmental selection but rather the joint outcome of intentionality and environmental effects. Thus, we are less pessimistic about the landscape that our review portrays of the adaptation-selection literature. It may, at first glance, resemble a weed patch, but we also discern a wide-open opportunity for research that takes advantage of complementary theoretical explanations and cross levels of analysis, incorporating reverse causalities and striving to achieve integration across the theoretical silos. Integration of multiple different views can better inform understanding of the complexities of organizational adaptation and change over time.

A closer examination reveals several points of overlap and common themes. For example, population ecology views organizational change as detrimental, disruptive, and a threat to organizational survival (Hannan and Freeman, 1977, 1989), and evolutionary economics views change as positive and firms as constantly evolving and outperforming each other through innovation (Nelson and Winter, 1982). While population ecology sees organizations as unlikely to change because of forces of structural inertia (Hannan and Freeman, 1977), change is a major driver of organizational learning (Levinthal and March, 1981, 1993), the behavioral theory of the firm (Cyert and March, 1963), and evolutionary economics (Nelson and Winter, 1982). In the sections that follow we attempt to highlight areas of overlap and opportunities for forging complementarity and a more integrative understanding of adaptation-selection phenomena.

Population ecology and institutional theory both inform aspects of population homogeneity, although their approaches differ markedly. Studying density dependence of populations over time, population ecology stresses variation, selection, and retention as processes by which populations, but not the individual organization, change. Change at the population level occurs through entry of new organizational forms that drive variation, which lead to increased selection

and culminate in homogeneity (Hannan and Freeman, 1984). Institutional theory focuses on accounting for the emergence of homogeneity, not variation. It views change as unidirectional and driven by the institutional environment. Institutional isomorphic pressures lead to greater homogeneity, conformity, and convergence (DiMaggio and Powell, 1983; Meyer and Rowan, 1977). Population ecology emphasizes the technical and competitive environment, in contrast to institutional theory, which emphasizes the importance of legitimacy for survival. While structural inertia is the source of maladaptation in population ecology (Hannan and Freeman, 1977), incompatibility with institutional norms represents the source of maladaptation in institutional theory (DiMaggio and Powell, 1983). Institutional theory predicts that the rate of adoption of institutional practices increases the more organizations adopt the new practices. The more similar to each other organizations become, the lower will be the variation in the population (Strang and Soule, 1998). The implication of institutional theory for managerial intentionality is to direct their efforts toward gaining legitimacy with their environment by continually aligning their organizational structure, strategy, and values with institutional norms and expectations.

Industrial organization economics also stresses the dominant influence of the population (industry) on individual firm survival and performance. Market structure (concentration, entry barriers, and product differentiation) determines industry and firm performance (Bain, 1968; Mason, 1959; Porter, 1981). However, industrial organization economics assumes static equilibrium and homogeneity of firms within an industry. Because IO economics assumes that firms cannot shape industry structure, positioning becomes crucial (Porter, 1980). Managerial implications of IO economics include selecting and entering attractive industries, reduction of intra-industry rivalry through collusion and implementation of barriers to entry (excess capacity, vertical integration, limit pricing, or product differentiation).

The resource-based view (RBV) has its roots in IO economics. In contrast to IO economics, which views industry membership as determinant of firm performance, RBV focuses on internal firm-unique resources and capabilities as the source of a sustainable competitive advantage (Barney, 1991; Wernerfelt, 1984). Moreover, RBV views managers as able to actively influence the destiny of their firm by their decision to invest in firm-specific inimitable capabilities. Furthermore, divestitures and diversification strategies are seen as means to acquire new capabilities (while reversing the structural inertia of obsolete capabilities) and determining the direction and timing of entry into new markets becomes a key strategic variable for managing adaptation (Ramanujam and Varadarajan, 1989). IO economics and RBV both inform the role of "isolating mechanisms" (Rumelt, 1984) as a means for sustaining competitive advantage. IO economics emphasizes entry into new lines of business (industry) and barriers to entry as an isolating mechanism. RBV stresses the inimitability of unique resources, their social complexity, and causal ambiguity as isolating mechanisms (e.g., intellectual property rights, patents, and learning asymmetries) that shelter firm strategic resources from imitation and maintain their rents. RBV also contributes to the elucidation of sources and causes of structural inertia. It argues that organizational survival is enhanced through resource-base differentiation. However, altering the firm resource endowment often requires reversing embedded investments, which requires considerable effort and takes longer than altering its market strategy through mergers and acquisition (Dierickx and Cool, 1989). This is in contrast to institutional theory, which views organizations as improving their survival chances through conformity and homogeneity.

Contrary to the underlying unidirectional assumptions of institutional theory, population ecology, and IO economics, resource-dependence theory (RDT) assumes that the organization can influence and shape its relationship with the environment. The central concern of RDT is how the organization can enact and negotiate its environment, reduce its dependence on the environment, and execute strategic choice within certain constraints (Pfeffer and Salancik, 1978). RDT emphasizes controlling dependencies through such means as interlocking directorates or trade organizations (Stearns and Mizruchi, 1993). It holds that scale matters (in this it is consistent with Fligstein [1996], which argues that large firms can exercise coercive isomorphic power over smaller firms).

A shared theme that underlies several theories— resource dependence theory, institutional theory, transaction cost theory, and the behavioral theory of the firm—involves the role of environmental uncertainty and the motivation of managers to avoid uncertainty. Resource dependence theory relies on restructuring dependence relationships by devising power constellations and interorganizational power relationships for reducing environmental uncertainty (Pfeffer and Salancik, 1978). Transaction cost economics (TCE) reduces transaction-specific risk by changing organizational boundaries and devising appropriate governance structures such as internalizing market transactions into the hierarchy (Williamson, 1975, 1979). The behavioral theory of the firm (Cyert and March, 1963) also views organizations as motivated to avoid environmental uncertainty by negotiating their environment (similar to RDT, which reintroduced the concept 15 years later) and accumulating organizational slack, which serves to buffer variability in performance and environmental uncertainty. For institutional theory, environmental uncertainty and ambiguity can be mitigated through mimetic and normative isomorphism, which increase legitimacy and perceived success (DiMaggio and Powell, 1983). Transaction costs economics and resource dependence theory share a focus on structuring interorganizational relationships. TCE, however, emphasizes alignment of governance structures and transactions as a function of transaction characteristics (Williamson, 1975, 1979). Competitive advantage derives from selecting the governance structure that maximizes efficiency and minimizes transaction costs. Several of the adaptation-selection theories summarized in table 5.1 inform change and adaptation over time and assume some role for managerial intentionality. These include the behavioral theory of the firm (Cyert and March, 1963), evolutionary economics (Nelson and Winter, 1982), strategic choice theory (Child, 1972), punctuated equilibrium (Gersick, 1991; Tushman and Romanelli, 1985), and organizational learning theories (Levinthal and March, 1981, 1993; March, 1991).

Punctuated equilibrium theories represent a more complex argument for managerial intentionality and the conditions under which intentionality could affect firm longevity and survival. In that respect, punctuated equilibrium research supplants strategic choice research (Child, 1972) or theories that espouse a more limited view of managerial intentionality: the achievement of fit with the environment (Donaldson, 1995, 1996b). Theories of evolutionary economics, organizational learning, and the behavioral theory of the firm establish a foundation for studying organizational adaptation and change over time. These theories have several features in common. They encompass multilevel phenomena, bidirectional causalities, micro and macro selection, the ever-present tension of balancing exploration and exploitation, and organization-specific idiosyncrasies. Collectively these theories begin to inform the analysis of organizational adaptation and change as the joint outcome of microselection.

While RBV views organizations as "bundle[s] of resources" (Penrose, 1959), the behavioral theory of the firm (BTOF) views organizations as coalitions (Cyert and March, 1963). As in resource dependence theory, BTOF views organizations as negotiating their environment; similar to strategic choice theory (Child, 1972), organizations possess "considerable latitude in selecting their strategies for dealing with their environments" (Cyert and March, 1963, p. 244). BTOF advises managers to accumulate slack to avoid uncertainty, allocate slack resources to innovation, and to adapt goals, shift attention, and search procedures as consequence of organizational learning. BTOF presents both a behavioral alternative to the classical theory of the firm (Cyert and March, 1963) and one of the bases for evolutionary economics (Nelson and Winter, 1982) and organizational learning (Levinthal and March, 1981, 1993).

In contrast to more static-oriented theories such as TCE, RBV, and IO economics, evolutionary economics is dynamic and process oriented. Similar to RBV and unlike IO economics, evolutionary economics stresses heterogeneity among firms. Heterogeneity is seen as the result of different rates and paths of adaptation over time. Evolutionary economics focuses on the intensity and direction of search and selection in the adaptation and change of organizational routines. The analysis takes place at the firm level for search processes and for the occurrence of selection decisions and at the industry level for imitation mechanisms (Nelson and Winter, 1973, 1974, 1982). Similar to population ecology and institutional theory, evolutionary economics explains how variation disappears. Successful routines that become dominant are copied at the industry level through the imitation mechanism, thereby reducing variation. In contrast to population ecology, evolutionary economics assigns a positive connotation to change—superior routines at the industry level drive innovations and change. Managerial implications of evolutionary economics include the replication and retention of successful practices and routines, the active management of routines for innovation, and the leveraging of past competencies.

Organizational learning views organizations as adaptive learning systems and takes a multilevel perspective, involving intra- and interorganizational learning, population-level, and individual-level learning. Similar to evolutionary economics and BTOF, learning is viewed as highly path-dependent and dynamic (Levinthal and March, 1981, 1993). Managerial implications include the continuous renewal of knowledge bases and management of incremental and radical innovation, the avoidance of competency traps and myopic learning by focusing on long-term adaptation.

In contrast to population ecology, punctuated equilibrium holds that organizations can overcome structural inertia through radical and discontinuous organizational evolution and transformation, and it argues that change positively correlates with performance (Gersick, 1991; Tushman and Romanelli, 1985). Punctuated equilibrium advises managers to be responsive to discontinuous changes in the environment and to overcome inertia through radical and discontinuous change.

Collectively, the competing theories reviewed in this chapter serve to inform various aspects of the phenomena of adaptation and selection. Rather than viewing the theories as incompatible with each other, we consider the various theories to inform different aspects and levels of analysis relating to adaptation and to selection. It is also evident that research on organizational mutation over time remains a wide-open area of research. More generally, we argue that the extent to which intentionality can affect adaptation has yet to be empirically investigated within dialectics and with data and methods equivalent to the power of selection research.

Population ecology, institutional theory, and evolutionary economics share an opportunity to link their perspectives to understand a small but unique class of firms. These are the firms that in the face of new entrants and intensifying selection rates are able to adapt and renew themselves by mutating and adopting the required attributes of the new entrants. Empirically it is altogether clear that most firms are selected out. But a few firms are successful in renewing themselves time and time again. Do such firms posses some unique regime of routines and capabilities that accounts for their ability to survive and adapt?

Evolutionary economics makes a strong assumption that environmental VSR processes mediate the internal VSR processes. In other words, superior best practices in the external environment are the stimulus for internal change processes of routines and imitation of the superior routines discovered in the external environment. The process of setting the level of adaptive tension (the performance gap that needs to be overcome) can be explained by level of aspiration theory (Lewin, Dembo, Festinger, and Sears, 1944; Festinger, 1954; Lewin and Massini, 2004; Greve, 2003). Levels of aspirations are a function of past experience combined with a comparison to a reference group. Most of the research on level of aspiration theory is found in social psychology. In organization theory it has a role in A *Behavioral Theory of the Firm* (Cyert and March, 1963) as a general process for changing performance goals. Thus, for example, Cyert and March assume that performance goals are adjusted based on firm-specific historical rate of improvement in performance and on the basis of comparison with the performance improvements of competitors. The theory and the empirical research are silent on how firms determine what weight to assign to past performance and how the competitor reference group is chosen. Lewin and Massini (2004) note that one important source of heterogeneity between firms is the weight they assign to their own experience relative to information on competitors. In addition, they note that choosing to compare against a composite of average competitors relative to competitors defining the performance frontier has significant implications for the firm's adaptation trajectory. A firm that routinely chooses an industry average comparison group is more likely to follow a micro level adaptation process that is consistent with mimetic and normative adaptation behaviors in institutional theory. Empirically such micro adaptation will be best explained by changes in the population average for the particular routine. Firms that routinely chose other industry frontier–defining firms for comparison are more likely to be early adopters of new innovations and to mutate in tandem with emergence and success of new entrants. Such firms also more consistently earn above-average returns that further increase their life chances over time. Lewin and Massini (2004) expect the presence of such firms in a population to be very small. This is because comparison to the average population seems to be a preferred behavioral norm in managerial practice and in social psychological research. It is also an outcome of the prevalent asymmetric incentive system in organizations (Schiff and Lewin, 1970) and of the dominant competitive analysis framework in use by managers who emphasize various industry-average performance measures. Identifying and studying such firms could present a new and significant approach for advancing research on adaptation-selection. Perhaps such firms express (in a genetic sense) certain routines (e.g., selecting frontier competitors for comparison and assigning significant weights to their performance) that distinguish their adaptation capabilities from other firms. However, the empirical challenge of designing prospective (as distinct from retrospective) case studies requires longitudinal analyses and research methods that seek to uncover the source (e.g., founding conditions or management intentionality), existence, and practice of metaroutines such as that for setting the level of adaptive tension. Anecdotally, it seems that this is what Jack Welch had in mind when he demanded that each GE business must be number one or two in its industry.

We agree with McKelvey (1998) and others (Anderson, 1999; Levinthal and Warglein, 1999; Lewin and Volberda, 1999) that the study of intentionality and mutation at the organizational level could be advanced by adopting coevolutionary systems of inquiry and new longitudinally-based empirical approaches. However, we also see high potential for research centering on firms that have successfully adapted in times of creative destruction by focusing their analysis on uncovering the nature and functioning of metaroutines, such as those that determine level of adaptive tension, drive internal variation and knowledge creation, or define internal and external absorptive capacity. If the last quarter-century can be characterized as documenting the many sources and causes of structural inertia and the futility of managerial intentionality, perhaps the next quarter-century will see a mushrooming of research traditions that focus on explicating joint micro and macro adaptation processes and change.

Notes

Many colleagues too numerous to thank individually have helped stimulate and direct our thinking as our ideas evolved over the past two years. We wish to acknowledge specifically the helpful suggestions of Pat Thornton, Bill McKelvey, Henk Volberda, Axel von Werder, Mitchell Koza, Silvia Massini, Tomoaki Sakano, and faculty colloquia participants at the Fuqua School of Business, Erasmus University, Technical University Berlin, IESE, Business Schook, University of

Navarra Barcelona, and the doctoral consortium on international research in strategy and new organizational forms. We also wish to acknowledge the financial support of the IBM Consulting Group, Coopers Lybrand, the Fuqua Center for International Education and Research, and the Center for Research on Consumer Finance at Waseda University. Finally, we would like to thank Billie Maciunas and Marybeth Lavrakas for their efforts in editing the text.

1. The term in italics is the authors' interpretation.

References

Abernathy, W. J. & Utterback, J. (1978). Patterns of industrial innovation. *Technological Review, 80,* 41–47.

Agrawal, A., Jaffe, J. F., & Mandelker, G. N. (1992). The post-merger performance of acquiring firms: A re-examination of an anomaly. *Journal of Finance, 47,* 1605–1621.

Alchian, A. A. & Demsetz, H. (1972). Production, information costs, and economic organization. *American Economic Review, 62,* 777–795.

Aldrich, H. E. (1979). *Organizations and environments.* Englewood Cliffs, NJ: Prentice-Hall.

Aldrich, H. E. & Auster, E. (1986). Even dwarfs started small: Liabilities of age and size and their strategic implications. *Research in Organizational Behavior, 8,* 165–198.

Amburgey, T. L. & Miner, A. S. (1992). Strategic momentum: The effects of repetitive, positional, and contextual momentum on merger activity. *Strategic Management Journal, 13,* 335–348.

Amburgey, T. L., Kelly, D., & Barnett, W. P. (1993). Resetting the clock: The dynamics of organizational change and failure. *Administrative Science Quarterly, 38,* 51–73.

Amel, D. F. & Rhoades, S. A. (1988). Strategic groups in banking. *Review of Economics and Statistics, 70,* 685–689.

Amit, R. & Schoemaker, P. J. H. (1993). Strategic assets and organizational rent. *Strategic Management Journal, 14,* 33–46.

Anderson (1999). Complexity theory and organization science. *Organization Science, 10,* 216–232.

Anderson, P. & Tushman, M. L. (1990). Technological discontinuities and dominant design: A cyclical model of technological change. *Administrative Science Quarterly, 35,* 604–633.

Andrews, K. R. (1971). *The concept of corporate strategy.* Homewood, IL: Irwin.

Argote, L., Beckman, S. L., & Epple, D. (1990). The persistence and transfer of learning in industrial settings. *Management Science, 36,* 140–154.

Argyres, N. S. & Porter-Liebeskind, J. P. (1999). Contractual commitments, bargaining power, and governance inseparability: Incorporating history into transaction cost theory. *Academy of Management Review, 24,* 49–63.

Argyris, C. & Schoen, D. A. (1978). *Organizational learning.* Reading, MA: Addison-Wesley.

Astley, W. G. (1985). The two ecologies: Population and community perspectives on organizational evolution. *Administrative Science Quarterly, 30,* 224–241.

Astley, W. G. & Van de Ven, A. H. (1983). Central perspectives and debates in organizational theory. *Administrative Science Quarterly, 28,* 245–273.

Bain, J. S. (1951). Relation of profit rate to industry concentration: American manufacturing, 1936–1940. *Quarterly Journal of Economics, 65,* 293–324.

Bain, J. S. (1956). *Barriers to new competition.* Cambridge, MA: Harvard University Press.

Bain, J. S. (1968). *Industrial organization.* New York: Wiley.

Balakrishnan, C. & Wernerfelt, B. (1986). Technical change, competition, and vertical integration. *Strategic Management Journal, 7,* 347–359.

Barnett, W. P. & Burgelman, R. A. (1996). Evolutionary perspectives on strategy. *Strategic Management Journal, 17,* 5–19.

Barnett, W. P. & Carroll, G. R. (1987). Competition and mutualism among early telephone companies. *Administrative Science Quarterly, 32,* 400–421.

Barnett, W. P. & Hansen, M. P. (1996). The red queen in organizational evolution. *Strategic Management Journal, 17,* 139–157.

Barnett, W. P., Greve, H. P., & Park, D. Y. (1994). An evolutionary model of organizational performance. *Strategic Management Journal, 15,* 11–28.

Barney, J. B. (1986). Strategic factor markets: Expectations, luck, and business strategy. *Management Science, 32,* 1231–1241.

Barney, J. B. (1988). Returns to bidding firms in mergers and acquisitions: Reconsidering the relatedness hypothesis. *Strategic Management Journal, 9,* 71–78.

Barney, J. B. (1991). Firm resources and sustained competitive advantage. *Journal of Management, 17,* 99–120.

Barney, J. B. (1999). How a firm's capabilities affect boundary decisions. *Sloan Management Review, 40,* 137–145.

Baum, J. A. C. (1996). Organizational ecology. In S. R. Clegg, C. Hardy, & W. R. Nord (Eds.), *Handbook of organization studies* (pp. 77–114). London: Sage.

Baum, J. A. C. & Ingram, P. (1998). Survival-enhancing learning in the Manhattan hotel industry, 1898–1980. *Management Science, 44,* 996–1016.

Baum, J. A. C. & Oliver, C. (1991). Institutional link-ages and organizational mortality. *Administrative Science Quarterly*, 36, 187–218.

Baum, J. A. C. & Oliver, C. (1992). Institutional em-beddedness and the dynamics of organizational po-pulations. *American Sociological Review*, 57, 540–559.

Baum, J. A. C. & Mezias, S. J. (1992). Localized com-petition and organizational failure in the Man-hattan hotel industry, 1898–1990. *Administrative Science Quarterly*, 37, 580–604.

Baum, J. A. C. & Singh, J. V. (1994). Organizational niches and the dynamics of organizational found-ing. *Organization Science*, 5, 483–501.

Baumol, W. J., Panzar, J. C., & Willig, R. D. (1982). *Contestable markets and the theory of industry structure*. New York: Harcourt.

Biggart, N. W. (1977). The creative destructive process of organizational change: The case of the post of-fice. *Administrative Science Quarterly*, 22, 410–426.

Boeker, W. P. (1988). Organizational origins: Entre-preneurial and environmental imprinting at the time of founding. In G. R. Carroll (Ed.), *Ecological models of organization* (pp. 33–52). Cambridge, MA: Ballinger.

Boeker, W. (1989). Strategic change: The effects of founding and history. *Academy of Management Journal*, 32, 489–515.

Bourgeois, L. J. I. (1981). On the measurement of or-ganizational slack. *Academy of Management Re-view*, 6, 29–39.

Bourgeois, L. J. I. (1984). Strategic management and determinism. *Academy of Management Review*, 9, 586–596.

Bresnahan, T. F. & Schmalensee, R. (1987). The em-pirical renaissance in industrial economics: An over-view. *Journal of Industrial Economics*, 35, 371–378.

Brush, T. H., Bromiley, P., & Hendrickx, M. (1999). The relative influence of industry and corporation on business segment performance: An alternative esti-mate. *Strategic Management Journal*, 20, 519–547.

Burgelman, R. A. (2002). Strategy as vector and the in-ertia of co-evolutionary lock-in. *Administrative Science Quarterly*, 47, 325–356.

Burns, T. & Stalker, G. M. (1961). *The management of innovation*. London: Tavistock.

Carroll, G. R. (1984). Organizational ecology. *Annual Review of Sociology*, 10, 71–93.

Carroll, G. R. (1985). Concentration and specialization: Dynamics of niche width in populations of organi-zations. *American Journal of Sociology*, 90, 1263–1283.

Carroll, G. R. & Hannan, M. T. (1989). Density depend-ence in the evolution of populations of newspaper organizations. *American Sociological Review*, 54, 524–541.

Carroll, G. R. & Wade, J. B. (1991). Density depend-ence in the evolution of the American brewing industry across different levels of analysis. *Social Science Research*, 20, 271–302.

Caves, R. E. & Porter, M. E. (1977). From entry barriers to mobility barriers: Conjectural decisions and contrived deterrence to new competition. *Quarterly Journal of Economics*, 91, 241–262.

Caves, R. E. (1980). Industrial organization, corporate strategy and structure. *Journal of Economic Litera-ture*, 18, 64–92.

Caves, R. E. (1984). Economic analysis and the quest for competitive advantage. *American Economic Re-view*, 74, 127–132.

Chandler, A. D. (1962). *Strategy and structure: chapters in the history of American industrial enterprise*. Cambridge, MA: MIT Press.

Chang, S. J. (1996). An evolutionary perspective on di-versification and corporate restructuring: Entry, exit, and economic performance during 1981–89. *Strategic Management Journal*, 17, 587–611.

Chang, S. J. & Singh, H. (1999). The impact of modes of entry and resource fit on modes of exit by multi-business firms. *Strategic Management Journal*, 20, 1019–1035.

Chatterjee, S. (1990). Excess resources, utilization costs, and mode of entry. *Academy of Management Journal*, 33, 780–800.

Chatterjee, S. & Wernerfelt, B. (1991). The link between resources and type of diversification: Theory and evidence. *Strategic Management Journal*, 12, 33–48.

Child, J. (1972). Organization structure, environment, and performance: The role of strategic choice. *Sociology*, 6, 1–22.

Child, J. (1977). Organization design and performance—Contingency theory and beyond. *Organization and Administrative Sciences*, 8, 169.

Child, J. (1997). Strategic choice in the analysis of ac-tion, structure, organizations and environment: Retrospect and prospect. *Organization Studies*, 18, 43–76.

Clark, K. B. (1989). Project scope and project perfor-mance: The effect of parts strategy and supplier involvement on product development. *Manage-ment Science*, 35, 1247–1263.

Coase, R. H. (1937). The nature of the firm. *Economica*, 4, 386–405.

Cohen, W. M. & Levinthal, D. A. (1990). Absorptive ca-pacity: A new perspective on learning and innova-tion. *Administrative Science Quarterly*, 35, 128–152.

Commons, J. R. (1934). *Institutional economics*. Madi-son, WI: University of Wisconsin Press.

Conner, K. R. (1991). A historical comparison of resource-based theory and five schools of thought within industrial organization economics: Do we have a new theory of the firm? *Journal of Management*, 17, 121–154.

Conner, K. R. & Prahalad, C. K. (1996). A resource-based theory of the firm: Knowledge versus opportunism. *Organization Science*, 5, 477–501.

Cool, K. O. & Schendel, D. (1987). Strategic group formation and performance: The case of the U.S. pharmaceutical industry, 1963–1982. *Management Science*, 33, 1102–1124.

Covaleski, M. A. & Dirsmith, M. W. (1988). An institutional perspective on the rise, social transformation, and fall of a university budget category. *Administrative Science Quarterly*, 33, 562–587.

Crossan, M. M., Lane, H. W., & White, R. E. (1999). An organizational learning framework: From intuition to institution. *Academy of Management Review*, 24, 522–537.

Cubbin, J. & Geroski, P. (1987). The convergence of profits in the long run: Inter-firm and inter-industry comparisons. *Journal of Industrial Economics*, 35, 427–442.

Cyert, R. M. & March J. G. (1963). *A behavioral theory of the firm*. Englewood Cliffs, NJ: Prentice-Hall.

Daft, R. L. & Weick, K. (1984). Toward a model of organizations as interpretation systems. *Academy of Management Review*, 9, 284–295.

Daily, C. M. (1995). The relationship between board composition and leadership structure and bankruptcy reorganization outcomes. *Journal of Management*, 21, 1041–1056.

Darr, E. D., Argote, L., & Epple, D. (1995). The acquisition, transfer, and depreciation of knowledge in service organizations: Productivity in franchises. *Management Science*, 41, 1750–1762.

D'Aveni, R. A. & Kesner, I. F. (1993). Top managerial prestige, power, and tender offer response: A study of elite social networks and target firm cooperation during takeovers. *Organization Science*, 4, 123–151.

Day, D. L., Lewin, A. Y., & Li, H. (1995). Strategic leaders or strategic groups: A longitudinal data envelopment analysis of the U.S. brewing industry. *European Journal of Operational Research*, 80, 619–638.

Delacroix, J. & Carroll, G. R. (1983). Organizational foundings: An ecological study of the newspaper industries of Argentina and Ireland. *Administrative Science Quarterly*, 28, 274–291.

Delacroix, J. & Swaminathan, A. (1991). Cosmetic, speculative, and adaptive organizational change in the wine industry: A longitudinal study. *Administrative Science Quarterly*, 36, 631–661.

Delacroix, J., Swaminathan, A., & Solt, M. E. (1989). Density dependence versus population dynamics: An ecological study of failings in the California

wine industry. *American Sociological Review*, 54, 245–262.

Demsetz, H. (1973). Industry structure, market rivalry, and public policy. *Journal of Law and Economics*, 16, 1–10.

DeSanctis, G. & Poole, M. S. (1994). Capturing the complexity in advanced technology use: Adaptive structuration theory. *Organization Science*, 5, 121–147.

Dierickx, I. & Cool, K. (1989). Asset stock accumulation and sustainability of competitive advantage. *Management Science*, 35, 1504–1511.

DiMaggio, P. J. (1988). Interest and agency in institutional theory. In L. G. Zucker (Ed.), *Institutional patterns and organizations: Culture and environment* (pp. 3–21) Cambridge, MA: Ballinger.

DiMaggio, P. J. & Powell, W. W. (1983). The iron cage revisited: Institutional isomorphism and collective rationality in organizational fields. *American Sociological Review*, 48, 147–160.

DiMaggio, P. J. & Powell W. W. (1991). Introduction. In W. W. Powell & P. J. DiMaggio (Eds.), *The new institutionalism in organizational analysis* (pp. 1–38). Chicago: University of Chicago Press.

Donaldson, L. (1985). Organization design and the life-cycles of products. *Journal of Management Studies*, 22, 25–37.

Donaldson, L. (1995). *American anti-management theories of organization: A critique of paradigm proliferation*. Cambridge, UK: Cambridge University Press.

Donaldson, L. (1996a). *For positivist organization theory*. London: Sage.

Donaldson, L. (1996b). The normal science of structural contingency theory. In S. R. Clegg, C. Hardy, & W. R. Nord (Eds.), *Handbook of organization studies* (pp. 77–114). London: Sage.

Dosi, G., Nelson, R. R., and Winter, S. G. (Eds.) (2000). *The nature of dynamics of organizational capabilities*. Oxford: Oxford University Press.

Dosi, G., Teece, D., and Winter, S. (1992). Towards a theory of corporate change: Preliminary remarks. In G. Dosi, R. Giannetti, & P. A. Toninelli (Eds.), *Technology and Enterprise in a Historical Perspective* (pp. 185–211). Oxford: Clarendon Press.

Doz, Y. L. (1996). The evolution of cooperation in strategic alliances: Initial conditions or learning processes? *Strategic Management Journal*, 17, 55–83.

Drazin, R. & Van de Ven, A. H. (1985). Alternative forms of fit in contingency theory. *Administrative Science Quarterly*, 30, 514–539.

Dutton, J. M., Thomas, A., & Butler, J. E. (1984). The history of progress functions as a managerial technology. *Business History Review*, 58, 204–233.

Dyer, J. H. (1996a). Does governance matter? Keiretsu alliances and asset specificity as sources of Japanese competitive advantage. *Organization Science*, 7, 649–666.

Dyer, J. H. (1996b). Specialized supplier networks as a source of competitive advantage: Evidence from the auto industry. *Strategic Management Journal*, 17, 271–291.

Dyer, J. H. (1997). Effective interfirm collaboration: How firms minimize transaction costs and maximize transaction value. *Strategic Management Journal*, 18, 535–556.

Eisenhardt, K. M. (1989). Making fast strategic decisions in high-velocity environments. *Academy of Management Journal*, 32, 543–576.

Fennell, M. L. & Alexander, J. A. (1987). Organizational boundary spanning in institutionalized environments. *Academy of Management Journal*, 30, 456–476.

Festinger, L. (1954). A theory of social comparison processes. *Human Relations*, 7, 117–140.

Fiegenbaum, A. & Thomas, H. (1990). Strategic groups and performance: The U.S. insurance industry, 1970–1984. *Strategic Management Journal*, 11, 197–215.

Fiegenbaum, A. & Thomas, H. (1995). Strategic groups as reference groups: Theory, modeling, and empirical examination of industry and competitive strategy. *Strategic Management Journal*, 16, 461–476.

Finkelstein, S. (1997). Interindustry merger patterns and resource dependence: A replication and extension of Pfeffer 1972. *Strategic Management Journal*, 18, 787–810.

Fiol, C. M. & Lyles, M. A. (1985). Organizational learning. *Academy of Management Review*, 10, 803–813.

Fligstein, N. (1985). The spread of the multidivisional form among large firms, 1919–1979. *American Sociological Review*, 50, 377–391.

Fligstein, N. (1996). Markets as politics: A political-cultural approach to market institutions. *American Sociological Review*, 61, 656–673.

Fombrun, C. J. (1986). Structural dynamics within and between organizations. *Administrative Science Quarterly*, 31, 403–421.

Foss, N. J., Knudsen, C., & Montgomery, C. A. (1995). An exploration of common ground: Integrating evolutionary and strategic theories of the firm. In C. A. Montgomery (Ed.), *Resource-based and evolutionary theories of the firm: Towards a synthesis* (pp. 1–42). Boston: Kluwer Academic.

Fox-Wolfgramm, S. J., Boal, K. B., & Hunt, J. G. (1998). Organizational adaptation to institutional change: A comparative study of first-order change in pro-spector and defender banks. *Administrative Science Quarterly*, 43, 87–126.

Freeman, J., Carroll, G. R., & Hannan, M. T. (1983). The liability of newness: Age dependence in organizational death rates. *American Sociological Review*, 48, 692–710.

Galaskiewicz, J. & Wasserman, S. (1989). Mimetic processes within an interorganizational field: An empirical test. *Administrative Science Quarterly*, 34, 454–479.

Garud, R. & Van de Ven, A. H. (1992). An empirical evaluation of the internal corporate venturing process. *Strategic Management Journal*, 13, 93–109.

Geroski, P. A. (1988). In pursuit of monopoly power: Recent quantitative work in industrial economics. *Journal of Applied Econometrics*, 3, 107–123.

Gersick, C. J. G. (1988). Time and transition in work teams: Toward a new model of group development. *Academy of Management Journal*, 31, 9–41.

Gersick, C. J. G. (1989). Marking time: Predictable transitions in task groups. *Academy of Management Journal*, 32, 274–309.

Gersick, C. J. G. (1991). Revolutionary change theories: A multilevel exploration of the punctuated equilibrium paradigm. *Academy of Management Review*, 16, 10–36.

Ginsberg, A. & Venkatraman, N. (1985). Contingency perspectives of organizational strategy: A critical review of the empirical research. *Academy of Management Review*, 10, 421–434.

Godfrey, P. C. & Hill, C. W. L. (1995). The problem of unobservables in strategic management research. *Strategic Management Journal*, 16, 519–533.

Goodstein, J. D. (1994). Institutional pressures and strategic responsiveness: Employer involvement on work-family issues. *Academy of Management Journal*, 37, 350–376.

Grandori, A. & Kogut, B. (2002). Dialogue on organization and knowledge. *Organization Science*, 3, 224–231.

Grant, R. M. (1996). Toward a knowledge-based theory of the firm. *Strategic Management Journal*, 17, 109–122.

Granovetter, M. (1985). Economic action and social structure: The problem of embeddedness. *American Journal of Sociology*, 91, 481–510.

Green, S. G. & Welsh, M. A. (1988). Cybernetics and dependence: Reframing the control concept. *Academy of Management Review*, 13, 287–301.

Greening, D. W. & Gray, B. (1994). Testing a model of organizational response to social and political issues. *Academy of Management Journal*, 37, 467–498.

Greenwood, R. & Hinings, C. R. (1996). Understanding radical organizational change: Bringing together the old and the new institutionalism. *Academy of Management Review, 21*, 1022–1054.

Greiner, L. E. (1972). Evolution and revolution as organizations grow. *Harvard Business Review, 50*, 37–46.

Gresov, C. (1989). Exploring fit and misfit with multiple contingencies. *Administrative Science Quarterly, 34*, 431–453.

Gresov, C. & Drazin, R. (1997). Equifinality: Functional equivalence in organization design. *Academy of Management Review, 22*, 403–428.

Grether, E. T. (1970). Industrial organization: Past history and future problems. *American Economic Review, 60*, 83–89.

Greve, H. R. (1995). Jumping ship: The diffusion of strategy abandonment. *Administrative Science Quarterly, 40*, 444–473.

Greve, H. R. (1998). Performance, aspirations, and risky organizational change. *Administrative Science Quarterly, 43*, 58–86.

Greve, H. R. (2003). *Organizational learning from performance feedback—A behavioral perspective on innovation and change.* Cambridge: Cambridge University Press.

Haleblian, J. & Finkelstein, S. (1999). The influence of organizational acquisition experience on acquisition performance: A behavioral learning perspective. *Administrative Science Quarterly, 44*, 29–56.

Hambrick, D. C. (1983). Some tests of the effectiveness of functional attributes of Miles and Snow's strategic types. *Academy of Management Journal, 26*, 5–26.

Hamel, G. (1991). Competition for competence and inter-partner learning within international strategic alliances. *Strategic Management Journal, 12*, 83–103.

Hannan, M. T. & Carroll, G. R. (1992). *Dynamics of organizational populations: Density, competition, and legitimation.* New York: Oxford University Press.

Hannan, M. T. & Freeman, J. (1977). The population ecology of organizations. *American Journal of Sociology, 82*, 929–964.

Hannan, M. T. & Freeman, J. (1984). Structural inertia and organizational change. *American Sociological Review, 49*, 149–164.

Hannan, M. T. & Freeman, J. (1987). The ecology of organizational founding: American labor unions, 1836–1985. *American Journal of Sociology, 92*, 910–943.

Hannan, M. T. & Freeman, J. (1989). *Organizational ecology.* Cambridge, MA: Harvard University Press.

Hannan, M. T., Carroll, G. R., Dundon, R. E., & Torres, J. C. (1995). Organizational evolution in a multinational context: Entries of automobile manufacturers in Belgium, Britain, France, Germany, and Italy. *American Sociological Review, 60*, 509–528.

Hansen, G. & Wernerfelt, B. (1989). Determinants of firm performance: The relative importance of economic and organizational factors. *Strategic Management Journal, 10*, 399–411.

Haveman, H. A. (1992). Between a rock and a hard place: Organizational change and performance under conditions of fundamental environmental transformation. *Administrative Science Quarterly, 37*, 48–75.

Haveman, H. A. (1993a). Organizational size and change: Diversification in the savings and loan industry after deregulation. *Administrative Science Quarterly, 38*, 20–50.

Haveman, H. A. (1993b). Follow the leader: Mimetic isomorphism and entry into new markets. *Administrative Science Quarterly, 38*, 593–627.

Hawley, A. (1968). Human ecology. In D. L. Sills (Ed.), *International encyclopedia of the social sciences* (pp. 328–337). New York: Macmillan.

Hedberg, B. (1981). How organizations learn and unlearn. In P. C. Nystrom & W. H. Starbuck (Eds.), *Handbook of organizational design* (pp. 3–27). London: Oxford University Press.

Henderson, R. M. & Clark, K. B. (1990). Architectural innovation: The reconfiguration of existing product technologies and the failure of established firms. *Administrative Science Quarterly, 35*, 9–30.

Hennart, J. F. (1993). Explaining the swollen middle: Why most transactions are a mix of "market" and "hierarchy." *Organization Science, 4*, 529–547.

Herriott, S. R., Levinthal, D., & March, J. G. (1985). Learning from experience in organizations. *American Economic Review, 75*, 298–302.

Hitt, M. A. & Ireland, R. D. (1985). Corporate distinctive competence, strategy, industry, and performance. *Strategic Management Journal, 6*, 273–293.

Hrebiniak, L. G. & Joyce, W. F. (1985). Organizational adaptation: Strategic choice and environmental determinism. *Administrative Science Quarterly, 30*, 336–349.

Huber, G. P. (1991). Organizational learning: The contributing processes and the literatures. *Organization Science, 2*, 88–115.

Hunt, M. S. (1972). *Competition in the major home appliance industry, 1960–1970.* Unpublished doctoral dissertation, Harvard University.

Ingram, P. & Baum, J. A. C. (1997a). Opportunity and constraint: Organizations' learning from the operating and competitive experience of industries. *Strategic Management Journal, 18*, 75–98.

Ingram, P. & Baum, J. A. C. (1997b). Chain affiliation and the failure of Manhattan hotels, 1898–1980. *Administrative Science Quarterly, 42*, 68–102.

James, W. L. & Hatten, K. J. (1994). Evaluating the performance effects of M&S strategic archetypes in banking, 1983–1987: Big or small. *Journal of Business Research, 31*, 145–154.

James, W. L. & Hatten, K. J. (1995). Further evidence on the validity of the self typing paragraph approach: Miles and Snow strategic archetypes in banking. *Strategic Management Journal, 16*, 161–168.

Johnson, J. L., Daily, C. M., & Ellstrand, A. E. (1996). Boards of directors: A review and research agenda. *Journal of Management, 22*, 409–438.

Kaplan, S. N. & Minton, B. A. (1994). Appointments of outsiders to Japanese boards: Determinants and implications for managers. *Journal of Financial Economics, 36*, 225–258.

Kelly, D. & Amburgey, T. L. (1991). Organizational inertia and momentum: A dynamic model of strategic change. *Academy of Management, 34*, 591–612.

Khandwalla, P. N. (1977). *The design of organizations.* New York: Harcourt Brace Jovanovich.

Kim, L. (1998). Crisis construction and organizational learning: Capability building in catching-up at Hyundai motor. *Organization Science, 9*, 506–521.

Klein, B. (1988). Vertical integration as organized ownership: The Fisher Body–General Motors relationship revisited. *Journal of Law, Economics, & Organization, 4*, 199–213.

Kogut, B. & Zander, U. (1992). Knowledge of the firm, combinative capabilities, and the replication of technology. *Organization Science, 3*, 383–397.

Korn, H. J. & Baum, J. A. C. (1999). Chance, imitative, and strategic antecedents to multimarket contact. *Academy of Management Journal, 42*, 171–193.

Koza, M. P. & Lewin, A. Y. (1998). The co-evolution of strategic alliances. *Organization Science, 9*, 255–264.

Kraatz, M. S. & Zajac, E. J. (1996). Exploring the limits of the new institutionalism: The causes and consequences of illegitimate organizational change. *American Sociological Review, 61*, 812–836.

Lane, P. J. & Lubatkin, M. (1998). Relative absorptive capacity and interorganizational learning. *Strategic Management Journal, 19*, 461–477.

Lang, J. R. & Lockhart, D. E. (1990). Increased environmental uncertainty and changes in board linkage patterns. *Academy of Management Journal, 33*, 106–128.

Lant, T. K. (1992). Aspiration level updating: An empirical exploration. *Management Science, 38*, 623–644.

Lant, T. K., Milliken, F. J., & Batra, B. (1992). The role of managerial learning and interpretation in strategic persistence and reorientation: An empirical exploration. *Strategic Management Journal, 13*, 585–608.

Lawless, M. W. & Finch, L. K. (1989). Choice and determinism: A test of Hrebiniak and Joyce's framework on strategy-environment fit. *Strategic Management Journal, 10*, 351–365.

Lawrence, P. R. & Lorsch, J. W. (1967). *Organization and environment: Managing differentiation and integration.* Cambridge, MA: Harvard University Press.

Leonard-Barton, D. (1992). Core capabilities and core rigidities: A paradox in manging new product development. *Strategic Management Journal, 13*, 111–125.

Levins, R. (1968). *Evolution in changing environments.* Princeton, NJ: Princeton University Press.

Levinthal, D. A. & Warglein, M. (1999). Landscape design: Designing for local action in complex worlds. *Organization Science, 10*, 342–357.

Levinthal, D. A. & March, J. G. (1981). A model of adaptive organizational search. *Journal of Economic Behavior and Organization, 2*, 307–333.

Levinthal, D. A. & March, J. G. (1993). The myopia of learning. *Strategic Management Journal, 14*, 95–112.

Levitt, B. & March, J. G. (1988). Organizational learning. *Annual Review of Sociology, 14*, 319–340.

Levitt, B. & Nass, C. (1989). The lid on the garbage can: Institutional constraints on decision making in the technical core of college-text publishers. *Administrative Science Quarterly, 34*, 190–207.

Levy, D. T. (1985). The transaction cost approach to vertical integration: An empirical examination. *Review of Economics and Statistics, 67*, 438–445.

Lewin, K., Dembo, T., Festinger, L., & Sears, P. (1944). Level of aspiration. In J. M. Hunt (Ed.), *Personality and the behavior disorder* (vol. 1). New York: Ronald.

Lewin, A. Y. & Volberda, H. (1999). Prolegomena on coevolution: A famework for research on strategy and new organizational forms. *Organization Science, 10*, 519–534.

Lewin, A. Y. & Massini, S. (2004). Knowledge creation capabilities of innovating and imitating firms. In H. Tsoukas & N. Mylonopoulos (Eds.), *Organizations as knowledge systems.* London: Palgrave.

Lewin, A. Y., Long, C. P., & Carroll, T. N. (1999). The coevolution of new organizational forms. *Organization Science, 10*, 535–550.

Lewis, P. & Thomas, H. (1990). The linkage between strategy, strategic groups, and performance in the U. K. retail grocery industry. *Strategic Management Journal, 11*, 385–397.

Lieberman, M. B. (1991). Determinants of vertical integration: An empirical test. *Journal of Industrial Economics, 39*, 451–466.

Lieberman, M. B. & Montgomery, D. B. (1988). First-mover advantages. *Strategic Management Journal, 9*, 41–58.

Lieberman, M. B. & Montgomery, D. B. (1998). First-mover (dis)advantages: Retrospective and link with the resource-based view. *Strategic Management Journal*, 19, 1111–1125.

Lincoln, J. R., Gerlach, M. L., & Takahashi, P. (1992). Keiretsu networks in the Japanese economy: A dyad analysis of intercorporate ties. *American Sociological Review*, 57, 561–585.

Lippman, S. A. & Rumelt, R. P. (1982). Uncertain imitability: An analysis of interfirm differences in efficiency under competition. *Bell Journal of Economics*, 13, 418–438.

Low, M. B. & MacMillan, I. C. (1988). Entrepreneurship: Past research and future challenges. *Journal of Management*, 14, 139–161.

MacDonald, J. M. (1985). Market exchange or vertical integration: An empirical analysis. *Review of Economics and Statistics*, 67, 327–331.

Madhok, A. (1997). Cost, value, and foreign market entry mode: The transaction and the firm. *Strategic Management Journal*, 18, 39–61.

Mahoney, J. T. & Pandian, J. R. (1992). The resource-based view within the conversation of strategic management. *Strategic Management Journal*, 13, 363–380.

Makadok, R. (1998). Can first-mover and early-mover advantages be sustained in an industry with low barriers to entry/imitation? *Strategic Management Journal*, 19, 683–696.

Makadok, R. & Walker, G. (1996). Search and selection in the money market fund industry. *Strategic Management Journal*, 17, 39–54.

Makhija, M. V. & Ganesh, U. (1997). The relationship between control and partner learning in learning-related joint ventures. *Organization Science*, 8, 508–527.

Malatesta, P. H. (1983). The wealth effect of merger activity and the objective functions of merging firms. *Journal of Financial Economics*, 11, 155–181.

March, J. G. (1966). The power of power. In D. Easton (Ed.), *Varieties of Political Theory* (pp. 39–70). Englewood Cliffs, N.J.: Prentice-Hall.

March, J. G. (1981). Footnotes to organizational change. *Administrative Science Quarterly*, 26, 563–577.

March, J. G. (1991). Exploration and exploitation in organizational learning. *Organization Science*, 2, 71–87.

March, J. G. & Olsen, J. P. (1975). The uncertainty of the past: Organizational learning under ambiguity. *European Journal of Political Research*, 3, 147–171.

March, J. G. & Olsen, J. P. (1976). Organizational choice under ambiguity. In J. G. March & J. P. Olsen (Eds.), *Ambiguity and choice in organizations* (pp. 10–29). Bergen: Universitetsforlaget.

March, J. G. & Simon, H. A. (1958). *Organizations*. New York: Wiley.

Marlin, D., Lamont, B. T., & Hoffman, J. J. (1994). Choice situation, strategy, and performance: A reexamination. *Strategic Management Journal*, 15, 229–239.

Martinez, R. J. & Dacin, M. T. (1999). Efficiency motives and normative forces: Combining transaction costs and institutional logic. *Journal of Management*, 25, 75–96.

Mascarenhas, B. & Aaker, D. A. (1989). Strategy over the business cycle. *Strategic Management Journal*, 10, 199–210.

Mason, E. S. (1959). *The corporation in modern society*. Cambridge: Harvard University Press.

Masten, S. E., Meehan, J. W., Jr., & Snyder, E. A. (1989). Vertical integration in the U.S. auto industry: A note on the influence of specific assets. *Journal of Economic Behavior and Organization*, 12, 265–273.

Masten, S. E., Meehan J. W., Jr., & Snyder, E. A. (1991). The costs of organization. *Journal of Law, Economics, and Organization*, 7, 1–25.

Mauri, A. J. & Michaels, M. P. (1998). Firm and industry effects within strategic management: An empirical examination. *Strategic Management Journal*, 19, 211–219.

McKelvey, B. (1998). Avoiding complexity catastrophe in coevolutionary pockets: Strategies for rugged landscapes. *Organization Science*, 10, 298–321.

Meyer, A. D., Brooks, G. R., & Goes, J. B. (1990). Environmental jolts and industry revolutions: Organizational responses to discontinuous change. *Strategic Management Journal*, 11, 93–110.

Meyer, J. W. & Rowan, B. (1977). Institutionalized organizations: Formal structure as myth and ceremony. *American Journal of Sociology*, 83, 340–363.

Meyer, M. W. & Zucker, L. G. (1990). Permanently failing organizations. *Academy of Management Review*, 15, 706.

Mezias, S. J. & Lant, T. K. (1994). Mimetic learning and the evolution of organizational populations. In J. A. C. Baum & J. V. Singh (Eds.), *Evolutionary dynamics of organizations* (pp. 179–198). New York: Oxford University Press.

Miles, R. E. & Snow, C. C. (1978). *Organizational strategy, structure, and process*. New York: McGraw-Hill.

Miles, R. E. & Snow, C. C. (1994). *Fit, failure, and the hall of fame: How companies succeed or fail*. New York: Free Press.

Miller, D. & Friesen, P. H. (1980). Momentum and revolution in organizational adaptation. *Academy of Management Journal*, 23, 591–614.

Miller, D. & Friesen, P. H. (1982). Structural change and performance: Quantum vs. piecemeal-incremental approaches. *Academy of Management Journal*, 25, 867–892.

Miller, D. & Friesen, P. H. (1984). *Organizations: A quantum view*. Englewood Cliffs, NJ: Prentice-Hall.

Miner, A. S. & Haunschild, P. R. (1995). Population level learning. *Research in Organizational Behavior*, 17, 115–166.

Miner, A. S. & Mezias, S. J. (1996). Ugly duckling no more: Pasts and futures of organizational learning research. *Organization Science*, 7, 88–99.

Mitchell, W. (1989). Whether and when? Probability and timing of incumbents' entry into emerging industrial subfields. *Administrative Science Quarterly*, 34, 208–230.

Mitchell, W. (1994). The dynamics of evolving markets: The effects of business sales and age on dissolutions and divestitures. *Administrative Science Quarterly*, 39, 575–602.

Mizruchi, M. S. & Fein, L. C. (1999). The social construction of organizational knowledge: A study of the uses of coercive, mimetic, and normative isomorphism. *Administrative Science Quarterly*, 44, 653–683.

Monteverde, K. (1995). Technical dialog as an incentive for vertical integration in the semiconductor industry. *Management Science*, 41, 1624–1638.

Monteverde, K. & Teece, D. J. (1982). Supplier switching costs and vertical integration in the automobile industry. *Bell Journal of Economics*, 13, 206–213.

Montgomery, C. A. & Hariharan, S. (1991). Diversified entry by established firms. *Journal of Economic Behavior and Organization*, 15, 71–89.

Montgomery, C. A. & Wernerfelt, B. (1988). Diversification, Ricardian rents, and Tobin's q. *Rand Journal of Economics*, 19, 623–632.

Nelson, R. R. (1991). Why do firms differ, and how does it matter? *Strategic Management Journal*, 12, 61–74.

Nelson, R. R. (1995). Recent evolutionary theorizing about economic change. *Journal of Economic Literature*, 33, 48–90.

Nelson, R. R. & Winter, S. G. (1973). Toward an evolutionary theory of economic capabilities. *American Economic Review*, 63, 440–449.

Nelson, R. R. & Winter, S. G. (1974). Neoclassical vs. evolutionary theories of economic growth: Critique and Prospectus. *Economic Journal*, 84, 886–905.

Nelson, R. R. & Winter, S. G. (1982). *An evolutionary theory of economic change*. Cambridge, MA: Harvard University Press.

Newman, H. H. (1978). Strategic groups and the structure-performance relationship. *Review of Economics and Statistics*, 60, 417–427.

Ohanian, N. K. (1994). Vertical integration in the U.S. pulp and paper industry, 1900–1940. *Review of Economics and Statistics*, 76, 202–207.

Oliver, C. (1991). Strategic responses to institutional processes. *Academy of Management Review*, 16, 145–179.

Oster, S. (1982). Intraindustry structure and the ease of strategic change. *Review of Economics and Statistics*, 64, 376–383.

Palepu, K. (1985). Diversification strategy, profit performance, and the entropy measure. *Strategic Management Journal*, 6, 239–255.

Palmer, D., Barber, B. M., & Zhou, X. (1995). The friendly and predatory acquisition of large U.S. corporations in the 1960s: The other contested terrain. *American Sociological Review*, 60, 469–499.

Palmer, D. A., Jennings, P. D., & Zhou, X. (1993). Late adoption of the multidivisional form by large U.S. corporations: Institutional, political, and economic accounts. *Administrative Science Quarterly*, 38, 100–131.

Pearce, J. A. & Zahra, S. A. (1992). Board composition from a strategic contingency perspective. *Journal of Management Studies*, 29, 411–438.

Pennings, J. M. (1987). Structural contingency theory: A multivariate test. *Organization Studies*, 8, 223–240.

Pennings, J. M., Barkema, H., & Douma, S. (1994). Organizational learning and diversification. *Academy of Management Journal*, 37, 608–640.

Penrose, E. T. (1959). *The theory of the growth of the firm*. White Plains, NY: M. E. Sharpe.

Peteraf, M. (1993). The cornerstones of competitive advantage: A resource-based view. *Strategic Management Journal*, 14, 179–191.

Pfeffer, J. (1972a). Merger as a response to organizational interdependence. *Administrative Science Quarterly*, 17, 382–394.

Pfeffer, J. (1972b). Size and composition of corporate boards of directors: The organization and its environment. *Administrative Science Quarterly*, 17, 218–228.

Pfeffer, J. (1982). *Organizations and organization theory*. Boston: Pitman.

Pfeffer, J. (1993). Barriers to the advance of organization science: Paradigm development as a dependent variable. *Academy of Management Review*, 18, 599–620.

Pfeffer, J. & Salancik, G. R. (1978). *The external control of organizations: A resource dependence perspective*. New York: Harper and Row.

Podolny, J. M. (1994). Market uncertainty and the social character of economic exchange. *Administrative Science Quarterly*, 39, 458–483.

Podolny, J. M. & Stuart, T. E. (1995). A role-based ecology of technological change. *American Journal of Sociology, 100,* 1224–1260.

Poppo, L. (1995). Influence activities and strategic coordination: Two distinctions of internal and external markets. *Management Science, 41,* 1845–1859.

Poppo, L. & Zenger, T. (1998). Testing alternative theories of the firm: Transaction cost, knowledge-based, and measurement explanations for make-or-buy decisions in information services. *Strategic Management Journal, 19,* 853–877.

Porter, M. E. (1979). The structure within industries and companies' performance. *Review of Economics and Statistics, 61,* 214–227.

Porter, M. E. (1980). *Competitive strategy: Techniques for analyzing industries and competitors.* New York: Free Press.

Porter, M. E. (1981). The contributions of industrial organization to strategic management. *Academy of Management Review, 6,* 609–620.

Porter, M. E. (1985). *Competitive advantage: Creating and sustaining superior performance.* New York: Free Press.

Porter, M. E. (1991). Towards a dynamic theory of strategy. *Strategic Management Journal, 12,* 95–117.

Prahalad, C. K. & Hamel, G. (1990). The core competence of the corporation. *Harvard Business Review, 68,* 79–91.

Pugh, D. S., Hickson, D. J., Hinings, C. R., & Turner, C. (1969). The context of organization structures. *Administrative Science Quarterly, 14,* 91–114.

Ramanujam, V. & Varadarajan, P. (1989). Research on corporate diversification: A synthesis. *Strategic Management Journal, 10,* 523–551.

Ranger-Moore, J., Banaszak-Holl, J., & Hannan, M. T. (1991). Density-dependent dynamics in regulated industries: Founding rates of banks and life insurance companies. *Administrative Science Quarterly, 36,* 36–65.

Reed, R. & DeFillippi, R. J. (1990). Causal ambiguity, barriers to imitation, and sustainable competitive advantage. *Academy of Management Review, 15,* 88–102.

Roberts, P. W. & Greenwood, R. (1997). Integrating transaction cost and institutional theories: Toward a constrained-efficiency framework for understanding organizational design adoption. *Academy of Management Review, 22,* 346–373.

Robins, J. & Wiersema, M. F. (1995). A resource-based approach to the multibusiness firm: Empirical analysis of portfolio interrelationships and corporate financial performance. *Strategic Management Journal, 16,* 277–299.

Robinson, W., Fornell, C., & Sullivan, M. (1992). Are market pioneers intrinsically stronger than later entrants? *Strategic Management Journal, 13,* 609–624.

Romanelli, E. & Tushman, M. L. (1994). Organizational transformation as punctuated equilibrium: An empirical test. *Academy of Management Journal, 37,* 1141–1166.

Rouse, M. J. & Daellenbach, U.S. (1999). Rethinking research methods for the resource-based perspective: Isolating sources of sustainable competitive advantage. *Strategic Management Journal, 20,* 487–494.

Rumelt, R. P. (1974). *Strategy, structure, and economic performance.* Cambridge, MA: Harvard University Press.

Rumelt, R. P. (1984). Towards a strategic theory of the firm. In R. B. Lamb (Ed.), *Competitive strategic management* (pp. 556–570). Englewood Cliffs, NJ: Prentice-Hall.

Rumelt, R. P. (1987). Theory, strategy, and entrepreneurship. In D. J. Teece (Ed.), *The competitive challenge: Strategies for industrial innovation and renewal* (pp. 137–158). Cambridge, MA: Ballinger.

Rumelt, R. P. (1991). How much does industry matter? *Strategic Management Journal, 12,* 167–185.

Schiff, M. and Lewin, A. V. (1970). The impact of people on budgets. *The Accounting Review, XLV,* 259–268.

Schmalensee, R. (1982). Product differentiation advantages of pioneering brands. *American Economic Review, 72,* 349–365.

Schmalensee, R. (1985). Do markets differ much? *American Economic Review, 75,* 341–351.

Schmalensee, R. (1988). Industrial economics: An overview. *Economic Journal, 98,* 643–681.

Schoenecker, T. S. & Cooper, A. C. (1998). The role of firm resources and organizational attributes in determining entry timing: A cross-industry study. *Strategic Management Journal, 19,* 1127–1143.

Schumpeter, J. A. (1934). *The theory of economic development.* Cambridge, MA: Harvard University Press.

Schumpeter, J. A. (1950). *Capitalism, socialism, and democracy.* New York: Harper.

Scott, W. R. (1987). The adolescence of institutional theory. *Administrative Science Quarterly, 32,* 493–511.

Scott, W. R. (1991). *Unpacking institutional arguments.* In W. W. Powell & P. J. DiMaggio (Eds.), *The new institutionalism in organizational analysis* (pp. 143–163). Chicago: University of Chicago Press.

Scott, W. R. (1998). *Organizations: Rational, natural, and open systems.* Englewood Cliffs, NJ: Prentice-Hall.

Selznick, P. (1948). Foundations of the theory of organization. *American Sociological Review*, 13, 25–35.

Selznick, P. (1949). *TVA and the grass roots*. Berkeley: University of California Press.

Selznick, P. (1957). *Leadership in administration*. New York: Harper & Row.

Sharma, A. & Kesner, I. (1996). Diversifying entry: Some ex ante explanations for postentry survival and growth. *Academy of Management Journal*, 39, 635–677.

Shelanski, H. A. & Klein, P. G. (1995). Empirical research in transaction cost economics: A review and assessment. *Journal of Law, Economics, & Organization*, 11, 335–361.

Shortell, S. M. & Zajac, E. J. (1990). Perceptual and archival measures of Miles and Snow's strategic types: A comprehensive assessment of reliability and validity. *Academy of Management Journal*, 33, 817–832.

Silverman, B. S. (1999). Technological resources and the direction of corporate diversification: Toward an integration of the resource-based view and transaction cost economics. *Management Science*, 45, 1109–1124.

Singh, H. & Montgomery, C. (1987). Corporate acquisition strategies and economic performance. *Strategic Management Journal*, 8, 377–386.

Singh, J. V. (1986). Performance, slack, and risk taking in organizational decision making. *Academy of Management Journal*, 29, 562–585.

Singh, J. V. & Lumsden, C. J. (1990). Theory and research in organizational ecology. *Annual Review of Sociology*, 16, 161–195.

Singh, J. V., House, R. J., & Tucker, D. J. (1986). Organizational change and organizational mortality. *Administrative Science Quarterly*, 31, 587–611.

Snow, C. C. & Hrebiniak, L. G. (1980). Strategy, distinctive competence, and organizational performance. *Administrative Science Quarterly*, 25, 317–335.

Solow, R. M. (1956). A contribution to the theory of economic growth. *The Quarterly Journal of Economics*, 70, 65–94.

Solow, R. M. (1957). Technical change and the aggregate production function. *The Review of Economics and Statistics*, 39, 312–320.

Stearns, L. B. & Mizruchi, M. S. (1993). Board composition and corporate financing: The impact of financial institution representation on borrowing. *Academy of Management Journal*, 36, 603–618.

Stinchcombe, A. L. (1965). Social structure and organizations. In J. G. March (Ed.), *Handbook of organizations* (pp. 142–193). Chicago: Rand-McNally.

Strang, D. & Meyer, J. W. (1993). Institutional conditions for diffusion. *Theory & Sociology*, 22, 487–512.

Strang, D. & Soule, S. A. (1998). Diffusion in organizations and social movements: From hybrid corn to poison pill. *Annual Review of Sociology*, 24, 265–290.

Stuart, T. E. & Podolny, J. M. (1996). Local search and the evolution of technological capabilities. *Strategic Management Journal*, 17, 21–38.

Sutton, R. I. & Callahan, A. L. (1987). The stigma of bankruptcy: Spoiled organizational image and its management. *Academy of Management Journal*, 30, 405–436.

Sydow, J. & Windeler, A. (1998). Organizing and evaluating interfirm networks: A structurationist perspective on networks and effectiveness. *Organization Science*, 4, 265–285.

Szulanski, G. (1996). Exploring internal stickiness: Impediments to the transfer of best practice within the firm. *Strategic Management Journal*, 17, 27–43.

Teece, D. J. (1992). Competition, cooperation and innovation: Organizational arrangements for regimes of rapid technological progress. *Journal of Economic Behavior and Organization*, 18, 1–26.

Teece, D. J., Pisano, G., & Shuen, A. (1997). Dynamic capabilities and strategic management. *Strategic Management Journal*, 18, 509–533.

Thompson, J. D. (1967). *Organizations in action*. New York: McGraw-Hill.

Thornton, P. H. & Ocasio, W. (1999). Institutional logics and the historical contingency of power in organizations: Executive succession in the higher education publishing industry, 1958–1990. *American Journal of Sociology*, 105, 801–843.

Tolbert, P. S. (1985). Institutional environments and resource dependence: Sources of administrative structure in institutions of higher education. *Administrative Science Quarterly*, 30, 1–13.

Tolbert, P. S. & Zucker, L. G. (1983). Institutional sources of change in the formal structure of organizations: The diffusion of civil service reform, 1880–1935. *Administrative Science Quarterly*, 28, 22–39.

Tolbert, P. S. & Zucker, L. G. (1996). The institutionalization of institutional theory. In S. R. Clegg, C. Hardy, & W. R. Nord (Eds.), *Handbook of organization studies* (pp. 175–190). Thousand Oaks, CA: Sage.

Tucker, D. J., Baum, J. A. C., & Singh J. V. (1992). The institutional ecology of human service organizations. In Y. Hasenfeld (Ed.), *Human service organizations* (pp. 47–72). Newbury Park, CA: Sage.

Tucker, D. J., Singh, J. V., & Meinhard, A. G. (1990). Organizational form, population dynamics, and institutional change: The founding patterns of voluntary organizations. *Academy of Management Journal*, 33, 151–178.

Tucker, D. J., Singh, J. V., Meinhard, A. G., & House, R. J. (1988). Ecological and institutional sources of change in organizational populations. In G. R. Carroll (Ed.), *Ecological models of organization* (pp. 127–152). Cambridge, MA: Ballinger.

Tushman, M. L. & Anderson, P. A. (1986). Technological discontinuities and organizational environments. *Administrative Science Quarterly, 31,* 439–465.

Tushman, M. L. & Romanelli, E. (1985). Organizational evolution: A metamorphosis model of convergence and reorientation. In L. L. Cummings & B. M. Staw (Eds.), *Research in organizational behavior* (pp. 171–222). Greenwich, CT: JAI Press.

Tushman, M. L., Newman, W. H., & Romanelli, E. (1986). Convergence and upheaval: Managing the unsteady pace of organizational evolution. *California Management Review, 29,* 1–16.

Utterback, J. M. & Abernathy, W. J. (1975). Dynamic capabilities and strategic management. *Strategic Management Journal, 18,* 509–533.

Varadarajan, P. & Ramanujam, V. (1987). Diversification and performance: A reexamination using a new two-dimensional conceptualization of diversify in firms. *Academy of Management Journal, 30,* 380–397.

Venkatraman, N. & Prescott, J. E. (1990). Environment-strategy coalignment: An empirical test of its performance implications. *Strategic Management Journal, 11,* 1–23.

Virany, B., Tushman, M. L., & Romanelli, E. (1992). Executive succession and organization outcomes in turbulent environments: An organization learning approach. *Organization Science, 3,* 72–91.

Von Werder, A. (2001). *A longitudinal study of Siemenes and AEG.* Paper prsented at the Academy of Management Annual Meeting. Washington, DC.

Walker, G. (1994). Asset choice and supplier performance in two organizations—US and Japanese. *Organization Science, 5,* 583–593.

Walker, G. & Poppo, L. (1991). Profit centers, single-source suppliers, and transaction costs. *Administrative Science Quarterly, 36,* 66–87.

Walker, G. & Weber, D. (1984). A transaction cost approach to make-or-buy decisions. *Administrative Science Quarterly, 29,* 373–391.

Walker, G. & Weber, D. (1987). Supplier competition, uncertainty, and make-or-buy decisions. *Academy of Management Journal, 30,* 589–596.

Walsh, J. P. (1995). Managerial and organizational cognition: Notes from a trip down memory lane. *Organization Science, 6,* 280–321.

Weick, K. E. (1969). *The social psychology of organizing.* Reading, MA: Addison-Wesley.

Weigelt, C. & Lewin, A. Y. (2000). *Performance effects of exploitation exploration merger patterns for U.S. Banks, 1982–1998* (Working paper, Fuqua School of Business). Durham, NC: Author.

Wernerfelt, B. (1984). A resource-based view of the firm. *Strategic Management Journal, 5,* 171–180.

Wernerfelt, B. (1989). From critical resources to corporate strategy. *Journal of General Management, 14,* 4–12.

Wernerfelt, B. & Montgomery, C. A. (1988). Tobin's q and the importance of focus in firm performance. *American Economic Review, 78,* 246–251.

Williamson, O. E. (1975). *Markets and hierarchies.* New York: Free Press.

Williamson, O. E. (1979). Transaction cost economics: The governance of contractual relations. *Journal of Law and Economics, 22,* 233–261.

Williamson, O. E. (1981). The economics of organization: The transaction cost approach. *American Journal of Sociology, 87,* 548–577.

Williamson, O. E. (1985). *The economic institutions of capitalism.* New York: Free Press.

Williamson, O. E. (1991). Strategizing, economizing, and economic organization. *Strategic Management Journal, 23,* 75–94.

Winter, S. G. & Szulanski, G. (2001). Replication as strategy. *Organization Science, 12,* 730–744.

Woodward, J. (1958). *Management and technology.* London: HMSO.

Woodward, J. (1965). *Industrial organization: Theory and practice.* New York: Oxford University Press.

Zahra, S. A. & Pearce, J. A., II (1990). Research evidence on the Miles-Snow typology. *Journal of Management, 16,* 751–768.

Zajac, E. J. & Shortell, S. M. (1989). Changing generic strategies: Likelihood, direction, and performance implications. *Strategic Management Journal, 10,* 413–430.

Zajac, E. J., Kraatz, M. S., & Bresser, R. K. F. (2000). Modeling the dynamics of strategic fit: A normative approach to strategic change. *Strategic Management Journal, 21,* 429–453.

Zander, U. & Kogut, B. (1995). Knowledge and the speed of the transfer and imitation of organizational capabilities: An empirical test. *Organization Science, 6,* 76–92.

Zucker, L. G. (1987). Institutional theories of organization. *Annual Review of Sociology, 13,* 443–464.

Zucker, L. G. (1989). Combining institutional theory and population ecology: No legitimacy, no history. *American Sociological Review, 54,* 542–545.

6

Dynamics of Structural Change

Robert Drazin, Mary Ann Glynn, & Robert K. Kazanjian

The 1960s and 1970s emerged as a critical period in the development of research related to the study of organization structure. The dominant perspective that emerged was structural contingency theory. Classical management theory, which held sway through the first half of the twentieth century, argued that there was a single organization structure that was highly effective in all settings (Donaldson, 1996). In contrast, proponents of contingency theory argued that there was no one best way, and that the appropriate structure must reflect the demands of the context. Burns and Stalker (1961) offered what emerged as one of the most widely cited examples of this perspective. Based on qualitative case studies, they found that stable settings did best with mechanistic structures, while settings characterized by high degrees of environmental and task uncertainty required organic structures. Equally important pioneering research was completed by Lawrence and Lorsch (1967), who proposed that the rate of environmental change should determine the degree of structural differentiation and integration within an organization. Based on a sample of firms in three industries, Lawrence and Lorsch (1967) also found that organizations whose structures fit their environment had higher performance (Donaldson, 1996), making them one of the first researchers to find

a tie between structure and efficiency. This work was consistent with that of Simon (1957) and March and Simon (1958) in relying heavily on an economic focus on markets and rational adaptation to market conditions (Fligstein and Freeland, 1995).

Subsequent research by others during this period expanded the range of contingency factors theorized to influence structure. For example, Chandler (1962) related structure to firm strategy; Woodward (1965) and Perrow (1967) investigated the effects of technology; Thompson (1967) and Galbraith (1973) studied the effects of task uncertainty; Khandwalla (1977) studied the effects of environmental hostility; Dewar and Duncan (1977) related strategies for innovation to structure; and Blau (1970) researched the effects of size on structure.

Also during this period, several centers of research emerged around topics related to organization design, most notably the Aston group (Pugh, Hickson, and Hinings, 1969; Pugh and Hinings, 1976), which concentrated on issues of research measurement and survey methods related to structure. The work of Chandler (1962), Lawrence and Lorsch (1967), and others contributed to a critical mass of research activity related to contingency theory at Harvard. Finally, work by Galbraith (1973), Trist (1963), Van de

Ven (Van de Ven and Delbecq, 1974) and Ferry (Van de Ven and Ferry, 1980) established the Wharton School as a recognized center for the study of organization design as well.

Beginning in the late 1970s and accelerating through the 1980s and 1990s, a marked shift occurred in research related to structure. Several streams of research emerged around the belief that environments are powerful determinants of organizational design. Researchers found that shifts in the environment did not have the straightforward effect on subsequent organizational changes predicted by contingency theory (Fligstein and Freeland, 1995). One such view argues that the power of decision makers within the firm to solve internal resource dependencies is a function of their abilities, knowledge, and links with the outside world. Population ecology (Hannan and Freeman, 1977, 1984) emerged as another perspective related to resource dependence but emphasizing market selection and efficiency principles. This view maintains that change occurs due to selection of organizational forms at the population level, while internal organization change is difficult due to structural inertia.

Institutional theory (DiMaggio and Powell, 1983; DiMaggio, 1988; Scott and Meyer, 1994; Zucker, 1977) represents the most complete conceptual transition away from models based on technical environments and strategic choice, focusing heavily on the socially constructed worlds of organizations (Fligstein and Freeman, 1995). Powell and DiMaggio (1991) explicitly reject rational actor models of organizing, instead arguing for cultural and cognition-based explanations that supercede the actions and motives of individuals. Tolbert and Zucker (1996) note that much of what emerged in the institutional literature as radical new thinking about structure and its role in decision making can be traced to the now classic paper by Meyer and Rowan (1977).

Their analysis was guided by a key insight, namely, formal structures have symbolic as well as action-generating properties. In other words, structures can become invested with socially shared meanings, and thus, in addition to their "objective" functions, can serve to communicate information about the organization to both internal and external audiences. Explaining formal structure from this vantage point offered organizational researchers the opportunity to explore an array of new insights into the causes and consequences of structure (Tolbert and Zucker, 1996, p. 177).

These research perspectives have dominated, if not completely appropriated, the study of structure in recent years. In much of this work, structure is reduced to a dependent variable determined by exogenous institutional forces. Such studies typically rely on large, longitudinal databases that often lack the richness and detail regarding structural change characterized by past research. Burrell and Morgan (1979) presaged this shift in theoretical dominance by identifying a duality across organizational theories. They argued that organization theories were predicated on one of two underlying assumptions—either organizations are socially determined, or they are chosen by autonomous decision makers. Similarly, Astley and Van de Ven (1983) elaborated on this tension in their discussion of the six critical debates implicit in the organization theory literature. One of these central debates centered on the question "Are organizations neutral technical instruments engineered to achieve a goal, or are they institutionalized manifestations of the vested interests of the power structure?" (Astley and Van de Ven, 1983, p. 264). Van de Ven and Poole (1988) labeled this the action-structure paradox. Most theories of organizational structure state that individuals take actions to pursue their own vested interests, but they also recognize that one role of structure is to contain and channel individuals' actions to serve broader goals. The theoretical paradox, according to Van de Ven and Poole, is mirrored in a methodological paradox: most researchers measure variables that reflect social structure but not action.

In summary, much of the research of the 1960s and 1970s assumed that organization structure was consciously designed through a rational decision process, and that the choice of structure was central to firm-level efficiency and performance. We categorize this research as the meso/strategy perspective, given its reliance on internal organizational and strategic determinants of structure. In contrast to this earlier period, subsequent research in the 1980s and 1990s demonstrates a loss of focus on agency and the central role structure plays in determining performance. Instead, current research views structure as the product of a social process emphasizing normatively based conformity and trait imitation. Further, structure is seen not as functional or central to organizational outcomes of efficiency, but rather as instrumental to effectiveness, which is operationalized solely as survival. We categorize this research as the macro/institutional perspective.

By the latter part of the 1990s, research on structure qua structure diminished rapidly with the ascendancy of the macro/institutional perspective. Pockets of interesting ideas within the meso/strategy have surfaced, but none has generated major streams of ongoing work (for example, see studies of gestalts [Miller and Friesen, 1982, 1984], fit [Doty and Glick, 1994; Doty, Glick and Huber, 1993; Van de Ven and Drazin, 1985], and equifinality [Gresov and Drazin, 1996]). No new major perspective related to endogenous organizational change has emerged to take the place of contingency theory. The macro/institutional perspective continues to dominate the literature on structural change.

We consider these trends in academic studies a dramatic counterpoint to the vast literature in the popular press that emphasizes the critical role of organization structure. Topics such as alternative structures (Dess, Rasheed, McLaughlin, and Priem, 1995), emerging organizational designs (Ashkenas, Ulrich, Jick, and Kerr, 1995; Miles, Snow, Matthews, Miles, and Coleman, 1997; Mitroff, Mason, and Pearson, 1994), the centerless corporation (Pasternak and Viscio, 1998), and organizational transformation (Miles, 1997; O'Toole, 1995) are representative of the vast body of work related to structure and directed at practicing managers. Innumerable books have been written on reengineering (Hammer and Champy, 1993), the impact of information technology on design (Lucas, 1996), horizontal organizing (O'Dell and Jackson, 1998; Ostroff, 1999), and "formless" organizations (Purser and Cabana, 1998). Additionally, many publications have appeared recently on specialized structures that deal with project management (Frame, 1994; Larson and Gobelli, 1987), new product development (Clark and Wheelwright, 1995; Imai, Nonaka, and Takeuchi, 1985), teams (Katzenbach and Smith, 1993), and innovation (Tushman and O'Reilly, 1997). This body of work has been oriented toward the organizational practices of the 1990s: downsizing, delayering, process improvement, process flow, organization innovation, e-commerce, virtual organizations, network organizations, and adaptation.

This introduction may seem to suggest the impending death of research on endogenous structural change. In the rest of this chapter, we argue that such a conclusion is premature. Instead, we propose that new perspectives on structure and structural change may lead to a resurgence of interest in mesolevels of organizational analysis. In the second section we

explore the outline of such an approach by introducing the concept of organizational "logics." We define "logics" as cognitions, or organizing principles, encoded in the minds of those who create organizations. These logics are then mapped onto actual organization designs; the cognitive map becomes the organizational territory. We argue that "logics" have a dual character. They simultaneously describe the techno-economic basis of the organization as well as its normative appropriateness. In sections 3 through 5 of the chapter we categorize the literature on structural change as consisting of three domains: (1) change as the establishment and elaboration of logics, (2) change as the breakdown of a previous logic, and (3) change as the logic of anticipation. In each of these three domains we review the existing literature to show how it is built around techno-economic and normative forms of logic. We do not review every theoretical and empirical article but instead examine exemplars. In the sixth section we speculate on what a logics-based approach to organizational change might imply for theories of structural dynamics.

The Concept of Organizational Logics

Logic, according to the dictionary (at www.dictionary. com), is a system of reasoning or formal, guiding principles that articulate "the relationship between elements and between an element and the whole in a set of objects, individuals, principles, or events." Logic can be understood as the underlying cognition or mental model that configures a coherent thought, orders an argument, or arranges a system. The link between logic and structure is hinted at in the very definition of structure, itself described as the "way in which parts are arranged or put together to form a whole; the interrelation or arrangement of parts in a complex entity" (www.dictionary.com). In computer science, logic describes the graphic representation of computer circuitry. In organizations, we argue, logic is the mental conception of how an organization should be structured and then how that conception is mapped onto practice.

In the management literature, the notion of logic has been an important part of theorizing about organizations. In the strategic management literature, Prahalad and Bettis (1986) articulated perhaps one of the earliest and most forceful arguments for considering the role of logic in explicating organizational performance. They advanced the construct of "dominant general management logic" (or more simply, dominant logic), which they define as "the way in which managers conceptualize the business and make critical resource allocation decisions—be it in technologies, product development, distribution, advertising, or in human resource management. These tasks are performed by managing the infrastructure of administrative tools like choice of key individuals, processes of planning, budgeting, control, compensation, career management, and *organizational structure*" (Prahalad and Bettis, 1986, p. 490, emphasis added).

In this formulation, the dominant logic is a cognitive construct, a "mind set or world view" (Prahalad and Bettis, 1986, p. 491) that conceptualizes both the business and the management of the business in order to make decisions, allocate resources, and realize goals. Thus, the notion of how an organization should be structured is embedded within the logic of the enterprise. For instance, Prahald and Bettis (1986, p. 494) note how the logic that drives a firm's diversification strategy also dictates its structure: organizations should be structured so as to reduce or contain the "strategic variety" that executives must manage, often "by creating an intermediate level of general management." Logic guides the development of structure; however, structures, once in place, tend to delimit the further development of managerial logic. Like any cognitive schema, the dominant logic develops and changes as a result of managerial learning, often from experience. If a structure limits the opportunities for more learning, and especially more varied learning, then change in the dominant logic is less likely over time. Changing the dominant logic is often triggered by crisis (Prahalad and Bettis, 1986), encouraging managers to unlearn routinized ways of thinking and behaving (Hedberg, Nystrom, and Starbuck, 1976). In some sense, then, the adaptive ability of the dominant logic hinges on organizational learning, in particular the ability to learn about learning or learn in a double-loop fashion (Argyris and Schon, 1996; Bateson, 1972).

In their original conceptualization, Prahalad and Bettis (1986) invoked the notion of dominant logic to explain the link between a firm's diversification strategy and performance. However, in revisiting their ideas almost a decade later (Bettis and Prahalad, 1994), they note its application is broader than that of diversification-driven organizational change. Arguing

that the dominant logic is "an emergent property of organizations as complex adaptive systems," Bettis and Prahalad (1994, p. 7) suggest that the dominant logic constitutes part of the "underlying structures and foundations" of organizational strategy, structure, and systems, and perhaps something akin to that of "deep structure." More specifically, they argue that "organizational structure and systems...are tightly coupled to the dominant logic and embody parts of it" (p. 10). Thus, change in an organization's structure shapes, and is shaped by, the dominant logic.

At the macro level, the construct of logic has also been used in institutionalists' constructions of organizations and organizational fields. In contrast to strategists, who look to the market and competitive environment for principles of organizing and structuration, institutionalists alert us to the importance of societal forces and institutionalized patterns of meaning, embedded at the interorganizational level of analysis, as key drivers of organizational behavior and form. Thus, institutionalists position the origin of organizational structure at a higher level of analysis, that of the institutional environment. In their influential chapter, Friedland and Alford (1991, p. 243) note that "organizational structures appear to be institutionally patterned in ways which cannot be explained by competitive interaction between organizations, technology, or organization-specific environmental conditions." According to institutional theorists, organizations are mimetic in their adoption of particular forms, practices, and structures because such conformity increases their legitimacy, which, in turn, enhances their ability to elicit and access resources from key sources. The effect has been demonstrated for organizational structures and practices (Abzug and Mezias, 1993; Meyer and Rowan, 1977; Tolbert and Zucker, 1996) as well as strategies (Deephouse, 1996; Fligstein, 1990). More generally, institutional researchers have demonstrated the normative aspects of organizational structures, noting such configurations as the diffusion of the multidivisional form (Fligstein, 1985).

Importantly, though, those institutional orders that characterize organizational fields, as well as specifying other important societal forms, embed a core or central logic, described as:

A set of material practices and symbolic constructions—which constitutes its organizing principles and which is available to organizations and individuals to elaborate. The institutional logic of capitalism is accumulation and the commodification of human activity. That of the state is rationalization and the regulation of human activity by legal and bureaucratic hierarchies. That of democracy is participation and the extension of popular control over human activity. That of the family is community and the motivation of human activity by unconditional loyalty to its members and their reproductive needs. That of religion, or science for that matter, is truth, whether mundane or transcendental, and the symbolic construction of reality within which all human activity takes place. These institutional logics are symbolically grounded, organizationally structured, politically defended, and technically and materially constrained, and hence have specific historical limits. (Friedland and Alford, 1991, pp. 238–249)

Society, then, is constituted by multiple, different, and sometimes conflicting institutional logics; for instance, capitalism, the state, democracy, family, religion, and science all tend to coexist within a society. In turn, organizations, as well as other institutional actors, interpret, manipulate, and codify these understandings in their key symbols and practices (Friedland and Alford, 1991). In a historical analysis of the higher education publishing industry, Thornton and Ocasio (1999) found that institutional logics shifted from an editorial to a market focus, which had important effects on the authority structures within firms, and, in particular, the type and occurrence of executive succession within corporations. Their work reveals a clear link between institutional logic and organizational structure. For instance, "publishing houses under the editorial logic were perhaps best described as quasi-professional firms, where the ideology of the profession is intermixed with a formal hierarchy.... With the shift to a market logic, the professional orientation of the publishing industry declined and was replaced by the logic of Wall Street investment bankers and the increasing concern with profitability and market orientation common to other US industries" (Thornton and Ocasio, 1999, p. 816). The authors note how the historical change in the dominant institutional logic in an industry, that is, from the logic of professions to the logic of markets, determined patterns of succession. Building upon the work of Friedland and Alford (1991), Thornton and Ocasio (1999, p. 803) concluded that institutional logics function as "supra-organizational patterns, both symbolic and material, that order reality and provide

meaning to actions and structure conflicts." More generally, then, institutional theorists conceptualize logics as providing the constitutive rules that shape the cognition of organizational members (DiMaggio, 1997; Powell and DiMaggio, 1991) and thus are regulative in that they specify governing norms, values, and routines for organizations (DiMaggio, 1994).

This is not to imply, however, that such interpretations are immune from environmental and institutional realities. DeSanctis and Poole (1994) alert us to the fact that organizational structures (logics) have a correspondence to reality. DeSanctis and Poole (1994, p. 126) note that social structures of advanced information technology can be described in terms of their "spirit," which they define as "the general intent with regard to values and goals underlying a given set of structural features." They relate spirit to normative frame and legitimation (citing Giddens) and contend that "spirit is a property of the technology as it is presented to users." Thus, social structures are themselves enacted and socially constructed (Weick, 1995), with learning and change promulgated through ongoing practice.

In summary, we view logic as a kind of underlying cognitive "glue" that lends meaning, rationality, and purpose to organizational structures. We define logics as those principles of organizing encoded in the minds of organizational actors (or agents) who create institutions. Moreover, logics have a teleological orientation; agents map out their logics onto real organizations. In turn, these real organizations provide the generative basis for the creation of alternative logics, which allow for change. Thus, there is an iterative and reciprocal process between logic and organizational structuration; each one shapes, contains, and births the other.

More broadly, different types of logic can arise from the competitive market environment and the embedded social and institutional order in which firms operate. Mechanisms that shape logic (and structure) arise from collective understandings, ideologies, and systems of rules that categorize and constitute institutions. This line of thought leads to the more general realization that logics are embedded in wider categories of authoritative classification systems that shape organizational and managerial action (Walsh, 1995).

Logic functions to define the normative appropriateness (legitimacy) of different organizational structures. Logic contains two identifiable components: one is a techno-economic logic, linking means and ends, and the second is a normative logic, binding individuals' values to the techno-economic logic. Both components are inseparably bound together. Normative logics activate production logics; members of an organization have to believe that organizational work and purposefulness are not simply instrumental, but that they also have moral value (Stinchcombe, 1965). Logics also imply agency; influential organizational leaders, a dominant coalition, and/or other collectives, such as work groups, functional departments, or project units, develop logics and interpret and reinterpret them to take action in times of change.

How do organizational logics form and change? How do they move from cognitive constructs to mapped-out structures and routines? Below, we review the literature on structural change through three lenses. First, we examine how change occurs through the establishment and elaboration of organizational logics. Second, given that an organization has an already formulated logic, we examine how change occurs when that logic breaks down. Third, we investigate how change can occur through an anticipatory logic of learning and continual renewal.

Change as the Establishment and Elaboration of Logics

Three research streams have examined how organizations establish and elaborate initial logics. Examining organizational logics was a mainstay of research conducted by the earliest institutional theorists. Essentially, early institutionalism was the study of how logics were initiated and became established. This stream of research was expanded upon by stage-of-growth theorists, whose work sought to understand how organizations started and the logic underlying their growth. Most recently, self-organizing and complexity theory examine the means by which logics come to be and endure.

Early Institutional Theorists

The research of institutionalists, best represented by the work of Selznick (1949) and heavily influenced by that of Barnard (1938), consists of understanding the interrelationship between the two forms of logics. The first logic is one of rationality, whereby organi-

zations are carefully designed according to bureaucratic principles of structuring activities to efficiently achieve desired ends. Here, the institutionalists can be seen as extending the basic principles of bureaucracy as outlined by Weber (1947), but in a less universalistic fashion, recognizing the interplay of an organization with its specific environment. The second logic relates to the centrality of values and principles to organizational legitimacy, constituting what might be considered a logic of morality. Barnard strongly argued that the central purpose of an organization must always be a moral one and that the task of executives is to develop a shared agreement of this purpose among all members throughout the entire organization (Perrow, 1986). Both Selznick (1957) and Parsons (1977) reinforce this notion, arguing that power can survive only if it is legitimate. This notion is built upon assumptions that organizations are cooperative systems and that individuals must be enticed to join voluntarily. As Perrow notes:

> People cooperate in organizations. They join voluntarily. They cooperate toward a goal, the goal of the organization. Therefore the goal must be a common goal, a goal of all participants. Such a goal could not fail to be moral, because morality emerges from cooperative endeavors. Society could not exist without cooperation, and the clearest form of cooperation may be seen in organizations. Thus, in this view, if people cooperate in pursuit of common goals there can be no problem with the output of organizations; they must be moral institutions. (1986, p. 66)

Several studies by early institutionalists emphasized the dual logic of organizational establishment. Selznick (1957) explicitly acknowledged the critical role of values and moral purpose in organizing processes. He recognized the requirement for organizations to be rational, means-oriented, efficient, and administratively capable entities. However, he contrasts purely efficiency-oriented organizations with what he calls "institutions," describing the latter as value-laden, adaptive, and responsive to the external environment. Selznick's widely referenced study of the Tennessee Valley Authority (TVA) is a strong case example of the initial struggle to establish a shared purpose and core values and of the interplay between techno-economic and moral logics. The TVA was created to build dams, control flooding, improve navigability of waterways, produce power, and manufacture fertilizer. In addition to such commercial activities, it was also intended to preserve forests, develop recreation areas, and help poor farmers. Selznick found that its design as a grassroots organization quickly led to its cooptation by land grant colleges, department of agriculture county agents, and local political and business leaders. As a result, all programs suffered. Ultimately, the TVA adopted flood control and electrification as its primary organizational goal. Although it survived and succeeded toward that end, it nonetheless largely abandoned its noncommercial mission and commitment to the poor farmers in the region. Selznick demonstrated through this case how values and purpose are established, challenged, or reinforced through internal processes and interaction with the environment.

Langton's (1984) study of Josiah Wedgwood and the British pottery industry provides another example of the role of rational bureaucracy and moral purpose as the twin logics guiding organization structuring. Langton examined the transformation of British potteries in the mid-eighteenth century from a small, fragmented craft industry to an industry composed of large, complex organizations with national, and in some cases, international markets. The focus of Langton's study is mostly on Wedgwood's firm and is based on historical descriptions.

Given the rise in the standard of living and the increasing consumption of coffee and tea around 1760, Josiah Wedgwood sensed the impending increase, of unprecedented proportions, of the market for pottery. He wanted his firm to "mass produce superior but affordable pottery so excellent in all respects as to be suited to the tables of the upper classes; and which when improvements and facility of production should enable the manufacturer to sell it at a cheaper rate, might reach those of the middle classes" (Langton, 1984, p. 340). With more than 150 potteries in existence in England at the time, his objective was to produce more pottery of higher quality, offered at less expensive prices. In his pursuit of these goals, Wedgwood developed and imposed on his organization carefully designed bureaucratic structures, coordination processes, expected behaviors and technological processes. That is, he initiated a techno-economic logic of a new form of pottery manufacture. Wedgwood elaborated this initial logic of organization, worker roles and production until he had

developed a complex of five specialized shops located adjacent to a commercial canal:

> The firm had been completely transformed into a large complex enterprise with a fairly elaborate administrative hierarchy and an intricate division of labor in which more than 200 men, women, and children performed a wide range of specialized tasks. Supervision of labor was rigorous and systematic; workers tended to be efficient, diligent, and reliable; production was carried on in accordance with detailed written rules, and, while nepotism was still practiced, hiring was based on contracts, and advancement was predicated on job performance and the acquisition of technical skills. (Langton, 1984, p. 345)

Wedgwood initially encountered stiff resistance to his introduction of a bureaucratic logic. As Bendix (1956) noted, the typical industrial worker of the time demonstrated values and behaviors antithetical to the pursuit of a common business goal.

> For the peasant, work varied with the season, involving long hours during the summer months and short hours during the winter. Moreover, many peasants were also occupied in the putting out system (also called domestic industries) but just as many workers in these industries had at least small strips of land that they cultivated. And the routine of their work entailed an unwitting adoption to a variety of tasks and to an irregularity of performance which were incompatible with the specialization and machine driven regularity of factory work. (Bendix, 1956, p. 38)

To deal with the problems of worker resistance, Wedgwood expounded a normative logic consistent with his techno-economic logic. At the time Wedgwood was establishing his factory, John Wesley began preaching locally in England, marking the advent of Methodism and the rise of the Protestant work ethic. Both Wesley and Wedgwood worked aggressively for the establishment of new values and rules of conduct such as dedication to work, frugality, and sobriety. More specifically, Wedgwood worked diligently to establish these new values and priorities among the employees of his pottery. This was reinforced through the application of a detailed and carefully administered system of rewards, punishments, and career advancement opportunities for employees. Langton

(1984) argues that this focus on values and behaviors, including the influence of Wesley, resulted in Wedgwood developing the most dedicated, skillful, efficient workforce in the pottery industry. Wedgwood succeeded in his endeavor by combing both techno-economic and normative forms of logic into a cohesive system.

Other examples of building organizations around the dual logics of bureaucratic rationality and morality abound. Bendix (1956) describes this process in detail in the development of the iron industry in England in the 1800s. Messinger (1955) studied how an old-age influence group, the Townsend organization, transformed itself from lobbying for the economic support of the aged into an organization directed toward goals of social fellowship and fiscal self-sufficiency. Zald and Denton (1963), in their study of the YMCA, demonstrated how the organization shifted its mission as the character of its urban environments changed. Clark (1960), in his study of a community college, and Perrow (1961), in his study of a private voluntary hospital, both capture similar transformations in the primary purpose and mission of these organizations. These studies all describe organizations that are deeply embedded in local communities to which they are tied by the multiple loyalties of personnel and by interorganizational agreements hammered out in face-to-face interaction (Powell and DiMaggio, 1991). All of this research served to highlight the dual importance of economic and normative logics to establish and maintain organizations.

The contribution of these early institutionalists was to extend our conception of bureaucracy beyond economic imperatives. They identified the critical role of values in the definition of the core mission of an organization and articulated an organization designed according to a logic of morality as well as a logic of rules. They showed us that the organizational founder, entrepreneur, or chief executive was central to the development and dissemination of these logics. These leaders were the architects of the technosocial designs of the formal structure as well as the advocate and proponent of the logic of moral values.

Stage-of-Growth Models

Over several decades, scholars have used biological analogies to explain a range of organizational phenomena. Examples include life-cycle or stage-of-growth perspectives on the career development of individuals (Levinson, 1978), group decision-making processes (Bales and Strodtbeck, 1951), organizational development (Kimberly and Miles, 1980; Kazanjian, 1988), and populations of organizations (Hannan and Freeman, 1984; McKelvey and Aldrich, 1983). A life-cycle or stage-of-growth model is one of the most common perspectives in the management literature used to explain how an organization moves from initial development to a position of ongoing viability (Van de Ven and Poole, 1995).

Although widely employed to explain the underlying process of development and change within new organizations, models of stages of growth in the life cycle of an organization are nonetheless controversial. Predicated on a developmental logic, a number of multistage models have been proposed that assume that predictable patterns exist in the growth of organizations and that these patterns unfold as discrete time periods best thought of as stages (Smith, Mitchell, and Summer, 1985). These models have different distinguishing characteristics. For example, several researchers have argued that stages are driven by the search for new growth opportunities, while Greiner (1972) sees stages as a response to internal crises. Some models suggest that organizations progress through stages sequentially while others (Adizes, 1979) argue that there may be multiple paths through the stages. Most models ignore the factors leading to the formal creation of the firm; others (Van de Ven, Hudson, and Schroeder, 1984) provide an explicit rationale as to how and why the firm was formed. Finally, authors differ in terms of the number of stages they explicate. Examples can be found of three-stage models (Smith, Mitchell, and Summer, 1985), four-stage models (Kazanjian, 1988; Quinn and Cameron, 1983; Rhenman, 1973), and five-or-more-stage models (Adizes, 1979; Miller and Freisen, 1984; Van de Ven, Hudson, and Schroeder, 1984).

Despite such variance, stage-of-growth models share a common underlying theoretical basis. Organizations are said to undergo structural change that enables them to face the new tasks or problems that growth elicits. For example, Greiner (1972) views the growth of organizations as a series of evolutions and revolutions precipitated by internal crises related to leadership, control, and coordination. Chandler (1962) viewed stages of growth as responses to the firm's search for new growth opportunities once prior strategies have been exhausted. Tushman and Moore

(1982) regarded stages of organizational growth as a response to changes in industry structure over the product life cycle. Starbuck (1971) captured the spirit of these stage models by referring to the implied and necessary sequential pattern of change as a form of organizational metamorphosis.

Empirical research related to a stage-of-growth progression of firms has been rather limited. Most data-based research on organizational growth models merely assumes a priori the existence of stages but does not test explicitly the progression of firms across stages of growth over time. Consequently, there is little in the way of empirical evidence to support either the prostage or antistage perspectives. There are only a few exceptions. Miller and Friesen (1984) studied the patterns of interstage transition of 36 firms and concluded that progression according to a five-stage growth model was roughly present in their data. Drazin and Kazanjian's (1990) reanalysis of Miller and Friesen's (1984) data reinforced their finding; they concluded that when allowances are made for the probability that some firms may stay in the same stage over varying periods of time, then there is good support for the stage-progression idea.

Based upon two case studies, Kazanjian (1988) found evidence to support a four-stage model of growth theorized to obtain for technology-based new ventures. The four stages are: (1) conception and development, (2) commercialization, (3) growth, and (4) stability. Each of these four stages of growth was seen to constitute a distinct configuration of organizational structure and process developed in response to a set of dominant problems that differed by stage. Kazanjian (1988) also found partial support for the link of dominant problems to stage of growth based upon a survey of 105 technology-based new ventures from a single industry. In a related study, Dodge, Fullerton, and Robbins (1994) assessed the relationship of life cycle stage and level of competition to perceived problems with a sample of 645 small businesses. Problems were collected and categorized from case statements in the files of the Small Business Administration. Of 16 identified problem areas, nine exhibited at least one material difference across categories of stage of life cycle and degree of competition. Although this finding reinforces the notion that problems differ by stage of growth, the authors also identified a set of problems that they characterized as "core" problems that do not seem to lessen or increase in importance across stages of growth. They

argue that these "core" problems remain relatively constant in importance independent of stage of growth or level of competition. It should be noted that the sample used by Dodge et al. was a cross-industry collection of small businesses from industries such as retailing, service and manufacturing. The firms studied were not necessarily new or young firms, and many of them faced demanding, constrained, competitive markets. This is a contrast to the single-industry sample of new firms studied by Kazanjian (1988) and Kazanjian and Drazin (1989), where demand was not seen as a limiting factor.

Much of the empirical research on stage of growth supports the notion that there is a rough central tendency for firms in certain settings to progress through predictable developmental stages. A major implication of this empirical research is the critical relationship of dominant problems to stage of growth. Although some core problems may demonstrate an enduring character (Dodge et al., 1994), others clearly do increase or decrease in importance by stage of growth. Kazanjian (1988) and Kazanjian and Drazin (1989) find that the theoretical role of dominant problems is important not only in defining and measuring discrete stages, but also in understanding the transition from stage to stage, which they viewed as an organizational learning process (Normann, 1977; Rhenman, 1973).

How are stage-of-growth models based in concepts of logic? Stage-of-growth models add to our understanding of organizational logics by taking us beyond logic imprinted during initial founding. They point our attention to the systematic need to resolve problems that emerge as the organization grows. The initial techno-economic logic used to establish the organization is not sufficient to carry the organization over time. Instead, it forms a basis, or blueprint, which is added to, as needed, to deal with growth. Indeed for the most part, stage-of-growth models imply an elaboration of the dual logics initialized when the organization was founded. This is especially salient in models that focus on resolving problems that occur as the organization grows. These problems emerge because the organization is only partially formed at its inception. In a sense, solutions to these problems focus an initial vision that was at best fuzzy when first put into place. This may explain why most stage-of-growth models imply little need to change normative logic. That is, they address only elaboration of techno-economic logics because the normative principles established at the founding of the organization are not called into question. (Of course, there are exceptions, such as Greiner's [1972] model.)

Complexity Theory and Self-Organizing Systems

Over the past two decades, new approaches to modeling the organizing processes of complex, open systems have emerged across the disciplines of mathematics, physics, chemistry, biology, organization theory, social psychology, economics, and sociology (e.g., Allen and McGlade, 1986; Brock and Sayers, 1988; Cohen, March, and Olsen, 1972; Day and Schafer, 1985; Devaney, 1987; Hayes, 1984; Krippendorff, 1971; Masuch and LaPotin, 1989; Miner, 1987, Rasmussen and Mosekilde, 1988; Weick and Berlinger, 1989). Despite differences of discipline, these researchers share common problems, language, perspectives, and methods geared toward understanding how organizing occurs. This emerging body of literature, grounded in the principles of complex systems theory, is not a theory per se, but rather a perspective for theorizing and modeling dynamic systems (Morel and Ramanujam, 1999). It has been termed the science of self-organizing by its major proponents (Ashby, 1968; Prigogine and Stengers, 1984; Schieve and Allen, 1982; Yates, 1987).

More recent work has applied these emerging ideas to the development of formal organizations, mostly under the labels of complexity theory (Anderson, 1999), but also with references to chaos theory (Brown and Eisenhardt, 1998; Dooley and Van de Ven, 1999). Drazin and Sandelands (1992) and Sandelands and Drazin (1989) provided a detailed development of these principles, applied to organization theory, through their discussion of self-organizing or "autogenesis." Their perspective, representative of much of the emerging research in this domain, is developed through three mainstay ideas central to complex systems theory.

Their central idea is that structure is emergent. A fundamental postulate of self-organizing is that structure or order emerges out of the interactions of discrete microscopic entities, without outside intervention by the environment or a designer. This concept is suggested most dramatically by recent findings that show that highly disordered systems, far from equilibrium, actually organize themselves in this manner (Nicolis and Prigogine, 1977; Prigogine and Stengers, 1984). One idea, central to the notion of

emergence, is that structure has primarily a conceptual or cognitive status, which exists in the mind of the observer as a representation of something more than interactions among individuals (Allport, 1962; Collins, 1981; Homans, 1950). Correspondingly, social structure is more than the aggregation of individual actions (Mayhew, 1980), but has unique properties not possessed by individuals alone. Finally, as Berger and Luckmann (1966) note, social structure is a mental construct that depends upon categorization schemes used by observers to abstract information and give meaning to the flow of experience. These conceptual abstractions can be shared, modified, and reproduced intersubjectively and transmitted intergenerationally. The structure that emerges is the product of the collective and cannot be inferred from the elements in isolation or from their interactions (Geertz, 1973; Poundstone, 1984).

The second theme of self-organizing is that the interactions among entities that generate structure are governed by rules. This idea is well illustrated by models of physical and social systems called "cellular automata" (Axelrod, 1984; Friedhoff, 1989; Hayes, 1984; Schelling, 1978; Von Neumann, 1951). Cellular automata are a uniform array of identical cells as in a matrix where each cell represents a discrete entity, such as a molecule in a snowflake or an individual in a social field. Each cell then interacts with its neighboring cells according to specific rules of interaction that operate recursively over time. Very complex structures can be explained as a result of the recursive application of simple rules that govern interactions of component parts (Hofstadter, 1985). Recursively applied rules are essential to self-organizing processes.

The final central idea of self-organizing is that structuring is a moment in time. Structure is not merely a static property of a system but rather a perceived moment in time in a dynamic organizing process. The depiction of the emergent structure unfolding over time is a challenge. Computer simulations have been developed by some researchers to produce both direct and indirect visual representations of self-organizing systems as they evolve over time (Abraham and Shaw, 1987; Gleick, 1987; Lorenz, 1987). An alternative approach is to plot key system parameters, such as performance, against each other or against time.

Based on these three central ideas of self-organizing, Drazin and Sandelands (1992) describe their theory of "autogenesis" as a process model of how organizing occurs: "Expressed simply, 'autogenesis' is the idea that organization can be explained by observation and categorization of the interactions of independent actors whose behavior is governed by a system of recursively applied rules. 'Autogenesis' is pre-eminently a process oriented perspective because it focuses on explaining how organization emerges, rather than why it emerges" (1992, p. 236).

Drazin and Sandelands (1992) relate self-organizing processes to logics of structuring at three levels. The first level of structure is deep structure, which consists of the rules that generate and govern individual behavior and the interaction of individuals. At this level, explicit task-related rules (such as the standard operating procedures in a manufacturing or engineering function) guide actions and behaviors of individuals. Assuming (1) that individuals have bounded knowledge of the social milieu and therefore must rely on their immediate environment for information about other actors (Berger and Luckmann, 1966), and (2) that rules are applied recursively, organizing processes emerge and social organizations are generated. Elemental structure, the second level, is captured in the actions and interactions of individuals observed by others. They change or unfold with each iteration of the recursively applied rules to produce a temporal stream of activity that is the explicated process of organizing. While logics are not observable, elemental structure is and exists in time and space. Finally, observed structure is more macroscopic, having global properties and characteristics that differ from the disaggregated behaviors and interactions of individuals and includes entities such as groups, teams, departments, business units, or whole organizations.

A self-organizing perspective on organizational change implies that a logic underlies the system as it develops. However, the form of the logic differs from that implied by institutionalists or stage-of-growth theorists. Here the logic exists as rules played out by a series of agents. Each agent in the self-organizing process follows his or her own cognitively encoded logic. The organizational systems that are generated cannot be explained by the actions of a single designer endogenous to the system being played out. The overall "logic" that emerges from the interplay of many is seen and intuited by sideline observers. These observers may attribute a "god in the machine" logic to the process; however, there is no designer in the system.

Critique of Initiation and Elaboration Models

We regard this approach to the study of change as having high potential, especially its earliest theoretical and empirical treatments. Early institutional researchers concentrated on the creation of logics of organizing and emphasized simultaneously the development of both techno-economic logics and normative logics. In doing so, they adopted a field study perspective seeking to understand deeply the processes of institutionalization.

Perhaps more so than any other tradition of organizational change, this perspective emphasized the simultaneous elaboration of techno-economic and moral logics. To the early institutionalists these were bound together as one. To create a producing organization required the creation of a set of moral principles that allowed all stakeholders to buy into the new organization.

The study of dual forms of logic and process was lost or at least diluted when research shifted to stage of growth progression models; a form of determinism crept into theory building. The first models in this stream considered agency, at least of leaders or entrepreneurs. Later models became more self-propelled in character. The argument offered is a convincing one—as organizations grow, they solve some problems, then others emerge in a predictable manner. What went missing was how agents dealt with the transitions between stages. Stages became an accepted fact and researchers sought only to chronicle the macro patterns of stage transitions. We know of no studies that approach the process of stage transitions in the same way that the early institutionalists studied organizational inception.

In effect, our major critique of this perspective is its treatment of agency. What was once important now no longer is. The study of change as logics of progression leaves out the role that informed agents, embedded in the structures in which they participate, take action to change those structures. Agency and structure are divorced when they should be co-equals (Giddens, 1979).

Change as the Breakdown of a Previous Logic

A dominant theme in the literature on organizational change is that change occurs through the breakdown of a previous organizational logic and the establishment of a new logic. In this perspective change is viewed as revolutionary rather than evolutionary (Mezias and Glynn, 1993). This theme has persisted from the earliest writings on change management and socio-technical systems to more recent models of change as a punctuated equilibrium. The threads common to all these models are:

1. The organization (whether group, sub-unit, or total organization) is in a state of homeostasis where there is alignment among environment and structure that produces an acceptable level of performance. This is the organization's current instantiation of its logic.
2. An exogenous change occurs that results in a decline in performance to an unacceptable level. The old logics no longer work.
3. Management attempts to rectify the situation by instituting a set of structural and technological changes that constitute a new logic.
4. The organization, or its employees and middle managers, resists change due to inertia or vested interests. The new techno-economic logic is at odds with the normative logic of the past.
5. Management overcomes the resistance or inertia through change management techniques, some drastic.
6. The organization is resurrected in a new form that better suits the needs of the environment and performance is restored. A new techno-economic and normative logic is in place.

Two related streams of literature have evolved that use this framework to explain organization change. They differ as to when they were popular, the focal level of analysis, and the methods used to develop or test the theory of change. First is the change management literature, published primarily prior to the 1980s, and second is the punctuated equilibrium model of change, a current mainstay of organizational-level analyses of change (Tushman and Romanelli, 1985).

Resistance to Change and Organization Development

Research on organizational change began in earnest in the postwar years. Much of the early research centered on analyses of working groups in industrial settings. Although the level of analysis was primarily groups, or departments, the units studied were central to the productivity and life of the entire company.

Students of organizational change were heavily influenced by social psychologists such as Kurt Lewin (1951), who developed the concept of force-field analysis. He suggested that organizations were normally in a state of stability caused by opposing forces and leading to a given level of output and performance. To effect change, management had to both increase the forces for change and overcome the resistance to change. If management didn't overcome the inertia of the present system, then conflict and strife were predicted.

Virtually all of the studies on planned change involved a process sequence that started with stability, was interrupted by the change itself, and ended (hopefully) with the system reaching a new equilibrium at a higher level of performance. Lewin introduced the now-famous three-step model of unfreezing, moving, and refreezing. The terms themselves indicate that a previous logic undergoes a breakdown and is supplanted with a new logic. Other authors offered similar, but slightly more complex models (Huse and Bowditch, 1973; Rice, 1958).

One of the early and best-known studies of resistance to change was published by Trist and Bamforth (1951) and Trist (1963). They described the impact of a technological change on the social structure of coal mining in the United Kingdom. The early approach, in force until the end of World War II, was known as the short-wall method of coal getting. It involved rudimentary technologies that revolved around teams of coal miners working in pairs to extract the coal. The team, usually of six workers, rotated around shifts and made their own decisions around which veins to mine. Each pair of workers would take over from the previous pair and continue the work process. The six-man group was paid according to its total productivity and was close to what we call a self-managed team today.

New technology resulted in what was termed the long-wall method of coal getting. This approach involved an assembly line of sorts, where the work previously done by 2 men was now divided into 5 specialized jobs spread across 40 men. Each specialized job was appraised as to the level of work and productivity involved, and wages were negotiated individually. Additionally, miners preferred the old job, which involved doing a complete task, instead of the new job that involved repetition due to specialization. This created a culture of individualism instead of cooperation. Resentment toward supervisors increased, status differences developed between old and new workers, and productivity declined while absenteeism increased.

The Tavistock Institute researchers suggested a composite system, where specialization was not complete. Instead the 40-man team was allowed to rotate workers among several of the specialized positions. This restored satisfaction and gave the workers a feeling of greater autonomy. Productivity increased by close to 100% and absenteeism declined significantly.

Most analyses of planned change and socio-technological change were based on in-depth case studies. These cases reported robust accounts of the details of the forces for change, managerial mistakes at implementing change, and the resolution of the resistance issues. This resulted in more detailed knowledge about how to intervene in change situations and the creation of the field of organizational development (Huse, 1975; Kotter and Schlesinger, 1979; Reichers, Wanous, and Austin, 1997; Schein, 1988). The enduring contribution of the socio-technological school of organization is its emphasis on normative as well as techno-economic logics.

Punctuated Equilibrium Models

One of the more recent advances in theories of organizational change has been in the area of punctuated equilibrium models. Advocates of this approach maintain that organizational change is best characterized as long periods of equilibrium punctuated by brief periods of major change and transformation. Borrowing from the fields of paleontology and evolutionary biology, researchers in this area maintain that change is not gradual and accumulative, but sudden and dramatic.

In their original work, Eldredge and Gould (1972) proposed a macroevolutionary theory they termed *punctuated equilibrium*. The theory is based on observation of the fossil record and states that (in geologic time) the appearance of a new species occurs relatively suddenly and without the continuous slow accumulation of small variations that characterize typical Darwinian models. Instead, Eldredge and Gould observed that evolution is not gradual, but instead moves quickly and sporadically. They suggest that studies of the fossil record found in geological layers reveal long periods in which nothing changes (stasis or equilibrium), and then shows punctuation in short, revolutionary transitions in which species become extinct and are replaced by new species.

Punctuated equilibrium models have been used to explain change in a wide variety of social settings. Gersick's thorough review (1991) lists representative work in the areas of individual life structures (Levinson, 1978), the pattern of progress in group projects (Gersick, 1988), organization theory (Sastry, 1997; Tushman and Romanelli, 1985), paradigm shifts (Kuhn, 1970), and general systems theory (Prigogine and Stengers, 1984). Gersick notes that these punctuated equilibrium theories are qualitatively different than other theories of change. Their most striking differences fall in two areas. First, most models of change suggest that change occurs gradually and that the system in question can absorb almost any change as long as it occurs gradually, primarily in subsystems of the overall system. Change is accommodated because it is nonthreatening, and emotional and political reactions are diffused over time. Second, many models of change assume some progress along a pre-defined path, as in models that are based on stages or cycles. Punctuated equilibrium theories do not emphasize predictable progress, instead maintaining that change matches shifts in the environment. Change occurs to meet a threat to system maintenance imposed by shifts outside the system.

Gersick (1991) makes the argument that one of the most important concepts for understanding punctuated equilibrium change models is that they involve change in "deep structure." Gersick (1991, p. 14) defines deep structure as "the set of fundamental choices a system has made of (1) the basic parts into which its units will be organized and (2) the basic activity patterns that will maintain its existence." To us, this implies that change occurs rapidly in both the techno-economic and normative logics that have heretofore been the mainstay of the organization.

Although punctuated equilibrium models are general enough to apply at multiple levels of analysis, our interest in this chapter is confined to organization-wide change dynamics. Here, Michael Tushman and his associates have applied punctuated equilibrium theory to develop a useful model of organizational change. First we briefly review Tushman's theory and empirical findings and show the extent to which his model incorporates dual forms of logic.

The centerpiece of the empirical work of Tushman and colleagues appears in Romanelli and Tushman (1994). Here, the authors provide the first full test of their theory. They noted that other research has been relevant in providing case studies of punctuated equilibrium models (Bartunek, 1984;, Tushman, Newman, and Romanelli, 1986) or in testing portions of the model (Miller and Friesen, 1982, 1984; Virany, Tushman and Romanelli, 1992), but that no single study has tested the complete model.

At its core, Tushman's model of punctuated equilibrium proposes that exogenous "jolts," coupled with concomitant performance declines and senior executive turnover, are the major pressures that force organizations to change or fail. Tushman and Romanelli (1994) developed five hypotheses central to testing the punctuated equilibrium model. The first two examine the underlying nature of change. They proposed that organizational transformation would occur in short, discontinuous bursts of change involving most, or all, key domains of organizational activity. They also hypothesize that small change in single domains of organizational activity will not accumulate to fundamental transformations. Taken together, these two hypotheses seek to establish that organizational change is not a gradual process, but rather a process wherein major change occurs rapidly at periodic points in an organization's history.

Romanelli and Tushman (1994) developed three additional hypotheses that link transformational change to external environmental shifts. They propose that major change is likely to occur in response to three antecedents: (1) short-term declines in performance, (2) major environmental changes that alter the external environment, and (3) the installation of a new CEO.

Data to test their theory was drawn from the life histories of 25 minicomputer producers. First, Romanelli and Tushman define transformational change as change that happens within a two-year period in three key domains of organizational activity—the strategy of the organization, the organization's structure, and the distribution of power in the organization. To be accounted for as a transformation, change had to occur in all three domains. If change occurred in one or two domains, then no transformation occurred. However, if change occurred in two domains, and then was followed by change in another domain some time later, a transformation was coded. In our view, the three domains of organizational activity comprise an organization's techno-economic and normative logic.

Based on their data, Romanelli and Tushman report that the types of changes observed in the minicomputer industry support a punctuated equilib-rium model. Revolutionary changes outnumbered nonrevolutionary changes 23 to 3. Further, the duration of the revolutionary changes was much shorter than the duration of the nonrevolutionary changes, thus supporting the idea that change occurs in small bursts rather than incrementally. The data also supported the notion that incremental change did not accumulate into revolutionary change. Romanelli and Tushman report that in no single case did small, incremental change lead to major and substantive change.

Taken together, these findings provide robust support for the underlying propositions of punctuated equilibrium theory. They recast organizational change as less of an incremental process as originally proposed by resistance to change and sociotechnical theorists. They convincingly show that change occurs in a manner similar to that proposed by biologists and paleontologists, introducing a powerful new metaphor for change into our organizational lexicon.

The Role of Executives

Other work by Tushman and associates examines the role of succession at the senior executive level in the change process. Two papers on the cement industry specifically look at CEO and senior executive team change. These papers are particularly noteworthy because they theorize and test for the effects of agency on structural change. This is an advance over static contingency theory research. Contingency theories assume that strategic choice is the motivating factor in bringing about congruence between environment and organization, but do little to test what role managers play in making this congruence happen. In contrast, this pair of articles specifically proposes a casual link between the external environment and structural change.

Keck and Tushman (1993) argued that executive teams act at the boundary between an organization and its environment. They mediate between environmental demands and internal political dynamics. Executive teams do so by substantively and symbolically shaping the organization's view of its external world. When significant change happens outside the organization, the CEO and the senior management team of the organization must reframe the organization's cognitive view by changing both means of production and the organization's value system. By emphasizing the role of the executive in change management, Tushman et al.'s model of punctuated equilibrium accounts for agency in the change process. Senior executives articulate or encode a new organizational logic.

Keck and Tushman (1993) hypothesized that technological change, environmental change (particularly legislative action), organizational reorientations, and CEO changes will all lead to alterations in the composition of the team (through processes of entry and exit), increased team heterogeneity, and decreases in team tenure. That is, that team members will leave and be replaced by new team members with greater differences in background. These changes lead to newness in the team. The new team members presumably bring with them the knowledge necessary to compete in a new environment and a freedom from past organization decisions and culture (inertia).

Keck and Tushman (1993) go beyond examining what happens to the top management team at the moment of a reorientation or environmental jolt. They also studied the effect of elapsed time as a factor influencing executive team composition. After a punctuating event, the organization adapts to that event and then enters into a period of incremental change. This period is characterized by small changes that elaborate the logic of the new organization form put in place during the reorientation. During this convergent period, the organization stabilizes and focuses inward on itself to develop routines that rationalize the new operating mode. Keck and Tushman argued that these processes of incremental change and innovation have an impact on the structure of the executive team. Their results show good support for the role of punctuated change in executive team structure. Technological discontinuities, reorientations, and environmental (regulatory) jolts have a significant impact on the composition of the executive team, as does CEO succession. Environmental jolts were found to be related only to mean team tenure, but not to the other characteristics of the team.

In a second article on the role of executive change in bringing about organizational change, Tushman and Rosenkopf (1996) maintain that the tasks of senior executives are to define and legitimate organizational change—that is, to develop and implement techno-economic and normative logics. Two types of change are discussed using an organizational learning framework. One type of learning occurs during periods of organizational stability. The organization invests in the development of incremental change

that centers on the elaboration of existing technologies and working within a given social-political framework. Another type of change occurs during periods of reorientation and turbulence. Here, the organization needs to focus on new ways of operation that are departures from past methods.

There are two approaches to change that top-management teams can bring about. In the first, the existing team can initiate change itself. In the second approach, the current top management team can be replaced and change will be initiated by a new team. Tushman and Rosenkopf (1996) argue that partial change of the executive team, or change of the entire team except the CEO, will lead only to incremental organizational change. Sweeping executive change, which they define as the succession of the CEO and a change of a majority of the senior executive team, is needed to make major, reorienting type of organizational change. They call these change efforts, respectively, first- and second-order change.

In general, the results support the model theorized but differ according to whether the turbulence was generated environmentally or internally by a decline in performance. For high environmental-turbulence conditions, there is a positive and significant relationship between subsequent organizational performance and succession among both the CEO and the executive team. This supports Tushman and Rosenkopf's arguments that turbulent times require sweeping forms of managerial change to be successful. When turbulence is defined as a performance crisis, the combined effect of CEO and top team change did not effect subsequent performance. Tushman and Rosenkopf comment that because these are fundamentally different kinds of events, different underlying processes may be at work.

Critique of the Breakdown of Logic Models

Again, early writers in this perspective focused on agency and process. Researchers who studied organizational development and resistance to change were keen on understanding what managers could do to overcome and limit the obstructions put in place by lower-level workers. This led to detailed case studies of actual change events, which examined the motivations and actions of managers and workers alike. But agency was only for managers. Employees were reduced to a homogenous group that resisted, but had no agency— that is, no power to enact an organization. However, an examination of the case studies reveals that non-managerial groups had a significant impact on the structures that emerged in the end. Students of organizational development forewent the opportunity to incorporate into the concept of agency the logics of groups other than managers. In doing so, they initiated a trend wherein agency was considered a property of only an elite coalition of senior executives.

Later writers, notably Tushman et al. (1986), continued in this fashion by conceptualizing agency only in terms of top managers. Tushman et al. presented a model where organizational logics reside with the current dominant coalition or with the successors to those who fail to adapt their logics to external jolts. Thus, adaptation and agency are clearly present in punctuated equilibrium models, but only in the form of the senior leaders and their ill-fated turnover. New leaders change techno-economic logics, but there is little discussion of normative logics.

What is most inviting about punctuated equilibrium models is that they formally introduce the concept of a crisis into models of change. Periods of substantive transformation involve changes in the organization's deep structure (Gersick, 1991). The earlier periods logic is overthrown in favor of a new logic more adaptive to major environmental or technological shifts. These shifts are accompanied by performance declines and the stress of managerial succession. A crisis occurs that threatens the organization's well being.

We believe that the concept of crisis extant in these models provides a basis for understanding organizational transformation. However, the methodologies used by punctuated equilibrium theorists allow only for a remote view of how crises unfold. Data often stretches over decades, if not a century. Such data afford researchers a macrolevel lens on crises. This approach allows researchers to examine the antecedents and consequences of change in multiple events over time, but does not permit an examination of the microlevel nature of a single crisis. By design, longitudinal methods set our attention solely on techno-economic logics, but not on normative logics. There appear to be prospects for developing a more robust concept of crisis in theories of organizational change.

Finally, all the work of Tushman and his associates refers to organizational learning. During relatively stable periods of time the organization engages in learning that is convergent. That is, this learning

goes on within the logic that dominates the organization. Here, learning is gradual and accumulative. During periods of turmoil, initiated by exogenous jolts, learning also occurs. But this learning is radical and reorienting in character. The cyclical nature of learning is reminiscent of March's (1991) model of exploration and exploitation. March suggests that organizations engage in periods of learning best described as exploratory in nature. During these periods they develop relatively new knowledge that leads to new products, services, and production processes. Once exploratory knowledge is developed, the organization engages in exploitation of that knowledge. In this learning phase, existing knowledge is leveraged through product and service extension and the replication of newly established routines. March and Tushman differ in identifying the forces that drive cyclical learning. Tushman argues that discontinuous learning takes place only under conditions of exogenous threat. March argues that agents who anticipate the need for change internally generate cycles of exploration and exploitation.

Change as a Logic of Anticipation

Bettis and Prahalad (1994, p. 11) note that organizational adaptation to the environment is predicated on the adaptive ability of the dominant logic; the dominant logic "provides a set of heuristics that simplify and speed decision making.... [The dominant logic] allows the organization to 'anticipate' the environment." Further, they note that the adaptability of the dominant logic is predicated upon the process of organizational learning and, in particular, unlearning.

Organizational learning is the process by which organizations notice, interpret, and manage experience (Glynn, Lant, and Milliken, 1994). The notion of the "learning organization" has become fairly ubiquitous both in academic theorizing and in business practice (e.g., Senge, 1990a). Part of the appeal of this perspective is that it offers an alternative to "rational choice assumptions" (Cohen and Sproull, 1991) and thus offers a framework for understanding some of the ways in which organizational logics and sense making can impact institutional change. From a learning perspective, there are two types of change that occur: first-order learning and second-order learning (Watzlawick, Weakland, and

Fisch, 1974). First-order learning involves incremental change or "single-loop" learning—that is, a conservative, incremental process that aims to stabilize organizations and maintain existing rules or logic (March, 1981; Lant and Mezias, 1992). It is basically the process of gaining competence in a particular routine or technology so as to increase efficiency; it is commensurate with what Tushman and Romanelli (1985) label "convergence." Second-order learning is "double-loop" learning with the realization that current logic, beliefs, or theories in use (Argyris and Schon, 1978) are no longer effective; a radical shift in existing practices, rules, technologies and goals occurs. Often motivated by unsatisfactory performance, second-order learning involves major change or innovation, a process Tushman and Romanelli (1985) call "reorientation."

The organizational learning literature has been characterized as having two thematic perspectives: an adaptive learning approach, best typified by the work of March and colleagues, and a knowledge development approach, best represented in the work of Argyris and Schon (Aldrich, 1999; Glynn, Lant, and Milliken, 1994). These two streams in the literature bifurcate the methods, focal levels of analysis, and theoretical assumptions embedded in studying organizational learning.

Typified by the behavioral theory of the firm (Cyert and March, 1963), the adaptive learning approach addresses explicitly the mechanisms by which organizations change over time. This perspective views organizations as experiential learning systems (Lant, 1992; Lant and Mezias, 1990; Levinthal and March, 1981; March and Olsen, 1976; Mezias and Glynn, 1993) that are "routine-based, history-dependent, and target-oriented" (Levitt and March, 1988, p. 319). Organizational change tends to be incremental in nature, in that successful behaviors are repeated and unsuccessful ones avoided or abandoned; thus, change is often motivated by failure, or an organization's performance below targets or aspiration levels. Thus, from an adaptive learning perspective, an established organizational logic tends to govern action and be fairly inert to major disruptive or transformational change. The organizational logic becomes embedded in routinized organizational roles, practices, and standard operating procedures that, in turn, constitute a structural imperative for the firm.

The dominant methodology used by researchers from this perspective tends to be that of the computer simulation examining the impact of different decision rules—or forms of logic—on the processes and outcomes of organizational learning. Organizations are modeled as experiential learning systems that can alter their routines in response to past experience. Lant and Mezias (1990) model routines in terms of three important categories: (1) search routines, or processes by which organizations attempt to discover adaptive opportunities under conditions of uncertainty, complexity, and ambiguity, (2) performance routines, or comparative processes that compare actual organizational outcomes against a moving target or aspiration level that adjusts in response to experience over time, and (3) change routines, or the organizational choice to refine current capabilities incrementally or attempt new, radically different capabilities for innovation. In making change to extant systems and capabilities, organizations follow the contours of the well-established learning curve such that performance improves with change (or the adoption of new practices or technologies), but at a decreasing rate (Argote, Beckman, and Epple, 1990; Argote and Epple, 1990; Epple, Argote, and Devadas, 1991; Yelle, 1979). Organizations experience myopia (Radner, 1975) and become mired in competency traps (Lave and March, 1975; Levinthal and March, 1981; Levitt and March, 1988). Organizational change, thus, tends to be incremental and slow or, as March (1981, p. 564) so cogently observed: "Most change in organizations results neither from extraordinary organizational processes nor forces, nor from uncommon imagination, persistence or skill, but from relatively stable, routine processes that relate organizations to their environments."

The knowledge development perspective on organizational learning tends to complicate the picture. This approach focuses more directly on the patterns of cognitive associations, knowledge structures, or beliefs about causal relationships that govern organizational behavior (Glynn, Lant, and Milliken, 1994) and grounds them in the contexts in which they are embedded. In contrast to modeling the organization as a homogenous entity or unitary actor, the knowledge development approach seeks to capture the complexities and intraorganizational dynamics that attend learning, to a greater extent than the abstracted simulations of the adaptive learning theorists. As Argyris (1993, p. 1) notes, the focus is on actionable knowledge—that is, not only knowledge relevant to the world of practice, but the knowledge that people use to create the world. More than abstracted espoused theories (Argyris and Schon, 1978) that simply assert claims, the focus is on theories in use or the enactment of the ideas that are espoused.

In this framework, organizational learning is viewed as the sharing of knowledge, cognition, or beliefs and organizational structures that enable such integration to constitute more favorable learning environments. Argyris and Schon (1978) demonstrate that organizations that encourage information sharing and a diversity of views enable learning. Jelinek (1979) corroborated this view in her study of administrative systems that enable innovation. Moreover, the establishment of learning strategies early in an institution's life has been shown to have profound effects on subsequent learning (Miles and Randolph, 1980), a view that is echoed in Cohen and Levinthal's (1990) demonstration of the impact of absorptive capacity.

Because the emphasis is on the intersubjective sharing of knowledge, learning theorists in this tradition focus on the processes of diffusion, a perspective that is not unlike other researchers modeling technological or innovation diffusion. Organizational members are modeled not only for their learning in terms of knowing how (work practices) but also in terms of becoming practitioners and belonging to communities of practice (Brown and Dugoid, 1991). Studies of technology transfer, for instance, have demonstrated how more permeable organizational boundaries, enabled by individual and systemic learning, are effective in knowledge accumulation and application (e.g., Argote, Beckman, and Epple, 1990; Epple, Argote, and Devadas, 1991; Kogut and Zander, 1992). Organizational knowledge plays a key role in developing organizational capabilities for change. Cohen and Levinthal (1989, 1990) demonstrated that "absorptive capacity"—a function of a firm's prior accumulations of relevant knowledge—lends innovative potential, learning, and competitive advantage. Subsequent research has validated their analysis and extended the construct of absorptive capacity to the organizational and interorganizational levels of analysis (e.g., Koza and Lewin, 1998; Lane and Lubatkin, 1998; Shenkar and Li, 1999; Szulanski, 1996).

Models of Organizational Design That Promote Innovation Adoption and Knowledge Assimilation

Innovation is simply the process of bringing any new, problem-solving idea into use in an organization (Kanter, 1983); its critical feature is that it be perceived as new to the adopting organization (Kimberly & Miles, 1980; Rogers and Shoemaker, 1971). Innovation tends to represent radical, "frame-breaking" change (Tushman, Newman, and Romanelli, 1986) and thus seems to necessitate a departure from extant logics and programmatic rules (Damanpour, 1991), particularly as they are encoded in organizational structures. This departure is highlighted in Galbraith's (1982, p. 14) argument that "innovating and operating are fundamentally opposing logics." This distinction is maintained not only in the form of logic but also in the form of organizational structures that are conducive to innovation and change.

Perhaps the most robust finding in the research relating innovation to organizational structure is that organizational size, formalization, and complexity are not conducive to innovation (e.g., Aiken and Hage, 1971; Brown, 1991; Burns and Stalker, 1961; Kanter, 1983; Nadler and Tushman, 1989; Pierce and Delbecq, 1977; Rogers, 1983; Thompson, 1965). As Kanter (1985, p. 54) cogently summarizes the key finding, when it comes to innovation, small is better. Researchers have demonstrated that structures designed for efficiency or production tend to be quite different from those that promote innovation. As opposed to operating organizations, which tend to have mechanistic (Burns and Stalker, 1961) or segmentalist structures (Kanter, 1983), innovating organizations tend to have organic (Burns and Stalker, 1961) or integrative structures (Kanter, 1983) that promote knowledge assimilation across group, functional, professional and/or organizational boundaries. Because radical change (or innovation) requires "frame-breaking" change in which institutionalized logic and habituated thinking are reformulated or discarded (Senge, 1990b) organizations need to be designed so as to separate and protect potential innovation champions or revolutionaries (Howell and Higgins, 1990) from enculturated routines.

An alternative approach to designing organizations for innovation acknowledges the probabilistic, chaotic character of innovation (Quinn, 1985). Instead of delineating different structures for innovating and operating, advocates of an evolutionary approach recognize the role of chance in most organizational innovation (Angle and Van de Ven, 1989). Thus, instead of partitioning the organizational structure into organistic or mechanistic, for example, Quinn (1985) argues for redundancies and parallel processes in routines and programs. Innovation is encouraged by a process of imperfect routine maintenance (Levitt and March, 1988), experimentation with slack resources (Cyert and March, 1963), and loose coupling (Weick, 1979). In general, the approach is to relax organizational and managerial controls (Angle and Van de Ven, 1989).

In their computer simulation study, Mezias and Glynn (1993) modeled corporate change in terms of the routines and rules that underscore organizational structure. Using a learning framework, they examined how the type and frequency of organizational innovation are affected by three different routines or logics: institution, revolution, and evolution. The first two involve intentional organizational efforts to increase innovation, either by working within the current paradigm or logic (institutional) or by departing from it (revolutionary); the third (evolutionary) involves less conscious efforts to manage innovation by varying routines and loosening controls.

Thus, organizational structures that enable learning seem to be key drivers of change and innovation. The underlying logic is one that is, as March and colleagues have described it, experientially based, historically grounded, and target-oriented. It is a logic that encourages vigilance—or perhaps heightened self-consciousness—about an organization's current and past performance history, as well as anticipation about future goals, articulated as aspirations for the next trial period. In a sense, organizations are designed or constructed purposefully to be adaptive. This research implies that norms of change permeate the organization.

Critique of Anticipatory Change Models

This view of change is promising in that it allows for change to occur all the time. It recognizes that change is not an episodic process, punctuated by jolts, but rather continuously evolving. Further, this perspective embraces core notions on structuration processes developed by Giddens (1979); structure is not an omnipresent force that continuously reproduces itself, but rather is structuration, a process where structure empowers agents, who then have the capacity and inclination to change that structure. In other words, structuring is an ongoing process that requires continual adjustment and adaptation, a view consonant with Adaptive Structuration Theory (AST), articulated by DeSanctis and Poole (1994). Moreover, it implies the need for active and empowered agents—

perhaps innovation champions (Howell and Higgins, 1990)—to take on the roles of interpreting and manipulating logics (Friedland and Alford, 1991).

A limitation of this view is that it applies, somewhat unrealistically, only to sets of organizations that are in highly turbulent environments. True, change begets turbulence, which begets further change. However, this view suggests that all organizations are in a constant state of flux and does an injustice to change theorizing by overemphasizing the propensity of organizations to change and underemphasizing the propensity of organizations to reproduce themselves.

Discussion

Throughout this chapter we have argued that organizations and organizational change can best be understood using a framework of organizational logic. To us, logics are principles of organizing resident in the minds of agents who use them to create and modify organizations. Logics have a teleological orientation. Agents map their logics onto real organizations in order to suit their purposes. These real organizations in turn provide the basis for the creation of alternative logics, which allow for change.

This chapter has distinguished the characteristics of three perspectives on structural change. We outlined brief chronologies of each of these perspectives and reviewed the key empirical literature. This review showed how techno-economic and moral logics of change were handled in each approach. Each point of view has its admirable qualities; each also makes assumptions about change that limit its potential contributions. A challenge for organization theorists is to build a model of structural change that accounts for agency (broadly defined), allows for the possibility of both structural reproduction and transformation, and also allows for endogenous change (coming out of the structure itself) as well as exogenous change. Future models of organizational change need to incorporate, simultaneously, the logic of technology and production as well as moral logic. Following, we present a few guiding principles to inform future theories of change.

Structures Can Contain Multiple and Interactive Logics

Perhaps with the exception of learning approaches to structural change, most researchers emphasize the holistic and homogenous nature of structure (Sewell, 1992). That is, they assume that the logics that are the basis of realized structures are shared and singular throughout the organization. The importance of this assumption is that it leads the change researcher to think of change as originating primarily outside the organization. If the current logic is pervasive throughout the organization, then the only source of disconfirming this logic is from without. This assumption cascades easily to others. If the logic that creates and sustains a structure is homogenous and shared, then "breaking" that logic requires a powerful external agency. The view of agency is then one of powerful external elites who substitute physically for former elites who embody old logics. No possibility is allowed for internally generated change or for multiple agents with different and potentially useful logics.

Instead of assuming structural homogeneity, we argue instead that organization structures contain a diverse set of coexistent and potentially interactive logics simultaneously. One of these logics may be dominant in one epoch of the organization's history while others are dormant, but full of change potential. Logics are multiple because different portions of the organization or different levels of the organization have different logics. Logics themselves are transformable. They can apply or be applied to different problems, moreover; when the assumptions and rules of different logics interact, they can recombine into new logics. Multiplicity endows the organization with potential for change (Sewell, 1992).

A shared logic may develop within a single organization; however, it is also likely that logics will differ across communities within an organization. As Goffman (1974) notes, even though two actors share a similar set of experiences, their frames of reference may differ based on their positions with respect to that activity. As a result, shared logics may not be neat, tidy, and polite, but rather marked by divergent and sometimes antagonistic frames of reference (Trice, 1993; Walsh and Fahey, 1986; Walsh, Henderson, and Deighton, 1988; Weick, 1995). Fine (1996, p. 111) argues this convincingly with respect to differences among professional groups domiciled in a single organization: "By the placement of an occupation within an organizational field, workers provisionally create occupational meanings, given the real constraints under which they work and in light of the evaluations of other actors who impinge on their claimed expertise." Thus, even in a single organiza-

tion, a multitude of diverse logics can exist, arising from, and characterizing, different job categories, functional departments, hierarchical levels, occupations, positions, status, ideologies, and paradigms (Trice, 1993; Weick, 1995).

When change occurs, it is a particularly ripe context for the playing out of divergent views of what the organization's logic should be. Change can create tension between different, and perhaps opposing, intraorganizational communities (Huff, 1988). For example, Dougherty (1992) notes that innovation and change require the insights of multiple "thought worlds," that is, the interpretive schemas of different communities of specialists who literally think differently from each other. She identifies four competing thought worlds—technical, field, manufacturing, and planning—and argues that, at best, each thought world views the other as esoteric, and, at worst, meaningless. These four communities likely have different views of what makes sense and therefore different views of what constitutes an appropriate organizational logic, each wishing that their own logic would be dominant.

Similarly, Trice (1993) views organizations as collections of diverse subcultures that subscribe to different systems of meanings. For him, there are two dominant subcultures—administrative and occupational—that compete over the control of work, access to power, resources, and credit; their inevitable clashes are resolved through adaptation and negotiation. Note that by highlighting two levels, Trice places agency in the hands of more than just the managerial elite. Daft and Becker (1978) demonstrate explicitly the link between different communities of meaning and change endeavors. In their study of high schools, they found that 71% of the administrative innovation proposals (e.g., changes in community/school relationships, registration systems, human resource management systems, and systems to control costs) originated from administrators and, conversely, 70% of the teaching innovation proposals (e.g., curriculum changes, new teaching techniques, and equipment to support instruction) were initiated by teachers. Daft's (1978) finding that different groups promulgated different types of innovations led him to conclude that there was a dual-core nature to change processes.

When an organization faces a crisis, the dominant logic, perforce, is no longer valid. As Tushman and associates have pointed out, a new dominant logic is needed that is better adapted to a shifted external environment. Tushman, and most change theorists, focuses solely on current senior managers or their successors as the source of new logics. Most change theorists ignore the possibility that new logics can arise from inside the organization, through the interaction of different sets of stakeholders, each of which maintains their own unique logics. As an example, the dominant logic of an organization may have marketing as its central element. If this logic fails, then manufacturing, technical, and financial communities may exploit the crisis opportunity to advance their community-specific logics, or, jointly develop a new or hybrid logic.

Other possibilities exist as well. An organization's dominant logic may be transposable (Sewell, 1992). That is, an organization's logic may be capable of being applied to a wide variety of problems and external landscapes. Change events have sociopsychological effects on an organization and its members; Poole, Gioia, and Gray (1989, p. 273) refer to these critical incidents as "organizational breakdowns." When a breakdown occurs, it causes members of the organizational community to suspend their existing logics and to look at the world differently. Goffman (1974) termed this process *re-keying*. While keying involves a transformation or transcription of experience from one meaning into another, re-keying means to reorganize meaning parenthetically by modifying (but not totally transforming) a current logic. Opposing logics may become united through the common experience of a change-engendered breakdown. Each side, usually carrying its own set of meanings, can alter or drop these meanings in recognition of the need to resolve the crisis.

How Multiple Logics Interact

Individuals or groups in organizations can have *agency*, the ability to map logics onto organizational resources and to produce new patterns of human and resource interaction. Agency exists in leaders, but also among other groups (such as those at different functions and levels). Because multiple logics exist, and because logics are transposable, agents are prepared to introduce new logics to create change.

Because they face different goals and tasks, and value different activities, communities within an organization are likely, at least on occasion, to have opposing views of how an organization should be managed. These views clash in organizational settings, with each group representing its opinions to the other in the form of an argument that stands for its unique logic of what makes sense. The argument each group proposes to others reveals the logic it holds to be the superior one. Although one outcome of a change event might be mutual accommodation (Poole, et al., 1989), another might be that each party sees the other as not making any sense (Dougherty, 1992).

How conflicts are adjudicated between communities of logic determines the process and direction the organization will take. Disputes are resolved politically (Walsh and Fahey, 1986), and whoever has the power to resolve a dispute owns the logic system that carries the day (Hickson, Hinings, Lee, Schneck, and Pennings, 1971). The cumulative resolution of many disputes, in turn, becomes events for interpretation themselves. As all communities witness a dispute resolved in favor of one party over another, interpretations develop about how the organization's political system affects change. These interpretations guide the extent to which each group sets goals for itself and the degree to which they become engaged in a process to bring about change.

A negotiated order is likely to emerge from the interaction of opposing communities of logic (Walsh and Fahey, 1986), with each community doing "whatever is necessary within their ability to achieve the ends of the organization" (Fine, 1996, p. 111). Similar to concepts introduced by Weick (1995), we use the term *collective logic* to reflect the simultaneous cognitive and sociopolitical underpinnings of the change process. The collective logic may not be completely shared, but political compromise between opposing groups will nonetheless guide future organizational behavior.

Crises and Changes in Organizational Logics

A *crisis* is a situation in which the techno-economic and normative logics of the organization diverge. When the organization, or portions of the organization, no longer sees the organization as valid, agents attempt to introduce new logics to realign production and values. Crises can occur due to exogenous jolts or be endogenously created by agents. Because logics are multiple and often in conflict, one may dominate while others wait to contest that domination. Exogenous jolts or created crises allow for one group's logic to (possibly) supplant another's or even to blend interactively to create a new logic.

In the life of an organization, crises can occur that will shift the collective logic between communities to allow for crisis resolution. A crisis may be framed as being capable of being solved by one function, rather than another. If politics favor this function and its proposed solution, the effect will be to shift power to those capable of solving the crisis. Those functions most capable of dealing with an organization's critical problems are the ones that acquire power (Hickson et al., 1971). The ability to solve a problem and, consequently, to help the organization cope with uncertainty, creates dependence on the function. In the case of a cost crisis, power may accrue to manufacturing and purchasing in lieu of marketing. The result is a shift in the negotiated order of the collective logic such that the logic associated with the manufacturing function becomes primary. This results in management's willingness to search for, and accept, change solutions that solve the cost problem. Alternatively, crises can arise in response to cost or schedule problems. Manufacturing managers may refocus the organization's attention on "the conservation of resources and tight control mechanisms" and the "maintenance of the status quo" (Thomas, Clark, and Gioia, 1993, p. 244). The effect on change behavior would be to favor simpler cost-effective solutions and to be biased against elaborate searches for creative marketing alternatives.

Such a classification may be oversimplified. A crisis might involve collaboration between multiple functions (Daft, 1978). A cost problem might be solved by R&D's development of less expensive technologies or by marketing's creative interface with a client. Further, depending on the nature of the crisis, all functions might simultaneously engage in proposing change behavior, and from this interaction, a new, perhaps integrative logic, can emerge and become dominant. Our overall point is that crises shift structures of power and meaning.

Our expectation is that crisis-engendered reframings are normally reversible and temporary. They are likely to be bounded in time by the recognition of the crisis and its subsequent resolution. The collective logic may simply revert to its previous balance of power and meaning (Trice, 1993). Alternatively, a new collective logic may emerge that rewards the community that resolved the crisis by according it relatively greater status. Lasting change may occur

when repeated crises leave organizational members with altered interpretive schemes (Poole et al., 1989). The effects may be cumulative over the course of the life of an organization, and the histories that develop may spill into the future.

Conclusion

The concept of organizational logic is a useful means to organize the literature on structural change. We have identified three clusters of logics and have shown how they have developed over time. Each of the three perspectives offers a portal into how organizations change. The strengths and limitations of each suggest new concepts to guide change research in the future. We have extended the view of logic that appears in the extant literature by introducing concepts of multiple logics, multiple agents, the transposibility of logics, and organizational crises. These additional concepts offer promising opportunities for extending logics-based models of organizational change.

Notes

We would like to thank Maureen Blyler for her extensive help in preparing this chapter.

References

Abraham, R. & Shaw, C. (1987). Dynamics: a visual introduction. In F. E. Yates (Ed.) *Self-organizing systems* (pp. 543–597). New York: Plenum Publishing.

Abzug, R. & Mezias, S. J. (1993). The fragmented state and due process protections in organizations: The case of comparable worth. *Organization Science, 4,* 433–453.

Adizes, I. (1979). Organizational passages—Diagnosing and treating lifecycle problems of organizations. *Organizational Dynamics, 8,* 3–25.

Aiken, M. & Hage, J. (1971). The organic organization and innovation. *Sociology, 5,* 63–82.

Aldrich, H. E. (1999). *Organizations evolving.* London: Sage.

Allen, P. & McGlade, J. M. (1986). Dynamics of discovery and exploitation: The case of the Scotian fisheries. *Canadian Journal of Fish and Aquatic Sciences, 43,* 1187–1200.

Allport, F. H. (1962). A structureconomic conception of behavior: Individual and collective. *Journal of Abnormal and Social Psychology, 64,* 3–30.

Anderson, P. (1999). Complexity theory and organization science. *Organization Science, 10,* 216–232.

Angle, H. L. & Van de Ven, A. H. (1989). Suggestions for managing the innovation journey. In A. H. Van de Ven, H. L. Angle, & M. S. Poole (Eds.), *Research on the management of innovation* (pp. 663–698). New York: Ballinger/Harper & Row.

Argote, L. & Epple, D. (1990). Learning curves in manufacturing. *Science, 247,* 920–924.

Argote, L., Beckman, S. L., & Epple, D. (1990). The persistence and transfer of learning in industrial settings. *Management Science, 36,* 140–154.

Argyris, C. (1993). Education for leading-learning. *Organizational Dynamics, 21,* 5–18.

Argyris, C. & Schon, D. A. (1978). *Organizational learning.* Reading, MA: Addison-Wesley.

Argyris, C. & Schon, D. A. (1996). *Organizational learning II: Theory, method, and practice.* Reading, MA: Addison-Wesley.

Ashby, W. R. (1968). Principles of self-organizing systems. In W. Buckley (Ed.), *Modern systems research for the behavioral scientist* (pp. 1–41). Chicago: Aldine.

Ashkenas, R., Ulrich, D., Jick, T., & Kerr, S. (1995). *The boundaryless organization: Breaking the chains of organizational structure.* San Francisco: Jossey-Bass.

Astley, W. G. & Van de Ven, A. H. (1983). Central perspectives and debates in organization theory. *Administrative Science Quarterly, 28,* 245–273.

Axelrod, R. (1984). *The evolution of cooperation.* New York: Basic Books.

Bales, R. F. & Strodtbeck, F. L. (1951). Phases in group problem-solving. *Journal of Abnormal and Social Psychology, 46,* 485–495.

Barnard, C. I. (1938). *The functions of the executive.* Cambridge, MA: Harvard University Press.

Bartunek, J. M. (1984). Changing interpretive schemes and organizational restructuring: The example of a religious order. *Administrative Science Quarterly, 29,* 355–373.

Bateson, G. (1972). *Steps to an ecology of mind.* New York: Ballantine.

Bendix, R. (1956). *Work and authority in industry.* New York: Wiley.

Berger, P. & Luckman, T. (1966). *The social construction of reality.* New York: Anchor Press.

Bettis, R. A. & Prahalad, C. K. (1994). The dominant logic: Retrospective and extension. *Strategic Management Journal, 16,* 5–14.

Blau, P. M. (1970). A formal theory of differentiation in organizations. *American Sociological Review, 35,* 201–218.

Brock, W. & Sayers, C. (1988). Is the business cycle characterized by deterministic chaos? *Journal of Monetary Economics, 22,* 71–90.

Brown, J. S. (1991). Research that reinvents the corporation. *Harvard Business Review, 67,* 102–111.

Brown, J. S. & Duguid, P. (1991). Organizational learning and communities of practice: Toward a unified view of working, learning, and innovation. *Organization Science, 2,* 40–57.

Brown, S. L. & Eisenhardt, K. M. (1998). *Competing on the edge: Strategy as structured chaos.* Boston: Harvard Business School Press.

Burns, T. & Stalker, G. M. (1961). *The management of innovation.* London: Tavistock.

Burrell, G. & Morgan, G. (1979). *Sociological paradigms and organizational analysis: Elements of the sociology of corporate life.* London: Heinemann.

Chandler, A. I. (1962). *Strategy and structure.* Cambridge, MA: MIT Press.

Clark, B. R. (1960). *The open door college: A case study.* New York: McGraw-Hill.

Clark, K. B. & Wheelwright, S. C. (1995). *Managing new product and process development: Text and cases.* New York: Free Press.

Cohen, M. D., March, J. G., & Olsen, J. P. (1972). A garbage can model of organizational choice. *Administrative Science Quarterly, 17,* 1–25.

Cohen, W. M. & Levinthal, D. A. (1989). Innovation and learning: The two faces of R & D. *Economic Journal, 99,* 569–596.

Cohen, W. M. & Levinthal, D. A. (1990). Absorptive capacity: A new perspective on learning and innovation. *Administrative Science Quarterly, 35,* 128–152.

Cohen, M. D. & Sproull, L. S. (1991). Editors' introduction: Special issue on organizational learning. *Organization Science, 2,* 119–135.

Collins, R. (1981). The microfoundations of macrosociology. *American Journal of Sociology, 86,* (984–1004).

Cyert, R. M. & March, J. G. (1963). *A behavioral theory of the firm.* Englewood Cliffs, NJ: Prentice-Hall.

Daft, R. L. (1978). A dual-core model of organizational innovation. *Academy of Management Journal, 21,* 193–210.

Daft, R. L. & Becker, S. W. (1978). *Innovation in organizations.* New York: Elsevier.

Damanpour, F. (1991). Organizational innovation: A meta-analysis of effects of determinants and moderators. *Academy of Management Journal, 34,* 555–590.

Day, R. & Schafer, W. (1985). Keynesian chaos. *Journal of Macroeconomics, 7,* 277–295.

Deephouse, D. L. (1996). Does isomorphism legitimate? *Academy of Management Journal, 39,* 1024–1039.

DeSanctis, G. & Poole, M. S. (1994). Capturing the complexity in advanced technology use: Adaptive structuration theory. *Organization Science*, 5, 121–147.

Dess, G. G., Rasheed, A. M. A., McLaughlin, K. J., & Priem, R. L. (1995). The new corporate architecture. *Academy of Management Executive*, 9, 7–18.

Devaney, R. (1987). Chaotic bursts in nonlinear dynamical systems. *Science*, 235, 342–345.

Dewar, R. & Duncan, R. B. (1977). Implications for organizational design of structural alteration as a consequence of growth and innovation. *Organization and Administrative Sciences*, 8, 203–225.

DiMaggio, P. (1988). Interest and agency in institutional theory. In L. Zucker (Ed.), *Research on institutional patterns and organizations* (pp. 3–21). Cambridge, MA: Ballinger.

DiMaggio, P. (1994). Culture and economy. In N. J. Smelser & R. Swedberg (Eds.), *Handbook of economic sociology* (pp. 27–57). Princeton, NJ: Princeton University Press.

DiMaggio, P. (1997). Culture and cognition. *Annual Review of Sociology*, 23, 263–287.

DiMaggio, P. D. & Powell, W. W. (1983). The iron cage revisited: Institutional isomorphism and collective rationality in organizational fields. *American Sociological Review*, 48, 147–160.

Dodge, H. R., Fullerton, S., & Robbins, J. E. (1994). Stage of the organizational life cycle and competition as mediators of problem perception for small business. *Strategic Management Journal*, 15, 121–134.

Donaldson, L. (1996). The normal science of structural contingency theory. In S. R. Clegg, C. Hardy, & W. R. Nord (Eds.), *Handbook of organization studies* (pp. 57–76). Thousand Oaks, CA: Sage.

Dooley, K. J. & Van de Ven, A. H. (1999). Explaining complex organizational dynamics. *Organization Science*, 10, 358–372.

Doty, D. H. & Glick, W. H. (1994). Typologies as a unique form of theory building: Toward improved understanding and modeling. *Academy of Management Review*, 19, 230–251.

Doty, H. D., Glick, W. H., & Huber, G. P. (1993). Fit, equifinality, and organizational effectiveness: A test of two configurational theories. *Academy of Management Journal*, 36, 1196–1250.

Dougherty, D. (1992). Interpretive barriers to successful product innovation in large firms. *Organizational Science*, 3, 179–203.

Drazin, R. & Kazanjian, R. K. (1990). A reanalysis of Miller and Friesen's life cycle data. *Strategic Management Journal*, 11, 319–325.

Drazin, R. & Sandelands, L. (1992). Autogenesis: A perspective on the process of organizing. *Organization Science*, 3, 230–249.

Eldredge, N. & Gould, S. J. (1972). Punctuated equilibria: An alternative to phyletic gradualism. In T. J. Schopf (Ed.), *Models in paleobiology* (pp. 82–115). San Francisco: Freeman Cooper & Company.

Epple, D., Argote, L., & Devadas, R. (1991). Organizational learning curves: A method for investigating intra-plant transfer of knowledge acquired through learning by doing. *Organization Science*, 2, 58–70.

Fine, G. A. (1996). Justifying work: Occupational rhetorics as resources in restaurant kitchens. *Administrative Science Quarterly*, 41, 90–115.

Fligstein, N. (1985). The spread of the multidivisional firm, 1919–1979. *American Sociological Review*, 50, 377–391.

Fligstein, N. (1990). *The transformation of corporate control*. Cambridge, MA: Harvard University Press.

Fligstein, N. & Freeland, R. (1995). Theoretical and comparative perspectives on corporate organization. *Annual Review of Sociology*, 21, 21–43.

Frame, J. D. (1994). *The new project management: Tools for an age of rapid change, corporate reengineering, and other business realities*. San Francisco: Jossey-Bass.

Friedhoff, R. M. (1989). *Visualization: The second computer revolution*. New York: Harry Abrahms.

Friedland, R. & Alford, R. B. (1991). Bringing society back in: Symbols, practices, and institutional contradictions. In W. W. Powell & P. J. DiMaggio (Eds.), *The new institutionalism in organizational analysis* (pp. 232–263). Chicago: University of Chicago Press.

Galbraith, J. R. (1973). *Designing complex organizations*. Reading, MA: Addison Wesley.

Galbraith, J. R. (1982). Designing the innovating organization. *Organizational Dynamics*, 11, 5–25.

Geertz, C. (1973). *The interpretation of cultures*. New York: Basic Books.

Gersick, C. J. G. (1988). Time and transition in work teams: Toward a new model of group development. *Academy of Management Journal*, 41, 9–41.

Gersick, C. J. G. (1991). Revolutionary change theories: A multilevel exploration of the punctuated equilibrium paradigm. *Academy of Management Review*, 16, 10–36.

Giddens, A. (1979). *Central problems in social theory: Action, structure, and contradiction in social analysis*. Los Angeles: University of California Press.

Gleick, J. (1987). *Chaos: Making a new science*. New York: Viking.

Glynn, M. A., Lant, T. K., & Milliken, F. J. (1994). Mapping learning processes in organizations: A multi-level framework linking learning and organizing. *Advances in Managerial Cognition and Organizational Information Processing*, 5, 43–83.

Goffman, E. (1974). *Frame analysis.* Cambridge, MA: Harvard University Press.

Greiner, L. E. (1972). Evolution and revolution as organizations grow. *Harvard Business Review, 50,* 37–46.

Gresov, C. & Drazin, R. (1996). Equifinality: Functional equivalence in organization design. *Academy of Management Review, 22,* 403–428.

Hammer, M. & Champy, J. (1993). *Reengineering the corporation: A manifesto for business revolution.* New York: Harper Business.

Hannan, M. & Freeman, J. (1977). The population ecology of organizations. *American Journal of Sociology, 82,* 929–966.

Hannan, M. & Freeman, J. (1984). Structural inertia and organizational change. *American Sociological Review, 49,* 149–164.

Hayes, B. (1984). The cellular automation. *Scientific American, 50,* 12–21.

Hedberg, B. L. T., Nystrom, P. C., & Starbuck, W. (1976). Camping on seesaws: Prescriptions for a self-designing organization. *Administrative Science Quarterly, 21,* 41–65.

Hickson, D. J., Hinings, C. R., Lee, C. A., Schneck, R. E., & Pennings, J. M. (1971). A strategic contingencies theory of inter-organizational power. *Administrative Science Quarterly, 16,* 216–229.

Hitt, M. A., Ireland, R. D., & Palia, K. A. (1982). Industrial firms' grand strategy and functional importance: Moderating effects of technology and uncertainty. *Academy of Management Journal, 25,* 265–298.

Hofstadter, D. C. (1985). *Metamagical themas: Questing for the essence of mind and pattern.* London: Penguin Books.

Homans, G. C. (1950). *The human group.* New York: Harcourt.

Howell, J. M. & Higgins, C. A. (1990). Champions of technological innovations. *Administrative Science Quarterly, 35,* 317–341.

Huff, A. S. (1988). Politics and argument as a means of coping with ambiguity and change. In L. R. Pondy, R. J. Boland, & H. Thomas (Eds.), *Managing ambiguity and change* (pp. 79–90). New York: John Wiley.

Huse, E. F. (1975). *Organization development and change.* New York: West.

Huse, E. F. & Bowditch, J. L. (1973). *Behavior in organizations: A systems approach to managing.* Reading, MA: Addison-Wesley.

Imai, K., Nonaka, I., & Takeuchi, H. (1985). Managing product development: How Japanese companies learn and unlearn. In K. Clark, R. Hayes, & C. Lorenz (Eds.), *The uneasy alliance: Managing the productivity-technology dilemma* (pp. 337–376). Boston: Harvard Business School.

Jelinek, M. (1979). *Institutionalizing innovations: A study of organizational learning systems.* New York: Praeger.

Kanter, R. M. (1983). *The change masters.* New York: Simon & Schuster.

Kanter, R. M. (1985). Supporting innovation and venture development in established corporations. *Journal of Business Venturing, 1,* 47–60.

Katzenbach, J. R. & Smith, D. K. (1993). *The wisdom of teams: Creating the high performance organization.* Boston: Harvard Business School.

Kazanjian, R. K. (1988). Relation of dominant problems to stages of growth in technology-based new ventures. *Academy of Management Journal, 31,* 257–279.

Kazanjian, R. K. & Drazin, R. (1989). An empirical test of a stage of growth progression model. *Management Science, 35,* 1489–1503.

Keck, S. L. & Tushman, M. L. (1993). Environmental and organizational context and executive team structure. *Academy of Management Journal, 36,* 1314–1344.

Khandwalla, P. N. (1977). *The design of organizations.* New York: Harcourt.

Kimberly, J. R. & Miles, R. H. (Eds.) (1980). *The organizational life cycle: Issues in the creation, transformation, and decline of organizations.* San Francisco: Jossey-Bass.

Kogut, B. & Zander, U. (1992). Knowledge of the firm, combinative capabilities, and the replication of technology. *Organization Science, 3,* 383–397.

Kotter, J. P. & Schlesinger, L. A. (1979). Choosing strategies for change. *Harvard Business Review, 57,* 106–114.

Koza, M. P. & Lewin, A. Y. (1998). The co-evolution of strategic alliances. *Organization Science, 9,* 255–264.

Krippendorff, K. (1971). Communication and the genesis of structure. *General Systems, 16,* 171–185.

Kuhn, T. S. (1970). *The structure of scientific revolutions.* Chicago: University of Chicago Press.

Lane, P. J. & Lubatkin, M. (1998). Relative absorptive capacity and interorganizational learning. *Strategic Management Journal, 19,* 461–477.

Langton, J. (1984). The ecological theory of bureaucracy: The case of Josiah Wedgwood and the British pottery industry. *Administrative Science Quarterly, 29,* 330–354.

Lant, T. K. (1992). Aspiration level updating: An empirical exploration. *Management Science, 38,* 623–644.

Lant, T. K. & Mezias, S. K. (1990). Managing discontinuous change: A simulation study of organizational learning and entrepreneurship. *Strategic Management Journal, 11,* 147–179.

Larson, E. W. & Gobelli, D. H. (1987). Matrix management: Contradictions and insights. *California Management Review, 29,* 126–138.

Lave, C. A. & March, J. G. (1975). *An introduction to models in the social sciences.* New York: Harper & Row.

Lawrence, P. W. & Lorsch, J. W. (1967). Organization and environment: Managing differentiation and integration. Boston: Harvard Business School Press.

Levinson, D. J. (1978). *The seasons of a man's life.* New York: Knopf.

Levinthal, D. A. & March, J. G. (1981). A model of adaptive organizational search. In J. G. March (Ed.), *Decisions and organizations* (pp. 187–218). New York: Basil Blackwell.

Levitt, B. & March, J. G. (1988). Organizational learning. *Annual Review of Sociology, 14,* 319–340.

Lewin, K. (1951). *Field theory in social science.* New York: Harper & Row.

Lorenz, H. (1987). Strange attractors in a multisector business model. *Journal of Economic Behavior and Organization, 8,* 397–411.

Lucas, H. C. (1996). *Information technology for management.* New York: McGraw-Hill.

March, J. & Simon, H. (1958). *Organizations.* New York: Wiley.

March, J. G. (1981). Footnotes to organizational change. *Administrative Science Quarterly, 26,* 563–577.

March, J. G. (1991). Exploration and exploitation in organizational learning. *Organization Science, 2,* 71–87.

March, J. G. & Olsen, J. P. (1976). *Ambiguity and choice in organizations.* Bergen, Norway: Universitetsforlaget.

Masuch, M. & LaPotin, P. (1989). Beyond garbage cans: An AI model of organizational choice. *Administrative Science Quarterly, 34,* 38–67.

Mayhew, B. (1980). Structuralism versus individualism: Shadow boxing in the dark. *Social Forces, 59,* 335–375.

McKelvey, B. & Aldrich, H. (1983). Populations, natural selection, and applied organizational science. *Administrative Science Quarterly, 28,* 101–128.

Messinger, S. L. (1955). Organizational transformation: A case study of declining social movement. *American Journal of Sociology, 20,* 3–10.

Meyer, J. W. & Rowan, B. T. (1977). Institutionalized organizations: Formal structure as myth and ceremony. *American Journal of Sociology, 83,* 340–363.

Mezias, S. V. & Glynn, M. A. (1993). The three faces of corporate renewal: Institution, revolution, and evolution. *Strategic Management Journal, 14,* 77–101.

Miles, R. E., Snow, C. C., Matthews, J. A., Miles, G., & Coleman, H. J., Jr. (1997). Organizing in the knowledge age: Anticipating the cellular form. *Academy of Management Executive, 11,* 7–20.

Miles, R. H. (1997). *Leading corporate transformation: An executive briefing.* San Francisco: Jossey-Bass.

Miles, R. H. & Randolph, W. (1980). Influence of organizational learning styles on early development. In J. H. Kimberly & R. H. Miles (Eds.), *The organizational life cycle* (pp. 44–82). San Francisco: Jossey-Bass.

Miller, D. & Friesen, P. H. (1982). Structural change and performance: Quantum versus piecemeal-incremental approaches. *Academy of Management Journal, 25,* 867–892.

Miller, D. & Friesen, P. H. (1984). A longitudinal study of the corporate life cycle. *Management Science, 30,* 1161–1183.

Miner, A. (1987). Idiosyncratic jobs in formalized organizations. *Administrative Science Quarterly, 32,* 327–351.

Mitroff, I. I., Mason, R. O., & Pearson, C. M. (1994). Radical surgery: What will tomorrow's organizations look like? *Academy of Management Executive, 8,* 11–22.

Morel, B. & Ramanujam, R. (1999). Through the looking glass of complexity: The dynamics of organizations as adaptive and evolving systems. *Organization Science, 10,* 278–293.

Nadler, D. A. & Tushman, M. T. (1989). Organizational frame bending: Principles for managing reorientation. *Academy of Management Executive, 3,* 194–204.

Nicolis, G. & Prigogine, I. (1977). Self-organization in nonequilibrium systems: From dissipative structures to order through fluctuations. New York: Wiley.

Normann, R. (1977). *Management for growth.* New York: Wiley.

O'Dell, C. S. & Jackson, C., Jr. (1998). *If only we knew what we know: The transfer of internal knowledge and best practice.* New York: Free Press.

O'Toole, J. (1995). Leading change: Overcoming the ideology of comfort and the tyranny of custom. San Francisco: Jossey-Bass.

Ostroff, F. (1999). *The horizontal organization: What the organization of the future actually looks like and how it delivers value to customers.* Oxford: Oxford University Press.

Parsons, T. (1977). *The evolution of societies.* Englewood Cliffs, NJ: Prentice-Hall.

Pasternak, B. & Viscio, A. (1998). *The centerless corporation: Transforming your organization for growth and prosperity in the new millennium.* New York: Simon & Schuster.

Perrow, C. (1961). The analysis of goals in complex organizations. *American Sociological Review, 26,* 854–865.

Perrow, C. (1967). A framework for the comparative analysis of organizations. *American Sociological Review, 32,* 194–208.

Perrow, C. (1986). *Complex organizations: A critical essay.* New York: Random House.

Pierce, J. L. & Delbecq, A. L. (1977). Organizational structure, individual attitudes, and innovation. *Academy of Management Review, 2,* 27–37.

Poole, P., Gioia, D., & Gray, B. (1989). Influence modes, schema change, and organizational transformation. *Journal of Applied Behavioral Science, 25,* 271–289.

Poundstone, W. (1984). *The recursive universe.* Chicago: Contemporary Books.

Powell, W. W. & DiMaggio, P. J. (Eds.) (1991). *The new institutionalism in organizational analysis.* Chicago: University of Chicago Press.

Prahalad, C. K. & Bettis, R. A. (1986). The dominant logic: A new linkage between diversity and performance. *Strategic Management Journal, 7,* 485–501.

Prigogine, I. & Stengers, I. (1984). *Order out of chaos: Man's new dialog with nature.* New York: Bantam Books.

Pugh, D. S. & Hinings, C. R. (1976). *Organizational structure in its context: the Aston programme II.* Farnsborough, Hants: Saxon House.

Pugh, D. S., Hickson. D. J., & Hinings, C. R. (1969). An empirical taxonomy of structures of work. *Administrative Science Quarterly, 14,* 115–126.

Purser, R. E. & Cabana, S. (1998). *The self-managing organization: How leading companies are transforming the work of teams for real impact.* New York: Free Press.

Quinn, R. E. & Cameron, K. (1983). Organizational life cycles and shifting criteria of effectiveness: Some preliminary evidence. *Management Science, 29,* 33–51.

Quinn, J. B. (1985, May–June). Managing innovation: Controlled chaos. *Harvard Business Review,* 73–84.

Radner, R. (1975). A behavioral model of cost reduction. *Bell Journal of Economics, 6,* 196–215.

Rasmussen, D. & Mosekilde, E. (1988). Bifurcations and chaos in a generic management model. *European Journal of Operational Research, 35,* 80–88.

Reichers, A. E., Wanous, J. P., & Austin, J. T. (1997). Understanding and managing cynicism about organizational change. *Academy of Management Executive, 11,* 48–57.

Rhenman, E. (1973). *Organization theory for long range planning.* London: Wiley.

Rice, A. K. (1958). *Productivity and social organization: The Ahmedabad experiment.* London: Tavistock.

Rogers, E. M. & Shoemaker, F. F. (1971). *Communication of innovation.* New York: Free Press.

Rogers, E. M. (1983). *Diffusion of innovations.* New York: Free Press.

Romanelli, E. & Tushman, M. L. (1994). Organizational transformation as punctuated equilibrium: An empirical test. *Academy of Management Journal, 37,* 1141–1166.

Sandelands, L. & Drazin, R. (1989). On the language of organization theory. *Organization Science, 10,* 457–477.

Sastry, M. A. (1997). Problems and paradoxes in a model of punctuated organizational change. *Administrative Science Quarterly, 42,* 237–275.

Schein, E. H. (1988). *Process consultation.* Reading, MA: Addison-Wesley.

Schelling, T. C. (1978). *Micromotives and macrobehavior.* New York: Norton.

Schieve, W. & Allen, P. (Eds.) (1982). *Self-organization and dissipative structures: Applications in the physical and social sciences.* Austin: University of Texas Press.

Scott, W. R. & Meyer, J. W. (1994). *Institutional environments and organizations: Structural complexity and individualism.* Thousand Oaks, CA: Sage Publications.

Selznick, P. (1949). *TVA and the grass roots.* Berkeley, CA: University of California Press.

Selznick, P. (1957). *Leadership in administration.* New York: Harper and Row.

Senge, P. M. (1990a, Fall). The leader's new work: Building learning organizations. *Sloan Management Review,* 7–23.

Senge, P. M. (1990b). *The fifth discipline.* New York: Doubleday Currency.

Sewell, T. H. (1992). A theory of structure: Duality, agency, and transformation. *American Journal of Sociology, 98,* 1–29.

Shenkar, O. & Li, J. (1999). Knowledge search in international cooperative ventures. *Organization Science, 10,* 134–143.

Simon, H. (1957). *Administrative behavior.* New York: Macmillan.

Smith, K. G., Mitchell, T. R., & Summer, C. E. (1985). Top-level management priorities in different stages of organizational life cycle. *Academy of Management Journal, 28,* 799–820.

Starbuck, W. (1971). *Organizational growth and development.* London: Penguin Books.

Stinchcombe, A. (1965). Social structure and organization. In J. March (Ed.), *The handbook of organizations* (pp. 142–193). Chicago: Rand McNally.

Szulanski, G. (1996). Exploring internal stickness: Impediments to the transfer of best practice within the firm. *Strategic Management Journal, 17,* 27–43.

Thomas, J., Clark, S., & Gioia, C. (1993). Strategic sensemaking and organizational performance: Linkages among scanning, interpretation, action, and outcomes. *Academy of Management Journal, 36,* 239–270.

Thompson, V. A. (1965). Bureaucracy and innovation. *Administrative Science Quarterly, 10,* 1–20.

Thompson, J. D. (1967). *Organizations in action.* New York: McGraw-Hill.

Thornton, P. H. & Ocasio, W. (1999). Institutional logics and the historical contingency of power in organizations: Executive succession in the higher education publishing industry, 1958–1990. *American Journal of Sociology, 105,* 801–843.

Tolbert, P. S. & Zucker, L. G. (1996). The institutionalization of institutional theory. In S. R. Clegg, C. Hardy, & W. R. Nord (Eds.), *Handbook of organizational studies* (pp. 175–190). Thousand Oaks, CA: Sage.

Trice, H. M. (1993). *Occupational subcultures in the workplace.* Ithaca, NY: ILR Press, Cornell University.

Trist, E. L. (Ed.) (1963). *Organizational choice: Capabilities of groups at the coal face under changing technologies.* London: Tavistock Institute.

Trist, E. & Bamforth, K. (1951). Some social and psychological consequences of the long wall method of goal-setting. *Human Relations, 4,* 1–8.

Tushman, M. L. & Moore, W. L. (Eds.) (1982). *Readings in the management of innovation.* Boston: Pitman Press.

Tushman, M. L. & O'Reilly, C. A. (1997). *Winning through innovation: A practical guide to leading organizational change and renewal.* Boston: Harvard Business School Press.

Tushman, M. L. & Romanelli, E. (1985). Organizational evolution: A metamorphosis model of convergence and reorientation. In L. L. Cummings & B. M Shaw (Eds.), *Research in organizational behavior* (pp. 171–222). Greenwich, CT: JAI Press.

Tushman, M. L. & Rosenkopf, L. (1996). Executive succession, strategic reorientation and performance growth: A longitudinal study in the U. S. cement industry. *Management Science, 42,* 939–953.

Tushman, M. L.; Newman, W. H., & Romanelli, R. (1986). Convergence and upheaval: Managing the unsteady pace of organizational evolution. *California Management Review, 29,* 1–16.

Van de Ven, A. H. & Delbecq, A. L. (1974). A task contingent model of work-unit structure. *Administrative Science Quarterly, 2,* 183–197.

Van de Ven, A. H. & Drazin, R. (1985). The concept of fit in contingency theory. *Research in Organizational Behavior, 7,* 333–365.

Van de Ven, A. H. & Ferry, D. (1980). *Measuring and assessing organizations.* New York: Wiley.

Van de Ven, A. & Poole, M. S. (1988). Paradoxical requirements for a theory of organizational change. In K. S. Cameron & R. E. Quinn (Eds.), *Paradox and transformation: Toward a theory of change in organization and management* (pp. 19–64). Cambridge, MA: Ballinger Publishing Company.

Van de Ven, A. H. & Poole, M. S. (1995). Explaining development and change in organizations. *Academy of Management Review, 20,* 510–540.

Van de Ven, A. H., Hudson, R., & Schroeder, D. (1984). Designing new business start-ups: Entrepreneurial, organizational, and ecological considerations. *Journal of Management, 10,* 87–108.

Virany, B., Tushman, M. L., & Romanelli, E. (1992). Executive succession and organization outcomes in turbulent environments: An organization learning approach. *Organization Science, 3,* 72–91.

Von Neumann, J. (1951). The general and logical theory of automata. In L. A. Jeffries (Ed.), *Servomechanisms and behavior* (pp. 1–41). New York: Wiley.

Walsh, J. P. (1995). Managerial and organizational cognition: Notes from a trip down memory lane. *Organization Science, 6,* 280–321.

Walsh, J. P. & Fahey, L. (1986). The role of negotiated belief structures in strategy making. *Journal of Management, 12,* 325–338.

Walsh, J. P., Henderson, C., & Deighton, J. (1988). Negotiated belief structures and decision performance: An empirical investigation. *Organizational Behavior and Human Decision Processes, 42,* 194–216.

Watzlawick, P., Weakland, J. H., & Fisch, R. (1974). *Change: Principles of problem formation and problem resolution.* New York: Norton.

Weber, M. (1947). *The theory of social and economic organization.* New York: Irvington.

Weick, K. (1979). *The social psychology of organizing.* Reading, MA: Addison-Wesley.

Weick, K. & Berlinger, L. (1989). Career improvisation in self-designing organizations. In M. Arthur, D. Hall, & B. Lawrence (Eds.), *Handbook of career theory* (pp. 313–328). New York: Cambridge University Press.

Weick, K. E. (1995). *Sensemaking in organizations.* Thousand Oaks, CA: Sage.

Woodward, J. (1965). *Industrial organization: Theory and practice.* Oxford, UK: Oxford University Press.

Yates, F. E. (Ed.) (1987). *Self organizing systems: The emergence of order.* New York: Plenum.

Yelle, L. E. (1979). The learning curve: Historical review and comprehensive survey. *Decision Sciences,* *10,* 302–328.

Zald, M. N. & Denton, P. (1963). From evangelism to general service: The transformation of the YMCA. *Administrative Science Quarterly,* 8, 214–234.

Zucker, L. G. (1977). The role of institutionalization in cultural persistence. *American Sociological Review,* *42,* 726–743.

7

Dynamics in Organizational Culture

Mary Jo Hatch

Cultures change, but they also stay the same. Sociologists and anthropologists have studied their evolution (e.g., Sahlins and Service, 1960; Sorokin, 1937; White, 1959), documented both their stability and changes, and theorized about their dynamics (Barnett, 1953; Herskovits, 1948, 1964; Kroeber, 1944; Malinowski, 1945; Redfield, 1953; Weber, 1924/1947). For some reason, however, little of this work has filtered into contemporary discussions of culture in the field of organization studies where the focus is on the cultures of business firms and other organizations. In fact, it seems fair to say that only a handful of organization studies since the 1980s, when organizational culture came into its own, mention the dynamic properties of culture (Brannen, 1998; Czarniawska and Sevon, 1996; Gagliardi, 1986; Hatch, 1993; Schein, 1985, 1992; Van Maanen and Schein, 1979).

For most organizational writers, culture is a stable, conservative, and resistant force that is likely to change only through management intervention. As recently as 1999, for example, Hendry stated: "Because of its deeply embedded nature any culture, societal, institutional, or organizational, is resistant to change" (Hendry, 1999, p. 563). There are literally hundreds of examples one might give of this attitude to orga-

nizational culture change, some of the earliest and most influential being Ouchi (1981), Pascale and Athos (1981), Deal and Kennedy (1982), and Kilmann, Saxton, and Serpa (1985). Nonetheless nearly all of this literature addresses the possibilities and benefits of intentionally altering organizational culture as a means to achieving greater managerial control or enhancing organizational performance. Thus, this literature pits the stability of organizational culture against managerial demands for organizational adaptability and change.

Those not adopting the managerial view of culture change will be found mainly in the interpretive organizational literature (see Schultz, 1995, or Hatch and Yanow, 2003, for discussions of the interpretive perspective in organization studies). Interpretivists, however, have tended to focus on meaning, sense making, and the symbolic and aesthetic aspects of culture rather than on its dynamic properties (see, e.g., Frost, Moore, Louis, Lundberg, and Martin, 1985, 1991; Gagliardi, 1990; Jones, Moore, and Snyder, 1988; and Turner, 1990, for compilations of interpretive organizational culture research, or Martin, 1992, for a comprehensive survey of the organizational culture literature). Although change is not a primary topic of concern for the interpretivists (cf.

Gagliardi, 1986; Hatch, 1993; Schein, 1985, 1992), resistance to change sometimes is, especially among those who adopt a critical orientation (e.g., Collinson, 1999; Hopfl and Linstead, 1993; Jermier, 1998; Knights and Willmott, 1987; Rosen, 1985; Stablein and Nord, 1985; Willmott, 1993). The critical camp views culture either as symbolic terrain to be contested (who will control meaning?), or as a resource (symbolism) used by both sides in the struggle for power and domination.

Both managerially and critically minded organizational researchers assume that resistance to change is rooted in cultural stability (or, in critical terminology, that resistance to managerial oppression can be rooted in the solidarity of working-class culture). Bate (1997, p. 1155) voiced the managerial side of this conundrum when he claimed that "debilitating cultural hangovers from the past" play "havoc" with day-to-day management processes. On the critical side, Jermier (1998, p. 238, paraphrasing Horkheimer) noted that "the project of the critical theorist is to think in the service of exploited and oppressed humanity and to work for the abolition of social injustice." Resistance, whether bemoaned by managerial organizational culture researchers or encouraged by critical theorists, reproduces the old standoff between the interests of management and those of the "resistance fighters." A similar standoff, branded the "organizational culture war games" by Martin and Frost (1996), is evident among academics.

Martin and Frost (1996) presented an analysis of the academic war among researchers adopting different perspectives on organizational culture. Drawing on Martin's (1992) classification of researchers into the factions of integrationists, differentiationists, and fragmentationists (roughly aligned with modern, interpretive, and postmodern perspectives), Martin and Frost claimed that, historically, the managerially-oriented integrationist perspective vied with the interpretivists in drawing battle lines between a view of culture that emphasized consistency, harmony, and consensus and a view that culture is essentially divided into subcultures. These battle lines were reinforced by differences of view concerning appropriate methodologies and their underlying epistemological positions, in particular the relative merits of quantitative and qualitative methods. As Martin and Frost (1996, p. 613) put it: "Every careful ethnography or qualitative study that tries to challenge integrationist assumptions is countered quickly by yet another

assertion that any culture can be a haven for homogeneity and harmony—a place where management's values are shared by all, and an employee's major task is simply to find a culture where he or she will 'fit in.' "

While the metaphor of war games may attract attention to key debates within organizational culture studies, it also distracts it from the bigger picture of cultural dynamics. This chapter marks a return to the seemingly lost project of explaining both stability and change, a project begun by evolutionary sociologists and early cultural anthropologists. In the following pages I will retrace the steps of these early scholars of cultural dynamics and follow their paths into organizational culture studies, suggesting where connections to the earlier work either have been or yet might be made. My purpose is to draw together theoretical support for the continued pursuit of a theory of the cultural dynamics of organizations that considers stability and change as dual products of the same cultural processes.

Cultural Dynamics in Evolutionary Sociology and Cultural Anthropology

In 1883, the evolutionary sociologist Lester Ward suggested that the mechanisms of evolution themselves evolve. According to Ward, cosmogenesis appeared at the birth of the universe, following which new evolutionary mechanisms evolved along with the appearance of life (biogenesis), humans (anthropogenesis), and social systems (sociogenesis), the latter including societies and organizations. Evolution-minded anthropologists then focused on sociogenesis, some interpreting this mechanism in relation to cultural evolution. For example, Leslie White (1959) proposed that the primary mechanism of cultural evolution was technological change. Taking a different approach, Sahlins and Service (1960) distinguished general from specific evolution on the grounds that general evolution defines "the overall direction of humanity, in which new cultural types constantly emerge," while specific evolution "comprises the concrete ways in which the new cultural types adapt themselves to specific environments" (Sztompka, 1993, p. 117).

In parallel with specific evolution theory, but often denying evolution as their theoretical foundation, cultural anthropologists similarly came to the conclusion that it is important to study concrete cultural change and define its underlying processes.

Although not all cultural anthropologists denigrated evolution, those who followed the lead of Boas and Malinowski argued against the evolutionary assumption that cultures evolve independently of each other. Instead of evolution, these anthropologists proposed mechanisms of cross-cultural influence such as diffusion. But there were other differences between these early cultural anthropologists and their colleagues in sociology who advocated an evolutionary view. One important difference was that the anthropologists did not restrict their interest to the processes of change involving adaptation to the environment; they were also interested in processes of cultural change that occurred within a culture. A second difference was that cultural anthropologists tended not to look only at mechanisms of change, but to look at these in relation to mechanisms of stability.

According to Robert Redfield (1953), the first cultural anthropologists left the false impression that so-called primitive cultures were conservative, stable, and unchanging. Redfield admitted that anthropologists were often a bit sentimental, mourning the passing of cultures and their forms. For example, in reaction to a journalist's comment that "indignation is felt when the monograph records that the rhythm of the old dances is now beaten out on a biscuit tin instead of a drum," he mused (1953, pp. 149–150):

I am sure that I have lamented the decline in folk arts in Mexico or in China. This tendency to betray some preference for the old ways in an exotic society is, I suppose, stimulated by the fact that the comparison of cultures, as unchanging systems, has been a principal task of anthropology until more recent times, when acculturation and the troubles of the personality have become matters for anthropologists to study. It is perhaps also induced by the attractiveness of a system of ideas that natives find convincing and satisfying and that anthropologists find logically coherent.

Alongside sentimentality, Redfield noted that emphasis on cultural conservatism and stability was at least partly a methodological artifact, and that the heavy theoretical influence of structuralism and the search for the universal laws of culture did not encourage paying attention to change either. Changes were annoying more than interesting. For example, when cultures changed, anthropologists were called on to defend the reliability of their methods and the validity of their theories and findings. Ultimately,

however, cultural change could not be denied, and by the 1940s questions of change were influencing the course of cultural anthropology dramatically.

Even with the shifting of focus onto cultural change, the importance of cultural stability was never forgotten. The early anthropologists of cultural dynamics clearly understood the need to theorize cultural change in relation to stability. For instance, under the heading "Culture is dynamic," Melville Herskovits (1948, p. 635) stated:

Change is a constant in human culture. It is, however, always to be studied against a backdrop of cultural stability. Even though changes may appear to be far-reaching to the members of a society where they occur, they seldom affect more than a relatively small part of the total body of custom by which a people live. The problems of cultural dynamics thus are seen to take on a positive and at the same time a negative aspect. Change, that is, must always be considered in relation to resistance to change.

Though the confounding of cultural stability and resistance to change in this passage may help to explain current standoffs in the culture war games, Herskovits also offered an important lead to understanding how stability and change can both be part of culture. As he astutely observed, you will "never find cultures that move at the same rate over the whole front" (Herskovits 1964, p. 148). Thus one key to unlocking the dynamics of organizational culture is to understand that, at a given moment, culture is changing only in parts; other parts remain stable.

Herskovits's idea that cultures vary at different rates "over the whole front" presents an early dynamic image of culture, which he metaphorized vividly in another passage by stating that "the broad stream which comprises any culture has varied currents, of which now some, now others will be the more rapid" (Herskovits 1964, pp. 205–206). This dynamic perspective was suggested to him, in part, by the work of Linton (1936) and Barnett (1942).

Linton had described similarities and differences in behavior within a culture in terms of four elements (Linton, 1936, pp. 272–275, cited in Herskovits 1964, p. 210):

1. Universals—those beliefs and forms of behavior to be expected of any normal member of a society (language, clothing, housing).

2. Specialties—particular aspects of behavior that characterize the members of specialized groups within the larger social whole (gendered activities, activities of different kinds of craftsmen)
3. Alternatives—forms of behavior recognized by a society as valid, but which cut across class or occupational or sex lines (color choice in decorations, word choice, ways of playing a game, different forms of marriage)
4. Individual peculiarities—experimental forms of behavior contributed by individualists (sources of innovation in a culture).

According to Linton, the universals of a culture explain similarities in behavior across all cultural members while specialties, alternatives and peculiarities (i.e., idiosyncrasies) account for differences. In addition, Linton (1936, p. 402) argued that all elements of culture possess four interrelated qualities—form, meaning, use, and function. Barnett (1942) later claimed that these qualities can vary independently as cultural elements change, thus rendering Linton's framework more dynamic. As will be seen below, specialties, peculiarities, and especially alternatives were later conceptualized as opportunities for cultures to change. What is more, the qualities of meaning and use (as opposed to form and function) presaged symbolic-interpretive developments in cultural anthropology (as typified for most by the work of Geertz, e.g., 1973).

As part of his attempt to theorize cultural dynamics, Herskovits (1964, pp. 152–158) categorized cultural change studies as being one of two types: change from within and change from outside. Thus we find the sources of change attributed either to innovation, discovery, and invention ("internal change" or "independent origin"), or to diffusion and cultural borrowing ("change from outside"). Herskovits claimed that the anthropological evidence supporting change from outside was much more readily available than that supporting independent origin due to the interests of anthropologists of his day. One of the most influential of these was Bronislaw Malinowski, though as we shall see below in connection with Weber's work, much of what Malinowski said about the dynamics of change from outside appears to generalize to change from within.

Malinowski was a leading figure in research on diffusion processes as they unfold through cultural contact and change. His efforts to describe and ex-

plain what happens to "primitive" cultures when they are "exposed" to "modern" ones were documented in his 1945 book *The Dynamics of Culture Change*, in which he wrote about the diffusion of European culture to Africa. In this book Malinowski (1945) presented cultural contact as occurring primarily between the institutions of the two cultures in question and argued that change was the consequence of the effect pairs of institutions had on one another. Malinowski (1945, p. 71) explained: "The ultimate reality in culture change hinges on the fact that corresponding institutions in two cultures satisfy analogous needs in different ways and with different techniques; but in the process they have to use the same human and natural resources: land, capital, labor, politically organized force, the impulses of human reproduction, and also the standardized emotions, values, and loyalties specific to each culture." Malinowski then analyzed the mutual influence of "corresponding" European and African institutions, such as European administrations and native tribal authority, Western enterprise and African labor, and organized missionary societies and African religion.

For our purposes in this chapter, the important point is not Malinowski's focus on institutions as media for cultural exchange, but his descriptions of the exchange process itself. Cultural contact and change for Malinowski were not a simple fusion or mixing together of two cultures. Instead of integration, Malinowski (1945, p. 26) proposed a dynamic of complex modification in which "the two impinge on each other" and thereby create "the phenomenon of autonomous change resulting from the reaction between two cultures." He described diffusion as dependent on prior cultures, but with no precedent in either of them. The result, he claimed, was "new cultural realities" that must be understood, not by direct reference to either parent culture, but as processes "running on their own specific lines" (Malinowski, 1945, p. 80).

Malinowski (1945, p. 52) also acknowledged stability as a counterforce to cultural change, noting, "While it may seem easy to replace a custom here and there or transform a technical device, such a change of detail very often upsets an institution without reforming it, because...beliefs, ideas, and practices are welded into bigger systems." According to Malinowski, the stabilizing force of the bigger systems into which institutions (as beliefs, ideas, and practices) are welded limits the integrative possibilities between two cultures. This limitation, according to Malinowski, leads to there being only three possible outcomes of cultural contact: conflict, cooperation, or compromise.

It was in relation to the alternatives of conflict, cooperation, and compromise that Malinowski became pragmatic and political in regard to deliberate efforts to change culture. His notion of selective giving shows clear evidence that he understood the role of domination in the culture changes that he observed in Africa (Malinowski, 1945, p. 58): "If power, wealth, and social amenities were given, culture change would be a comparatively easy and smooth process. It is the absence of these factors—our selective giving—which makes culture change such a complicated and difficult process. The real forces for effective assimilation are to be found in the advantages offered by us to the accepting culture.... Selective giving influences the process of change perhaps more than any other element in the situation." In this passage Malinowski interprets culture change that occurs through planned incursions into others' cultures as domination on the part of one group relative to another (i.e., the withholding of power, wealth, and social amenities). Resistance to such efforts may be rooted in cultural resources but is directed at the struggle for power and domination between two competing groups. Thus, following Malinowski, I would argue that it is not culture per se that should be held accountable for resistance, but rather acts of domination inscribed within cross-cultural relationships (such as have been the primary focus of those taking the critical ethnographic approach to the management of culture, e.g., Van Maanen, 1991; Rosen, 1988; and Kunda, 1992).

In taking a cross-cultural perspective on resistance to selective giving, Malinowski (1945) approximated the cultural dynamic that the sociologist Max Weber earlier described as the routinization of charisma (see Hatch, 2000, for further discussion of Weber and cultural dynamics). That is, if we conceptualize leaders and followers as members of different cultures (or subcultures), the powerful forms of resistance that Malinowski observed operating between cultures are paralleled by Weber's discussion of routinization.

Weber had been interested in explaining how, under extraordinary conditions including "suffering, conflicts or enthusiasm," revolutionary change in worldviews and their consequent influence on social action occurs within society (Weber, 1968/1978, pp. 241–249). However, Weber found that even in revolutionary change the effects of charismatic influence are routinized to serve the needs and interests of everyday life. To explain routinization, Weber proposed the processes of systematization and accommodation. With systematization, "disciples" of the charismatic leader link and extend charismatic influence to everyday life. As Weberian scholar Ralph Schroeder (1992, p. 10) explained it, "A stratum of interpreters elaborates the belief-system so that it constitutes a coherent whole and its tenets are extended to apply to various aspects of everyday life." Accommodation involves the interpretations and implementations of new beliefs and obligations. These new beliefs and obligations then shape and alter the charismatic influence in ways that bring it into line with the mundane and familiar aspects of everyday life and cause it to conform, more or less, to existing power relations. Schroeder (1992, p. 10) explained: "There is an accommodation of the belief-system to the interests of various strata of believers. As a result, its content corresponds more and more closely with what these strata, on the basis of their social position, had already been predisposed to believe or with their everyday conduct."

It is through routinization, Weber argued, that new ideas introduced by charismatic individuals constitute culture change but are also transformed (routinized) by that very process (i.e., via systematization and accommodation). The transformation occurs because followers not only wish to participate in the worldview of the charismatic leader, but also wish to maintain their social position and their material well-being (e.g., serve their family obligations and their political and economic interests). Thus routinization accomplishes both change and stability.

It is in terms of routinization that I see Malinowski's description of cross-cultural exchange to be comparable to Weber's theory of charisma. Under conditions of selective giving (i.e., domination), the wish to participate in the worldview of the change agent is absent or severely limited, and as a result the processes of systematization and accommodation described by Weber are never put fully into play. When domination is not an issue (either for the dominating culture, or for both cultures in a power-balanced exchange), the worldviews of the other may offer enticements that engage systematization and accommodation processes, just as do enticing ideas put forward by a charismatic leader.

The notion of selective giving suggests that culture change may involve the definition of the situation as either including domination or not. When resistance fighters invoke a frame of domination they socially construct a cultural orientation best suited to maintaining resistance to imposed change. Ironically, in accusing others of hegemonic practices, such actions themselves are hegemonic. On the other hand, managers invite such resistance, particularly when they practice selective giving—for example, when they promote employee empowerment schemes, not for the welfare of the employees, but to maximize their own wealth or that of their shareholders. When this attitude is combined with downsizing, the resultant fear of loss only magnifies the sense of domination that shuts down the very change process that the manager was hoping to lead. Clear examples of this phenomenon have been found by researchers studying the cultural aspects of mergers and acquisitions (e.g., Bastien, 1989; Mirvis and Marks, 1992).

According to the work that I have done on cultural dynamics (Hatch, 1993, 2000; see also the synopsis below), a better approach to changing culture would be to acknowledge and participate in the culture's own dynamic processes, fitting one's ambition into the flow of stability and change from which the culture itself is constituted. This involves, perhaps above all else, a simultaneous focus on what will be preserved (and how) and what will be changed. The present either-or mentality hampers the dynamics of culture and undermines ability to influence either outcome.

In his theory of the routinization of charisma, Weber presented a dynamic view of culture, that is, a theory capable of explaining both stability and change. However, his theory depended upon the dual assumptions of extraordinary conditions and the presence of charismatic leadership. Malinowski's ideas can be used to extend Weber's theory to cross-cultural situations. But what of everyday cultural dynamism occurring within an organizational culture without the benefit of charisma? Here Herskovits made a significant contribution, not only focusing on the mundane aspects of cultural dynamics, but also highlighting additional processes by which culture change takes place.

Herskovits noted that "small changes begin immediately on the introduction of an innovation, and the process of alteration never ceases" (1964, p. 158). The same is true, Herskovits also pointed out, for an introduction of new material or meaning via borrowing from other cultures. But regardless of whether the source of change is internal or external, symbolic or technological, the point Herskovits stressed time and again is the need to focus on process. For example, Herskovits (1948, p. 640) wrote:

> The laws . . . must be laws of process; the cultural forms which represent their end-results must be regarded not as fixed, but as variables whose limits are set by the probabilities that a given type will emerge from a given concatenation of circumstances. . . . In these terms, prediction is quite possible. It is achieved in everyday life when, all unconsciously, we predict within fairly narrow limits how a man or woman of a given society will behave in a given situation. Prediction of a broader sort can be made with considerable confidence about how certain dynamic processes will operate under cross-cultural contact.

In this passage we can see the positivist bent of the scientific discourse in which Herskovits participated—the language of variables, laws, probabilities, and predictions. But through his positivist vocabulary, we can also hear Herskovits proposing a special kind of prediction—unconscious prediction—and along with promoting laws of process we might imagine that he was moving quite a distance from what positivists meant when they used terms like *prediction* and *law*. Specifically, with his "all unconsciously" Herskovits opened the door to intuitive knowledge, while with his "laws of process" he pushed us toward dynamic understanding. In the next section of this chapter, I review the processes of cultural change and stability documented and described by the early cultural anthropologists and discuss contemporary organization studies that feature these processes. Following this is a section discussing three organizational culture theories that consider stability and change as outcomes of the same processes, thus bringing us closer to a dynamic understanding of organizational culture.

Processes of Cultural Change and Stability

At this point it may be worth noting that some postmodern culture theorists have rejected the work of the early cultural anthropologists that I review below. Zygmunt Bauman (1999), for example, recently claimed that processes such as diffusion and accommodation are irrelevant in the face of recent changes in transportation and communication that render cultural borders permeable and thus obsolete. In Bauman's (1999, p. xliv) words:

> The concept of diffusion makes sense only when it is seen as a traffic between wholesome, well-defined entities; when, in other words, the treating of cultures as separate wholes itself makes sense. It is doubtful, however, whether it (still) does. If there are no rules, there are no exceptions; if there are no comprehensive and self-enclosed totalities, there is no diffusion. The idea of diffusion or cross-cultural exchange does not help understanding of contemporary culture. Neither do other traditional concepts of cultural analysis, like, for instance, assimilation or accommodation.

My view is that Bauman considerably overstated his case. In particular, the changes he alluded to only make processes like diffusion and accommodation more important by increasing their penetration among all members of a culture. Thus, while the changes Bauman described intensify and extend cross-cultural relationships, this does not imply total boundary collapse, or what equates to the loss of cultural identity. This leaves us with something still to learn from the early anthropologists who studied cultural change in cross-cultural contexts, though admittedly we should proceed with caution in view of

the different contexts in which contemporary cultures are defined as existing.[1]

While contemporary society is not tribal in the sense once meant by cultural anthropologists, contemporary issues in organization studies suggest that at least some of the processes first articulated by cultural anthropologists remain relevant today. Although they rarely make mention of the work of the early anthropologists, cultural researchers working within and between contemporary organizational cultures describe similar processes. It is informative to look at what the early cultural anthropologists said about the processes of change and stability and compare their ideas to some contemporary studies of organizational culture (see table 7.1).

Evolutionary Patterns: Variation, Growth, and Decline

Many early theories of cultural change were founded on an aspect of culture commonly regarded to be universal—cultural variation. Closely linked to the notion of pattern associated with the work of Ruth Benedict (1934), cultural variation articulated one major theme of Darwinian evolutionary theory (two others being selection and retention, whose shadows can be seen below in the discussion of cultural growth and decline.)

In the variation process, change comes from adding new alternatives to the culture. Herskovits

Table 7.1 The processes of cultural stability and change

Source	Cultural Processes Described in Anthropology and Sociology	Similar Process Described in Organizational-Culture Studies
Evolutionary patterns of culture	• pattern maintenance (Benedict, 1936) • variation, growth, and decline (Herskovits, 1948, 1964) • exhaustion of possibilities, decline, decay (Sorokin, 1937) • florescence (Kroeber, 1944)	• institutionalization (transmission) of cultural norms (Zucker, 1977) • imitation as variation (Sevon, 1996)
From outside	• idea transmission (Kroeber, 1944) • diffusion, contact and exchange, resistance, selective giving (Malinowski, 1945) • acculturation, selective borrowing, focus and reinterpretation (Herskovits, 1948, 1964)	• materialization of ideas, translation (Czarniawska and Joerges, 1996) • negotiation, recontextualization, salience (Brannen, 1992, 1998)
From within	• enculturation, reenculturation (Herskovits, 1948, 1964) • innovation (Barnett, 1953; White, 1959) • individual peculiarities (Linton, 1936)	• organizational socialization (Schein, 1971; Van Maanen and Schein, 1979; Louis, 1980)

(1964, p. 26) provided an example of culture change via the learning of a new alternative from another culture:

A man or woman knows the ways of behavior that are traditionally acceptable to his group in a given situation—in one society, that he must step off a path and turn his back on a passing elder to show respect, in another, that the thing to do with the property of a dead person is to burn it.... But should he have contact with another people who hold that respect is shown by facing a superior rather than by turning away from him, then even with the greatest freedom of choice, an alternative has been presented that must be grappled with. If he accepts the new mode for himself he may meet with resistance at home. But unless he is prevented from carrying on the new way of showing respect, his persistence will make of him a center from which a possible deviation from the sanctioned form of polite behavior radiates, and his fellows will be continuously faced with making the choice he has already made.

But alternatives (along with specialties and peculiarities) are often already part of culture, for as Herskovits (1964, p. 202) also noted: "No two persons, even those who do not question their culture at all, will perform the same operation, or conceive the same accepted belief, in identical terms." According to Herskovits (1964, p. 200): "The larger the number of persons who react to a given situation in similar—not identical—ways, the wider the effectiveness of that pattern over the society where it is found. Consensus of cultural behavior is thus but another expression of cultural variation. A culture, considered in this way, becomes an aggregate of differing individual patterns." Herskovits continued: "The extreme deviant widens the range of variation in a culture... This, in turn, may set up a dynamic reaction that leads to other deviations which push the frontiers of accepted convention ever further" (p. 203). He concluded, "Change is brought about by a process whereby certain deviations from established norms are taken over by a number of people, thus initiating and continuing a tendency that becomes a trend" (p. 205). Of course, Herskovits (1948, p. 639) also noted: "Most of the random variations in culture disappear with the individual who manifests them. Those that do not disappear, that are taken up by other members of a society, tend to be cumulative."

Thus Herskovits brings down to a mundane level what Kroeber had earlier proposed as an account of cultural growth and decline. About growth Kroeber (1944, p. 763–764) stated:

The patterns which we adjudge as of higher quality are selected from among a number of potentialities. They cannot remain undifferentiated and attain quality. As they begin to select, early in their formation, they commit themselves to certain specializations, and exclude others. If this arouses conflict with other parts of the culture in which the pattern is forming, the selection and exclusion may be abandoned, the pattern as something well differentiated be renounced, and nothing of much cultural value eventuate. If, however, this does not happen, but the other patterns of the culture reinforce the growing one, or at least do not conflict with it, the pattern in question tends to develop cumulatively, in the direction in which it first differentiated, by a sort of momentum. Finally, either a conflict with the rest of its culture arises and puts an end to the pattern, or it explores and traverses the new opportunities lying in its selective path, until less and less of these remain, and at last none.

About decline Kroeber said:

The pattern can be said to have fulfilled itself when its opportunities or possibilities have been exhausted. Or more exactly, the value culmination comes at the moment when the full range of possibilities within the pattern is sensed; the decline, when there remain only minor areas of terrain to be occupied. After this, development may quietly subside, the results achieved being retained as institutions, but with repetitive instead of growth activity; the quality atrophies. Or again, energy still being vigorous in the field of culture in question, the limitations imposed on itself by the growing or culminating pattern are felt as restraints, and there is an effort to disrupt them. Such efforts may end in incoherent conflicts which sooner or later level out in undifferentiation.

Kroeber labeled this dynamic of growth and decline *florescence*, which he defined as growth patterns in cultural forms (for Kroeber, these forms were restricted to philosophy, science, philology, sculpture, painting, drama, literature, music, and politics). About the decline stage of florescence, Kroeber (1944,

p. 774) explained: "Soon after culmination, . . . [the cultural form, such as drama] usually becomes fairly repetitive at a constant low level of quality; but it continues on this level. It has become a fairly fixed or institutionalized activity, well rooted in its culture and affording unquestionable satisfactions; an activity which does not aim at, nor can longer achieve, high values, though it may be practiced with genuine competence."

Kroeber's perspective, by today's standards, seems out of date. His unreflective stance toward applying his particular criterion of aesthetic value grates on postmodern pluralist sensibilities. What is more, his interest in "high" culture (drama, poetry, philosophy, etc.) marks him as elitist. Nonetheless, he made an important point about the role of institutions in explaining cultural dynamics. As static remains of once dynamic cultural patterns, institutions are like cultural fossils that can only suggest clues to past states of consciousness and meaning. In Kroeber's view, institutions are rote repetitions of the past that do not accommodate new learning.

Kroeber offered an interesting challenge to contemporary institutional theory in sociology and organization studies. Whereas institutional theory presents institutions as explanations of cultural conservatism, Kroeber maintained that they are merely artifacts. Moreover, most institutionalists argue that institutions maintain and transfer knowledge and meaning from one generation to the next (see Zucker's 1977 experiments on the institutionalization of norms in work groups), whereas Kroeber's views suggest that institutionalization is a process by which knowledge and meaning are lost. Kroeber's theory makes institutions complicit in the decline of particular cultural patterns. When you look at institutions you look into the past without much hope of recovering the meanings that once made these fossilized cultural patterns flourish. While such a view is perhaps unnecessarily contentious, it does suggest distinguishing between cultural meaning and the institutions (i.e., structures or forms) a society produces. It is in this sense that Kroeber offers a dynamic view of culture in which certain practices move from the domain of change (florescence) to that of stability (institutionalization).

Sevon (1996) made a good case for resolving this tension between institutional theory and cultural change. Her work on processes of imitation among organizations reintroduced variation into the discussion of pattern maintenance. Citing Merton (1985), Sevon (1996, p. 66) claimed that:

> We live in a world where nothing is absolute[ly] new, where there are no absolute original ideas or actions. In such a world, every act is related to one's own and others' ideas, experiences and actions. At the same time, however, no idea or action is completely a copy from other organizations, as organizations pick up ideas and translate them into something that fits their own context. In this way, action, although imitated, may become different. Imitation is an ongoing and never-completed action. Through imitation, ideas, experiences and actions are constructed and spread over time and space thereby transforming ideas, mental models, actions, organizational forms, and organization fields.

Sevon's concept of imitation reminds me of contemporary anthropologist Joseph Roach's (1995) notion of "repetition with a difference." Roach (p. 46) built this concept by extending Richard Schechner's (1985, pp. 35–116) idea of restored behavior. Schechner defined restored behavior as "that which can be repeated, rehearsed and above all recreated." In describing Louisiana jazz funerals as restored behaviors, Roach noticed that while each repetition restores a cultural form, it also changes it. In the specific case of the jazz funeral, the change aspect is apparent in that these cultural events involve the playing of jazz. This means that improvisation and difference—hence change—are characteristics of the restored cultural form of the Louisiana jazz funeral. Studying jazz funerals made Roach aware of the potential for variation lying within the process of restoring behavior, an observation that seems to parallel Linton's concept of peculiarities and Barnett's observation that the form and meaning of cultural elements can vary independently. As a process, repetition with a difference thus creates the conditions for the simultaneous enactment of stability and change. Thus, institutions as restored behaviors may accommodate change even as they provide stability.

Change from Outside: Diffusion, Acculturation, and Selective Borrowing

Early anthropologists found much evidence that groups in close proximity share more cultural traits and complexes than do those that are geographically distant. They generally explained this finding by alluding to processes of diffusion and acculturation.[2] According to Herskovits (1964, p. 170, emphasis in the original), "diffusion is the study of *achieved cultural transmissions*; while acculturation is the study of *cultural transmission in process*." Both diffusion and acculturation embrace the phenomenon of cultural borrowing.

Like cultural variation, borrowing from other cultures is a universal phenomenon. Borrowing results from cultural contact in which dominant groups are often deeply influenced by the customs of those over whom they rule. An example would be the adoption of elements of Native American culture such as maize cultivation, the use of tobacco, and many place names by those who migrated to North America following Columbus's "discovery" (Herskovits, 1964, p. 58).

Acculturation studies consistently show that borrowing is selective. In borrowing, people typically accept what promises to be rewarding and reject what seems unworkable or disadvantageous (Herskovits, 1964, p. 143). That is, while some elements may be taken over wholesale from another culture, others are resisted, often completely. Herskovits (1964, p. 177) interpreted cultural borrowing in relation to the dynamics of acculturation processes: "The arithmetic of culture-contact is never a process of addition. The borrowed element is always merged with what was present before the contact. As a result, a culture of multiple origins is different from any of the bodies of tradition that have contributed to it. The dynamics of acculturation, they say, are creative. To study the result of acculturation by tracing traits to their origin is to distort the picture and falsify the results."

Two mechanisms that determine what will be selectively borrowed are focus and reinterpretation. According to Herskovits, those areas of culture that are focal at a given time (i.e., in which cultural members take immediate and often self-interest) are more likely to be receptive to borrowing than are other aspects not in focus. That is, elements from outside are more readily accepted if they fall within a focal area of the culture (the same can be said about the acceptance of innovations within a culture). This is because "the concerns of the persons who go to make up the group at a given time are more centered in some aspects of their culture than in others" (Herskovits, 1964, p. 183). According to Herskovits

(187), "in circumstances of acculturation where cultures are in free contact, the focal aspect will be the one where the new elements are most hospitably received."

Mary Yoko Brannen (1998, p. 12) proposed that, in bicultural contexts, cultures change through contact as a result of negotiation processes involving conflict and compromise "because it is in such situations that assumptions get inspected." These negotiation processes involve "the construction and reconstruction of divergent meanings and actions by individual organizational actors." Within these processes, Brannen, Liker, and Fruin (1999, p. 31) claimed, "only those cultural attributes that become salient in the organization's course of doing business become docket items for cultural negotiations." Thus, similar to Herskovits, Brannen argued that focus (or salience) directs culture change.

The idea of focus as a mechanism that directs culture change has implications for the role of top management in organizational change processes. If cultures change most readily in their foci, then leaders who are conversant with their cultures are likely to be able to pinpoint and intensify the cultural focus inside their organizations in order to facilitate culture change processes. Leaders who are isolated from their cultures will be disabled in this function and hence be unlikely to serve as effective change agents. It is in relation to focus that the vast majority of managerial writings about culture change in organizations seem to fit. What is absent in these writings, however, is any direct reflection on the contextualized nature of leadership in relation to culture change. The predominant view in this highly prescriptive literature is that leaders are in charge of their cultures rather than the other way around, so I would say that a relatively naive view of cultural focus is adopted in the managerial literature on culture change. One exception is the work done on the widespread failure of mergers and acquisitions to achieve their expected performance outcomes. Studies of these situations focused on cultural mismatch have shown that the way the cultures of the two original organizations react to one another explains the negative outcomes (e.g. Bastien, 1989; Nahavandi and Malekzadeh, 1988; Sales and Mirvis, 1984).

However, as Herskovits showed, there is more to change than focus. Whenever elements of another culture are borrowed, reinterpretation is likely to occur. In reinterpretation, the element is given a meaning that assimilates it into the existing cultural pattern with minimal disruption. As Herskovits (1948, p. 637) explained, the same process occurs within a culture: "It is the reactions of individuals to any innovation that determine what will be taken over and what will not, and the forms in which the reinterpretation process will shape innovations. These reactions, however, stem from the cultural conditioning of the individuals who are the agents of change."

Cultural reinterpretation can involve the reading of old meaning into new forms, but it can also involve the retention of old forms that have been given new meanings. In Herskovits's (1964, p. 190) words, reinterpretation is "the process by which old meanings are ascribed to new elements or by which new values change the cultural significance of old forms." Reinterpretation operates internally from generation to generation (see the discussion of enculturation below, and of accommodation above) although cultural anthropologists have most often studied it as a means of integrating a borrowed element into a receiving culture. As Herskovits put it: "The earlier pattern, with the passage of time, is reinterpreted so as to be in accord with change in the total setting of the culture as a whole" (p. 193).

Recently, Brannen (1992) developed a concept similar to reinterpretation that, following the practice of recent anthropologists, she has labeled "recontextualization." She developed this idea on the basis of her study of what she argued was the Japanese appropriation of Disneyland in Tokyo. Her claim was that, in insisting on building a precise replica of the original Disneyland (even though they did not ultimately do this, incorporating several changes such as transforming Main Street into a World Bazaar that operates as a huge shopping center), the Japanese investors in the project gave Japanese meanings to borrowed artifacts of American culture. This recontextualization assimilated Tokyo Disneyland into Japanese culture in a way that meant minimal disruption to existing cultural patterns in Japan.

In contrast to the Japanese model, Euro-Disneyland developers decided to redesign the original park to try to accommodate European sensitivities to the imposition of an American cultural icon. Euro-Disneyland (now renamed Disneyland Paris) originally met with far less success in attracting visitors and currying public favor, being the brunt of enormous cultural resistance to this symbol of "American Imperialism." Brannen argued that the recontextualiza-

tion of Disneyland by Japanese culture, as opposed to French resistance to it, accounts for the difference in outcomes.

While recontextualization is focused mainly on material exchanges between cultures (the Disneyland amusement park), Kroeber saw diffusion in ideal terms. Kroeber proposed "idea transmission" as a mechanism of diffusion that is "distinct from diffusions of specific culture contents or forms." He thereby extended the diffusion concept to "seemingly independent inventions or growths." According to Kroeber (1944, p. 423), "the receiving civilization becomes conscious, in spots at least, of a potentiality which had been realized elsewhere before and then the receiving culture achieves the potentiality out of its own materials and in its own way." As examples, Kroeber cited:

- Porcelain making in Europe—Kroeber claimed this developed as the result of conscious experiments to reproduce porcelain imported from China.
- Drama in Japan—Kroeber suggested that it may have been mere knowledge of the fact that a theater could exist that was imported into Japan.
- Cherokee invention of writing by Sequoya.
- Chinese discovery of tones in their language— Kroeber suggested this may have been the result of exposure to the Buddhist-carried philology of Sanskrit, though Sanskrit is a toneless language.
- Elizabethan theater—Kroeber claimed this was an indigenous formulation but that there must have been knowledge in England of the ancients and of the Renaissance Italians.

In organization studies Barbara Czarniawska-Joerges and Bernward Joerges (1996) proposed a version of idea transmission that they called "travels of ideas." These scholars were interested in providing a counter-explanation to planned organizational change as a manifestation of rational managerial intervention. Czarniawska-Joerges and Joerges proposed that the process of materialization of ideas is a means of producing conventionality that "can be observed when, out of the myriads of ideas floating in the translocal organizational thought-worlds, certain ideas catch and are subsequently translated into substance in a given organization, often barely touching the bureaucratic apparatus of planned change. More likely than not, it is the same ideas which materialize in similar organizations around the same time, indicating that mechanisms are at work which are best seen as akin to fashion" (p. 16).

Czarniawska-Joerges and Joerges presented a series of examples drawn from the worlds of municipal government and technology transfer. They concluded that:

These are cases where a set of actions is already in the offing and an idea is needed to legitimately trigger it. A technology arrives, first as a nebulous idea, something only vaguely, in some minds, related to some actions, which then lands heavily on the ground, showing its nasty side, requiring still new investments and additional commitments. At worst, a new technology can break down a whole social system . . . At best, in the course of the fitting process, the idea and the set of actions will get adjusted to each other in a new, unique combination. (p. 19)

While Czarniawska-Joerges and Joerges preferred to use the term *translation* to label the process they studied, in the main they articulated what Malinowski and Kroeber called diffusion, and in fact they noted the similarity themselves. They justified their preference for the translation metaphor (which they borrowed from Latour, 1986) on the basis of its textual associations, seeing diffusion as a scientific (chemical) metaphor having to do with the movement of molecules from more to less saturated environments. For them, ideas are more like texts than chemical substances, and therefore translation, as a mechanism for carrying texts across cultural (i.e., language) borders, is a more fitting metaphorization of the process.

Change from Within: Enculturation, Re-enculturation, and Cultural Innovation

Enculturation is often given as part of the explanation for cultural stability. It accounts for how symbols, practices, and meanings are transferred from one generation to another, thus it has clear parallels to pattern maintenance, discussed above. However, Herskovits distinguished between the early enculturation of childhood and later enculturation or re-enculturation.

According to Herskovits (1964, p. 27), in the early years of life, enculturation mostly involves

conditioning to fundamentals, and much of it occurs below the level of conscious thought. Enculturation involves absorption of intangibles such as right and wrong, normal and abnormal, beautiful and plain (or ugly). Beyond these ethical and aesthetic judgments, early enculturation experiences transfer the conventions of a group, such as those that mediate their perceptions of time, distance, weight, size and other "realities."

In later life, however, enculturation is used differently. According to Herskovits (1964, p. 25): "By the time he has reached maturity, a man or woman has been so conditioned that he moves easily within the limits of accepted behavior set by his group. Thereafter, new forms of behavior presented to him are largely those involved in culture change—new inventions or discoveries, or new ideas diffused from outside his society about which, as an individual, he has to 'make up his mind' and thus play his role in reorienting his culture."

Herskovits concluded that enculturation in early life leads to cultural stability while in maturity it can also lead to cultural change. This Herskovits (1964, p. 627) explained in terms of re-enculturation:

The reconditioning process we call later enculturation . . . provides the mechanism that makes possible the changes that mark the history of every body of custom. Culture, being learned, can be relearned. Hence when an individual has reached maturity and some new mode of behavior, some new technique or concept is presented to him, he reacts to it in terms of his previous experience. If he accepts it, he must to that extent recondition his responses. In other words, he must to that degree reenculturate himself.

What is more, when enculturation occurs on the conscious level, as it often does in re-enculturation, it opens the gate to change via examination of alternative possibilities that permit reconditioning to new modes of thought and conduct (Herskovits, 1964, p. 152).

Organization theorists come closest to a discussion of re-enculturation when they talk about organizational socialization. For example, Louis (1980) discussed how sense-making processes enable newcomers to an organizational setting to learn its culture and adapt to its values, norms, and practices. Like most organizational socialization researchers, Louis did not concern herself with the implications of socialization for the organization and its culture. However, Schein and Van Maanen (Schein, 1971; Van Maanen, 1976; Van Maanen and Schein, 1979) addressed this issue when they theorized three possible recruit responses to socialization: custodianship, content innovation, and role innovation.

Two of Van Maanen and Schein's (1979) recruit responses to socialization imply cultural change: the role of the newcomer is adopted, but the strategy for carrying out the role is altered by the incumbent (content innovation), and the newcomer alters the basic mission served by the assigned role (role innovation). Thus, their ideas form a link with Linton's (1936) work on the effects of individual peculiarities that are sources of innovation within a culture. In this regard socialization can be seen as a process through which individuals contribute to cultural pattern maintenance as well as change. Although Schein and Van Maanen mainly concerned themselves with aspects of the socialization process that limit or enhance the likelihood of content or role innovation, their ideas about socialization suggest that newcomers are an important source of change within a culture and that socialization must be included among the processes that constitute cultural dynamics as relating to both stability and change.

Barnett (1953, p. 10) described innovation as "qualitative departures from habitual patterns." Barnett claimed that innovation occurs when existing cultural materials are brought together in original ways and that these materials come both from the cultural inventory and from nature (including the innovator him- or herself). He summarized the link between innovation and culture change this way: "Human beings have an infinite capacity for responding divergently ... in this ultimate sense of being deviant every individual is an innovator many times over" (Barnett, 1953, p. 19). His view of the link between individual divergence and cultural dynamics was:

> Individuals do react differently to the same situation, and some are certain to respond with greater originality than are others. Given any set of circumstances, some individuals will be constrained to the orbit of the customary more certainly and more securely than will others. Individual variability in this respect is unquestioned. At the same time, it is only a special aspect of the more general and universal phenomenon of idiosyncratic deviation. Within conventional limits individual

deviation is inevitable; for excursions beyond those limits special conditions are necessary. (Barnett, 1953, p. 21)

Barnett (1953, p. 46) also claimed that "difference itself induces change" in that it produces the conjunctions of cultural materials that inspire innovations. Among the examples of ways in which conjunctions are culturally encouraged Barnett (pp. 46–48) included: markets, missionary endeavor, trade relations, intermarriage, ambassadorial exchange, emigration, expatriation, slavery, wage labor (especially involving cross-ethnic recruiting, as in seasonal use of Mexican labor in the United States), exploration, adventure, conquest, and colonization.

While Barnett raised the important issue of innovation in relation to cultural change, his focus was primarily on innovation and not on culture. His work on processes was concerned with processes of innovation (e.g., recombination, substitution), not with processes of culture change, of which he saw innovation as the basis. By way of contrast, two studies by organizational culture researchers have taken innovative organizations as their subjects and examined organizational processes surrounding innovation from a cultural perspective. Kreiner and Schultz (1995) examined the symbolic use of the name Eureka (a European program for cross-national collaborative ventures) to categorize project activities, to magnetize external interests, and to license innovation teams to pursue new opportunities as they emerged. Kunda (1992) studied the mechanisms of normative (cultural) control that he discovered in a large and well-respected high-technology organization known for innovation. Though neither of these studies looks at innovation processes such as recombination and substitution of cultural forms and meanings as dynamic processes of cultural change, studies such as those of Kunda and Kreiner and Schultz suggest the possibilities inherent in applying Barnett's processes to the field of business.

Cultural Dynamics in Organization Studies

There are three theories of organizational culture that implicate both cultural stability and change, and each accommodates both change from within and change from outside. Schein's (1985/1992) relatively managerialist theory of culture change came first and the other two built on his work. Gagliardi's (1986) typology of culture change maintained Schein's strong managerial focus in its emphasis on the links between culture and strategy but took a more organizationally centered point of view of the effects of strategic intervention. Hatch's (1993) cultural dynamics model is the most organizationally and least managerially oriented in that it situates top managers within cultural processes. Since both Gagliardi and Hatch built on Schein, we will begin with Schein's contribution.

Schein's Theory of Organizational Culture and Leadership

Schein was one of the first organizational theorists to borrow ideas directly from cultural anthropology. In his case, he borrowed the idea of basic assumptions from Kluckhohn and Strodtbeck (1961). These anthropologists identified seven types of assumptions that Schein reinterpreted as organizational: the organization's relationship with its environment, the nature of human activity, the nature of reality and truth, the nature of time, the nature of human nature, the nature of human relationships, and homogeneity vs. diversity (Schein, 1985, p. 86).

Schein argued that basic assumptions lie at the taken-for-granted core of an organization's culture (see figure 7.1). In his theory this deep, nearly impenetrable core underpins a middle level of cultural consciousness where cultural values reside. Values, then, are sandwiched between assumptions and the more superficial and accessible level of cultural artifacts. According to Schein, assumptions, values, and artifacts are linked in that artifacts are manifes-

tations of values, while values are manifestations of assumptions.

Schein considered cultures to be stable until leaders act to change them. He claimed that leaders change a culture by changing its value set. They do this by demonstration, providing public displays of new values, which they must work hard to make successful in the context of the organization's task and environment. Schein argued that if the leader's actions are successful, others in the culture will accept the new values on which these actions were based. If and when sufficient support is generated to make the new values an accepted part of everyday life, the new values will have sunk below consciousness and become taken-for-granted assumptions. It is thus that change reaches the deepest level of culture.

Schein's theory of how cultures change is similar to Weber's notion of charismatic leadership described earlier in this chapter. Both propose that culture change occurs via the direct influence of a leader. One difference between Schein and Weber is that Weber carefully described the stabilizing counterforces to leader-induced change (i.e., systematization and accommodation, or what Weber called the "routinization of charisma"), while Schein only noted the moderating effect of the success of the leader's actions on the uptake of his or her influence within the culture. Another pronounced difference is that, where Weber marked "suffering, conflicts or enthusiasm" as conditions for change through charismatic influence, Schein placed no conditions on his model, other than the success factor noted above.[3]

Gagliardi's Three Types of Cultural Change

Building on Schein's basic model of culture as assumptions, values, and artifacts, Pasquale Gagliardi focused his attention on the relationship between culture and strategy, suggesting that different strategic moves have different effects on organizational cultures. His theory depicted stability and change as counterforces whose interaction presented three possible outcomes: apparent change, incremental change, and revolutionary change (see table 7.2).

Apparent change occurs within culture, but without changing it in any fundamental way. Gagliardi claimed that this is what happens when strategies align with existing organizational assumptions and values. That is, new problems are confronted by choosing from the range of strategies permitted by

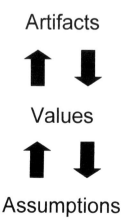

Figure 7.1 Schein's three level model of culture.

Table 7.2 Gagliardi's three types of culture change

Change Type	Stability Maintained?	Change Introduced?	Description of Change
apparent	yes	no	superficial
incremental	yes	yes	deep
revolutionary	no	yes	destructive but potentially renewing

existing assumptions and values. Implementation of these strategies may produce change at the level of artifacts (see figure 7.2), but these cultural changes are superficial; the organization adapts only within the confines of its existing identity. Gagliardi claimed that, paradoxically, cultures within this pattern change in order to stay the same.

Incremental change comes closest to Schein's model of culture change via management influence. According to Gagliardi, cultural incrementalism is the only type of change that reaches the deep level of values and assumptions. In this case a strategy that implies different, but not incompatible, values stretches the organizational culture to include new values alongside its old ones. According to Gagliardi, when strategies are different but not incompatible with assumptions and values, culture expands by the assumptions, values, and artifacts inherent in the new strategy (see figure 7.3).

Gagliardi's incremental change might be compared to Kroeber's notion of cultural growth. Recall Kroeber's (1944, pp. 763–764) description: "If . . . the other patterns of culture reinforce the growing one, or at least do not conflict with it, the pattern in question tends to develop cumulatively." What Kroeber brings to the discussion of incremental change is his notion of florescence in cultural patterns. Applying Kroeber's idea suggests equating strategy with a new cultural pattern whose incorporation hinges on reinforcement by the existing cultural patterns. This suggests that successful incremental strategies do not rest merely on assumption and value compatibility, but rather on a process resulting in resonance with the entire web of cultural meaning.

In revolutionary change, a strategy incompatible with at least some key assumptions and values is imposed upon the organization, usually through the entry of outsiders who destroy old symbols and create

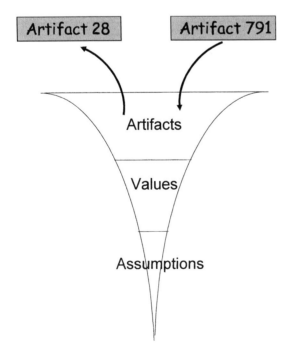

Figure 7.2 A representation of Gagliardi's notion of apparent change.

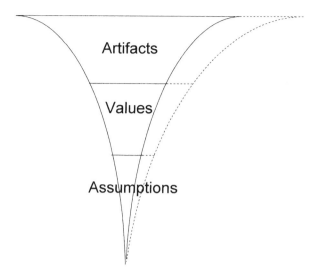

Artifacts

Values

Assumptions

Figure 7.3 A representation
of Gagliardi's notion of
incremental change.

new ones. This can occur, for example, when a new
CEO is brought into a company from the outside, or
when a company is merged, acquired, or downsized.
When strategies are in conflict with assumptions and
values, either culture is replaced or destroyed (revolutionary change), or the strategy is resisted and
never implemented (no change). However, in cases
of revolutionary change, Gagliardi argued, it is "more
correct to say that the old firm dies and that a new
firm, which has little in common with the first, was
born (1986 p. 130)." Here culture is not changed so
much as it is displaced.

Although he did not build his model on Kroeber's
work, Gagliardi's category of revolutionary change
echoed Kroeber's (1944, p. 765) views of revolt
against cultural patterns, or pattern rupture:

Harmony or rhyme or symmetry can be used until
they have become mechanical and dull. The
choice then is between going on with them per-
functorily, or revolting against them. Of the two,
revolt is not necessarily the worse course. Certainly
in the last half-dozen decades far more energy and
imagination have been developed by the pattern
wreckers than by the pattern preservers still trying
to travel in the channels of a century ago. And
therefore extravagances like the horizon line carried in front of a tree, a piano struck with full
forearm length, lines of verse beginning with small
letters or full of stammers, can be accepted as
neither wicked nor insane. In part they represent
the zeal of the revolutionist who needs first
to wreck everything, whether significant or not,

before he can reconstruct; in part, responses to a
condition in which, accepted patterns having gone
stale, any upsetting novelty is rewarded for being
startling, and the shrewd exploit the situation. The
fundamental fact is that while twentieth-century
Occidentals can still write in the manner of Goethe
and compose in the manner of Beethoven, they
evidently cannot do so with the same quality, else
presumably some of them would be doing it. That
is, the pattern possibilities of the Goethe and
Beethoven configurations are obviously exhausted.
Such being the case, does it matter much whether
the successors revolt and wreck or peacefully
atrophy into senility? Revolution may at least be
followed by new growth; and whether this is to be
greater or less, no one can foretell.

Kroeber painted a somewhat romantic or heroic
picture of revolutionary change, but one worth considering as a broad explanation of what has happened
in industry after industry in the West. If manufacturing has been exhausted as an economic pattern
for the cultures of the West, then the destruction of
organizational cultures as a means to renewal may be
justified on the basis of new economic growth. In this
metaphor certain managers are pattern wreckers in
the mold of Picasso or Thelonious Monk.

Using artists as models of cultural change agents,
as the application of Kroeber's ideas to managerial
action suggests, sets some (aesthetic) criteria by which
we might judge the managerial pattern wreckers—
some form of cultural enrichment should follow their
destructive acts. Using aesthetic criteria, it should be

possible to discern which pattern wreckers have replaced exhausted cultural patterns with more viable ones that enrich rather than simply destroy, and which joined the revolution merely as an excuse to pillage and plunder. What recent experiences of restructuring confirm, however, is that cultural destruction is possible, and subsequent growth in industries and economies hard hit by downsizing does not argue against the proposition that, at least in some cases, renewal has followed.

Hatch's Dynamics of Organizational Culture

Herskovits (1948, p. 640) argued that cultural dynamics includes both socialization and self-expression, because the individual is enculturated both to "the social structures which make of society an organized unit" and to "patterns of music and art and dancing... [and]... speculation about the universe and the powers that govern it." He continued, suggesting that the dynamic pattern is a circular one: "The process of adjustment is circular and never-ending; it is a process of interaction between the individual and his group in terms of his enculturation to its pre-existing patterns. This adjustment is furthered by the creativeness which, as a fundamental expression of the restlessness of the individual in the face of the ways of his group, permits him to exercise various modes of self-expression, and thus to extend the scope of his culture without breaking down its basic orientations" (Herskovits, 1948, p. 641).

Hatch's model of the dynamics of organizational culture described four processes underlying both cultural change and stability (Hatch, 1993; see figure 7.4). In developing this model I followed Herskovits's suggestion to think in a circular (or what I interpreted to be a hermeneutic) way about processes able to explain both stability and change. This approach was then applied to Schein's model of culture as assumptions, values, and artifacts. It also added symbols in order to accommodate the interpretivism that was sweeping through organization studies at the time the model was developed. Unlike Schein's theory, this model focused not on the elements of culture per se (i.e., assumptions, values, artifacts, and symbols), but on the processes linking these elements.

The top half of the cultural dynamics model shown in figure 7.4 describes the manifestation and realization processes by which artifacts are created; the bottom half describes what happens once artifacts

are made part of the organization's cultural inventory and become available for symbolization and interpretation. In the domain of the top half of the model, assumptions and values shape activity such that artifacts of these influences are created and maintained within the culture. In the domain of the lower half of the model, organizational members choose some (but not all) of the artifacts available to them and use the selected artifacts to symbolize their meanings in communication with others.

The idea of cultural focus mentioned earlier could offer a means to better understand management's role in cultural dynamics. If cultures change more readily in areas of focus, then managers who are aware of and can intensify attention within this focus have an important part to play in culture change. Because they themselves are readily attended to and so often symbolized (as a consequence of their power, authority and access to others), managers who allow themselves to represent focal issues within the culture can act as lightning rods for change.

The processes described by the cultural dynamics model are ongoing. Active attempts by managers to change organizations would therefore also be described as a part of these processes. Attempts to intentionally introduce change usually begin in the domain of realization and symbolization when management (or contact with another culture) introduces a new idea through language or other artifacts (don't forget that physical objects and behavioral manifestations are also powerful communicators), which then may be symbolized and interpreted by those who will either carry the change forward or deny it any

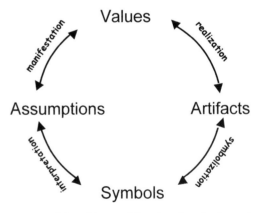

Figure 7.4 Hatch's model of cultural dynamics. *Source*: Hatch (1993).

influence. If the symbols made are in alignment with existing organizational assumptions and values, change should be relatively easy but not very deep (this is Gagliardi's notion of apparent change).

However, change in line with existing assumptions and values may not be what management wants. Some change may involve introducing "foreign" ideas into the system. Cultural processes of acculturation, accommodation, and reinterpretation then come into play, and change initiators must recognize that their sense of control over the process will be diminished as others confront the new artifacts, construct symbols with them and make their own interpretations of the meaning of the change and intent of the change agent. This is how the cultural dynamics model places the manager within the organizational culture. It suggests that control of the power of leadership lies in the sensitivity of managers to their own symbolic meaning. Furthermore, this symbolic meaning shifts and changes in relation to a symbolic world constituted by the interpretive acts of others. Leaders have tremendous influence within organizations, but their ability to effectively mobilize this influence depends upon their knowledge of, and relationship with, the culture.

Meanwhile, regardless of acts of leadership and change interventions, the dynamic processes of culture produce continuous stability and change. This is because the processes of culture are in constant motion. Furthermore, what appears to be stability and what change is an interpretation given to events after the fact, and this propensity to interpret and

label likewise needs to be part of the theory of cultural dynamics. This means that we need to incorporate leaders and other agents of change into our theories not only of culture, but of ourselves as students and observers of culture.

Some Comparisons

Looking at the three dynamic theories presented by Schein, Gagliardi, and Hatch as a progression highlights a few important changes in thinking about culture. First, tracking the three models in this way shows a move from managerial to organizational theorizing about cultural dynamics with a commensurate decentering of management and its significance in the explanations of these processes. In each of the theories leaders become less central to, yet still a part of, the processes described. Second, there is the principle of return in Hatch's model (a fundamental circularity in the relationships between the processes of culture) not present in the other two models. Schein's is a top-down model of change flowing through the hierarchy, while Gagliardi's is a model of unidirectional change over time. Hatch's model depicts change as cycles of interaction infused with power of various and interrelated sorts (i.e., to influence and to interpret that influence). Third, the three models show a growing sensitivity to the symbolic-interpretive aspects of culture (expressive strategies in Gagliardi and the processes of symbolization and interpretation in Hatch). As has been shown in this chapter, all of these developments were either

Table 7.3 The processes of cultural dynamics

Dynamic Models of Organizational Culture	Related Concepts/Theories from Cultural Anthropology and Sociology
Schein (1981, 1984, 1985, 1992): Culture as assumptions, values, and artifacts; leaders change culture by introducing new values	Basic assumptions underpin cultures (Kluckhohn and Strodtbeck, 1961) How a charismatic leader influences a culture (Weber, 1968/1978)
Gagliardi (1986): Three types of cultural change relating strategy to culture: apparent, incremental, and revolutionary	Pattern growth as a model for cultural incrementalism (Kroeber, 1944) Pattern rupture as a means of cultural renewal (Kroeber, 1944)
Hatch (1993): Cultural dynamics as processes of manifestation, realization, symbolization, and interpretation	Stability and change as processes; focus and reinterpretation (Herskovits, 1948, 1964) Influence of charisma and its routinization specifies power dimension in cultural stability and change (Weber, 1968/1978; see Hatch, 2000)

anticipated in or can be extended by the work of the early anthropologists reviewed in this chapter.

As discussed above and summarized in table 7.3, there are numerous links between the ideas of the early cultural anthropologists and evolutionary sociologists and contemporary organizational culture theory as it pertains to the dynamics of culture. As already mentioned, Schein built directly on the work of Kluckhohn and Strodtbeck and also made observations in line with Weber's theory of charismatic leadership. Gagliardi's work is enriched by comparison with Kroeber's, perhaps not least because both of these theorists evidenced a strong aesthetic sensibility through their work. Finally, Hatch's reliance on Herskovits and her own comparisons of her cultural dynamics model with Weber's routinization of charisma (Hatch, 2000), suggest strong links to earlier theory.

Conclusion

It has been my contention in this chapter that organizational culture researchers often unwittingly replicate and extend some of the processes of cultural stability and change described earlier by cultural anthropologists and hinted at by a few evolutionary sociologists. Thus it would seem that much early anthropology and some evolutionary sociology is restored within contemporary organization theory. But if this is correct, it is restoration with a difference, since organizational researchers have redescribed some of the key processes (e.g., institutionalization, imitation, translation, recontextualization). This chapter traced these connections and highlighted both similarities and differences.

I realize that I may be accused of practicing revisionist history in constructing connections between the work of early anthropologists and sociologists and present-day organization theorists that were not part of the original record. In my own defense I would like to say two things. First, at the start of the contemporary period of organizational culture studies in the late 1970s, much reading of anthropology and sociology occurred mainly because culture was so rarely mentioned in the organizational literature. Though there was an occasional reference to this reading, by and large the work of these scholars was not immediately and directly applicable to organizations, and though anthropological and sociological thought inspired much organizational theorizing about culture, it was

difficult to demonstrate the relevance to readers, most of whom were unfamiliar with these fields. What connections existed were lost through the conservative referencing practices of professional journals that sanctioned inclusion of only direct references. Second, the similarities between early anthropology and sociology and contemporary organizational culture theory support making connections between them; the insights summarized in this chapter and extended to contemporary business and organizational issues, I believe, indicate the value of further developing our thoughts about the dynamics of culture in organizations.

The most important development in the field of organizational culture studies is the specification of processes. Whether done singly, as is the case for the processes of imitation, materialization, translation, negotiation, and recontextualization; or severally, as in the dynamic theories of Schein, Gagliardi, and Hatch, this development promises to advance organizational culture theory significantly. What is more, organization theorists have given culture theory a new and highly relevant context by examining these processes within formal organizations, which are arguably the most influential human structures to appear in modern times.

Though the organizational work commented upon in this chapter has barely begun, it is my view that its continuities with the prior theory offered by anthropologists and by Weberian and evolutionary sociology indicate its nascent possibilities. This chapter attempts to articulate this potential and to challenge current thought in postmodern culture studies that suggests that these earlier works are no longer relevant. While some of the expressions of understanding that accompanied these earlier works have proven to be sadly deficient, the knowledge contributed by the authors of the period can be separated from the opinions of the day and thereby retained for posterity. Doing so enriches our present understanding of the dynamics of culture that I have endeavored to describe in this chapter.

Notes

I want to thank Michael Owen Jones for so generously sharing with me his extensive appreciation for cultural anthropology and folklore studies. His influence on all of my work in the field of organizational culture was keenly felt throughout the preparation of this chapter. James Rubin helped me to understand this chapter as an act of historicizing, which added depth to my writing. I am grateful to both for their persistent efforts to broaden my perspective.

1. A different argument mustered against Malinowski in particular is that his personal attitudes toward his subjects of study, as revealed by the publication of his field journals, render his work highly suspicious. While I certainly hope that no one would model what in contemporary Western society is considered racist bigotry, I also hope that we have the wisdom to separate Malinowski's private struggles from his public contribution to social science.

2. This is where Bauman argued that cultures are now in such close contact as to no longer be interpretable as distinct cultures, with a commensurate loss of the meaning of diffusion.

3. But then, perhaps, he did not need to. Observation of the many change programs undertaken by Western organizations during the 1980s and 1990s suggest that leaders instinctively turn to suffering and conflict (e.g., as created by downsizing) to obtain cultural change when enthusiasm fails. It would appear that practitioners intuitively understand and take advantage of the conditions that Weber placed on his theory of charismatic leadership. Perhaps within managerial cultures these conditions are taken-for-granted assumptions, and thus Schein, who worked within these cultures, was unable to surface them.

References

Barnett, H. G. (1942). Invention and culture change. *American Anthropologist, 44,* 14–30.

Barnett, H. G. (1953). *Innovation: The basis of cultural change.* New York.

Bastien, D. T. (1989). Communication, conflict, and learning in mergers and acquisitions. In A. H. Van de Ven, H. L. Angle, & M. S. Poole (Eds.), *Research on the management of innovation* (pp. 367–396). New York: Ballinger/Harper & Row.

Bate, P. (1997). Whatever happened to organizational anthropology? A review of the field of organizational ethnography and anthropological studies. *Human Relations, 50,* 1147–1175.

Bauman, Z. (1999). *Culture as praxis.* London: Sage.

Benedict, R. (1934). *Patterns of culture.* Boston: Houghton Mifflin.

Brannen, M. Y. (1992). Bwana Mickey: Constructing cultural consumption at Tokyo Disneyland. In J. J. Tobin (Ed.), *Re-made in Japan: Everyday life and consumer taste in a changing society* (pp. 216–234). New Haven, CT: Yale University Press.

Brannen, M. Y. (1998). Negotiated culture in binational contexts: A model of culture change based on a Japanese/American organizational experience. *Anthropology of Work Review, 18* (2–3), 6–17.

Brannen, M. Y., Liker, J. K., & Fruin, W. M. (1999). Recontextualization and factory-to-factory knowledge transfer from Japan to the U.S.: The case of NSK. In J. K. Liker, W. M. Fruin, & P. S. Adler (Eds.), *Re-made in America: Transplanting and transforming Japanese management systems* (pp. 117–154). New York: Oxford University Press.

Collinson, D. L. (1999). "Surviving the rigs": Safety and surveillance on North Sea oil installations. *Organization Studies, 20,* 579–600.

Czarniawska-Joerges, B. (1992). Exploring complex organizations: A cultural perspective. Newbury Park, CA: Sage

Czarniawska, B. & Joerges, B. (1996). Travels of ideas. In B. Czarniawska-Joerges & G. Sevon (Eds.), *Translating organizational change* (pp. 13–48). Berlin: W. de Gruyter.

Czarniawska, B. & Sevon, G. (Eds.) (1996). *Translating organizational change.* Berlin: W. de Gruyter.

Deal, T. E. & Kennedy, A. A. (1982). *Corporate cultures: The rites and rituals of corporate life.* Reading, MA: Addison-Wesley.

Frost, P. J., Moore, L. F., Louis, M. R., Lundberg, C. C., & Martin, J. (1985). *Organizational culture.* Newbury Park, CA: Sage.

Frost, P. J., Moore, L. F., Louis, M. R., Lundberg, C. C., & Martin, J. (1991). *Reframing organizational culture.* Newbury Park, CA: Sage.

Gagliardi, P. (1986). The creation and change of organizational cultures: A conceptual framework. *Organization Studies, 7,* 117–134.

Gagliardi, P. (Ed.) (1990) *Symbols and artifacts: Views of the corporate landscape.* Berlin: W. de Gruyter.

Geertz, C. (1973). *Interpretation of cultures.* New York: Basic Books.

Hatch, M. J. (1993). The dynamics of organizational culture. *Academy of Management Review, 18,* 657–63.

Hatch, M. J. (2000). The cultural dynamics of organizing and change. In N. Ashkanasy, C. Wilderom, & M. Peterson (Eds.), *Handbook of organizational culture and climate* (pp. 245–260). London: Sage.

Hatch, M. J. & Yanow, D. (2003). Organization studies as an interpretive science. In C. Knudsen & H. Tsoukas (Eds.), *The handbook of organization theory: Meta-theoretical perspectives* (pp. 63–87). Oxford: Oxford University Press.

Hendry, J. (1999). Cultural theory and contemporary management organization. *Human Relations*, 52, 557–577.

Herskovits, M. J. (1948). *Man and his works*. New York: Knopf.

Herskovits, M. J. (1964). *Cultural dynamics*. New York: Knopf.

Hopfl, H. & Linstead, S. (1993). Passion and performance: Suffering and the carrying of organizational roles. In S. Fineman (Ed.), *Emotion in organizations* (pp. 76–93). London: Sage.

Jermier, J. (1998). Introduction: Critical perspectives on organizational control. *Administrative Science Quarterly*, 43, 235–256.

Jones, M. O., Moore, M. D., & Snyder, R. C. (1988). *Inside organizations: Understanding the human dimension*. Newbury Park, CA: Sage.

Kilmann, R. H., Saxton, M. J., Serpa, R., & Associates. (1985). *Gaining control of the corporate culture*. San Francisco, CA: Jossey-Bass.

Knights, D. & Willmott, H. (1987). Organizational culture as management strategy. *International Studies of Management and Organization*, 17, 40–63.

Kluckhohn, F. R. & Strodtbeck, F. L. (1961). *Variations in value orientations*. New York: Harper & Row.

Kreiner, K. & Schultz, M. (1995). Soft cultures: The symbolism of cross-border organizing. *Studies in Cultures, Organizations, and Societies*, 1, 63–81.

Kroeber, A. L. (1944). *Configurations of culture growth*. Berkeley: University of California Press.

Kunda, G. (1992). *Engineering culture*. Philadelphia: Temple University Press.

Latour, B. (1986). The powers of association. In J. Law (Ed.), *Power, action, and belief* (pp. 264–280). London: Routledge and Kegan Paul.

Linton, R. (1936). *The study of man*. New York.

Louis, M. R. (1980). Surprise and sense making: What newcomers experience in entering unfamiliar organizational settings. *Administrative Science Quarterly*, 25, 226–250.

Malinowski, B. (1945). *The dynamics of culture change*. New Haven, CT: Yale University Press.

Martin, J. (1992). *Cultures in organizations: Three perspectives*. New York: Oxford University Press.

Martin, J. & Frost, P. (1996). The organizational culture war games: A struggle for intellectual dominance. In S. Clegg, C. Hardy, & W. Nord (Eds.), *Handbook of organization studies* (pp. 599–621). London: Sage.

Merton, R. K. (1985). *On the shoulders of giants: A Shandean postscript*. New York: Harcourt and Jovanovich.

Mirvis, P. & Marks, M. L. (1992). *Managing the merger: Making it work*. Englewood Cliffs, NJ: Prentice Hall.

Nahavandi, A. & Malekzadeh, A. R. (1988). Acculturation in mergers and acquisitions. *Academy of Management Review*, 13, 79–90.

Ouchi, W. G. (1981). *Theory Z: How American business can meet the Japanese challenge*. Reading, MA: Addison-Wesley.

Pascale, R. T. & Athos, A. G. (1981). *The art of Japanese management*. New York: Simon & Schuster.

Redfield, R. (1953). *The primitive world and its transformations*. Ithaca, NY: Cornell University Press.

Roach, J. (1995). Culture and performance in the circum-Atlantic world. In A. Parker & E. K. Sedgwick (Eds.), *Performativity and performance* (pp. 45–63). New York: Routledge.

Rosen, M. (1985). Breakfast at Spiros: Dramaturgy and dominance. *Journal of Management*, 11, 31–48.

Rosen, M. (1988). You asked for it: Christmas at the bosses' expense. *Journal of Management Studies*, 25, 463–480.

Sahlins, M. & Service, E. (Eds.) (1960). *Evolution and culture*. Ann Arbor: University of Michigan Press.

Sales, A. & Mirvis, P. (1984). When cultures collide: Issues in acquisition. In J. R. Kimberly & R. E. Quinn (Eds.), *Managing organizational transitions* (pp. 107–133). Homewood, IL: Richard Irwin.

Schechner, R. (1985). *Between theater and anthropology*. Philadelphia: University of Pennsylvania Press.

Schein, E. H. (1971). Occupational socialization in the professions: The case of the role innovator. *Journal of Psychiatric Research*, 8, 521–530.

Schein, E. H. (1985). *Organizational culture and leadership*. San Francisco, CA: Jossey-Bass.

Schein, E. H. (1992). *Organizational culture and leadership* (2nd ed.). San Francisco, CA: Jossey-Bass.

Schroeder, R. (1992). *Max Weber and the sociology of culture*. London: Sage.

Schultz, M. (1995). *On studying organizational cultures: Diagnosis and understanding*. Berlin: W. de Gruyter.

Sevon, G. (1996). Organizational imitation in identity transformation. In B. Czarniawska & G. Sevon (Eds.), *Translating organizational change* (pp. 49–67). Berlin: W. de Gruyter.

Sorokin, P. A. (1937). *Social and cultural dynamics* (Vols. 1–4). New York: American Book Company.

Stablein, R. & Nord, W. (1985). Practical and emancipatory interests in organizational symbolism. *Journal of Management*, 11, 13–28.

Sztompka, P. (1993). *The sociology of social change*. Oxford, UK: Blackwell.

Turner, B. R. (1990). Introduction. In B. R. Turner (Ed.), *Organizational symbolism* (pp. 1–11). Berlin: W. de Gruyter.

Van Maanen, J. (1991). The smile factory. In P. J. Frost, L. F. Moore, M. R. Louis, C. C. Lundberg, &

J. Martin (Eds.), *Reframing organizational culture* (pp. 58–76). London: Sage.

Van Maanen, J. & Schein, E. (1979). Toward a theory of organizational socialization. *Research in Organizational Behavior, 1,* 209–264.

Ward, L. (1883). *Dynamic sociology.* New York: D. Appleton and Company.

Weber, Max (1924/1947) *The theory of social and economic organization,* ed. A. H. Henderson and T. Parsons. Glencoe, IL: Free Press.

Weber, M. (1968/1978). *Economy and society.* Berkeley: University of California Press.

White, L. (1959). *The evolution of culture.* New York: McGraw Hill.

Willmott, H. (1993). Strength is ignorance; slavery is freedom: Managing culture in modern organizations. *Journal of Management Studies, 30,* 515–52.

Zucker, L. (1977). The role of institutionalization in cultural persistence. *American Sociological Review, 42,* 726–743.

8

Evolutionary Dynamics of Organizational Populations and Communities

Joel A. C. Baum & Hayagreeva Rao

The ability of societies to respond to social problems may hinge crucially on the diversity of organizational forms, and in the long run, in a dynamic environment, diversity can be maintained or increased by the rise of new forms. Moreover, new forms are vital engines of organizational evolution. Indeed, an important component of organizational change, at the macro level, consists of the selection and replacement of existing organizational forms by new organizational forms. Furthermore, since new organizational forms are structural incarnations of technologies, beliefs, values, and norms, they emerge in tandem with social movements, new institutions, and new technologies and help to foster and reflect cultural and technical change in societies. For these reasons, where new organizational forms come from is a central question for organization theorists.

New organizational forms are novel recombinations of goals, authority relations (including governance structures), technologies and client markets. The evolution of a new organizational form involves a complex interplay between ecological and historical (i.e., genealogical) processes. A new form's emergence and character are shaped both by opportunities to create new resource spaces and by the characteristics and creativity of, and competition among, existing organizations and entrepreneurs. It begins with the differential proliferation of variations within existing populations that lead, ultimately, to an organizational founding, the product of innovative thought, that jumps out of an established form to create a new one. New organizational forms congeal as the result of processes that isolate or segregate one set of organizations from another, including technological incompatibilities, institutional actions such as government regulations, and imprinting. The rise of new organizational forms is an essential source of organization variation, playing a vital role in the creation of organizational diversity.

Organizational populations—local, coevolving groupings of organizations that embody the same organizational form—develop relationships with organizational populations engaged in other activities that bind them into organizational communities. Organizational communities constitute functionally integrated systems of interacting organizational populations (Hawley, 1950). Organizational populations, not organizations, interact to shape communities. In an organizational community, the outcomes for organizations of any one population are fundamentally intertwined with those of organizations in other populations that belong to the same community system. At a still higher level, organizational communities interact to form organizational ecosystems, including national economies (Baum and Korn, 1994).

Although Hannan and Freeman (1977) called for research at the population level as a first step toward the study of community-level phenomena, research in organizational ecology remains focused primarily on population-ecology models of the growth and decline of local populations of established organizational forms. Community-ecology models emphasize processes of creation (i.e., speciation) and demise (i.e., extinction) of organizational populations and forms and address the evolution of community structures that bind together a set of organizational populations and affect the persistence and stability of the community as a whole. The original question of organizational ecology—why there are so many kinds of organizations—has thus yet to be pursued fastidiously. Consequently, we still know too little about processes leading to the emergence of new organizational forms, or the structures of organizational inheritance that foster their persistence and transformation over time.

If, however, the current diversity of organizations is to be conceived as a reflection of the "cumulative effect of a long history of variation and selection" (Hannan and Freeman, 1989, p. 20), then an explanation of how new organizational forms arise, become different, and remain different through time is required. In this chapter, we attempt to answer these questions by analyzing population and community-level dynamics through an evolutionary variation-selection-retention (VSR) lens (Aldrich, 1979, 1999; Campbell, 1965). We offer a view of organizational populations and communities as residing in a nested hierarchy where they coevolve and present a general framework—the "dual-hierarchy" model (Baum and Singh, 1994a)—that identifies and interconnects the elements and processes we think are basic to organizational evolution. After presenting this framework, we turn to more detailed analyses of evolutionary dynamics at two levels of organization:

- Micro-evolutionary processes that shape persistence and change over time among organizations within a particular lineage or organizational form;

- Macro-evolutionary processes that shape persistence and change over time within a community of organizational forms, and through which new organizational forms arise.

Our analysis of population- and community-level evolution emphasizes the roles of institutional change (e.g., industry deregulation, globalization, market reforms), technological innovation cycles (e.g., technological discontinuities, dominant designs), entrepreneurs, and social movements as triggers of organizational variation. We explore how institutional and technological change transforms the dynamics of organizational communities by shifting the boundaries of organizational forms, destabilizing or reinforcing existing community structures, giving rise to consensus-and/or conflict-oriented social movements, and creating opportunities for entrepreneurs and venture capitalists to shape new organizational forms. Our analysis of population-level VSR aims to consolidate and refine earlier treatments of these processes; our analysis of community-level VSR, in contrast, represents one of the first comprehensive treatments of these processes (see also Aldrich, 1999; Hunt and Aldrich, 1998), and so will be, by necessity, more speculative in nature. We will conclude by highlighting some basic connections between evolutionary dynamics at population and community levels that emerge from our analysis.

Evolutionary Dynamics of Organizations

Organizational evolution can be conceptualized as the interplay between two kinds of processes, interaction and replication, acting on two kinds of entities, ecological and genealogical, at a variety of levels of organization (Baum and Singh, 1994a). Genealogical entities pass on their information largely intact in successive replications. Ecological entities, the structural and behavioral expressions of the genealogical entities, interact with the environment, and this interaction causes replication to be differential. "Organizational evolution is the result of genealogical entities replicating, ecological entities interacting, the net effect of these interactions being the differential persistence of the genealogical entities that produced them" (Baum and Singh, 1994a, p. 4).

A theory of organizational evolution, indeed any evolutionary system, minimally requires these two kinds of processes (i.e., interaction and replication) and two kinds of entities (i.e., ecological and genealogical). No theory of evolution can be complete without careful consideration of the structure and function of moment-by-moment ecological systems. Neither is a theory of evolution complete without consideration of the source of the information that supplies the entities to the ecological arena. In the evolutionary view, history and current function are intricately related. We need an understanding of the integration of interactive processes of resource exchange and transformation on the one hand, and historical processes of information conservation and transmission on the other.

Although research in organizational ecology has informed us about interaction processes within populations (for a review, see Baum, 1996), it has yet to deal comprehensively with the community-level problem of the emergence and disappearance of organizational forms and has only rarely attempted to link ecological processes of interaction and genealogical processes of replication. Consequently, we still know very little about the genealogical side of organizational evolution—the structures of organizational inheritance and speciation. Whereas biological inheritance is based primarily on propagation of genes, inheritance processes for social organizations appear very different, suggesting more equivocal organizational genealogies and evolutionary dynamics perhaps strikingly different from those expected with purely genetic transmission.

Fortunately, Darwin's idea of evolution—descent with modification—is not tied to particular features of biological inheritance. Natural selection is a very general mechanism likely to operate in any system of inheritance that meets two conditions: (1) there is heritable (blind) variation in form, and (2) the variation in form is related to variation in survival and replication. Whenever these two conditions are met, the forms with the highest probability of being transmitted to the next generation will tend to increase in number (Campbell, 1965).

The Dual Hierarchy of Organizational Evolution

Organizational evolution is frequently conceived to take place simultaneously at multiple hierarchical levels (e.g., face-to-face group, organization, population, community) (Aldrich, 1979, 1999; Baum and Singh, 1994a). The hierarchies relevant to organiza-

tional evolution are inclusive, with levels nested one within the other. Wholes are composed of parts at lower levels of organization and are themselves parts of more extensive wholes. Organizational communities, for example, are composed of populations of organizational forms, which themselves are composed of organizations, and so on. The nesting of entities into larger entities at a higher level of organization creates a system of levels. Each level constitutes a "node of selection" at which organizational entities are either retained or eliminated (Baum and Singh, 1994a; Campbell, 1974, 1994).

Ecological and Genealogical Entities

These entities form the various levels of two inclusive hierarchies, one genealogical and the other ecological, summarized in table 8.1 (Baum and Singh, 1994a). The genealogical hierarchy is formed by components of institutional memory engaged in the preservation and dissemination of production and organizing information. It is composed of lineages, entities that persist over time through replication in the same or a similar state. The ecological hierarchy reflects the economic structure and integration (i.e., resource exchange and transformation) of organizational systems. It is composed of historical entities, the result of the cumulative effect of variation and selection over time, and the structural and behavioral expressions of entities of the genealogical class.

Organizations constitute a level in both hierarchies (Baum and Singh, 1994a). As members of organizational forms (genealogical entities), organizations are packages of routinized competence, temporary repositories of production and organizing know-how (McKelvey, 1982; Winter, 1990). As members of populations (ecological entities), organizations are the external manifestation of the production and organizing competence they carry at any given time (McKelvey, 1982). As such, organizations are transmitters of the routines that embody the knowledge, capabilities, beliefs, values, and memory of the organization and its decision makers, bearers of adaptations, and expressors of variation in populations. And organizations, varying among one another, are shuffled as units as selection. Organizations thus have both ecological and genealogical roles: they are the nexus of environmental interaction and the conservation of lineages of production and organizing routines and competencies.

Table 8.1 Genealogical and ecological entities

Genealogical Hierarchy	Ecological Hierarchy
	Ecosystem: a group of coevolving communities and its natural, social, technical, and economic environment, between which resources are regularly cycled
Polythyletic grouping: an aggregate of one or more organizational forms descended from two or more immediate common ancestors, though ultimately from a common ancestor	**Community:** a group of coevolving organizational populations connected and integrated by a network of commensalistic and symbiotic interdependencies
Organizational form: a polythyletic group of competence sharing populations. A set of highly probable combinations of routines temporarily housed among all its included members at any given time.	**Population:** a group of coevolving organizations connected by commensalistic interdependencies that embody similar combinations of competences and routines
Organization: a temporary repository of routines embodied in the organization's employees and technologies at any given time	**Organization:** a group of coevolving work groups and jobs. External expression of competences and routines embodied in the organization's employees and technologies at any given time
Competence: an integrated set of interdependent routines	**Work group:** a group of coevolving jobs. External expression of competences and routines embodied by group members at any given time.
Routine: an element of production and organizing knowledge and skill	**Job:** a coevolving set of tasks or pattern of activity performed by a single individual. External expression of routines held by the employee at any given time

Source: Adapted from Baum and Singh (1994a, p. 10).

Interaction and Replication Processes

Two classes of processes, interaction and replication, distinguish the ecological and genealogical hierarchies, respectively (Baum and Singh, 1994a). Processes in the ecological hierarchy are concerned with the mutual interactions between ecological entities at the same level of organization (e.g., between organizations within populations, and populations within communities) that are connected to the resource exchanges that propel ecological entities. Social, technical, and economic environmental conditions strongly implicated in patterns of organizational persistence and change shape organizational evolution through their influence on ecological entities, and by forming part of the ecological hierarchy at the ecosystem level.

Dynamic interactions at each level hold together entities at the next-higher level of the nested ecological hierarchy. Interactions among jobs bind work groups together, which in turn bind organizations together. Interactions among organizations of the same form constitute populations. Competition, mutualism, collective action, collective learning, and other ecological processes at this level are the char-

acteristic phenomena responsible for producing the variables most frequently studied by organizational ecologists—organizational density, rates of founding, failure, and growth. When we become concerned with the interactions of populations of different organizational forms, we have moved up to the community level. Populations, not organizations, interact to shape communities. Ecological processes at this level include interpopulation competition, symbiotic interactions, institutional entrepreneurship and social movements related to new organizational forms, and changes in environmental carrying capacities. Finally, organizational communities interact to form ecosystems.

In the genealogical hierarchy, processes are those related to the production of new entities from old: the replication of lineages of routines, organizations, and organizational forms. Each level of the genealogical hierarchy is maintained by production of lower-level entities: routines must reproduce themselves for organizations to persist, organizations must produce more organizations for organizational forms to persist, and organizational forms must fragment for polyphyletic groupings to endure. Polyphyletic groupings are historical entities comprised of one or more organizational forms and formed by the production of new organizational forms from old; they constitute the highest level of organization in the genealogical hierarchy. Although reproduction occurs at all levels of the genealogical hierarchy, replication appears to be concentrated primarily at the lower levels of the genealogical hierarchy. That is, because they have short generation lengths compared to higher-level entities, most replication is replication of lower-level entities (e.g., routines, organizations) (see, e.g., Miner, 1990, 1991). As a result, time scales are shorter and the rate of evolution faster at lower levels of organization (Baum, 1999; Campbell, 1994).

VSR Processes

Evolution at all these levels of organization reflects the operation of three basic processes: variation, selection, and retention, or VSR (Aldrich, 1979, 1999; McKelvey, 1982, 1997). This view of change, which is derived from Campbell's (1965) seminal article, is based upon an analogy between "natural selection in biological evolution and the selective propagation of cultural forms" (Campbell, 1965, p. 26). The three key elements of Campbell's model are (p. 27):

1. The occurrence of variations: heterogeneous, haphazard, "blind," "chance," "random," but in any event variable. (The mutation process in organic evolution, and exploratory responses in learning.)
2. Consistent selection criteria: selective elimination, selective propagation, selective retention, of certain types of variations. (Differential survival of certain mutants in organic evolution, differential reinforcement of certain responses in learning.)
3. A mechanism for the preservation, duplication, or propagation of the positively selected variants. (The rigid duplication process of the chromosome/gene system in plants and animals, memory in learning.)

Campbell emphasized "blindness" to capture the accidental nature of variation and emergent nature of consequent behavior, processes, functions, and structure:

"Deliberate" or "intelligent" variations would do as well as "blind," "haphazard," "chance," "random," or "spontaneous" ones. They might be better insofar as they could be pre-selected. But they might be worse in that they could be restricted to the implications of already achieved wisdom and would not be likely to go beyond it. One of the services of terms like "blind" and "haphazard" . . . is that they emphasize that elaborate adaptive social systems . . . could have emerged, just as did termite societies, without any self-conscious planning or foresightful action. It provides a plausible model for social systems that are "wiser" than the individuals who constitute the society, or than the rational social science of the ruling elite. It provides an anticipation of powerful "inadvertent" social change processes in our own day, which may be adaptive in unforeseen or unwanted ways. (Campbell, 1965, p. 28)

Campbell settled on the term *blind variation* to emphasize the danger of basing variations on a priori understanding or knowledge of their adaptive outcomes. Selection does not operate by comparing any one variation to some hypothetical best variation; it chooses among presented variations that which most improves an organization's fitness (Romanelli, 1999). As Campbell (1988, p. 173) observed, "Being a purposeful problem solver . . . does not make one clairvoyant or prescient." Adaptation involves exploring the unknown, going beyond existing knowledge and recipes, and "fumbling in the dark" (Campbell, 1974, p. 147).

In organizations, however, whether due to institutionalized understandings about right and appropriate forms of activity (Zucker, 1977), or evolution of formal control systems (e.g., employment or accounting systems), members tend to develop preferences for certain responses or variations. Trial-and-error learning over the history of an organization's trials of variations may thus predispose its members to future trial or avoidance of certain kinds of variations. Such "vicarious selectors" act to shortcut purely blind variation by eliminating dangerous or inadequate actions before they are executed (Campbell, 1965). As a result, variations may be differentially probable, limited to certain forms, and not independent of one another over successive trials. As long, however, as any regularity in exploration is independent of foreknowledge of the correct response, VSR processes will continue to operate effectively. Thus, new variations need not be blind with respect to outcomes of prior variations—but they must be blind with respect to their own outcomes. So, while vicarious selectors channel evolution in certain directions, evolution will occur as long as they are subject to selection themselves (Campbell, 1965).

In the VSR model, simultaneous interaction of (blind) variation, (competitive) selection, and retention processes, termed a *Darwin machine* (Plotkin, 1993), unfold endlessly, moving systems toward greater fitness over time. Variation generates the raw material from which selection is made. Retention processes preserve the selected variation. Combined (blind) variation and (competitive) selective retention generate "evolution in the direction of better fit to the selective system" (Campbell, 1965, p. 27). If any of the three components is missing, however, no fit or order will occur.

Within and Cross-Level Processes

Darwin machines operate at each level of organization, setting the evolutionary process in motion by searching over time for more effective variations. This search can be envisioned as an ongoing exploration of possible configurations (variations) with differing values on some measure of goodness or fitness, where fitness is a function of the entity and its environment, and entities that have the highest fitness are selected and retained. At each level of organization, multiple Darwin machines operate simultaneously and interactively (e.g., multiple employees and work groups search for more effective routines or combinations of routines). Their explorations can be visualized as movement through a fitness landscape, where configurations correspond to points in a two-dimensional (horizontal) space and fitness corresponds to the configuration's value on a third (vertical) dimension (Kauffman, 1993). Local fitness maxima correspond to peaks in the landscape, local minima to valleys.

Processes within each level of each hierarchy (e.g., innovation, replication, competition), when taken alone, each constitute only one element of the overall evolutionary process, however. There are also interactive effects among levels within each hierarchy. Organizational evolution is above all a product of these coupled interactions. Although there is a degree of autonomy of event and process within each hierarchical level, and each level is taken to operate quasi-independently as a dynamic VSR system in its own right, there is also both upward and downward causation (Campbell, 1974, 1990). Interactions across levels limit the kinds of processes that can occur at a given level and regulate those that do. For example, people constitute, and are acted upon by, organizations and interactions among organizations. Their understanding of, beliefs about, and attitudes toward organizations help shape the decisions from which organizations are formed. These decisions (variations) are injected into the higher level of the populations, where selection, random drift, and entrepreneurship take over as dynamics. More generally, upward causation implies that, at each level, persistent features of the previous level constrain what emerges at the next level. Downward causation operates as follows:

> Where natural selection operates through life and death at a higher level of organization, the laws of the higher level selective system determine in part the distribution of lower level events and substances. Description of an intermediate-level phenomenon is not complete by describing its possibility and implementation in lower level terms. Its presence, prevalence, or distribution . . . will often require reference to laws at a higher level of organization as well. . . . all processes at the lower levels of a hierarchy are restrained by, and act in conformity to, the laws of the higher levels. (Campbell, 1990, p. 4)

Selection among higher-level entities thus shapes and constrains subsequent lower-level VSR processes. As a result, VSR processes at one level (e.g., organizational learning) can dramatically affect variability at lower levels (Tyre and Orlikowski, 1994). Such cross-level interactions are likely to be strongest across contiguous levels, with their significance declining as the levels involved become increasingly remote. Thus, what goes on at one level of the evolutionary hierarchy shapes processes and events at other levels, with dynamics connected most strongly at adjacent lower and upper levels. Systems of this type, hierarchical structures with feedback in which underlying components comprise and react to the overall organization, are termed *heterarchies* (Hofstader, 1979).

Importantly, higher-level adaptation does not arise automatically from lower-level adaptation. It would be highly unusual in the evolution of nested hierarchical systems for a competence or routine that optimizes fitness for components of the system to optimize prospects for the higher levels of the system or the system as a whole (Baum, 1999; Campbell, 1994, March, 1994). While selection among organizations can cause them to become well designed to survive, for example, adaptation at the level of individual organizations need not lead to adaptation at the level of populations. Selection within an organizational population acts on organizations' relative fitness and is insensitive to the fitness of the population per se. A competence or routine that decreases the fitness of the entire population will be favored if it yields individual organizations a bigger slice of the smaller pie. Similarly, one that benefits the entire population but involves a cost for individual organizations will be selected against. What is best for organizational entities at one level is not, however, generally best for those at other levels. As a result, while attempting to improve their own fitness, entities at different levels compete for resources across (as well as within) levels, complicating organizational evolution. Competitive saturation can serve to tighten relationships among levels, triggering positive and negative feedback and influencing the mix of selection and adaptation events (Van de Ven and Grazman, 1999).

A population of well-adapted individuals (in the sense of maximizing relative fitness) thus need not also be a well-adapted population. A well-adapted population might regulate its size to avoid overexploiting its resources, cooperate to defend itself against rival populations, or improve its common core technology, but none of these traits is likely to evolve when selection is insensitive to the welfare of the population per se. Functional organization at any level of the organizational hierarchy requires a corresponding process of selection at that level. Populations can become well designed only by a process of between-population selection, and communities can become well designed only by a process of between-community selection (Baum, 1999; Campbell, 1994; Sober and Wilson, 1998). Relatedly, Van de Ven and Grazman (1999) suggest that the relationships among the various levels can be positive or negative, and that stability results from a balance between positive selection at one level (e.g., population) and negative selection at a higher level (e.g., community). Even if selection among entities at a given hierarchical level enhances their fitness, however, because the rate of evolution is faster at lower levels of organization, the fitness achieved at the higher level may be eroded constantly by lower-level entities that "out-evolve" their higher-level counterparts.

Ecological and Genealogical Interactions

In the dual-hierarchy framework, however, it is interactions between ecological and genealogical hierarchies that integrate all the entities taking part in the process of organizational evolution. The elements of these two hierarchies interact, regulating change within one another, and, as by-products, create the patterns and events of organizational evolution: the persistence and the modification of the entities comprising the ecological and genealogical hierarchies over time (Baum and Singh, 1994a).

At any point in time, organizations, the members of populations, operate with other populations of organizations in more or less integrated communities. From a genealogical point of view, these ecological communities are integrated collections of populations drawn from various lineages of organizational forms. Polyphyletic groupings provide the organizational forms, which in turn provide the populations observed in each community, which are themselves integrated into the larger ecosystems of the ecological hierarchy. Thus, the genealogical hierarchy supplies the entities of the ecological hierarchy, and their continued existence and characteristic features are dependent on what is available in the genealogical hierarchy.

However, it is ecological entities, the visible structural and behavioral expressions of genealogical entities, that are shuffled as units of selection. For example, within populations, the ongoing selection of organizations results in valuable configurations of routines (i.e., competencies) being retained and less valuable configurations being rejected. And it is the unequal results of the interactions among ecological entities that determine what exists in the genealogical hierarchy in the next generation—which particular lineages of routines, organizations, and organizational forms survive over time, and in what form. In general, the ecological interactions that result in the differential perpetuation of genealogical entities occur at the same level or higher levels of the ecological hierarchy. Thus, most of the regulation of retention and modification of production and organizing competence over time results not from processes in the genealogical hierarchy, but from those in the ecological hierarchy responsible for the changing composition of ecological entities over time. Consequently, anything contributing to the differential birth, death, and persistence of ecological entities is material to an understanding of evolutionary processes. Of course, this does not mean that one hierarchy is causally prior to the other; both are necessary for a theory of organizational evolution.

Figure 8.1 overlays VSR processes on the dual hierarchy framework to depict one possible version of ecological-genealogical interactions. At each level of organization, Darwin machines connect ecological and genealogical hierarchies, continuously producing variations in genealogical entities, whose external expressions are shuffled as units of selection in the ecological hierarchy, with selected variations in turn retained as genealogical entities. Thus, "V" and "R" map onto replication processes and operate on genealogical entities, while "S" maps onto interaction processes and operates on ecological entities. In the scheme presented, Darwin machines operate at five levels of the dual hierarchy: job-routine, competence–work group, organization-organization, population-organizational form, and community-polyphyletic group. In other words, ongoing selection of jobs

within work groups, work groups within organizations, organizations within populations, populations within communities and communities within ecosystems is conceived to directly affect replication of entities in the genealogical hierarchy, which in turn directly affects the variation among jobs, organizations, and populations.

Figure 8.1 also illustrates patterns of upward and downward interaction that constrain and regulate processes at adjacent levels within each hierarchy. Across levels of organization, Darwin machines interact through retention within the genealogical and selection within the ecological hierarchy. In the genealogical hierarchy, retention at each level affects variation at other levels both up (e.g., the pool of available routines limits the range of organizational variation expressed within an organizational form) and down (e.g., integrating multiple interdependent routines into competencies rules out many lower-level combinatorial possibilities) the hierarchy. In the

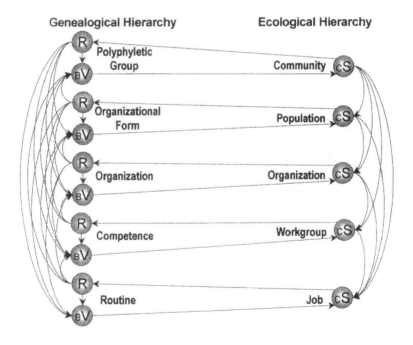

BV = (Blind) Variation

CS = (Competitive) Selection

R = Retention

Figure 8.1 Multilevel VSR.

ecological hierarchy, the interactions that result in the differential selection of ecological entities cascade downward with the selection of organizations, dependent on the selection of their populations, which in turn depend on the selection of the communities to which they belong. Thus, the ecological fates of organizations are tied inextricably to the fates of the populations and communities within which they are nested.

Although figure 8.1 presents a detailed "snapshot" of the content, levels, and processes that constitute the dual-hierarchy model, it does not explicitly depict the implications of the model's dynamics over time. In the genealogical hierarchy, the result is a set of lineages tracing the temporal progression of changes in routines, competencies, organizations, and organizational forms (Van de Ven and Grazman, 1999). In the ecological hierarchy, the result is a shifting distribution (e.g., changes in variability and average characteristics) of jobs, work groups, organizations, and organizational populations.

Micro-Evolutionary Dynamics of Organizational Populations

Most new organizations constitute replications—with variation—of existing organizational forms (Aldrich and Kenworthy, 1999). Such foundings are central to micro-evolutionary processes that produce persistence and change within lineages of established organizational forms. On occasion, however, an organizational founding, the product of innovative entrepreneurial initiative, jumps out of an established form to create a new one (i.e., "speciates"). The emergence of new forms is the domain of macroevolution. The emergence and character of new organizational forms are shaped by both opportunities to create new resource spaces (Hannan and Freeman, 1989; Schumpeter, 1934) and the characteristics and creativity of, and competition among, existing organizations and entrepreneurs (Lumsden and Singh, 1990). New organizational forms represent novel recombinations of core organizational features (Rao and Singh, 1999), which include:

Stated goals—the basis on which legitimacy and other resources are mobilized (including not-for-profit, for-profit, cooperative, religious, and charitable orientations);

Authority relations—the basis of exchange within the organization and between the organization and its members (including governance structures—e.g., market, hierarchy, and clan);

Core technology—as encoded in capital investment, infrastructure, and the skills and knowledge of employees;

Market strategy—the kinds of clients or customers to which the organization orients its production, and the ways in which it attracts resources from the environment.

These core organizational features, which are difficult and hazardous to change (Hannan and Freeman, 1984) and which play central roles in the mobilization of resources and legitimacy, comprise a four-dimensional space in which new organizational forms appear or disappear over time (Baum, 1989; Rao and Singh, 1999).[1] Hannan and Freeman (1984) distinguish these core features from more peripheral attributes of organizations, which are more amenable to change and serve to protect an organization's core from uncertainty by buffering it from, and broadening its connections to, the environment. Peripheral features include number and sizes of subunits, number of hierarchical levels, span of control, patterns of communication, and buffering mechanisms such as interlocking directorates and strategic alliances (Hannan and Freeman, 1984, p. 157). Although these and other organizational features (e.g., organizational culture) can be central to the character and identity of individual organizations, core features are intended to serve as a basis for characterizing the identities of organizational forms.

An advantage of using core features to identify and describe organizational forms is that they provide a compact list of relatively stable and adaptively significant attributes on which to base relatively stable and vital distinctions between organizational forms. These four features can also help assess how an organizational form is connected to ancestral forms and direct our attention to processes by which new discontinuities in configurations of goals, authority, technology, and market strategy arise. Organizational forms, then, are defined in terms of their core characteristics, and one form differs from another primarily according to core characteristics of the form. Organizational forms constitute polyphyletic groupings (McKelvey 1982); that is, each member of a form shares common core characteristics but may differ with respect to peripheral features.

There are considerable obstacles to the emergence of new organizational forms. Unless a new organizational form can rapidly acquire mechanisms that isolate it from its parent population(s) and external legitimacy that helps overcome a liability of newness (Stinchcombe, 1965), its distinctive characteristics are unlikely to be maintained over time. Before we tackle the macro-evolutionary problem of the emergence of new forms, however, we must first characterize the ongoing, micro-evolutionary within-lineage dynamics of replication with variation within organizational forms.

Variation: Exploring Organizational Fitness Landscapes

Organizational variations are the result of human behavior. Any kind of change, intentional or blind, is variation. Individuals intentionally produce variations in, for example, technical and management competencies in their efforts to adjust their organization's relationship to the environment. Blind variations, in contrast, are accidental, the product of chance, luck, or unforeseen product of creative exploration. Most variations are small, serving mainly to perpetuate the existing order rather than displace it. Organizational variations provide the raw material from which selection can be made. Some variations prove more beneficial to organizations than others in acquiring resources in a competitive environment and are thus selected positively—not by some amorphous environment, but by managers inside organizations and investors, customers, and government regulators (McKelvey, 1994; Meyer, 1994a; Miner, 1994).

Selection criteria are set through operation of competitive and institutional processes, as well as the logic of technologies in use and organizational structures and incentives. Retention occurs when selected variations are routinized, reproduced, and carried forward into future actions and organizations. Internal criteria for selection (and retention) of variations are often more salient to people inside organizations than external, environmental criteria. Compared to the strong situations that characterize organizations' internal environments (Davis-Blake and Pfeffer, 1989), their external environments are often inchoate and rarely provide feedback with sufficient speed, frequency, or detail to yield clear cues about effective behavior. Most selection of variation within organizations, then, is driven by internal criteria defined by

organizations including goals, subgoals, and organizationally based rewards for attaining these goals (Meyer, 1994a).

When successful variations are known, or when environmental trends are identifiable, organizations can attempt to copy and implement these successful variations, or they can attempt to forecast, anticipate, plan, and implement policies in the context of the predictable trends (DiMaggio and Powell, 1983; Nelson and Winter, 1982). But when successful variations are unknown, because, for example, the behavior of consumers and competitors is unpredictable, the probability of choosing the correct variation and implementing it successfully is very low. Even when effective variations are identifiable, ambiguity in the causes of success may frustrate attempts at imitation. Under such conditions, variations can be viewed as experimental trials, some of which are consciously planned and some of which are accidental, some of which succeed and some of which fail (McKelvey, 1994; Miner, 1994). Whether or not they are known, over time, selected variations are retained as surviving organizations come to be characterized by them.

If the survival odds are low for organizations with a particular variant, it does not mean that these organizations are destined to fail. Rather, it means the capacity of their members to change them successfully is of utmost importance to their performance and survival. However, individuals cannot always (or even often) determine in advance which organizational variations will succeed, and there are constraints on the capacity of individuals to change their organizations successfully, including established practices, norms, and incentives, competition for scarce resources, and limits to individual rationality. Consequently, in addition to variations introduced by members of ongoing organizations, evolutionary approaches also highlight the creation of new organizations as an important source of variation.

Intraorganizational Sources of Organizational Variation

The persistent centrality of issues of coordination and control in organization theory is a testament to the commonness of variation inside organizations (Aldrich, 1999). New ideas—variations—emerge all the time and are tried out as a result of the inventiveness as well as the mistakes of an organization's fallible members. Organizational members forget standard routines and invent new ones while fulfilling their roles, or pursue their own creative (or destructive) insights when discouraged or bored. Random drift results as organizational members fulfill their roles independently of one another over time. Copying mistakes occur and information is imperfectly transmitted in attempts to transfer routines to new organizational members. Transferred personnel create hybrid routines, mixing ideas from their prior and current roles (Miner, 1990, 1991). The problem is that not all this variation is beneficial: Although many variations turn out to be benign, some may prove harmful. While required variations cannot be specified in advance, and outcomes of enacted variations are difficult to determine without a trial, organizations can still affect the types and level of variation they produce (Miner, 1994).

Several organizational practices facilitate variation. One is institutionalized experimentation (Miner, 1994). This includes formal research and development, introduction of "champion" and "intrapreneur" roles, adoption of total quality management and other continuous improvement practices, as well as use of parallel projects in which several teams work on solving the same general problem, generating intentional variation among potential solutions. A second is provision of direct and indirect incentives for producing variations. Many organizations use total quality, continuous improvement, and suggestion programs to establish innovation as a regular facet of work. Organizations also establish competitions between individuals or work groups, rewarding winners with resources and status. Others provide specific monetary incentives for discoveries, such as a percentage of licensing fees from patents produced by the new ideas. Sometimes, full-scale venture divisions or spin-off companies are established with participants sharing an equity interest in new products developed, or the venture itself (Burgelman, 1983). A third is for organizations to officially tolerate unfocused variation or playfulness (March, 1981). Research labs are purposely informal to encourage unplanned interactions and variations in ideas. A certain level of slack resources is tolerated to support informal work on unapproved projects.

Some organization theorists have come to view complexity theory as providing a general framework for understanding intraorganizational sources of variation (e.g., Baum, 1999; Brown and Eisenhardt, 1998; McKelvey, 1998; Stacey, 1995, 1996; Thietart and

Forgues, 1995; see chapter 12 in this volume). Complexity theory suggests that adaptive systems tend to steer themselves to "the edge of chaos" or "region of emergence" by regulating their level of autonomy/mutual dependence, both among components and between a system as a whole and other systems in the environment with which it interacts. Such regulation of interdependence is hypothesized to benefit an organizational system by admitting order and change, structure and surprise. Organizational complexity theorists conceive organizations as "complex adaptive systems" and emphasize how individuals, organizational subunits, and organizations "self-organize" into emergent aggregate structure.

Consider, for example, a large organization in need of a turnaround. If subunits comprising the organization are too tightly coupled, there may be excessive interdependence and rigidity—if every act of each subunit influences others throughout the organization, then the repercussions of any given action have the potential to destabilize the entire system. Coupling that is too tight leaves no room for desirable individual autonomy. If, in contrast, the organizational subunits are too loosely coupled, there is no coherence. Coordination is problematic, knowledge fails to diffuse and accumulate, and confusion sets in. In short, "too much structure creates gridlock . . . too little structure creates chaos" (Brown and Eisenhardt, 1998, p. 14). The edge of chaos lies between these extremes, where partially connected organizational subunits never quite reach equilibrium, but never quite disintegrate either. It is a transitional realm in which emergent structures (e.g., new network formations, informal or formal group activities, departments, entrepreneurial ventures, technologies, and routines), resulting from responses to changing environmental conditions, form and produce new variations to resolve adaptive tensions and then dissipate (McKelvey, 1999). Such activity is very sensitive to small differences in initial conditions, leading to path-dependent behavior in which historical accidents "tip" outcomes strongly in a particular direction. As a result, complex behavior amplifies any initially random variation among organizational routines, which can follow radically divergent paths over time, providing a basis for a range of innovative behavior on which selection can act.

In the end, however, the source of variation does not matter as long as many blind variations are tried on a more or less regular basis.

Balancing Organizational Variation and Internal Selective Retention

There is an inherent tension in the VSR model: "Variation and retention are at odds in most exemplifications of the model. Maximizing either one jeopardizes the other. Some compromise of each is required" (Campbell, 1974, p. 27). Too much retention restricts the kinds of variations that can occur; too much variation prevents the system from systematically harvesting effective variations. Within organizations, although March (1981), Miner (1994), and others suggest that variation can be promoted through institutionalized experimentation and incentives that reward playfulness, over time a self-reinforcing bias toward preservation of current routines appears, inevitably, to tip the balance in favor of retention.

All organizations face the question of how to allocate energy between the exploration of new routines and the exploitation of old ones (March, 1991). Exploitation refers to refinement and reproduction of existing routines. Exploration refers to search for new routines through concerted variation, planned experimentation, and play. March (1991) advocates striking a balance between the two: too much emphasis on exploitation (retention) can lead to the adoption of suboptimal routines and stagnation; too much emphasis on exploration (variation) can lead to incurring the high costs of experimentation without harvesting any of the value of its benefits. In practice, however, sure short-run rewards of exploitation distract organizations from exploration, since each increase in competence at an activity increases the likelihood of obtaining rewards for engaging in that activity, while returns from exploration are systematically less certain.

Given initial success at applying a routine, organizations are likely to retain and reuse it because they know increasingly well how to, and because it is less risky and costly to apply an existing, proven routine than alternatives with which organizations have limited experience. Managers' attributions of success to their own abilities, and to the policies and practices (correct or not) they previously adopted, limits the likelihood that they will initiate experimentation. This is especially true if there are few negative results, tempting managers to go just a little bit farther, and increasing the likelihood that any false or superstitious beliefs that managers hold will be reinforced (Levinthal and March, 1993; Miller, 1993). These managerial beliefs serve as powerful vicarious selectors within organizations, leading organizations to concentrate on what they believe they are good at, get worse at other things, attribute success to what they think they are good at, and attribute failure to not trying hard enough (Levitt and March, 1988).

In the face of ambiguity and uncertainty, an emphasis on reproducing routines honed in the past can prevent organizations from adjusting their routines too quickly and detrimentally to idiosyncratic events and from engaging in costly explorations into highly uncertain domains. Exploitive learning may also enhance performance by reducing variability in the quality or efficiency of task execution (Argote and Epple, 1990; Hannan and Freeman, 1984). Exploitation can become harmful, however, if the criteria for organizational success and survival change after the organization has learned. Then the organization may perform poorly by doing well what it learned in the past; it may suffer the so-called competency trap (Levitt and March, 1988). Organizations may thus often reduce exploratory activity prematurely and, in the case of a changing environment, may not renew exploratory search and learning activities despite the fact that new opportunities and threats are present (Starbuck, 1983). This path dependency limits evolutionary possibilities, potentially overriding exploratory search and learning activities despite the fact that new opportunities and threats are present. Managers' internal selection criteria come to dominate external ones, leading organizations to employ routines of the past well beyond their point of usefulness to consumers and investors (Miller, 1990, 1999; Starbuck, 1983).

As noted above, there is nothing inherently problematic with limiting variations to certain forms, and nonindependence over successive trials. However, internal vicarious selectors that develop through mutual positive feedback between experience and competence are often not subject to selection (Miller, 1999). They also engender managerial confidence in their prescience about the outcomes of variation. Managers come to rely on inductive analysis to determine which variation will be best. Given an improvement, they conclude that the outcome was best based on comparison with presumed results of other variations that were never tried. Thus, rather than variations in routines and competencies that are subject to selection, internal vicarious selectors tend to produce singular changes that are not subject to selection. Ultimately, excessive attention to internal selection criteria that are not themselves subject to selection erodes an organization's competence as its goals become ends in themselves, and its members find easier (but not more effective) ways to achieve them (Meyer, 1994b). This situation fundamentally and detrimentally reduces the ability of the organization to evolve: If multiple variations are not tried blindly, selection will not operate or will operate through extreme failure, the result of organizational selection at a higher evolutionary level (Baum and Ingram, 1998).

Although the threat exploitation and internal vicarious selectors pose for individual organizational survival is substantial, the resulting cycle of "specialization and replacement" may well be efficient for the organization's population (Levinthal and March, 1993, p. 103). By combining advantages of learning at the organization level and advantages of selection at the population level, the "self-destructive" properties of organizational learning make the replacement of obsolescent organizations easier. Rigidities in one organization serve to exploit current knowledge and simultaneously make old markets vulnerable to new organizations with new capabilities.

Interorganizational Sources of Organizational Variation

Organizations' own experience is not the only source of variation, however. Organizations also learn vicariously or more directly from the experiences of other organizations, imitating or avoiding specific actions or practices based on their perceived impact (Cyert and March, 1963; Miner and Haunschild, 1995).

Interorganizational learning occurs when one organization learns by observing, exchanging knowledge, or generating knowledge through joint interaction with other organizations in its own or a different population. This learning may be either strictly vicarious, when one organization observes but does not interact with another, or interactive, when the learning process arises from active contacts between two or more organizations (e.g., strategic alliances, research consortia). Vicarious interorganizational learning is a ubiquitous feature of contemporary organization theory (DiMaggio and Powell, 1983) and in strategic management is the basis for the second-mover advantage (Lieberman and Montgomery, 1988). Interactive interorganizational learning is widely held to be the primary incentive for (and benefit of) strategic alliances (Powell, Koput, and Smith-Doerr, 1996) and research consortia (Aldrich and Sasaki, 1995; Mowery, Oxley, and Silverman, 1996).

Interorganizational learning can also occur when members of one organizational population collectively observe members of other organizational populations or forms and draw on their shared experience to enact or inform organizational routines (Miner and Anderson, 1999). Members of one population might, for example, develop a formal collective entity after watching another population do so, as U.S. semiconductor producers did after observing Japanese research consortia (e.g., SEMATECH; Mowery et al., 1996). An emerging industry's development of a trade association group in response to a common external threat also represents collective learning.

The experience of other organizations has some unique advantages over an organization's own experience. Of particular significance, while individual organizations tend to engage in too much exploitation, in the aggregate, they may explore the fitness landscape thoroughly. Unlike organizations, any one severely limited in how much it can explore, organizational populations and forms are nonhierarchical, face limited demands for integration, and therefore can be more varied in their experience than individual organizations. The general lack of cohesion, the diversity of organizational goals, and the absence of any systematic harvesting or censoring of newly created routines all contribute to the proliferation of new ideas and routines as opposed to one that encourages incremental learning. Compared to individual organizations, then, organizational populations can explore a great deal of variation without violating internal or external standards for consistency and reliability (Baum and Ingram, 1998).

Consequently, other organizations may offer a source of fresh variation for organizations that have fallen into competency traps. With such an approach, organizations mired in their own past can potentially learn the strategies, production and organizing competencies, and technologies employed by other successful organizations in their industry. A good strategy for any individual organization may thus often be to emphasize exploitation of the successful explorations of others (Levinthal and March, 1993).[2] Although the politics of ingrained internal vicarious selectors can limit the potential of this strategy by channeling interorganizational search, widespread identification and imitation of "best practices" and the practice of "benchmarking" both typify this strategy (Imai, 1986). More generally, Haunschild and Miner (1997) identify three "modes" of interorganizational imitation: frequency imitation (copying the most common organizational routine), trait imitation (copying the routine of some organization based on a trait of that organization such as size, prestige, similarity to self, etc.), and outcome imitation (copying routines that appear to have good consequences for other organizations).

"And what could be more efficient? The observing organization acquires the trial-and-error experience of another organization without ever investing resources in its own trial. What could be less risky? The chosen routine or practice, from among those observed, has demonstrated its ability to improve an organization's environmental fit" (Romanelli, 1999, p. 87). The problem is again prescience, which is typically the main objective of interorganizational learning. Organizations learning in this manner do not invest in learning without an expectation that they will discover new routines that will improve performance, and they try to infer in advance which among possible variations will provide the greatest improvement. As long as no immediate decline in performance occurs that can be traced to the variation introduced, the action is likely to be interpreted as a success, but selection has had no chance to work (Romanelli, 1999).

Selection: Defining Criteria and Organizational Fitness Landscapes

The contours of fitness landscapes that members of an organizational form must navigate, as well as the values of particular organizational variations they conjure, are shaped by three main processes: competitive isomorphism, institutional isomorphism, and the r-K transition. Competitive and institutional isomorphism focus on how exogenous environmental processes in the surrounding environment affect the "spatial" characteristics of selection criteria—how selection criteria affect the variability within organizational forms. The r-K transition captures processes endogenous to an organizational form's evolution that affect the "temporal" characteristics of selection criteria—how selection criteria change systematically as an organizational form ages and grows.

Competitive Isomorphism

Organizational ecologists contend that the degree of similarity or isomorphism among organizations is determined by competition among them (Hannan and Freeman, 1977, 1989). Ecological models of competition focus on the importance of organizational niche similarity for intrapopulation competition. Niche overlap—the confrontation by organizations of a similar set of resources and constraints—is predicted to lead to competition, and the intensity of competition is expected to be a function of relative niche location. In particular, the more similar organizations' niche locations (i.e., the greater the degree of niche overlap), the more they require similar resources to thrive—raw materials, labor, financial support, institutional support, and customer demand—and the more intensely they compete (Hawley, 1950; Hannan and Freeman, 1977, 1989; McPherson, 1983). At one extreme, if organizations' niches overlap completely, the potential for competition will be fierce. At the other extreme, if organizations' niches do not overlap at all, they will require entirely different resources and there will be no potential for competition.

In general, the niche is a location in multidimensional space defined by the resources in the environment. Although the niche is a concept well known in organizational ecology, the usual focus is on the niches of organizational forms (Hannan and Freeman, 1977, 1989). In addition to the macro-niche of the form, however, individual organizations have micro- or organizational niches as well (Baum and Singh, 1994b, 1994c; McKelvey, 1982; McPherson, 1983). Thus, organizational forms can encompass multiple organizational niches, and depending on the organizational niches they occupy, organizations face different competitive landscapes, and organizational niches provide a way to account for intraform heterogeneity in capabilities and resource requirements (Baum and Singh, 1994b, 1994c). Competition among organizations within and among organizational niches sets the evolution of organizational forms in motion. Variation in adaptive capacities at the organizational niche level is the raw material based on which organizations in competition are differentially selected for retention. Organizations with variations that are less proficient at adapting to and acquiring resources from the environment tend to be eliminated. Retention processes preserve the selected variation, setting the range of organizational variation that can be expressed within an organizational form—and its fitness relative to rival forms. Such competition can affect variability within organizational forms in several ways.

According to the principle of competitive isomorphism in organizational ecology (Hannan and Freeman, 1977), selection processes link the variability of organizations to the variability of environments. Organizations are specialized and these specializations, which follow from environmental selection pressures, create homogeneous organizational groupings that compete in different ways for different resources and rely on different strategic and operational competencies. The more uniform the demands (e.g., consumer and investor) of an organizational environment, the greater the convergence of selection pressures on particular organizational variations and the greater the similarity of surviving organizations. This is because in homogeneous environments, few differentiated resources exist, and organizations prevail by virtue of their specialization to common environmentally imposed constraints. As a result, selection pressures reduce variation by eliminating organizations that deviate from those most proficient at acquiring the undifferentiated resources from the environment. Two different selection processes operate in homogeneous environments to lower organizational variability (Amburgey, Dacin, and Kelly, 1994; Baum, in press; McPherson, Popielarz and Drobnic, 1992).

Stabilizing selection directs pressures against organizations whose features vary from the "optimum." Stabilizing selection leaves the features of the average organization unchanged and reduces organizational variation. Organizational forms undergoing stabilizing selection are in the process of specializing. Organizational size, for example, might be subject to stabilizing selection that favors organizations close to some "optimum" size while systematically selecting larger and smaller organizations out of the environment. Directive selection favors organizations at one tail of a distribution of organizational variation, while subjecting those at the other tail to negative selection pressures. For example, larger airlines (or, alternatively, labor unions, or life insurance companies) might be favored while smaller airlines are systematically eliminated, resulting in a larger mean size of airlines. Directive selection thus simultaneously reduces organizational variability and moves the features characterizing the average organization toward the favored tail of the distribution.

In contrast, heterogeneous environments contain many distinct resources and constraints, leading organizations to face varied circumstances and requiring local adaptations. Under these conditions, differentiated organizations, adept at acquiring differentiated resources and carving out distinct niches, are favored by competitive selection, increasing organizational variation. Diversifying or disruptive selection increases variability by favoring organizations at the tails of the distribution, while discriminating against those in the middle, producing a bimodal or multimodal distribution of variation (Hannan and Freeman, 1977). For example, if large and small hotels (alternatively, banks, book publishers, or brewers) depend on different mixes of resources (e.g., conventions versus individual travelers), then patterns of resource use will be specialized to particular segments of the size distribution, hotels' niche location will vary with size, and similar-sized hotels will compete most intensely. As a result, large hotels pose a threat to medium-sized hotels but not small ones. Whatever strategy medium-sized hotels adopt to compete with large hotels makes them more vulnerable to competition from small hotels and vice versa. Therefore, the emergence of large hotels is accompanied by a decline in the number of medium-sized hotels, while small hotels flourish as their most intense competitors are removed from the environment (Baum and Mezias, 1992).

Institutional Isomorphism

Neoinstitutional theorists agree with organizational ecologists that organizational variability is a function of environmental heterogeneity. The central issue from the institutional perspective, however, is the level of fragmentation in the structure of the institutional environment (Scott, 1995). Institutional theory emphasizes that environments are characterized by the elaboration of institutionalized beliefs, rules, and requirements to which organizations must conform if they are to receive support, acquire needed resources, and be perceived as legitimate. In contrast to ecologists' focus on competitive isomorphism, neoinstitutionalists stress the degree of interdependence and connection among organizations. Institutional isomorphism is seen to result from powerful social forces—coercive, normative, and mimetic—in the interorganizational context that leads organizations to conform to institutionalized patterns (DiMaggio and Powell, 1983).

Coercive isomorphism results from formal or informal pressures exerted by one organization on another. For example, organizations may conform to rules and regulations prescribed by superordinate environmental agents, such as the state, that are sufficiently powerful to impose particular structures or practices on them. Although conformity to such pressures may not increase a subordinate organization's ability to achieve its ends, it will at least enhance its legitimacy. Scott (1987) identifies two additional related mechanisms. Authorization involves legitimation of an organization's structural features or qualities by a superordinate institution (e.g., an accreditation agency). In this case, the subordinate organization is not compelled to conform but voluntarily seeks out attention and approval of the authorizing agent. Inducement creates isomorphism by providing incentives to subordinate organizations willing to conform to the conditions of a superordinate agent, when the agent lacks the power or authority to impose its stipulations on subordinate organizations. Examples include venture capitalists and funding agencies that specify conditions for acquiring and remaining eligible for funding or being reimbursed for work performed.

Normative isomorphism is derived from professionalization and the belief systems promulgated by professional membership. Organizations may adhere to the norms and standards of business and professional circles that define routine or acceptable solutions to professional, managerial, and organizational problems. These solutions are institutionalized in the business, academic, or professional subcultures and are transmitted through vehicles including educational institutions, conferences, training workshops, industry and professional journals, and the movement of the members of business or professional circles among organizations.

When influence in the institutional environment is centralized, coercive and normative institutional pressures are homogeneous and easily coordinated and imposed on subordinate organizations. In contrast, fragmented institutional structures suffer from ambiguity, coordinated action to influence organizations is difficult, and room for organizational discretion is created by the resulting uncertainty (Goodrick and Salancik, 1996). In his study of the influence of government regulation on the evolution of the American life insurance industry, Lehrman (1994, p. 631), for example, observes: "The preferences of the institutional environment were initially neither stable nor uniform but over time shifted toward more technical, sober, and uniform standards. This resulted in decreased diversity of viable forms and increased conformity with a definition of life insurance as a financial service conceived and administered in a fairly specific manner." Thus, consistent with the principle of competitive isomorphism in organizational ecology, the greater the number of distinct institutional resources and constraints in an organizational field (i.e., the greater the fragmentation of institutional structures), the greater the diversity of organizations that can be sustained in the field.

Mimetic isomorphism results from processes that induce the imitation of "normal" structures and practices. Faced with environmental uncertainty, organizations imitate or model themselves after other organizations in their field—especially similar organizations perceived to be more effective or successful, or with which they are in direct contact. Such imitation may be unrelated to goal attainment. Instead, becoming identified with the practices and characteristics of "successful" or "high-status" organizations is more critical. Like coercive and normative processes, mimetic processes also depend on the homogeneity of the institutional environment. When a widely accepted "normal" model exists, mimicry will tend to speed the predominance of the model and reduce organizational diversity. However, when such a "normal" model does not exist, mimicry tends to impede a "normal" model's rise (DiMaggio and Powell 1983, p. 155–156) and can increase organizational diversity if several qualitatively different alternatives, each with its own prestigious adopters and supporters, are the focus of imitation (Baum, in press).

The role of such institutional processes has figured with increasing prominence in recent ecological theory and research, and increasingly it is recognized that institutional processes are contextual to ecological processes (e.g., Aldrich and Fiol, 1994; Barnett and Carroll, 1993; Rao and Singh, 1999; Tucker, Baum, and Singh, 1992). In this view, institutional processes constitute the broader social context for ecological processes, prescribing the selection criteria on which ecological processes operate. Moreover, as an organizational form grows and its social impact becomes more widely recognized, community advocacy groups, government agencies, professional associations, and other social actors increasingly take an active role in monitoring its members' activities,

compared to their "host" organizations. As a result, information about organizing and production can potentially be inherited from diverse sources and the flow of information continues throughout the life of individual organizations as generations of its members come and go (McKelvey, 1982; Miner and Haunschild, 1995).

Organizational inheritance occurs through different processes at each level of the evolutionary hierarchy. At the organization level, an organization's current routines serve as templates for producing copies, making their replication through observation, formal training and education, or hiring proficient new employees possible with some precision from day-to-day and over generations of organizational employees (Bandura, 1977; McKelvey, 1982; Nelson and Winter, 1982).[5] Organizational routines not only record history, however, they also shape its future course. Each time an organization uses a certain routine, it becomes more proficient at that routine and more likely to repeat it again in the future (Levitt and March, 1988). Although this self-reinforcing process contributes to organizational stability, efficiency and reliability, as described above, it can lead to competency traps that make the exploration of potentially adaptive alternatives difficult.

Other organizations' routines can also be inherited though selective copying or vicarious learning (e.g., reverse engineering, benchmarking); however, routines inherited in this manner may constitute substantial mutations because the "target" is often unavailable for direct observation and may be accompanied by unobservable subtle subroutines and tacit knowledge. More direct transmission of routines also occurs through personal and formal relationships between organizations and their members (e.g., personal ties, board-of-directors interlocks, interorganizational relations), and still more directly when an organization hires employees from other organizations judged to possess knowledge of superior routines or absorbs a whole organization. Information can also be inherited in many different directions among generations of organizational members and organizations: vertically forward (i.e., young copy old); horizontally (i.e., young copy young, old copy old); and even vertically backward (i.e., old copy young) (Baum and Singh, 1994a). Trial-and-error learning as well as more elaborate methods of adaptation (i.e., rational calculation based on collection of information, estimation of outcomes of various alternatives, and evaluations of the desirability of estimated outcomes according to some preference criteria) are forces that guide patterns of organizational inheritance. These features of organizational inheritance suggest evolutionary effects and levels of diversity and variation within organizational forms that are strikingly different from those expected with purely genetic transmission.

For one, the pace of organizational evolution is often likely to be very much faster than biotic evolution,[6] and quantum or punctuated evolutionary patterns may be more readily applicable to organizational than biotic evolution (McKelvey, 1982; Miller and Friesen, 1980; Tushman and Romanelli, 1985).[7] In combination, transmission after birth and organizational learning may result in a preponderance of Lamarckian (versus Mendelian) inheritance in the sense that production and organizing competence acquired through learning can be retransmitted (Boyd and Richerson, 1985; McKelvey, 1982; but see Hull, 1988, pp. 452–457). Such social learning–driven inheritance mechanisms have the added advantage of easily admitting change in individual organizations and attending to the hierarchical nature of organizational evolution (Baum and Singh, 1994a). Consequently, the genealogies of organizational forms may often be equivocal and direct genetic analogies infeasible (Hannan and Freeman, 1989; McKelvey, 1982; but see Van de Ven and Grazman, 1999).

Nevertheless, inheritance is certainly not completely unrestrained among organizational forms. The emergence and maintenance of distinctions among organizational forms requires barriers to the exchange of production and organizing competence. Without such barriers, organizational forms could not become or remain meaningfully different from each other over time. Instead, they would fall into a normal distribution of slightly varying forms with some average properties that are not heritable. In the world of organizations, although probably not rooted in a system of inheritance in the biological sense, it is obvious that differences can and do become deep enough that the gaps between them are rarely (if ever) bridged (Baum and Singh, 1994a; McKelvey, 1982).

Within organizational forms, organizations retaining similar bundles of production and organizing competence are reproduced over generations of employees and organizations as the result of barriers to inheritance from other organizational forms (Baum, 1989; Boyd and Richerson, 1985; Hannan and

Freeman, 1989; McKelvey, 1982).[8] These "segregating" mechanisms include:

- *Technological interdependencies.* The dependence for successful performance of one element of organizational competence on the successful completion of others means the introduction of new kinds of production and organizing competence is potentially disruptive. As a result, gaps appear between organizational forms because certain combinations of goals, authority relations, market strategies, and modes of production are inconsistent technologically (Hannan and Freeman, 1989; McKelvey, 1982).
- *Transaction costs.* Transaction cost considerations (e.g., asset specificity, small numbers) lead to distinctive clusters of transactions within organizations engaged in different kinds of production (Williamson, 1975, 1991). For example, integration into retailing occurs only for organizations whose products require considerable point-of-sale information and follow-up service, while integration into wholesaling occurs only for organizations whose products are perishable and branded.
- *Collective action.* Organizations working together (e.g., as a lobbying association) create distinctions between those engaged in collective action and those not so engaged (Hannan and Freeman, 1989).
- *Institutional processes.* Coercive, normative, and mimetic processes (DiMaggio and Powell, 1983) and the taken-for-grantedness of established organizational forms (Hannan and Freeman, 1989) operate to accentuate and maintain the diversity of organizations. In either case, potentially arbitrary differences between organizations are transformed into differences with real social consequences, so that nominal classifications become substantive.
- *Social, professional, and personnel network closures.* Groups of organizations that repeatedly hire either each other's employees or employees from the same educational or training institutions (because they possess required skill and knowledge) develop a high degree of inbreeding with respect to production and organizing competence as well as language and culture and tend to become separate and different from other groups of organizations (Hannan and Freeman, 1989; McKelvey, 1982).

- *Complexity of learning.* The more difficult an organization's production and organizing competence is to learn and socially transmit (as a function of its complexity and distinctness), the less likely it is that organizations in different organizational forms will be able to acquire and comprehend enough of the competence to successfully implement it (McKelvey, 1982).
- *Resistance to learning.* Organizations tend to prefer employing routines of the past (even beyond their point of usefulness) or to focus on refining current routines (e.g., updating and or managing more effectively the routines already held) rather than trying out new (potentially superior) ideas invented elsewhere (March, 1991; McKelvey, 1982; Nystrom and Starbuck, 1984).
- *Conformist transmission.* Interorganizational imitation is biased toward adoption of majority or plurality practices when several competing beliefs are transmitted by different organizations (Boyd and Richerson, 1985). Organizational inheritance is thus a strong homogenizing force that is frequency-dependent, varying with the commonness or rarity of organizational practices and structures, and trait- and outcome-dependent, with the most successful, similar organizations the most attractive models for imitation (Miner and Haunschild, 1995).
- *Imprinting.* The features acquired by organizations at the time of their founding—for example, by mimicking those features that are taken as the natural way to organize a particular form of collective activity, or as the result of environmental conditions—are retained into the future (Stinchcombe, 1965).

These mechanisms foster stability of organizational forms, prevent breakdown of adaptive combinations of production and organizing knowledge, and keep worthless combinations from forming. However, they also decrease variability, limiting the ability of an organizational form and its members to explore new ways and means of adapting. Thus, organizational forms too can experience competency traps. As described earlier, however, compared to individual organizations, organizational forms can explore a great deal of variation without violating internal or external standards for consistency and reliability, and therefore are more likely to experience a proliferation of new ideas and competencies as opposed to incremental learning (Baum and Ingram, 1998).

Inheritance is not nearly as effectively isolated socioculturally as it is biotically, however. As a result, "speciation" of organizational forms is likely to be more frequent among organizational than biotic forms. Indeed, Campbell (1979) views the extent of "cross-lineage" borrowing that occurs in sociocultural evolution as the major disanalogy between it and biological evolution.

Macro-Evolutionary Dynamics of Organizational Communities

Now that we have explored micro-evolutionary VSR processes shaping the persistence and transformation over time within an existing organizational form, we are ready to begin our examination of the macro-evolutionary VSR processes through which new organizational forms arise, and the considerable challenges associated with their establishment. This requires us to shift from population-level thinking to community-level thinking. Community ecology examines the ways in which similar and dissimilar populations interact attending in particular to the ways in which they develop collective modes of adaptation to the environment (Hawley, 1950) and to the emergence of new kinds of organizational forms. It is only at this level that the creation of new populations and the erosion of boundaries of existing populations can be observed.

The idea of the community as a functionally organized unit has a troubled history in biology. The naturalists who preceded Darwin envisioned all of nature as part of a grand design. Darwin's theory, however, justified only limited functionalism: Natural selection can cause individuals to become well designed to survive and reproduce but, as we noted above, adaptation by individuals does not generally lead to the adaptation of populations, much less multipopulation communities. Nevertheless, functionalism persisted, even flourishing after being recast in superficially Darwinian terms, and communities were compared to single individuals in their functional organization. These ideas were scrutinized and dismissed by evolutionary biologists in the 1960s (e.g., Williams, 1966). As a result, most bioecologists with an evolutionary background regard the concept of community "superorganisms" dubiously.

Whether organizational communities have sufficient coherence as entities to be selected as entire units has also been argued (Baum and Singh, 1994a; Hodgson, 1993) and contested (Campbell, 1994) in organization theory. Recently, Aldrich (1999) suggested that selection at the organizational-community level depends upon the existence of a very tight coupling among populations, a condition most likely requiring strong centralized dominance by political authorities, as in authoritarian political regimes. Our hierarchical approach and analysis of organizational communities, which is informed by multilevel selection theory, does not require strong coupling for community-level selection. Below, we first describe the community concept in more detail and then elaborate the VSR engines shaping evolutionary dynamics within organizational communities.

Defining Organizational Communities

An organizational population built around an organizational form develops relationships with other populations engaged in other activities, but related to a common technical or institutional core, that bind them into organizational communities (Aldrich, 1999; Astley, 1985; Fombrun, 1986; Hannan and Freeman, 1989). A typical organizational form interacts with many different kinds of organizations. These include states and professions that regulate and monitor organizational activity, schools that train potential employees, suppliers of technical and material inputs, producers of similar and related (complementary and competitive) products and services, and consumers of the products and services (Baum and Korn, 1994; Scott, Ruef, Mendel, and Caronna, 2000). An organizational community is a set of populations, linked by ecological ties of commensalism and symbiosis, that coevolve with each other and their environment. The set of populations may inhabit a local geographic area (e.g., Silicon Valley, Route 128), or may encompass entire national, regional, or global economies, depending on its technical or institutional core (e.g., "Wintel" PCs). *Commensalism* refers to competition and cooperation between similar units, and *symbiosis* to mutual interdependence between dissimilar units (Hawley, 1950). The resources that define these interdependencies vary across populations but generally include raw material, labor, technical knowledge, and market share (Baum and Korn, 1994).

Community ecology attends explicitly to the structure and evolution of these ecological ties among organizational populations and considers the community-level implications of these interactions for coacting sets of populations. One consequence of adopting a community-level approach is that relationships among populations can begin to be understood as a dynamic system. Changes in interacting populations result not only from their direct interactions, but also from indirect interactions and feedback processes. Consequently, a change in one population may produce a series of changes in other populations. As a result, the effects of change in one population may not follow the logic of direct cause-and-effect relations between populations (Baum and Korn, 1994).

Community emergence and evolution depends on a steady stream of organizational foundings for the establishment of new populations and the reproduction (or revitalization) of established ones (Baum and Singh, 1994a; Hunt and Aldrich, 1998). Often, new organizational forms come into existence in organizational communities as a result of social movements led by institutional entrepreneurs—ideological activists who combine previously unconnected routines and competencies into an organizational solution to a problem—catalyzed by technological and institutional change that disrupts the status quo (Rao, 1998). Within a community, processes of commensalism and symbiosis sort populations into differentiated niches, and dominant populations drive others into subordinate positions and ancillary roles, resulting in community-level differentiation and integration, and a hierarchical ordering emerges (Astley, 1985).[9] Hawley (1950, p. 221) felt that inequality was an inevitable result of functional differentiation because "certain functions are by their nature more influential than others; they are strategically placed in the division of labor and thus impinge directly upon a larger number of other functions." Populations occupying central locations are well positioned to play coordinating roles (Aldrich, 1979). For example, the largest CPA firms in the United States molded the structure of the entire accounting community because they attracted the largest clients. Subsequently, their practices were imitated by middle-sized accounting firms and also used in standards-setting activity (Han, 1994).

As community relationships stabilize, competition may shift from the population to the community level. What was once competition between populations becomes rivalry between communities. In Silicon Valley, symbiotic relationships developed among entrepreneurs, educators, venture capitalists, and other local residents that promoted "collective learning and flexible adjustment among specialist producers of a complex of related technologies" (Saxenian, 1994, p. 2). Law firms played a particularly important symbiotic role in the emergence of Silicon Valley's organizational community brokering financing agreements between venture capital firms and startups (Suchman, 1995). In contrast, firms in the Route 128 region around Boston perpetuated a competitive system in which large, independent firms looked to their own internal resources for much of what they needed, rather than developing links with other firms in the area. The region's culture encouraged stability and self-reliance, promoting competition based on secrecy and corporate loyalty (Saxenian, 1994, p. 3). The major universities in the Boston area, MIT and Harvard, kept their distance from smaller companies, preferring ties to large firms that could fund the universities' own research priorities. DEC and other large firms experienced financial difficulties in the 1980s, as the bottom fell out of the minicomputer market. Route 128's lack of a network-based symbiotic community structure and culture dealt it a severe blow from which it had trouble recovering, in contrast to Silicon Valley's rapid recovery after its troubles in the 1980s.

Silicon Valley and Route 128 illustrate the concept of shared fate that is central to community ecology and multilevel selection theory (Sober and Wilson, 1998; Wilson and Sober 1989, 1994). The activities of an organization can affect its performance relative to other organizations in the same and different populations in the local community, but they can also affect the abundance of all organizations in the local community as a unit. When multiple local communities exist that vary in their population composition, patterns of interaction, beliefs and customs, and social-organizational structures, those that function well as a unit contribute differentially to the next generation of local communities. Routines, beliefs, and norms can therefore spread, not by virtue of their advantage within local communities, but by virtue of the advantage that they bestow on their local community relative to other local communities. If the process of between-community selection is sufficiently strong, then, over time, local communities become functionally organized, increasing their contribution to future communities. Under such conditions, the often apparently functional forms of organizational communities can be seen as adaptations that have evolved because communities expressing them outcompete other groups (Sober and Wilson, 1998).

Of course, all of this requires an appropriate community structure. If there is only one local community, then the shared effect becomes irrelevant. If many groups are present but community-level selection is weak, then the activities that would turn the community into a functional unit will largely succumb to activities that succeed within the local community. Organizational communities frequently consist of a mosaic of semi-isolated patches, however. Some are geographically localized communities including Silicon Valley and Route 128, as well as North Carolina's Research Triangle, the U.S. manufacturing belt, the tile cluster and textile district in northern Italy, and the German Machine-Tool District. The geographic localization of these (and other) organizational communities may derive from the nature of the community's technological core (Sorenson and Audia, 2000). Others may not be geographically localized but instead linked by shared technologies or markets (Astley and Fombrun, 1983). Ferguson (1998), for example, chronicles the gastronomic community in nineteenth-century France comprised of restaurants, critics, culinary magazines, and aristocratic consumers and connected by the traditions of classical cuisine. Von Burg and Kenney (2000) describe the local area networking (LAN) industry as an organizational community comprising mainframe, micro-, and minicomputer manufacturers, which was initially driven into two groups championing Token ring and Ethernet systems until the latter triumphed. Ingram and Simons (2000) show how Israeli kibbutzim were located in a community of populations consisting of credit cooperatives, banks and political parties, and Scott et al. (2000), offer a detailed account of the agencies, associations, hospitals, health maintenance organizations (HMOs), and insurance companies constituting the San Francisco Bay area health care organization community. Regardless of the basis for their patchiness, local variations—either in physical or technological space—promote a process of natural selection at the community level.

Notably, the positive feedback inherent in conformist transmission of organizational practices, which biases imitation toward majority or plurality practices, implies that small differences in initial distributions of practices between communities will be reinforced, and variations within them erased (Boyd and Richerson, 1985; DiMaggio and Powell, 1983). This observation suggests a potentially important role for complexity theory, introduced earlier, in understanding community evolution. When community interactions are complex, sensitive dependence on initial conditions magnifies initially random variation among local communities, while simple interactions reduce it. Since selection at any level requires variation among entities, local communities characterized by complex interactions may be more prone to community-level selection than communities governed by simple interactions (Wilson, 1997). Thus, in the same way that complex behavior produces variation within organizations, complex interactions among populations of organizations can produce variation among organizational communities.

Although the resulting homogeneities within groups and sharp differences between groups need not be interpreted as adaptive products of selection, they do, however, provide a basis for community selection. The community whose set of beliefs and social organization are most group-beneficial will have a higher global fitness and tend to replace communities with less adaptive beliefs and organization. In this context, "beneficial" implies beliefs that promote a synergetic pattern of interaction within the community. The more communities vary in fitness, the stronger such group selection becomes. Thus, the often-functional form of organizational communities can be seen as adaptations that have evolved because groups expressing them outcompete other groups (Sober and Wilson, 1998). Consider, for example, returns to research activity within an organizational community. If other organizations in an organization's community invest in a high level of R&D activity, the pool of new knowledge into which the organization can tap will be quite rich. And, since research performs the dual role of both generating new knowledge as well as absorbing new knowledge generated by other firms (Cohen and Levinthal, 1990), the organization will find it attractive to invest in R&D as well. Of course, low-level R&D equilibria in which the level of new knowledge is too limited to motivate individual organizations to invest are also possible. Thus, at the community level, there are increasing returns to R&D investment, and communities settling at high-level equilibria will tend to outcompete those settling at low-level equilibria.

Community Structure

Organizational communities thus emerge as sets of populations become interlinked by commensalism and symbiosis, and those linkages become increasingly important determinants of outcomes for members of the populations that comprise the community. Understanding the structure of these relationships, which define the community context, is a crucial step in understanding processes that govern the emergence and selection of new organizational forms: as organizational communities evolve, community structure changes, altering environmental opportunities and constraints facing potential entrepreneurs.

In our earlier discussion of competitive selection processes within organizational populations, we introduced the following logistic population growth function to model competitive selection acting on the growth of a single population (recall that K is the carrying capacity of the population's environment, r is the natural growth rate of the population, N is population density—the number of organizations in the population, and t is a time interval):

$$\frac{dN}{dt} = rN\left(\frac{K-N}{K}\right),$$

Of course, when a population interacts with other populations as part of a community, it is difficult to understand the population's behavior and evolution without attending to the nature of its ecological relationships with those other populations. This single-population formulation is easily modified to account for a population's ecological interactions with other populations in the same community. Consider first the case of a two-population community:

$$\frac{dN_A}{dt} = r_A N_A\left(\frac{K_A - N_A - \alpha_{AB}N_B}{K_A}\right)$$
$$\frac{dN_B}{dt} = r_B N_B\left(\frac{K_B - N_B - \alpha_{BA}N_A}{K_B}\right)$$

The community represented by this pair of equations is composed of two populations, A and B, which affect each other's rates of growth and decline through their interdependence. The second equation is the mirror of the first. The coefficients α_{AB} and α_{BA} represent the interdependence of populations A and B. These coefficients represent the proportional effect each member in one population has on the carrying capacity of the other. Thus when $\alpha > 0$, the presence

of a member of population A (B) reduces by the fraction α_{AB} (α_{BA}) the resources available for population B (A), slowing Bs (As) growth or speeding its decline. When $\alpha < 0$, however, the presence of one population increases the resources available to the other, speeding its growth or slowing its decline. The two-population model can be generalized to a community of J populations as:

$$\frac{dN_i}{dt} = r_i N_i\left(\frac{K_i - N_i - \sum_{j\neq i}^{J}\alpha_{ij}N_j}{K_i}\right), \quad \alpha_{ii}=1.$$

Symbiotic relations (i.e., $\alpha_{AB} < 0$, $\alpha_{BA} < 0$) involve mutual "interdependence of unlike forms, i.e. units of dissimilar functions" (Hawley, 1950, p. 209) and imply that populations occupying different niches benefit from each other's presence, each enhancing the resource availability and growth prospects of the other. In the "information economy" interacting populations of "complementors" abound (Shapiro and Varian, 1999). The populations of software vendors and original equipment manufacturers each producing and selling one component of the Wintel PC standard is perhaps the most visible example. Commensalism, in contrast, involves "co-action of like forms, i.e. units of similar functions" (Hawley, 1950, p. 209) and implies potential competition between interacting populations. The degree of competition between populations depends on the degree of similarity or overlap of the niches they occupy. Aldrich (1999: 302) has identified six scenarios of commensalism (see also Baum, 1996, pp. 91–92; Brittain and Wholey, 1988).

- *Full competition* (i.e., $\alpha_{AB} > 0$, $\alpha_{BA} > 0$): growth in each population leads to a decline in the other because their niches overlap. For example, an increase in the number of day care centers in Toronto stimulated the failure of nursery schools in Toronto, and an increase in the number of nursery schools stimulated failure of day care centers in return (Baum and Oliver, 1991).
- *Partial competition* (i.e., $\alpha_{AB} > 0$, $\alpha_{BA} = 0$): inter-population relations are asymmetric, with only one having a negative effect on the other. For example, an increase in the number of U.S. craft labor unions both suppressed founding and increased failure of U.S. industrial unions, but the number of industrial unions did not

affect either the founding or the failure of craft unions (Hannan and Freeman, 1989).

- *Predatory competition* (i.e., $\alpha_{AB} > 0$, $\alpha_{BA} < 0$): one population expands at the expense of another. For example, in the United States, the population of television stations grew at the expense of the population of radio stations (Dimmick and Rothenbuhler, 1984).
- *Partial mutualism* (i.e., $\alpha_{AB} < 0$, $\alpha_{BA} = 0$) obtains when interpopulation relations are asymmetric, with only one population benefiting from the presence of the other. For example, an increase in the number of brewpubs in the United States stimulated the founding of microbreweries, but the number of microbreweries did not affect brewpub founding (Carroll and Swaminathan, 1992).
- *Full mutualism* (i.e., $\alpha_{AB} < 0$, $\alpha_{BA} < 0$) means that two populations are in overlapping niches and benefit from the presence of the other. For example, an increase in the number of single-exchange telephone companies lowered the failure rate of multi-exchange telephone companies, and an increase the number of multi-exchange companies lowered failure of single-exchange companies in return (Barnett, 1990).
- *Neutrality* (i.e., $\alpha_{AB} = 0$, $\alpha_{BA} = 0$) means that two populations have no influence on each other, although they do affect other populations in the community. For example, the numbers of commercial and savings banks in Manhattan were unrelated to each other's founding rates (Ranger-Moore, Banaszak-Holl, and Hannan, 1991), and the numbers of group and IPA HMOs were unrelated to each other's failure rates (Wholey, Christianson, and Sanchez, 1992).

Aldrich (1999) suggests that the apparent commonness of neutrality in organizational communities is a result of evolutionary selection favoring loosely coupled social systems whose various subparts can adapt autonomously. An alternative explanation is that when we attempt to detect competition in a community structure that contains the effects of competition, we fail to detect it because we observe an evolved set of interactions reflecting the effects of past competition. Another is coevolution. Although *coevolution* has become an umbrella term for a variety of processes and outcomes, it is important to distinguish the reciprocal evolution of coevolution from the mutual causation of systems theory and ecology. This basic difference helps account for observing neutrality. Given similar resource requirements (ecological similarity), but absent coevolution, one population in a predator/prey interaction will outcompete the other—the inferior population either migrates or disappears. But with coevolution, organizations comprising two ecologically similar populations might evolve toward different niches such that both survive. Thus, "rapid-coevolution" can alter nature of ecological interactions (McKelvey, 1999).

Caveats about Communities

Three cautions are in order here to avoid mistaken inferences about community-level structural organization and evolution. First, discussions of organizational communities often equate higher-level functional organization with evidence of strong ecological interactions and dynamic equilibria. However, these features are properties of many chemical, physical, biological, and social systems, and they do not imply functional organization. An organizational population can have a carrying capacity, regardless of whether it manages or overexploits its resources. Even the most dysfunctional communities can be stable, responding in ways that resist perturbation—stability at the community level occurs when the overall system of interpopulation interactions is characterized by negative feedback (Puccia and Levins, 1985). In general, the fact that organizational populations have strong effects on each other and on the environment should not be confused with higher-level functional organization.

Second, although mutualism certainly plays an important role in community-level functional organization, and may be more common in functional than dysfunctional organizational communities, the proportion of interactions in a community that are mutualistic says little about its functional organization. Functional community-level organization can involve competition and predation in addition to mutualism. Indeed, mutualism is an inevitable byproduct of indirect effects, which will exist even in highly dysfunctional communities (Baum and Korn, 1994).[10] Community-level functional organization must be studied by investigating the properties that contribute to functional design. Whether functional properties are created by mutualistic or competitive interactions among members of the community is a secondary issue.

Third, it is sometimes claimed that complex system dynamics can produce higher-level functional organization in the absence of natural selection (Kauffman, 1993; McKelvey, 1998, 1999). Although it is certainly true that complex systems dynamics can produce striking patterns in the absence of natural selection, similar to the often-striking "strange attractor" patterns that can be generated by complex systems of equations, a pattern is not the same as functional organization. An object that is designed to do something well must be structured in a particular way. Complex system dynamics are no more likely than simple system dynamics to produce the right combination of properties in the absence of natural selection. As we noted earlier, however, the variability fostered by complex system dynamics may be highly relevant to community-level functional organization when combined with multilevel selection theory (Wilson, 1997).

Variation: Entrepreneurs and New Organizational Forms

How do new organizational forms arise within communities? Although, as we noted above, segregating mechanisms isolate organizational forms from inheriting one another's production and organizing competence, they are not so strong and stable that they are never bridged, and organizational forms do "speciate" to produce new organizational forms. Social boundaries separating organizational forms are subject to blending processes that may weaken segregating mechanisms, causing boundaries among organizational forms to erode and become blurred as organizations once clearly distinguishable become more interpenetrated and alike (Hannan and Freeman, 1989). Some social forces—for example, stable technologies and strong regulatory systems—work to maintain organizational forms as discrete, easily recognized entities. Such technological and institutional barriers can be established and dismantled quickly, however, increasing the pace of divergence or convergence in the evolution of organizational forms.

Neoinstitutional theorists emphasize entrepreneurs' recombination of existing templates as the primary source of variation in organizational forms. More generally, recombination involves working with routines and competencies. Preexisting routines and competencies are thus seen as the building blocks with which entrepreneurs build new organizational forms. The creation of new forms through recombination implies that structure shapes action, and in turn, action shapes structure (DiMaggio and Powell, 1991; Friedland and Alford, 1991). It also implies that entrepreneurs shortcut natural selection using vicarious selectors (Campbell, 1965): fit knowledge retained in the form of preexisting templates accelerates organizational evolution by eliminating dangerous or inadequate actions before they are executed and increasing chances for survival of new forms.

Imitative and Innovative Entrepreneurship

Although the popular press portrays the typical entrepreneur as an innovator—a Michael Dell or a Jeff Bezos—in fact entrepreneurs mostly reproduce existing organizational structures (Aldrich and Kenworthy, 1999). There is a crucial difference between the first instance of a new form, the act of speciation—innovative entrepreneurship—and the emulation of a new form—imitative entrepreneurship. Founding a new organization is always a risky business, but especially so when entrepreneurs have few precedents for the kinds of activities they want to found. Innovative entrepreneurs in the early years of a new organizational form face a greater set of challenges than imitative entrepreneurs who carry on a tradition pioneered by their many predecessors. The first instance of a new form represents an innovation that requires integration into the prevailing community social order to be viable. Building institutional context and institutional entrepreneurship, including but not limited to acquiring legitimacy, are thus far more crucial challenges for innovative entrepreneurs.

Rao and Singh (1999) present a simple typology of recombinations that effectively captures the organizing processes involved in the construction of new forms through recombination. In their typology, new organizational forms represent novel incarnations of core features—goals, authority relations, technologies, and markets. Entrepreneurs can add or delete existing organizing elements from existing organizational forms, both add and delete elements, or they can neither add nor delete elements, the final case representing imitative entrepreneurship. Table 8.2 summarizes the four possibilities. Rao and Singh also distinguish between recombinations based on the number of changes. Strong speciation occurs when all four of the core features differ from existing forms. Weak speciation occurs when only one or two core attributes differ. Strategic groups within an industry, differing in markets served or technologies, illustrate weak speciation.

Table 8.2 A typology of new organizational forms

	No Addition of Organizing Elements	*Addition of New Organizing Elements*
No deletion of organizing elements	cell I imitative entrepreneurship	cell III partial enlargement
Deletion of organizing elements	cell II partial contraction	cell IV radical recombination

Source: Adapted from Rao and Singh (1999, p. 72).

Cell 1 exemplifies imitative entrepreneurship. Such organizations, which reproduce an existing form, are likely to be accommodated easily into the current institutional order and legitimated on a nearly automatic basis because of existing precedents and tradition (Delacroix and Rao, 1994). Many new organizations replicate existing forms because the entrepreneurs who found them use simple, conformist imitation rules that are frequency-dependent, varying with the commonness of organizational routines and capabilities, and trait- and outcome-dependent, with the most successful, similar organizations the most attractive models for imitation (Haunschild and Miner, 1997). Faced with insufficient information and uncertainty, entrepreneurs turn to the actions of established organizations for clues about how to proceed. However, because it is not often possible to gauge the true value of other organizations' routines and competencies, more frequent use is taken as evidence that others find it valuable and appropriate, increasing its likelihood of entrepreneurial adoption. Entrepreneurs are also selective about which organizations to imitate, discriminating among organizations and imitating those that achieve the most desirable outcomes (e.g., high-status and superior performance). Organizational founders thus adopt institutionalized designs and attempt to model their new venture's structures and practices on patterns thought to be more modern, appropriate, and professional. As noted above, however, entrepreneurs who reflexively copy "industry recipes" (Spender, 1989) not only reproduce existing organizational forms, they also fail to explore potentially superior alternatives (Romanelli, 1999).

Coercive and normative processes at various levels of organizations also produce strong downward pressure to conform, reinforcing imitative behavior. At the organization level, parent companies pressure new branches and franchises to conform to their internal standards. At the population level, structuring of the immediate environment within which

innovative entrepreneurs must operate, by standard designs and operating procedures, for example, can stand in the way of novelty. At the community level, interpopulation relations affect the distribution of resources in the environment and the terms on which they are available to entrepreneurs. Resource providers, for example, reward entrepreneurs who signal their conformity to proven past predictors of success with easier (and cheaper) access to financial capital and social capital (Aldrich and Fiol, 1994). At the institutional level, government regulations and policies, dominant professional models, and the skills and knowledge emphasized in educational curricula produce similar pressures for conformity (DiMaggio, 1991; Sutton and Dobbin, 1996). Cultural rules and norms also create powerful pressures toward conformity and cultural rigidity that can severely fetter innovative individual initiatives.

Although following conformist imitation rules can lead to a preponderance of imitative entrepreneurship that reproduces established populations, conformist imitation can, under certain conditions, produce eclectic recombinations of routines that bloom into innovative organizations (Miner and Raghavan, 1999). For example, if entrepreneurs combine different modes of conformist imitation (frequency, trait, and outcome) in different mixes, they may bring about novel combinations of routines. Imperfect imitation can also introduce variety (Lippman and Rumelt, 1982; Nelson and Winter, 1982). For example, entrepreneurs can make copying errors, implementing imitated routines in different ways—for better or worse—or, lacking complete information, they may base their imitation on different samples of the outcomes for prior adopters, giving rise to novel combinations. Other important sources of variation in new organizations include the hiring and training of new employees from across several "training" populations. As a result of experiential learning processes, chance variations in the temporal sequences that entrepreneurs adopt or sampling other organizations' actions or outcomes may also produce new mixes of routines.

Another path to nonconformity is ignorance of existing cultural norms and industry practices (Aldrich and Kenworthy, 1999). Some individuals will simply be unaware of prevailing conformity-inducing forces. For entrepreneurs ignorant of the norms, rules, and practices that dictate organizational forms within a community or population, any conformity would be purely accidental. Perhaps only "outsiders," unencumbered by industry norms, practices, and recipes, are able to blindly (in Campbell's terms) assemble truly innovative organizations. This conjecture is at odds with the observation of highly visible habitual innovative entrepreneurs in many industries (Aldrich and Kenworthy, 1999). What gives rise to habitually innovative entrepreneurs, and why is their success not contagious? Entrepreneurs' accumulation of tacit knowledge and social capital over a series of innovative successes provides one possible explanation for this phenomenon—innovative entrepreneurs with a track record become highly valued for their abilities and may gain superior access to sources of capital and other forms of support. For them, "nonconformity" becomes a legitimate activity.

Regardless of how they "break the bonds" of conformity, innovative entrepreneurs can recombine core organizational features in three ways. Partial contraction (cell 2) results when organizational elements are deleted. Point-to-point airlines are the result of innovative entrepreneurs eliminating key elements of core technology from the value chain, including hub-and-spoke route networks, ticketing agents, transfer agreements with other airlines, and in-house maintenance. Cell 2 resembles imitative entrepreneurship to the extent that external endorsement may not be problematic because the new form entails eliminating some elements from preexisting organizational forms, and so can readily draw on available institutional understandings. It may also be welcome by resource providers and consumers to whom it may represent a leaner, low-cost version of an existing form. Recombination through partial enlargement (cell 3), in contrast, creates new forms as entrepreneurs consciously add elements. Examples of such recombination are leading business schools' active involvement in executive education or, more recently, U.S. hospitals' entry into the managed care business. Although in some instances legislative barriers may exist that

prevent some types of enlargement, in other cases, regulators may—through deregulation, for example—encourage existing forms to add elements. Even when sanctioned by the state, however, new forms created by adding new elements may experience an external liability of newness because they are intelligible to resource providers and the general public. For example, diversified firms that combine unfamiliar elements may face poor market valuations, while nonprofits that pursue multiple causes may find it difficult to gain philanthropists' support.

Radical recombination (cell 4) involves both the addition and deletion of core organizing elements, resulting in new forms that embody new beliefs, values, goals, authority relations, technology, and new products or services to consumers. One illustration of such a recombination includes health maintenance organizations. On the one hand, HMOs add elements that come with a profit orientation and greater cost consciousness, such as preventative care and careful review of referrals to specialists. On the other hand, routine access to sophisticated (and costly) diagnostic procedures and the availability of significant discretion to physicians are typically curtailed. Such new forms cannot draw on existing institutional understandings and so must create new understandings and new cognitive frames that establish a rationale for a new form (Meyer and Scott, 1983). As a result, organizing challenges are likely to be greatest here, but may also offer the greatest potential rewards—if the challenges are successfully met (Rao and Singh, 1999).

Imitation is thus the least disruptive form of entrepreneurship but is also likely to secure the fewest rewards (Henderson, 1999). New forms created through partial contraction of elements, and spawned by the addition of elements, are more disruptive and may gain substantial rewards. The relative advantages of leaner forms premised on the deletion of elements, and fatter forms composed of new elements, hinge on consumer preferences and institutional tolerances for costs and service. New forms produced through these processes also face more significant challenges, and their proponents have to go the distance in erecting segregating mechanisms, gaining legitimacy, and buffering the new form from selection pressures.

Selection: Ecological Opportunity

The isolation of new organizational forms from their parent population(s) will succeed in establishing new populations only under certain ecological conditions. "Ecological opportunity" must be available for a novel form to establish itself successfully (Stanley, 1981, p. 96). Such opportunities exist where competitive saturation of the environment is low enough to weaken selection pressures. The environment must approximate an "unfilled ecospace," unoccupied by other populations (Gould and Eldredge, 1977, p. 144). Otherwise, the novel form will be crowded out, as it would in its parent population. Organizational communities are the contexts that govern the extent of ecological opportunity and the selection of new organizational forms (Astley, 1985).

Within populations, the familiar r-to-K transition unfolds (see "r-K Transition," above). While competition runs its course within populations, symbiotic interdependencies emerge between them. New populations branch out from established ones to fulfill ancillary roles in which they are dependent on but noncompetitive with their ancestors and each other (Hawley, 1950, p. 203). Horizontal and vertical interdependencies among populations result from underlying technologies that define resource consumption patterns. As organizations struggle either to increase their autonomy (Burt, 1980) or to stabilize their interdependence (Pfeffer and Salancik, 1978), they develop relationships with organizations in other neighboring populations, which, in part, serve to define the community's social structure (Fombrun, 1986). This social structure itself unfolds nested within a set of institutionalized beliefs and understandings about competition and cooperation (DiMaggio and Powell, 1983; Meyer and Rowan, 1977).

In the early stages of community evolution, branching occurs frequently as competition at carrying capacity within populations initiates a process of functional and territorial differentiation that pushes entrepreneurs to seek distinct functions in which they hold a competitive advantage. Complementary functionalities and interpopulation dependencies can thus multiply rapidly as entrepreneurs create many novel organizational forms, some of which initiate new populations (Astley, 1985; Hunt and Aldrich, 1998; Romanelli, 1989). Because communities contain multiple populations, each potentially at a different stage of the r-K transition, rates of entrepreneurship will differ across populations, as will—as a result—the favored organizational forms (Hunt and Aldrich, 1998). The community evolves through a process of ecological succession in which change unfolds

simultaneously in the structure of relationships within and between populations comprising the community along two axes—commensalistic and symbiotic (Hawley, 1950, pp. 201–203). As possible niches are progressively filled, the growth of internal complexity fosters community stability (Astley, 1985; Hawley, 1950).

Elaboration continues until the complexity of internal relationships can no longer increase without reducing the community's effectiveness as a functional unit (Hawley, 1950, p. 203). At this stage, the community is "full"; it is a closed, self-contained, self-maintaining, dynamic equilibrium system (Astley, 1985). Tight integration of populations within the community makes it more likely that a new form will encounter a competitor that prevents it from being successful. New populations cannot be added without disturbing the system, and the size of each population is balanced against the needs of other populations in the community. Thus, community closure coincides with competitive saturation within its constituent populations, and its approach is a major factor regulating the extent of ecological opportunity. It also sets the stage for community collapse, however. If complex systems experience disturbances beyond a certain threshold, they may disintegrate as the result of a domino effect (Astley, 1985; Pimm, 1991). Thus, tightly coupled community systems can be fragile and prone to collapse and simplification when confronted with disturbances (e.g., technological and institutional change) that upset their equilibrium, and although they may be reestablished though ecological succession, they also may not (Kauffman, 1993; Pimm, 1991).

Community Disruption

Stable technologies and strong regulatory systems work to maintain organizational forms as discrete, easily recognized entities. At the same time, however, such technological and institutional barriers between forms can be erected and dismantled quickly, increasing the pace of divergence and convergence in the evolution of organizational forms. As a result, ecological opportunities and the potential for innovative entrepreneurship are closely tied to technological and institutional dynamics. Technological conditions shape the boundaries around organizational forms, determining the relative importance of resources and values of organizational routines and capabilities, and so the nature of interdependencies among organizational forms.

Institutional conditions also define the boundaries around organizational forms and the criteria for judging whether an organization or an organizational form is worthy of continued support and survival. Technological and institutional changes, which disrupt previously stable communities, are thus major catalysts for the creation of new organizational forms and the evolution of new community structures that bind new forms sharing a common orientation toward novel technological, normative, or regulatory conditions. Of course, communities experiencing major technological or institutional change present challenging contexts. Rules are disputed, technologies are contested, and social actors competing to create a new social order receive little guidance.

Technology Cycles

Technological disruptions spawn new forms by opening up spaces for new core technologies and possibilities for novel marketing strategies. Technological models of creative destruction through innovation (Schumpeter, 1934; Tushman and Anderson, 1986) hold that technological discontinuities create opportunities for entrepreneurs to establish new organizational forms as existing populations' sources of competitive advantage decay, freeing up resources for new organizations to take advantage of new opportunities for establishing competitive positions. Evolutionary models of technological change portray organizations as genealogical repositories of skills, routines, assets, and information (Nelson and Winter, 1982; Winter, 1988; Dosi, 1988). Technological innovation produces new organizational forms through an ongoing recombinatory process of variation, selection, and retention (Abernathy and Utterback, 1978; Basalla, 1988; Bijker, Hughes, and Pinch, 1987; Dosi, 1982, 1984; Sahal, 1985).

Anderson and Tushman (1990) integrate these diverse evolutionary analyses and outline how cycles of technological change affect entries and exits of organizations. They suggest that cycles of technological change are triggered by technological discontinuities—that is, radical product and process innovations that result in significant cost, performance, and quality improvements. Competence-enhancing discontinuities build on technologies of existing organizational forms, making possible order-of-magnitude improvements in their efficiency and changes in the core technological characteristics of organizations. Competence-destroying discontinuities, in contrast, render existing organizational forms' know-how, skills, and resources obsolete, creating new possibilities for new actors (entrepreneurs and organizations from other domains) to enter and novel organizational forms to emerge. By redefining the value and importance of organizational resources and capabilities, competence-destroying change alters the relational structure of an organizational community substantially, transforming exchange and power relationships, unraveling status orders, and fostering new types of linkages. Population boundaries give way as new actors enter, activities are reshuffled among organizations, and personnel blend and blur. Even the borders of the community may be realigned as the new technology in use redefines what types of activities and which types of actors are legitimate and which are more or less central or peripheral to those activities.

Competence-destroying technological discontinuities unleash an era of ferment characterized by variation and competition among multiple versions of the same technology and potential substitutes. Product diversity is high, and products tend to be made to customer specifications. The production process is nascent, labor-intensive, and poorly codified. Performance criteria are ambiguous, the evaluation of technological alternatives is costly, and the trajectory of technological change is uncertain (Abernathy and Utterback, 1978; Zuscovitch, 1986). Eras of ferment culminate with the emergence of one design or technology as the *dominant design*, a set of engineering ideas that constrain future technological progress. Dominant designs consist of the core product idea, the functions the product is to perform, and the processes by which it is to be manufactured, and they enable product standardization and generate stable linkages among firms, personnel, and capital markets (Clark, 1985). A design becomes dominant as a result of its efficiency, legitimacy, or political support, often entailing intense political activity by entrepreneurs and organizations championing different ideas (Tushman and Rosenkopf, 1992). The advent of a dominant design signals the start of an era of incremental technological change, which, as we noted earlier, can trigger an *r*-to-*K* transition within populations that create or use the technology. Innovations cumulate and refine the dominant design. Productivity and process improvements become more central, price competition becomes more important, and internal coordination in firms becomes formalized and routinized.

The era of incremental change lasts until it is broken by another product- or process-based technological discontinuity that restarts the cycle. Product innovations are likely to be embodied in new organizational forms because the structure, decision making, and learning processes of existing forms inhibit them from perceiving and effectively capitalizing on opportunities to modify subsystems and the linkages among subsystems (Baum, Korn, and Kotha, 1995; Henderson and Clark, 1990). Thus, as we noted earlier, the "self-destructive" properties of organizational learning make the replacement of obsolescent organizations easier by making old markets vulnerable to new organizations with new capabilities. By contrast, process innovations are likely to inhibit new forms because they presuppose and capitalize on organizations' learning through doing and create entry barriers (Abernathy and Utterback, 1978; Kamien and Schwartz, 1982).

Institutional Dynamics

Organizations exist not only in technical-resource environments, but also in worlds of beliefs, rules, and ideas that are referred to as *institutional environments*. The concept of the institutional environment refers to the cultural-cognitive belief systems and regulatory and normative structures that prevail in a given organizational community, constituting its organizing principles and providing a basis for its coherence, meaning, and stability (Friedland and Alford, 1991; Scott, 1995). Although it is possible to separate material-resource and institutional environments analytically, what constitutes a "resource" and whether and how it can be used and combined are determined, in part, by institutional beliefs and rule systems (Scott, 1995). In addition to such indirect influence, institutional environments influence organizations directly through the logics they legitimate, and the governance systems and rules of social action they support. Institutional environments specify what goals or values are to be pursued within a domain and indicate appropriate means for pursuing them. Organizational forms embody and enact the institutionally defined structures, practices, and identities.

Social actors—individuals as well as organizations—are capable of exercising their power to create and modify their institutional environments to have their interests reflected. Once institutional environments are in place, however, they operate as an external force, regulating and empowering social actors.

Institutional arrangements, by their nature, are unlikely to change abruptly. Even when change appears sudden, it is usually possible to find evidence of earlier forces at work, undermining current arrangements, or precursors to new institutional logics and organizational forms (Scott, 1995). Thus, although there is often a "dominant" institutional logic that reflects the consensus of powerful institutional actors in a given community, secondary or repressed logics representing other, subordinated interests also exist that may, over time, become more influential, and even superordinate (Fombrun, 1986). These secondary logics may serve as precursors to institutional change, but of course not all vying will be successful.

Institutional models stress environmental imprinting, through which social conditions at the time of founding limit organizational inventions (Stinchcombe, 1965), the importance of political upheavals, entrepreneurs' access to resources and power, and the role of the state in enabling (or constraining) competition and competence sharing between organizational forms (Aldrich, 1979, 1999). The state and professions, for example, shape organizational communities and the potential for new organizational forms by providing cognitive and legal frameworks and spawning formal structures to create and defend jurisdictional claims (Abbott, 1988; Rao, 1998). When legal or other rules responsible for the emergence or governing the maintenance of differences between groups of organizations are relaxed, or other forms of institutional pressures (e.g., normative rules, taken-for-granted assumptions) are removed, the existing distinctions among organizations may become blurred.

For example, for a number of decades the U.S. telecommunications industry experienced steady development, measured growth, and relative stability. But, suddenly, the onset of deregulation fostered an accelerating curve of new technologies and reshaping of industry structures (Astley and Fombrun, 1983). This restructuring of telecommunications is now unfolding globally as countries around the world deregulate their telecommunications industries. Other industries (e.g., banking, airlines, and electric utilities) are also now experiencing or beginning to experience similar effects of deregulation. Beyond deregulation, perhaps most salient institutions to arise in the final decades of this century are the institutions of market reform in Latin American and European economies (e.g., Chile, Poland), and trade agreements giving rise to regionalization and globalization of economic organization (e.g., EEC and NAFTA).

More generally, Scott et al. (2000) identify a range of outcomes of such institutional changes vital to community evolution:

- *New logics.* The logics that direct, motivate and legitimate the behavior of actors in the community are changed. The types of ends pursued and/or means-ends chains that guide action undergo change, as do the types of justifications that are given for action.
- *New actors.* New types of social actors, both individual and collective, appear, sometimes representing new combinations or hybrids of existing organizational forms, sometimes representing new entrants from other [communities]. Existing actors may transform their identities. The cast of characters undergoes change.
- *New meanings.* The meanings associated with the attributes of behavior of actors in the community or the effects associated with them (that is, changes in the causal relations among variables) are modified. Old attributes are viewed in new ways or are observed to have different effects.
- *New relations among actors.* The nature and extent of relations among actors in the community, including, in particular, exchange and power relations, are transformed. New types of linkages are created and the relational structure of the community exhibits substantial alterations.
- *Modified population boundaries.* Boundaries once containing and separating organizational populations, organization, customary activities, and personnel blend and blur.
- *Modified [community] boundaries.* The borders of [the community] are expanded, reduced, or realigned. New definitions determine what types of activities and which types of actors are legitimate and which are more or less central or peripheral players.

Changes in logics are likely to occur first, creating conditions for the construction of new roles and new types of organizations: "Logics lead the way because they are largely based on ideas. Ideas are often generated within a [community] by the 'creative odd ones' who formulate new concepts, models, and designs" (Scott et al., 2000, p. 174). The introduction of new actors can alter patterns of interaction, providing participants with a new perspective on their situation that can precipitate changes in interpretation (i.e., logic). If new ideas and interpretations diffuse and gain acceptance—often they do not—they can become the basis for social movements. If successful, over time, logics become taken for granted as "how things are" and the "way things are done." Because they require a buildup of pressure and political will, changes in regulatory and normative structures (e.g., professional association policy) tend to lag the introduction of new logics and actors, but nevertheless, open up spaces for new core features—organizational goals, authority systems, client markets—and promote organizational diversity.

By dismantling segregating barriers, technological and institutional change creates ecological opportunities for innovative entrepreneurs to construct new technical and institutional ideas, models, and designs and found new organizations that represent new combinations of interests, personnel, and technical capabilities. Technological and institutional change are thus essential, though not sufficient, preconditions for the birth of new organizational forms. New types of actors cannot come into existence in the absence of a supportive ideological base (Stinchcombe, 1965; Aldrich and Fiol, 1994). Social visionaries, intellectuals, inventors, and entrepreneurs create new possibilities—new designs for structures and new ways of acting. They propose new templates or archetypes for roles, groups, and organizations (Greenwood and Hinings, 1993). But these ideas must find a receptive audience. More importantly, the new ideas must be instantiated in routines, roles, and social organizations if they are to persist over time.

Retention: The Institutionalization of New Organizational Forms

Although necessary, ecological opportunity is not sufficient for the creation of a new organizational form. Resources do not "preexist" as free-floating niches waiting to be filled with new forms; they have to be mobilized and niches carved out through individual and collective efforts (McKelvey, 1982; Van de Ven and Garud, 1989). Institutional entrepreneurship is needed to carve out a space for new organizational forms within a community of populations, either by creating a new niche for itself or by invading an already occupied niche. Entrepreneurs must mobilize resources, legitimate the goals, structures, and competencies embodied in their new forms, and integrate them within the organizational community. They must also rapidly acquire mechanisms that isolate their new form from its parent forms(s), or its distinctive characteristics are unlikely to be maintained over time. The balance of competition and symbiosis the new population achieves vis-à-vis other populations in the community ultimately determines its boundaries. Innovative entrepreneurs and their early imitators must learn and respond to constraints and opportunities as they construct their population's boundaries. Their struggle is very much a collective one, though not necessarily a collaborative one (Aldrich, 1999). For new organizational forms, then, the burden of selection may stem more from the realm of institutional selection than from competitive selection (Rao and Singh, 1999). Central to the retention of any new organizational form, therefore, is the process by which the logic, technology, and values underpinning the new form are legitimated (Rao and Singh, 1999; Stinchcombe, 1968).

Organizational Legitimacy and the Liability of Newness

All new organizational forms face external and internal liabilities of newness (Stinchcombe, 1965). Externally, new forms require the endorsement of the state and markets for capital and personnel. Internally, they must develop routines to perform and coordinate their work effectively. New organizational forms must also rapidly acquire mechanisms that isolate them from their parent form(s), or their distinctive characteristics are unlikely to be maintained over time.

Among these challenges, a lack of legitimacy is especially critical: crucial stakeholders do not fully understand the nature of the new ventures, and their conformity to established institutional rules remains in doubt. These two entrepreneurial challenges reflect two forms of legitimacy: cognitive and sociopolitical (Aldrich and Fiol, 1994; Hannan and Carroll, 1992; Scott, 1995). Cognitive legitimacy stresses conformity to institutionalized archetypes and schemas and emphasizes the legitimacy reflected in actors' taken-for-granted assumptions, conceiving an organizational form as legitimate when actors view it as the natural way to effect some kind of collective action. Sociopolitical legitimacy emphasizes how embeddedness in relational and normative contexts influences an organizational form's legitimacy by signaling its conformity to social and institutional expectations, rules, and practices. An organizational form achieves sociopolitical legitimacy when it becomes regarded as obligatory, buttressed by legal mandate or by widely shared cultural, professional, and political norms and values. Legitimacy is thus not merely a resource to be possessed or exchanged but a condition reflecting the alignment of an organization to normative, regulatory, and cultural-cognitive rules and beliefs prevailing in its organizational community and wider social environment (Scott, 1995). The extent to which an organization or organizational form is judged to be legitimate has critical implications for the level of support and sanction conferred on it by its environment and thus for its survival.

Aldrich and Fiol (1994) suggest that social contexts not only pattern established meaning to which imitative entrepreneurs conform, but also create opportunities for institutional entrepreneurs to initiate renegotiation of meanings. Aldrich and Fiol identify four nested levels of social context within which institutional entrepreneurs must progressively build trust, reliability, reputation, and, ultimately, cognitive and sociopolitical legitimacy for their novel forms. Table 8.3 shows the levels in their framework and strategies for institutional entrepreneurship at each level. The levels are tightly coupled. Gaining stakeholder trust at the organization level provides a basis on which to develop a codified knowledge base at the population level, which, in turn, makes it easier to organize collectively and establish a reputation facilitating interaction at the community level and cooptation of institutional actors. Legitimation of a new organizational form thus depends on individual efforts of institutional entrepreneurs to frame their new form and build trust in it, and on collective efforts of early imitative entrepreneurs to establish standards, promote reliability, and advance the interests of the new form through institutional linkages (Friedland and Alford, 1991).

Absent cognitive legitimacy, institutional entrepreneurs face the hurdle of winning approval for their activities from key stakeholders, who are unlikely to offer their unconditional support to the novel venture—and who may actively oppose it. Institutional entrepreneurs must cognitively frame their new venture to foster others' trust in their competence and efforts. Cognitive frames are explanations that

Table 8.3 Strategies for institutional entrepreneurship

Level	Cognitive Legitimacy	Sociopolitical Legitimacy
Organization	develop knowledge base via symbolic language and behavior	develop trust by constructing internally consistent cognitive frames
Population	develop knowledge base by encouraging convergence on a standard	develop perceptions of reliability by mobilizing collective action
Community	develop knowledge base by promoting activity through third parties	develop reputation by negotiating and compromising with other populations
Institutional	develop knowledge base by creating linkages with educational institutions and professions	develop legitimacy by organizing collective marketing and lobbying

Source: Adapted from Aldrich and Fiol (1994, p. 649).

mobilize capital, personnel, and legitimacy by providing an institutional logic for the institutional entrepreneur's novel organizational solution (Rao, 1998). Frames define the scope of the new organizational form and justify it as indispensable, valid, and appropriate. They also define the interests of various constituencies, identify threats, and provide a vision (Snow and Benford, 1992). Frames must be compatible with the established institutional order while at the same time concealing the new form's radical nature (Aldrich and Fiol, 1994; Hunt and Aldrich, 1998). Given the lack of externally validated frames, institutional entrepreneurs must construct a coherent case for their venture by recombining elements from existing cultural repertoires and organizational myths (Douglas, 1986; Meyer and Rowan, 1977). Institutional entrepreneurs are thus conduits though which new forms are infused with cultural and normative content.

Not only must institutional entrepreneurs convince various stakeholders of their novel venture's legitimacy, they must also fend off rival entrepreneurs offering alternate versions of their products and services and competing with them for legitimacy by appealing to customers and investors to accept and endorse their version. When different institutional entrepreneurs champion incompatible frames, the choice between them hinges on power and social structure (Friedland and Alford, 1991; DiMaggio, 1991; Rao, 1998). The fate of alternative frames depends on the relative sizes of the political coalitions that form around them, the attitudes of government actors, and levels of support from professionals. In such cases, stakeholder and institutional endorsements are critical if a new form is to take hold and proliferate.

Once institutional entrepreneurs have developed a basis of understanding and trust in their new form,

they must develop strategies to enhance its performance reliability and establish stable relationships with early imitative entrepreneurs attempting to reproduce the new form. Intense competition among early entrants slows the growth of all ventures by reducing the chances that a champion will emerge and inspire efforts toward collective action, and by increasing confusion about what standards should be followed (Aldrich and Fiol, 1994). Convergence is critical to establishing the new form's identity, boundaries, and role in the interorganizational community. Collective action and convergence toward a standard version are facilitated if entrepreneurs choose early on to imitate innovators, rather than seek further innovation.[11] Convergence is more likely if the original innovation is imitable, creating incentives for cooperating to stabilize competitive conditions (Aldrich and Fiol, 1994). The likelihood of convergence also depends on the rate at which payoffs to new adopters accumulate; increasing returns to adoption stimulate imitative adoption (Arthur, 1989). As we discuss below, institutional entrepreneurs' efforts to convince others to accept and adopt their version of the new form often resemble social movements (Haveman and Rao, 1997; Rao, 1998). Social movements are collective attempts to construct the boundaries of new organizational forms and integrate them with the prevalent social order. Industry or trade associations, frequently founded by innovative entrepreneurs themselves, are often the centerpiece of such movements, taking leadership in formulating product and process standards, founding trade journals, running educational trade fairs, and representing the form to government agencies (Aldrich and Fiol, 1994).

Although early imitative entrepreneurs will inevitably make frequent mistakes because so much of the knowledge about the new form is uncodified, repeated imitation and borrowing from earlier foundings fosters codification of knowledge about the form, promoting its spread and contributing to convergence on an organizational standard. Industry associations and other collective actors can facilitate codification and convergence by instituting accreditation procedures or certification contests to evaluate organizations and their products or services according to performance on preset criteria (Rao, 1994). Increasingly, accreditation has become a formalized process as professional associations establish criteria and assessment regimes to evaluate organizations' conformity to their standards. Accreditation and certification offer standard social tests of an organizational form and its products and services. They also serve as knowledge diffusion mechanisms that help to establish the identity and cognitive legitimacy and accountability of the new form and the reliability of its products or services and its producers. What is good for the organizational form is not necessarily good for the innovative entrepreneur, however (Aldrich and Fiol, 1994). Codification and convergence facilitate replication, stimulating further imitative founding and lowering failure rates, but easy imitability also makes organizational survival more problematic as the market crowds with competitors whose survival depends on small differences. Under such circumstances, imitative entrepreneurs often survive at the expense of the original innovator (Delacroix and Rao, 1994).

Converging on a common, well-codified definition helps create consumer awareness (e.g., though media attention) and provides financial institutions an opportunity to assess the credit-worthiness of the form. It also familiarizes government authorities with the form and facilitates educational institutions' development of training programs. This familiarization in turn facilitates development of cognitive legitimacy—establishing the form as the taken-for-granted and natural way to organization a collective activity. Emergence of a consistent body of knowledge also provides entrepreneurs a basis on which to build a reputation for their new form as a taken-for-granted member of the larger interorganizational community, facilitating stable relationships and economic transactions with other established populations and raising the likelihood of sociopolitical approval. A new form becomes "established" when powerful actors endorse its claims by enacting rules and defining

social and technical boundaries around the form, ensuring that its distinctive character—a novel incarnation of goals, authority relations, technology, and market strategy—will be preserved over time. The development of a regulatory framework of rules and guidelines (e.g., licensing) makes conditions conducive to the creation of organizations (Meyer and Rowan, 1977).

Social Movements and Legitimation

Under certain conditions, social movements may also play a vital role in establishing new organizational forms. Social movements are collective endeavors to solve social problems. Social movement theory identifies processes through which actors translate shared interests into collective action. In the same way that organizations working together (e.g., as lobbying association) can serve as a segregating mechanism, maintaining distinctions between those engaged in collective action and those not so engaged, collective action is also a vehicle through which such boundaries can be constructed in the first place. Contemporary social movement theory views the ability of institutional entrepreneurs to bring about change to depend on framing processes, mobilizing structures, and political opportunities (McAdam, McCarthy, and Zald, 1996).

Institutional entrepreneurs can mobilize legitimacy, finances, and personnel only when they are able to elaborate collective action frames that enable collective attribution processes to operate (Snow and Benford, 1992). Opportunities to elaborate such frames are provided by major institutional and technological disruption and instability that undermines the status quo, increasing chances for a shared interpretation that a social system has lost legitimacy and is vulnerable to new demands from groups who seek to have their interests taken into account (McAdam, 1994). Collective vehicles through which people mobilize and engage in collective action are also essential for social movements. Such structures include formal social movement organizations (McCarthy and Zald, 1977), work and neighborhood organizations, and informal friendship networks (Tilly, 1978) that shape the common identity and social ties linking individuals and organizations. The recognition of a shared identity, coupled with previously existing social ties, greatly increases the ability of a group to translate common interests into mobilization (Tilly, 1978). Social connections are the conduits through which individuals join movements, and those most central in social networks are most likely to join social movements or otherwise become active and to do so early on. Homogeneous interests and dense social networks increase a group's capacity to mobilize its resources the likelihood of the formation of a movement. Because organizations are the critical units in governmental policymaking, creating formal organizations to represent the movement is vital (Laumann and Knoke, 1987).

Organized attempts to establish new structures also require political opportunity on which to thrive. Social movements thrive in times of social or political instability because the status quo is more vulnerable to successful challenge by outsiders. Disruptions change power relations and thus create opportunities for insurgency (McAdam, 1994). While the social movements we focus on are aimed at institutionalization of new organizational forms, some are "counter-movements" aimed at unraveling some perceived regulatory or institutional injustice and so may themselves underlie institutional changes that create fertile conditions for new organizational forms to emerge. Political opportunity, mobilization structures, and framing processes are reciprocally intertwined such that skillful framing of an issue can create an opportunity and reduce mobilization costs, just as strong mobilization structures can broaden opportunity and reduce the need for an awe-inspiring frame. The background of conditions that creates new possibilities for the rise of social movements often consists of a priori organizational and market failures (Rao, Morrill, and Zald, 2000). We consider three: influence costs, positive externalities, and negative externalities.

When a new organizational form involves a radical recombination (table 8.2, cell 4), it can jeopardize vested interests. It must acquire endorsements from powerful collective actors, such as the state, and must be transformed from a novel artifact into a social fact. A common presumption is that instances of a new organizational form can garner legitimacy by banding together through trade associations to secure governmental support and gain standing in consumer and financial markets. Trade associations can, however, be crippled by influence costs (Milgrom and Roberts, 1982). When decisions affect the distribution of wealth or benefits among constituents of trade associations and elite coalitions, affected individuals can attempt to influence decisions to their benefit. As a result, agreements may be hard to negotiate, thus blocking sustained coordination among producers. When producers are unable to coordinate action because of influence costs, social movements can play vital roles in the legitimation of a new organizational form. For example, automobile clubs played an important role in legitimating the automobile in the United States due to the failure of collective action by trade associations for producers (Rao et al., 2000). As a novel product, the automobile was unfamiliar to prospective consumers, who were confused because the source of power, the number of cylinders, systems of steering and control, and the mode of stopping were topics of considerable controversy. Sporadic opposition from vigilante antispeed organizations constrained the use of the automobile by forcing municipal governments to impose speed ordinances. Firms within the new industry could not successfully band together to legitimate the automobile. The National Association of Automobile Manufacturers was established in 1900 in a bid to assure product quality, but was superseded by the Association of Licensed Automobile Manufacturers, formed in 1903, and then challenged by a rival, the American Motor Car Manufacturer's Association, established in 1905. Both associations had collapsed by 1911 following a legal battle. It was in this context that automobile fans banded together into automobile clubs and sought to legitimate the automobile as a reliable and safe means of transportation.

Positive externalities arise when those who incur the costs of an action are not the sole beneficiaries of the action and those who benefit have necessarily not shared in its costs. Standard economic theory holds that industry "pioneers" incur the costs of establishing a trade association, formulating technical standards, and setting up supply and distribution networks, as well as playing key roles in familiarizing investors, personnel, consumers, and government agencies with the new organizational form. However, the benefits of these activities also extend to later entrants to the industry and not just to pioneers. In principle, pioneers should balk at incurring the costs of legitimating a new organizational form, but, as standard economic theory points out, they bear these costs because they have an opportunity to gain a large share of the market. Normal incentives can be inadequate, however, to motivate pioneers to incur these costs when collective goods such as technical standards are the result. In such cases, actors have incentives to ride free. New organizational forms may thus rely on social movement processes when "normal" incentives are insufficient to create public goods (Moe, 1980; Olson, 1965). For example, although technical standards benefit both producers and consumers, neither took the lead in creating standard setting organizations in the United States. Activists such as James Chase and Frederick Schlink (both employees of the National Bureau of Standards) wrote pamphlets that railed against the evils of wasteful variety, preached the virtues of standards, recruited members from the ranks of private corporations, and established standard-setting bodies. Their efforts peaked during World War I, when activists in the War Industries Board pushed producers to standardize products and conserve resources, leading to the formation of the American Standards Association in 1919.

Negative externalities obtain when some parties draw all the benefits of an action, while others face all of the costs. For example, steam locomotives, as Coase (1960) observed in a famous example, can emit sparks that set fire to fields, or deceptive advertising can harm the image of the advertising agencies and defraud consumers. In principle, one could claim that social costs can be reduced wholly through market mechanisms: for example, farmers can sell rights to emit sparks on their fields, or purveyors of deceptive advertisements can be eliminated because they acquire a bad reputation. However, market mechanisms may not work when transactions span large distances, and victims are uninformed and lack recognized legal rights. Steel firms, for instance, can pollute air in another country. Consumers may not be able to discern honest from dishonest advertisers, and may even lack the right of legal redress. In such cases, social movements can arise to establish new firms to reduce social costs. New organizational forms may thus also rely on social movements for their legitimation when market mechanisms are inadequate to reduce negative externalities. For example, at the turn of the twentieth century in the United States, deceptive advertising may have benefited some firms but harmed consumers and the image of advertising. Consumers were uninformed, free-rider problems prevented advertising agencies from engaging in collective action, and a social movement emerged to promote truth in advertising. Activists began forming advertising clubs in 1896, merging in 1904 to form the Associated Advertising Clubs of America. John Romer, publisher of Printers'

Ink, urged these clubs to establish vigilance committees to ascertain the truthfulness of advertisements issued by members, to discipline errant members, or even to take them to court. A National Vigilance Committee formed in 1912, and by 1914, twenty-four cities had founded vigilance committees in a bid to signal the advertising community's commitment to probity and professional conduct. In 1916, vigilance committees were renamed as Better Business Bureaus, and by 1930 more than 10,000 businesses supported these bureaus in numerous cities (Samson, 1980, p. 343).

Micro-Macro Evolutionary Interactions

To this point, our examination of micro-evolutionary VSR processes within particular organizational forms and macro-evolutionary VSR processes that give rise to new organizational forms has emphasized primarily genealogical ("V" and "R") and ecological ("S") processes and their interactions within each level. What have remained implicit in our analyses are the interactions between VSR processes across micro and macro levels. Although process at population and community levels operate quasi-independently, each a dynamic VSR system in its own right, as we noted earlier there is also both upward and downward causation across hierarchical levels (Campbell, 1974, 1990). These interactions constrain and enable the kinds of processes and events that can occur at a given level and regulate, in part, those that do occur. As a result, VSR processes at the population level (e.g., organizational learning, isomorphism) can dramatically affect VSR processes at the community level, while, at the same time, VSR processes at the community level (e.g., community disruption, co-evolution, social movements) shape and constrain those at the population level. To help us illustrate these cross-level interactions, figure 8.2 overlays the main micro- and macro-evolutionary VSR processes that we identified at the population and community levels on the dual hierarchy model.

Across levels of organization, VSR processes interact through variation and retention within the genealogical hierarchy and selection within the ecological hierarchy. In the genealogical hierarchy, retention processes at each level affect variation at other levels both up and down the hierarchy. For example, organizational learning and imitative

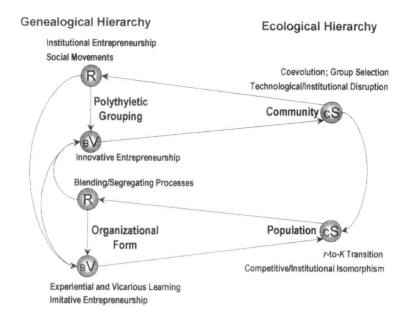

Figure 8.2 Micro-macro evolutionary interactions.

entrepreneurship at the population level limit the range of organizational variation that is expressed within an organizational population, while institutional entrepreneurship and social movements within organizational communities foster new specializations that reshape competitive processes at the population level. Each of these upward and downward effects can, in turn, echo back and forth up and down the hierarchy as processes and events at each level react to each other (Hofstader, 1979).

Within the ecological hierarchy, interactions that result in differential selection cascade downward, determining the fates of organizations, dependent on the selection of their populations, which in turn depends on the selection of the communities to which they belong. Technological innovations at the community level, for example, may alter competitive selection and segregating mechanisms at the popu-

lation level, reshaping the boundaries of populations. The convergence of telecommunications technologies, for instance, has created opportunities (and nightmares) for new kinds of organizations (e.g., cable companies) in the telecommunications community. More generally, the emergence of a dominant design or technological discontinuity can alter the basis of competition at the population level by, for example, triggering an r-to-K transition or altering the relative importance of various competencies and resources.

Conversely, upward causation means that retained features of the lower level constrain what can emerge at the higher levels. Thus, organizations in one population can learn vicariously routines employed by organizations in another population belonging to the same organizational community, and the increasing homogeneity resulting from such imitation may, in turn, alter the structure of commensalisms within their community. Credit unions can, for example, imitate the practices and products of commercial banks, intensifying competition between them. Alternately, organizations in one population may establish cooperative relationships with organizations in another population, and in doing so alter the structure of symbiosis in their community. Hotels, car rental agencies, and airline companies, for example, are now bound together through a web of frequent-flyer programs. Community structures can also be reshaped as disruptive competitive selection or r-to-K transitions within populations promote new specializations and symbiotic relations as new populations emerge to fulfill ancillary roles (Hawley, 1950).

Complications of Hierarchical Evolution

These cross-level interactions of micro- and macroevolutionary VSR processes complicate organizational evolution considerably. Units of organizational evolution are nested and overlapping so that some entities (organizations and populations) are integral parts of other adapting entities (communities). The structure of relations among them arises from interaction among various nested levels, each responding to its own and each other's VSR dynamics. As a result, selection pressures are often in conflict across levels, with adaptations that are beneficial for entities at one level harmful at others. Union power, for example, may enable some classes of jobs to be retained through industry-wide agreements but may jeopardize the fates of individual organizations and the overall population. It is also possible for two entities to both compete and cooperate, depending on the level at which their interaction takes place. For example, a population of firms may band together into an effective trade association designed to ward off competition from other populations—but at the cost of more intense competition within the population. Analogously, what is good for an organizational form is not necessarily good for its innovative entrepreneur: While codification and convergence facilitate legitimation, easy imitability can result in imitative entrepreneurs surviving at the expense of the original innovator (Delacroix and Rao, 1994).

Higher-level adaptation thus does not arise automatically from lower-level adaptation. Indeed, it would be very unusual in the evolution of a nested hierarchical system for an adaptation that optimizes fitness for components of the system to also optimize prospects for the higher levels of the system or the system as a whole (Baum, 1999; Campbell, 1994, March, 1994). What is best for entities at one level is thus not generally best for those at other levels. As a result, while attempting to improve their own fitness, entities at different levels of organization compete for resources across (as well as within) levels, complicating organizational evolution. As we noted earlier, functional organization at any level of the organizational hierarchy requires a corresponding process of selection at that level. Populations can become well designed only by a process of between-population selection, and communities can become well designed only by a process of between-community selection (Baum, 1999; Campbell, 1994; Sober and Wilson, 1998). Even if selection among entities at a given hierarchical level enhances their fitness, however, because the rate of evolution is faster at lower levels, the fitness achieved at the higher level may constantly be undermined by lower-level entities that "out-evolve" their higher-level counterparts.

Conclusion

Our goal in this chapter has been to provide a comprehensive framework and account of evolutionary dynamics in organizational populations and communities. We outlined the core premises of an evolutionary-ecological view of organizations drawing on core research findings amassed during twenty-five years of empirical research. After presenting our framework, we presented more detailed analyses of evolutionary dynamics at two levels of organization: (1) Micro-evolutionary processes that shape persistence and change over time among organizations within a particular lineage, or organizational form; and (2) Macro-evolutionary processes that shape persistence and change over time within a community of organizational forms, and through which new organizational forms arise.

Our analysis of population- and community-level evolution highlighted the roles of institutional change, technological innovation cycles, entrepreneurs, and social movements as triggers of organizational variation. We explored how institutional and technological change transforms the dynamics of organizational communities by shifting the boundaries of organizational forms, destabilizing or reinforcing existing community structures, giving rise to social movements, and creating opportunities for entrepreneurs to shape new organizational forms. Our analysis of population-level VSR serves to consolidate and refine earlier treatments of these processes; our analysis of community-level VSR, in contrast, represents one of the first comprehensive treatments of these processes (see also Aldrich, 1999). We concluded by highlighting some basic connections between evolutionary processes at population and community levels that emerge from our analysis.

Although we have attempted to be comprehensive in our treatment, in closing, we would like to point out two avenues for research into the evolutionary dynamics of populations and communities: spatial processes and endogenous sources of change.

Our review finessed the issue of whether populations and communities change due to exogenous events or endogenous processes. Although our discussion depicted how organizations themselves are sources of variations and could learn from other organizations in populations, and hinted at the endogenous foundations of population change, we need systematic research, because seemingly exogenous shocks such as new laws or economic crises could themselves well be the outcome of organizational action. For example, Edelman (1999) described how new laws often are the outcomes of best practices in organizations, and therefore have endogenous origins. Similarly, boom-bust phenomena in a given industry or a community may themselves be the outcomes of firms expanding capacity recklessly or exiting the market in droves (Fombrun, 1986).

Our review also glossed over spatial aspects of population and community evolution. Spatial dimensions of population- and community-level change are likely to become a rich avenue for work not only because of the growing importance of industrial districts and multiunit chain organizations for which space is a vital strategic variable, but also because of the promise of joining hands with economic and social geographers to understand variation, selection, and retention at the level of regions. A growing line of research (Baum and Greve, 2001; Baum and Haveman, 1997; Baum, Li and Usher, 2000; Baum and Sorenson, 2003; Greve, 1999a, 1999b; Ingram and Baum, 1997) bodes well for a deeper understanding of why many different kinds of organizations dot the landscape of our contemporary organizational society.

Notes

An early version of this chapter was presented at the Macro-Level Perspectives on Organizational Change and Development Symposium, Academy of Management, Chicago, August 1999. We are most grateful to Kim Bates, Scott Poole, and Andy Van de Ven for conversations, comments, and ideas that helped us to improve this chapter.

1. There is considerable disagreement on how to define organizational forms and multiple definitions premised on different approaches to organizational classification have been discussed (see Baum, 1989; McKelvey, 1982, pp. 35–65; Rao and Singh, 1999; Rich, 1992; Romanelli, 1991).

2. Of course, if all organizations follow such a strategy, the population may produce no variations to imitate.

3. Here, we do not consider Hannan and Carroll's (1992) version of the density dependence model, which focuses on the dynamics of legitimation and competition to explain the growth trajectories of organizational populations, because it is cast at the population level. As a result, density-dependent legitimation captures relative fitness of populations but does not address relative fitness of organizations within a population. Hannan and Carroll's formulation of density-dependent competition, which treats all organizations in a population as equal competitors, is similarly silent on relative fitness of organizations within a population. Therefore we present Brittain and Freeman's earlier formulation, which incorporates within-population variation among organizations.

4. Biological transmission is not so simple either. Hull (1988, pp. 397–431) suggests that while familiar with the complexities of sociocultural transmission, social scientists may have an overly simple view of biological transmission.

5. For a detailed account of organizational routines and their replication, see Nelson and Winter (1982, pp. 96–136).

6. Of course, in terms of "generation time," organizational evolution occurs at the same rate as biological evolution. In "physical time," however, organizational evolution falls somewhere in the middle—between viruses on the one hand and sequoia trees on the other (see, e.g., Hull, 1988).

7. Use of these terms by some organizational scholars differs from their meanings in biology. In biology, the punctuation hypothesis is that rates of evolution are accelerated by rapidly divergent speciation. Species are conceived to change little during most of their history, but events of rapid speciation occasionally punctuate this stability, resulting in concentrated periods of change

(Eldredge and Gould, 1972). The punctuation model explains the rapid speciation as a result of the rapid appearance of new attributes in emergent populations (Stanley, 1979). By comparison, organizational conceptions of the punctuation hypotheses typically entail the progression of single organizations (Miller and Friesen, 1980; Tushman and Romanelli, 1985) through a pattern of alternating periods of sustained inertial and discontinuous revolutionary change.

8. For more detailed discussions of isolation mechanisms, see Baum (1989, pp. 25–33; 44–48), McKelvey (1982, pp. 196–202), and Hannan and Freeman (1989, pp. 53–57).

9. Community dynamics have much in common with processes of organizational field (de)structuration (DiMaggio and Powell, 1993; Oliver, 1992). Organizational fields, "those organizations that, in aggregate, constitute a recognized area of institutional life: key suppliers, resource and product consumers, regulatory agencies, and other organizations that produce similar services or products" (DiMaggio and Powell, 1983: 148). Indeed, as Scott (1994, pp. 207–208, cf. Scott 1995) notes, "the notion of a field connotes the existence of a community of organizations that partakes of a common meaning system and whose participants interact more frequently and fatefully with one another than with actors outside of the field." The primary difference appears to us to be one of levels, with organizational fields frequently constituted by multiple local organizational communities that vary in their degree and form of functional integration.

10. For example, competition between two populations, A and B, which benefits a third population, C, because it also competes with B, would appear as mutualism between populations A and C even if A and C did not interact directly.

11. If, however, the organizational definition is settled before early entrepreneurs have had the chance to discover effective routines, the standard itself will be suboptimal, and this may prove disastrous for the form (Baum and Berta, 1999).

References

Abbott, A. (1988). *The system of professions: An essay on the division of expert labor.* Chicago: University of Chicago Press.

Abernathy, W. J. (1978). *The productivity dilemma.* Baltimore: Johns Hopkins University Press.

Abernathy, W. J. & Utterback, J. M. (1978). Patterns of industrial innovation. *Technology Review,* 80, 40–47.

Aldrich, H. E. (1979). *Organizations and environments.* Englewood Cliffs, NJ: Prentice-Hall.

Aldrich, H. E. (1999). *Organizations evolving.* London: Sage.

Aldrich, H. E. & Fiol, C. M. (1994). Fools rush in? The institutional context of industry creation. *Academy of Management Review,* 19, 645–670.

Aldrich, H. E. & Kenworthy, A. L. (1999). The accidental entrepreneur: Campbellian antinomies and organizational foundings. In J. A. C. Baum & B. McKelvey (Eds.), *Variations in organization science: In honor of Donald T. Campbell* (pp. 19–34). Thousand Oaks, CA: Sage.

Aldrich, H. E. & Sasaki, T. (1995). R & D consortia in the United States and Japan. *Research Policy,* 24, 301–316.

Amburgey, T. L., Dacin, T., & Kelly, D. (1994). Disruptive selection and population segmentation: Interpopulation competition as a segregating process. In J. A. C. Baum & J. V. Singh (Eds.), *Evolutionary dynamics of organizations* (pp. 240–254). New York: Oxford University Press.

Anderson, P. & Tushman, M. L. (1990). Technological discontinuities and dominant designs: A cyclical model of technological change. *Administrative Science Quarterly,* 35, 604–633.

Arthur, B. (1989). Competing technologies, increasing returns, and lock-in by historically small events. *Economic Journal,* 99, 116–131.

Argote, L. & Epple, D. (1990). Learning curves in manufacturing. *Science,* 247, 920–924.

Astley, W. G. (1985). The two ecologies: Population and community perspectives on organizational evolution. *Administrative Science Quarterly,* 30, 224–241.

Astley, W. G. & Fombrun, C. J. (1983). Collective strategy: Social ecology of organizational environments. *Academy of Management Review,* 8, 576–587.

Bandura, A. (1977). *Social learning theory.* Englewood Cliffs, NJ: Prentice-Hall.

Barnett, W. P. (1990). The organizational ecology of a technological system. *Administrative Science Quarterly,* 35, 31–60.

Barnett, W. P. & Carroll, G. R. (1993). How institutional constraints affected the organization of early American telephony. *Journal of Law, Economics, and Organization,* 9, 98–126.

Basalla, G. (1988). *The evolution of technology.* Cambridge: Cambridge University Press.

Baum, J. A. C. (1989). *A population perspective on organizations: A study of diversity and transformation in childcare service organizations.* Unpublished doctoral dissertation, University of Toronto, Canada.

Baum, J. A. C. (1996). Organizational ecology. In S. Clegg, C. Hardy, & W. Nord (Eds.), *Handbook of organization studies* (pp. 77–114). London: Sage.

Baum, J. A. C. (1999). Whole-part coevolutionary competition in organizations. In J. A. C. Baum & B. McKelvey (Eds.), *Variations in organization science: In honor of Donald T. Campbell* (pp. 113–135). Thousand Oaks, CA: Sage.

Baum, J. A. C. (in press). Competitive and institutional isomorphism in organizational populations. In W. W. Powell & D. L. Jones (Eds.), *Institutional dynamics and processes.* Chicago: University of Chicago Press.

Baum, J. A. C. & Berta, W. B. (1999). Sources, dynamics, and speed: Population-level learning by organizations in a longitudinal behavioral simulation. In A. S. Miner & P. Anderson (Eds.), *Population-level learning and industry change: Advances in strategic management,* vol. 16 (pp. 155–184). Stamford, CT: JAI Press.

Baum, J. A. C. & Greve, H. R. (Eds.) (2001). *Multiunit organization and multimarket strategy—Advances in strategic management,* vol. 18. Oxford: JAI/Elsevier.

Baum, J. A. C. & Haveman, H. A. (1997). Love thy neighbor? Differentiation and agglomeration in the Manhattan hotel industry. *Administrative Science Quarterly, 42,* 304–338.

Baum, J. A. C. & Ingram, P. (1998). Survival-enhancing learning in the Manhattan hotel industry, 1898–1980. *Management Science, 44,* 996–1016.

Baum, J. A. C. & Korn, H. J. (1994). The community ecology of large Canadian companies, 1984–1991. *Canadian Journal of Administrative Sciences, 11,* 277–294.

Baum, J. A. C. & Oliver, C. (1992). Institutional embeddedness and the dynamics of organizational populations. *American Sociological Review, 57,* 540–599.

Baum, J. A. C. & Mezias, S. J. (1992). Localized competition and organizational failure in the Manhattan hotel industry, 1898–1990. *Administrative Science Quarterly, 37,* 580–604.

Baum, J. A. C. & Singh, J. V. (1994a). Organizational hierarchies and evolutionary processes: Some reflections on a theory of organizational evolution. In J. A. C. Baum & J. V. Singh (Eds.), *Evolutionary dynamics of organizations* (pp. 3–20). New York: Oxford University Press.

Baum, J. A. C. & Singh, J. V. (1994b). Organizational niche overlap and the dynamics of organizational founding. *Organization Science, 5,* 483–501.

Baum, J. A. C. & Singh, J. V. (1994c). Organizational niche overlap and the dynamics of organizational mortality. *American Journal of Sociology, 100,* 346–380.

Baum, J. A. C. & Sorenson, O. (Eds.) (2003). *Geography and strategy—Advances in strategic management,* vol. 20. Oxford: JAI/Elsevier.

Baum, J. A. C., Korn, H. J., & Kotha, S. (1995). Dominant designs and population dynamics in telecommunications services: Founding and failure of facsimile service organizations, 1969–1992. *Social Science Research, 24,* 97–135.

Baum, J. A. C., Li, S. X., & Usher, J. M. (2000). Making the next move: How experiential and vicarious learning shape the locations of chains' acquisitions. *Administrative Science Quarterly, 45,* 766–801.

Bijker, W., Hughes, T., & Pinch, T. (1987). *The social construction of technological systems.* Cambridge, MA: MIT Press.

Boyd R. & Richerson, P. J. (1985). *Culture and the evolutionary process.* Chicago: University of Chicago Press.

Brittain, J. W. & Freeman, J. H. (1980). Organizational proliferation and density dependent selection. In J. Kimberly & R. Miles (Eds.), *The organizational life cycle* (pp.291–388). San Francisco, CA: Jossey-Bass.

Brittain, J. W. & Wholey, D. H. (1988). Competition and coexistence in organizational communities: Population dynamics in electronics components manufacturing. In G. R. Carroll (Ed.), *Ecological models of organizations* (pp. 195–222). Cambridge, MA: Ballinger.

Brown, S. L. & Eisenhardt, K. M. (1998). *Competing on the edge.* Boston, MA: Harvard Business School Press.

Burgelman, R. A. (1983). A process model of internal corporate venturing in the diversified major firm. *Administrative Science Quarterly, 28,* 223–244.

Burt, R. S. (1980). Models of network structure. *Annual Review of Sociology, 6,* 79–141.

Campbell, D. T. (1965). Variation and selective retention in socio-cultural evolution. In H. R. Barringer, G. I. Blanksten, & R. W. Mack (Eds.), *Social change in developing areas: A reinterpretation of evolutionary theory* (pp. 19–48). Cambridge, MA: Schenkman.

Campbell, D. T. (1974). Evolutionary epistemology. In P. A. Schlipp (Ed.), *The philosophy of Karl Popper* (pp. 413–463). Lasalle, IL: Open Court.

Campbell, D. T. (1979). Comments on the sociology and ethics of moralizing. *Behavioral Science, 24,* 37–45.

Campbell, D. T. (1988). A general "selection theory" as implemented in biological evolution and in social belief-transmission-with-modification in science. *Biology and Philosophy, 3,* 171–177.

Campbell, D. T. (1990). Levels of organization, downward causation, and the selection-theory approach to evolutionary epistemology. In G. Greenberg & E. Tobach (Eds.), *Theories of the evolution of knowing* (pp. 1–17). Hillsdale, NJ: Lawrence Erlbaum Associates.

Campbell, D. T. (1994). How individual and face-to-face-group selection undermine firm selection in organizational evolution. In J. A. C. Baum & J. V. Singh (Eds.), *Evolutionary dynamics of organizations* (pp. 23–38). New York: Oxford University Press.

Carroll, G. R. (1985). Concentration and specialization: Dynamics of niche width in populations of organizations. *American Journal of Sociology*, 90,1262–1283.

Carroll, G. R. & Swaminathan, A. (1992). The organizational ecology of strategic groups in the American brewing industry from 1975 to 1990. *Industrial and Corporate Change, 1*, 65–97.

Clark, K. B. (1985). The interaction of design hierarchies and market concepts in technological evolution. *Research Policy, 14*, 235–251.

Coase, R. H. (1960). The problem of social cost. *Journal of Law and Economics, 3*, 1–44.

Cohen, W. M. & Levinthal, D. A. (1990). Absorptive capacity: A new perspective on organizational learning and innovation. *Administrative Science Quarterly, 35*, 128–152.

Cyert, R. M. & March, J. G. (1963). *A behavioral theory of the firm.* Englewood Cliffs, NJ: Prentice-Hall.

Davis-Blake, A. & Pfeffer, J. (1989). Just a mirage: The search for dispositional effects in organizational research. *Academy of Management Review, 14*, 385–400.

Delacroix, J. & Rao, H. (1994). Externalities and ecological theory: Unbundling density dependence. In J. A. C. Baum & J. V. Singh (Eds.), *Evolutionary dynamics of organizations* (pp. 255–268). New York: Oxford University Press.

DiMaggio, P. J. (1991). Constructing an organizational field as a professional project: U. S. art museums, 1920–1940. In W. W. Powell & P. J. DiMaggio (Eds.), *The new institutionalism in organizational analysis* (pp. 276–292). Chicago: University of Chicago Press.

DiMaggio, P. J. & Powell, W. W. (1983). The iron cage revisited: Institutional isomorphism and collective rationality in organizational fields. *American Sociological Review, 48*, 147–160.

DiMaggio, P. J. & Powell, W. W. (Eds.) (1991). Introduction. In W. W. Powell & P. J. DiMaggio (Eds.), *The new institutionalism in organizational analysis* (pp. 1–38). Chicago: University of Chicago Press.

Dimmick, J. & Rothenbuhler, E. (1984). Competitive displacement in communication industries: New media in old environments. In R. Rice & Associates (Eds.), *The new media: Communication research and technology* (pp. 287–308). Beverly Hills, CA: Sage.

Dosi, G. (1982). Technological paradigms and technological trajectories. *Research Policy, 11*, 147–162.

Dosi, G. (1984). *Technical change and industrial transformation.* New York: St. Martin's.

Dosi, G. (1988). Sources, procedures, and microeconomic effects of innovation. *Journal of Economic Literature, 26*, 1120–1171.

Douglas, M. (1986). *How institutions think.* Syracuse, NY: Syracuse University Press.

Edelman, L. (in press). On the endogeneity of law. In W. W. Powell & D. L. Jones (Eds.), *Institutional dynamics and processes.* Chicago: University of Chicago Press.

Eldredge, N. & Gould, S. J. (1972). Punctuated equilibria: An alternative to phyletic gradualism. In T. J. M. Schopf (Ed.), *Models in paleobiology* (pp. 82–115). San Francisco: Freeman Cooper.

Ferguson, P. (1998). A cultural field in the making: Gastronomy in 19th century France. *American Journal of Sociology, 104*, 197–641.

Fombrun, C. J. (1986). Structural dynamics within and between organizations. *Administrative Science Quarterly, 31*, 403–421.

Friedland, R. & Alford, R. R. (1991). Bringing society back in: Symbols, practices, and institutional contradictions. In W. W. Powell & P. J. DiMaggio (Eds.), *The new institutionalism in organizational analysis* (pp. 232–263). Chicago: University of Chicago Press.

Goodrick, E. & Salancik, G. R. (1996). Organizational discretion in responding to institutional practices: Hospitals and cesarean births. *Administrative Science Quarterly, 41*, 1–28.

Gould, S. J. & Eldredge, N. (1977). Punctuated equilibria: The tempo and mode of evolution reconsidered. *Paleobiology, 3*, 115–151.

Greenwood, R. & Hinings, C. R. (1993). Understanding strategic change: The contribution of archetypes. *Academy of Management Journal, 36*, 1052–1081.

Greve, H. R. (1999a). Branch systems and nonlocal learning in organizational populations. In A. S. Miner & P. C. Anderson (Eds.), *Population level learning and industry change—Advances in strategic management* (Vol. 16, pp. 57–80). Greenwich, CT: JAI Press.

Greve, H. R. (1999b). *Organizational location decisions: Competition, learning, and strategy in Tokyo banking, 1894–1936.* Unpublished manuscript, Institute of Policy and Planning Science, University of Tsukuba, Tsukuba, Japan.

Han, S.-K. (1994). Mimetic isomorphism and its effect on the auditor services market. *Social Forces, 73*, 637–664.

Hannan, M. T. & Carroll, G. R. (1992). *Dynamics of organizational populations: Density, competition, and legitimation.* New York: Oxford University Press.

Hannan, M. T. & Freeman, J. H. (1977). The population ecology of organizations. *American Journal of Sociology, 83,* 929–984.

Hannan, M. T. & Freeman, J. H. (1984). Structural inertia and organizational change. *American Sociological Review, 49,* 149–164.

Hannan, M. T. & Freeman, J. H. (1989). *Organizational ecology.* Cambridge, MA: Harvard University Press.

Haunschild, P. R. & Miner, A. S. (1997). Modes of interorganizational imitation: The effects of outcome salience and uncertainty. *Administrative Science Quarterly, 42,* 472–500.

Haveman, H. A. & Rao, H. (1997). Structuring a theory of moral sentiments: Institutional and organizational coevolution in the early thrift industry. *American Journal of Sociology, 102,* 1606–1651.

Hawley, A. H. (1950). *Human ecology.* New York: Ronald.

Henderson, A. D. (1999). Firm strategy and age dependence: A contingent view of the liabilities of newness, adolescence and obsolescence. *Administrative Science Quarterly, 44,* 281–314.

Henderson, R. M. & Clark, K. B. (1990). Architectural innovation: The reconfiguration of existing product technologies and the failure of established firms. *Administrative Science Quarterly, 35,* 9–30.

Hodgson, G. (1993). *Economics and evolution.* Cambridge: Polity Press.

Hofstader, D. R. (1979). *Gödel, Escher, Bach: An eternal golden braid.* New York: Basic Books.

Hull, D. L. (1988). *Science as a process.* New York: Oxford University Press.

Hunt, C. S. & Aldrich, H. E. (1998). The second ecology: Creation and evolution or organizational communities. In B. Staw & L. L. Cummings (Eds.), *Research in organizational behavior* (Vol. 20, pp. 267–302). Greenwich, CT: JAI Press.

Ijiri, Y. & Simon, H. A. (1977). *Skew distributions and the sizes of business firms.* New York: North Holland.

Imai, K. (1986). *Kaizen: The key to Japan's competitive success.* New York: Random House.

Ingram, P. & Baum, J. A. C. (1997). Opportunity and constraint: Organizational learning from operating and competitive experience. *Strategic Management Journal, 18,* (Summer Special Issue), 75–98.

Ingram, P. & Simons, T. (2000). State formation, ideological competition, and the ecology of Israeli worker cooperatives. *Administrative Science Quarterly, 45,* 25–54.

Kamien, M. L. & Schwartz, N. L. (1982). *Market structure and innovation.* New York: Cambridge University Press.

Kauffman, S. A. (1993). *The origins of order: Self-organization and selection in evolution.* New York: Oxford University Press.

Laumann, E. O. & Knoke, D. (1987). *The organizational state: Social choice in national policy domains.* Madison: University of Wisconsin Press.

Lehrman, W. G. (1994). Diversity in decline: Institutional environment and organizational failure in the American life insurance industry. *Social Forces, 73,* 605–635.

Levinthal, D. A. & March, J. G. (1993). The myopia of learning. *Strategic Management Journal, 14,* 94–112.

Levitt, B. & March, J. G. (1988). Organizational learning. *Annual Review of Sociology, 14,* 319–340.

Lieberman, M. B. & Montgomery, D. B. (1988). First-mover advantages. *Strategic Management Journal, 9,* 41–58.

Lippman, S. A. & Rumelt, R. P. (1982). Uncertain imitability: An analysis of interfirm differences in efficiency under competition. *Bell Journal of Economics, 13,* 418–438.

Lumsden, C. J. & Singh, J. V. (1990). The dynamics of organizational speciation. In J. V. Singh (Ed.), *Organizational evolution: New directions* (pp. 145–163). Newbury Park, CA: Sage.

March, J. G. (1981). Footnotes on organizational change. *Administrative Science Quarterly, 26,* 563–597.

March, J. G. (1991). Exploration and exploitation in organizational learning. *Organization Science, 2,* 71–87.

March, J. G. (1994). The evolution of evolution. In J. A. C. Baum & J. V. Singh (Eds.), *Evolutionary dynamics of organizations* (pp. 39–49). New York: Oxford University Press.

McAdam, D. (1994). Culture and social movements. In E. Larana, H. Johnston, & J. R. Gusfield (Eds.), *New social movements* (pp. 36–57). Philadelphia: Temple University Press.

McAdam, D., McCarthy, J. D., & Zald, M. N. (1996). Introduction: Opportunities, mobilizing structures, and framing processes—Toward a synthetic, comparative perspective on social movements. In D. McAdam, J. D. McCarthy, & M. N. Zald (Eds.), *Comparative perspectives on social movements: Political opportunities, mobilizing structures, and cultural framings* (pp. 1–20). Cambridge: Cambridge University Press.

McCarthy, J. D. & Zald, M. N. (1977). Resource mobilization and social movements: A partial theory. *American Journal of Sociology, 82,* 1212–1241.

McKelvey, B. (1982). *Organizational systematics*. Los Angeles, CA: University of California Press.

McKelvey, B. (1997). Quasi-natural organization science. *Organization Science*, 8, 351–380.

McKelvey, B. (1998). Complexity vs. selection among coevolutionary firms: Factors affecting Nash equilibrium fitness levels. *Comportamento Organizacional e Gestão*, 4, 17–59.

McKelvey, B. (1999). *Dynamics of new science leadership: An OB theory of the firm, strategy, and distributed intelligence*. Unpublished manuscript, Anderson School of Management, UCLA.

McPherson, J. M. (1983). An ecology of affiliation. *American Sociological Review*, 48, 519–532.

McPherson, J. M., Popielarz, P. A., & Drobnic, S. (1992). Social networks and organizational dynamics. *American Sociological Review*, 57, 153–170.

Meyer, J. W. & Rowan, B. (1977). Institutionalized organizations: Formal structure as myth and ceremony. *American Journal of Sociology*, 83, 340–363.

Meyer, J. W. & Scott, W. R. (1983). Centralization and the legitimacy problems of local governments. In J. W. Meyer & W. R. Scott (Eds.), *Organizational environments: Ritual and rationality* (pp. 199–215). San Francisco, CA: Sage.

Meyer, M. W. (1994a). Turning evolution inside organizations. In J. A. C. Baum & J. V. Singh (Eds.), *Evolutionary dynamics of organizations* (pp. 109–116). New York: Oxford University Press.

Meyer, M. W. (1994b). Measuring performance in economic organizations. In N. J. Smelser & R. Swedberg (Eds.), *The handbook of economic sociology* (pp. 556–578). Princeton, NJ: Princeton University Press.

Milgrom, P. & Roberts, J. (1982). Predation, reputation, and entry deterrence. *Journal of Economic Theory*, 27, 280–312.

Miller, D. (1990). *The Icarus paradox: How exceptional companies bring about their own downfall*. New York: HarperCollins.

Miller, D. (1993). The architecture of simplicity. *Academy of Management Review*, 18, 116–138.

Miller, D. (1999). Selection processes inside organizations: The self-reinforcing consequences of success. In J. A. C. Baum & B. McKelvey (Eds.), *Variations in organization science: In honor of Donald T. Campbell* (pp. 93–109). Thousand Oaks, CA: Sage.

Miller, D. & Friesen, P. H. (1980). Momentum and revolution in organizational adaptation. *Academy of Management Journal*, 22, 591–614.

Miner, A. S. (1990). Structural evolution through idiosyncratic jobs: The potential for unplanned learning. *Organization Science*, 1, 195–210.

Miner, A. S. (1991). The social ecology of jobs. *American Sociological Review*, 56, 772–785.

Miner, A. S. (1994). Seeking adaptive advantage: Evolutionary theory and managerial action. In J. A. C. Baum & J. V. Singh (Eds.), *Evolutionary dynamics of organizations* (pp. 76–89). New York: Oxford University Press.

Miner, A. S. & Anderson, P. (1999). Industry and population level learning: Organizational, interorganizational, and collective learning. In A. S. Miner & P. Anderson (Eds.), *Population level learning and industry change: Vol. 17. Advances in Strategic Management* (pp. 1–30). Stamford, CT: JAI Press.

Miner, A. S. & Haunschild, P. R. (1995). Population level learning. In B. Staw & L. Cummings (Eds.), *Research in Organizational Behavior* (Vol. 17, pp. 115–166). Greenwich, CT: JAI Press.

Miner, A. S. & Raghavan, S. V. (1999). Interorganizational imitation: A hidden engine of selection. In J. A. C. Baum & B. McKelvey (Eds.), *Variations in organization science: In honor of Donald T. Campbell* (pp. 35–62). Thousand Oaks, CA: Sage.

Moe, T. M. (1980). *The organization of interests*. Chicago: University of Chicago.

Mowery, D. C., Oxley, J. E., & Silverman, B. S. (1996). Strategic alliances and interfirm knowledge transfer. *Strategic Management Journal*, 17, 77–92.

Nelson, R. R. & Winter, S. G. (1982). *An evolutionary theory of economic change*. Cambridge, MA: Harvard University Press.

Nystrom, P. C. & Starbuck, W. H. (1984). To avoid organizational crisis, unlearn. *Organizational Dynamics*, 12, 53–65.

Oliver, C. (1992). The antecedents of deinstitutionalization. *Organization Studies*, 13, 563–588.

Olson, M. (1965). *The logic of collective action*. Cambridge, MA: Harvard University Press.

Pfeffer, J. & Salancik, G. R. (1978). *The external control of organizations*. New York: Harper and Row.

Pimm, S. L. (1991). *Balance of nature?* Chicago: University of Chicago Press.

Plotkin, H. (1993). *Darwin machines and the nature of knowledge*. Cambridge, MA: Harvard University Press.

Powell, W. W., Koput, K. W., & Smith-Doerr, L. (1996). Interorganizational collaboration and the locus of innovation: Networks of learning in biotechnology. *Administrative Science Quarterly*, 41, 116–145.

Puccia, C. J. & Levins, R. (1985). *Qualitative modeling of complex systems*. Cambridge, MA: Harvard University Press.

Ranger-Moore, J., Banaszak-Holl, J. J., & Hannan, M. T. (1991). Density-dependent dynamics in regulated industries: Founding rates of banks and life insurance companies. *Administrative Science Quarterly, 36,* 36–65.

Rao, H. (1994). The social construction of reputation: Certification contests, legitimation, and the survival of organizations in the American automobile industry; 1895–1912. *Strategic Management Journal, 15,* 29–44.

Rao, H. (1998). Caveat emptor: The construction of non-profit consumer watchdog organizations. *American Journal of Sociology, 103,* 912–961.

Rao, H., Morrill, C., & Zald, M. N. (2000). Power plays: Social movements, collective action and new organizational forms. In B. Staw & R. Sutton (Eds.), *Research in organizational behavior* (Vol. 22, pp. 237–282). Greenwich, CT: JAI.

Rao, H. & Singh, J. V. (1999). Types of variation in organizational populations: The speciation of new organizational forms. In J. A. C. Baum & B. McKelvey (Eds.), *Variations in organization science: In honor of Donald T. Campbell* (pp. 63–77). Thousand Oaks, CA: Sage.

Rich, P. (1992). Organizational taxonomy: Definition and design. *Academy of Management Review, 14,* 758–781.

Romanelli, E. (1989). Organizational birth and population variety: A community perspective on origins. In B. Staw & L. L. Cummings (Eds.), *Research in organizational behavior* (Vol. 11, pp. 211–246). Greenwich, CT: JAI Press.

Romanelli, E. (1991). The evolution of new organizational forms. *Annual Review of Sociology, 17,* 79–103.

Romanelli, E. (1999). Blind (but not unconditioned) variation: Problems of copying in sociocultural evolution. In J. A. C. Baum & B. McKelvey (Eds.), *Variations in organization science: In honor of Donald T. Campbell* (pp. 79–91). Thousand Oaks, CA: Sage.

Sahal, D. (1985). Technological guideposts and innovation avenues. *Research Policy, 14,* 61–82.

Samson, P. (1980). *The emergence of a consumer interest in America.* Unpublished Ph.D. thesis, University of Chicago.

Saxenian, A. (1994). *Regional advantage: Culture and competition in Silicon Alley and Route 128.* Cambridge, MA: Harvard University Press.

Schumpeter, J. A. (1934). *The theory of economic development.* Cambridge, MA: Harvard University Press.

Scott, W. R. (1987). The adolescence of institutional theory. *Administrative Science Quarterly, 32,* 493–511.

Scott, W. R. (1994). Conceptualizing organizational fields: Linking organizations and societal systems.

In H-U. Derlien, U. Gerhardt, & F. W. Scharpf (Eds.), *Systemrationalität und partialinteresse* [Systems rationality and partial interests] (pp. 203–221). Baden, Germany: Nomos Velagsgesellschaft.

Scott, W. R. (1995). *Institutions and organizations.* Thousand Oaks, CA: Sage.

Scott, W. R., Ruef, M., Mendel, P. J., & Caronna, C. A. (2000). *Institutional change and organizations.* Chicago: University of Chicago Press.

Shapiro, C. & Varian, H. (1999). *Information rules.* Boston, MA: Harvard Business School Press.

Singh, J. V. & Lumsden, C. J. (1990). Theory and research in organizational ecology. *Annual Review of Sociology, 16,* 161–195.

Snow, D. A. & Benford, R. D. (1992). Master frames and cycles of protest. In A. D. Morris & C. McClung Mueller (Eds.), *Frontiers in social movement theory* (pp. 133–155). New Haven, CT: Yale University Press.

Sober, E. & Wilson, D. S. (1998). *Unto others: The evolution and psychology of unselfish behavior.* Cambridge, MA: Harvard University Press.

Sorenson, O. & Audia, P. G. (2000). The social structure of entrepreneurial activity: Concentration of footwear production in the United States, 1940–1989. *American Journal of Sociology, 106,* 424–462.

Spender, J.-C. (1989). *Industry recipes: The nature and sources of managerial judgment.* Oxford, UK: Blackwell.

Stacey, R. D. (1995). The science of complexity: An alternative perspective for strategic change processes. *Strategic Management Journal, 16,* 477–495.

Stacey, R. D. (1996). *Complexity and creativity in organizations.* London: Berrett-Koehler.

Stanley, S. M. (1979). *Macroevolution: Pattern and process.* San Francisco: W. H. Freeman.

Stanley, S. M. (1981). *The new evolutionary timetable.* New York: Basic Books.

Starbuck, W. H. (1983). Organizations as action generators. *American Sociological Review, 48,* 91–102.

Stinchcombe, A. L. (1965). Social structure and organizations. In J. G. March (Ed.), *Handbook of organizations* (pp. 153–193). Chicago: Rand McNally.

Stinchcombe, A. L. (1968). *Constructing social theories.* Chicago: University of Chicago Press.

Suchman, M. C. (1995). Localism and globalism in institutional analysis: The emergence of contractual norms in venture finance. In W. R. Scott & S. Christensen (Eds.), *The institutional construction of organizations* (pp. 39–63). Thousand Oaks, CA: Sage.

Sutton, J. R. & Dobbin, F. (1996). The two faces of governance: Responses to legal uncertainty in U.S.

firms, 1955 to 1986. *American Sociological Review*, 61, 794–811.

Thietart, R. A. & Forgues, B. (1995). Chaos theory and organization. *Organization Science*, 6, 19–31.

Tilly, C. (1978). *From mobilization to revolution*. Reading, MA: Addison-Wesley.

Tucker, D. J., Baum, J. A. C., & Singh, J. V. (1992). The institutional ecology of human service organizations. In Y. Hasenfeld (Ed.), *Human service organizations* (pp. 47–72). Newbury Park, CA: Sage.

Tushman, M. L. & Anderson, P. (1986). Technological discontinuities and organizational environments. *Administrative Science Quarterly*, 31, 439–465.

Tushman, M. L. & Romanelli, E. (1985). Organizational evolution: A metamorphosis model of convergence and reorientation. *Research in Organizational Behavior* (Vol. 7, pp. 171–222). Greenwich, CT: JAI Press.

Tushman, M. L. & Rosenkopf, L. (1992). Organizational determinants of technological change: Toward a sociology of technological evolution. In *Research in organizational behavior* (Vol. 14, pp. 311–347). Greenwich, CT: JAI Press.

Tyre, M. J. & Orlikowski, W. J. (1994). Windows of opportunity: Temporal patterns of technological adaptation in organizations. *Organization Science*, 5, 98–118.

Van de Ven, A. H. & Garud, R. (1989). A framework for understanding the emergence of new industries. In R. Rosenbloom (Ed.), *Research on technological innovation, management, and policy* (pp. 195–225). Greenwich, CT: JAI Press.

Van de Ven, A. H. & Garud, R. (1993). Innovation and industry development: That case of cochlear implants. In R. Burgelman & R. Rosenbloom (Eds.), *Research on technological innovation, management, and policy* (Vol. 5, pp. 1–46). Greenwich, CT: JAI Press.

Van de Ven, A. H. & Grazman, D. N. (1999). Evolution in a nested hierarchy: A genealogy of twin cities' health care organizations, 1853–1995. In J. A. C.

Baum & B. McKelvey (Eds.), *Variations in organization science: In honor of Donald T. Campbell* (pp. 185–209). Thousand Oaks, CA: Sage.

Von Burg, U. & Kenney, M. (2000). Venture capital and the birth of the local area networking industry. *Research Policy*, 29, 1135–1155.

Wholey, D. R., Christianson, J. B., & Sanchez, S. M. (1992). Organizational size and failure among health maintenance organizations. *American Sociological Review*, 57, 829–842.

Williams, G. C. (1966). *Adaptation and natural selection: A critique of some current evolutionary thought*. Princeton, NJ: Princeton University Press.

Williamson, O. E. (1975). *Markets and hierarchies*. New York: Free Press.

Williamson, O. E. (1991). Comparative economic organization: The analysis of discrete structural alternatives. *Administrative Science Quarterly*, 36, 269–296.

Wilson, D. S. (1997). Biological communities as functionally organized units. *Ecology*, 78, 2018–2024.

Wilson, D. S. & Sober, E. (1989). Reviving the superorganism. *Journal of Theoretical Biology*, 136, 337–356.

Wilson, D. S. & Sober, E. (1994). Re-introducing group selection to the human behavioral sciences. *Behavioral and Brain Sciences*, 17, 585–654.

Winter, S. G. (1988). On Coase, competence and the corporation. *Journal of Law, Economics, and Organization*, 4, 163–180.

Winter, S. G. (1990). Survival, selection, and inheritance in evolutionary theories of organization. In J. V. Singh (Ed.), *Organizational evolution: New directions* (pp. 269–297). Newbury Park, CA: Sage.

Zucker, L. G. (1977). The role of institutionalization in cultural persistence. *American Sociological Review*, 42, 726–743.

Zuscovitch, E. (1986). The economic dynamics of technological development. *Research Policy*, 15, 175–186.

9

Social, Technical, and Institutional Change

A Literature Review and Synthesis

Andrew H. Van de Ven & Timothy J. Hargrave

What explains the dramatic technical and social changes observed in much of the world during the past century? Responses to this kind of question vary, depending on the degree to which one assumes that social life is a product of individualism or institutionalism. Individualists view social and economic change as the product of individual agency, where purposeful and goal-directed individuals exercise their free wills to construct social arrangements that satisfy their self-interests and values. Institutionalists take a more macro and structural view. While not necessarily denying the agency of individuals, they see human action as largely conditioned by institutions. Institutions are social structures that are constructed by humans to provide stability and meaning to life. They are the "rules of the game" (North, 1990) that both enable and constrain human behavior.

The tension and interplay between the utility-maximizing behavior of individuals and the deterministic effects of institutions—i.e., between action and structure—have been constant themes in social and economic theorizing (Hirsch and Lounsbury, 1997; Poole and Van de Ven, 1989). In economics,

institutionalism emerged at the end of the nineteenth century in reaction to the assumptions of methodological individualism of classical economics that viewed human beings as rational, utility maximizing, and atomized (Dorfman, 1963). Some of the "old" institutional economists—Veblen, Mitchell, Ayres— were primarily interested in the emergence and diffusion of "taken for granted" customs and habits, while others such as Commons focused on social movements (e.g., labor unionization and monopoly busting) and examined how institutional working rules are created to address disputes and injustices among parties and classes with unequal power and diverse interests.

In the last quarter of the twentieth century, a new school of institutionalism emerged among organizational sociologists to address questions of how and why organizations adopt similar institutional arrangements. Powell and DiMaggio (1991) note that this new institutionalism was built on the foundation laid by the "cognitive revolution" in sociology, ethnomethodology (Garfinkel, 1967), and social construction theory (Berger and Luckmann, 1967). It viewed institutionalization as a collective framing process that treated rules, values, and conflict as peripheral and less important than cognitive processes. The new institutionalists viewed the social construction of scripts, norms, and classifications as the "stuff of which institutions are made" (Powell and DiMaggio, 1991, p. 15). Some also adopted a population-level evolutionary approach that marginalized the purposive actions and frames of divergent interest groups in changing institutions. As we shall see, some neoinstitutional scholars have begun to address this shortcoming by examining the interplay between structural determinism and individual agency.

Scholars in two other areas have studied institutional change. Social movement scholars have focused on the institutional changes that occur through protests, political action, and grassroots mobilization campaigns to address racism, war, atomic weapons, gender issues, environmental degradation, and other social issues. Technology scholars have called attention to the interdependence of technical, social, and institutional change in their studies of technological innovations, entrepreneurship, and industry emergence. Scholars in both of these areas have focused on processes of collective action, as well as interest-seeking actions that actors take to influence these processes.

Recently scholars have observed striking similarities in the literatures on social, technical, and institutional change (Campbell 2002; McAdam and Scott, 2002; Ruttan, 2001). They have called for a broader and more systematic mapping of the common ground shared by these fields. By way of a literature review, this chapter attempts to provide such a mapping. We discuss the major conceptual and empirical works from the old school of institutional economics, the new school of institutional theory found in organization theory and sociology, the work on technology innovation and industry emergence in the management literature, and the social movements literature produced by sociologists and political scientists. Our focus is on the work that examines the dynamic interactions among institutions, technological innovations, and social movements. We identify similarities and differences among these fields of scholarship and reveal some of the value-added contributions that each field makes to understand institutional change.

Our emphasis is on institutional change rather than on institutional theory per se. We see the study

of institutional change as particularly important for several reasons. First, institutions become important when crucial matters are at stake. In reading Meyer and Rowan (1977) one might mistakenly conclude that institutions are symbolic myths that serve no useful purpose other than to provide a camouflage that makes an organization appear legitimate because its practices conform to societal expectations. On the contrary, Stinchcombe (1997) argued that institutional formality and rituals increase with the substantive importance of the issue or decision being determined, because the reason for having things institutionalized is that they matter.

> Or to put it the other way around, when the value system informing an institution ranks something as of high priority, it is more likely that the keepers of the institution will formalize conformity with the institution in a ritual designed to monitor, enforce, and enact the value of that something. The higher the priority is, the higher the formality and ritual. The more ritualized a thing is in an institution, the less it is merely a ritual because the more substantively important it is.... example in evidence law: the more justice depends on a bit of evidence, the more formal evidence law there is about the introduction of that evidence. (Stinchcombe, 1997, p. 10)

A second important reason to study institutional change is that it provides a plausible alternative way to understand processes of change in the emerging new economy that traditional theories of organization are ill equipped to explain. Davis and McAdam (2000) argue that increasingly, "boundaryless" production processes, the predominance of evaluative standards based in financial markets, and the social and political processes shaping the structure and evolution of organizations are undermining the explanatory usefulness of organization theories such as resource dependence and population ecology. Theories of institutional change and social movements may provide explanations better suited for cooperative and competitive collective action among networks of organizations and other institutional actors in this postindustrial economy. To realize this potential, however, neoinstitutional theory's static view of institutions as immutable, persistent structural forces must be revised and extended. A focus on institutional change has been relatively neglected in the recent institutional literature.

The next sections of this introduction define basic concepts and provide a framework for analyzing institutional change. We identify four distinct perspectives on institutional change, which we define as institutional design, institutional adaptation, institutional diffusion, and collective action. Part 2 of the chapter reviews the works associated with each of these perspectives. We cover both seminal theoretical pieces and empirical studies. The concluding part of the chapter discusses major themes in the literature on institutional change and a synthesis of the perspectives.

Definitions

North (1990, p. 3) defines institutions as "the rules of the game in a society, or more formally,...the humanly devised constraints that shape human interaction." They are socially constructed to make life stable and meaningful, and they both constrain and enable action. Scott (2001) describes institutions as being composed of cultural-cognitive, normative, and regulative elements or "pillars." Although Scott emphasizes the cultural-cognitive aspects of institutions, he views "institution" as being a multidimensional concept. That is, the cognitive, normative, and regulative pillars represent three different dimensions of a single institution. The relative salience of these dimensions varies with the questions being addressed. For example, because the old institutionalists (such as Commons, 1934/1961; 1950) addressed questions of designing enforceable institutional rules for settling disputes and injustices among opposing parties, they focused on the regulative dimension of institutions.

Neoinstitutionalists focus on the cognitive-cultural dimension of institutions largely because it fits their research question of how institutions reproduce and spread. They have been most concerned with how institutions become taken-for-granted mental frameworks that ease information processing and decision-making and enable actors to make sense of the world. They view institutions, once formed, as powerful forces that shape the behavior of individuals and organizations. They establish how the actor's world must be, should be, and even the cognitive view of what the world is. Neoinstitutional theorists such as Tolbert and Zucker (1996) have focused on institutionalization, which is the process by which institutions are diffused and formalized—that is, the

process by which institutions become taken for granted and experienced by institutional actors as objective reality rather than socially constructed.

Following Leonid Hurwicz (1993), we distinguish institutional actors (or entities) from institutional arrangements, with the term *institution* referring to the latter. This is a distinction that not all institutional scholars make. We think that this distinction is important, particularly in light of a tendency in the literature to overlook or not examine the institutional and legal bases of organizations. It is only by virtue of an institutional arrangement that an organization can act as though it is a person with specifically designated rights and duties.

Part of the difficulty in understanding institutions is their pervasiveness and diversity. An institutional arrangement may be very simple (e.g., a stoplight or school bell) or complex and highly contested (e.g., stem-cell cloning, environmental laws, auditing and consulting practices by accounting firms). The institutional arrangement may apply to a single institutional actor (e.g., a firm's internal hiring and promotion policies), to organizations in an industry or population (e.g., technology standards, rules of market competition, or a particular organizational form), to all citizens of a country (e.g., taxation, property rights, civil liberties laws), or to people in multiple countries (e.g., human rights laws, tariff and trade agreements, international environmental treaties, foreign currency values).

We define institutional change as the difference in form, quality, or state over time in an institution. Change in an institutional arrangement can be determined by observing the arrangement at two or more points in time on a set of dimensions (e.g., cognitive, normative, or regulative clarity) and then calculating the differences over time in these dimensions. If there is a noticeable difference, we can say that the institutional arrangement has changed. Much of the voluminous literature on institutional change focuses on the nature of this difference, what produced it, and its consequences. Somewhat less attention has been given to the processes of institutional change.

Two different definitions of process are often used in the literature: (1) a category of concepts or variables that pertain to actions and activities, and (2) a narrative describing how things develop and change (Van de Ven, 1992). When the first definition is used, process is typically associated with a "variance theory" (Mohr, 1982) of change, in which a set of independent variables statistically explains variations in some outcome criteria (dependent variables). The second meaning of process is often associated with a "process theory" explanation of the temporal order and sequence in which a discrete set of change events occurs based on a story or historical narrative (Abbott, 1988; Pentland, 1999; Poole, Van de Ven, Dooley, and Holmes, 2000). In this usage, the issue of "how change unfolds" is addressed by narrating the temporal sequence of events that unfold in an institutional arrangement.

In our literature review, we identify particular works as process theories or variance theories. While examples of process theories and variance theories can be found in each of the four perspectives on change identified in this chapter, most work to date on institutional change has been concerned with variance theory. While a single study will typically employ either a variance theory or a process theory but not both, the two approaches are not theoretically mutually exclusive and in fact can be complementary. Poole et al. (2000, chapter 2) provide further discussion of the important distinctions between variance and process theories.

Institutional scholars have an ongoing debate about whether institutional change is continuous and evolutionary or discontinuous and revolutionary (e.g., Rutherford, 1994; Greenwood and Hinings, 1996; Meyer, Goes, and Brooks, 1993; Tushman and Romanelli, 1985). We agree with Campbell (2001) that the distinction between evolutionary and revolutionary change is largely a function of level of analysis and time scale of the change process. What appears to be discontinuous change from a distance may upon closer inspection be found to be gradual and continuous. For example, in their study of post-communist Eastern Europe and the former Soviet Union, Campbell and Pedersen (1996) demonstrate that seemingly revolutionary changes in national governance structures were in fact the result of more evolutionary changes in discursive structures that came about through bricolage.

Some scholars have developed different models for distinguishing continuous (incremental, evolutionary) from discontinuous (punctuated equilibrium) patterns of change. We question whether these different models are useful. Whether change proceeds at incremental (slow, gradual) or radical (fast, sudden) rates is an empirical question. Adopting different models to explain different magnitudes of change observed along a distribution does not appear to be a good strategy for building a general and parsimonious theory. A single theory would be much more useful and robust. In fact, punctuated equilibrium theory has been found to be a member of a much broader class of nonlinear dynamics reflecting an inverse power function (Dooley and Van de Ven, 1999; Poole et al., 2000). This is quite exciting, for it suggests that it may be possible to develop a single theory (with a common generating mechanism) that can explain the wide distributions in the magnitudes and rates of changes observed in the empirical world.

A Framework for Guiding the Literature Review

Unfortunately, our review of the sprawling interdisciplinary literature on institutional change cannot be integrated into a single perspective. Scholars have not converged on a single question or theory of change. Instead, we think they have converged on four distinct perspectives of institutional change. Each perspective addresses different questions and relies on a unique generative mechanism or motor to explain change. We label the four perspectives institutional design, institutional adaptation, institutional diffusion, and collective action. The distinguishing dimensions of these four perspectives are outlined in table 9.1 and summarized below.

The institutional design perspective focuses on the purposeful creation or revision of institutions to address conflicts or social injustices. The generative mechanism for addressing questions of how institutions are created and emerge is a purposeful enactment and social construction. In this view, institutions reflect the pursuit of conscious choices and behavior that society judges to be prudent and reasonable.

The institutional adaptation perspective seeks to explain how and why organizations conform to forces in the institutional environment. Scott (2001) notes that since Meyer and Rowan's seminal 1977 work, organizational sociologists have focused their attention on the issue of how the institutional environment shapes organizational structure. The work of these new institutionalists can be characterized as taking an institutional adaptation perspective.

The institutional diffusion perspective focuses on how and why specific institutions are adopted (selected) and diffused (retained) in a population.

Table 9.1 Distinguishing dimensions of four perspectives on institutional change

Dimension	Institutional Design	Institutional Adaptation	Institutional Diffusion	Collective Action
Question	What actions and roles do individual actors undertake to create or change an institutional arrangement?	How do individual organizations adapt to their institutional environment? Why do organizations adopt similar institutions?	How do institutional arrangements reproduce, diffuse, or decline in a population or organizational field? Why are organizations so alike?	How do institutions emerge to facilitate or constrain social movements or technological innovations?
Focal institutional actors	Individual entrepreneurial actor(s) with bounded agency: affordance and partisan mutual adjustment	Individual organizational actors adapting (proactively or reactively) to institutional environments	Population or industry of organizations exposed to same institutional environment	Networks of distributed and partisan actors in an interorganizational field who are embedded in a collective process of creating or revising institutions
Generative mechanism	Purposeful social construction and strategies by actor to solve a problem or correct an injustice	Institutional environmental beliefs, pressures, or regulations to which organizational actor must adapt to be legitimate	Competition for scarce resources forces actors to imitate and conform to legitimate institutional practices	Recognition of an institutional problem, barrier, or injustice among groups of social or technical entrepreneurs
Process: event sequence	A dialectical process of creating working rules that resolve conflicts or address unprecedented cases	Coercive, normative, and mimetic processes of internal organizational adaptation and change	Evolutionary processes of variation, selection, and retention of institutional forms	Collective political events dealing with processes of framing and mobilizing structures and opportunities for institutional reform
Outcome	New "rules of the game" that enable and constrain actors by changing their rights, duties, or roles	Organizational legitimacy by adopting isomorphic institutional arrangements	Institutionalization or deinstituitionalization of institutional arrangements in a population of actors	Institutional precedent, a new or changed working rule, an institutional innovation

Here institutional theory has borrowed and extended organizational ecology and evolution. Population ecologists have used density dependence arguments to explain the legitimacy and competitive selection of certain institutional forms.

Collective action models focus on processes of institutional change at the interorganizational field level. These processes are initiated by social movements and entrepreneurs pursuing technological innovations. Scholars working from this perspective are primarily concerned with how new institutional arrangements emerge from interactions among interdependent partisan agents.

We will review these four perspectives of institutional change in the historical sequence in which they emerged, beginning with institutional design, then institutional adaptation, diffusion, and collective action. Once they emerged historically, the perspectives have progressed simultaneously and occasionally in reaction to each other.

Before launching into the four perspectives, we confess that our literature review is not comprehensive. We focus only on those works that we believe represent the leading theoretical contributions and exemplary empirical studies in each perspective. The literature is too extensive to cover completely. We also caution that our classification of theories and research studies does not apply to their authors. We wish to avoid typecasting individual scholars. Many have written about and studied institutional change from multiple perspectives. With time their thinking evolves. In the conclusion we suggest that initially the distinctions between the four perspectives were sharp and crisp, but they are becoming more blurred as scholars recognize the shortcomings of each perspective and grope for a more general theory of institutional change.

Perspectives on Institutional Change

Institutional Design

Scholars taking an institutional design perspective have been concerned with the actions that individual actors take to create or change institutional arrangements. They view institutions to be a reflection of conscious, intentional decisions and actions. These scholars have tended to focus their attention on injustice and unequal power relations; consequently, they have given attention to the dialectical processes by which working rules are developed to resolve conflicts. These working rules are not necessarily rational but rather reflect consensus on what is prudent and reasonable. They are the "rules of the game" that enable and constrain actors by changing their rights, duties, or roles.

Institutional Design and the Old Institutionalists

The institutional design perspective was introduced by the old institutional economists, and in particular by John R. Commons. In *The Economics of Collective Action* (1950), in which Commons attempts to simplify the arguments he made in *Legal Foundations of Capitalism* (1924/1968) and *Institutional Economics* (1934/1961), Commons presents a "pragmatic and volitional theory of institutions" (Van de Ven, 1993) that seeks to reconcile power and freedom. Commons argued that individuals are not self-sufficient independent entities, and society is not the simple aggregation of individual members. The norms, customs, and laws that regulate and provide security of expectation to the actions of individuals and organizations are the "working rules" of collective action. These institutional working rules control, liberate, and expand individual action by specifying the rights and duties of individuals and organizations. Institutions control individual behavior through physical, moral, or economic sanctions. Institutions do not simply constrain, however; they also liberate and expand individual action. Liberation for some individuals (e.g., from coercion, duress, or discrimination) may be achieved by constraining the acts of others. Commons emphasized that individual freedom is not a natural right; he viewed it as a collective achievement. "The only way in which 'liberty' can be obtained is by imposing duties on others who might interfere with the activity of the 'liberated' individual" (Commons, 1950, p. 35). Thus, Commons viewed institutions as literally the means to individual liberty.

Just as institutions constrain, liberate, and expand individual action, individuals construct and change institutions. Commons rejected natural selection and replaced it with artificial (i.e., purposeful) selection, noting that individuals adapt their environments to their own needs and purposes. He argued that individuals have capabilities, in their own nature, of molding natural and institutional forces around them. As a consequence, institutional change is subject to individual volition, purpose, and will.

Commons provided three operational concepts for examining the human will in action: performance, avoidance, and forbearance. "In choosing, which includes acting, the will is purposeful—forward looking. The will is always up against something. It is always performing, avoiding, forbearing, that is, always moving along lines . . . with a purpose looking toward the future" (Commons, 1950, p. 79). An individual performs by undertaking a behavioral act, which is limited or constrained by avoidance and forbearance. Avoidance is a choice to omit all alternative courses of action other than the one chosen. Although some alternatives may be avoided because of institutional rules or constraints of nature, the individual has freedom to choose from a remaining set of alternatives available to him or her. Within the direction of the alternative chosen, performance is further modified by forbearance, or the degree of power exercised at the "right" time, place, and degree. Forbearance is self-restraint in action either with nature or in transactions with others. "The human will does not override natural laws, but makes use of them in accomplishing its purposes" (Commons, 1950, p. 193). Unlike physical forces (e.g., gravity) that always go to the limit, individuals place limits on their own performances by forbearing in the exercise of their full power, except in times of crises. In Commons's framework, these times of crisis were the "limiting factors" that triggered opportunities for institutional change. They occurred when individuals were engaged in strategic (novel or disputed) transactions to gain control over the "limiting factors" that prevented otherwise routine transactions from working to bring about intended results.

Commons offered a dialectical and pragmatic view of institutional change. Changes to the working rules come from customs, norms, and laws that evolve historically in a society, which in turn are produced by an accretion of numerous common practices and by decisions among contestants and ultimately by courts in resolving disputes. Institutional working rules change incrementally over time as a result of precedents that are established when the validity of transactions among contesting parties is questioned and judged by arbitrators or courts of law to be legal or illegal, given what a "prudent reasonable man" would do under the new set of circumstances. Procedures for due process and appeal not only resolve disputes between plaintiffs and defendants, but they more significantly set precedents for resolving future similar disputes. Precedents thereby become the customs and laws for the repetition of activities by which expectations are made secure.

To Commons, the institutions existing at a specific time represent nothing more than imperfect and pragmatic solutions to reconcile past conflicts. These institutional solutions consist of a set of rights and duties for individuals, an authority for enforcing them, and some degree of adherence to societal norms of prudent reasonable behavior. Commons thought of institutional history as a process of willful selection of one set of institutional practices over alternative sets—a process of pragmatic decision making involving "the discovery through investigation and negotiation of what is the best practicable thing to do under the actual circumstances of conflicting interests, organized as they are, to impose their collective wills on individuals and each other" (Commons, 1950, p. 25). Without an institutional system of working rules to create a degree of order and predictability for individuals, there could be "little or no present value, present enterprise, present transactions, or present employment" (p. 104).

The economist who has most clearly carried on the tradition of Commons is Douglas C. North. In *Institutions, Institutional Change, and Economic Performance* (1990), North argues that the economic success achieved in some countries is attributable to the establishment of institutions that facilitate complex exchange. He writes that institutions, which he defines as the formal and informal "rules of the game," reduce the costs of exchange and production by defining opportunities and directing effort. North states that the institutional framework must be stable if complex exchange is to occur, and he argues that stability is normally obtains because the rules of the game—routines, customs, norms, laws—are complex and interdependent. Because the web of constraints is so dense and complex and because a symbiotic relationship develops between institutions and organizations, institutional change is overwhelmingly incremental. Discontinuous change to a substantially different set of institutions therefore would be extremely costly.

North views changes in real prices—changes in material conditions—as the most important source of institutional change. For North, organizations respond to changes in real prices by either adapting or by trying to change the institutional framework; they choose the latter when doing so is efficient and when they have sufficient bargaining power. North believes that changes in tastes—ideas—are also an important source of institutional change. Like Commons, North argues that institutions make freedom possible. But reflecting more of a rational-choice perspective, North argues that the desire for individual freedom precedes and motivates the establishment of institutions. For North it is the demand for freedom that drives the creation and maintenance of the appropriate institutional form.

Two additional economists who contribute to our understanding of institutional design are Vernon Ruttan and Leonid Hurwicz. In *Toward a Theory of Induced Institutional Innovation* (1984), Ruttan and Yujiro Hayami present a model of institutional change that considers the relationships between resource endowments, technology, cultural endowments, and institutions. Ruttan and Hayami draw on agricultural history to argue that changes in the demand for institutional innovation are induced by changes in relative resource endowments and by technical change, and that the supply of institutional change is a function of the cost of achieving consensus or suppressing opposition. Ruttan (2001) views institutional change as endogenous to the system under investigation, and as induced by technological and resource factors. However, he takes issue with an "institutional determinism" perspective, such as North's, arguing that discussions of the relative impact of technical, institutional, and social forces on one another are pointless because these forces are highly interdependent and coevolve.

Leonid Hurwicz (1987) has taken a game-theoretic approach to institutional change in which he models the moves or strategies of actors as shaped by institutional rules. Hurwicz views macro processes of institutional change as both deliberate and evolutionary, writing that "some institutional changes may be viewed as purely evolutionary phenomena, induced (as analyzed by Ruttan) by changes in external factors.... But often these changes contain an important element of conscious design and produce an institutional framework different from anything that existed before. It may not be incorrect to view the new institutions as invented" (1987, p. 395). Hurwicz links design and evolutionary processes of change, asserting that "when underlying conditions (e.g., technology, tastes, or attitudes) change, this may create a need, and demand, for institutional innovation, and the process of satisfying this demand may involve conscious design activities. Legislation is one example of such a process" (1993, p. 58).

The sociologist Philip Selznick extended the institutional design tradition initiated by Commons. In *Leadership in Administration* (1957), in which he draws on his classic 1949 *TVA and the Grass Roots*, Selznick wrote that an organization is an expendable tool that becomes an institution only when its leader infuses it with value. Through the process of institutionalization the organization acquires a unique identity, special values, and a distinctive competence; at the same time, individuals absorb a way of perceiving and evaluating experience. For Selznick, institutional change occurs in organizations through processes that are intentionally initiated and shepherded by organizational leaders.

Institutional Design and the New Institutionalists

More recently, neoinstitutionalists have begun to challenge their own view that institutions are unyielding structures that condition the characteristics and actions of organizations (Powell and DiMaggio, 1991; Scott, 2001). Stinchcombe (1997) urged sociologists to "put the guts"—the people—back into institutional theory, arguing that institutions—by which he means institutional entities, using our definitions—work well when they are staffed by people who make moral commitments, conduct their business with integrity, and are held to the standards that they were created to uphold. Stinchcombe reviews John Henry Wigmore's work on appellate courts, which emphasized that institutional legitimacy comes not through demanding obedience but through upholding deep values. Stinchcombe also discusses the emergence of capitalism in Eastern Europe and the former Soviet Union, asserting that capitalism is not serving society well there due to a lack of institutions, which cannot be created because of a lack of commitment to values of commercial honesty. Stinchcombe sees the expression of deep values as the motor driving institutional change.

Barley and Tolbert (1997) adopt Giddens's (1984) structuration model to remedy the lack of agency in neoinstitutional theory. Barley and Tolbert write that institutions and actions exist in separate realms of social order that are mediated by "modalities" (stocks of practical knowledge that include interpretive schemes, resources, and norms adapted to a particular setting). These modalities "influence how people communicate, enact power, and determine what behaviours to sanction and reward" (p. 98).[1] Barley and Tolbert propose four stages to the process of institutionalization: encoding, which frequently takes place during socialization; enactment, which "may or may not entail conscious choice or an awareness of alternatives"; revision or replication, which they believe occurs more frequently as a result of intentional choice rather than unconscious, unintended deviations from scripts; and objectification or externalization, which "involves the disassociation of patterns with particular actors and particular historical circumstances" (p. 102). At this stage, the patterns take on a factual quality. Barley and Tolbert write that institutions "set bounds on rationality by restricting the opportunities and alternatives we perceive" but that "through choice and action, individuals and organizations can deliberately modify, and even eliminate institutions" (p. 94). They see institutional change as primarily endogenous to the system of study, and as more likely to be intentional rather than unconscious.

Oliver (1991) seeks to redress neoinstitutional theory's early lack of attention to human agency by describing five strategic responses to institutional pressures, each with its own set of tactical options (noted in parentheses): acquiescence (habit, imitation, compliance), compromise (balance, pacification, bargaining), avoidance (concealment, buffering, escape), defiance (dismissal, challenge, attack), and manipulation (co-optation, influence, control). Oliver argues that the response of an organization to institutional pressure will depend on the cause of the pressure, the constituents imposing pressure, the content of the pressure, the method of control being imposed, and the context. She suggests that organizations do not simply conform to institutional pressures but respond purposively to them and in some cases modify them.

Brint and Karabel (1991) provide empirical evidence of institutional design. They found that the "vocationalization" of community colleges is explained not by consumer choice or business domination of the colleges but instead by the intentional actions of community college leaders in response to environmental pressures and opportunities. Brint and Karabel found that the leaders of community colleges first began to pursue vocationalization in the 1920s, but that their interests were constrained by the predominance of four-year colleges as training grounds; by business organizations, which often prefer to train their employees themselves; and by governmental bodies, which accredited the junior colleges. Gradually, however, community college leaders became aware that an opportunity existed for them to become the training ground for midlevel quasi-professionals. They were able to realize their interests when the college labor market declined in 1970.

Strategies and Tactics

Several scholars have contributed to our understanding of institutional design by describing strategies and tactics that actors employ in trying to effect change. In *The Intelligence of Democracy* (1965), Charles E. Lindblom provides an account of the inner workings of the process of "partisan mutual adjustment." This is the public policy-making process by which interdependent, opposing forces reach mutual decisions. Lindblom describes the methods that an individual actor may employ when facing policy opponents. Adaptive methods are those where one actor does not seek a response from the other (e.g., deference), while manipulative methods are those where one actor does seek a response from the other. These manipulative methods include bargaining, compensation, reciprocity, and unconditional manipulation, among others. Lindblom wrote that participants in the process of partisan mutual adjustment manipulate each other though persuasion, authority, appeals to conventions, votes, and wealth.

Saul Alinsky, the noted labor organizer, also provided very specific advice for actors engaged in dialectical conflict. In *Rules for Radicals: A Practical Primer for Realistic Radicals* (1971), Alinsky enumerated thirteen political tactics for social activists struggling against powerful opponents. These tactics stress attack much more than forbearance. Fligstein (1997) echoes Alinsky, describing the social skills that the institutional entrepreneur needs to effect institutional change. Some of these, such as "setting the agenda for others," can be characterized as manipulative, while others can be characterized as adaptive or as a form of affordance—that is, "taking what the system gives."

Summary

Commons and economists that have followed him such as North, Ruttan, and Hurwicz have viewed institutions as working rules that emerge to address human problems and that change through the interaction of agents. Commons and North both have described institutional change as gradual, incremental, and deliberate, occurring through processes of collective action that resolve conflicts among individuals that are brought into opposition by resource scarcity. North and others have also argued that ideas and not just material conditions can bring about dialectical change.

Recently, some new institutional scholars have begun to take a design perspective on institutional change, albeit with a focus on the cognitive rather than on norms and values. For them, designed institutional change is not so much about the need to address social problems and remedy injustices, as it was for Commons, but instead occurs when actors question taken-for-granted "scripts." One especially notable work in this area is Barley and Tolbert's (1997) process model of institutional change. This paper, which is one of the few process-oriented works that takes an institutional design perspective, builds off of Giddens's structuration theory, which seeks to reconcile deterministic institutional pressures with conscious, intentional action.

Finally, we note that some scholars have "zoomed in" on the tactics and strategies employed by social change agents. These commentators have identified both manipulative and adaptive methods that actors have used in their pursuit of institutional change.

Institutional Adaptation

Much of the work of the new organizational institutionalists can be characterized as taking an institutional adaptation perspective. The central question being addressed by neoinstitutionalists is, Why do organizations look so similar? Their answer is that organizations look alike because they must conform to norms, beliefs, and rules in the institutional environment in order to achieve legitimacy, which enables them to acquire resources and improve their chances of survival. Unlike the other three perspectives, the institutional adaptation perspective is primarily concerned with changes in the characteristics of institutional actors in response to institutional arrangements in organizational environments.

Scott (2001) notes that Weber (1924/1968) was "among the first social theorists to call attention to the central importance of legitimacy in social life" and that Parsons (1960) was the first to link legitimacy to organizational goals. Scott interprets the emphasis of neoinstitutionalists on conformity with the institutional environment as an extension of open-systems theory, which transformed the organizations and strategic management literatures "by insisting on the importance of the wider environmental context as it constrains, shapes, penetrates, and renews the organization" (p. xx). Researchers first recognized that the technical environment imposed pressures on the organization and then in the 1970s came to see that organizations were also affected by their institutional environments (Scott, 2001).

Meyer and Rowan's (1977) *Institutionalized Organizations: Formal Structure as Myth and Ceremony* was the first work to put forth the thesis that organizations adapt their structures to conform to the pressures of the institutional environment. Meyer and Rowan argue that modernization drives the development and rationalization of institutionalized rules and elements of organizational structure, and that the organization's concern for legitimacy and survival causes it to adopt these institutional arrangements. Meyer and Rowan trace the origin of rational institutional myths to the elaboration of complex relational networks, the degree of collective organization of the environment, and the leadership efforts of local organizations. They argue that because conformity with institutionalized rules can conflict with technical efficiency considerations, organizations must decouple their structures from technical activities so that institutional "myths" are upheld and legitimacy is attained, yet at the same time technical efficiency is achieved. While Meyer and Rowan emphasize the conditioning effect of the institutional environment on organizational structure, they also write that powerful organizations often impose their practices and procedures on other organizations as well as actively attempt to build their goals and procedures directly into society as institutional rules. Thus their deterministic theory does not deny agency.

Another seminal contribution is DiMaggio and Powell's (1983) *The Iron Cage Revisited: Institutional Isomorphism and Collective Rationality in Organizational Fields*. DiMaggio and Powell argue that in modern societies, the rationalization of organizations proceeds not so much because of the demands of the marketplace but because of homogenizing pressure from the state and professions. They describe the coercive, normative, and mimetic processes that cause organizations to adopt similar structural characteristics. Coercive pressures are those which come in the form of force, persuasion, or the invitation to collude; mimetic isomorphic pressures are found when an organization feels compelled to respond to uncertainty by mimicking another organization; and normative pressures are exerted by professional networks, which diffuse organizational norms developed at universities and other training institutions. Scott (1987) expanded on DiMaggio and Powell's categorization of institutional pressures, identifying seven distinct ways that institutions exert pressures on organizational structure. They include the imposition, authorization, inducement, acquisition, imprinting, incorporation, and bypassing of organizational structures.

Most empirical studies have found that organizations conform to pressures of their prevailing institutionalized environments (Leblebici and Salancik, 1982; Mezias, 1990; Perrow, 1991; Hoffman, 1997; Thornton, 2002). Under conditions of uncertainty, organizational decision makers will mimic the behavior of other organizations, particularly those to which they are strongly linked in their network (Galaskiewicz and Wasserman, 1989). Moreover, Deephouse (1996) found that organizational isomorphism (the degree to which organizations adopt similar structures, strategies, and processes) is a significant predictor of organizational legitimacy (the acceptance of an organization by its external environment).

Hoffman (1997) provides strong empirical evidence of institutional isomorphism with his analysis of how petroleum and chemical companies moved from strongly resisting environmentalism to proactive environmental management from 1960 to 1993. He argues that shifts in the constituency of the organizational field drove changes in the field's institutions, which in turn led to changes in organizational structure and culture. Hoffman describes four stages in corporate environmentalism: industrial environmentalism (1960–1970), regulatory environmentalism (1970–1982), environmentalism as social responsibility (1982–1988), and strategic environmentalism (1988–1993). During the period of industrial environmentalism, industry viewed pollution as a problem that it could handle itself. After government and

activists entered the organization field, regulative institutions came to dominate the field and technical compliance with regulations became the dominant principle in industry. The third stage was marked by a decline in the credibility of regulators due to scandal, a change that led to the emergence of normative institutions as the dominant institutional pressure facing industry. The final stage, strategic environmentalism, emerged because investors and insurance companies entered the organizational field. This last stage was marked by the dominance of a cognitive frame in which environmental management had come to be taken for granted by industry.

Kraatz and Zajac (1996) found evidence that conflicts with the organizational adaptation perspective. They concluded that organizations make changes in response to the technical environment rather than conform to the demands of the institutional environment. Kraatz and Zajac examined the degree to which U.S. liberal arts colleges adopted professional and vocational programs during the period 1971 to 1986. Based on neoinstitutional theory, they hypothesized that to maintain legitimacy, the colleges under study would conform to prevailing norms and values that dictate that liberal arts colleges maintain their purity and resist the professionalization of their curricula. Kraatz and Zajac found support for none of their hypotheses, however. Instead, they found that colleges made changes that violated institutional norms; that they responded to their technical environments rather than institutional norms; that their structures diverged rather than converged; that less prestigious colleges did not emulate elite ones; that local conditions affected behavior more than institutional pressures did; and that colleges making illegitimate changes did not suffer harmful performance impacts. Kraatz and Zajac express surprise at their findings because they view the liberal arts college organizational field as a supportive testing ground for neoinstitutional theory.

Variable Organizational Responses to Institutional Pressures

While new institutional theorists initially expected to witness isomorphic behavior among organizations, many scholars have since recognized that organizational responses to the institutional environment are contingent upon a variety of factors, such as organizational attributes (e.g., size, performance, CEO background, and degree of unionization), linkages with other actors in the environment, and the location and status of an organization's reference group. Scott (2001) notes that institutional pressures vary with respect to their sources (for example, which agencies or publics confer legitimacy), the mechanisms by which they are transmitted (e.g., norms, laws), and their power to shape organizational structure. Finally, they also vary over time and space. Scott cites works by Dobbin, Edelman, Meyer, Scott, and Swidler (1988), Edelman (1992), Mezias (1990), Tolbert and Zucker (1983), and Fligstein (1985) as examples of studies that document variable institutional pressures.

Greenwood and Hinings (1996) explicitly address the interaction of organizational context and action. They argue that: (1) "organizational resistance to change derives from the normative embeddedness of an organization within an institutional context"; (2) the incidence and pace of radical organizational change will vary across institutional sectors because of differences in the structure of those sectors (the extent of tight coupling and the extent of sectoral permeability); and (3) the incidence and pace of institutional change will vary within sectors because of internal organizational dynamics. In particular, the level of "interest dissatisfaction" within an organization and the level of value commitments determine the organization's response to environmental pressure.

In a paper on the Canadian accounting profession, Greenwood, Suddaby, and Hinings (2002) document the shift in the profession from an "accounting and tax services only" business model to one of providing a broader array of business services. They present a process model of institutional change that includes the following stages:

1. A *precipitating jolt* that disturbs existing practices.
2. *Deinstitutionalization*, in which the socially constructed consensus is challenged and new actors and practices enter.
3. *Pre-institutionalization*, in which organizations innovate independently.
4. *Theorization*, in which deviations from prevailing conventions become abstracted and made available for wider adoption.
5. *Diffusion*, which occurs after successful theorization.
6. *Reinstitutionalization*, the stage at which new ideas, practices, and so on become fully institutionalized (taken for granted).

Greenwood et al. highlight the importance of stage 4, theorization, in this process. They argue that theorization is likely to be more important in highly institutionalized settings; further, they write that in settings in which instrumental logic dominates, legitimation is likely to take place during the diffusion process, whereas in more normative settings, legitimation must take place during the theorization stage. If it does not, then diffusion will not follow.

While Greenwood, Suddaby, and Hinings emphasize environmental pressure to change, they also call attention to the importance of deliberate collective action in the process of institutional change. They find that in the Canadian accounting industry, professional associations played an important role in endorsing institutional change by hosting intraprofessional discourse and representing the profession to the outside world. While change was initiated by the large accounting firms, the professional associations played a key role in legitimating change by making change seem normal and resistance to change unnatural. In chapter 10 of this volume, Hinings, Greenwood, Reay, and Suddaby offer a more general theoretical process model of institutional change at the level of the organizational field. This model is largely consistent with that of Greenwood, Suddaby, and Hinings (2002) but places even greater emphasis on collective action by theorizing the importance to the process of institutional change of conflict between competing institutional regimes.

Meyer et al. (1993) provide a fascinating account of the interplay between institutional pressure and strategic response. In a study of the San Francisco Bay Area hospital industry, they write that "distinct temporal shifts occur in modes of change and levels of change." They classify the 1960s as a period of evolution, the 1970s as a period of organizational adaptation, and the 1980s as a period of industry revolution and firm metamorphoses induced by resource scarcity. They find that in the California hospital industry, strategic reorientations were initiated in response to poor performance relative to competitors and that poor performers who made fundamental changes in response to "hyperturbulent" environments outperformed those who "displayed strategic persistence." However, they also found that strategic reorientations hurt the performance of formerly strong performers. Meyer and colleagues found that reorientations were more common when the industry was undergoing major change.

Another major longitudinal study of organizational adaptation to the institutional environment was conducted by Scott, Ruef, Mendel, and Caronna (1999). They assess the nature and extent of changes in health care delivery systems in the San Francisco Bay Area during the period 1945–1995. They identify three distinct institutional eras in health care delivery, each with its own dominant logic, institutional actors, and governance structure. Scott and colleagues describe the health care field during the period of study as being in the throes of destructuration, characterized by a breakdown in organizational forms, the dismantling of governance structures, and the dislodging of belief systems. They demonstrate that in the era of professional dominance hospitals were primarily independent, but by the era of managerial control they had become associated with integrated health care systems. Scott and colleagues view these changes as having occurred because of both pressures from the material environment—rising health care costs and technological developments—and institutional pressures such as federal legislation. With regard to institutional pressures, Scott et al. also note that it was not the transition from a logic of "professional authority" to a logic of "equity of access" per se that caused changes in organizational form; rather, it was new logics that resulted in a new governance and funding structure, which necessitated new organizational forms. Scott and his collaborators rely on the concept of structuration to explain their findings: "Structuration is the master process operating at the level of the organizational field as it relates to its wider environments—both material-resource and institutional" (p. 362). They argue that in a more structured organizational field, there is less room for autonomy and innovation.

Innovation scholars have also studied organizational responses to external environmental pressures for change. In comparison with the neoinstitutional studies summarized above, they have focused more directly on the activities and difficulties that adopters experience as they attempt to implement technical or institutional innovations that were developed externally and mandated on host organizations. Rogers (1995) emphasizes that it is misleading to assume that externally mandated innovations can be implemented by adopting organizations without their "reinvention." Reinvention is a process in which adopters modify an innovation to fit their local implementation setting. Rice and Rogers (1980) found

that reinvention is positively related to the adoption and implementation of innovations. They indicate that reinvention facilitates the transition of innovation ownership from developers to implementers and permits tailoring an innovation to the adopting organization's specific needs and constraints.

For example, Marcus and Weber (2001) describe the implications for organizational effectiveness of two different types of reactions by American electric power companies to new nuclear safety procedures mandated by the U.S. Nuclear Power Commission. They found that the nuclear power plants with relatively poor safety records tended to respond in a rule-bound manner that perpetuated their poor safety performance. Conversely, plants with relatively strong safety records tended to retain their autonomy by adapting the standards to their local situations, a response that reinforced their strong safety performance. They observed that those least ready or willing to adopt the innovation needed it the most.

Marcus and Weber (2001) point out an important implication of their study for managing externally imposed innovations: be forewarned of the possible consequences of passive acceptance of external dictates by those who strictly follow the letter of the law—they may be doing so in "bad faith" and may not achieve the results intended. Some autonomy is needed for an adopting unit to identify with and internalize an innovation; formal compliance is insufficient for innovation adoption. The disposition of innovation adopters is likely to be negatively affected if they are not granted a sufficient level of autonomy, and their disposition is often critical in assuring successful adoption. This evidence emphasizes the importance of overcoming resistance to change when imposing, or even suggesting, the adoption of innovations that did not originate in the adopting organization. The "not invented here" syndrome is well known in all sorts of organizations. Adopting organizations that have not developed a commitment to those innovations may behave "bureaupathically" by simply doing what the "letter of the law" stipulates (Kerr, 1975; Lawler and Rhode, 1976).

Lindquist and Mauriel (2001) compared two common alternative strategies for adopting and implementing a site-based management institutional innovation in public schools. One is a "depth" strategy, in which the innovation is implemented and "debugged" in a demonstration site before it is generalized to other organizational units. The other is a "breadth" strategy, in which the innovation is implemented through successive hierarchical levels across all organizational units simultaneously. Lindquist and Mauriel found that the school district that implemented the Site-Based Management innovation in "breadth"—across all schools in the district—was more successful in implementing and institutionalizing more components of the innovation than the school district that adopted the "depth" strategy within a school selected as the demonstration site. This finding is contrary to conventional wisdom that successfully implemented innovations start small and spread incrementally with success (Greiner, 1970). Lindquist and Mauriel (2001) provide several important generalizable explanations for this finding.

1. When the depth strategy is introduced and heralded by top management, the demonstration project soon loses visible attention and institutional legitimacy from top-level managers, as their agendas become preoccupied with other pressing management problems.
2. With a breadth strategy, top management stays in control of the innovation implementation process, increasing, rather than decreasing, its power. Moreover, slack resources within the control of top management can ensure success better than limited budgets for innovation to a demonstration site.
3. There is a tradeoff between implementing a few components of an innovation in breadth versus implementing all components in depth in a particular demonstration site. Fewer hurdles and resistances to change are encountered when a few—presumably the easy—components of an innovation are implemented across the board to a few supportive stakeholders, than when all components of a program are implemented in depth with all partisan stakeholders involved.
4. With a depth strategy, it is easier for opposing forces in other parts of the organization to mobilize efforts to sabotage a "favored" demonstration site than it is to produce positive evidence of the merits and generalizability of an innovation.

Bryson and Roering (2001) examined the introduction of an institutional innovation—the adoption of new planning systems—in six local governmental agencies. They found that each attempt at implementation was prone to disintegration. They identified several implementation impediments:

1. External events and crises frequently occur, distracting participants' attention and priorities and absorbing resources that are available to adopt the innovation.
2. The adoption process itself is partially cumulative: What occurred before was sometimes remembered and had to be accounted for, even though past actions and decisions became inconsistent with, or contradicted, subsequent turns of events.
3. Participants get bogged down with information, conflicting priorities, and divergent issues that fall outside of their decision jurisdictions or domains.

Based on these observations, Bryson and Roering (2001) make the following recommendations for managing innovation:

1. Have a powerful innovation sponsor and an effective process facilitator committed to continuing with the adoption process, particularly when difficult hurdles and setbacks arise.
2. Structure the adoption process into key junctures—deadlines, conferences, and peak events—because disruptions and setbacks cause delays and interest wanes with time. These structured junctures in the adoption process establish key deadlines to perform planned intermediate tasks and facilitate learning of key ideas among participants.
3. Be flexible not only about what constitutes acceptable innovation adoption but also in constructing arguments geared to many different evaluation criteria. In the final analysis, innovation-adoption success represents a socially constructed reality more often than an objective reality.

Summary

Since the seminal papers by Meyer and Rowan (1977) and DiMaggio and Powell (1983), new institutionalists have conducted a variety of studies that examine how organizations adapt to their institutional environments. As Scott (2001) notes, the institutional adaptation perspective represents a natural extension of open systems theory, which first identified the sensitivity of the organization to its technical environment. Research has focused on the impact of the external institutional arrangements (the independent variable) on the structure of organizational entities (the dependent variable). The central idea of those taking the institutional adaptation perspective is that in order to achieve legitimacy, which is crucial to survival, organizations must conform to pressures from the institutional environment.

Most institutional adaptation studies have focused on the causes rather than the processes of adaptation. However, recently organizational scholars have begun to explore the interplay between agency and environmental pressures (Greenwood and Hinings, 1996; Greenwood et al., 2002; Meyer et al., 1993; Scott et al., 1999). Organizations do not simply react and succumb in uniform ways to institutional environmental pressures; their responses vary and are contingent on various strategic and organizational conditions. Rogers (1995) reviews numerous studies of innovation adoption that provide important insights for understanding processes of organizational adaptation. In comparison with the neoinstitutional studies, innovation adoption studies have focused more directly on the activities and difficulties that adopters experience as they attempt to implement technical or institutional innovations that were developed externally and imposed on host organizations.

Institutional Diffusion

The institutional diffusion perspective examines how institutional arrangements reproduce, diffuse, and decline in the organizational field. Studies tend to focus on the diffusion of a particular institutional form or practice within a population of organizations that are all subject to the same institutional environment. An evolutionary theory of variation, selection, and retention processes is often used to explain the institutionalization or deinstitutionalization of an institutional form or arrangement in a population (Aldrich, 1999). Institutional diffusion studies tend to specify the conditions under which reproduction of an institutional form occurs, the rate at which it happens, and the degree to which it permeates a field of organizations or movement. Theorists have described coercive, normative, and mimetic mechanisms of institutional diffusion (DiMaggio and Powell, 1983). Scott (2001) asserts that institutional diffusion can be usefully categorized with respect to whether diffusion occurs through regulative, normative, or culture/cognitive processes of change.

The institutional diffusion perspective was first evident in the work of the old institutionalists, and in particular in the work of Veblen (1914/1964), who stated that societies hold particular "organizing principles" that relate to their means of pursuing material improvement. At first these principles take hold in one realm of activity but then they are "crossed and grafted" into many other activities (Veblen, 1914/1964; Rutherford, 1994). "Crossing and grafting" is analogous to the processes described in Mendelian genetics. Veblen emphasized that the diffusion of new thoughts and practices is often unintended by their innovators; he saw institutionalization at the societal level as involving at first a series of deliberate decisions by individual actors and eventually the unconscious adoption of practices. Wesley C. Mitchell also emphasized the spontaneous, unintended nature of institutional diffusion at the societal level (Rutherford, 1994). In *The Rationality of Business Activity* (1910), Mitchell argued that "pecuniary concepts" had resulted in a vast, elaborate business system that "produces consequences which no man willed."

More recently, organizational sociologists have studied institutional diffusion from a population ecology perspective. This view argues that competition for scarce resources forces actors to imitate and conform to legitimate institutional practices. For population ecologists, competition sets into motion evolutionary processes of variation, selection, and retention of institutional forms (Campbell, 1969). The first researchers to link population ecology with institutional theory were Carroll and Hannan (1989). They argued that the rates of founding and mortality of a particular institutional form within a population is a function of the cognitive legitimacy of that form, which in turn depends on the form's organizational density (the degree to which it has already infused the population). Carroll and Hannan observed that at first increases in density increase legitimacy and cause more organizational foundings and fewer organizational failures, but that at some point the greater competition associated with increased density outweighs legitimacy benefits, resulting in a decrease in foundings and an increase in mortality (Carroll and Hannan, 1989; Hannan, Carroll, Dundon and Torres, 1995).

Zucker (1989) questioned Carroll and Hannan's (1989) linking of density and legitimacy by arguing that they assume but do not provide evidence of such a link. Further, Baum and Powell (1995) take issue with Hannan and Carroll's conception of legitimacy.[2] They argue that Hannan and Carroll miscast legitimacy as a process that is controlled by organizational density and that explains rates of organizational founding and mortality. They call for a more historically oriented examination of legitimation and the relationship between legitimacy and density. They cite Baum and Oliver's (1992) empirical study of Toronto day care centers, which examined the relationship between organizational foundings and failures and both population density and relational density, a measure of institutional embeddedness. Baum and Oliver find that institutional embeddedness increases founding rates and decreases failure rates of all organizations in the early stages of population growth, and that organizations with institutional ties have higher survival rates than those without. Their conclusions suggest that, contrary to Hannan and Carroll's thesis, organizational survival is a function of institutional embeddedness rather than legitimacy.

Westphal, Gulati, and Shortell (1997) test the theory that legitimacy drives diffusion. They integrate institutional and network perspectives to examine the diffusion of an organizational practice, total quality management (TQM), among U.S. hospitals during the period 1985–1993. Westphal and colleagues address the question of whether TQM adoption occurred for efficiency reasons or due to isomorphic pressures. They develop a contingency-network approach in which social network ties either facilitate customization of TQM in response to internal efficiency needs or promote conformity in response to external legitimacy pressures, depending on the stage of institutionalization and the attendant motivation for adoption. They find that later adoption of TQM is associated with greater levels of conformity to the normative pattern of quality practices introduced by other adopting organizations and, further, that late adopters have higher levels of conformity to normative patterns when the level of adoption by alliance members and other system members is higher. Westphal et al. argue that network ties play an important role in institutional diffusion. These ties enable early adopters of an organizational practice to learn about alternative practices so that they can customize their own practices, and they enable late adopters to learn about and adopt accepted practices so that they can achieve legitimacy.

In a study of the diffusion of human resources practices of law firms, Sherer and Lee (2002) also investigate the relative contributions of institutional

(legitimacy) and technical (resource scarcity) pressures to institutional diffusion. They argue that legitimacy enables institutional change and that resource scarcity drives such change. They find that prestigious firms innovate first because they can get away with deviance due to their greater legitimacy, and that less prestigious firms adopt the innovative practices only after these practices have been legitimated.

In their examination of the diffusion of the partner-associate structure among Dutch professional service firms during the period 1925–1990, Lee and Pennings (2002) also study the interplay of technical and institutional pressures. They find evidence that the partner-associate organizational structure became associated with better performance, which in turn led to a change in managers' cognitive maps, which led to diffusion of the new form. Their study suggests that market feedback (a signal from the technical environment) can foster the legitimacy and therefore diffusion of a new form (a change in the institutional environment). Lee and Pennings note that diffusion of the organizational innovation depended on size similarity, geographic proximity, and network ties.

Wade, Swaminathan, and Saxon (1998) studied the impact of state-level prohibitions on alcohol production and consumption on the founding and mortality rates of breweries in adjacent, prohibition-free states. They use a population ecology approach to examine the interactions between organization-level and population-level institutional change. They find that prohibitions in a focal state at first lead to increased brewery foundings in adjacent states due to economic leakage. However, they also find that when the number of adjacent states adopting prohibition is greater than three, then brewery foundings decline and mortality rates increase. They conclude that government regulations create resource-flow opportunities for organizations not directly affected by the regulations (breweries in adjacent states) but also impose normative pressures on those organizations. The overall impact on organizations not directly affected by the regulations depends on the organization's location, its age, and the time elapsed since the passage of the legislation. Wade et al. trace out a process of institutional diffusion in which norms in one state lead to the passage of regulations in that state, which in turn catalyzes the adoption of the norms and eventually regulations in adjacent states.

Clemens and Cook (1999) developed a conceptual model of institutionalization that describes institutional diffusion as a function of the institution's characteristics and of network density. They view institutions as both external constraints (rules to be followed) and models for behavior that are internalized by actors. They argue that these two views of institutions complement rather than contradict one another. They conceptualize institutions as schemas that are embedded in, sustained by, or enacted through resources and/or social networks. They argue that the reliable reproduction of an institution depends on that institution's mutability (whether it promotes or squelches the development of alternative institutions), its degree of internal contradictions, and its degree of multiplicity (contradictions between institutions). The interaction of schemas with social networks and other resources also affects the degree of institutional change. Reproducibility is affected by network density, which affects the degree of containment/diffusion of variations, and the degree to which the institution can mediate exogenous shocks. Clemens and Cook's model explains both the durability of institutions and institutional change and calls attention to endogenous forces of change while not denying the possibility of exogenous shocks.

Christine Oliver examines deinstitutionalization, the process by which institutions erode and are replaced. In *The Antecedents of Deinstitutionalization* (1992), Oliver argues that political, functional, and social pressures, both endogenous and exogenous, can result in the dissipation or rejection of existing organizational practices. Political pressures essentially are changes in power distributions; functional pressures exist when the functional utility of a practice is questioned—for example, due to demands for greater technical efficiency; and social pressures include social fragmentation (e.g., high turnover), external forces such as changes in societal norms, and structural disaggregation, which reduces opportunities for interaction. Oliver also notes that entropy pressures and inertial pressures, which have countervailing effects, affect the rate of deinstitutionalization. She concludes that changing government regulations are likely to be the most powerful external force of institutional change and that performance problems are likely to be the most powerful internal force of change.

In a 1986 study of trust in the American business sector, Zucker investigates processes of institutionalization and deinstitutionalization. She distinguishes three central modes of trust production: (1) process-based, which is tied to past or expected exchange (e.g.,

trusting one due to reputation); (2) characteristics-based, where one trusts another due to that person's characteristics (e.g., family or race); and (3) institutional-based, where trust is tied to formal societal structures (e.g., CPA certification). Zucker's economic history shows that process-based trust was initially dominant in American business but then was disrupted by high rates of immigration, internal migration, and instability in business enterprises. She argues that process-based trust was replaced by institutional-based trust, which takes root when there is significant social distance between groups, exchange occurs across great geographic distances, and transactions are interdependent. Zucker finds that the spread of rational bureaucratic organizations, professional credentialing, the service economy, and regulation/legislation were critical to the early production of institution-based trust.

Galaskiewicz (1997) examined the influence of personal networks and community institutions on corporate charitable contributions in the Twin Cities during the periods 1979–1981 and 1987–1989. He found that informal social relationships (e.g., old-boy networks) were more durable than institutional structures (e.g., tithing clubs) in explaining philanthropic giving in 1987–1989. But Galaskiewicz insightfully notes that while interpersonal networks were crucial to sustaining the Twin Cities' urban grants economy, an institutional infrastructure of civic and voluntary institutional associations and practices was crucial to building and nurturing these informal ties. Galaskiewicz (1997, p. 468) concludes that "without this institutional infrastructure, the networks would have atrophied and had a difficult time surviving."

Structure and Agency in the Diffusion Literature

Scholars have begun to view institutional diffusion at the field level as a function of the interplay between environmental pressures and strategic choice at the organizational level. This work has been done in response to the criticism that population ecology takes a "bird's-eye view" of events and does not describe the mechanics and dynamics of change. Campbell (2002, p. 14) states that the "problem with diffusion studies is that we are left with a black box in which the processes whereby new practices are actually adopted and institutionalized on a case-by-case basis are left unspecified. In this sense, diffusion appears to be a mindless mechanical transfer of information from one place to another" (Rao, Morrill, and Zald, 2000; Haveman, 2000, p. 477).

Tolbert and Zucker (1996) develop a conceptual process model of the institutionalization process that addresses the lack of agency they perceive in the new institutionalism. Their model describes four stages in the institutionalization process: *innovation*, in which new varieties are generated for efficiency or political reasons; *habitualization*, during which others try out the new innovation; *objectification*, which is the process by which the new structural element moves toward a more permanent and widespread status; and *sedimentation*, when full institutionalization takes place. Sedimentation depends on the conjoint effects of relatively low resistance by opposing groups, continued cultural support and promotion by advocacy groups, and positive correlation with desired outcomes. Tolbert and Zucker's model brings purposive institutional design into institutional theory by explicitly viewing interest groups as consciously playing a role in the institutionalization process, by either supporting or opposing the sedimentation of an innovation.

Van de Ven and Grazman (1999) examine the relative influences of managerial, organizational, and industry-level events on the evolution of institutional arrangements in the Minnesota Twin Cities health care community from 1853 to 1995. Adopting a Mendelian genetics approach in a nested hierarchy, they study how new generations of managerial practices, organizational structures, and institutional arrangements emerge and evolve in lineages from ancestral forms through the crossing of existing arrangements and entities. Events when these crossings or recombinations occur are examined in terms of *branching* (the creation of novel forms) and *persistence* (incremental changes that enable existing branches to adapt and reproduce) in each lineage. Their "nested hierarchy" approach views managers as nested in organizations, which are nested in industries. By analyzing event time series in the historical genealogies at each level in this nested hierarchy, Van de Ven and Grazman found the following process patterns: (1) selection and adaptation processes work simultaneously and differently at each level in the nested hierarchy, (2) relationships between levels may be both positive and negative and the relative dominance of evolutionary processes at macro levels on micro levels is a matter of time scale

and spatial variation, and (3) coevolutionary processes between levels were evident during periods of environmental resource scarcity, while path-dependent processes within lineages occurred during periods of resource munificence. Van de Ven and Grazman found temporal waves of both structural diversification and structural consolidation in response to environmental institutional pressures. They conclude that the creation of new organizational forms (new branches in a lineage) and the diffusion and adaptation of particular forms (persistence of branches) must be understood as a coevolutionary function of influences from institutional environment events, managerial agency, and the accumulated history of an organization's culture, structure, and competencies.

Rosenkopf and Nerkar (1999) also take a nested hierarchy view of the evolution of optical disc technology. They describe the product hierarchy as including component, product, and system levels, one nested in the next, and they view the evolution of product hierarchies as involving processes of variation, selection, and retention at each of the levels. They argue that the battle between competing optical disc technologies (CD, AHD, and MD) was settled in favor of the CD not so much because of technological superiority but because Sony, a major proponent of the CD, was also in the entertainment industry, which was looking for a new music format to increase sales. Noting that evolutionary forces at one level may conflict with those at another level, they found that efforts to achieve consensus on a system-level optical disc standard (i.e., to choose between the CD, AHD, and MD approaches) was stymied by the lower-level efforts of firms to promote their own technologies.

Kraatz and Moore (2002) study the intersection of environmental institutional pressure and strategic choice. They examine the adoption of professional programs by liberal arts colleges during the 1970s and 1980s, finding that the spread of professional programs was associated with the migration of leaders from one organization to another. While they do not deny social and economic drivers of institutional change, they argue that more attention should be given to actors as the carriers who promulgate the diffusion of institutional forms. This study follows the tradition of Selznick and his students, who focused on the leader as the agent of change, and directly takes up Stinchcombe's (1997) challenge to bring people back into institutional theory.

Finally, in their studies of organizational band-wagons and fads, Abrahamson and colleagues theorize both the rise (institutionalization) and fall (deinstitutionalization) of various organizational practices, such as TQM (Abrahamson and Fairchild, 1999; Abrahamson and Rosenkopf, 1993).

Summary

Institutional diffusion studies examine the reproduction and spread of institutional arrangements within a population or organizational field, as well as processes of deinstitutionalization by which institutional arrangements erode and disappear. While the institutional diffusion literature began with Veblen over one hundred years ago, organizational population ecologists have more recently focused on the spread of organizational forms as resulting from organizations' quests for legitimacy. The link between organizational density and legitimacy, first proposed by Carroll and Hannan (1989), has been challenged by Tolbert and Zucker (1996), Baum and Powell (1995), and Baum and Oliver (1992) on the grounds that organizational legitimacy was not directly measured.

Institutional scholars have also begun to examine the conditions under which institutionalization occurs. Some have seen reproducibility as a function of institutional characteristics and network characteristics. Others have studied the relative contributions of technical and institutional pressures to the diffusion of new organizational forms and practices in the organizational field. Examples include studies by Westphal et al. (1997) and Lee and Pennings (2002). Both find that technical and institutional considerations will dominate at different times in the institutionalization process.

Institutional diffusion research has also begun to examine the joint influences of institutional pressures and strategic choice, resulting in a blurring of the boundaries between the diffusion perspective and the institutional design perspective on institutional change. Tolbert and Zucker (1996) present an adaptation of the variation-selection-retention model that makes room for agency by theorizing interest group conflict during the retention stage. Based on their genealogical study of the Twin Cities health care community, Van de Ven and Grazman (1999) propose organizational genetic engineering and "managerial stewardship" as two important roles for the exercise of managerial agency. Kraatz and Moore's

2000 study of the professionalization of U.S. liberal arts colleges supports Selznick's (1957) view that organizational leaders are the agents of institutional change.

Finally, Rogers (1995) notes that few topics in the social sciences have received more study than the diffusion of innovative practices. He reviews over 4,000 studies that have examined the diffusion of innovations. An understanding of the processes of institutional diffusion can be significantly enhanced by incorporating the theories and methods of this extensive body of research knowledge.

Collective Action

Collective action scholars of institutional change focus on the social and political processes that facilitate and constrain the development of a technological innovation or a social movement, and through which institutions emerge or are altered. They examine the political opportunity structures and framing processes surrounding institutional arrangements, as well as the networks of distributed, partisan, and interdependent actors who become embedded in these collective processes. While the collective action literature shares with the institutional design literature an emphasis on intentional efforts to produce change, it takes as its unit of analysis the industry or inter-organizational field rather than the individual actor. Major conceptual and empirical advances to the collective action perspective have been made by scholars who study social movements and technological innovation and industry emergence. Social movement scholars have addressed collective political efforts to achieve institutional changes that remedy perceived social and ecological problems, barriers, or injustices. Technology scholars have taken a more proprietary and economic view by examining the institutional arrangements (such as property rights, standards, regulations, trade policies, legitimating practices, research and development efforts, financing arrangements, consumption patterns, market structure, etc.) that help and hinder the development and commercialization of new products, services, and technologies.

Social Movements

Rucht (1999, p. 207) defines a social movement as "an action system comprised of mobilized networks of individuals, groups and organizations which, based on a shared collective identity, attempt to achieve or prevent social change, predominantly by means of collective protest." McAdam, McCarthy, and Zald (1996) point out that social movement scholars are converging on three broad sets of factors to explain the emergence and development of social movements. They refer to these as *mobilizing structures*, which are the forms of organizations or collective vehicles (informal and formal) that are available to insurgents and through which people mobilize and engage in collective action; *political opportunity structures*, which are the institutional arrangements or the structure of political opportunities and constraints confronting the movement; and *framing processes*, the collective processes of interpretation, attribution, and social construction that mediate between political opportunities/structures and collective action. We will now summarize the basic model of social movements discussed by McAdam et al. (1996). This model is illustrated in figure 9.1.

Framing Processes Drawing on McAdam et al. (1996) and Zald (1996), Campbell (2002) notes that framing involves the strategic creation and manip-

ulation of shared understandings and interpretations of the world, its problems, and viable courses of action. Frames mediate between opportunity structures and action because they provide the means with which people can interpret the political opportunities before them and, thus, decide how best to pursue their objectives. Viewing pluralistic settings, Morrill, Zald, and Rao (2003) note that a dominant frame is seldom a consensual frame and that frames are "contested terrains" over control and power (Edwards, 1982). Frame settlements are temporary truces to political conflict and struggle among opposing coalitions. A frame consists of at least two parts: a diagnostic part that concerns how problems are defined and who is to blame for them, and a prognostic part that defines solutions and appropriate strategies for attaining them (Benford and Snow, 2000; McCarthy, Smith, and Zald, 1996). Social movements scholars have noted that frames are rarely constructed out of whole cloth and instead are normally fabricated from already available repertoires and cultural artifacts (Tarrow, 1994, pp. 130–131; Strang and Bradburn, 2001).

Clemens and Cook (1999) argue that the reproducibility of institutional entities depends on their

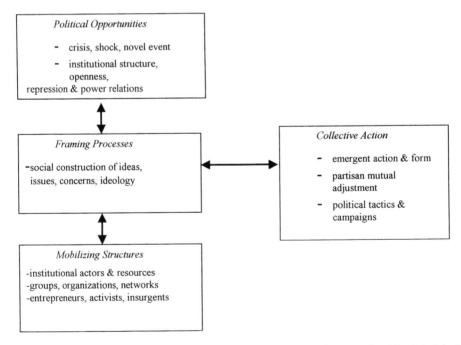

Figure 9.1 Social movements theory. Adapted from McAdam, D., McCarthy, J., and Zald, M. (eds.), *Comparative Perspectives on Social Movements: Political Opportunities, Mobilizing Structures and Cultural Framings.*

ability to create organizational and mental structures that embody them. They argue that institutions seek not only to impose their schemas but also to transform the world to fit their schemas. Institutional entities reproduce themselves when they are able to frame issues in ways that support their reproduction and eliminate the possibility of creating or reproducing alternative institutions. While Scully and Creed (2002) do not dispute that the contest to control meaning is important, they question whether the emphasis placed on framing and identity has sapped or diverted activists of their power to change material causes, such as the redistribution of wealth, poverty, and the wage gap.

Although his work is not typically cited by social movement scholars, Donald Schon (1971) presented a process model of how public policies emerge that includes all three factors of social movements analysis. He argues that new public policies emerge through a process involving the following stages:

1. A disruptive event threatens the social system and triggers a new appreciation of the problem or opportunity.
2. Ideas gestating in peripheral areas are carried into the mainstream by their adherents.
3. Networks and media galvanize around ideas, give them catchy slogans, and propel them into public scrutiny and debate.
4. Ideas are not potent to change public policy unless they win out in political debate and are used to gain influence and resources.
5. Winning ideas gain the legitimacy and power needed to change institutions.
6. Ideas remain current for only as long as they address critical problems, and the administrative regime remains in power, or both.

In addition to this reactive sequence to disaster events, Braithwaite and Drahos (2000) discuss a proactive process model in which individual entrepreneurship with regulatory innovation was much more important in launching global regulatory changes. But in both reactive and proactive process models, the essential work of social movements is the same. It is to enroll and mobilize the resources needed to push and ride ideas into good currency— i.e., to win the battle over framing.

In an investigation of the adoption of innovations in the treatment of HIV/AIDS, Maguire (2002) presents evidence of the importance of framing to social movement success. He presents a political model of innovation adoption that sees adoption as a negotiated settlement emerging from a contested discursive struggle. Maguire documents how AIDS activists were able not only to change the outcomes emanating from the FDA's drug approval process but also to force a negotiation of both the structure of the system guiding that process and the nature and role of evidence used in the process. He shows how AIDS activists inserted themselves into the drug approval process and won the establishment of a fast-track drug approval process that made possible the widespread adoption of new treatments prior to the conclusion of efficacy research. This "parallel track" supplemented the slower, traditional drug approval process that is guided by academic researchers' demands for universal scientific knowledge. Activists succeeded by raising, in addition to ethical concerns, epistemological and methodological questions about the conduct of clinical trials, the drug approval process, and the criteria on which approval was based, arguing that these were matters of life and death that should not be guided solely by an abstract imperative of scientific purity. Maguire shows that activists changed the institutional process through which treatments are adopted in the United States by framing critical questions about the structure and function of the process in resonant ethical terms.

Numerous scholars have discussed the importance of framing processes, or social construction, in the establishment of new laws. McCann (1994), Stryker (1994), and Boyle (2000) found that law is rarely an "exclusive" or unilateral "force" in social practice, especially related to social change. Zald, Morrill, and Rao (2002) argue that because actors—lawyers, activists, and government officials—are embedded in different social practices and contexts, they may interpret any single law in very different ways and consequently may make very diverse claims about the appropriate distribution of social benefits and burdens. Similarly, Kelly (2002) argues that while tax policy may appear concrete and unambiguous, it is still open to the collective construction of the law by consultants, organizations, and regulators. Braithwaite and Drahos (2000) found contests of principles to be a key phenomenon in the process of globalization of a wide variety of business regulations.

Fligstein (1996) argues that markets are social constructions that reflect the unique political-cultural constructions of firms and nations and emerge through political processes to provide stability and solutions to competition. Fligstein views market development as occurring in three stages and the nature of politics as varying with the stage of development. The three stages are:

1. *The formation stage*, in which actors in firms try to create a status hierarchy that enforces noncompetitive forms of competition. During this stage political action resembles social movement activity.
2. *Stable markets*, during which incumbent firms defend their positions against challengers and invaders.
3. *Transformation periods*, during which invaders can reintroduce more fluid social-movement-like conditions.

Fligstein points out that the state facilitates economic growth because it supports the interests of powerful elites by building an infrastructure that facilitates wealth creation. This infrastructure consists of institutions—property rights, governance structures, and rules of exchange—that establish stable and reliable conditions under which firms organize, compete, cooperate, and exchange. Fligstein asserts that the content of laws, their applicability to given firms and markets, and the extent and direction of state intervention into the economy are always disputed, and that laws always favor certain groups of firms. He writes that as they first emerge, markets resemble social movements in that there is a battle over "conceptions of control," which are shared cognitive structures that enable actors to interpret events.

Resource Mobilization   Mobilizing structures are the forms and vehicles through which people engage in collective action. McAdam and Scott (2002) view mobilizing structures as the institutional actors that are the building blocks of social movements and revolutions. An issue or idea becomes an "opportunity" only when defined as such by a group of actors that is sufficiently well organized to act on this shared definition of the situation.

Campbell (2002, p. 20) states that the formal and informal networks that connect individuals and organizations (Tilly, 1978, chap. 3) are among the most important aspects of mobilizing structures and that bricolage is critical to mobilization as well, because the tactics and organizational practices employed by activists are formed through bricolage. Campbell

(2002) sees networks as the conduits though which new models, concepts, and practices diffuse and become part of an organization's repertoire, and therefore become available for use in framing and translation by bricoleurs. Networks thus provide the foundation for organizational innovation and activity.

McAdam et al. (1996) note that resource mobilization theorists focus on the critical role of resources and formal organizations in the rise of movements. They assert that "movements may largely be born of environmental opportunities, but their fate is heavily shaped by their own actions" (p. 15).

Perhaps more than any other scholar, the anthropologist Luther Gerlach has articulated the organizational form of social movements. Gerlach and Palmer (1981) argue that resource development is a key driver of societal evolution and that this evolution need not proceed toward higher degrees of interdependence and concentration because of the benefits of polycentrism. They describe four types of networks that affect resource and technoeconomic development: *developer networks* that promote innovation and development; *manager networks* that plan and manage development and distribution and deal with social and environmental impacts; *resister networks*, such as social movements; and *mediator networks* that tie people together and mediate disputes. They make the case that the "segmented, polycentric, integrated network" (SPIN) model may be the appropriate model for all of these networks, including social movements, because it is highly adaptive. Gerlach (2001) describes SPINs as neither bureaucratic and centralized nor amorphous, but rather composed of many diverse yet networked groups that follow no single leader. The groups are united by their opposition to a shared enemy and by their shared ideology. SPINs are adaptive because their multiplicity prevents effective suppression by the opposition, enables penetration into a variety of social niches, permits division of labor and adaptation to circumstances, contributes to system reliability (in that one part can fail without harming the others) and escalates the level of effort (due to competition among groups). Further, the SPIN model facilitates trial and error learning and promotes innovation and experimentation in generating and implementing sociocultural change.

Political Opportunity Structures   As they attempt to bring about social change, social movements must engage in dialectical political struggle with entrenched interests over the "shape" and governance of institutionalized systems of power" (McAdam, Tarrow, and Tilly, 2001, pp. 342–343). Change will be easier to bring about in some instances than others, however. Campbell (2002, p. 4) views the political opportunity structure as a set of formal and informal political conditions that encourage, discourage, channel, and otherwise affect movement activity. In studying political opportunity structures, social movements scholars have examined the degree to which formal political institutions are open or closed to challengers of the status quo, the degree to which political elites are organized in stable or unstable coalitions and alignments, the degree to which movements have allies within the political elite, and the degree to which political authorities are willing to use repression against challengers (McAdam et al., 1996; Tarrow, 1996; Campbell, 2002, p. 4).

Clemens and Cook (1999) and Stryker (2000) address how the characteristics of the political opportunity structure influence legitimacy, defined in terms of collective orientation to binding rules. Stryker explains institutional change as produced by political conflicts that arise from institutional contradictions. As Clemens and Cook argue, the reliable reproduction of an institution depends on the institution's mutability, its degree of internal contradictions, and its consistency with other institutions; its ability to mediate exogenous shocks; and its network density, which determines whether variations are diffused. One can interpret Clemens and Cook's argument to suggest that a social movement is more likely to be successful if the political opportunity structure is dense, permits the generation of new ideas, and is internally inconsistent with other institutions.

Recently social movements scholars have undertaken a number of empirical studies that integrate analysis of framing processes, resource mobilization, and political opportunity structures. Lounsbury (2002) tells a story that demonstrates the impacts of framing on the political opportunity structure and ultimately on the ability of local activists to organize. He describes how a shift in logics created changes in the drivers of state-level recycling advocacy group creation. Lounsbury shows that these groups first emerged in states that were conducive to ecological activism, and that in these states advocates envisioned recycling as a means of restructuring economic re-

lations and of addressing problems such as mass consumerism. Once this "holistic" recycling logic was replaced by a more "technocratic" logic, however, recycling advocacy groups began to emerge at a faster rate and in states that had incineration capacity, because in this second period recycling was viewed as an alternative to incineration. Lounsbury argues that the shift in logics occurred due to the establishment of a national recycling association that was allied with major solid waste haulers, who saw recycling as a new market opportunity. Lounsbury argues that a focus on institutional logics is preferable to a focus on institutionalization because it "restores attention to broader social structures of resources and meanings and how those social structures themselves change and mediate flows of practices" (p. 22). A focus on logics also enables one to get away from the determinism inherent in institutional theory, Lounsbury argues, because it allows one to see that social movements were not simply co-opted but rather continued to struggle for change, albeit in new ways.

In a study that examines the structuration, or crystallization, of the lesbian/gay movement in San Francisco during the period 1969–1973, Armstrong (2002) proposes that even when a field appears to be in crisis, its future stable form will likely resemble its prior stable form due to the efforts of elites to perpetuate existing working rules; that the form a field ultimately takes depends on the rules governing related fields; that the more intense and generalized the crisis in a field, the less likely the new stable form of the field will resemble the prior form; and that the more intense, general, and contentious an institutional crisis, the more the resulting institutional settlement will depend on the social skills of actors, the quality and diversity of available cultural models, and historically specific conditions. Armstrong argues that the convergence of the lesbian/gay organizations in San Francisco on a "gay rights" model focused on pride and identity cannot be explained through structuralist arguments but rather must be seen as emerging from the collision of existing homosexual organizing with the dynamism of the New Left. The decline of the New Left in the early 1970s made clear that the more radical homosexual agenda of "gay liberation" was not tenable, yet at the same time provided the homosexual movement with new symbols, social skills, and organizational models, leading to a burst of "intense cultural creativity" that produced the gay movement's political strategy centered around "coming out." Armstrong asserts that the moderation of the gay/lesbian movement's agenda from gay liberation to gay identity was not inevitable but rather occurred because gay activists drew on the tools provided by the New Left and then pragmatically assessed what the system would offer.

Holm (1995) explores the interplay among all three foundations of social movements theory by investigating the process of institutional change in the Norwegian fishing industry. Holm documents the emergence and decline of the mandated sales organization (MSO), essentially a fishermen's cartel that when established gave the fishermen market power vis-à-vis fish merchants. Holm demonstrates that policy outcomes related to fisheries can be explained in terms of the efforts of different interest groups to mold national policy to their interests. These groups were simultaneously constrained by the political institutional environment and for practical reasons sought to change it. Holm shows that in the 1930s, Norwegian fishermen were able to mobilize government support for MSOs but that by the 1990s, MSOs met their demise as a result of a new ideological climate that favored deregulation and privatization, the influence of European integration, and resistance to central authority, which Holm calls "a basic theme in Norwegian politics."

Holm's model of institutional change employs a nested-systems perspective, which views practical action at the first-order level as taking place in a political, second-order context. Holm argues that institutional change may originate at either of the two levels, that the two levels are interconnected in practice, and that because forces of change at one level are mediated by internal dynamics at the other level, the outcome of the process of institutional change can take unexpected forms. Holm states that just as there is feedback between actors and institutions, ideas and interests shape one another.

Technological Innovation and Industry Emergence

A significant trend in the literature on technological innovation and industry emergence during the past fifteen years has been the adoption of a broader, more dynamic, institutional and political view of innovation. Increasingly, technical and institutional innovations are viewed as coevolving. They are collective achievements in constructing an industrial infrastructure for economic development among actors who are distributed, partisan, and become embedded in a path-dependent process. Studies have found that processes of technological innovation and entrepreneurship have many similarities to social movements. Moreover, these studies elaborate and extend the social movement concepts of framing processes, political opportunity structures, and mobilizing processes.

Framing Processes   In the context of technological innovation, *framing* refers not only to creating resonant understandings of issues (as it does in the social movements literature), but also to understanding the framework in which technology innovation unfolds—in other words, understanding that technology development is a political and social process involving a broad community of actors and not simply a proprietary technical activity. Notwithstanding common folklore of the independent entrepreneur working alone to develop his or her innovation, numerous historical studies have demonstrated that innovation and entrepreneurship are a collective achievement. New technologies and new businesses are seldom developed by a single firm in the vacuum of an institutionalized environment (see, e.g., Jewkes, Sawers, and Stillerman, 1958; Nelson, 1982; Chandler, 1990). Usher (1929/1954, p. 60) insisted that the history of mechanical inventions in the nineteenth century is not the history of single inventors or random chance events. Gilfillan (1935, p. 5) observed a perpetual accretion of little details—having no clear beginnings, completions, or definable limits—in the gradual evolution of shipbuilding. Constant (1980) found that advances in aircraft propulsion emerged not from flashes of disembodied inspiration but from many incremental changes and recombinations of existing technology and organizational arrangements, which add up to what might be called a technological revolution.

Moreover, there is a systemic nature to technological advances, as demonstrated in studies by Hughes (1983) of electrical power, Ruttan and Hayami (1984) of agricultural innovations, Kuhn (1962/1982) and Hull (1988) of scientific advances, Tushman and Anderson (1986) of technological revolutions in cement, minicomputers, and glass, and by Powell (1998) and Zucker and Darby (1997) of biotechnology. Many complementary innovations in technical and institutional arrangements are usually required before a particular technology is suitable for commercial application (Binswanger and Ruttan, 1978). Developments in other complementary technologies and institutions often explain bottlenecks and breakthroughs in the development of a given technology. Thus, as Rosenberg (1983, p. 49) says, "What is really involved is a process of cumulative accretion of useful knowledge, to which many people make essential contributions, even though the prizes and recognition are usually accorded to the one actor who happens to have been on the stage at a critical moment."

Murmann and Tushman (2001) describe technological systems as consisting of multiple levels of subsystems, linking mechanisms, and basic components. Echoing Henderson and Clark's (1990) discussion of the architectural design of technologies, Murmann and Tushman note that subsystems become "core" if they serve as the link to many other subsystems or when they represent bottlenecks in the overall performance of the system. Within the nested hierarchy, a dominant design may arise in a subsystem, causing technological discontinuities in lower-level subsystems and components. There is also uneven development among subsystems, as components and subsystem technologies often will not be in the same stage of the technology cycle. Murmann and Tushman note that their description of technological subsystems can also be applied to institutional systems.

Numerous scholars have noted that technological development and entrepreneurship have striking similarities with social movements. Swaminathan and Wade (2001) observe that like social movements, entrepreneurs in emerging industries face the key task of gaining cognitive and sociopolitical legitimacy. Dowell, Swaminathan, and Wade (2002) make the link between social movements theory and industry emergence in their account of how proponents and opponents of high definition television (HDTV) engaged in collective framing processes to influence the trajectory of HDTV in the United States. Rao (2001) writes that neoinstitutionalists have begun to take the view that the creation of new organizational forms entails an institutionalization project that resembles a social movement (Fligstein, 1996, pp. 663–664) and that new organizational forms become validated through a bottom-up process of institutional entrepreneurship (Rao, 2001). Miner, Eesley, DeVaughn and Rura-Polley (2001) also note in their study of university-led venture developments that

university officers resembled social movements leaders in that their efforts were motivated by deeply held convictions and shared internalized visions of the university as an engine for regional economic development and new jobs. Like social movements, the research ventures under study mobilized resources for a specific cause.

Porac, Thomas, Wilson, Paton, and Kanfer (1995) emphasize the framing of the interorganizational field, arguing that market boundaries and the interorganizational field are socially constructed around a collective cognitive model. They develop their model in the context of the Scottish knitwear industry, finding that managers compare their firms with others and that rivalry occurs "when one firm orients toward another and considers the actions and characteristics of the other in business decisions, with the goal of achieving a commercial advantage over the other" (p. 204). Porac et al. conclude, "Rather than being an exogenous force acting on managerial minds, market structure is an endogenous product of managerial minds" (emphasis in original).

Schoonhoven and Romanelli (2001) give attention to the community in which entrepreneurial activity is embedded. They write, "Entrepreneurial activity arises from the collective activity of entrepreneurs and others, such as venture capitalists, lawyers, and industry professionals, who together actively create and sustain legitimate market space for new products, services, and technologies" (p. 384). They define "community" as a set of interdependent organizational populations, and they assert that a shared mental model, a coherent idea, or the cognitive instantiation of institutionalized understandings emerges among members of an entrepreneurial community. This assertion is supported by other contributions to the same volume, including that of Suchman, Steward, and Westfall (2001), who show that the mental models that Silicon Valley law firms present to their entrepreneur clients constitute a package of routinized methods for efficiently dealing with questions common to those starting companies.

Political Opportunity Structures Technology scholars have also elaborated and extended the social movement's concept of political opportunity structures for technological innovation and entrepreneurship at the interorganizational field. Figure 9.2 sketches an institutional framework that incorporates the various components of an industrial infrastructure

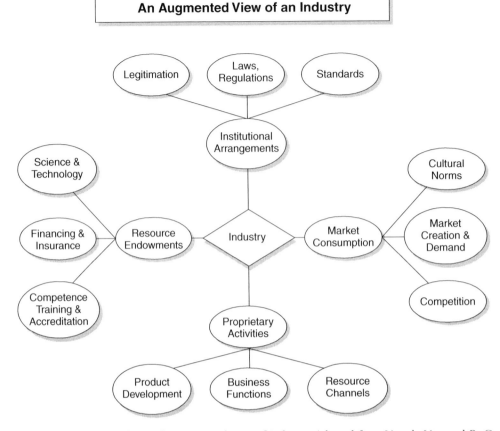

Figure 9.2 Van de Ven and Garud's augmented view of industry. Adapted from Van de Ven and R. Garud (1989).

for technological innovation. This framework adopts an augmented view of an industry as consisting not only of the set of firms producing similar or substitute products (Porter, 1980), but also of many other public and private sector actors who perform critical functions to develop and commercialize a new technology. The industrial infrastructure at the interorganizational field includes the following four subsystems (see figure 9.2):

1. *Institutional arrangements*, the governmental agencies, professional trade associations, and scientific/technical communities that legitimate, regulate, and standardize a technology.
2. *Resource endowments*, which include advancements in basic scientific and technological knowledge, financing and insurance arrangements, and training of competent professionals.

3. *Consumer demand*, which is essential to a market economy. For new-to-the-world technologies, informed, competent, and responsible consumers do not preexist; the market must be created.
4. *Proprietary activities*, which transform the available supply of public resources (scientific knowledge and work force competence) into proprietary products and services to meet customer demand.

This framework, developed initially from studies of the development of the cochlear-implant technology by Van de Ven and Garud (1989; 1993), has been extended in studies of technological communities by Garud and Rappa (1994); new business start-ups by Aldrich and Fiol (1994), the U.S. health-care provider industry by Van de Ven and Lofstrom (1997), the American film industry by Mezias and

Kuperman (2000), flat-panel display technologies by Murtha, Lenway, and Hart (2001); and Java technology standards by Garud, Jain, and Kumaraswamy (2002). Powell (1998) addresses institutional change specifically, arguing that the organizational field of an emerging industry is not only multidisciplinary but also multi-institutional. He writes that all the necessary skills and organizational capabilities needed to compete are not readily found under a single roof and that technological process goes hand in hand with the evolution of the industry and its supporting institutions (p. 233).

In their study of cochlear implants, Van de Ven and Garud (1993) found clear statistical evidence that the institutional arrangements, resource endowments, and proprietary commercial events were reciprocally related and coproduced each other over time. Uneven developments in complementary technologies, institutions, and resource endowments created bottlenecks as well as breakthroughs in the development and commercialization of cochlear implants. Van de Ven and Garud (1989; 1993; 1994) and Aldrich and Fiol (1994) note that in technology-intensive industries fragmented interests across industry participants often complicate the collective action process. Such competition can hinder collective action as industry participants promote their own interests and fail to advance the interests of the overall industry in obtaining legitimacy.

Other researchers have studied the development of selective components of the institutional infrastructure for technological innovation. With respect to proprietary channel activities, Stuart (2000) determined that a focal firm's level of innovation in the semiconductor industry increased after the firm entered an alliance with a very innovative firm, and similarly, that a firm's sales growth rate increased after that firm entered an alliance with a large firm. He found that the benefits of allying with an innovative or larger firm were more pronounced for young or small firms because it signaled legitimacy for the smaller firms. These findings are consistent with the idea that young and small firms suffer "liabilities of newness" (Stinchcombe, 1965), which include the lack of legitimacy as viewed by financial and labor markets, governments, consumers, and other key actors in the environment (Rao, 2001; Aldrich, 1999; Hannan and Freeman, 1989).

Several researchers have studied the development of standards for evaluating new technologies and the emergence of dominant technological designs among competing designs. Bijker, Hughes, and Pinch (1987), Anderson and Tushman (1990), and Das and Van de Ven (2000) observed that technology selection occurs through a process of negotiation among relevant social groups and reflects the extent to which evaluation criteria are influenced in favor of the technology. Existing evaluation policy for a technological application plays a role analogous to that played by an accepted paradigm in an area of scientific explanation. It comprises a system of judgments as to which factors are important, how each is measured, and how they are to be valued (Wojick, 1979).

For example, the revolutionary turbojet technology, which replaced the older piston engine and propeller system, not only required development of entirely new testing techniques and construction of new test facilities, but also necessitated the redefinition of the way aeroengine output is measured, thrust for shaft horsepower. Initial metaphors that are used to describe and evaluate a new system are based on the preceding established system, because means and concepts to articulate the new system are not yet developed. Automobiles were first called "horseless carriages," a turn of phrase that facilitated comparison with an existing choice instead of highlighting the unique features of the new product.

Green (1992) discussed how a market may not exist for a new technology and may have to be shaped. For a market to exist, institutions must first be in place to establish prices, to inform customers and suppliers, and to provide distribution arrangements. Entrepreneurs developing radically new technologies must often engage in collective action with others to create these institutions. Bower and Christensen (1995) discuss the case of disruptive technologies where information about potential customers, dimensions of product performance of importance to customers, and pricing level can be acquired only by experimenting with the product and the market.

When the institution of market does not exist, a firm sponsoring a radically new product technology has to "run in packs" (Van de Ven, Polley, Garud, and Venkataraman, 1999) with other cooperating and competing firms in the public and private sectors to create this and other institutions. Murmann and Tushman (2001) discuss the collective decision process, stating that except in the case of simple technologies, uncertainty about the potential of certain technological designs cannot be adjudicated by technology alone; rather, dominant designs emerge out of a sociopolitical process of compromise and accommodation played out in the community (Rosenkopf and Tushman, 1994; Van de Ven and Garud, 1994). The "best" technology does not necessarily win the competition between alternative designs.

Studies provide evidence that firms sponsoring new technologies can influence the outcome of the selection process through a variety of strategies. David (1987) examined the actions of business firms that had invested in either alternating current (AC) or in direct current (DC) to influence selection of one of these technologies for generating and distributing electricity. These actions included debates over technical factors and social factors. DeLamarter (1986) discussed how IBM used its market power to influence selection of its own mainframe computer as the dominant design in its category. Rosenkopf and Tushman (1994) discussed the effect of firm participation in cooperative groups to influence the process of technological evolution. Cusumano, Mylonadis, and Rosenbloom (1992) concluded that the selection of the VHS format over Betamax format for video-cassette recorders was due mainly to the use of "strategic alliances" by the JVC company, which sponsored VHS format. Das and Van de Ven (2000) conducted a longitudinal study of leading firms that were sponsoring new and competing product technologies in the video player and medical diagnostic imaging industries. They found that the nature of the product technology, whether novel or evolved, and the market, whether concentrated or dispersed, influence when firms use technical or institutional strategies to get their new product technologies accepted by the market.

Garud, Jain, and Kumaraswamy (2002) study Sun Microsystems' sponsorship of the Java technological standard. They argue that organizations socially construct institutions, sponsor their creation, and try to catalyze their legitimation, yet they also show that institutional entrepreneurship (in this case sponsorship of a new standard) is fraught with challenges. One obstacle is that agency in the structuration of the field creates oppositions and mobilizes collective action; the institutional entrepreneur must both overcome inertia and take on vested interests. Further, mobilizing collective action is itself made difficult by "legitimacy traps"—the fact that others will view entrepreneurship as self-interested and not in the best

interests of the field as a whole. Garud and colleagues also document the problem of "coopetition"—the difficulty of achieving cooperation among competitors. They note that maintaining collective action may be difficult because others may want to start departing from the standard (challenging the newly formed institution) even as it is emerging.

Recent studies emphasize that learning is at the heart of the social nature of innovation and industry emergence. Murtha, Lenway, and Hart (2001) trace the emergence of the flat-panel display (FPD) industry. They argue that the industry emerged through the efforts of an international community of companies that each leverage unique, national capabilities from several countries. In the race to create new knowledge and learn, companies seek close relationships to gain access to specialized capabilities that they can leverage in combination with their own. These include both direct and indirect relationships with competitors and potential competitors, as well as relationships with universities, research labs, suppliers, and customers. Critical bodies of new knowledge and technology accumulate in shared rather than proprietary domains of activity, such as interactions with equipment and materials makers whose customer base includes multiple competitors in the same industry.

Studies in the biotechnology industry by Liebeskind, Oliver, Zucker, and Brewer (1996); Powell, Koput, and Smith-Doerr (1996); Powell (1998); and Zucker and Darby (1997) also emphasize the importance of collaboration for learning. Powell (1998, p. 117) states that when there is a regime of rapid technological development, research breakthroughs demand a range of intellectual and scientific skills that far exceed the capabilities of any single organization. Hence, Powell et al. (1996) observe that the locus of innovation is found in networks of learning rather than in individual firms. This is true not only of R&D but also for other components of the institutional infrastructure that are highly uncertain and changing rapidly.

Liebeskind et al. (1996) argued that the collective nature of innovation is a function of uncertainty about technology and competition. They write that new biotechnology firms (NBFs) cannot determine in advance if any particular research program in which they invest will lead to a valuable discovery and further, that the locus of innovation in biotech is constantly changing because university-based expertise diffuses rapidly and innovation is accelerated by strict property-rights regimes. To be successful, NBF's must devise institutional arrangements that enable them to source their critical input—patentable scientific knowledge—at minimum sunk costs while overcoming problems of uncertainty, appropriability, and intellectual resource immobility. Liebeskind et al. study two NBF's and report that social networks provide opportunities for learning and flexibility.

Zucker and Darby (1997) argue that new institutional structures for biotechnology development must not only be viewed as legitimate but also have net performance benefits. They observe that some institutional financial arrangements, such as NBF's and money-market mutual funds, result from successful attempts of extraordinarily creative, innovative, and productive individuals who resourcefully accept or fine-tune existing institutional arrangements rather than engage in collective institutional reconstruction projects. They view a society's inherited set of institutions as important for two reasons. First, having been created for other environments, inherited institutions may pose impediments and create vested interests that retard or block adoption of other, more productive institutions in a change environment. Second, inherited institutions themselves define the available, off-the-shelf, dominant designs for organizations that any contemplated innovation must be expected to sufficiently outperform in order to cover the costs of creating a new organizational form. The latter provides a powerful reason why even with perfect foresight, a cost-benefit analysis may conclude that the use of an existing institutional infrastructure may be pragmatically preferable to the efforts of mobilizing collective actions to create a better-fitting infrastructure. Because the development costs of existing institutional arrangements have been borne by others and the entrepreneurs must bear the costs of creating new institutional forms, only where substantially better outcomes are expected can the cost differential be justified (Zucker and Darby, 1997, p. 503).

Process Theories of Technology Emergence

Whereas social movements scholars discuss resource mobilization in terms of the organizations that seek to make change, technology scholars go farther, describing not only actors that construct change but also the processes through which this change is constructed. The institutional infrastructure just discussed represents the political opportunity structure that enables and constrains the innovation efforts of individual entrepreneurs and firms. There is a convergence of thought among most technology and entrepreneurship scholars that actors construct and change this institutional infrastructure. This infrastructure does not emerge and change all at once due to the actions of one or even a few key individuals but instead is built through a process that consists of an accretion of numerous events involving many actors who transcend boundaries of public and private sector organizations (Van de Ven et al., 1999).

The sequence of events in which individual actors become engaged in collective action to construct the institutional infrastructure can begin any number of ways and varies with the technology being developed. For example, it can begin with the inventive ideas of entrepreneurs, who undertake a stream of activities to gain the resources, competencies, and endorsements necessary to develop an economically viable enterprise. As they undertake these activities, the paths of independent entrepreneurs, acting out their own diverse intentions and ideas, intersect. These interactions provide occasions for recognizing areas for establishing cooperative and competitive relationships (Romanelli, 1992).

Cooperative relationships emerge among the actors who can achieve complementary benefits by integrating their functional specializations or institutional roles. Competitive relationships emerge as alternative technological paths become evident and different entrepreneurs or firms "place their bets on" and pursue alternative paths. During this initial period, applied research and development activities are highly uncertain and often dependent on basic science and technology. Depending on the technological alternative chosen, entrepreneurs become highly dependent on different clusters of basic research institutions, such as universities and laboratories, that have been producing and directing the accumulation of basic knowledge, techniques, and experience associated with a given technological alternative.

By engaging in cooperative and competitive relationships and by interacting in the same networks, groups of entrepreneurs in the public and private sectors increasingly isolate themselves from traditional industries by virtue of their interdependencies and growing commitments to and unique knowledge of a new technology. Isolation frees an emerging system from institutional constraints of existing technologies and industries (Astley, 1985) and permits it to develop its own distinctive institutional forms (Rappa, 1987). Coordination among actors takes place not so much by a central plan, hierarchy, or price mechanism but mostly through interactions (Mattsson, 1987) and partisan mutual adjustments among actors (Lindblom, 1965).

As the number of organizational units and actors gains a critical mass, a complex network of cooperative and competitive relationships begins to accumulate. Like a social movement, this network itself becomes recognized as a new "industrial sector" and takes the form of a hierarchical, loosely coupled system. This emerging network consists of the key entrepreneurs and firms that govern, integrate, and play diverse roles in transforming a technological community into a commercially viable industry. The structure of this network consists of the institutional and market arrangements, resource endowments, and proprietary arrangements, as illustrated in figure 9.2.

Technology scholars have proposed a variety of process theories for explaining this developmental sequence. They have given more attention to the processes of technical and institutional change than to the other literatures discussed in this chapter. One of the earliest and richest models is the process of partial cumulative synthesis introduced by Abbott Payson Usher. In his "History of Mechanical Invention" (1929, p. 1954), Usher presented a model of change, illustrated in figure 9.3, in which invention is viewed as "a cumulative synthesis of a relatively large number of individual items" or events (p. 60). Usher views insight as a four-step process involving pattern completion in response to particular conditions. The four steps are (1) perception of a problem; (2) the "setting of the stage," in which all the tools and data needed for a solution are presented; (3) the act of insight; and (4) critical revision, in which the solution is studied, understood, learned, and mastered. Usher emphasizes that the conditions for the finding of a solution cannot be deliberately arranged by the actor seeking a solution and that the time of a solution cannot be preordained. Further, he argues that

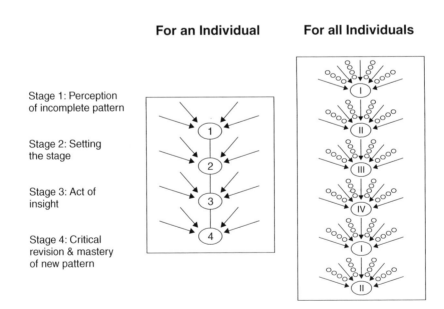

For an Individual

Stage 1: Perception of incomplete pattern

Stage 2: Setting the stage

Stage 3: Act of insight

Stage 4: Critical revision & mastery of new pattern

For all Individuals

Figure 9.3 Usher's model of cumulative synthesis. Left: The emergence of novelty in the act of insight: synthesis of familiar items: 1, perception of an incomplete pattern; 2, the setting of the stage; 3, the act of insight; 4, critical revision and full memory of the new pattern. Right: The process of cumulative synthesis. A full cycle of strategic invention, and part of a second cycle. Large figures I–IV represents steps in the development of a strategic invention. Small figures represent individual elements of novelty. Arrows represent familiar elements included in the new synthesis. *Source*: Usher (1929/1954).

"emergent novelty becomes truly significant only through cumulation" (p. 67) because strategic invention is a social process which blends "many individual items as well as many familiar elements" (p. 68). Insight on the part of the individual emerges from the recombination of familiar items and is embedded in and contributes to a social process of recombination. Usher's model of cumulative synthesis clearly depicts invention as a collective process in which the efforts of many embedded bricoleurs, each working on his or her own particular problem, are synthesized.

In a 1991 study of changes in organizational practices in the U.S. radio broadcasting industry during the period 1920 to 1965, Leblebici, Salancik, Copay, and King (1991) provide evidence that changes in the interorganizational field result from a process of cumulative synthesis. Leblebici et al. provide a rich historical analysis of the radio broadcasting interorganizational field and develop a four-stage model of the cycle of institutional change:

In the first stage, a choice is made in the interorganizational field as to *how to organize the field's fundamental interdependence* (in this case, the interdependence of broadcasters and listeners). How this choice is made defines "the relationships between actors [as well as] what resources are critical, what defines success, and what positions in the field are pivotal" (p.358).

In the second stage, new practices are introduced by fringe players who through trial and error develop solutions to "the problem of realizing value from transactions." Leblebici et al. show that many of the innovative practices in the radio broadcasting industry were introduced by "shady traders, small independent stations, renegade record producers, weaker networks, or enterprising advertising agencies." The powerful organizations in the field were not the innovators, because they had invested their resources in maintaining the status quo or in establishing new practices that confirmed established conventions.

In the third stage, the new institutionalized conventions produce distributional consequences and set off a new round of intensified competition for resources.

In the fourth stage, the intensified competition causes the dominant players in the field to adopt the new practices, in the process legitimating those practices.

Finally, the institutionalization of the innovative practice transforms relationships, positions in the field, and definitions of critical resources. Thus we return to stage one of the cycle.

Leblebici and his colleagues found that institutionalized organizational practices are introduced at the micro level by fringe players and then later adopted by more prestigious players. They found that while adoption by established actors provides legitimacy to new practices, both fringe and prestigious actors are motivated by instrumental reasons.

Garud, Jain, and Kumaraswamy's (2002) study of Sun Microsystems' sponsorship of the Java technological standard illustrates that multiple key actors involved in the technological development process are distributed, partisan, and become embedded in the technological and institutional trajectories that they are pursuing. The actors are distributed in the sense that many different public and private actors play roles in developing the institutional infrastructure that supports and enables technological development and that no single actor controls the technology development process. New technologies and related institutions are socially constructed and coevolve. Actors are embedded in the sense that because the technology development process is a collective one, their actions are constrained by and must be taken in concert with the actions of other actors in the process. Thus technology development is partially a path-dependent process in which both initial context and conditions matter. At the same time, however, the trajectory of actions is not completely determined by the process because learning can occur as the process unfolds. Actors invent new technologies and institutions and achieve legitimacy by recombining existing skills and knowledge; they are bricoleurs. Finally, actors are partisan in the sense that they participate from their own frames of references and often have different, even conflicting, interests. These interests are worked out through collective action processes in which actors use strategies and tactics of partisan mutual adjustment and political entrepreneurship, such as those described by Lindblom, Alinsky, and Fligstein (reviewed above in the institutional design section).

Garud and Karnøe (2003) attest to the importance of bricolage in their examination of the development of wind turbines in Denmark and the United States. The Danes developed reliable, cost-effective turbines by taking a "low-tech," incremental path that emphasized constant interaction and feedback among actors, a number of scale-up steps with product development efforts in between scale-ups, and government policies that strategically steered the activities of the various actors. In contrast, firms in the United States took a "high-tech" approach that was intended to but failed to achieve a technological breakthrough that would "leap-frog" Danish technology. U.S. engineers sought to apply lessons from aerospace engineering that turned out to be inapplicable and even misleading in the context of wind technology. Further, U.S. engineers and researchers paid little attention to product development and engaged in little information sharing with each other and with wind turbine users. Garud and Karnøe conclude that the Danes succeeded in developing viable wind turbine technology and in dominating the world wind turbine market because they recognized that technological innovation involves distributed, embedded agency among multiple actors, in this case designers, users, research centers, and regulators. Each of the actors in the Danish system focused on solving a small problem that was shaped by and embedded in the larger technology path, and although the actors had differing interpretive frames, their efforts fused through a process of creative synthesis. Garud and Karnøe provide very clear evidence of bricolage and the process of cumulative synthesis involving distributed, embedded, and partisan actors.

Hunt and Aldrich (1998) take a coevolutionary view of community change, writing that "the coevolution of an organizational community depends on the simultaneous processes of variation, selection, retention and struggle at the population level." They define the organizational community as a "set of coevolving organizational populations joined by ties of commensalism and symbiosis through their orientation to a common technology" (p. 272). They argue that community evolution involves three factors: (1) technological innovation, which acts as a catalyst for the creation of new organizational forms and new populations; (2) entrepreneurial activities that promote and sustain the growth of populations and communities; and (3) processes of legitimation at multiple levels. Like Usher and Rosenblom, Hunt and Aldrich argue that one can rarely identify a single event that triggers the creation of a new population. They take an evolutionary view that sees innovation as cumulative and incremental. They illustrate their

arguments with examples related to the evolution of the Internet.

In their study of technological change in the cement, glass, and minicomputer industries, Anderson and Tushman (1990) propose a cyclical, evolutionary model of technological change in which a technological breakthrough initiates an era of industry ferment that is marked by competition for dominance. This era of ferment culminates in convergence on a single dominant design that enables standardization; increased efficiency and volume; more stable relations with customers, suppliers, and vendors; and systemwide compatibility and integration. Because standard technologies are difficult to dislodge, periods in which a single technology dominates are marked by incremental change and order in the industry; nevertheless, these periods eventually are punctuated by new technological discontinuities that usher in new eras of ferment.

While Anderson and Tushman's view is an ecological one that sees technological change as a process of variation, selection, and retention, it also emphasizes that technological change emerges from collective processes marked by conflict among opposing interests. Anderson and Tushman write that during eras of ferment, competition takes place both between old and new technological regimes and within the new regime. Further, they note that "competence-destroying" technological breakthroughs face more stubborn opposition from entrenched interests than "competence-enhancing" breakthroughs" (Tushman and Anderson, 1986). Tushman and Anderson conclude that the "actions of individuals, organizations, and networks of organizations shape dominant designs" and that "the closing on an industry standard is an inherently political and organizational phenomenon constrained by technical possibilities. The passage of an industry from ferment to order is not an engineering issue as much as a sociological one" (p. 627).

In a 2001 study of knowledge industries—sets of organizations that produce substitutable knowledge (e.g., publishing, education, consulting, mass media)—Abrahamson and Fairchild observe a coevolution of a body of knowledge and the organizational communities that supply such knowledge. They focus their attention on idea entrepreneurs such as journalists, scholars, and technical experts, noting that when these entrepreneurs cause a body of knowledge to evolve, they also create a fertile soil in which new types of idea entrepreneurship and new knowledge organizations flourish and old ones wither. Like Murtha et al. (2001), Abrahamson and Fairchild note that because most ideas are consumed once or only a few times, idea entrepreneurs must continuously invent, reinvent, and repackage ideas. Further, because the shelf life of an idea is short, idea entrepreneurs must sow the seeds of new ideas, harvest them as long as they are being consumed, and be ever prepared to sow the next crop of progressive ideas. Abrahamson and Fairchild also describe the coevolution of knowledge and the community of idea entrepreneurs, writing that "organizing templates may emerge on the demand side of the management-knowledge markets and flow back to these markets, where they create opportunities for entrepreneurs, as well as new organizational templates for entrepreneurial activity" (p. 174).

Collective Action Summary

Both the social movements and technology emergence literatures document efforts to make institutional change through intentional collective action. Like the institutional design literature, these literatures see institutional change as constructed by actors; unlike the design literature, however, they analyze the industry or interorganizational field rather than the individual actor.

A number of key themes emerge from the social movements and technology emergence literatures. First, change is produced through collective efforts in which no single actor has the power or authority to produce change by itself. Second, change results from a process of cumulative synthesis in which actors contribute to a larger solution by recombining inherited practices, technologies, and institutions to address their own unique and particular problems. This vision of institutional change as collective and emergent provides a sharp contrast to the popular notion of innovation and change as resulting from a flash of brilliance by an inspired individual.

Third, the process of partial cumulative synthesis is path-dependent but not deterministic. Usher avoided determinism by viewing the steps involved in partial cumulative synthesis as occurring stochastically. While Campbell (2002) states that institutional change is path-dependent because high start-up costs impede the development of new ways, institutions are designed so that they are hard to dismantle, actors accumulate knowledge about how things work, and

beneficiaries of the status quo reinforce existing institutions, he also argues that path-dependence theories are too deterministic and fail to recognize learning and bricolage. In a 1996 study of institutional change in postcommunist Europe, Campbell and Pedersen argue that history and existing institutions do not simply lock actors into particular paths but also enable new possibilities by providing templates for recombination. Campbell and Pedersen find that in some former Soviet Union countries, actors created new institutions by drawing on long dormant ideologies from the past.

Scholars have begun to notice the similarities between social movements and technology emergence processes. Specifically, they have discovered that technology entrepreneurs must not only develop new technologies but also, like social movements leaders, engage in framing contests and mobilize resources while taking advantage of the opportunities presented by the political environment. While the framing/resource mobilization/political opportunity structure framework provided by social movements scholars is beginning to prove useful to technology researchers, social movements analysts could learn from technology scholars with respect to characterizing the processes of change. The technology/industry emergence literature is replete with descriptions of processes of cumulative synthesis that generates technology innovation (Usher 1929/1954), processes of variation, selection, and retention (Hunt and Aldrich, 1998; Rosenkopf and Nerkar, 1999), the coevolution of technology and institutions (e.g., Van de Ven and Garud, 1994) and cycles of change (Anderson and Tushman, 1990). Social movement theory has lacked such attention to process.

Technology scholars have also paid more attention than social movements scholars to the structure and characteristics of the organizational field. Noteworthy here are Van de Ven and Garud's (1993) augmented view of an industry and the work of scholars such as Stuart (2000), who draws explicitly on network theory.

Concluding Discussion

From this literature review we conclude that the study of institutional change is diverse, paradoxical, and healthy. Diversity is reflected in the different perspectives taken to explain institutional change.

Paradox is evident in the seemingly incompatible views taken to explain change, particularly as reflected in the long-standing tension between structure and action. Fortunately, our literature review provides a way to address this structure-action paradox: While institutional structures enable and constrain the behavior of individuals, it is the motivations and strategic actions of individuals and groups that create and change these institutions. The health of this scholarly community is reflected in its openness and cross-fertilization of theories and empirical findings with related fields of study—particularly social movements and technological innovation. As a result, it is evident that learning is occurring. Initially one-sided, somewhat naïve and static perspectives on institutional structure and action are becoming more nuanced, richly textured, and dynamic. This concluding section discusses these observations.

A Typology of Institutional Change Theories

Our literature review surfaced four distinct perspectives on institutional change: institutional design, institutional adaptation, institutional diffusion, and collective action. Each perspective addresses different questions about institutional change and relies on a different generative mechanism or motor (Van de Ven and Poole, 1995) to explain the change process.

Institutional design examines the purposeful creation or revision of institutions to address conflicts or social injustices. The generative mechanism for addressing questions of how institutions are created and emerge is teleology. It locates the motor of change in the purposeful strategic action and social construction of individual actors. In this view, institutional arrangements reflect the pursuit of conscious choices and behavior within the bounds that society judges to be prudent and reasonable.

Institutional adaptation explains how and why organizations conform to forces in the institutional environment. Relying on the metaphor of organic growth, a life cycle motor is used to prescribe how change unfolds in programmed or regulated directions. The adaptation perspective views institutional environmental pressures as the motor that shapes the structure and actions of organizational actors. The work of these new institutionalists can be characterized as taking an institutional adaptation perspective.

Institutional diffusion focuses on how and why specific institutional arrangements are adopted (selected) and diffused (retained) among institutional actors in a population. Density dependence arguments of population ecologists have been used to explain the legitimacy and competitive selection of certain institutional forms. These arguments rely on an evolution motor, where change is driven by competition for scarce environmental resources among entities inhabiting a population.

Collective action models examine the construction and change of institutions through the political behaviors among many actors who play diverse and partisan roles in the interorganizational field or network that emerges around a social movement or technical innovation. Scholars working from this perspective are primarily concerned with how new institutional arrangements emerge from interactions among interdependent partisan agents. This perspective relies on a dialectical motor of change, where confrontations emerge between conflicting entities espousing opposing thesis and antithesis that collide to produce a synthesis, which in time becomes the thesis for the next cycle of a dialectical progression of change.

Each of these four perspectives provides an internally consistent account of institutional change processes. When and where might each perspective apply to explain various facets of institutional change? Figure 9.4 presents a typology that is useful to address this question. Like Van de Ven and Poole's (1995) typology of four process theories of organizational change, the typology in figure 9.4 distinguishes the four perspectives of institutional change in terms of the mode of change and the focus of analysis.

Mode of change: The institutional design and collective action perspectives focus on the construction of institutional arrangements, while the institutional adaptation and diffusion perspectives focus on the reproduction of institutional arrangements among institutional actors through evolutionary and/or adaptive processes. The design and collective action perspectives emphasize strategic and political agency as the basis of action, while the adaptation and diffusion perspectives emphasize the conditioning effects of institutional structures and pressures on actors. In other words, the construction mode of change examines how institutional actors change institutional arrangements, while the reproduction mode examines how institutional arrangements change institutional actors. Correspondingly, the construction mode of change relies on individual agency, while the reproduction

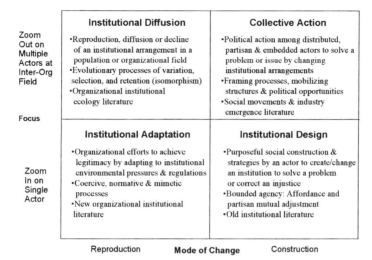

	Institutional Diffusion	Collective Action
Zoom Out on Multiple Actors at Inter-Org Field	•Reproduction, diffusion or decline of an institutional arrangement in a population or organizational field •Evolutionary processes of variation, selection, and retention (isomorphism) •Organizational institutional ecology literature	•Political action among distributed, partisan & embedded actors to solve a problem or issue by changing institutional arrangements •Framing processes, mobilizing structures & political opportunities •Social movements & industry emergence literature
Focus		
	Institutional Adaptation	Institutional Design
Zoom In on Single Actor	•Organizational efforts to achieve legitimacy by adapting to institutional environmental pressures & regulations •Coercive, normative & mimetic processes •New organizational institutional literature	•Purposeful social construction & strategies by an actor to create/change an institution to solve a problem or correct an injustice •Bounded agency: Affordance and partisan mutual adjustment •Old institutional literature
	Reproduction **Mode of Change** Construction	

Figure 9.4 Perspectives on institutional change.

mode of change emphasizes structural constraints on actors.

Focus: The institutional design and adaptation perspectives "zoom in" on the behavior of focal actors who are engaged in designing or adopting an institutional arrangement, while the diffusion and collective action perspectives "zoom" out to observe the construction or diffusion of an institutional arrangement among multiple actors at the level of the industry, population, or interorganizational field. This distinction is similar to the more common "micro versus macro" (intraorganizational versus interorganizational) levels of analysis.

We think that the metaphor of an optical lens that zooms in and out on the subject matter provides flexibility in describing the behavior of focal actors—be they people, units, organizations, or fields. A researcher needs to be able to observe processes of institutional change at close and distant degrees of magnification because change in any particular institution under investigation is typically embedded in a nested hierarchy of institutional actors and arrangements. The behaviors that a researcher observes when zooming in on the behavior of an individual actor will be conditioned by what he or she observes when zooming out to the interorganizational field, network, or population of actors, and vice versa. For example, behavior that appears at first to reflect the reproduction and impact of environmental pressures on actors may show upon closer scrutiny that entrepreneurial

actors are strategically engaged in constructing different kinds of institutional arrangements not evident from a distance. Another advantage of the optical lens metaphor is that it may reconcile questions about whether institutional change is caused by endogenous factors or exogenous shocks. Many factors or events that are outside of one's purview when looking up close become evident when one zooms out to a more distant view of the subject. Whether the motor or source of change is located within or outside of a theory is often a function of the degree or level of focus.

Relations among Change Perspectives

Our literature review has shown that the process of institutional change is more complicated than any one of the four perspectives. This is so for several reasons. First, we have seen that institutional change is not a unitary concept. There are many different forms of institutional change, and each perspective in figure 9.4 captures one of these forms of change. While each perspective in the typology provides a coherent perspective on institutional change, it is a one-sided perspective. As Poggie (1965, p. 294) said, "A way of seeing is a way of not seeing." The factors and events considered in other perspectives are useful to remedy the incompleteness of any single model of institutional change. Seeing the strengths in other perspectives to address the weaknesses in another is crucial for addressing theoretical tensions between action and structure among the four perspectives in the typology.

Hirsch and Lounsbury (1997) and Poole and Van de Ven (1989) point out that an action-structure paradox has fueled a long-standing debate between the old and new institutionalists. Hirsch and Lounsbury praise Powell and DiMaggio (1991) for stating clearly the dimensions that distinguish the action and structure perspectives (see table 9.2). They state that the action orientation of the old institutionalists to design institutions leads them to focus on dynamics, change, social construction, and values, as discussed in the institutional design and collective action perspectives. In contradistinction, the structuralist orientation of the new institutionalists focused on convergent processes of institutional adoption and diffusion that emphasized organizational isomorphism, cognition, and the dominance and continuity of the institutional environment on organizations (Hirsch and Lounsbury, 1997, p. 407).

Each perspective in the typology views the action-structure debate from a particular level of analysis and mode of change. Examining the strengths and limitations of each perspective provides the key ingredients for addressing this action-structure debate. Poole and Van de Ven (1989) discuss four ways to address opposing statements in this action-structure debate: (1) accept and constructively use the paradoxical nature of social institutions to appreciate their fragile structure and susceptibility to changing cultural beliefs and values; (2) clarify levels of analysis, for the purposeful strategic actions by individuals often appear at a distance to represent unexplained evolutionary variations; (3) separate the temporal periods when different poles of the tension between institutional structure and individual agency exert their forces and produce different forms of institutional change; and (4) introduce new terms, such as structuration theory, to dissolve apparent inconsistencies or oppositions. Poole and Van de Ven's (1989) four methods provide useful ways to address these and other oppositions among the four perspectives in the typology. Working out these conceptual oppositions and inconsistencies between the different perspectives in the typology can significantly advance and strengthen our understanding of institutional change in its different forms and periods.

Several scholars have used Giddens's (1984) structuration theory to bridge different perspectives dealing with the interaction of action and structure on environmental forces and the teleological pursuit of individual interests. Barley and Tolbert's (1997) model of institutionalization both describes a diffusion process and gives great weight to the efforts of actors to enact their environments. So also, Scott et al. (1999) apply the concept of structuration to explain their findings regarding changes in health care delivery systems in the San Francisco Bay Area. Scott et al. argue that structuration explains the coevolution of the organizational field with both its technical and institutional environments. These works pick up the assertions of Powell and DiMaggio (1991), who state that structuration theory accommodates both intentionality and adherence to routine.

Another reason why processes of institutional change are often more complicated than any one of

Table 9.2 Comparison of action in "old" and structure in "new" institutionalisms

Dimension	Old Institutionalism	New Institutionalism
conflicts of interest	central	peripheral
source of inertia	vested interests	environmental legitimacy
level of analysis	focal organizations	field, sector, society
institutional locus	organizational values, culture	abstracted, societal
behavioral emphasis	commitment	habits, rules
organizational dynamics	change	persistence
key forms of cognition	values, norms, attitudes	classifications, scripts, schemas
social psychology	socialization	attribution
goals	negotiable	symbolic
structural emphasis	informal networks	formal administration

Source: Adapted from DiMaggio and Powell (1991), p. 13, and Hirsch and Lounsbury (1997), p. 408.

the four perspectives in figure 9.4 is because change in any particular institution tends to be located in a nested hierarchy of institutional actors and arrangements. Since these other entities in the nested hierarchy are influenced by different actors and conditions, more than one change motor may operate and influence the change process. This is especially likely with the passage of time as different motors play prominent roles during an institution's temporal duration—its creation, ratification, adoption, diffusion, and demise. The resulting observed process may therefore be multilayered and multimodal, whereas each perspective in the typology pertains to only one layer and mode of change. As a result two or more perspectives in the typology need to be joined together to explain observed processes of institutional change.

Our literature review suggests that scholars are increasingly beginning to work across and integrate different perspectives on institutional change. For example, we notice that the more recent work of longstanding scholars who were early proponents of one perspective–such as Scott, McAdam, Clemens, Cook, Fligstein, Powell, Zucker, Campbell—was used to exemplify elements in more than one perspective. The fact that much of the work used to exemplify multiple perspectives is fairly recent indicates that scholars are increasingly crossing and integrating perspectives. In other words, perhaps it is the case that while the distinctions between perspectives were once sharp and crisp while they were forming initially, today they are becoming more blurred as scholars recognize the shortcomings of each one and grope toward a common and perhaps more general theory of institutional change.[3] For instance, chapter 10 in this volume, by Hinings, Greenwood, Reay, and Suddaby, presents a multimotor theory of institutional change that gives attention to both collective action processes and the efforts of individual actors to enact their environments. They recognize that actors intentionally interpret and recast institutions even as they respond to them, sometimes reproducing existing institutions and in other cases modifying them and creating new institutions.

Integrating Themes and Trends

A final concluding observation from our literature review is that institutional change is a healthy domain of scholarship. There appears to be a growing recognition and appreciation of the contributions of different scholarly communities—particularly social movements, technological innovation and entrepreneurship, and industry emergence. As Lounsbury and Ventresca (2002) observe, much learning appears to be occurring as a result of this "cross-pollination." Whereas early definitions and perspectives tended to be somewhat one-sided, naive, and static, the more recent literature on institutional change is becoming more nuanced, richly textured, and dynamic. In particular, the following four themes are noteworthy.

First, a more agency-oriented and social constructionist view of strategic action is emerging. As noted in our literature review, institutionalism was itself a reaction to the assumptions of methodological individualism in classical economics that viewed human beings as rational, utility maximizing, and atomized. However, with the exception of Commons and his followers, many institutional scholars became overly influenced by the elegance of rational expectation theory, which views strategic agency as having rational, free, and independent actors. Only recently have institutional scholars begun to recognize that strategic agency is itself a social construction that is contextually conditioned by institutional frames, norms, and regulations.

Institutions are "based fundamentally on a cognitively shared social reality which, in turn, is a human construction, being created in social interaction" (Scott, 1987, p. 495). Ironically, while neoinstitutional theorists have staunchly advanced this cognitive social construction of institutions, Stinchcombe (1997) criticizes them for having left "the guts out" of institutional theory by not addressing the exercise of power and politics in social construction. The process of institutionalization cannot be solely an emergent product of the shared cognitive belief systems of interacting individuals. Commons (1950) emphasized that in a society of scarcity, interdependence, and conflict, this social construction process can produce an unworkable neomodernist world of irreconcilable belief systems. Order to the institutionalization process, Commons argued, also requires collective sovereign action. The state and its delegates (officials, courts, boards, and police) can exercise their monopoly powers (including violence) in direct and indirect ways without specific individual consent. It can directly constrain, liberate, and expand certain belief systems through its collective working rules. Indirectly, it can promulgate and enforce its own belief system of the "official collective will."

Second, a more political view of institutional change is emerging that recognizes that this change is mobilized and driven by politically savvy institutional entrepreneurs. Increasingly, researchers are studying institutional change at a more macro level of the interorganizational field. They have begun to notice and describe how technical and institutional change coevolve in path-dependent processes that resemble social movements, and they have begun to integrate their study of interorganizational pressures, mechanisms, and processes with an examination of how diverse, partisan, and embedded actors engage in these movements to construct and change institutions. Lindblom (1965), Fligstein (1997), and Alinsky (1971) described the political strategies and tactics that entrepreneurs employ to pursue their interests while navigating environmental pressures. These works identify both political tactics and strategies for taking advantage of what the environment provides. In addition, as already noted, neoinstitutionalists including Kraatz and Zajac (1996); Oliver (1991); Greenwood et al. (2002); and Meyer et al. (1993) have begun to challenge their own assumptions about the immutability of institutions by describing creative efforts to change those institutions. In the technology innovation literature, Cusumano et al.'s 1992 study of the emergence of the videocassette recorder market, Garud et al.'s 2002 account of Sun Microsystems' efforts to spur the adoption of Java as a technological standard, Van de Ven and Garud's 1993 study of the emergence of the cochlear implant industry, and Van de Ven and Grazman's 1999 study of the genealogy of Minnesota Twin Cities health care organizations all provide evidence of the importance of institutional entrepreneurship in institutional change.

Third, few if any institutional changes begin with a clean slate; instead they begin with the existence of an inherited set of institutional actors and arrangements that were themselves produced historically through a bricolage process of crossing, grafting, or recombining existing institutional arrangements in novel ways. The fact of inheritance was discussed by Commons (1950), Fligstein (1996), Zucker and Darby (1996) and Van de Ven and Grazman (1999), and the importance of bricolage has been noted in the institutional diffusion (Czarniawska and Sevon, 1996; Rice and Rogers, 1980; Dobbin and Sutton, 1998; Edelman, Uggen, and Erlanger, 1999), social movements (Armstrong, 2002; Campbell, 2002) and technology emergence (Usher, 1929/1954; Garud

and Karnøe, 2003) literatures. One could say that recombinative efforts to reproduce existing institutions result in institutional diffusion, while recombinative efforts to create new institutions lead to institutional design.

A final trend that we see emerging across the literatures is increased emphasis on the processes of institutional change. Many of the process models that examine the sequence of events in which institutions change come from the technology literature, where researchers have been systematically studying the coevolution of technical and institutional changes. Although there are notable exceptions, institutional sociologists and social movements scholars have paid less attention to process. As we discussed in the first section of the chapter, process theories are important because they specify the mechanisms through which change unfolds over time rather than finding associations that exist at one time (but may not be found later). In their discussion of entrepreneurship and innovation, Schoonhoven and Romanelli (2001) amplify this argument, noting that a lack of attention to origins is a continuing problem in the literature on entrepreneurship. They write that it is difficult to study something before it comes about, especially with cross-sectional surveys or population counts. Longitudinal process studies are needed to observe the sequence of events in which institutions are constructed and reproduced (Poole et al., 2000).

Notes

We greatly appreciate useful comments on an earlier draft of this chapter from Elizabeth Boyle, John Campbell, Joseph Galaskiewicz, Raghu Garud, Luther Gerlach, Stephen Maguire, Alan Meyer, Scott Poole, Vernon Ruttan, Richard Scott, Arthur Stinchcombe, Robin Stryker, and Pamela Tolbert.

1. Note the consonance between the elements of Giddens's institutional realm (signification, domination, and legitimation) and Scott's three institutional pillars (cultural/cognitive, regulative, and normative.)

2. As it is presented in Hannan et al. (1995).

3. We appreciate John Campbell (Dartmouth College) for making this comment.

References

Abbott, A. (1988). Transcending general linear reality. *Sociological Theory*, 6, 375–392.

Abrahamson, E. & Fairchild, G. (1999). Management fashion: Lifecycles, triggers, and collective learning processes. *Administrative Science Quarterly, 44,* 708–740.

Abrahamson, E. & Fairchild, G. (2001). Knowledge industries and idea entrepreneurs: New dimensions of innovative products, services and organizations. In C. B. Schoonhoven & E. Romanelli (Eds.), *The entrepreneurship dynamic: Origins of entrepreneurship and the evolution of industries* (pp. 147–177). Stanford, CA: Stanford University Press.

Abrahamson, E. & Rosenkopf, L. (1993). Institutional and competitive bandwagons: Using mathematical modeling as a tool to explore innovation diffusion. *Academy of Management Review, 18,* 487–517.

Aldrich, H. E. (1999). *Organizations evolving.* Thousand Oaks, CA: Sage.

Aldrich, H. E. & Fiol, C. M. (1994). Fools rush in? Institutional context of industry creation. *Academy of Management Review, 19,* 645–670.

Alinsky, S. (1971). *Rules for radicals: A practical primer for realistic radicals.* New York: Random House.

Anderson, P. & Tushman, M. L. (1990). Technological discontinuities and dominant designs: A cyclical model of technological change. *Administrative Science Quarterly, 35,* 604–633.

Armstrong, E. (2002). *From struggle to settlement: The crystallization of a field of lesbian/gay organizations in San Francisco, 1969–1973.* Paper presented at the Social Movements and Organization Theory conference, Ann Arbor, MI. http://webuser.bus. umich.edu/organizations/smo/2002paper.html.

Astley, W. G. (1985). The two ecologies: Population and community perspectives on organizational evolution. *Administrative Science Quarterly, 30,* 224–241.

Barley, S. R. & Tolbert, P. S. (1997). Institutionalization and structuration: studying the links between action and institution. *Organization Science, 18,* 93–117.

Baum, J. A. C. & Oliver, C. (1992). Institutional embeddedness and the dynamics of organizational populations. *American Sociological Review, 57,* 540–559.

Baum, J. A. C. & Powell, W. W. (1995). Cultivating an institutional ecology of organizations: Comment on Hannan, Carroll, Dundon, and Torres. *American Sociological Review, 60,* 529–538.

Benford, R. D. & Snow, D. A. (2000). Framing processes and social movements: an overview and assessment. *Annual Review of Sociology, 26,* 611–639.

Berger, P. L. & Luckmann, T. (1967). *The social construction of reality.* New York: Doubleday Anchor.

Bijker, W. E., Hughes, T. P., & Pinch, T. J. (Eds.) (1987). *The social construction of technological systems: New directions in the sociology and history of technology.* Cambridge, MA: MIT Press.

Binswanger, H. P. & Ruttan, V. W. (1978). *Induced innovation.* Baltimore, MD: Johns Hopkins University Press.

Bower, J. L. & Christensen, C. M. (1995). Disruptive technologies: Catching the wave. *Harvard Business Review, 73,* 43–53.

Boyle, E. H. (2000). Is law the rule? Using political frames to explain cross-national variation in legal activity. *Social Forces, 79,* 385–418.

Braithwaite, J. & Drahos, P. (2000). *Global business regulation.* New York: Cambridge University Press.

Brint, S. & Karabel, J. (1991). Institutional origins and transformations: The case of American community colleges. In W. W. Powell & P. J. DiMaggio (Eds.), *The new institutionalism in organizational analysis* (pp. 337–360). Chicago, IL: University of Chicago Press.

Bryson, J. & Roering, W. (2001). Mobilizing innovation efforts: The case of government strategic planning. In A. H. Van de Ven, H. L. Angle, & M. S. Poole (Eds.), *Research on the management of innovation: The Minnesota studies* (pp. 583–610). New York: Oxford University Press.

Campbell, D. T. (1969). Variation and selective retention in socio-cultural evolution. *General Systems, 14,* 69–85.

Campbell, J. L. (2001). The problem of change in institutional analysis. Unpublished manuscript.

Campbell, J. L. (2002, May). *Where do we stand? Common mechanisms in organizations and social movements research.* Paper presented at the Social movements and Organization Theory conference, Lansing, MI. http://webuser.bus.umich.edu/organizations/smo/2002paper.html.

Campbell, J. L. & Pedersen, O. K. (1996). The evolutionary nature of revolutionary change in post-communist Europe. In J. L. Campbell & O. K. Pedersen (Eds.), *Legacies of change: Transformations of postcommunist European economies.* New York: Aldine de Gruyter.

Carroll, G. R. & Hannan, M. T. (1989). Density dependence in the evolution of populations of newspaper organizations. *American Sociological Review, 54,* 524–548.

Chandler, A. D. (1990). *Scale and scope: The dynamics of industrial capitalism.* Cambridge, MA: Harvard University Press.

Clemens, E. S. & Cook, J. M. (1999). Politics and institutionalism: Explaining durability and change. *Annual Review of Sociology, 25,* 441–466.

Commons, J. R. (1968). *The legal foundations of capitalism.* Madison, WI: University of Wisconsin Press. (Original work published 1924)

Commons, J. R. (1961). *Institutional economics: Its place in political economy.* Madison, WI: University of Wisconsin Press. (Original work published 1934)

Commons, J. R. (1950). *The economics of collective action.* Madison, WI: University of Wisconsin Press.

Constant, E. W. (1980). *The origins of the turbojet revolution.* Baltimore, MD: Johns Hopkins University Press.

Cusumano, M. A., Mylonadis, Y., & Rosenbloom, R. S. (1992). Strategic maneuvering and mass market dynamics: The triumph of VHS over Beta. *Business History Review, 66,* 51–93.

Czarniawska, B. & Sevon, G. (1996). Introduction. In B. Czarniawska & G. Sevon (Eds.), *Translating organizational change* (pp. 1–12). New York: Aldine de Gruyter.

Das, S. S. & Van de Ven, A. H. (2000). Competing with new product technologies: A process model of strategy. *Management Science, 46,* 1300–1316.

David, P. (1987). The hero and the herd in technological history: Reflections on Thomas Edison and the battle of the systems. In P. Higonnet, D. Landes, & H. Rosovsky (Eds.), *Favorites of fortune.* Cambridge, MA: Harvard University Press.

Davis, G. F. & McAdam, D. (2000). Corporations, classes, and social movements after managerialism. In B. Staw & R. Suttan (Eds.), *Research in Organizational Behavior* (Vol. 22, pp. 193–236). Greenwich, CT: JAI Press.

Deephouse, D. L. (1996). Does isomorphism legitimate? *Academy of Management Journal, 39,* 1024–1039.

DeLamarter, R. (1986). *Big Blue: IBM's use and abuse of power.* New York: Dodd, Mead.

DiMaggio, P. J. & Powell, W. W. (1983). The iron cage revisited: Institutional isomorphism and collective rationality in organizational fields. *American Sociological Review, 48,* 147–160.

Dobbin, F. R. & Sutton, J. R. (1998). The strength of a weak state: The rights revolution and the rise of human resources management divisions. *American Journal of Sociology, 104,* 441–476.

Dobbin, F. R., Edelman, L., Meyer, J. R., Scott, W. R., & Swidler, A. (1988). The expansion of due process in organizations. In L. G. Zucker (Ed.), *Institutional patterns and organizations: Culture and environment* (pp. 71–100). Cambridge, MA: Ballinger.

Dooley, K. & Van de Ven, A. H. (1999). Explaining complex organizational dynamics. *Organization Science, 10,* 358–372.

Dorfman, J. (1963). The background of institutional economics. In J. Dorfman, C. E. Ayres, N. W.

Chamberlain, S. Kuznets, & R. A. Gordon, *Institutional economics: Veblen, Commons, and Mitchell reconsidered.* Berkeley: University of California Press.

Dowell, G., Swaminathan, A., & Wade, J. (2002, May). *Pretty pictures and ugly scenes: Political and technological maneuvers in high definition television.* Paper presented at the Social Movements and Organization Theory Conference, Ann Arbor, MI. http://webuser.bus.umich.edu/organizations/smo/2002paper.html.

Edelman, L. B. (1992). Legal ambiguity and symbolic structures: organizational mediation of civil rights law. *American Journal of Sociology, 97,* 1531–1576.

Edelman, L. B., Uggen, C., & Erlanger, H. S. (1999). The endogeneity of legal regulation: Grievance procedures as rational myth. *American Journal of Sociology, 105,* 406–454.

Edwards, R. (1982). *Contested terrain: The transformation of the workplace in the twentieth century.* New York: Basic Books.

Fligstein, N. (1985). The spread of the multidivisional form among large firms. *American Sociological Review, 50,* 377–391.

Fligstein, N. (1996). Markets as politics: A political-cultural approach to market institutions. *American Sociological Review, 61,* 228–244.

Fligstein, N. (1997). Social skills and institutional theory. *American Behavioral Scientist, 40,* 397–405.

Galaskiewicz, J. (1997). An urban grants economy revisited: Corporate charitable contributions in the Twin Cities, 1979–81, 1987–89. *Administrative Science Quarterly, 42,* 445–471.

Galaskiewicz, J. & Wasserman, S. (1989). Mimetic processes within an interorganizational field: An empirical test. *Administrative Science Quarterly, 34,* 454–479.

Garfinkel, H. (1967). *Studies in ethnomethodology.* Englewood Cliffs, NJ: Prentice-Hall.

Garud, R., Jain, S., & Kumaraswamy, A. (2002). Institutional entrepreneurship in the sponsorship of common technological standards: The case of Sun Microsystems and Java. *Academy of Management Journal, 45,* 196–214.

Garud, R. & Karnøe, P. (2003). Bricolage vs. breakthrough: Distributed and embedded agency in technology entrepreneurship. *Research Policy.*

Garud, R. & Rappa, M. (1994). A socio-cognitive model of technology evolution. *Organization Science, 5,* 344–362.

Gerlach, L. P. (2001). The structure of social movements: Environmental activism and its opponents. In J. Arquilla & D. Ronfeldt (Eds.), *Networks and netwars: The future of terror, crime, and militancy* (pp. 300–320). Santa Monica, CA: RAND.

Gerlach, L. P. & Palmer G. B. (1981). Adaptation through evolving interdependence. In P. C. Nystrom & W. B. Starbuck (Eds.), *Handbook of organizational design* (pp. 323–381). Oxford: Oxford University Press.

Giddens, A. (1984). *The constitution of society.* Berkeley: University of California Press.

Gilfillan, S. G. (1935). *The sociology of invention.* Cambridge, MA: MIT Press.

Green, K. (1992). Creating demand for biotechnology: Shaping technologies and markets. In R. Coombs, P. Saviotti & V. Walsh (Eds.), *Technological change and company strategies: Economic and sociological perspectives* (pp. 164–184). San Diego, CA: Harcourt Brace Jovanovic.

Greenwood, R. & Hinings, C. R. (1996). Understanding radical organizational change: Bringing together the old and the new institutionalism. *Academy of Management Review, 21,* 1022–1054.

Greenwood, R., Suddaby, R., & Hinings, C. R. (2002). Theorizing change: The role of professional associations in the transformation of institutionalized fields. *The Academy of Management Journal, 45,* 58–80.

Greiner, L. E. (1970). Patterns of organizational change. In G. Dalton, P. R. Lawrence, & L. E. Greiner (Eds.), *Organizational change and development* (pp. 213–229). Homewood, IL: Irwin-Dorsey.

Hannan, M. T., Carroll, G. R., Dundon, E. A., & Torres, J. C. (1995). Organizational evolution in a multinational context: Entries of automobile manufacturers in Belgium, Britain, France, Germany, and Italy. *American Sociological Review, 60,* 509–528.

Hannan, M. T. & Freeman, J. (1989). *Organizational ecology.* Cambridge, MA: Harvard University Press.

Haveman, H. (2000). The future of organizational sociology: Forging ties among paradigms. *Contemporary Sociology, 29,* 476–486.

Henderson, R. M. & Clark, K. B. (1990). Architectural innovation: The reconfiguration of existing product technologies and the failure of established firms. *Administrative Science Quarterly, 35,* 9–30.

Hirsch, P. M. & Lounsbury, M. (1997). Ending the family quarrel: Toward a reconciliation of "old" and "new" institutionalisms. *American Behavioral Scientist, 40,* 406–418.

Hoffman, A. J. (1997). *From heresy to dogma: An institutional history of corporate environmentalism.* San Francisco, CA: The New Lexington.

Holm, P. (1995). The dynamics of institutionalization: Transformation in Norwegian fisheries. *Administrative Science Quarterly, 40,* 398–422.

Hughes, T. P. (1983). *Networks of power: Electrification in western societies, 1880–1930.* Baltimore, MD: Johns Hopkins University Press.

Hull, D. L. (1988). *Science as a process: An evolutionary account of the social and conceptual development of science.* Chicago: University of Chicago Press.

Hunt, C. S. & Aldrich, H. E. (1998). The second ecology: Creation and evolution of organizational communities. In B. Staw & L. L. Cummings (Eds.), *Research in organizational behavior* (pp. 267–302). Greenwich, CT: JAI Press.

Hurwicz, L. (1987). Inventing new institutions: The design perspective. *American Journal of Agricultural Economics, 69,* 395–402.

Hurwicz, L. (1993). Toward a framework for analyzing institutions and institutional change. In S. Bowles, H. Gintis, & B. Gustafsson (Eds.), *Markets and democracy: Participation, accountability, and efficiency* (pp. 51–67). Cambridge: Cambridge University Press.

Jewkes, J., Sawers, D., & Stillerman, R. (1958). *The sources of invention.* New York: MacMillan.

Kelly, E. L. (2002). *The strange history of employer-sponsored childcare: Ambiguity, access, and transformation of law in organizational fields.* Manuscript in preparation.

Kerr, S. (1975). On the folly of rewarding A, while hoping for B. *Academy of Management Journal, 18,* 769–783.

Kraatz, M. S. & Moore, J. H. (2002). Executive migration and institutional change. *Academy of Management Journal, 45,* 120–143.

Kraatz, M. S. & Zajac, E. J. (1996). Exploring the limits of the new institutionalism: The causes and consequences of illegitimate organizational change. *American Sociological Review, 61,* 812–836.

Kuhn, T. S. (1982). The structure of scientific revolutions. Homewood, IL: Richard Irwin. (Original work published 1962)

Lawler, E. E. & Rhode, J. G. (1976). *Information and control in organizations.* Pacific Palisades, CA: Goodyear.

Leblebici, H. & Salancik, G. R. (1982). Stability in interorganizational exchanges: Rulemaking processes of the Chicago Board of Trade. *Administrative Science Quarterly, 27,* 227–242.

Leblebici, H., Salancik, G. R., Copay, A., & King, T. (1991). Institutional change and transformation of interorganizational fields. *Administrative Science Quarterly, 36,* 333–363.

Lee, K. & Pennings, J. M. (2002). Mimicry and the market: Adoption of a new organizational form. *Academy of Management Journal, 45*(1), 144–162.

Liebeskind, J. P., Oliver, A. L., Zucker, L., & Brewer, M. (1996, July–August). Social networks, learning, and flexibility: Sourcing scientific knowledge in new biotechnology firms. *Organization Science*, 7, 428–443.

Lindblom, C. E. (1965). *The intelligence of democracy: Decision making through mutual adjustment.* New York: Free Press.

Lindquist, K. & Mauriel, J. (2001). Depth and breadth in innovation implementation: The case of school-based management. In A. H. Van de Ven, H. L. Angle, & M. S. Poole (Eds.), *Research on the management of innovation: The Minnesota studies* (pp. 561–582). New York: Oxford University Press.

Lounsbury, M. (2002). *Institutional variation in the evolution of social movements: The spread of recycling advocacy groups.* Paper presented at the Social Movements and Organization Theory conference, Lansing, MI. http://webuser.bus.umich.edu/organizations/smo/2002paper.html.

Lounsbury, M. & Ventresca, M. J. (Eds.) (2002). Social structure and organizations revisited. *Elsevier Science, Ltd.*, 19, 3–36.

Maguire, S. (2002). Discourse and the adoption of innovations: A study of HIV/AIDS treatments. *Health Care Management Review*, 27, 74–88.

Marcus, A. & Weber, M. (2001). Externally induced innovation. In A. H. Van de Ven, H. L. Angle, & M. S. Poole (Eds.), *Research on the management of innovation: The Minnesota studies* (pp. 537–60). New York: Oxford University Press.

Mattsson, L. G. (1987). Management of strategic change in a "markets-as-networks" perspective. In A. Pettigrew (Ed.), *The management of strategic change* (pp. 234–256). London: Basil Blackwell.

McAdam, D. & Scott, W. R. (2002, May). *Organizations and movements.* Stanford University working paper. Paper presented at the Social Movements and Organization Theory conference, Lansing, MI. http://webuser.bus.umich.edu/organizations/smo/2002paper.html.

McAdam, D., McCarthy, J. D., & Zald, M. N. (1996). Introduction: Opportunities, mobilizing structures, and framing processes—Toward a synthetic, comparative perspective on social movements. In D. McAdam, J. D. McCarthy, & M. N. Zald (Eds.), *Comparative perspectives on social movements: Political opportunities, mobilizing structures and cultural framings* (pp. 1–20). New York: Cambridge University Press.

McAdam, D., Tarrow, S., & Tilly C. (2001). *Dynamics of contention.* New York: Cambridge University Press.

McCann, M. W. (1994). *Rights at work: Pay equity and the politics of legal mobilization.* Chicago: University of Chicago Press.

McCarthy, J. D., Smith, J., & Zald, M. N. (1996). Accessing public, media, electoral, and governmental agendas. In D. McAdam, J. D. McCarthy, & M. N. Zald (Eds.), *Comparative perspectives on social movements: Political opportunities, mobilizing structures, and cultural framings* (pp. 291–311). New York: Cambridge University Press.

Meyer, A. D., Goes, J. B., & Brooks, G. R. (1993). Organizations reacting to hyperturbulence. In G. Huber & Glick (Eds.), *Organizational change and redesign* (pp. 66–111). New York: Oxford University Press.

Meyer, J. R. & Rowan, B. (1977). Institutionalized organizations: Formal structure as myth and ceremony. *American Journal of Sociology*, 83, 340–363.

Mezias, S. J. (1990). An institutional model of organizational practice: Financial reporting at the Fortune 200. *Administrative Science Quarterly*, 35, 431–457.

Mezias, S. J. & Kuperman, J. C. (2000). The community dynamics of entrepreneurship: The birth of the American film industry, 1895–1929. *Journal of Business Venturing*, 16, 209–233.

Miner, A. S., Eesley, D. T., DeVaughn, M., & Rura-Polley, T. (2001). The magic beanstalk vision: Commercializing university inventions and research. In C. B. Schoonhoven & E. Romanelli (Eds.), *The entrepreneurship dynamic: Origins of entrepreneurship and the evolution of industries* (pp. 109–146). Stanford, CA: Stanford University Press.

Mitchell, W. C. (1910). The rationality of economic activity: II. *Journal of Political Economy*, 18, 197–216.

Mohr, L. B. (1982). *Explaining organizational behavior: The limits and possibilities of theory and research.* San Francisco, CA: Jossey-Bass.

Morrill, C., Zald, M. N., & Rao, H. (2003). Covert political conflict in organizations: Challenges from below. *Annual Review of Sociology*, 29, 391–415.

Murmann, J. P. & Tushman, M. L. (2001). From the technology cycle to the entrepreneurship dynamic: The social context of entrepreneurial innovation. In C. B. Schoonhoven & E. Romanelli (Eds.), *The entrepreneurship dynamic: Origins of entrepreneurship and the evolution of industries* (pp. 178–203). Stanford, CA: Stanford University Press.

Murtha, T., Lenway, S., & Hart, J. (2001). *Managing new industry creation: Global knowledge formation and entrepreneurship in high technology.* Stanford, CA: Stanford University Press.

Nelson, R. N. (1982). *Government and technical progress: A cross-industry analysis.* New York: Pergamon Press.

North, D. C. (1990). *Institutions, institutional change, and economic performance.* New York: Cambridge University Press.

Oliver, C. (1991). Strategic responses to institutional processes. *Academy of Management Review, 16*, 145–179.

Oliver, C. (1992). The antecedents of deinstitutionalization. *Organization Studies, 13*, 563–588.

Parsons, T. (1960). A sociological approach to the theory of organizations. In T. Parsons (Ed.), *Structure and process in modern societies*. Glencoe, IL: Free Press.

Pentland, B. T. (1999). Building process theory with narrative: From description to explanation. *Academy of Management Review, 24*, 711–724.

Perrow, C. (1991). A society of organizations. *Theory and Society, 20*, 725–762.

Poggie, G. (1965). A main theme of contemporary sociological analysis: Its achievements and limitations. *British Journal of Sociology, 16*, 283–294.

Poole, M. S. & Van de Ven, A. H. (1989). Using paradox to build management and organization theories. *Academy of Management Review, 14*, 562–578.

Poole, M. S., Van de Ven, A. H., Dooley, K., & Holmes, M. E. (2000). *Organizational change and innovation processes*. Oxford: Oxford University Press.

Porac, J. F., Thomas, H., Wilson, F., Paton, D., & Kanfer, A. (1995). Rivalry and the industry model of Scottish knitwear producers. *Administrative Science Quarterly, 40*, 203–229.

Porter, M. E. (1980). *Competitive strategy: Techniques for analyzing industries and competitors*. New York: Free Press.

Powell, W. W. (1998, Spring). Learning from collaboration: Knowledge and networks in the biotechnology and pharmaceutical industries. *California Management Review, 40*, 228–240.

Powell, W. W. & DiMaggio, P. J. (Eds.) (1991). *The new institutionalism in organizational analysis*. Chicago: University of Chicago Press.

Powell, W. W., Koput, K. W., & Smith-Doerr, L. (1996). Interorganizational collaboration and the locus of innovation: Networks of learning in biotechnology. *Administrative Science Quarterly, 41*, 116–145.

Rao, H. (2001). The power of public competition: Promoting cognitive legitimacy through certification contests. In C. B. Schoonhoven & E. Romanelli (Eds.), *The entrepreneurship dynamic: origins of entrepreneurship and the evolution of industries* (pp. 262–282). Stanford, CA: Stanford University Press.

Rao, H., Morrill, C., & Zald, M. N. (2000). Power plays: How social movements and collective action create new organizational forms. In B. Staw & R. Suttan (Eds.), *Research in organizational behavior* (Vol. 22, pp. 237–281). Greenwich, CT: JAI Press.

Rappa, M. (1987). *The structure of technological revolutions: An empirical study of the development of III-V compound semiconductor technology*. Un-

published doctoral dissertation, Carlson School of Management, University of Minnesota, Minneapolis.

Rice, R. & Rogers, E. (1980). Reinvention in the innovation process. *Knowledge: Creation, Diffusion, and Utilization, 1*, 499–514.

Rogers, E. M. (1995). *The diffusion of innovations* (4th ed.). New York: Free Press.

Romanelli, E. (1992). Review of *The new institutionalism in organizational analysis*. *Academy of Management Review, 17*, 612–615.

Rosenberg, N. (1983). *Inside the black box: Technology and economics*. Cambridge: Cambridge University Press.

Rosenkopf, L. & Nerkar, A. (1999). On the complexity of technological evolution: Exploring coevolution within and across hierarchical levels in optical disc technology. In J. A. C. Baum & B. McKelvey (Eds.), *Variations in organization science: In honor of Donald T. Campbell* (pp. 169–184). Thousand Oaks, CA: Sage.

Rosenkopf, L. & Tushman, M. L. (1994). The coevolution of technology and organization. In J. A. C. Baum & J. V. Singh (Eds.), *Evolutionary dynamics of organizations* (pp. 403–424). New York: Oxford University Press.

Rucht, D. (1999). The transnationalization of social movements: Trends, causes, problems. In D. Della Porta, H. Kriesi, & D. Rucht, *Social movements in a globalizing world* (pp. 206–222). London: MacMillan.

Rutherford, M. (1994). *Institutions in economics: The old and the new institutionalism*. Cambridge: Cambridge University Press.

Ruttan, V. W. (2001). *Technology, growth, and development: An induced innovation perspective*. New York: Oxford University Press.

Ruttan, V. W. & Hayami, Y. (1984). Toward a theory of induced institutional innovation. *Journal of Development Studies, 20*, 203–223.

Schon, D. (1971). *Beyond the stable state*. New York: Norton.

Schoonhoven, C. B. & Romanelli, E. (2001). Emergent themes and the next wave of entrepreneurship research. In C. B. Schoonhoven & E. Romanelli (Eds.), *The entrepreneurship dynamic: Origins of entrepreneurship and the evolution of industries* (pp. 383–408). Stanford, CA: Stanford University Press.

Scott, W. R. (1987). The adolescence of institutional theory. *Administrative Science Quarterly, 32*, 493–511.

Scott, W. R. (2001). *Institutions and organizations* (2nd ed.). Thousand Oaks, CA: Sage.

Scott, W. R., Ruef, M., Mendel, P. J., & Caronna, C. (1999). *Institutional change and healthcare organization: From professional dominance to managed care.* Chicago: University of Chicago Press.

Scully, M. A. & Creed, W. E. D. (2002, May). *Subverting our stories of subversion.* Paper presented at Social Movements and Organization Theory conference, Lansing, MI. Manuscript in preparation. http://webuser.bus.umich.edu/organizations/smo/2002paper.html.

Selznick, P. (1949). *TVA and the grass roots.* Berkeley: University of California Press.

Selznick, P. (1957). *Leadership in administration.* New York: Harper and Row.

Sherer, P. D. & Lee, K. (2002). Institutional change in large law firms: A resource dependency and institutional perspective. *Academy of Management Journal, 45,* 102–120.

Stinchcombe, A. L. (1965). Social structure and organizations. In J. G. March (Ed.), *Handbook of organizations* (pp. 142–193). Chicago: Rand McNally.

Stinchcombe, A. L. (1997). On the virtues of the old institutionalism. *Annual Review of Sociology, 23,* 1–18.

Strang, D. & Bradburn, E. M. (2001). Theorizing legitimacy or legitimating theory? Neoliberal discourse and HMO policy, 1970–89. In J. L. Campbell & O. K. Pedersen (Eds.), *The rise of neoliberalism and institutional analysis* (pp. 129–158). Princeton, NJ: Princeton University Press.

Stryker, R. (1994). Rules, resources, and legitimacy processes: Some implications for social conflict, order, and change. *American Journal of Sociology, 99,* 847–910.

Stryker, R. (2000). Legitimacy processes as institutional politics: Implications for theory and research in the sociology of organizations. *Research in the Sociology of Organizations, 17,* 179–223.

Stuart, T. (2000). Interorganizational alliances and the performance of firms: A study of growth and innovation rates in a high-technology industry. *Strategic Management Journal, 21,* 791–811.

Suchman, M. C., Steward, D. J., & Westfall, C. A. (2001). The legal environment of entrepreneurship: Observations on the legitimation of venture finance in Silicon Valley. In C. B. Schoonhoven & E. Romanelli (Eds.), *The entrepreneurship dynamic: Origins of entrepreneurship and the evolution of industries* (pp. 109–146). Stanford, CA: Stanford University Press.

Swaminathan, A. & Wade, J. B. (2001). Social movement theory and the evolution of new organizational forms. In C. B. Schoonhoven & E. Romanelli (Eds.), *The entrepreneurship dynamic: Origins of entrepreneurship and the evolution of*
industries (pp. 286–313). Stanford, CA: Stanford University Press.

Tarrow, S. (1994). *Power in movement: Social movements, collective action, and politics.* New York: Cambridge University Press.

Tarrow, S. (1996). States and opportunities: The political structuring of social movements. In D. McAdam, J. D. McCarthy, & M. N. Zald (Eds.), *Comparative perspectives on social movements: Political opportunities, mobilizing structures and cultural framings* (pp. 41–61). New York: Cambridge University Press.

Thornton, P. (2002). The rise of the corporation in the craft industry: Conflict and conformity in institutional logics. *Academy of Management Journal, 45,* 102–120.

Tilly, C. (1978). *From mobilization to revolution.* Reading, MA: Addison-Wesley.

Tolbert, P. S. & Zucker, L. G. (1983). Institutional sources of change in the formal structure of organizations: The diffusion of civil service reform, 1880–1935. *Administrative Science Quarterly, 28,* 22–29.

Tolbert, P. S. & Zucker, L. G. (1996). The institutionalization of institutional theory. In S. R. Clegg, C. Hardy, & W. R. Nord (Eds.), *The handbook of organization studies* (pp. 175–190). London: Sage.

Tushman, M. L. & Anderson, P. (1986). Technological discontinuities and organizational environments. *Administrative Science Quarterly, 31,* 439–465.

Tushman, M. L. & Romanelli, E. (1985). Organizational evolution and revolution. In B. Staw & L. L. Cummings (Eds.), *Research in organizational behavior* (pp. 171–222). Greenwich, CT: JAI Press.

Usher, A. P. (1954). *A history of mechanical invention.* (Rev. ed.) Cambridge, MA: Harvard University Press. (Original work published 1929)

Van de Ven, A. H. (1992). Suggestions for studying strategy process: A research note. *Strategic Management Journal, 13,* 169–188.

Van de Ven, A. H. (1993). The institutional theory of John R. Commons: A review and commentary. *Academy of Management Review, 18,* 129–152.

Van de Ven, A. H. & Garud, R. (1989). A framework for understanding the emergence of new industries. In R. S. Rosenbloom & R. Burgelman (Eds.), *Research on technological innovation, management, and policy* (Vol. 4, pp. 195–225). Greenwich, CT: JAI Press.

Van de Ven, A. H. & Garud, R. (1993). Innovation and industry emergence: The case of cochlear implants. In R. S. Rosenbloom & R. Burgelman (Eds.), *Research on technological innovation, management, and policy* (Vol. 5, pp. 1–46). Greenwich, CT: JAI Press.

Van de Ven, A. H. & Garud, R. (1994). The coevolution of technical and institutional events in the development of an innovation. In J. A. C. Baum & J. V. Singh (Eds.), *Evolutionary dynamics of organizations* (pp. 425–443). New York: Oxford University Press.

Van de Ven, A. H. & Grazman, D. N. (1999). Evolution in a nested hierarchy: A genealogy of Twin Cities health care organizations, 1853–1995. In J. A. C. Baum & B. McKelvey (Eds.), *Variations in organization science: In honor of Donald T. Campbell* (pp. 185–212). Thousand Oaks, CA: Sage.

Van de Ven, A. H. & Lofstrom, S. M. (1997). The diffusion and adoption of innovations in health care. Public testimony before Subcommittee on Quality Improvement and Environment, President's Advisory Committee on Consumer Protection and Quality in Health Care Industry, Chicago, IL.

Van de Ven, A. H. & Poole, M. S. (1995). Explaining development and change in organizations. *Academy of Management Review, 20,* 510–540.

Van de Ven, A. H., Polley, D. E., Garud, R., & Venkataraman, S. (1999). *The innovation journey.* Oxford: Oxford University Press.

Veblen, T. B. (1964). *The instinct of workmanship and the state of the industrial arts.* New York: Augustus M. Kelley. (Original work published 1914)

Wade, J. B., Swaminathan, A., & Saxon, M. S. (1998). Normative and resource flow consequences of local regulations. *Administrative Science Quarterly, 43,* 905–935.

Weber, M. (1968). Economy and society: An interpretive sociology. Three volumes. G. Roth & C. Wittich (Eds.) New York: Bedminister Press. (Original work published 1924)

Westphal, J. D., Gulati, R., & Shortell, S. M. (1997). Customization or conformity? An institutional and network perspective on the content and consequences of TQM adoption. *Administrative Science Quarterly, 42,* 366–394.

Wojick, D. (1979). The structure of technological revolutions. In G. Bugilarello & D. Doner (Eds.), *The history and philosophy of technology* (pp. 238–257). Urbana: University of Illinois Press.

Zald, M. N. (1996). Culture, ideology, and strategic framing. In D. McAdam, J. D. McCarthy, & M. N. Zald (Eds.), *Comparative perspectives on social movements: Political opportunities, mobilizing structures, and cultural framings* (pp. 261–274). New York: Cambridge University Press.

Zald, M. N., Morrill, C., & Rao, H. (2002, May). *How do social movements penetrate organizations? Environmental impact and organizational response.* Paper presented at the Social Movements and Organization Theory conference, Lansing, MI. http://webuser.bus.umich.edu/organizations/smo/2002paper.html.

Zucker, L. G. (1986). Production of trust: Institutional sources of economic structure, 1840–1920. In B. Staw & L. L. Cummings (Eds.), *Research in organizational behavior* (Vol. 8, pp. 53–111). Greenwich, CT: JAI Press.

Zucker, L. G. (1989). Combining institutional theory and population ecology: No legitimacy, no history (comment on Carroll-Hannan). *American Sociological Review, 54,* 542–545.

Zucker, L. G. & Darby, M. R. (1996). Costly information: From transformation, exit or persistent failure. *American Behavioral Scientist, 39,* 959–974.

Zucker, L. G. & Darby, M. R. (1997). Individual action and the demand for institutions. *American Behavioral Scientist, 40,* 502–513.

10

Dynamics of Change in Organizational Fields

C. R. (Bob) Hinings, Royston Greenwood, Trish Reay, & Roy Suddaby

This chapter proposes a process model for understanding institutional change at the organizational field level of analysis. This process model consists of five overlapping stages of institutional change: (1) pressures for change; (2) the sources of new practices from institutional entrepreneurs; (3) the processes of deinstitutionalization and reinstitutionalization; (4) the dynamics of deinstitutionalization and reinstitutionalization; and (5) reinstitutionalization and stability. We see this process model as useful for integrating much of the literature on institutional change. While this literature has been criticized for its static focus on convergence toward similar and stable states, it has always included an interest in change, and we use the process model to indicate the specific contributions of existing studies.

At the heart of institutional theory is the notion of institutions as "socially constructed, routine-reproduced programs or rules systems" (Jepperson, 1991, p. 149). Ways of organizing and acting become taken-for-granted because of their embeddedness and legitimacy. Institutional change, therefore, is the movement from one institutionally prescribed and legitimated pattern of practices to another. As such it involves processes of de- and reinstitutionalization. According to Scott (2001), organizational fields are

instrumental in disseminating and reproducing these socially constructed expectations and practices. Organizational fields are "sets of organizations that, in the aggregate, constitute an area of institutional life" (DiMaggio and Powell, 1983, p. 148) and those patterns of interaction are defined by shared systems of meaning (Scott, 1994).

According to Seo and Creed (2002, p. 222), "during the past two decades, institutional theorists have been able to offer more insights into the processes that explain institutional stability than those that explain institutional change." That is, institutional theory has had a primary emphasis on showing how and why organizations adopt institutionalized practices and systems—the question of why organizations come to be more and more like each other—so there has been an emphasis on the dynamics of convergence and institutionalization. The presumed endpoint of much of this theoretical work has been the steady state, a mature organizational field that has stronger forces holding it together than forces that tend to disruption and change. As Holm (1995, p. 398), put it, "The processes by which institutions are formed and reformed, which tend to be interest-driven and highly political, have been ignored. The result is an institutional theory that cannot explain how institutions are created and how they change." However, this focus is changing (Barley and Tolbert, 1997; Dacin, Goodstein, and Scott, 2002; Lawrence, Winn and Jennings, 2001; Oliver, 1992; Tolbert and Zucker, 1996), and recent theorizing has begun to point out the potential for addressing radical as well as convergent change. Indeed, Dacin et al. (2002, p. 45) suggest that "the topic of institutional change has emerged as a central focus for organizational researchers."

We believe that there is a need for a process model that explains how and why institutions change. Little attention has been given to understanding how the effects of isomorphism are brought about (rather than to the outcome itself), so that little is known of how and why institutionalized practices within a field atrophy or change. Tolbert and Zucker (1996, p. 175), in their excellent review of institutional theory, point out that, "despite the sizeable body of work defined as part of this tradition, there has been surprisingly little attention given to conceptualizing and specifying the processes of institutionalization." Similarly, Seo and Creed (2002) argue the processes that provide an essential understanding of institutional change "have not been adequately delineated in several recent efforts to explain institutional change" (p. 223). It is our challenge and object to provide that adequate delineation.

The paper presents a stage circular model of the processes and dynamics of institutional change. In developing the model, we draw on, and extend, the discussion and model presented in Greenwood, Suddaby, and Hinings (2002). Before describing the model, we review the literature on change in organizational fields. We then outline the role of institutional archetypes. Subsequently, each of the five stages is discussed. We conclude with a discussion of what this model means for future research.

Change in Organizational Fields

DiMaggio and Powell (1983, pp. 148–149) define an organizational field as: "Sets of organizations that, in the aggregate, constitute an area of institutional life: key suppliers, resource and product consumers, regulatory agencies, and other organizations that produce similar services or products." As Scott (2001, p. 137) puts it, "most analysts adopt a commonsense definition of field, a set of diverse organizations engaged in a similar function." In his earlier work, Scott (1994) suggests that patterns of interaction between organizational communities are defined by shared systems of meaning. Meaning systems establish the boundaries of communities of organizations, defining appropriate ways of behaving, membership, and appropriate relationships between these communities of organizations (Lawrence, 1999).

The notion of organizational field thus draws on a social constructionist view (Berger and Luckman, 1967; Zucker, 1977, 1987). Collective beliefs and values emerge from repeated interactions between organizations. Organizations develop typifications of their exchanges, which are objectified, thus constituting social reality. Behaving in accordance with this socially constructed reality reduces ambiguity and uncertainty for organizations. Reciprocally shared understandings of appropriate practice permit ordered exchanges. Over time, these shared understandings, or collective beliefs, become reinforced by isomorphic processes (coercive, normative, and mimetic), which both disseminate and reproduce coded prescriptions of social reality, thus pressing conformity upon constituent communities. Deviations from such prescriptions trigger attempts to justify (i.e., legitimize) departures from the social norm (Deephouse, 1999; Elsbach, 1994; Lamertz and Baum, 1997; Miller and Chen, 1995) or, perhaps, set in train new social constructions and their consequential change and transformation of the organizational field.

The concept of structuration captures this process of gradual maturity and specification of roles, behaviors, and interactions of organizational fields. But boundaries and behaviors are not fixed: structuration does not produce perfect reproduction (Goodrick and Salancik, 1996; Ranson, Hinings, and Greenwood, 1980). The boundaries of organizational communities are constantly under review and subject to redefinition and defense; they are the outcome of ongoing claims and counterclaims (Greenwood, Suddaby, and Hinings, 2002).

Institutional processes may, generally, work toward field stability. However, there are always differences of interpretation and emphasis that may be temporarily resolved by socially negotiated consensus. The appearance of stability is thus probably misleading (e.g. Sahlin-Andersson, 1996, p. 74) and fields should be seen "not as static but evolving" (Hoffman, 1999, p. 352). There may be times when fields may even "resemble institutional war" (p. 352). Boundaries

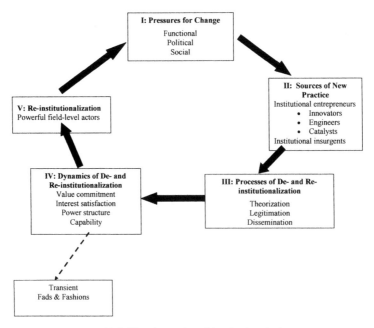

Figure 10.1 The dynamics of institutional change.

between organizations often exhibit phases of iso-morphic stability. But there is always likely to be at least implicit contestation.

We take up and develop these indications of change in our processual model of the dynamics of institutional change. Figure 10.1 outlines the stages of that model. Initially, there have to be events ("jolts," according to Meyer, Brooks, and Goes, 1990) that destabilize established practices (stage I). At stage II these events allow the entry and operation of in-stitutional entrepreneurs. But the new ideas and practices that these entrepreneurs put forward have to be formulated and gain legitimacy, constituting stage III of the model. Stage IV suggests conflict and contestation that takes place at both field and orga-nizational levels with attempts to formalize the new patterns of activity. Fields then achieve a degree of stability as they become reinstitutionalized (stage V). It is important that the model is circular, as re-institutionalization will be the subject of both on-going and further challenges as it evolves.

Institutional Archetypes

Organizations receive pressures from the institutional context to organize in prescribed ways (and not to organize in proscribed ways). These prescriptions, we suggest, constitute organizational design templates, or "archetypes." An archetype is a configuration of struc-tures and systems that are consistent with an under-lying interpretive scheme. Institutional theory stresses that archetypes originate outside an organization: "Or-ganizational environments are composed of cultural elements, that is, taken for granted beliefs and widely promulgated rules that serve as *templates for organiz-ing*. Institutional reproduction has been associated with the demands of powerful central actors, such as the state, the professions, or the dominant agents within organizational fields. This emphasis has highlighted the constraints imposed by institutions and stressed the ubiquity of rules that guide behavior" (DiMaggio and Powell, 1991, p. 278, emphasis added).

Kikulis, Slack, and Hinings (1995) show how the overall pattern of practices in organizations, estab-lished in structures and systems of organizing, are underpinned by core values and ideas—that is, an interpretive scheme (Ranson et al., 1980). Blau and McKinley (1979) analyze architectural practices as "work motifs," while Pettigrew (1985) describes ICI Corporation's organizational and managerial prac-tices in terms of "dominating rationalities or core beliefs." Haveman and Rao (2002) conceptualize the organizing force of "moral sentiments."

As fields develop, the processes of structuration produce an isomorphism in organizational forms, which are exhibited in a unity of interpretive scheme, organizational structures, and systems of activities—that is, there develops an institutionally defined and legitimated archetype. Organizations in the mature field adopt the same prescribed archetypal template. As fields mature they become increasingly stable, as they become more interconnected through common structures, interactions, and beliefs (Scott, 2001). Organizations within the field become more like each other through the consequences of coercive, normative, and mimetic processes that press adoption of the prescribed archetype (DiMaggio and Powell, 1983).

The evolution of technologies and industries has been described in similar terms. After an initial phase of technological ferment, socially constructed "dominant designs" provide greater stability of relationships between suppliers and producers: specialized professional communities develop, and regulatory agencies such as industry associations and the state enforce industry "standards." The technological "regime" becomes more "routinized and rigid" (Tushman and Rosenkopf, 1992, p. 324; see also Dosi, 1982; Nelson, 1994;[4] Utterback, 1994).

Institutional change, therefore, involves at least three things: the emergence of an alternative archetype, the delegitimizing of the existing archetype, and the legitimizing of the new one. These concurrent processes involve the adoption of the new archetype by a wider and wider range of organizations, together with the attendant changes in patterns of interaction and structures in the field. The five stages of figure 10.1 outline these processes. We will deal with each in turn.

Stage I: Pressures for Change

According to institutional theory, organizations become isomorphic to survive, with expectations embedded in the institutional context (Deephouse, 1996; Meyer and Rowan, 1977; but see Kraatz and Zajac, 1996). This institutional context is made up of interacting agencies (such as the state, regulatory agencies, and the professions) and of ideas and normative expectations. That is, the institutional context contains both ideas and mechanisms through which ideas are disseminated and reinforced (Scott, Ruef,

Mendel, & Caronna, 2000). Various mechanisms, or "multiple routes" (Greve, 1996), have been identified, such as interlocking directorates (e.g. Davis, 1991; Davis and Powell, 1991; Davis and Greve, 1997; Haveman, 1993; Palmer, Jennings, and Zhou, 1993), networks (e.g., Galaskiewicz, 1985; Kraatz, 1998; Westphal, Gulati, and Shortell, 1997), the knowledge base of these mechanisms (e.g. Oakes, Townley, and Cooper, 1999; Power and Laughlin, 1996), or the role models of imitation (e.g. Galaskiewicz and Wasserman, 1989; Greve, 1995, 1996; Haunschild and Miner, 1997; Havemann, 1993). The role of state and professional agencies in articulating and regulating organizational arrangements has also been documented (e.g. Baum and Oliver, 1991; Davis and Greve, 1997; Dobbin and Dowd, 1997; Kikulis et al., 1995).

Such an emphasis suggests that institutionally prescribed archetypes may change as contextual circumstances alter. Figure 10.1 starts with the idea of pressures on a field and organizations within it to change. There are two aspects to this process. First, there have to be pressures external to the field in question. But such pressures do not, in and of themselves, produce change. A second aspect is how actors in the field interpret and respond to these pressures and the changing or competing prescriptions that they contain. Actors see and act upon pressures as opportunities.

Meyer, Brooks, and Goes (1990) discuss the form that contextual changes might take and suggest that "jolts" destabilize established practices. Jolts may take the form of social upheaval (e.g., Zucker, 1987), technological disruptions, competitive discontinuities, or regulatory change (Fox-Wolfgramm, Boal, and Hunt, 1998; Lounsbury, 2002; Powell, 1991). Their effect is to disturb the socially constructed field-level consensus by introducing new ideas and thus to open up the possibility of change. Oliver (1992), in her analysis of the antecedents of deinstitutionalization, systematizes these various jolts or pressures. Focusing on the dissipation of institutionalized practices, she suggests three pressures, or *antecedents of deinstitutionalization*. While Oliver was working at the level of the organization, her antecedents of *political*, *functional*, and *social pressures* are easily transferable to the level of the organizational field and interorganizational dynamics.

Political pressures are threats to established resource flows in the field, together with changing power distributions, including the formation or breaking of alliances. Holm (1995) shows how alliances between producers, suppliers, trade unions, and governments can alter, changing the power relationships between field-level actors. In his study of the Norwegian fisheries field, these changes were backed up in legislation that altered resource flows. Scott et al. (2000) also draw attention to the importance of political pressures and the role of the rhetoric of crisis in producing deinstitutionalization of a stable, mature field. Thornton and Ocasio (1999) suggest that altered political processes occurred in higher education field-level change. Part of the political pressures in a field come from regulatory changes, something that is emphasized by Hoffman (1997) in researching changing attitudes toward environmental practices. A similar point is argued by both DiMaggio and Powell (1983, 1991) and Greenwood and Hinings (1996). D'Aunno, Succi, and Alexander (2000) argue that within health care, institutional actors have multiple and often inconsistent interests that, through their heterogeneity, produce pressures for institutional change.

Functional pressures occur from changes in technology and markets. Technological change can result in pressures to deinstitutionalize specific practices or to decompose the field. Similarly, markets for products and services change over time, sometimes in a hyperturbulent way, producing strong pressures for change in the field. For both Thornton and Ocasio (1999) and Scott et al. (2000), new technologies and market pressures led to deinstitutionalization. Greenwood and Hinings (1996) and Greenwood, Hinings, and Cooper (forthcoming) point to the way in which changing markets for professional services deinstitutionalize the field and encourage the emergence of new archetypes. Davis, Diekmann, and Tinsley (1994) argued that deinstitutionalization of the multidivisional form among the Fortune 500 occurred through a variety of processes including economic/market pressures. D'Aunno et al. (2000) point to the factors of geographical proximity to competitors and competitive disadvantage in product and service mix that produce divergent organizational change. Thornton (2002) demonstrates the way in which market capitalism produced a new institutional logic in higher education publishing and suggests that this has become common in other craft and professional industries, which transform from a professional logic to a market logic. Lee and Pennings (2002) utilize the concepts of market-level selection and market feedback to understand the emergence and diffusion of the partner-associate model in professional service firms. Competitive pressures led decision makers in accounting firms to search for a new organizational form, and feedback from the market on the successful economic performance of adopters of the partner-associate form produced a wave of mimetic adoption.

Oliver proposes that critical social pressures increase social fragmentation and decrease historical continuity. The tendency for a field to decompose or recompose can result from: (1) an initial fragmentation among the views of actors within the field; (2) the imposition of values from outside the field; and (3) changing opinions of actors about their involvement in a common enterprise. The concepts of fragmentation and changing opinions can be found in the studies of institutional transformation and the idea of changing institutional logics. Scott et al. (2000) make this idea central to their analysis of the changing institutional field of health care in the Bay Area, showing the movement from medical to administrative logics as actors change their views of involvement in the field. Greenwood et al. (2002) discuss how new views of the monopoly position of professions altered the organizational field of accounting firms. Haveman and Rao (1997) point to the changing nature of society in the late-nineteenth-century and early-twentieth-century United States that altered conceptions of thrift. Denis, Lamothe, Langley, and Valette (1999) argue that social pressures have produced an ideological shift away from a "provider-driven" system to a "population-driven" system in health care. The former emphasizes professional and organizational autonomy and the latter community-based services, integrated system design, local management, and democratic citizen control. Thus "there is wide agreement among policy elites that health services should no longer be organized as a loosely coupled set of autonomous providers but should become an integrated system capable of providing continuous care across organizational and professional boundaries and accountable to the populations served" (p. 107). This new ideology of health care is associated with archetypal structural changes demanding greater collaboration and integration.

The question of the emergence of an alternative view of the field, of new actors, and new archetypes is not directly addressed by most writers. Greenwood and Hinings (1988, 1993, 1996) and Hinings and

Greenwood (1988) address this issue by arguing that the processes of de- and reinstitutionalization are, in fact, linked or simultaneous, although the adoption of those new logics and structures is not straightforward. These different pressures precipitate the appearance of institutional entrepreneurs (DiMaggio 1988; Garud, Jain, and Kumaraswamy, 2002; Lawrence, 1999; Leblebici, Salancik, Copay, and King, 1991; Thornton, 1995). The effect of such changes is to disturb the field-level consensus through the introduction of new ideas, thus opening the possibility of change. Those ideas are formulated as a new archetype in terms of new ways of organizing and different institutional practices, that is, a new archetype.

Stage II: Sources of New Practices

Some form of pressure, either causing difficulties or creating opportunities, is necessary for change, but pressures alone are not sufficient; there has to be at least the outline of a set of alternative practices and an organizational form for diffusion. As McAdam, McCarthy, and Zald (1996, p. 5) phrase it, change requires "the critical catalytic effect of new ideas." There also have to be processes of legitimation, establishing the new form and practices as the valued, expected, and important ones for the institutional field. From where, then, do such new archetypes arise and how do they become legitimized and established within a field? Stage II of figure 10.1 suggests that institutional entrepreneurs are a source of emerging alternative practices. Such entrepreneurs may be existing actors, internal to the field, or new players, external to the organizational field.

DiMaggio (1988) identified "institutional entrepreneurship" as an important element in the dynamics of institutional change. He suggested that new institutions arise when "organized actors with sufficient resources see in them an opportunity to realize interests they value highly" (p. 14). They act entrepreneurially to alter institutional forms and practices to their own benefit. For DiMaggio, such action is critical to the process by which new institutions are formed. For example, DiMaggio (1991) pointed to the role of art professionals in reshaping the field of art museums. Thornton (1995) identified large conglomerates, outside the field, as significant actors who refashioned the publishing industry. And Leblebici et al. (1991) described the critical innova-

tions of small, fringe players in initiating field-level change in the radio broadcasting industry.

Since DiMaggio's initial formulation there have been other attempts to illustrate and clarify the concept (Dorado, 1999; Garud et al., 2002; Lawrence, 1999; Suddaby, 2001). A particularly useful classification is offered by Dorado (1999), who argues that there are three types of institutional entrepreneur: innovators, catalysts, and engineers. Innovators are already located within the organizational field and they introduce new ideas, organizational forms, or institutional practices. An example is Leblebici et al.'s (1991) account of the emergence of the radio broadcasting field. Their argument is that those on the periphery can engage in unorthodox practices that gradually become accepted, leading to field-level change. In a similar vein, Suddaby (2001) shows that it was marginalized actors within the field of law who originally introduced the notion of multidisciplinary practices to the legal profession, thus performing the role of innovators.

However, other studies emphasize that innovators are likely to be prestigious and powerful existing actors. Sherer and Lee (2002, p. 104) suggest "the prestige of an organization is important to the initiation of change in many organizational fields, particularly where prestige matters." Organizations with prestige are more able to act entrepreneurially because they have the legitimacy to act. Thus, in Sherer and Lee's study, it was highly regarded New York and Chicago law firms that introduced the senior attorney and staff attorney promotion tracks in the field of law. Similarly, it was Sun Microsystems, a prestigious computer firm, who championed Java, using their overall prestige and legitimacy as an important part of introducing the innovation (Garud et al., 2002). Others who have drawn attention to the actions of leading, powerful actors in institutional innovation are Brint and Karabel (1991), Galaskiewicz (1991), Fligstein (1997) and Greenwood et al. (2002).

Engineers are also found within the institutional field and are critical to the ultimate legitimation of innovations, once introduced. They are powerful gatekeepers who affect the flow of resources in a field. Their power can thus direct and control the content of discourse and debate. In DiMaggio's (1991) study of art museums, cultural and social elites were such engineers. Suddaby (2001), in his study of the legal profession, identifies several such actors in the emergence of multidisciplinary firms in law, including the U.S. Securities Exchange Commission as it attempted to restructure the rule system to preserve old boundaries between the professions of law, auditing, and management consulting. Legal academics also had a significant "engineering" function, as they organized testimony to the American Bar Association and provided commentary on proposed changes to the organization of legal practice.

Innovators and engineers are both part of the existing field and present new forms and practices from an insider perspective. Catalysts, on the other hand, operate from outside the organizational field, providing exogenous shocks. Outside actors are less subject to the conforming influences of an organizational field as they have, most likely, been socialized to different normative expectations. As a result they are able to provide fresh interpretations of events and bring alternative organizational practices.

Political, social, and functional changes precipitate the entry of new players (Garud et al., 2002; Reay and Hinings forthcoming; Thornton, 1995). Political pressures are often quite direct. For example, Reay and Hinings show how a governmental intervention in health care completely restructured the field over a one-year period by removing more than 200 hospital and public health boards and replacing them with 17 regional health authorities. These health authorities were new actors with a mandate to be "businesslike" in their approach to the delivery of health care. As such they represented a new archetype, structured around the integrated delivery of services, business planning, and an institutional logic emphasizing efficiency and effectiveness. Regulatory changes may have similar affects as shown in the action of the SEC in the United States, forcing the "Big Five" accounting firms to divest themselves of their consulting practices, thus restructuring the organizational field of business services and introducing new players. A major result was the emergence of the limited liability consulting company with a primary responsibility to shareholders, as against the partnership and its base in partners and clients. Again, new organizational forms and practices emerged that already have a high degree of legitimation from the SEC.

Functional pressures have been important in the deinstitutionalization of organizational fields, in particular through changes in markets. Indeed, there has been considerable interaction between political and functional pressures in many fields over the past two decades as right-of-center governments have introduced more and more deregulation with the aim of producing greater competition. This involves changing the actors in a field, introducing new ones, and transforming existing ones, for example, as described by Scott et al. (2000) in the Bay Area health system. Alongside such deregulation of markets has occurred the restructuring of already competitive markets. Thornton (1995) and Thornton and Ocasio (1999) show how market pressures in the college-publishing industry led to new actors entering the industry, bringing with them new management practices and organizational structures. Hinings, Greenwood, and Cooper (1999) similarly argue that the market changes in the demand for accounting services led to a move away from the professional partnership form of organization to a more market-oriented, managed professional bureaucracy.

An important way in which social pressures produce institutional transformation is through the emergence of new values challenging existing institutional logics. Changing social conceptions allow new actors to enter a field. The move from medical to administrative to efficiency logics in health care changed the providers of services, culminating, in the United States, with the HMO (Caronna and Scott, 1999). The HMO is a new organizational archetype for delivering health care with quite different practices from the professionally based, medical organizational form. Scott et al. (2000) point to the succession in the last 60 years of three different dominant institutional logics: the medical, governmental, and market, each representing different sets of social values about the nature of health care.

New actors introduce new ideas and new ways of doing things into an organizational field. Of course, "newness" has two meanings. Political, functional, and social pressures may either allow established actors from other fields to enter (as in Thornton's example of the publishing industry), or they may produce completely new actors. Both can happen at the same time. In the field of technology consulting it has primarily been the former (Greenwood et al., 2002). As information technology (IT) has become a more and more important part of business practice, so a convergence has occurred as, on the one hand, management consulting firms such as Cap Gemini Ernst and Young have moved strongly into IT work and, on the other hand, IT companies such as IBM have become consulting companies. The result is a transformation of the field as previously separate kinds of organizations begin to compete with each other. And the corporate form becomes the emerging appropriate form for delivering IT consulting services. Within health care, it has been much more a process of completely new actors emerging, such as HMOs and Regional Health Authorities (Reay and Hinings, forthcoming; Scott et al., 2000). In this situation the new actors invent new archetypes.

Why actors within a field should seek change is an interesting issue. It has at least in part to do with whether change is seen, by those introducing it, as radical or incremental. One perspective is that "peripheral" players are more likely to seek change (Powell, 1991). Not benefiting from the allocative benefits of the field, nor having extensive sunk investments in prevailing arrangements, peripheral players stand to benefit more than central actors from change. Therefore, they are more likely to contemplate and push for change where opportunities emerge. As Leblebici et al. (1991, p. 358) put it, radically new practices are more likely to be introduced by organizations "for whom experimentation is less costly in final outcomes." Similar examples come from technology studies, when competence-destroying innovation is associated with peripheral or external agencies because they have less reason to support the status quo (Anderson and Tushman, 1990). For example, Hargadon and Douglas (2001) describe how gas companies strongly resisted Edison's pioneering experiments with electricity generation for residential and business use. Moreover, as Greenwood and Suddaby (2002) note, peripheral players are less embedded within, and thus less effectively captured by, the socializing routines of a field.

The term *institutional entrepreneur* is useful because it depicts the idea of actors wittingly responding to opportunities in order to capture advantage. But in one sense, the term is misleading, because it conceals that initiators of change are more like the "insurgents" described by social movement theory. Social movement theory (McAdam et al., 1996) is concerned with how disadvantaged individuals and groups within society mobilize and challenge prevailing institutionalized structures and outcomes. According to McAdam et al., there is an "emerging consensus" that three factors are of importance when analyzing social movements: "political opportunities," "mobilizing structures," and "framing processes" (of which more later). Political opportunities, notes McAdam (1996, p. 23), are openings "afforded

insurgents by the shifting institutional structure and the ideological disposition of those in power" (emphasis added).

Social movement theory complements institutional theory because it reminds us that not all actors within a field are equally privileged by prevailing institutionalized practices and may confront them. In this sense, they resemble the peripheral players referred to earlier. But in one sense they are different. Institutional entrepreneurs as described by institutionalists are motivated by essentially *technical* considerations, i.e., prevailing practices are unsuccessful in coping with the challenges and circumstances of the field and alternatives are seen as more efficient. Indeed, the language of "entrepreneur" lends itself to that portrayal. But some changes are championed for *political* reasons, as groups seek to break through their disadvantage and gain ascendance and privilege. Such change agents are more like the "insurgents" of social movement theory. Examples would be consumer movements resisting private hospitals within health systems, or women's movements challenging inequality of treatment, or trade unions opposing primacy of shareholders.

In summary, we are suggesting that when (1) there are political, functional, and social pressures, (2) institutional entrepreneurs, both internal and external, emerge as important actors, and (3) the role of these actors is to initiate change. Institutional entrepreneurs and insurgents are important in triggering a process of change. They disrupt existing ideas and practices (thus precipitating deinstitutionalization) and put forward alternative ways of organizing (reinstitutionalization). Suddaby (2001) suggests that this accurately characterizes the actions of the "Big Five" in the process of creating multidisciplinary practices in accounting and law. However, as Greenwood and Hinings (1996) have argued, pressures for change, even in combination with local experimentation, do not automatically lead to the uniform and smooth diffusion of a new archetype. We thus need to turn to the processes by which diffusion is enabled.

Stage III: Processes of De- and Reinstitutionalization

There are three aspects to processes of de- and reinstitutionalization: theorization, legitimation, and dissemination. *Theorization* is the development and specification of abstract categories and the elaboration of chains of cause and effect; that is, it involves both building a model of how new practices and organizational forms work, and, providing a justification for them in the current and future contexts (Strang and Meyer, 1993, p. 492). *Legitimation* is the process of linking new ideas, forms and practices to sets of values and logics that are held in esteem by field actors and by the surrounding societal context. New organizational forms will not reach the archetypal status of "taken-for-granted" unless they are accepted as legitimate. *Dissemination* spreads the new archetype throughout the field, through the mechanisms of coercive, normative, and mimetic isomorphism.

Theorization

Theorization involves a process of abstraction (Abbott, 1988), taking specific, locally set instances of new ideas and generalizing them to other contexts. In the previous stage, stage II, new practices are essentially localized. That is, specific organizations experiment in an attempt to improve upon existing practices, or they unwittingly stumble upon a superior practice. The process of experimentation might be deliberate or an unwitting deviation. Critically, the experiments and deviations are associated with a minority of players within the field. Theorization lifts these localized experiments and provides a general story of how they are relevant to, and appropriate for, wider audiences. Theorization thus does two things. First, it *informs* wider audiences of localized experiments. Second, it *justifies* abandoning old practices in favor of new ones. Widespread adoption depends upon successfully presenting new ideas to potential adopters (Strang and Meyer, 1993, p. 494). New ideas and practices have to be seen, and seen as more compelling than existing practices. As Strang and Meyer (1993, p. 495) put it, "models must make the transition from theoretical formulation to social movement to institutional imperative." Through this, new organizational ideas are provided with "moral legitimacy" (Suchman, 1995) that increases their compelling quality.

Legitimation

Mizruchi and Fein (1999) point out that most writings in institutional theory have largely ignored how new ideas become legitimated, except where it occurs through mimetic isomorphism. However, there are some accounts of the construction of legitimacy for new organizational forms in nonisomorphic institutional change. Holm (1995) identified the state as a critical actor in the legitimation of the reforms in his study of Norwegian fishing. In his study, Holm deals with shifts in ideologies, social structures, and power at various levels that result in the replacement of existing legitimacies by new ones. Leblebici et al. (1991) suggest that legitimation occurs when innovations made by fringe players are adopted by established actors. DiMaggio (1991) adds the observation that legitimation of a new form of museum empowered the museum reform movement, thus permitting the delegitimation of existing forms. These select studies of institutional change identify legitimacy as essential to the establishment of new forms of organizing (Scott, 2001).

Institutional change involves broad based claims to legitimacy that are made to a variety of audiences by linking changes in archetypal practices to broader social values. The discourse of legitimacy aligns (or claims to align) the values and attributes of new ideas, forms, and practices to those held in society at large, that is, to broader values beyond the particular organizational field. Institutional change is initially organized around debates about the appropriateness of particular organizational forms, with actors trying to "insert their interests into the mainstream of societal values and, hence, to create or safeguard the legitimacy of their definition of the 'right' social order" (Miles, 1982, p. 23). Gaining legitimacy for new ways of organizing confers the right (authority) for certain actors to control existing and future processes of institutionalization.

Dissemination

New institutional practices that have been theorized and legitimated (these two processes interact with each other) can then be disseminated to other actors through the processes of coercive, normative, and mimetic isomorphism. Many writers have explored the patterns (Greve, 1995, 1996) and mechanisms (Baron, Dobbin, and Jennings, 1986; Burns and Wholey, 1993; Davis, 1991; Davis and Greve, 1997; Furusten, 1995; Gulati, 1995; Haveman, 1993; Haunschild and Miner, 1997; Kraatz, 1998; Mizruchi, 1996; Palmer, Jennings, and Zhou, 1993; Tolbert and Zucker, 1983; Westphal et al., 1997; Westphal and Zajac, 1997) by which ideas are transported within organizational communities. Indeed, a prime focus of institutional theory has been on how mimetic processes work to maintain structures, interactions, and cognitions within an institutional field. We suggest that these very same processes come into play in the dissemination of new ideas and practices at the field level, as it deinstitutionalizes and then reinstitutionalizes.

Tolbert and Zucker (1983) derive a two-stage process from their study of municipal reform in the United States, starting with functional, political, and social pressures. The first wave of adoption was contingent on various kinds of performance gaps; the second (our stage III) saw a rising tide of mimetic isomorphism following theorization and legitimation of the new organizational forms. Similarly, Lee and Pennings (2002) suggest an increasing acknowledgement that competitive and institutional processes interact with each other in producing convergence in structure. The template of the partner-associate model adopted in law firms gained legitimacy through market feedback endorsing the behavior (and thus the legitimacy) of adopting firms. There was then an amplification of dissemination through the increased legitimacy of the new form.

Westphal et al. (1997) confirm and extend the Tolbert and Zucker model. They examined adoption by hospitals of total quality management (TQM) practices and found that early adopters customize TQM practices, thus improving performance. Later adopters, in contrast, adopted more general TQM practices, even though adoption had adverse consequences for hospital performance. Westphal et al. conclude that late adopters pursue legitimacy because of normative pressures, despite performance consequences.

Greenwood and Hinings (1996) suggest that these mechanisms of dissemination vary across institutional fields. It is part of the definition of a mature organizational field that structures, patterns of interactions, and common meaning systems are well established. In effect, they are tightly coupled and relatively impermeable. This situation has two implications. One is that the processes of theorization and legitimation of new ideas are difficult to get underway. Greenwood et al. (2002) show that it took a decade for the idea of multidisciplinary partnerships to be accepted within the field of accounting, even though its proponents were the larger, powerful players. However, the second implication is that

because of the existence of normative and mimetic mechanisms in that particular case, dissemination, once triggered, can take place rapidly. In a less tightly coupled and more permeable field, more ideas can be theorized—as social movement theorists would put it, there are more "framing contests" (McAdam et al., 1996, p. 17), and as a result dissemination will be more difficult because of the lack of enabling mechanisms.

Of course, there are organizational fields in all countries that are strongly subject to legislation and regulation and thus where transformational change may occur "at a stroke." Dobbin (2000) and Dobbin and Dowd (1997) analyze how different policy regimes—public capitalization, pro-cartel, and antitrust—between 1825 and 1922 affected the founding and form of railroads in Massachusetts. Hinings and Greenwood (1988) showed how the field of local government in the United Kingdom was transformed through legislation emanating from a combination of political, social, and functional pressures within the system. On April 1, 1974, approximately 1,300 organizations became 430 with major redistributions of tasks, new geographical boundaries, and altered relationships, all underpinned by a different set of beliefs about the ways in which local services should be delivered. Reay (2000) demonstrated a similar legislated transformation in the delivery of health care in Alberta, Canada. More than 200 hospital and health boards were folded into 17 regional health authorities (RHAs). Again, this involved a major redistribution of tasks, new geographical boundaries, and altered relationships. The whole change was centered around a set of values that emphasized a "businesslike" approach to the delivery of health care, highlighted by the introduction of a business planning process for each RHA and favoring the appointment of board members with business experience rather than health care knowledge.

In some respects, stage III is one of the most studied areas of institutional dynamics; in other respects it is relatively underresearched. The *occurrence* of dissemination and (not the same thing) the *patterns* of diffusion are well understood. As noted above, the pace and the shape at which new practices disseminate have been topics of interest to numerous scholars. But only recently has attention turned to the processes of theorization and legitimation (Strang and Soule, 1988; Suchman, 1995). Theorization is a pivotal factor in stage III. It links the occurrence of local variations (stage II) with the process of diffusion. Theorization "sharpens . . . out-of-focus mutations into recognizable models, and . . . proclaims their functionality" (Greenwood and Suddaby, 2002, p. 4). Given that institutionalized practices are robust and resistant to change, theorization is an important enabling factor, but one that is relatively little understood. The work of Snow and his colleagues (Snow and Benford, 1992; Snow, Rochford, Worden, and Benford, 1986) in social movement theory offers some possible insights. Snow et al. (1986) are interested in how social movements attract participants. Drawing upon Goffman's (1974) notion of "framing," Snow et al. suggest ways by which social movements render events and occurrences so as to appeal to "untapped . . . sentiment pools" (1986, p. 468). Four aspects of framing are outlined: bridging (linking separate but ideologically congruent pools), amplification ["classification and invigoration" (1986, p. 469)], extension (extending the core frame to make it appealing), and transformation (reconfiguration of values). Central to this work is the use of language and dramatic imagery in order to "frame" issues so that they resonate with the values of important audiences. Unless the framing process is successful in doing this, it fails to attract participation: "Many framings may be plausible, but we suspect that relatively few strike a responsive chord and are thus characterized by a high degree of frame resonance" (Snow et al., 1986, p. 477). The provision of resonance through language that appeals to values we see as an important mechanism of theorization.

Better understanding of how theorization occurs requires that we afford more attention to how issues and practices are framed—to how prevailing organizational forms become defined as deficient and problematical, and to how alternatives are presented as solutions and pressed upon both potential adoptees and key players who can approve them.

Stage IV: Dynamics of De- and Reinstitutionalization

The picture we have presented so far deals primarily with what happens at the level of the organizational field, emphasizing the processes that produce pressures to deinstitutionalize and for new institutional archetypes to arise through institutional entrepreneurs or institutional insurgents, and how that archetype begins to be secured by means of theorization, legitimation, and dissemination. Following Tolbert and Zucker (1983), much of institutional theory has presented these processes as somewhat uniform, following an S-curve. But new archetypes are adopted by actors, usually organizations, within a field in differing ways and at differing rates. Greenwood and Hinings (1996) provide a framework for understanding these processes internal to organizations in a field, emphasizing the roles of value commitment, interest dissatisfaction, power, and capability.

Their argument is that there are two, interlinked, levels of field transformation. One level is that of the field, per se. At the field level new archetypes arise in response to pressures for change, as discussed above. The second level is that of the actors/organizations in the field. Organizations are not passive recipients of the new archetypes that transform the field. First, they may be the institutional entrepreneurs (innovators and engineers) active in developing and advancing these new ideas, structures, and processes. Even if they are not, they may be involved in the processes of theorization and legitimation. Second, organizations respond to the newly legitimated archetypes by interpreting (what do we understand by them?) and evaluating (should we adopt?) them. There is unlikely to be a simple (even though it may be an uncritical) process of adoption. Even in the situation outlined by Hinings and Greenwood (1988), where a field transformation was legislated and a new archetype given strong legitimation, after 10 years many organizations had still not adopted that archetype. The explanation for why, when, and how organizations adopt a new archetype resides in the internal dynamics of each organization. The essential dynamic elements of this process are presented in stage IV of figure 10.1. Our current aim is not to repeat their model in detail, merely to draw attention to its key components.

Greenwood and Hinings (1996) suggested that the pace and extent of adoption of a new institutional archetype by individual organizations within a field is dependent on four interrelated elements:

1. The extent to which different groups in an organization are *committed to the values* that underpin the new archetype. In many organizations there are competing commitments to the old and the new that make adoption difficult.
2. The extent to which there is *interest dissatisfaction*. Are there groups in the organization

who feel materially disadvantaged by existing practices and who see advantage in new arrangements, or, on the other hand, groups who will fight to maintain their advantage?

3. The ways in which the *power structure* of an organization is related to value commitment and interests. Are those in power committed to the new ways and do they see advantages in moving to a new archetype? Thus, can the support of the powerful be brought to bear to ensure adoption?

4. The *capability* of an organization to implement change. Groups within an organization may have the appropriate value commitment and material interest in moving to a new archetype. Those in power may be in favor. But do they understand how to implement the new design, both technically and socially? Does the organization have the necessary skills, in both change management and in the particular technical components of the new archetype, to ensure its successful implementation?

These four elements interact to allow dissemination and adoption of change or to impede it. Certainly, this framework suggests that the dynamics of reinstitutionalization are fraught with difficulty when examined from the perspective of the ways in which new organizational templates flow through the field on an organization-by-organization basis. Lawrence, Hardy, and Phillips (2002) pursue this theme of difficulty by referring to *proto-institutions*, by which they mean "practices, technologies, and rules that are narrowly diffused and only weakly entrenched, but that have the potential to become widely institutionalized" (p. 202). They espouse a process or stage model of institutional development. Seo and Creed (2002), in critiquing and extending Greenwood and Hinings (1996), emphasize the need to incorporate interests, agency, and power into institutional theory: "Institutional formation and change are the outcomes of political struggle among multiple social constituencies with unequal power" (p. 223). Drawing on Benson (1977), they suggest that institutional contradictions are key, leading to political struggles among participants with divergent interests and asymmetric power. Social actors, such as organizations and institutional entrepreneurs, are active exploiters of these contradictions, mobilizing other actors and resources for change. Similarly, in examining the temporal characteristics of institu-tionalization, Lawrence et al. (2001) emphasize the modes and targets of power that affect the pace of change and the stability of the emergent institution.

Stage V: Reinstitutionalization

Stage V of figure 10.1 is concerned with re-institutionalization, to which very little attention has been given (Tolbert and Zucker, 1996). Suchman (1995) argues that reinstitutionalization has occurred when the density of adoption provides ideas with cognitive legitimacy to the extent that they are taken for granted as the natural and appropriate arrangements for all organizations within the field. This may be thought of as "strong" reinstitutionalization, producing a transformed field that looks like the mature field defined by DiMaggio and Powell (1983, 1991). This raises the question, "How dense is dense"?

There are two aspects to this issue. First, as our theory suggests, there is a distinction to be made between density at the level of field institutions and density at the level of individual organizations. Second, is density at the level of organizations numerical, or is it in some way related to power?

At the field level, there are regulatory agencies such as the state, quasi-legal bodies such as the U.S. Securities and Exchange Commission, and professional associations. These can be critically important in the processes of de- and reinstitutionalization because they enable the expression and reproduction of shared meanings. They also adjudicate between competing claims, enhancing the legitimacy of certain views and practices over others. Hinings and Greenwood (1988) argue that the process of field transformation in British local government was moved forward considerably when all of the professional associations and municipal sector associations agreed with the same new prescription for function and organization. These field-level actors play an important role in monitoring compliance with normatively and coercively sanctioned expectations. New beliefs and the practices associated with them are reproduced through processes such as training and education, hiring and certification, and ceremonies of celebration. Field-level regulatory bodies are active in these processes (e.g., Rueff and Scott, 1998) and, as such, "define or enforce" (Oliver, 1997, p. 102) collective beliefs (see Freidson, 1970, 1986; Starr, 1982).

Because of the reflexive and iterative nature of field transformation, it is possible to argue that at least the first level of transformation has taken place when central, powerful actors adopt new beliefs and practices. As Leblebici et al. (1991) point out, even when new practices come from the margin, at some point they have to receive legitimation from those actors who control such processes. An important reason for emphasizing the important role of the powerful is because, as noted earlier, it is often other field members, acting as institutional entrepreneurs or insurgents, who are part of the source for such new ideas and practices. Once adopted by powerful agencies, the process of implementation within a field has already begun. It is not usually—or ever—a top-down process. Even in the situation described by Hinings and Greenwood (1988), where local government reform was legislated, the organizational ideas underlying that reform came from a group of municipalities committed to promoting a new archetype, which they had already implemented. Central bodies are not usually "disembodied" from other organizational actors; those actors, at least in part, frequently comprise the membership of those bodies.

The power aspect enters because central actors are not necessarily homogeneous communities (Barker, 1998; Powell, 1991). Decision making in any field is a political process (Van Hoy, 1993; Dezalay and Garth, 1996) in which the competing interests of subcommunities are reconciled on an ongoing basis. Some actors are more powerful than others and thus have greater opportunities to theorize, legitimate, and disseminate. For example, in the last decade, the role of the SEC in the United States has been particularly powerful in restructuring the field of accounting and management consulting.

We suggest that the same arguments apply with regard to density at the level of organizations. That is, central, powerful actors and groups are important in judging the degree of institutionalization; it is not purely a matter of numbers. Stage IV of our model emphasizes how power interacts with value commitments and material interests to allow, direct, and control the introduction of a new archetype. While much of the literature on organizational change emphasizes the importance of widespread commitment, the actuality is that large-scale, radical organizational change tends to occur, and become institutionalized, from the initiatives and activities of

the powerful, whether we label them as transformational leaders or visionaries or not. Thus, we are saying that the role of power, in the processes of both de- and reinstitutionalization, is profound (Clegg, 1989). Lawrence et al. (2001), for example, suggest that domination, where there is systemic rather than episodic power and the target of that power is seen as an object rather than a subject, will produce a high level of stability in the resultant institutionalization. More episodic power attempts coupled with high levels of agency by subjects will produce an unstable institutionalization.

However, there are two other issues that deserve consideration, namely, the occurrence of fads and fashions, and the idea of sedimentation. There is a growing body of work on fads and fashions in management thought and practices (cf. Abrahamson, 1991, 1996; Clark and Fincham, 2001). This work suggests that institutionalization often does not take place even though there may be occasions when it seems incipient. The question is raised, "How long does a new archetype or practice have to exist to be institutionalized?" A practice like total quality management may reach a point of widespread dissemination and even seem to have a high degree of legitimacy, yet after a few years the density of adoption declines dramatically. Rao, Greve, and Davis (2001) examined the processes by which securities analysts selected the firms that they would analyze in depth. Not surprisingly, given the uncertainty surrounding the choice, mimetic processes were observed (consistent with previous neoinstitutional findings). However, Rao et al. also found that analysts were prone to overestimating the future prospects of firms and were quick to abandon coverage. That is, mimetic processes were operant but did not necessarily result in institutionalized behavior. Practices that have achieved widespread adoption may perhaps be better classified as a fad or fashion (Abrahamson, 1996) or as a proto-institution (Lawrence et al., 2002).

The other issue in reinstitutionalization is the extent to which there is actually radical, archetypal change—a shift from one archetype to another—or whether there is more often a mixture of continuity and change (Child and Smith, 1987; Pettigrew, 1985, 1987). Cooper, Hinings, Greenwood, and Brown (1996) used the metaphor of "sedimentation." As they phrased it, "the geological metaphor of sedimentation allows us to consider a dialectical rather than a linear view of change" (p. 624). Cooper et al.'s basic argument is that institutional change represents a layering of archetypes rather than a shift from one archetype to another. Sedimentation points to the residual persistence of values, ideas, and practices, even when the formal structures and processes seem to change, and even when there may be a measure of incoherence. This approach takes up the theme of continuity and change working concurrently, which is echoed by Morris and Pinnington (1999). Thus, even in a situation where one can speak of an institutional change, this does not mean that previously institutionalized practices have disappeared, rather that they have been relatively delegitimized and no longer have the sufficient support of powerful actors in the field. But, as so much recent work has emphasized, there will still be competing institutional logics at the organizational-field level (Garud et al., 2002; Seo and Creed, 2002; Scott et al., 2001; Thornton, 2002; Townley, 2002). The imagery of sedimentation reminds us, again, that the stability of an organizational field is always temporary, and that dormant tensions frequently rest beneath even the most mature fields.

Conclusions

Our attempt has been to provide a more coherent and consistent account of the dynamics of change in an institutional field, one that involves interorganizational relations, and also the reactions of individual organizations and groups within organizations. Change in institutionalized fields can only be understood as constant interactions between these various levels of analysis. The causal directions are not one-way but reciprocal. Reflexive agents are involved in any kind of change at any level of analysis, whether these are catalysts bringing in new ideas from outside the field, innovators seeing opportunities within the field to move in new directions, or even well-established, powerful engineers who see their interests being served by pushing for the adoption of new beliefs and practices.

This process model points to some important implications and directions for theory and research. First, institutional change needs to be understood through the iterative action of the processes and dynamics depicted in the model (figure 10.1). It is presented as a circular process with the implication that

de- and reinstitutionalization is a constant activity. Aldrich (1999) has produced a masterful account of organizational evolution; we similarly have to conceptualize institutional fields as evolutionary. Typically, institutional theory has been about demonstrating the strength of institutional forces. More recently the question has been raised of how deinstitutionalization can take place, but it is always seen as followed by reinstitutionalization. And while this is a quite viable process, given the emphasis within organization theory generally on the continuous nature of change, it is important to bring that emphasis to the study of institutional fields. So, research should be focused less on how a particular institutional template is transformed into an alternative template, and more on the processes by which that happens and how those processes are constant, ongoing, and evolutionary. Endpoints, stability, and reinstitutionalization are relative terms.

Second, it is important to emphasize the multilevel interactions in the model between the field and organizational level and within organizations. Institutional innovations can occur within individual organizations or clusters of organizations that have implications for the field level of analysis. Similarly, innovations may occur at a field level that impacts individual organizations and interorganizational relations. By definition, an institutional field has a variety of components to it, including field-level structure and meanings, institutional archetypes, organizational systems, and interpretive schemes and actors within organizations. Not only can any of these emerge as institutional entrepreneurs, they can be involved in the processes and dynamics of de- and reinstitutionalization in different ways. Research needs to take these intralevel processes and dynamics seriously to tease out the relative roles and impacts of different levels at different points in the evolution of an institutional field.

These first two directions raise a third. The model is presented as a series of stages. This is a reasonable analytical representation in terms of the necessary movement from de- to reinstitutionalization. However, as with all stage models, there are problems with presenting them as cut and dried. There are likely to be degrees of overlap and nonlinearity in working out these stages. Thus, a very important research direction is to untangle the sequences that develop in particular cases of institutional dynamics. What happens when institutional entrepreneurs run into difficulties in legitimizing and disseminating their ideas? Do they give up, or do they co-opt other institutional players (Selznick, 1949)? That is, is there a "recycling" from processes (stage III) to sources (stage II)? Similar questions can be asked about the relationships between all stages. In the dynamics of stage IV, how are the pressures in stage I drawn upon to deal with problems in securing value commitment or interest satisfaction? We would expect stages III and IV to be intimately linked and interactive, as the clarity of theorization and legitimation has strong implications for the ways in which the dynamics of acceptance or rejection work out at the organizational level. The point is that the model should be seen as highly interactive, and research should concentrate on dealing with these interactions and the reflexivity that underlies them.

A fourth point is that the role of power in institutional change, as a key component, requires further exploration. Power and politics are at work throughout the model. We see institutional change as a highly political process at both the field and the organizational level (Greenwood and Hinings, 1996; Greenwood et al., 2002; Lawrence et al., 2002). This is a particularly important point because, generally, institutional theory tends not to say a great deal about power, in spite of the work of Selznick (1949) and Meyer and Rowan (1977). Power, of course, operates at a variety of levels (Clegg, 1989); in this case, field, organization, and intraorganizational group. Research should focus on the instrumental nature of power in allowing the achievement of both de- and reinstitutionalization, the extent to which the sources of new practices are evaluated in power terms, and the role of power in both the processes and dynamics of institutional change.

A fifth point relates to the speed of change. We have defined an institutional change as being from one institutional archetype to another. One of the questions that all theories of change raise, although few answer, concerns the speed of a particular change. While many of the studies of change report time periods, they tend not to examine this issue as an important part of our understanding. The research questions ask how long it takes to get from stage I of the model to stage V, and in what way the intervening stages affect that time period. Time is a necessary concept and variable in research in institutional change (Scott et al., 2001; Zaheer, Albert, and Zaheer, 2000).

A final point is that there are strong methodological implications from the questions that we are raising. It is unlikely that most, or indeed, any, of what we are suggesting could be done through large-scale, quantitative studies. Scott et al. (2001) come closest to what we are advocating, but even their excellent study does not cover many of the conceptual areas that we regard as vital (and their study took many people considerable time!). Issues of relationships between levels, of the reflexive roles of actors, and of processes and dynamics require detailed work with archival documents, interviews with current and past actors, surveys of practices, and observations of activities. And, of course, this needs to be done over considerable periods of time. As in the work of Scott et al. (2001) and Van de Ven, Polley, Garud and Venkataraman (1999), research into the dynamics of change in institutional fields has to be visualized and implemented as a long-term program, involving researchers in commitments that extend over many years. Thus, carrying out research on this most important topic within institutional theory represents a major challenge both theoretically and methodologically.

In closing, we reiterate that the dynamics of change in organizational fields is an increasingly central issue for institutional theory, and also that institutional theory represents a more than promising basis for understanding change. To quote Dacin et al. (2002, p. 48): "Institutional change can proceed from the most micro interpersonal and sub-organizational levels to the most macro societal and global levels. It can take place in relatively brief and concentrated periods or over time measured in decades or centuries. And it can take place incrementally, so that observers and participants are hardly aware of any change, or abruptly, in dramatic episodes that present large discontinuities with former patterns." We hope and expect that the model we have outlined will provide a promising approach for dealing with these very significant issues.

Note

The development of the ideas in this chapter was made possible by grants from the Social Sciences and Humanities Research Council, the Canadian Health Services Research Foundation, and the Alberta Heritage Foundation for Medical Research.

References

Abbott, A. (1988). *The system of professions*. Chicago: University of Chicago Press.

Abrahamson, E. (1991). Managerial fads and fashions: The diffusion and rejection of innovations. *Academy of Management Review, 16*, 586–612.

Abrahamson, E. (1996). Technical and aesthetic fashions. In B. Czarniawska & G. Sevon (Eds.), *Translating organizational change* (pp. 117–137). Berlin: W. de Gruyter.

Aldrich, H. (1999). *Organizations evolving*. Thousand Oaks, CA: Sage.

Anderson, P. & Tushman, M. (1990). Technological discontinuities and dominant designs: A cyclical model of technological change. *Administrative Science Quarterly, 35*, 604–633.

Barker, K. (1998). Women physicians and the gendered system of professions. *Work and Occupations, 25*, 229–255.

Barley, S. & Tolbert, P. (1997). Institutionalization and structuration: Studying the links between action and institution. *Organization Studies, 18*, 93–117.

Baron, J. N., Dobbin, F., & Jennings, P. D. (1986). War and peace: The evolution of modern personnel practice in US industry. *American Journal of Sociology, 92*, 250–283.

Baum, J. A. C. & Oliver, C. (1991). Institutional linkages and organizational mortality. *Administrative Science Quarterly, 36*, 187–218.

Benson, K. (1975). The interorganizational network as a political economy. *Administrative Science Quarterly, 20*, 229–249.

Berger, T. & Luckmann, P. (1967). *The social construction of reality*. New York: Doubleday Anchor.

Blau, J. R. & McKinley, W. (1979). Ideas, complexity, and innovation. *Administrative Science Quarterly, 24*, 200–219.

Brint, S. & Karabel, J. (1991). Institutional origins and transformations: The case of American community colleges. In W. W. Powell & P. J. DiMaggio (Eds.), *The new institutionalism in organizational analysis* (pp. 337–360). Chicago: University of Chicago Press.

Burns, L. R. & Wholey, D. R. (1993). Adoption and abandonment of matrix management programs: Effects of organizational characteristics on interorganizational networks. *Academy of Management Journal, 36*, 106–138.

Caronna, C. & Scott, W. R. (1999). Institutional effects on organizational governance and conformity: The case of the Kaiser Permanente and the United States health care field. In D. Brock, M. Powell, & C. R. Hinings (Eds.), *Restructuring the professional organization* (pp. 68–86). London: Routledge.

Child, J. & Smith, C. (1987). The context and processes of organizational transformation. *Journal of Management Studies, 24*, 565–593.

Clark, T. & Fincham, R. (Eds.) (2001). *Critical consulting: Perspectives on the management advice industry*. Oxford: Basil Blackwell.

Clegg, S. R. (1989). *Frameworks of power*. London: Sage.

Cooper, D., Hinings, C. R., Greenwood, R., & Brown, J. (1996). Sedimentation and transformation in organizational change: The case of Canadian law firms. *Organization Studies, 17*, 623–647.

Dacin, M. T., Goodstein, J., & Scott, W. R. (2002). Institutional theory and institutional change: Introduction to the special research forum. *Academy of Management Journal, 45*, 45–57.

D'Aunno, T., Succi, M., & Alexander, J. A. (2000). The role of institutional and market forces in divergent organizational change. *Administrative Science Quarterly, 45*, 679–703.

Davis, G. F. (1991). Agents without principles? The spread of the poison pill through the intercorporate network. *Administrative Science Quarterly, 36*, 583–613.

Davis, G. F. & Powell, W. W. (1991). Organization-environment relations. In M. Dunnette & L. Hough (Eds.), *Handbook of industrial and organizational psychology* (Vol. 3, pp. 315–376). Palo Alto, CA: Consulting Psychologists Press.

Davis, G. F. & Greve, H. R. (1997). Corporate elite networks and governance changes in the 1980s. *American Journal of Sociology, 103*, 1–37.

Davis, G. F., Diekmann, K. A., & Tinsley, C. H. (1994). The decline and fall of the conglomerate firm in the 1980s: The deinstitutionalization of an organizational form. *American Sociological Review, 59*, 547–570.

Deephouse, D. (1996). Does isomorphism legitimate? *Academy of Management Journal, 39*, 1024–1039.

Deephouse, D. (1999). To be different or to be the same? It's a question (and theory) of strategic balance. *Strategic Management Journal, 20*, 147–166.

Denis, J.-L., Lamothe, L., Langley, A., & Valette, A. (1999). The struggle to redefine boundaries in health care systems. In D. Brock, M. Powell, & C. R. Hinings (Eds.), *Restructuring the professional organization* (pp. 105–130). London: Routledge.

Dezalay, Y. & Garth, B. (1996). Fussing about the forum: Categories and definitions as stakes in a professional competition. *Law and Social Inquiry, 21*, 285–312.

DiMaggio, P. J. (1988). Interest and agency in institutional theory. In L. Zucker (Ed.), *Institutional patterns and organizations: Culture and environment* (pp. 3–21). Cambridge, MA: Ballinger.

DiMaggio, P. J. (1991). Constructing an organizational field as a professional project: U. S. Art Museums, 1920–1940. In W. W. Powell & P. J. DiMaggio (Eds.), *The new institutionalism in organizational analysis* (pp. 267–292). Chicago: University of Chicago Press.

DiMaggio, P. J. & Powell, W. W. (1983). The iron cage revisited: Institutional isomorphism and collective rationality in organizational fields. *American Sociological Review, 48,* 147–160.

DiMaggio, P. J. & Powell, W. W. (1991). Introduction. In W. W. Powell & P. J. DiMaggio (Eds.), *The new institutionalism in organizational analysis* (pp. 1–38). Chicago: University of Chicago Press.

Dobbin, F. & Dowd, T. J. (2000). The market that antitrust built: Public policy, private coercion, and railroad acquisitions, 1825–1922. *American Sociological Review, 65,* 631–657.

Dobbin, F. & Dowd, T. J. (1997). How policy shapes competition: Early railroad foundings in Massachusetts. *Administrative Science Quarterly, 42,* 501–529.

Dorado, S. (1999, August). *Institutional entrepreneurs: Engineers, catalysts, and innovators.* Paper presented at the Academy of Management Conference, Chicago, IL.

Dosi, G. (1982). Technological paradigms and technological trajectories. *Research Policy, 11,* 147–162.

Elsbach, K. (1994). Managing organizational legitimacy in the California cattle industry: The construction and effectiveness of verbal accounts. *Administrative Science Quarterly, 39,* 57–88.

Fligstein, N. (1997). Social skill and institutional theory. *American Behavioral Scientist, 40,* 397–405.

Fox-Wolfgramm, S. J., Boal, K. B., & Hunt, J. G. (1998). Organizational adaptation to institutional change: A comparative study of first-order change in prospective and defender banks. *Administrative Science Quarterly, 43,* 87–126.

Freidson, E. (1970). *Profession of medicine: A study of the sociology of applied knowledge.* New York: Dodd, Mead.

Freidson, E. (1986). *Professional powers: A study of the institutionalization of formal knowledge.* Chicago: University of Chicago Press.

Furusten, S. (1995). *The managerial discourse: A study of the creation and diffusion of popular management knowledge.* Doctoral thesis no. 60, Department of Business Studies, Uppsala University.

Galaskiewicz, J. (1985). Professional networks and the institutionalization of a single mind-set. *American Sociological Review, 50,* 639–658.

Galaskiewicz, J. (1991). Making corporate actors accountable: Institution-building in Minneapolis–St.

Paul. In W. W. Powell & P. J. DiMaggio (Eds.), *The new institutionalism in organizational analysis* (pp. 293–310). Chicago, IL: University of Chicago Press.

Galaskiewicz, J. & Wasserman, S. (1989). Mimetic processes within an interorganizational field: An empirical test. *Administrative Science Quarterly, 34,* 454–479.

Garud, R., Jain, S., & Kumaraswamy, A. (2002). Institutional entrepreneurship in the sponsorship of common technological standards: The case of Sun Microsystems and Java. *Academy of Management Journal, 45,* 196–214.

Goffman, E. (1974). *Frame analysis: An essay on the organization of experience.* New York: Harper Colophon.

Goodrick, E. & Salancik, G. (1996). Organizational discretion in responding to institutional practices: Hospitals and caesarean births. *Administrative Science Quarterly, 41,* 1–28.

Greenwood, R. & Hinings, C. R. (1988). Organizational design types, tracks and the dynamics of strategic change. *Organization Studies, 9,* 293–316.

Greenwood, R. & Hinings, C. R. (1993). Understanding strategic change: The contribution of archetypes. *Academy of Management Journal, 36,* 1052–1081.

Greenwood, R. & Hinings, C. R. (1996). Understanding radical organizational change: Bringing together the old and the new institutionalism. *Academy of Management Review, 21,* 1022–1054.

Greenwood, R. & Suddaby, R. (2002). *Institutional entrepreneurship and the dynamics of field transformation.* Paper presented at the European Group for Organizational Studies annual meeting, Barcelona, Spain.

Greenwood, R., Hinings, C. R., & Cooper, D. J. (forthcoming). An institutional theory of change: Contextual and interpretive dynamics in the acounting industry. In W. W. Powell & D. Jones (Eds.), *How institutions change.* Chicago: University of Chicago Press.

Greenwood, R., Suddaby, R., & Hinings, C. R. (2002). Theorizing change: The role of professional associations in the transformation of institutionalized fields. *Academy of Management Journal, 45,* 58–80.

Greve, H. R. (1995). Jumping ship: The diffusion of strategy abandonment. *Administrative Science Quarterly, 40,* 444–473.

Greve, H. R. (1996). Patterns of competition: The diffusion of a market position in radio broadcasting. *Administrative Science Quarterly, 41,* 29–60.

Gulati, R. (1995). Social structure and alliance formation patterns: A longitudinal analysis. *Administrative Science Quarterly, 40,* 619–654.

Hargadon, A. & Douglas, Y. (2001). When innovations meet institutions: Edison and the design of the electric light. *Administrative Science Quarterly, 46,* 476–501.

Haunschild, P. R. & Miner, A. (1997). Modes of interorganizational imitation: The effects of outcome salience and uncertainty. *Administrative Science Quarterly, 42,* 472–500.

Haveman, H. (1993). Follow the leader: Mimetic isomorphism and entry into new markets. *Administrative Science Quarterly, 38,* 593–627.

Haveman, H. & Rao, H. (1997). Structuring a theory of moral sentiments: Institutional and organizational co-evolution in the early thrift industry. *American Journal of Sociology, 102,* 1606–1651.

Haveman, H. & Rao, H. (in press). Hybrid forms and institutional change in the early California thrift industry. In W. W. Powell & D. Jones (Eds.), *Bending the bars of the iron cage: Institutional dynamics and processes.* Chicago: University of Chicago Press.

Hinings, C. R. & Greenwood, R. (1988). *The dynamics of strategic change.* London: Blackwell.

Hinings, C. R., Greenwood, R., & Cooper, D. J. (1999). The dynamics of change in large accounting firms. In D. Brock, M. Powell, & C. R. Hinings (Eds.), *Restructuring the professional organization* (pp. 131–153). London: Routledge.

Hoffman, A. J. (1997). *From heresy to dogma: An institutional history of corporate environmentalism.* Stanford, CA: Stanford University Press.

Hoffman, A. J. (1999). Institutional evolution and change: Environmentalism and the U.S. chemical industry. *Academy of Management Journal, 42,* 351–371.

Holm, P. (1995). The dynamics of institutionalization: Transformation processes in Norwegian fisheries. *Administrative Science Quarterly, 40,* 398–420.

Jepperson, R. L. (1991). Institutions, institutional effects, and institutionalism. In W. W. Powell & P. J. DiMaggio (Eds.), *The new institutionalism in organizational analysis* (pp. 143–163). Chicago: University of Chicago Press.

Kikulis, L., Slack, T., & Hinings, C. R. (1995). Sector-specific patterns of organizational design change. *Journal of Management Studies, 32,* 67–100.

Kraatz, M. (1998). Learning by association: Interorganizational networks and adaptation to environmental change. *Academy of Management Journal, 41,* 621–643.

Kraatz, M. S. & Zajac, E. J. (1996). Exploring the limits of the new institutionalism: the causes and consequences of illegitimate organizational change. *American Sociological Review, 61,* 812–836.

Lamertz, K. & Baum, J. (1998). The legitimacy of organizational downsizing in Canada: An analysis of explanatory media accounts. *Canadian Journal of Administrative Sciences, 15,* 93–107.

Lawrence, T. B. (1999). Institutional strategy. *Journal of Management, 25,* 161–187.

Lawrence, T., Hardy, C., & Phillips, N. (2002). Institutional effects of interorganizational collaboration: The emergence of proto-institututions. *Academy of Management Journal, 45,* 281–290.

Lawrence, T., Winn, M., & Jennings, P. D. (2001). The temporal dynamics of institutionalization. *Academy of Management Review, 26,* 624–644.

Leblebici, H., Salancik, G. R., Copay, A., & King, T. (1991). Institutional change and the transformation of interorganizational fields: An organizational history of the U. S. radio broadcasting industry. *Administrative Science Quarterly, 36,* 333–363.

Lee, K. & Pennings, J. M. (2002). Mimicry and the market: Adoption of a new organizational form. *Academy of Management Journal, 45,* 144–162.

Lounsbury, M. (2002). Institutional transformation and status mobility: The professionalization of the field of finance. *Academy of Management Journal, 45,* 255–266.

McAdam, D. (1996). Conceptual origins, current problems, future directions. In D. McAdam, J. D. McCarthy, & M. N. Zald (Eds.). *Comparative perspectives on social movements* (pp. 23–40). Cambridge: Cambridge University Press.

McAdam, D., McCarthy, J. D., & Zald, M. N. (1996). *Comparative perspectives on social movements.* Cambridge: Cambridge University Press.

Meyer, A. D., Brooks, G. R., & Goes, J. B. (1990). Environmental jolts and industry revolutions: Organizational responses to discontinuous change. *Strategic Management Journal, 11,* 93–110.

Meyer, J. W. & Rowan, B. (1977). Institutionalized organizations: Formal structure as myth and ceremony. *American Journal of Sociology, 83,* 340–363.

Miles, R. H. (1982). *Coffin nails and corporate strategies.* Englewood Cliff, NJ: Prentice Hall.

Miller, D. & Chen, M.-J. (1996). Nonconformity in competitive repertoires: A sociological view of markets. *Social Forces, 74,* 1209–1234.

Mizruchi, M. S. (1996). What do interlocks do? An analysis critique, and assessment of research on interlocking directorates. *Annual Review of Sociology, 22,* 271–298. Palo Alto, CA: Annual Reviews.

Mizruchi, M. S. & Fein, L. C. (1999). The social constitution of organizational knowledge: A study of the uses of coercive, mimetic and normative isomorphism. *Administrative Science Quarterly, 44,* 653–683.

Nelson, R. (1994). The coevolution of technology, industrial structure, and supporting institutions. *Industrial and Corporate Change*, 3, 47–64.

Oakes, L. S., Townley, B., & Cooper, D. J. (1998). Business plans as pedagogy: Language and control in a changing institutional field. *Administrative Science Quarterly*, 43, 257–292.

Oliver, C. (1992). The antecedents of deinstitutionalization. *Organization Studies*, 13, 563–588.

Oliver, C. (1997). The influence of institutional and task environment relationships on organizational performance: The Canadian construction industry. *Journal of Management Studies*, 34, 99–124.

Palmer, D. A., Jennings, P. D., & Zhou, X. (1993). Late adoption of the multi-divisional form by large U. S. corporations: Institutional, political, and economic accounts. *Administrative Science Quarterly*, 38, 100–131.

Pettigrew, A. (1985). *The awakening giant*. Oxford: Basil Blackwell.

Pettigrew, A. (1987). Context and action in the transformation of the firm. *Journal of Management Studies*, 24, 649–670.

Powell, W. W. (1991). Expanding the scope of institutional analysis. In W. W. Powell & P. J. DiMaggio (Eds.), *The new institutionalism in organizational analysis* (pp. 183–203). Chicago, IL: University of Chicago Press.

Power, M. K. & Laughlin, R. C. (1996). Habermas, law, and accounting. *Accounting Organizations and Society*, 21, 441–467.

Ranson, S., Hinings, C. R., & Greenwood, R. (1980). The structuring of organizational structures. *Administrative Science Quarterly*, 25, 1–7.

Rao, H., Greve, H., & Davis, G. (2001). Fool's gold: Social proof in the initiation and abandonment of coverage by Wall Street analysts. *Administrative Science Quarterly*, 46, 502–526.

Reay, P. (2000). *The reorganization of health care in Alberta: Change in an organizational field*. Unpublished doctoral dissertation, University of Alberta, Edmonton, Canada.

Reay, P. & Hinings, C. R. (2004). The recomposition of an organized field: Health care in Alberta. *Organization Studies*, forthcoming.

Ruef, M. & Scott, W. R. (1998). A multidimensional model of organizational legitimacy: Hospital survival in changing institutional environments. *Administrative Science Quarterly*, 43, 877–904.

Sahlin-Andersson, K. (1996). Imitating by editing success: The construction of organizational fields. In B. Czarniawska & G. Sevon (Eds.), *Translating organizational change* (pp. 69–92). Berlin: W. de Gruyter.

Scott, W. R. (1994). Conceptualizing organizational fields: Linking organizations and societal systems. In H. U. Derlien, U. Gerhardt, & F. W. Scharpf (Eds.), Systemrationalitat und partialinteresse [Systems rationality and partial interests] (pp. 203–221). Baden-Baden, Germany: Nomos Verlagsgesellschaft.

Scott, W. R. (2001). *Institutions and organizations*. Thousand Oaks, CA: Sage.

Scott, W. R., Ruef, M., Mendel, P. J., & Caronna, C. A. (2000). *Institutional change and healthcare organizations*. Chicago: University of Chicago Press.

Selznick, P. (1949). *TVA and the grass roots*. Berkeley: University of California Press.

Seo, M.-G. & Creed, W. E. D. (2002). Institutional contradictions, praxis, and institutional change: A dialectical perspective. *Academy of Management Review*, 27, 222–247.

Sherer, P. D. & Lee, K. (2002). Institutional change in large law firms: A resource dependency and institutional perspective. *Academy of Management Journal*, 45, 102–119.

Snow, D. A. & Benford, R. D. (1992). Master frames and cycles of social protest. In A. Morris & C. R. Mueller (Eds.), *Frontiers in social movement theory* (pp. 13–155). New Haven, CT: Yale University Press.

Snow, D. A., Rochford, E. B., Jr., Worden, S. K., & Benford, R. D. (1986). Frame alignment processes, micromobilization, and movement participation. *American Sociological Review*, 51, 464–481.

Starr, P. (1982). *The social transformation of American medicine*. New York: Basic Books.

Strang, D. & Meyer, J. W. (1993). Institutional conditions for diffusion. *Theory and Society*, 22, 487–511.

Strang, D. & Soule, S. A. (1998). Diffusion in organizations and social movements: From hybrid corn to poison pills. *Annual Review of Sociology*, 24, 265–309.

Suchman, M. (1995). Managing legitimacy: Strategic and institutional approaches. *Academy of Management Review*, 20, 571–611.

Suddaby, R. (2001). *Field level governance and the emergence of new organizational forms: The case of multidisciplinary practices in law*. Unpublished doctoral dissertation, University of Alberta, Canada.

Thornton, P. H. (1995). Accounting for acquisition waves: Evidence from the U. S. publishing industry. In W. R. Scott & S. Christensen (Eds.), *The institutional construction of organizations* (pp. 199–225). Thousand Oaks, CA: Sage.

Thornton, P. H. (2002). The rise of the corporation in a craft industry: Conflict and conformity in institutional logics. *Academy of Management Journal*, 45, 81–101.

Thornton, P. H. & Ocasio, W. (1999). Institutional logics and the historical contingency of power in organizations: Executive succession in the higher education publishing industry, 1958 to 1990. *American Journal of Sociology, 105,* 801–843.

Tolbert, P. S. & Zucker, L. G. (1983). Institutional sources of change in the formal structure of organizations: Diffusion of civil service reform, 1880–1935. *Administrative Science Quarterly, 28,* 22–39.

Tolbert, P. S. & Zucker, L. G. (1996). Institutionalization of institutional theory. In S. Clegg, C. Hardy, & W. Nord (Eds.), *The handbook of organization studies* (pp. 175–190). Thousand Oaks, CA: Sage.

Townley, B. (2002). The role of competing rationalities in institutional change. *Academy of Management Journal, 45,* 163–179.

Tushman, M. & Rosenkopf, L. (1992). Organizational determinants of technological change: toward a sociology of technological evolution. In B. M. Staw & L. L. Cummings (Eds.), *Research in Organizational Beahvior* (Vol. 14, pp. 311–347). Greenwich, CT: JAI Press.

Utterback, J. (1994). *Mastering the dynamics of innovation.* Cambridge, MA: Harvard Business School Press.

Van de Ven, A. H., Polley, D., Garud, R., & Venkataraman, S. (1999). *The innovation journey.* New York: Oxford University Press.

Van Hoy, J. (1993). Intraprofessional politics and professional regulation. *Work and Occupations, 20,* 90–109.

Westphal, J. D. & Zajac, E. J. (1997). Defections from the inner circle: Social exchange, reciprocity, and the diffusion of board independence in U. S. corporations. *Administrative Science Quarterly, 42,* 161–183.

Westphal, J. D., Gulati, R., & Shortell, S. M. (1997). Customization or conformity: An institutional and network perspective on the content and consequences of TQM adoption. *Administrative Science Quarterly, 42,* 366–394.

Zaheer, S., Albert, S., & Zaheer, A. (1999). Time scales and organizational theory. *Academy of Management Review, 24,* 725–741.

Zucker, L. G. (1977). The role of institutionalization in cultural persistence. *American Sociological Review, 42,* 726–743.

Zucker, L. G. (1987). Institutional theories of organization. *Annual Review of Sociology, 13,* 443–464.

11

The Nation-State and Culture as Influences on Organizational Change and Innovation

Arie Y. Lewin & Jisung Kim

Social science disciplines have explored or implied the thesis that cultural, historical, political, social, and economic dimensions of a nation-state influence managerial practices and organizational strategic adaptation (Adler, Doktor and Redding, 1986; Badie and Birnbaum, 1983; Chandler, 1990; Clegg and Reddings, 1990; Djelic, 1998; Fligstein, 1996; Hickson and McMillan, 1981; Lammers, 1978; Lange and Regini, 1989; Meyer, 1994; Nelson, 1993; Putnam, 1993; Skocpol, 1985; Stinchcombe, 1965; Warner, 1997; Weber, Hsee, and Sokolowska, 1998; Whitley, 1999). However, much of the research centers on partial relationships reflecting disciplinary orientations and often involves historical accounts without theoretical underpinnings of explored events. The result is a fragmented literature on comparative management (Redding, 1997).

The underlying implicit assumption of adaptation selection theories reviewed in Lewin, Weigelt, and Emory (chapter 5 of this volume) is their universal applicability for explaining phenomena of adaptation and selection. The theories of adaptation and selection reviewed in this volume, for example, are not specifically concerned with possible contingencies due to the moderating effect of the nation-state with few exceptions (e.g., institutional theory). Although institutional theory incorporates the role of the state in organizational change (coercive and normative isomorphism), the focus is on institutional processes as primary universal forces of change. Institutional theory, however, provides useful frameworks for generating, testing, and further developing sociological and organizational theories of organizational change (Elder, 1976; Kohn, 1987).

In this chapter, building on a coevolutionary perspective (Lewin, Long, and Carroll, 1999) and a multilevel approach (Lammers, 1978), we review the dynamics and complexities of the relationships among institutional configurations, managerial practices, and organizational change and innovation. Understanding evolutionary changes at the institutional level is necessary for explaining some of the causes and sources of change and innovation at the firm level. Combining ecological and institutional perspectives, researchers propose that institutional and technological processes should be considered as important environmental processes that shape organizational forms and behavior and constitute the selection criteria for organizational survival (Baum, 1996; Singh and Lumsden, 1990). We argue that the specific nation-state configuration legitimizes and is reflected in particular managerial practices of business enterprises and public institutions that show the moderating effect of nation-state forms of capitalism on organizational change and innovation. The discourse on whether managerial practices reflect specific nation-state configurations as determined by historical, cultural, political, economic, and social factors involves a well-established and growing literature in the social sciences (e.g., developmental economics, political science, sociology, international management, strategy, social psychology, etc.). The basic argument found in this literature is that nation-states evolve unique configurations of political and economic institutions, social compacts, and educational systems that reflect the collective enactment of a nation's culture, values, and history. With the "globalization" of business activities, the question of whether and how factors specific to a nation-state affect managerial practices has emerged as an important contingency.

We consider the range of theoretical arguments and empirical studies involving institutional configurations and the influence of institutional configurations on managerial practices. We adopt previous research on institutional and managerial factors (Lewin et al., 1999; Whitley, 1996) in choosing the dimensions of institutional configuration and managerial practices. We develop a framework integrating the institutional configuration and managerial practices to structure our arguments and explore the dynamics of the relationships. Specifically, we argue that managerial practices such as governance structures, authority and control, employment relationships, and strategic paradigms reflect institutional configurations of a nation-state such as founding conditions of the nation, role of government, legal system, capital market, education system, and culture, which act as constraints on population- and organizational-level change and innovation (see figure 11.1). The managerial practices evolve as a consequence of the never-ending interplay between changes in the institutional configuration within which organizations are embedded, the dynamics of population level, and the macro environment.

For the purposes of this chapter, we use nation, country, and culture alternatively for the moderating effect of a nation-state on strategic management and organizational change. Similarly, cross-national, cross-country, cross-cultural, and comparative studies are used alternately. We use the term *moderating* to frame our view that country-specific effects create contingencies that moderate the effects of general theoretical relationships among concepts (Child and Kieser 1981; Fligstein 1996).

We focus on the United States, Japan, and Germany in our review because the specific discussions give substance to our arguments, because each of the three countries represents a leading economy in its

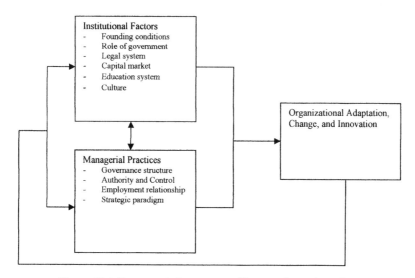

Figure 11.1 Framework for country effects on firm adaptation.

own continent that can be a source of institutional differences, and because a significant and growing comparative literature blueprints the countries' specific nation-state configurations. We do not argue that countries in the same continent are not different from each other. In fact, they could be as different as those in different continents (Kim, 1998; Whitley, 1996). The three countries we focus on are well represented in both academic and practitioner literature, so examples and cases are relatively easier to obtain than those of other countries. However, when it is necessary, we include the cases of other countries to help illustrate how countries that look similar can have different effects on managerial practices.

Conceptual Foundations for Institutional Configurations

The state and its relationship to society have gained increasing interest (Badie and Birnbaum, 1983; Hickson and McMillan, 1981; Warner, 1997). The "founding fathers" of sociological theories—Marx, Durkheim, and Weber—bring to light differences among states and their influence on society. However, the dominant paradigm of the state as a discrete system among others, as well as the notion that nationality is just an affiliation (i.e., arbitrary as club membership) had confined research on the role of the state. These views began to change rapidly in the 1960s, when the state emerged as a major line of inquiry by Anglo-American sociologists (Badie and Birnbaum, 1983; Skocpol, 1985; Steinmetz, 1999). The modernization of the Third World, led by powerful authoritarian states, the emergence of neo-Marxism, and a continuing reference to the influence of the state on the economy and society in most countries of the West, obliged scholars to revisit the role of the state (Mitchell, 1999). In addition, as the old balance between market economy and power of the state began shifting toward the latter, sociologists began to emphasize the increasing importance of governmental influence and structure (Parsons, 1971).

The influence of state on society is integral to recent perspectives. The "embeddedness" of economic action in society that Granovetter (1985, p. 481) articulates has gained support from various sources (e.g., Clegg and Reddings, 1990; Djelic, 1998). Viewing neoclassical economics as undersocialized, Granovetter argues that economic activity can be properly understood only in the context of social institutions and relations. The argument has led to a more pointed and urgent renewal of interest in how alternative modes of organizing economic activities are embedded in broader contexts (Callon, 1998; Redding and Whitley, 1990). In the studies of population dynamics, legitimacy was explained in terms of institutional embeddedness and was found to affect the founding and failure rates of a population (Baum and Oliver, 1992). Similarly, the new institutional theory (DiMaggio and Powell, 1983; Powell and DiMaggio, 1991) argues that organizational change must be examined in terms of the role of the state as a source of rationalization and coercive isomorphic pressure on managerial logic and organizational adaptation over time, and as a complement to the analysis of industry-competitive dynamics.

Nation-state institutional configurations are founded in historical and cultural conditions different from one another (Maddison, 1991; Redding, 1997; Stinchcombe, 1965). Studying the drivers in the development of capitalist countries, Maddison proposes that the economic performance of a country is to a significant extent affected by country-level factors such as institutions, ideologies, pressures of socioeconomic interest groups, economic policy at the national level, and historical accidents. He traces the evolution of economic leadership in the world as it shifts from the Netherlands to the United Kingdom and eventually to the United States, arguing that institutional factors drive the transitions. History tells us also that states are different in their reactions to certain economic actions of firms. For example, in the late 1800s and early 1900s, when large industrial firms joined cartels to mitigate environmental uncertainty by fixing prices, limiting production, and discouraging new entrants into the business, European and U.S. governments differed in their responses to cartelization (Barfield and Schambra, 1986; Djelic, Koza, and Lewin, 2000; Fligstein, 1990). For example, interfirm networks in the form of cartels were given official sanction and support in Germany; in the United States, antitrust legislation was enacted, followed by precedent-setting lawsuits breaking up the so-called trusts. As Djelic et al. discuss, a belief in market competition was prevalent in the United States, and an antimonopoly tradition had deep roots in English common law.

In the study of Italian regional reform from 1970s to 1990s, Putnam (1993) traces the influence of

Italy's social context and history on the effectiveness of institutions. Dense networks of local associations, active engagement in community activities, and egalitarian patterns of politics traditionally characterized the northern region, seen as trustworthy and law abiding. Here, the local government became more civic in orientation and its performance was constantly superior to institutions in the southern region. The southern region was characterized by vertical, political, and social participation, mutual suspicion, and corruption, all regarded as normal. Here, involvement in civic associations was scanty. Putnam further contends that changing formal institutions can change political practices, but institutional changes are slow, reflecting the influence and nature of path dependence. Advances in scientific and technological innovations are also influenced by the institutional configuration of national innovation systems (Nelson, 1993). Nelson and his colleagues demonstrated that countries evolve different configurations of national innovation systems consisting of a similar set of "institutional actors" (p. 9), such as national research laboratories and institutes, universities, and corporate laboratories. Moreover, the configurations of these "institutional actors" vary by country due to historical political, social, and economic factors.

Institutional configurations can be defined as constellations of formal and informal constraints that shape human interaction (North, 1990). Formal constraints include the government, the legal system, rules governing and enabling competition, capital market, and the education system. Informal constraints include history, culture, the value system, and social compacts. The formal system of constraints reflects and is embedded (Granovetter, 1985) in the informal constraints. Formal institutional arrangements evolve in ways consistent with, and reflective of, the social ideology or value system of the nation-state (Lewin et al., 1999). Changes in formal institutionalized constraints often lag behind changes emerging at the level of the popular culture and the emergence of de facto informal constraints. For example, the emergence and crystallization of social movements like environmental protection and civil rights preceded the enactment of new laws that signified changes to formal constraints.

Even though some nation-states share certain democratic philosophies (e.g., a system of popularly elected parliaments), the differences in their formal constraints reflect unique historical and cultural backgrounds (Badie and Birnbaum, 1983). Moreover, although the institutional configurations of developed countries have many formal constraints in common, the way both formal and informal constraints are treated by social actors can be significantly different and contribute to differences in the competitive advantage of a nation-state (Hill, 1995; Porter, 1990). In the remainder of this section we discuss key elements of institutional configurations, including founding conditions (Stinchcombe, 1965), the role of government (Murtha and Lenway, 1994), the legal system (Baron, 1996), capital markets (Chandler, 1980), the education system (Calori, Lubatkin, Veri, and Veiga, 1997), and culture (Hampden-Turner and Trompenaars, 1993).

Founding Conditions

Stinchcombe (1965) asserts that "organization forms and types have a history, and that this history determines some aspects of the present structure of organizations of that type" (p. 153). He also argues that the distinctive characteristics of the organization form persist over time. Depending on the level of analysis, the operationalization of founding conditions may vary. For example, at the organizational level, founding conditions could be represented as founder preference for organizational structure or initial gender mix (Baron, Hannan, and Burton, 1999). At the organization population level, the founding conditions could include government policy or ecological factors such as number of incumbents and capital availability (Dobbin and Dowd, 1997). Boeker (1988), in an empirical study on the effects of founding conditions on semiconductor manufacturing firms, finds that early strategic decisions and patterns of organizing are bound by both the preferences and beliefs of the founder entrepreneur and the environment. Within specific nation-state configurations, national history, geographical conditions, and specific historical accidents can act as constraints on the behavior of organizations and people. Following Stinchcombe (1965), we rely on historical context for relating founding conditions of a nation to organizational forms and managerial practices.

Although modern Japanese managerial practices originated in the period after World War II, several important dimensions have antecedents in the old

Tokugawa era (1603–1868), which continues to deeply influence the Japanese management system (Allen, 1981; Ito, 1996; Whitehill, 1990). Strong national identity established during the Tokugawa era still accounts for Japanese businessmen's identity with and loyalty to the nation. Confucianism underlies the beliefs, thinking, and behavior of managers. The teachings of Confucianism include unquestioned obedience to family, total loyalty to one's superior, respect for elders, and a reverence for education. Groupism or collectivism, evolved from the Tokugawa era, is antithetical to the legacy of American frontier spirit or rugged individualism. Thus, the Japanese enterprise system developed around networks of relatively small, specialized firms that cooperated with each other (Fruin, 1992), while in the United States, following the legislation of the antitrust statutes, firms developed large, diversified, multidivisional forms. Unlike in the United States, where the creation and consolidation of private railroad networks resulted in new managerial hierarchies composed of line and staff functions (Chandler, 1990), consolidation of the railway network in Japan took place, for the most part, under government ownership and control without challenging existing business forms.

In an analysis of U.S. economic leadership, Maddison (1991) argues that the emergence of the United States as the leading economy in the late nineteenth century was largely a result of intensive capital investments, abundant natural resources in land and minerals, and a vast internal market. The level of capital stock per person employed in the United States was twice as high as that in the United Kingdom in 1890. Increasingly abundant natural resources were available with improvements in transportation, including railroads and highways. The population of the United States in the late nineteenth century was bigger than that of any advanced country in Europe, and it was growing at faster rates because of immigration and high fertility rates. The continuing developments in transportation, mining, and manufacturing, the huge U.S. domestic market, and the constant pressure on founder-owners to raise capital led to the separation of shareholder ownership from control and the emergence of large diversified corporations with professional management (Berle and Means, 1932; Chandler, 1990; Maddison, 1991). Work ethics rooted in Puritanism provided the foundation of early entrepreneurial thought in the United

States (Guillén, 1994). The Puritans were early settlers in the United States, and their teaching promoted rational systematic profit seeking and presented the frontiersman and the self-made man as role models. This ideology was consistent with the political values of the new nation—liberty, equality of opportunity, and individualism.

As in the United States, the German modern business enterprise was greatly influenced by the development of modern industrialism. During the mid–eighteenth century, railroads and manufacturing and mining developments brought massive investments to the industrial sector (Kocka, 1980). After Bismarck united the German states under Kaiser Wilhelm I in 1873, German business firms continued to grow, diversify, and integrate under founding conditions both similar to and distinctive from those of the United States. Developments in transportation and the distribution of the largest manufacturing firms among industrial groups were similar in Germany and the United States in the early 1900s. However, the way firms were managed was significantly different in the two countries. In Germany, banks played the central role as sources of capital (Prowse, 1994). Through long-term loans and investments, which enabled banks to place their representatives on boards of directors, large banks could influence the strategic decisions of business firms (Kocka, 1980). Unlike in the United States, the German government was supportive of interim networks, such as cartels and syndicates, through which German manufacturing firms could grow in scale and adopt strategies of forward integration (Djelic et al., 2000; Kocka, 1980).

Another important aspect of German founding conditions is the development of trade unionism and worker participation distinct from those of other countries and rooted in early labor organizations (Leminsky, 1980). Prior to World War I, Germany was an authoritarian monarchy where workers were suppressed by legal means and through government action. Trade unions were established during the 1860s as a result of a socialist movement. To discourage workers from joining unions and to counter socialist influence, Chancellor Otto von Bismarck established laws, such as health and accident insurance and old age and disability pensions, that marked a breakthrough in social policy. Union members participated in the administration of these pensions. In 1918, when a parliamentary system was introduced and the monarchy was overthrown, unions were recognized as the representative of labor, and shop-level works councils were introduced by law. Since then, worker participation at both shop-floor level and company level (codetermination legislation) has become a distinctive feature of German employment relationships.

The Role of Government

It is widely accepted that national government is responsible for public welfare, guides the nation's economy, mediates and buffers environmental uncertainties, and enacts collective ideologies through legislation and regulatory mechanisms (Badie and Brinbaum, 1983; Callon, 1998; Conekin, Mort, and Waters, 1999; Djelic, 1998; Maddison, 1991; Putnam, 1993; Evans, Rueschemeyer, and Skocpol, 1985). As the key institutional player, the government is expected to create opportunities and establish constraints for organizational actions (Baron 1996; Whitley 1999). One dimension of government involves its impact on the economic activities of industries and firms. Government intervention in the economy can range from maximal reliance on free markets to central control and planning of all economic activities. Most governments belong somewhere on a continuum between the two extremes. Eisner (1993) asserts that the degree of intervention characteristic of a "regulatory regime" can change as the economy and political interests of a country change. Regimes are "political, institutional arrangements that define the relationship between social interests, the state, and economic actors such as corporations, labor unions, and agricultural associations" (p. 2). Furthermore, Eisner documents that the United States has evolved through four types of regimes, depending on economic and political situation. From 1880 to 1920, when large-scale corporations and markets emerged, the U.S. government followed a market regime, in which the policy goal was promotion of market governance and the creation of marketlike results through administrative means. During the Great Depression, an associational regime promoted industrial stability and redistribution of national income. Concerned with post–World War II economic development and quality of life, the government implemented a two-decade societal regime. Major goals addressed the prevention of hazards to health and environment that occur as a consequence of advanced industrial production. In the 1970s and 1980s, economic stagflation and growing foreign competition helped create an efficiency regime to roll back policies that interfered with market mechanisms or imposed large compliance costs.

Baron (1996) notes that the degree of government intervention also differs by industry. Governments may exercise control over nationally important industries such as power generation and distribution, transportation, or oil processing through creation of state-owned enterprises (Stanbury and Thompson, 1982). The motives for government ownership of business enterprises are varied and include political ideology (e.g., socialism), maintaining industries that the private sector is unable to sustain, developing certain regions of a country, and protecting nascent industries from foreign competition (Lewin, 1982). State ownership and management not only shape the context of the controlled industry but affect private firms. The behavior of managers in state-owned enterprises is different from that of managers in private firms (Aharoni, 1981) as a result of the dual obligations of managing for profit while also satisfying national political objectives in state-owned enterprises. Thus, the feasible set of activities in which both state-owned and private firms can engage depends on the degree of control and intervention by the government, resulting in different opportunities for strategic and organizational adaptations.

Other dimensions of the role of government in affecting managerial practices and organizational changes are transactional governance and property rights allocations. Murtha and Lenway (1994) develop a taxonomy of government systems that defines transactional governance as the proportion of inter-organizational transactions governed by the price mechanism, relative to the proportion of transactions governed by plan. Property rights are the proportional allocation of real assets between private and state ownership. The resulting four prototypical government systems are command economy (planned transaction and public property rights), transitional economy (market transaction and public property rights), corporatist private enterprise (planned transaction and private property rights), and pluralist private enterprise (private transaction and private property rights). Murtha and Lenway recognize that pure forms do not exist and that most political economies involve some hybrid form. In addition they argue that the strategic capabilities of government affect the strategies of domestic firms, their customers, collaborators and competitors, and foreign direct investors. Thus, in command and transitional economies, for example, state ownership leads to ambiguous property rights regimes that retard development of firm-specific advantages and overemphasize cost-based advantages. Conversely, in corporatist and pluralist capitalist economies, private property-right regimes foster development of firm-specific advantages that drive firms to focus on innovation and compete in international markets by investing abroad.

The U.S. government has the least incentive, compared with other countries, to develop national industrial policies as a consequence of its cultural heritage of individualism and a popular-culture belief in free markets (Hitt, Dacin, Tyler, and Park, 1997). Therefore, the national government's role is to develop institutional and legal structures that define property rights, including intellectual property, and to develop commercial and contract laws. This institutional structure is intended to promote selection mechanisms based on strong market competition, encouraging product innovation and exploration of new opportunities (Fligstein, 1990). The state has also been important in the development of certain nascent industries in the U.S. economy such as airlines, railroads, and telecommunications industries, and in establishing the regulatory regimes that shape the relationship among social interests, state, and economic actors (Eisner, 1993).

In Japan, labor and business interact with government through officially recognized associations to promote consensus on economic and social policies. For example, the Ministry of International Trade and Industry (MITI) and the association of business enterprises (Keidanren) work through joint committees to address issues affecting the economy, industry sector, and product market (Murtha and Lenway, 1994). Moreover, the Japanese government structure matches key sectors of the economy to specific ministries (e.g., construction, telecommunications, transportation, health, agriculture, and energy). In addition to the key sectors of the Japanese economy, other sectors are guided by the Ministry of International Trade and Industry or Ministry of Finance (MOF),

the two central and most influential ministries (Ito, 1996; Whitehill, 1990).

The government's role in the business sector is much stronger in a corporatist economy than in a pluralist-based political economy. In a corporatist economy, the government affects firm goals and strategies under the jurisdiction of specific government regimes (Fruin, 1992; Plenert, 1990). In Korea, for example, government industrial policies have emphasized the growth of exports as drivers of economic development. The primary influence of those policies on Korean firms is their focus on long-term growth and sales volume rather than on profitability or profit maximization (Chang and Chang, 1994; Ungson, Steers, and Park, 1997). Corporate growth is financed through extension of bank credits provided by government-controlled banks. A major consequence has been a high debt ratio and the prevalence of unrelated diversification (Ursacki and Vertinsky, 1995; Haggard, Kim, and Moon, 1991).

In Germany, the direct intervention of government is bounded by vertically and horizontally fragmented sovereignty and by constitutional limitations on the unilateral action of government. As a consequence, institutional changes can be very slow, and public policies, while stable and predictable, tend to be slow to respond to emerging interests of the public or other environmental discontinuities. Under this institutional structure, firms can develop stable expectations, pursue long-term objectives, and build lasting relationships with one another (Streek, 1997). Although the German government does not initiate strong industrial policies, a wide range of general infrastructural supports are facilitated by the government (Randlesome, 1994). The role of government in West Germany after World War II can be divided into three different periods. During the post–World War II reconstruction period (1948–1965), the goal was high growth rates, price stability, regaining of full employment, and re-establishment of strong positions in international trade. A state interventionist period (1966–1979) followed, characterized by applying the Keynesian principle of guaranteed full employment and extending the welfare state. A period of liberalization (1980–1990) emerged as the state faced difficulties sustaining the welfare state and began to replace full employment policies with policies for long-term growth, deregulation and privatization, and decreasing the growth rate of social welfare expenditures, such as social security and various subsidies (Kurz, 1991).

The Legal System

The structure of the legal system of a country significantly shapes how business is done with others (transparency) and how fast business practices can change (flexibility) (Baron, 1996; Randlesome, 1994). When the legal system is transparent, issues related to business are codified in statutes such as commercial law, intellectual property law, or contract law, and firms can carry on business activities with greater certainty than in a country where government guidance supplants legal rights. In guidance regimes, laws are not codified into detailed regulations and procedures, and government or its agent has vast discretion to interpret laws, issue private rulings and guidelines for conducting business, or establish regulations. The result is higher uncertainty in the conduct of business under a guidance regime than under a transparent one. Thus, for example, under a guidance legal system, it would be more difficult for a firm to form a strategic alliance with a previously unknown transaction partner than under a transparent legal system. Rule-making flexibility determines the effort and time required to change a legal statute. In a relatively inflexible rule-making environment, firms face a stable, reliable, and predictable legal environment and can pursue long-term strategic planning. However, when rules can be radically changed with every change in political regime (e.g., the post–World War II United Kingdom), firms face an unstable environment that causes them to resort to short-term adaptation (Kurz, 1991; Randlesome, 1994).

German laws have followed the prescriptive pattern of Roman law (Foster, 1996; Tricker, 1990) and are characterized by very detailed codification of regulations that, while cumbersome, make laws and legal procedures highly transparent. The high degree of codification in German laws distinguishes them from the U.K. system (Foster, 1996). The precise and transparent German rules allow firms to rely on the laws and procedures in their conduct of business (Randlesome, 1994). German laws, however, are less flexible because the processes for changing laws or enacting new laws require time and effort. Moreover, changes to basic statutes require the support of both major political parties. An example of the transparent and inflexible characteristics of German rules can be found in the retailing industry in connection with shop opening hours. Kurz (1991) says, "Shops are

allowed to open from Monday to Friday from 7 A.M. to 6.30 P.M. and on Saturday from 7 A.M. to 2 P.M. (the first Saturday of each month until 4 P.M.). After lengthy debate this has been liberalized and shops may now remain open until 8.30 P.M. every Thursday. A more comprehensive liberalization is unlikely to take place because unions and small and medium-sized enterprises (SMEs) are opposed to it" (p. 27). Kurz's observation shows that, in part, German rule-making inflexibility reflects a particular view of fairness that accords a certain quality-of-life protection to small shop owners and their families in the face of "predatory" competitive practices of large corporate retailers.

The Japanese legal system is patterned after the civil code systems of continental Europe rather than the adversarial system of the United States. The system relies heavily on dispute conciliation. Since the Japanese place great value on harmony and the absence of confrontation and conflict, they seek to resolve disputes without recourse to legal processes or the courts (Baron, 1996; Namiki and Sethi, 1988). Juries are not common and lawyers are viewed as counselors rather than as advocates. Although Japan has antimonopoly statutes, enforcement differs from the United States. Frequently, when the enforcer (the Fair Trade Commission, or FTC) concludes that a company has violated the antimonopoly law, the FTC issues a warning and relies on remedial action through guidance. Criminal charges are rarely brought against executives found to have violated fair-trade laws (Baron, 1996).

In the United States, detailed codification of laws and the reliance on case law create transparency in the conduct of business activities. Moreover, because legal procedures are based on an adversarial system, laws must be further clarified and justified. The tradition of relying on case law as a means to updating and interpreting legal statutes increases the flexibility of the U.S. legal system. Consequently, high transparency and flexibility foster an institutional environment in which firms can undertake transactions with unknown transaction partners (Baron, 1996).

Capital Markets

The development and characteristics of the capital market in a country play an important role in shaping firms' strategic paradigms. Although the causal relationship between the development of the capital market and the managers' focus on stock performance is not clear, the United States exemplifies a high correlation between the two (Chandler, 1980). The early development of the U.S. capital market is owed chiefly to government financing needs and rapidly growing basic industries, including railroad companies; the absence of a national banking system; abundant capital from foreign investors; the development of intermediaries such as investment bankers; and the increasing separation of ownership and control (Berle and Means, 1932; Carosso, 1970). The federal government had to finance participation in wars, including the Civil War. In the early history of the United States, corporations and businesses increasingly used the capital markets because individual owners could not afford growing investments. For example, as railroad construction expanded geographically and required vast capital investments, businessmen raised capital by issuing stocks and bonds and began to hire professional managers (Chandler, 1977; Neal, 1997). Investors relied on the stock market to monitor the performance of professional managers, who managed businesses separate from founding families and shareholders. Brokerage firms in New York and London traded the stocks of firms in the United States. They were also involved in the trading activities of regional exchanges, which usually concentrated on trading shares of locally known and operated firms. New York and London exchanges used regional exchange markets to monitor local firm performance for the benefit of distant investors (Neal, 1997). Lewin et al. (1999) argue that the scale, diversity, efficiency, liquidity, and highly competitive nature of capital markets in the United States lead managers to focus on maximizing shareholder value. The strong U.S. capital market has been dominated by institutional and individual stockholders (Hitt et al., 1997; Sakano and Lewin, 1999), and managers have been evaluated by stock performance since the early days of industrialization (Ito and Rose, 1994). Thus, the U.S. capital market is widely accepted as a market for corporate control in which capital markets ensure management discipline and shareholder orientation. In the event managers fail to maximize the value of a firm, any individual or organization with sufficient capital can purchase the firm's shares and replace the firm's managers, policies, or strategies to maximize shareholder value (Prowse, 1994).

Unlike managers in the United States, Japanese managers are concerned with all stakeholders, including employees, customers, society, and shareholders. Ozaki (1992) notes that Japanese managers do not have confidence in the efficiency of the capital market, and equity investments are considered by many investors to be gambles (Ozaki, 1992). Stock market evaluation is only one measure of managerial capability. Ito and Rose (1994) argue that since the Japanese venture capital market is very small in comparison with the U.S. market, the combination of large established firms and the ability to spin off subsidiaries may function as a substitute for an efficient venture market. The highly concentrated patterns of share ownership and cross-holding have made hostile takeovers practically impossible, reduced the liquidity, and produced the stability of the capital market (Macey and Miller, 1995). Cross-holdings of equity, keiretsu-type firm networks, main bank relationships, and an almost nonexistent market for financing mergers, acquisitions, and divestitures reinforce a long-term orientation, evolutionary adaptation, and strategic continuity (Aoki, 1994; Hundley and Jacobson, 1998; Sakano and Lewin, 1999).

Chandler (1980) points out that, in Europe, owners continue to manage enterprises at the highest level because they make less extensive use of mass-production techniques. In addition, coordination of the flow of goods is less complex than in the United States. Founder-owners and their families continue to make critical policy decisions, and as a result, the managerial class remains much smaller than in the United States (Djelic et al., 2000). German capital markets are not "markets for control" (Prowse, 1994; Streck, 1997). Many companies are privately held, shareholding is highly concentrated, and only a small part of equity capital is traded on the stock exchange (Jürgens, Naumann, and Rupp, 2000; Neal, 1997). Firms tend to finance themselves through long-term bank credit rather than through equity. According to Neal, in 1993 the capitalization of domestic equities amounted to only 26 percent of German GDP, compared to 62 percent and 120 percent for the United States and the United Kingdom, respectively. A mere 10 out of the nearly 800 companies publicly listed in Germany accounted for 63% of the trading volume. Only a little over 5% of the German population actually held any stocks, compared to over 16% in France, 21% in the United States and UK, and 35% in Sweden. Jürgens et al. argued that Germany's relatively small stock market in relation to the national economy led shareholders to play a minor role in the

German economy. Since firms depend on long-term credit from banks, which has been the alternative mode of financing for German firms for nearly two centuries (Neal, 1997), managers tend to adopt a long-term perspective and not speculate with stocks (Streek, 1997).

The Education System

The education system can exercise an important role in creating, transferring, and reinforcing social values and beliefs (Calori et al., 1997; Warner, 1996). It is considered to be a source of high quality human resources (Chandler, 1990; Tung, 1988; Warner, 1996). Chandler (1990) emphasizes the role of an education system as influencing the training and recruitment of managers and workers and affecting both day-to-day operating and long-term strategic decisions. Differences in education systems between nations can be significant and can affect organizational adaptations such as the development of industrial enterprises, technological innovations in organizations, and centralization or decentralization of decision-making preferences (Albach, 1994; Calori et al., 1997; Chandler, 1990). In an attempt to classify national education systems using statistical data, Wolhuter (1997) suggests constructing typologies based on aspects of education systems such as modes or degrees of educational privatization or administration on a centralized-decentralized continuum. Wolhuter points out that this approach might be theoretically driven rather than inductively driven. In the comparative study of technical innovation, Albach (1994) finds a strong relationship between knowledge of a subject and risk assessment of an innovation. He argues that risk aversion declines with education level, which he argues should be true of any culture. A review of the literature illustrates that the level and content of a national education system, as well as the degree of centralization, can be determining factors in organizational adaptation and strategies processes.

Following the beginning of the industrial age, German higher education in science and technology greatly helped German business enterprises. German universities became centers for serious research and scholarship in science and technology long before their British and American counterparts (Chandler, 1990). Since the establishment of the Federal Republic of Germany, the government has guaranteed people the right to freely develop and choose their profession and occupation. Education is the responsibility of individual states for the most part.

Germany is known for its highly developed system of vocational education and training (VET). The German education system is a dual system that encompasses both university-level and industry-based education and provides nationally standardized courses for occupations, from the apprenticeship level to the master craftsman and engineer levels (Lane, 1992; Randlesome, 1994). The dual system, which has its roots in the craft tradition of guilds and artisan associations, manifests organizational cooperation for the efficient and effective use of the labor pool and of the market (Neary, 1993). Quite distinctly from other countries, education and vocational training are closely linked in the German system. When children reach the age of 10, they choose between general schools, where the dual system prevails, and grammar schools, which lead to university education (Randlesome, 1994). The graduates of vocational training enter clearly prescribed professions (e.g., fireman, waiter, plumber, roofer, machinist, etc.) with strict paths for advancement and specialization. In Germany, unlike Japan, the education philosophy tends to reduce competition in the school system and postpone competition until entry into the employment system (Albach, 1994).

In Japan, the curriculum for all public schools is standardized by the Ministry of Education and even minor revisions require elaborate, time-consuming processes (Ito, 1994). Textbooks and course contents are prescribed. These standards are also followed by private schools (Whitehill, 1990). Getting into the right university is critical because education is highly correlated with point of entry on the socioeconomic ladder. Graduates of prestigious universities have a much greater opportunity of joining the governmental and corporate elite (Briggs, 1991; Dore, 1994; Warner, 1996; Wiersema and Bird, 1993).

The Japanese education system is highly meritocratic; entrance to universities is almost entirely based on entrance examination. Consequently, most Japanese parents push their children to prepare for passing entrance examinations of top universities to maximize opportunities for lifetime careers with Japan's largest, most prestigious companies. Since competition for entry into a good school is very intense (Bracey, 1998), and the education system is centralized and homogeneous (Whitehill, 1990), many Japanese students attend extra preparatory classes or learn math and science from private tutors in addition to regular school programs. Private teaching institutes aimed to help high school students enter specific prestigious universities are found in most Japanese cities.

The United States has achieved a high level of education since the early stage of industrialization. Chandler (1990) notes that the U.S. higher education system at the turn of the century was catching up to the German education system in technology. Similarly, higher education for business appeared in both the United States and Germany at the turn of the twentieth century. German business education focused on accounting, finance, and generalized business economics and law, while U.S. management education emphasized functional areas such as marketing and general management. These business schools, together with engineering schools, became a vital source of scientific, technical, and commercial knowledge. Since the Carnegie and Ford Foundation reports of the early 1950s, U.S. business schools have become a major source of highly educated professional managers. Germany, however, never developed professional graduate schools of business (Randlesome, 1994).

Unlike Japan and Germany, U.S. education is highly decentralized, with 15,000 independent local school boards with diverse interests and orientations (Thurow, 1992). Parents expect their children to become involved in extracurricular activities, to mature and develop social skills, and work in after-school jobs (Bracey, 1998). The pluralistic U.S. system creates an environment where getting into the top university is not the only way to join the corporate elite. Although graduating from a top school can offer a better start, there are multiple points of entry to jobs and experience over time. Demonstrated skills, motivation, and past performance increase in importance when employers evaluate job candidates. The decentralized education system, however, creates high variance in academic achievement, which has been documented in international comparisons of academic competitions. Debates on the quality of U.S. education go back as far as the 1950s, led by media and the federal government. Students' poor performance in international tests has been widely publicized (Bracey, 1998). In defending the U.S. education system, Bracey argues that the performance differences in the competition are primarily the result of the different characteristics of nations' formal and informal education

systems. Although Thurow (1992) recognizes that U.S. K–12 education must improve in terms of intensity of study in mathematics and science, he argues that graduate education in the United States has no equal elsewhere in the world.

A nation's cultural values are embedded in its education systems and can influence the structure and direction of organizational adaptation. Comparing French and British education systems, Calori et al. (1997) argue that the nations' education policies and content influence managers' preference for centralization and decentralization. The French secondary education system emphasizes that all students should have equal access to same educational opportunities, and the Ministry of National Education exercises tight control over the school system. Not unlike Japan, the ministry oversees most of the nation's teachers and determines the curriculum, pedagogical methods, and textbooks to be used in public schools. The highly centralized French education system and its meritocratic focus on selecting the few who enter the Grandes Écoles—and thus the political and corporate elite—accounts for French manager preference for centralized decision making in their organizations. In contrast, the British school system is much less centralized and more individualistic. In the United Kingdom, local educational authorities have some autonomy in designing the curriculum and making decisions. More important, the content of the education in the two nations is different. French education, based on "rationalism" and natural sciences and mathematics, focuses on constructing reality in orderly hierarchies, whereas the British education philosophy is based on "pragmatism" and more individualistic learning approaches (Calori et al., 1997). Calori et al. (1997) find that, as a consequence of the British education philosophy, British managers develop a greater preference for delegation of decision making and decentralized organizational structures.

Culture

Culture is closely related to the history of a country and influences managerial practices as well as other aspects of nation institutional configuration, such as government, legal system, and education system (Adler et al., 1986; Allen, Miller, and Nath, 1988; Besser, 1993; Bigoness and Blakely, 1996; Cray and Mallory, 1998; Hamada and Sibley, 1994; Joynt and

Warner, 1996; Newman and Nollen, 1996; Triandis, 1994). Culture, however, is also an aggregate phenomenon resulting from such characteristics. We view culture as an informal institution (Hill, 1995; North, 1990) and one dimension of the societal structure (Stinchcombe, 1965). Adler et al. (1986) argue that culture influences the form and function of the other aspects of societal structures. Ruigrok and Achtenhagen (1999) find an overarching effect of national culture in German-speaking organizations, which have their own unique organizational culture. Chui, Lloyd, and Kwok (2002), using data from 22 countries, show that national culture is related to the capital structure of firms operating in the nation. Researchers argue that there is a high congruence between national culture and management practices because mutually reinforcing management practices and national cultural values are more likely to yield predictable behavior, self-efficacy, and high performance (Hill, 1995; Newman and Nollen, 1996; Tayeb, 1991).

The issue of culture is examined in many disciplines and involves diverse concepts and methods. There are over 160 definitions of culture, and a great deal of new research has been published in recent years (Darlington, 1996; Kroeber and Kluckhohn, 1985). It is beyond the scope of this chapter to integrate all of these perspectives or present an exhaustive literature review. Instead, we try to illustrate how cultural differences may affect firm adaptation paths. Identifying country differences that result from cultural differences is very complex, because the observed national difference could be due to situational differences, which are not the same as cultural differences, such as socioeconomic development and democratization (Child, 1981; Schneider, 1989; Schwartz and Sagie, 2000; Triandis, 1994; Weber et al., 1998). Schwartz and Sagie find that the importance of certain values, such as self-direction, stimulation, universalism, benevolence, and hedonism, is positively related to both socioeconomic levels and degree of democratization. The consensus about values among people in a country was influenced by the two factors. While socioeconomic development was positively related to value consensus, democratization was negatively associated with the value consensus. Considering that value consensus can vary from country to country, we note that the discussion of cultural differences is also criticized for stereotyping people of a particular national culture and for not considering individual differences. Cultural differences, however, have been observed and studied by many researchers, and the consequences of culture differences have been reported repeatedly.

Although measuring cultural dimensions is problematic, there have been efforts to classify the cultures of different countries (Hampden-Turner and Trompenaars, 1994; Hofstede, 1980, 1983, 1991; Joynt and Warner 1996; Schwartz, 1994; Triandis, 1994; Trompenaars, 1993). Hofstede's arguments and findings on cultural dimensions are reviewed and replicated repeatedly in empirical studies (Triandis, 1994). Hofstede surveyed IBM employees from more than 60 countries, asking questions on four dimensions of culture. Hofstede's four cultural dimensions include: (1) individualism versus collectivism—the extent to which people emphasize personal or group goals, (2) power distance—the extent to which members of a culture accept inequality and whether they perceive much distance between those with power and those with little power, (3) uncertainty avoidance—the extent to which people try to avoid uncertainty and an emphasis on ritual behavior, rules, and stable employment, and (4) masculinity versus femininity—the degree of gender differentiation in the culture (Hofstede, 1980).

Triandis (1994) reports convergence among empirical research testing Hofstede's dimensions and suggests that Hofstede's framework can serve as a theoretical foundation for predictions of numerous attributes of organizational or managerial behaviors. Triandis also argues that since Hofstede's work is based on a static, cross-sectional, single-method approach, his findings could be method bound and future research must adopt dynamic perspectives that examine how cultural values are negotiated in environments over time. Culture research should be based on multiple approaches, with observations, responses to attitude and value systems, reactions to scenarios describing a variety of social situations, and responses in experimental settings (Triandis 1994).

Hampden-Turner and Trompenaars (1994) use seven valuing processes to compare and discuss the cultures of seven developed countries: the United States, Japan, Germany, France, Britain, Sweden, and the Netherlands. Hampden-Turner and Trompenaars use a survey methodology asking managers in those countries questions along the seven valuing processes: (1) universalism versus particularism, (2) analyzing versus integrating, (3) individualism versus communitarianism, (4) inner-directed versus outer-directed orientation, (5) time as sequence versus time as synchronization, (6) achieved status versus ascribed status, and (7) equality versus hierarchy. The data consistently show that the United States and Japan are at the opposite ends of each dimension. The analysis of manager responses from different countries reflects underlying and different cultural values. For example, 92% of U.S. managers, when asked which considerations are more important in the process of hiring a new employee, indicated "the new employee must have the skills, the knowledge, and a record of success in a previous job." At the other end of the scale, only 49% of Japanese managers chose that answer. German managers were in the middle with 87%. Sixty-one percent of the Japanese managers felt that "the new employee must fit into the group or team in which he or she is to work (Hampden-Turner and Trompenaars, 1994, p. 56).

Using data obtained from 41 cultural groups, Schwartz (1994) develops six value types: conservatism, autonomy, hierarchy, mastery, egalitarian commitment, and harmony. These six values form two broad cultural dimensions: (1) conservatism versus autonomy and (2) hierarchy and mastery versus egalitarian commitment and harmony. Conservatism is associated with whether an individual is viewed autonomous or constrained by the society. In the conservative culture, harmonious relationship within the society is emphasized. Autonomy is at the opposite side of conservatism. In the culture where mastery and hierarchy values are high, people are concerned more with individual interests than the interests of groups. On the other hand, with high egalitarian commitment and harmony, people view the group interests as more important than individual interests. According to the data, the United States and Japan are more conservative and less autonomous than Germany. An empirical study using these cultural dimensions as predictors of firm capital structure finds that high conservatism is associated with low debt ratio (Chui et al., 2002).

According to Weber et al. (1998), culture is associated with risk-taking behavior. Individualism emphasizes personal freedom and responsibility, whereas collectivism stresses the values of social relatedness and interdependence. Compared with individualistic cultures, members of collectivist societies will more likely receive support from others when needed. Comparing proverbs in the U.S.,

German, and Chinese cultures, Weber et al. (1998) find that Chinese and German proverbs advocate greater risk taking than American proverbs. Their finding is consistent with the notion that social network connections offset the consequences of an individual's taking risks.

Cultural differences embedded in the history of a nation mediate different emphases on the development of business. U.S. culture is often dubbed "rugged individualism," embodying a strong belief in the "free market" (Hitt et al., 1997, p. 160). The individualistic culture, pioneering spirit, and sense of limitless opportunity that pervaded American society in the late nineteenth and early twentieth centuries influenced the management of U.S. companies. Faced with the need to finance geographic expansion and extensive and rapid growth, business owners found it necessary to delegate the authority of running the business to professional managers, and they raised capital by issuing securities to the public. These measures weakened ownership and control in favor of professional managers (Berle and Means, 1932; Chandler, 1990). Thus, monitoring the performance of managers became an overriding issue and led to the implementation of corporate governance mechanisms and stock market monitoring. As we mentioned earlier, at the root of the pioneering spirit in the United States is a strong Protestant ethic that emphasizes honesty and helping others, as well as hard work, profit seeking, and individualism (Guillén, 1994). In a comparative study on voluntary association membership in fifteen countries, Curtis, Grabb, and Baer (1992) find that the United States has the highest level of voluntary association memberships, which is inconsistent with individualism. They conclude that U.S. society, which is based on the Protestant work ethic, balances in various ways free-market competition and nonmarket social transactions, which are the basis for supporting individuals who have failed in the competitive arena.

Japanese homogeneity, agrarian traditions, isolationism during the Tokugawa era (1603–1868), being an island nation, and the influence of Eastern religions and philosophies such as Confucianism and Buddhism have reinforced Japanese cultural norms that emphasize group identification, collective responsibility, and interpersonal harmony, called "Wa" (Barlett and Ghoshal, 1998; Fruin, 1992; Hill, 1995). Low mobility, stable social networks, and mutual assistance characterize agrarian traditions during sowing and harvest (Fruin, 1992). Collective responsibility, which as Hill (1995) argues is the source of cooperation, lowers the potential for opportunism with guile, reduces monitoring transaction costs incurred during business activities, and facilitates decentralized organizational forms and specialized investments. Another implication of collectivism is emphasis on group identification. Collectivist culture makes a greater distinction between in-group and out-group members and encourages conformity among group members. Group composition is usually based on family, schools, and universities, and often group membership becomes the basis of individual social network (Wiersema and Bird, 1993).

The Effects of Institutional Configurations on Managerial Practices

Organizations evolve through interplay with institutional configurations, which are reflected in distinct aspects of managerial practices in different nation-states (Franke, Hofstede, and Bond, 1991; Fruin, 1992; Orru, Hamilton, and Suzuki, 1989; Schneider and De Meyer, 1991; Shane, 1994; Whitley, 1996). As a consequence, organizations embedded in different countries can be expected to manifest different organizational configurations, or implement alternative structures or managerial practices intended to achieve equivalent goals. From this perspective, markets can be seen as politics (Fligstein, 1996) or cultures (Abolafia, 1998). Fligstein (1996) contends that states play an important role in the formation and ongoing stability of market institutions. Property rights, governance structures, and rules of exchange are arenas in which modern states establish rules for economic actors. Markets exhibit their own distinctive sets of mutual understandings (Abolafia, 1998). Market participants rely on these mutual understandings to pursue their interests and at the same time limit the range of alternatives available to each other. Thus, companies operating in different countries or cultures follow distinctive rules and sets of actions to continue their activities in each market.

In a comparative study of large firms in the United States, Great Britain, and Germany, Chandler (1990) concludes that because the institutional context in which firm-level decisions are made differs greatly, the content of managerial decisions also differs greatly from country to country, industry to industry,

and one time period to the next. Chandler (1990) notes cultural reasons for the differences in operational and strategic decision making, arguing that national differences in educational systems influence the recruiting and training of managers and workers, while national legal systems define the basic rules of competition differently. Although Chandler's conclusions are based on pre–World War II data, cultural differences that reflect historical roots continue to affect managerial practices (Cusumano and Takeishi, 1991; Kogut, 1991). In a study of the fashion industry in France, Italy, and the United States, Djelic and Ainamo (1999) show that the trajectories of new organizational forms in response to environmental turbulence were different in the three countries because of institutional constraints and firm-specific historical legacies.

Focusing on country capabilities, Kogut (1991) expands Chandler's observation to contemporary issues of international competitiveness and argues that countries differ not only in technological capabilities but also in their application of underlying principles for organizing work. As a result, technological capabilities and organizational routines develop within the constraints of a path dependent trajectory. Kogut further develops arguments for why different national trajectories arise and persist and why institutional or organizational changes may be slower than technological changes. According to Kogut, the required change may be legally and politically impossible to enforce; a new way of organizing may take levels of commitment and performance that are not acceptable in some cultures and countries and may require unacceptable levels of labor mobility. Firm-specific capabilities are affected or constrained by the country capabilities, as shown in the case of the Japanese enterprise system. Fruin (1992) argues that countries that adopted the Japanese general trading company model have not fully benefited from the system because of institutional differences. Porter (1990) argues that competitive advantage at a national level stems from culturally and technologically based continuous innovation. Emphasizing the importance of industry clusters in which firms in related industries are clustered and exchange resources and information, Porter (1990) contends that nations can gain important national advantage when national attributes are supportive of the emergence and growth of industry clusters.

Whitley (1996) argues that as a result of their different institutional configurations, European economies continue to show considerable variation in the way firms coordinate activities. Business groups in East Asia (i.e., Chinese family business, Japanese *keiretsu*, and Korean *chaebols*) demonstrate that Anglo-Saxon conceptions of the legally bound form as the basic unit of economic action are inadequate to explain the economic actions and structure of those businesses (Hamilton, Zeile, and Kim, 1990; Redding and Whitley, 1990). Nation-states, through their institutional configuration and policy regimes, can influence enterprises to make irrational investment decisions that can have irrational outcomes such as overemployment, building global overcapacity, and excessive competition (Brahm, 1995). The ways firms make strategic decisions in markets are affected by country-specific factors. For example, Boisot and Child (1996) contend that China is treading a path toward modernization that differs from Western experience, and the organization of economic activity in China is different from that of Western nations because China has distinctive historical, political, institutional, and cultural characteristics.

Institutions provide structure to economic exchange by defining the set of acceptable and unacceptable individual and organizational behaviors (Hill, 1995; North, 1990) and by shaping the paths or trajectories for organizations (Djelic and Ainamo, 1999). Thus, organizations embedded in a nation-state share a common institutional backdrop that shapes a distinctive set of managerial practices. Drawing from theoretical and empirical studies, we examine in the remainder of this section managerial practices related to governance structure, authority and control, employment relationship, and dominant strategic paradigm.

Governance Structure

With the increasing trend toward the separation of ownership from control and the rise of a managerial elite, monitoring the performance of a company and those who lead it is an increasingly important issue for shareholders and owners. In general, corporate governance in most countries refers to the relationships between the firm's capital providers and the firm's managers, as mediated by the board of directors, which oversees the firm on behalf of the capital providers (Bradley, Schipani, Sundaram, and Walsh, 1999; Lorsch, 1996; Scott, 1997). However, the meaning of *corporate governance* can be expanded to encompass the interests of the many constituencies (e.g., employees, creditors, suppliers, customers, and host communities) that serve and are served by the corporation (Bradley et al., 1999). Corporate boards are internal corporate control mechanisms designed to align the interests of managers and shareholders (Walsh and Seward, 1990).

Although basic governance structures are similar across different countries (e.g., the board of directors), the importance and function of governance structures varies greatly. Scott (1997), focusing on patterns of ownership and control, demonstrated the four main patterns of capitalist development: (1) the Anglo-American model, in which intermediate financial institutions are the principal shareholders, and an intercorporate network is central to control through a constellation of interests, (2) the Germanic model, in which capital is mobilized through banking mechanisms, and the intercorporate network is vertically integrated around corporate affiliates with the big banks, (3) the Japanese model, in which capital is circulated within a clustering of enterprises to sustain the long-term investment strategy of the group as a whole (Orru et al., 1989), and (4) the Latinic model, which uses corporate webs in which the shareholdings of families, banks, and investment companies interact in mutually supportive ways to form patterns of control that allow family influence (Wright and Chiplin, 1999).

In the United States, ownership and management tend to be separate and significant share ownership is under the control of financial institutions and wealthy individuals as parts of investment portfolios whose overall returns are to be maximized (Scott, 1997; Thurow, 1992; Whitley, 1994). There are significant differences in the ownership structure of the United States, Germany, and Japan. The percentages of corporate ownership of common stocks in 1990 were 44.5% in the United States, 64.0% in Germany, and 72.9% in Japan, whereas the percentages of individual ownership of common stocks in the same year were 50.2% in the United States, 17.0% in Germany, and 22.4% in Japan (Prowse, 1994). A high percentage of individual ownership implies the importance of the capital market as a monitoring tool in the United States. The separation of ownership and control, a distinctive characteristic of the U.S. governance system, can be traced back to early stages of modern enterprises. The first modern enterprises in the United States appeared in the 1850s with the emergence of railroads, the telegraph, and the availability of coal. The founding owners of the enterprises could not self-finance growth and mass production. They needed to raise capital in the market and also had to hire managers to monitor and coordinate divisions or departments (Berle and Means, 1932; Chandler, 1980). The increasing use of professional managers continued as enterprises grew rapidly. Salaried managers planned and carried out strategies for growth. The number of executives at all managerial levels within the enterprise increased. At the same time, salaried managers had to be accountable for strategy and operation. Owners monitored and supervised managers through the board of directors and the stock market. The discipline of the capital markets was expected to ensure that firms were effectively managed, and the board of directors was expected to represent the interests of owners.

Japanese firms tend to form groups, called "intermarket groups" and "independent groups" (Orru et al., 1989, p. 554) or *keiretsu*. There are two general stock ownership control mechanisms in these groups: horizontal control and vertical control. In horizontal control, power and influence are exercised through cross-holding or reciprocal shareholding, interlock ties, trade links, bank loans, business associations, and informal communications. Vertical control uses the unilateral flow of power and influence through the ownership of shares. From the viewpoint of capital allocation and corporate governance, *keiretsu* is a perfect substitute for the holding company (Dietl, 1998). As a delegated monitor on behalf of the *keiretsu*, a main bank or parent company exercises approximately the same amount of control over each member corporation as the headquarters of a holding company exercises over each subsidiary (Ozaki, 1992).

In most continental European countries, shareowners do not manage economic activities directly. Rather, they retain fairly close relationships and share some of the risks with the firms in which they invest. In Germany, banks significantly affect managerial decisions by exercising voting rights of their own share and proxy votes. Under the German proxy voting system, private shareholders automatically grant banks that hold their shares in custody, to represent their interests and vote for them at the general meetings of the companies (Jürgens et al., 2000). Low percentage of the capitalization of domestic equities relative to German GDP indicates that German firms are much less likely to finance themselves through issuing equity to the public. Instead, most firms raise capital through long-term bank credit. Moreover, banks can cast proxy votes on behalf of shares they hold on deposit. They thereby effectively monitor management performance (Streck, 1997).

One significant difference between Germany and the United States is the German two-board system (Chandler, 1990; Randlesome, 1994). In 1884, Germany enacted a dual board structure of a management board and a supervisory board. The management board is responsible for the operational decision of the business, and the supervisory board is responsible for monitoring major decisions made by the management board, including long-term strategies. Thus, for example, the supervisory board annually examines the reported financial results as prepared by the management board (Tricker, 1990).

From 1952 to 1976, various amendments to the codetermination statues were enacted. In companies with more than 500 employees, the plant constitution law of 1952 mandates representation of workers on the supervisory board. The Codetermination Act of 1976 required companies with more than 2,000 employees to provide for a fifty-percent employee representation on the supervisory board. Since 1952 the management board of companies in the iron, steel, and coal industries included a labor management director. The 1976 law required the appointment of a labor management director in all large public companies (Jürgens et al., 2000; Lawrence, 1991). Another distinctive dimension of corporate governance in Germany relates to the importance of publicly enabled associations (Lane, 1992). Power is delegated either to individual associations or to collective negotiations between them. The associations guide individual firm adaptation activities. For example, business associations have been pivotal in redirecting price competition into quality and product competition by promoting product specialization and setting and enforcing high quality standards. The employers' associations cooperate to prevent low-wage competition by negotiating uniformly high labor standards with national industry unions.

Authority and Control

Authority and control refers to the nature of relationships between employees and management and to the source of influence on behavior and organizational change within the organization. Authority and control determine the importance placed on the hierarchy, the individuals versus the group, and social versus task orientation. National culture and other managerial practices, such as corporate governance and employment relationship, influence authority and control patterns. For example, paternalistic cultures (e.g., Southeast Asia) favor very hierarchical authority and emphasize groups and societies. In individualistic cultures (the United States), hierarchy is somewhat less important, and emphasis is placed on individuals and tasks. The emphasis on hierarchy in Japan is midrange between Southeast Asia and the United States because power and status differences are defined by both role and seniority in an organization (Schneider, 1989).

Managers' attitudes toward authority vary among nations (Child and Kieser, 1981; Tayeb, 1991). For example, Germans have been viewed as having greater respect for authority and an inclination toward accepting and following directives in contrast to egalitarian, participative relationships (Neary, 1993). In a comparative study of German and British firms, Child and Kieser (1981) found that the size of British firms accounted for about three times the variation in their level of decentralization than did the size of German firms. Although the size of a firm is positively related to the level of decentralization in both countries, the average scale of decentralized German firms was significantly higher than for British firms. The separation of ownership and control, which accounts for decentralization in British firms, does not predict decentralization in German firms. Also, the tendency toward greater centralization in operational decision making among German firms led Child and Kieser to accept the predictions and descriptions of writers who argue that German firms prefer hierarchical authority structures.

Japanese firms emphasize total-quality principles of responsibility, accountability, flexibility, and teamwork (Fruin, 1992). Rules on the shop floor are strict but accepted by workers. Wilkinson and Oliver (1990) describe extreme cases of bell-to-bell working rules: "Employees will be prepared for work at the start and end of their normal working day/shift" (p. 336). Employees are expected to be dependable, flexible, dedicated, and loyal to the company rather than to the union or craft. Rigorous selection emphasizing attitude, employee orientation programs, embedded training and skill development, lifetime employment,

and frequent and direct communications all contribute to the Japanese control system (Briggs, 1991). The use of suggestion systems and intimate quality circles and management circles expected to enhance quality of products indicates the application of bottom-up management (Nonaka and Takeuchi, 1995; Plenert, 1990). Quality circles provide suggestions to the foreman, and he or she is expected to implement most of them. Whether the suggestion originates from the shop floor of the plant or from groups of white-collar employees, suggestions are generally accepted immediately and implemented as fast as is practicable. Japanese plants also show the characteristics of top-down, hierarchical management. In an empirical comparative study of the U.S. and Japanese control systems and employee commitment, Lincoln and Kalleberg (1990) find that Japanese plants had more levels of authority than their U.S. counterparts.

Employment Relationship

Employees are the source of quality, productivity, and tacit knowledge, and at the same time constitute a significant element of direct and indirect costs. As a consequence of cultural and historical differences, managers have developed distinct views on the employment relationship. The employment relationship philosophy of a firm affects the strategic and organizational adaptations available to the firm. At one extreme, employees are viewed as cogs in a machine, replaceable at will. In this case, organizational change is implemented through layoffs and replacements. At the other extreme, employees are viewed as a critical asset unique to the organization. Under the latter philosophy, organization change involves training and development of current employees for new demands. Layoffs and replacements are considered too difficult because of dependence on tacit and idiosyncratic knowledge (Miner, 1987) at the level of individuals, groups, and communities of practice (Brown and Duguid, 2001). Another aspect of the employment relationship is employee commitment to the organization (Lincoln and Kalleberg, 1990). When organization commitment to employees is high, employees are more likely to give higher priority to company needs and would be more willing to sacrifice self for company. When organization commitment to employees is low, employees act as free agents and put self-interest ahead of the company.

Commitment can be derived from different motives. In a survey measuring organizational commitment, when commitment was measured as working hard "because it is their responsibility to the company and coworkers," American employees scored higher than Japanese employees, despite the reputed high commitment behavior of Japanese employees (Besser, 1993). Japanese employees reported higher scores in working hard "to live up to the expectations of family, friends, and society" (p. 875). Which employees are more committed? Based on a review of comparative studies on employee commitment, researchers find that that commitment measurement is inconclusive (Besser, 1993; Briggs, 1991). This may be because of the different meanings of "commitment" in different cultural contexts (countries), or the result of inadequate measurements. Some studies find that Japanese employees are more committed to their organization than American employees (Lincoln and Kalleberg, 1990). A lifetime employment practice, social norms, and seniority-based compensation have been considered as reasons for Japanese employee commitment to the company in spite of declining performance (Briggs, 1991; Hill, 1995).

U.S. employment philosophy is based on the doctrine of "employment-at-will," which accords employers the freedom to hire and fire employees at will with relatively few constraints (e.g., racial, gender, and age discrimination) compared with other countries (Quinn and Rivoli, 1991). This perspective is close to the view in which labor is a factor of production not different from raw materials or equipment. Consequently, in the United States, human resource management is not traditionally seen as central to the competitive survival of the firm (Thurow, 1992). Firms are managed to be independent of any employee and with the expectation of staffing any position from the external labor market. The consequences are detailed job descriptions, proliferation of job families, greater specialization, and highly developed external labor markets. The dependence on external labor market and specialization of employee skills results in very specific job classifications compared with those of Japan (Plenert, 1990). Reliance on highly developed external labor markets and the expectation that employees may leave at any time leads American managers to underinvest in human resource development and training.

Japanese firms view their employees as critical, hard-to-replace assets. Lifetime employment systems keep employees until their retirement, and employees are willing to remain in the organization and not seek alternative employment opportunities (Fruin, 1992; Ozaki, 1992; Quinn and Rivoli, 1991). In Japan, firms rely on highly articulated internal labor markets, whereby managers rotate or promote current employees to new positions and employees are expected to be flexible, learn new skills, and stay with the same firm over a long period of time (Sako, 1994; Westney, 1994). Ito (1994) lists possible reasons for long-term employment relationships and the development of firm-specific internal labor market in Japan. They include seniority-based compensation, firm-specific training, collusion among large firms not to hire employees from each other, negative reputational effects on current employees from hiring outsiders, and negative social view of job changers. The long-term employment relationship in Japan is symbolized by the lifetime employment system (Fruin, 1992; Plenert, 1990). However, lifetime employment practices were adopted by Japanese employers only after World War II. Japanese employers adopt internal human resource development combined with a no-layoff policy as a more effective means of raising firm productivity and enhancing employee morale (Fruin, 1992; Ito, 1996; Ozaki, 1992). According to Ozaki (1992), in the 1950s and early 1960s, most firms did not yet thoroughly practice the Japanese-style management system, and layoff was not uncommon. Long-lasting and extremely costly strikes in the 1950s and 1960s, which were caused by mass layoffs in the coal, steel, and other industries, taught managers that keeping employees for the long term and training them internally is a more effective way of managing human resources. Hill (1995) argues that the phenomenon of group identification and loyalty helped the success of the new Japanese employment relationship model. Since Japanese firms rely on long-term employee relationships and an internal labor market, they rotate employees within the firm to acquire and learn new skills. According to Plenert (1990), a Japanese employee changes positions about every two years. By rotating employees and equipping them with diverse skills, Japanese firms avoid being stuck with unnecessary, hard-to-lay-off employees.

The long-term-employment view may lead employees to higher commitment to their company.

Dore (1973) argues that the strong commitments of Japanese employees to their organization result from Japanese culture, in which employees subordinate their private lives and the claims of family to the claims of the organization and "welfare corporatism," which includes factory- and company-based trade union and bargaining structures, enterprise welfare and security, and greater stability of employment. Contrary to an individualist culture, a collectivist culture emphasizes fulfilling others' expectations and collective responsibility (Hill, 1995), rather than individual responsibility.

In Germany, employees are also viewed as critical assets with valuable skills. A system of codetermination, a major characteristic of the German employment relationship, is part of the constitution (Plenert, 1990). With collective bargaining and worker legal rights, codetermination supports the German employment relationship, which inhibits employers from dismissing employees (Streek, 1992). By law, every employee who has worked for more than six months in a firm may not be laid off without good reason (Kurz, 1991). Moreover, laid-off employees must receive severance pay calculated according to specific formulas (Kurz, 1991). Labor is considered as a fixed production factor on a par with capital. This leads employers to invest in labor skills (Streek, 1997). As part of the reconstruction process after World War II, trade unionism was reaffirmed as a legitimate mechanism for the representation of employees' interests (Hollinshead and Leat, 1995). The freedom to design individual labor contracts is restricted by the existence of national collective agreements between unions and employers, from which individual labor contracts may deviate only if such deviation is to the advantage of the employee (Kurz, 1991). Employees participate in the decision making both at the shop-floor level, through works councils, and at the company level, through supervisory board representations. Employers cannot fire employees at will (Leminsky, 1980). Works councils, councils of employees elected by all employees, date from 1950 (Lawrence, 1991). The councils have various rights of participation or involvement in management decision making, including promotions, transfers, dismissals, working conditions, and pay-related matters (Hollinshead and Leat, 1995). The supervisory board, which oversees management boards under the statutes of codetermination, includes worker representatives.

The compensation system represents the means by which employees are financially compensated for joining organizations, staying in them, and accomplishing certain levels of work performance (Ferris and Buckley, 1995). Compensation can take the form of wages and salaries and a wide range of legally required and agreed-upon benefits. Compensation and reward systems motivate employees and managers to perform in their organizations. Since compensation systems can be implemented differently depending on the strategy of business units or corporations (Gomez-Mejia and Welbourne, 1988), and firm strategies can be affected by institutional factors, we observe a wide variety of different compensation practices in different countries.

Comparing the impact of U.S. and Japanese employment and compensation systems on innovation, Quinn and Rivoli (1991) emphasize that the American-style system has relatively high fixed wages that are invariant with firm performance, and the firm may terminate the employee at will. The Japanese-style system has a lower fixed wage, plus a bonus that is dependent on firm performance. Quinn and Rivoli (1991) argue that, under unstable environments, the U.S. system—in which employees are risk averse and wages are high, but job-loss risk is high and gains from innovation is low—leads firms to anti-innovative tendencies. However, under stable environments with full employment, the U.S. system may lead to more innovations because firms can get higher profits at high volumes, high-cost labor can be replaced by capital, and full employment policies can reduce the consequences of job loss.

The compensation system in Japanese firms is commonly known as the "seniority-based system" (Ozaki, 1992, p. 102). Seniority is a significant factor in calculating compensation. A typical Japanese compensation system is comprised of basic pay, merit pay, and job-related pay (Ozaki, 1992; Quinn and Rivoli, 1991; Whitehill, 1990). Seniority-based pay is the largest of the three, since it increases in proportion to the number of years worked at the firm. The seniority-based compensation system makes sense in the context of an internalized labor market. It assumes that employees learn and accumulate firm-specific skills as they stay in the firm longer and their productivity increases on average. The seniority-based system also reflects the Japanese culture of age-based hierarchy, in which seniors, cohorts, and juniors are considered in terms of age (Briggs, 1991;

Ozaki, 1992). Japanese firms compensate young talented employees, who get relatively smaller salaries compared to old employees, by giving important and responsible assignments. Thus, young workers get psychological satisfaction. Ozaki (1992) noted that the salary gap between top managers and bottom-line employees is strikingly modest compared to that of the United States: "In contemporary Japan top executive's after-tax salary is only about six times as large as the lowest starting salary of newly recruited worker" (Ozaki, 1992, p. 23).

Strategic Paradigm

A firm's strategic paradigm, like other managerial practices, will be affected by institutional configurations such as founding conditions of the nation, the role of government, the legal system, the capital market, the education system, and culture (Gatley, Lessem, and Altman, 1996). By strategic paradigm, we mean a framework by which top managers pursue their strategies. Strategic paradigms can be compared in terms of the strategy time horizon, main goals, and the contents of strategy. Strategic paradigms can be viewed as the joint outcome of institutional factors and other managerial factors. The assessment of environments and organizations in strategic planning is not necessarily "objective" but is a function of perceptions and interpretations that affect firm strategy (Schneider, 1989). Many of our observations and discussions are based on comparative studies done in the 1970s through the 1990s.

Market-based competition, a relatively low level of government interference in the economy, highly developed capital markets, widely accepted practices of separation of ownership and control, and highly developed external labor markets are the primary reasons that U.S. managers exhibit an asymmetric preference for short-term strategies and for managing shareholder value (Plenert, 1990; Thurow, 1992). American managers tend to focus on short-term profitability and prefer short-term formal contracts when structuring a deal (Cusumano and Takeishi, 1991; Gatley et al., 1996; Plenert, 1990). Profitability is considered the most critical measure of firm performance and profit is used by corporate boards and investors to determine management performance. When strategic decisions are directly affected by specific short-term evaluation and compensation strategies, managers tend to improve short-term profitability

rather than invest in longer term, high-risk/high-return projects. Thurow (1992) argues that the United States must change its capital markets, ownership structure (e.g., reform taxation of capital appreciations to favor long-term holdings), and education system to remain competitive with other developed countries. He argues that institutional shareholders influence the strategic paradigm of U.S. firms:

> In the absence of dominant shareholders, corporations are effectively run by their professional managers. Unlike founding fathers, the professional chief executive officers of large corporations usually reach that exalted position just a few years before they retire. Long-run careers at the top are very unusual. As short-term CEOs, they not surprisingly organize compensation packages for themselves that emphasize bonuses and salaries keyed to current profits or sales. These short-run compensation packages are unfortunately completely congruent with the short-run perspective of the institutional shareholders. Neither the manager nor the shareholder expects to be around very long. (Thurow, 1992, pp. 283–284)

Although the short-term perspective can lead to myopic decisions, close monitoring of firm financial performance permits early corrective actions in the event of any abnormality in firm performance. U.S. managers also prefer external growth diversification over internal growth. Mergers and acquisitions of related and unrelated businesses are the preferred growth strategies of U.S. firms (Whitley, 1994). In the United States, strategic adaptations involving mergers and acquisitions or divestiture are common and relatively easy to execute, not only because managers prefer short-term, external growth but also because huge U.S. capital markets and the highly articulated investment banking industry facilitate such transactions. In addition, individualistic culture and less intervention by the federal government may lead managers to more risk aversion because of the low likelihood of government bailouts in the event of failure (Weber et al., 1998). American managers seek to reduce uncertainty through investments in specialized knowledge and through task orientation (Schneider, 1989).

Although mindful of shareholder interests, U.S. managers have more discretion in implementing strategies and organizational changes than Japanese managers. Sakano and Lewin (1999) note that dramatic strategic and organizational changes occur within the first year of CEO succession in the United States, whereas no dramatic changes are observed in Japan for two years following CEO succession. Yet, low competition as a result of industrial policies and government protection, a close relationship between shareholders and managers, and a strong internal labor market allow Japanese corporate managers to focus on long-term growth of the company and making deals anchored on long-term relationships (Aoki, 1994; Fligstein, 1990; Gatley et al., 1996; Plenert, 1990). In Japan, the dominant strategic goal of a company is sales growth rather than profitability. Japanese manufacturers prefer long-term supplier contracts, and they exchange more information with each other (Cusumano and Takeishi, 1991). Firms are specialized and grow incrementally through internal expansion and restrict diversification to technologically related fields (Whitley, 1994; Sakano and Lewin, 1999). Unlike U.S. capital markets, Japanese capital markets are not highly developed. A collectivist culture and greater government guidance also contribute to Japanese managers' greater risk-seeking behavior relative to their counterparts in the United States (Weber et al., 1998). Uncertainty and ambiguity are actively managed by engaging in information generating and sharing activities (Schneider, 1989). In the study of strategic changes following CEO succession, Sakano and Lewin (1999) argue that Japanese firms favor evolutionary adaptation, strategic continuity, and preferred exploration alliances with other companies in their *keiretsu*. Simultaneously, operational efficiencies are achieved through measures such as ongoing product redesign and improvement, mass customization, and reduced cycle times.

Like Japanese managers, German managers adopt a long-term perspective in their strategic decisions. The stability of the institutional configuration (including the legal system), allied with slow and very deliberate change processes, allows firms to rely on long-term relationships with their main banks, which leads to the long-term strategies adopted by the firm (Jürgens et al., 2000; Kocka, 1980). Codetermination, trade unions, trade associations, dual education systems, and government sanctioning of interorganizational arrangements lead German managers to pursue cooperative strategies among stakeholders and even competitors, and to focus on more demanding value-added, quality production strategies and inter-

nal growth and diversification rather than external growth (Streck, 1992).

Implications for Organizational Change and Innovation

What implications does the interplay between country-specific institutional configuration and managerial practices provide for organizational change and innovation? We noted that the new institutional theory (DiMaggio and Powell, 1983; Powell and DiMaggio, 1991) argued that organizational change must be understood in terms of the role of the state as a source of rationalization and coercive isomorphic pressure on managerial logic and organizational adaptation over time. We further argue that understanding the nation-state's institutional configuration and managerial practices should provide useful insights in explaining and predicting the effectiveness and efficiency of organizational change in the nation. In discussing how organizational change and innovation can be manifested in different countries, we focus on the issues of corporate restructuring, downsizing, and technical (product/process) innovation.

Organizational change in terms of corporate restructuring or downsizing is easier and faster in the United States than in Japan or Germany. The U.S. capital market, viewed as a market for control of ownership rather than stability of ownership, facilitates relatively easy and frequent mergers and acquisitions. The highly developed large U.S. capital market encourages firms to pursue external growth strategies, which is considered to be a faster way of entering a new business. When a U.S. firm needs to restructure its business portfolio, it tends to look outside of its boundary to either buy into an attractive new business opportunity or dispose of a business deemed not to have future potential. Similarly downsizing a business through spin-offs or carve-outs is more easily accomplished on the U.S. capital markets than in Germany or Japan. The highly developed and adaptable external labor market in the United States and the employment-at-will doctrine, combined with a management philosophy of human capital as infinitely replaceable in the market, gives U.S. firms the latitude to replace employees relatively more easily in comparison with German or Japanese firms. On the other hand, in Japan or Germany, the capital market is viewed as the market for stability of ownership that facilitates the internal growth of businesses. German and Japanese firms tend to prefer internal growth strategies such as greenfield investments that take longer to grow than external growth strategies such as mergers and acquisitions preferred by U.S. companies. Similarly, divestiture of business units in Germany and Japan is more difficult to accomplish on the domestic capital markets because the markets are not sufficiently developed to accommodate such transactions when compared to the capital markets in the United States. Furthermore, the employees of Japanese firms are viewed as critical assets and, when combined with management philosophy of lifetime employment and fewer job specialties, it is more difficult for firms to achieve cost reductions through staff downsizing strategies. Instead, Japanese firms are more likely to counteract the pressure for downsizing staffs by investing in related businesses where excess staff can be employed productively. Moreover, because of the generalist multifunctional nature of Japanese employees, indiscriminant downsizing of employees in Japan raises the specter of losing important employee-specific idiosyncratic knowledge. Collective bargaining, legal rights of employees, and codetermination statutes also inhibit German firms from downsizing employees at will. Dual education and the professionalization of vocational education and training system make it difficult for German firms to change employees' skill sets. Recent debates in Germany regarding whether to open its door to immigrants with high technology skills has been attributed to the slow adaptation of a German labor force that is organized in professions with clear ladders of advancement and specialization and protective legislation. For example, a laid-off employee can reject job offers that do not exactly match the employee's specialized professional status (Kurz, 1991).

Technological advances show different trajectories among nation-states depending on their institutional configuration of innovation, or "national innovation system" (Nelson, 1993). Nelson and his colleagues argue that the different trajectories are the consequences of institutional characteristics such as research and development organizations, higher education systems, and government policy that are unique to the nation. Albach's (1994) research on culture and technical innovation provides details and useful insights on the issues of technical innovation in the United States, Germany, and Japan. He de-

fined technical innovations as "the introduction into the market of a new physical product or of a new technological production process, both based on invention and development" (p. 14). He further distinguishes improvement innovations that include new solutions to an old problem or creative imitations, fundamental innovations, internal innovations based on inventions and development by the innovative firm, and external innovations based on ideas generated in another organization.

Considering that innovation comes from both fundamental changes and incremental changes, externally and internally, and products and processes, managing innovation is managing consistency and control as well as variability (Tushman, Anderson, and O'Reilly, 1997). Although firms may endeavor to achieve the balance between the two, we note that some institutional configurations are more suited for a certain type of innovation. The United States provides a more fertile environment for innovation and entrepreneurship than Germany and Japan. The U.S. environment facilitates entrepreneurship, loose culture, and R&D resources necessary for radical innovations (Tushman et al., 1997). The highly developed capital market, the availability of large venture-capital pools, and a culture of individualism and market competition encourage experimentation and risk taking with new ideas and rapid commercialization of innovation. The mode of innovation of the United States is based on competitive behavior and a winner-take-all philosophy (Frank and Cook, 1995). In contrast, Japanese culture eschews competitive in favor of mutual evolution. This is an outcome of a homogenous culture, Confucianism, and its respect for elders over individualism. Japanese firms emphasize tight processes and continuous improvements and incremental innovation. Because human capital is considered to be critical and a source of competitive advantage, Japanese firms believe in the imperative of investing in human capital through education, training, and development of staff through formal and extensive on-the-job training programs.

The national centralized education system, commitment to lifetime employment, and directed industrial policies may enable speedier diffusion of knowledge and collective learning. However, in the face of discontinuous technological advances and rapidly evolving technological frontiers, Japan is likely to fall behind in the race to shape and adapt the new technologies. However, as the new technologies mature, Japanese firms may catch up and perhaps pull ahead with incremental and process improvements. This could explain why the new technological innovations emerge faster in the United States but the adoption, extension, and continuous improvement of products, applications, and processes is more organic and faster among Japanese than U.S. and German firms (Albach, 1994). Changing the skill set and professional expertise of German employees is greatly constrained by Germany's dual education system and the fine-grained professional status of technical and vocational trained workers. As a consequence the emergence and evolution of new job families and new professional specialties will take longer in Germany. German firms' ability to adopt a new technology is slowed because of the long lead times required for effecting changes and approving new training programs before the vocational education system can gear up to produce employees with new skills. In contrast, U.S. firms rely on market forces to induce individuals to learn and acquire new specialized skills and on flexible immigration policies that adjust supply of new skills. In Japan this task is largely the responsibility of firms that retrain current employees as well as recruit new entry-level employees with needed new skills.

Conclusion

We have reviewed and integrated a diverse theoretical and empirical literature that informs analysis of the moderating effects of the nation-state on organizational adaptation. It is clear that the effect of country institutional configuration is both exogenous and endogenous. Our focus has been on the United States, Japan, and Germany. We argued that differences in both formal and informal institutional configurations of a nation-state are the consequence of unique characteristics of the country. We also argued that organizational adaptation is affected by institutional configuration of the nation-state in which the organization is embedded. Table 11.1 summarizes key features of the institutional configurations and their reflection in the managerial practices of the three countries under study.

Does one national institutional configuration give rise to superior managerial strategies, practices, or wealth-creating firms? We have not examined this

question directly in this chapter. However, any listing of the 1,000 global firms clearly has significant representation of firms from every industrialized country. More research is needed on how different national institutional configurations evolve equifinal corporate organizational forms. In other words, how and why do equivalently effective world-class firms, distinguished by unique bundles of capabilities, emerge from distinctly different country-specific variation, selection, and retention processes as constrained by institutional configuration of their country?

The transition to the Internet Age raises further issues. In times of discontinuous, increasingly turbulent macro change forces, how will firms within each country system adapt? Which institutional configuration is better prepared for evolving new configurations and new organizational forms? How is the organizational ecology of a country evolving in response to forces driving the transition to the age of the Internet? For example, we would conjecture that the mean size of new entrants in the United States, measured by number of initial employees, will be significantly lower in the United States relative to Germany. It takes only a few days to incorporate a new firm in the United States, whereas in Germany it takes upward of 90 days. Moreover, we would conjecture that in the face of success, U.S. firms are likely to add new employees at a pace that exceeds the growth rate of top-line revenue. In contrast, we expect that German firms at founding would be larger entities (as measured by number of founding employees) and in the face of success grow their work force at a slower rate than the rate of growth in top-line revenue. The primary explanation for the differential entry rate of new firms and their different mean size and growth rates is due to availability of venture capital in the United States relative to Germany, the stigma associated with bankruptcy in Germany, and the high costs of scaling back permanent employees in Germany in the event of disappointed expectations.

We also conjecture that within each country's institutional configuration, the rate of change at the level of the individual firm is higher than the industry rate of change, and that changes to the institutional configuration are the slowest. This should hold true for any population of firms within any institutional configuration. However, the rate of adaptation can vary significantly from country to country. In the case of the United States, Germany, and Japan we would

Table 11.1 Dimensions of country differences: United States, Japan, Germany

	United States	Japan	Germany
Institutional Factors			
Founding conditions	• diversity • abundant resource • huge domestic market • puritanism • market competition	• homogeneity • Tokugawa era (1603–1868) • Confucianism • strong government	• early industrialization • financing through banks • cartelization • worker participation
Role of government	• encourage market competition • low industrial policy	• encourage agreement • high industrial policy	• encourage stability • direct intervention
Legal system	• common law • transparent • flexible • adversarial litigation • facilitates impersonal transactions	• civil law • guiding • flexible • conciliatory litigation • facilitates relationship-based transactions	• civil law • transparent • inflexible • facilitates both types of transactions
Capital market	• market for control of ownership • highly developed	• market for stability of ownership • moderately developed	• market for stability of ownership • moderately developed
Education system	• decentralized • diverse	• centralized • homogeneous • strong meritocracy	• centralized • vocational system
Culture	• individualism • heterogeneous	• collectivism • homogeneous	• moderate collectivism • homogeneous
Managerial practices			
Governance system	• separation of ownership from management • strong institutional holdings • shareholder oriented • one-board system	• cross-holdings among firms • stakeholder-oriented • one-board system • formation of group	• bank holdings • stakeholder-oriented • dual-board system
Authority and control	• emphasis on roles and tasks • top-down	• emphasis on both authority and roles • top-down and bottom-up	• emphasis on power and authority • top-down
Employment relationship	• employment-at-will • external labor market • nonparticipative • performance- and market-based • largest gap between top and bottom	• lifetime employment • internal labor market • participative • seniority-based • smallest gap between top and bottom	• long-term employment • participative • performance- and seniority-based • moderate gap between top and bottom
Strategic paradigm	• short-term oriented • external growth • high managerial autonomy	• long-term oriented • internal growth • incremental growth • low managerial autonomy	• long-term oriented • internal growth • moderate managerial autonomy

argue that the U.S. institutional configuration capacity for timely change is higher than for Germany and Japan. Therefore, new organizational forms are more likely to initially emerge in the United States with less disruption and upheaval than in Germany and Japan. This was the experience of Germany, Japan, and the United States during the transition to the Industrial Age. The M-form of organization first emerged in the United States, but subsequent adoption and diffusion of the M form in other countries was about the same (Fligstein, 1985). However, as Chandler (1990) noted, within each country the nature and character of managerial practices evolved to produce distinctly different operational capabilities. We would expect similar outcomes to obtain in the transition to the age of the Internet. More generally, we believe that the transition period to the Internet Age offers an important window for investigating the dynamic coevolution of technological advances (such as the Internet), as well as firm-, industry-, and country-level institutional configuration. Although the transition may have some parallels to the transition that ushered in the Industrial Age, it already has given rise to new organizational forms such as a new class of nongovernmental organizations (NGOs) as well as to rethinking of the imperative that companies had to become global and local (transnational). Instead, a more prevalent form of the regional firm may be emerging as the dominant international corporate form.

Note

Many colleagues too numerous to thank individually have helped stimulate and direct our thinking as our ideas evolved over the past two years. We wish to acknowledge specifically the helpful suggestions of Pat Thornton; Bill McKelvey; Henk Volberda; Axel von Werder; Mitchell Koza; Tomoaki Sakano and faculty colloquia participants at the Fuqua School of Business; Erasmus University; Technical University Berlin; IESE; and the doctoral consortium on international research in strategy and new organizational forms. We also wish to acknowledge the financial support of the IBM Consulting Group, Coopers Lybrand, the Fuqua CIBER, and the Center for Research on Consumer Finance at Waseda University. Finally, we would like to thank Billie Maciunas and Marybeth Lavrakas for their efforts in editing the text.

References

Abolafia, M. Y. (1998). Markets as cultures: An ethnographic approach. In M. Callon (Ed.), *The laws of the markets* (pp. 69–85). Oxford: Blackwell Publishers.

Adler, N. J., Doktor, R., & Redding, S. G. (1986). From the Atlantic to the Pacific century: Cross-cultural management reviewed. *Yearly Review of Management, 12*(2), 295–318.

Aharoni, Y. (1981). Managerial discretion. In R. Vernon & Y. Aharoni (Eds.), *State-owned enterprise in the western economies* (pp. 184–193). New York: St. Martin's Press.

Albach, H. (1994). *Culture and technical innovation: A cross-cultural analysis and policy recommendations.* New York: W. de Gruyter.

Allen, D. B., Miller, E. L., & Nath, R. (1988). North America. In R. Nath (Ed.), *Comparative management: A regional view* (pp. 23–54). Cambridge, MA: Ballinger.

Allen, G. C. (1981). A short economic history of modern Japan. New York: St. Martin's.

Aoki, M. (1994). The Japanese firm as a system of attributes: A survey and research agenda. In M. Aoki & R. Dore (Eds.), *The Japanese firm: Sources of competitive strength* (pp. 11–40). Oxford: Oxford University Press.

Badie B. & Birnbaum, P. (1983). *The sociology of the state.* Chicago: The University of Chicago Press.

Barfield, C. E. & Schambra, W. A. (Eds.) (1986). *The politics of industrial policy.* Washington, DC: American Enterprise Institute for Public Policy Research.

Bartlett, C. A. & Ghoshal, S. (1998). *Managing across borders: The international solution.* Boston, MA: Harvard Business Press.

Baron, D. P. (1996). *Business and its environment.* Upper Saddle River, NJ: Prentice Hall.

Baron, J. N., Hannan, M. T., & Burton, M. D. (1999). Building the iron cage: Determinants of managerial intensity in the early years of organizations. *American Sociological Review, 64*, 527–547.

Baum, J. A. C. (1996). Organizational ecology. In S. R. Clegg, C. Hardy & W. R. Nord (Eds.), *Handbook of organization studies* (pp. 77–114). London: Sage.

Baum, J. A. C. & Oliver, C. (1992). Institutional embeddedness and the dynamics of organizational populations. *American Sociological Review, 57*, 540–559.

Berle, A. A. & Means, G. C. (1932). *The modern corporation and private property.* New York: Macmillan.

Besser, T. (1993). The commitment of Japanese workers and U.S. workers: A reassessment of the literature. *American Sociological Review, 58*, 873–881.

Bigoness, W. J. & Blakely, G. L. (1996). A cross-national study of managerial values. *Journal of International Business Studies, 27*, 739–752.

Boeker, W. P. (1988). Organizational origins: Entrepreneurial and environmental imprinting at the time of founding. In G. R. Carroll (Ed.), *Ecological models of organizations* (pp. 33–52). Cambridge, MA: Ballinger Publishing Company.

Boisot, M. & Child, J. (1996). From fiefs to clans and network capitalism: Explaining China's emerging economic order. *Administrative Science Quarterly, 41*, 600–628.

Bracey, G. W. (1998, March–April). Are the U.S. students behind? *American Prospect*, 64–70.

Bradley, M., Schipani, C. A., Sundaram, A. K., & Walsh, J. P. (1999). The purposes and accountability of the corporation in contemporary society: Corporate governance at a crossroads. *Law and Contemporary Problems*, 62, 9–86.

Brahm, R. (1995). National targeting policies, high technology industries, and excessive competition. *Strategic Management Journal*, 16, 71–91.

Briggs, P. (1991). Organizational commitment: The key to Japanese success? In C. Brewster & S. Tyson (Eds.), *International comparisons in human resource management* (pp. 33–43). London: Pitman Publishing.

Brown, J. S. & Duguid, P. (2001). Knowledge and organization: A social-practice perspective. *Organization Science*, 12, 198–213.

Callon, M. (Ed.) (1998). *The laws of markets*. Oxford: Blackwell Publishers.

Calori, R., Lubatkin, M., Very, P., & Veiga, J. F. (1997). Modeling the origins of nationally-bound administrative heritages: A historical institutional analysis of French and British firms. *Organization Science*, 8, 681–696.

Carosso, V. P. (1970). *Investment banking in America: A history*. Cambridge, MA: Harvard University Press.

Chandler, A. D., Jr. (1977). *The visible hand: The managerial revolution in American business*. Cambridge, MA: Harvard University Press.

Chandler, A. D., Jr. (1980). The United States: Seedbed of managerial capitalism. In A. D. Chandler, Jr. & H. Daems (Eds.), *Managerial hierarchies: Comparative perspectives on the rise of the modern industrial enterprise* (pp. 9–40). Cambridge, MA: Harvard University Press.

Chandler, A. D., Jr. (1990). *Scale and scope*. Cambridge, MA: Harvard University Press.

Chang, C. S. & Chang, N. J. (1994). *The Korean management system: Cultural, political, economic foundations*. Westport, CT: Quorum Books.

Child, J. (1981). Culture, contingency and capitalism in the cross-national study of organizations. In L. L. Cummings & B. M. Staw (Eds.), *Research in Organizational Behavior*, 3, 303–356.

Child, J. & Kieser, A. (1981). Organization and managerial roles in British and West German companies: An examination of the culture-free thesis. In D. J. Hickson & C. J. McMillan (Eds.), *Organization and nation: The Aston Programme IV* (pp. 51–73). Hampshire, England: Gower Publishing Co.

Chui, A. C. W., Lloyd, A. E., & Kwok, C. C. Y. (2002). The determination of capital structure: Is national culture a missing piece to the puzzle? *Journal of International Business Studies*, 33, 99–128.

Clegg, S. R. & Reddings, S. G. (Eds.) (1990). *Capitalism in contrasting cultures*. Berlin: W. de Gruyter.

Conekin, B., Mort, F., & Waters, C. (1999). *Moments of modernity: Reconstructing Britain, 1945–1964*. New York: Rivers Oram Press.

Cray, D. & Mallory G. (1998). *Making sense of managing culture*. London: International Thompson Business Press.

Curtis, J. E., Grabb, E. G., & Baer, D. E. (1992). Voluntary association membership in fifteen countries: A comparative analysis. *American Sociological Review*, 57, 139–152.

Cusumano, M. A. & Takeishi, A. (1991). Supplier relations and management: A survey of Japanese-transplant and U.S. auto plants. *Strategic Management Journal*, 12, 563–588.

Darlington, G. (1996). Culture: A theoretical review. In P. Joynt & M. Warner (Eds.), *Managing across culture: Issues and perspectives* (pp. 33–55), London: International Thompson Business Press.

Dietl, H. M. (1998). *Capital markets and corporate governance in Japan, Germany, and the United States: Organizational response to market inefficiencies*. London: Routledge.

DiMaggio, P. J. & Powell, W. W. (1983). The iron cage revisited: Institutional isomorphism and collective rationality in organizational fields. *American Sociological Review*, 48, 147–160.

Djelic, M. (1998). *Exporting the American Model: The Postwar Transformation of European Business*. New York: Oxford University Press.

Djelic, M. & Ainamo, A. (1999). The coevolution of new organizational forms in the fashion industry: A historical and comparative study of France, Italy, and the United States. *Organization Science*, 10, 622–637.

Djelic, M., Koza, M. P., & Lewin, A. Y. (2000). *Are networks new forms of organizations? The coevolution of interfirm relationships in Germany, France, and the United States in the late nineteenth century*. Working paper: Department of Management, Duke University.

Dobbin, F. & Dowd, T. J. (1997). How policy shapes competition: Early railroad foundings in Massachusetts. *Administrative Science Quarterly*, 42, 501–529.

Dore, R. (1994). Equality-efficiency trade-offs: Japanese perceptions and choices. In M. Aoki & R. Dore (Eds.), *The Japanese firm: Sources of competitive strength* (pp. 379–391). Oxford: Oxford University Press.

Eisner, M. A. (1993). *Regulatory politics in transition*. Baltimore, MD: Johns Hopkins University Press.

Elder, J. W. (1976). Comparative cross-national methodology. *Annual Review of Sociology*, 2, 209–230.

Evans, P. B., Rueschemeyer, D., & Skocpol, T. (Eds.) (1985). *Bringing the state back in*. Cambridge: Cambridge University Press.

Ferris, G. R. & Buckley, M. R. (1995). *Human resource management: Perspectives, context, functions, and outcomes*. Englewood Cliffs, NJ: Prentice Hall.

Fligstein, N. (1990). *The transformation of corporate control*. Cambridge, MA: Harvard University Press.

Fligstein, N. (1996). Markets as politics: A political-cultural approach to market institution. *American Sociological Review*, 61, 656–673.

Foster, N. G. (1996). *German legal system and laws*. London: Blackstone Press Limited.

Frank, R. H. & Cook, P. (1995). *The winner-take-all society*. New York: Free Press.

Franke, R. H., Hofstede, G., & Bond, M. H. (1991). Cultural roots of economic performance: A research note. *Strategic Management Journal*, 12, 165–173.

Fruin, W. M. (1992). *The Japanese enterprise system: Competitive strategies and cooperative structures*. Oxford: Oxford University Press.

Gatley, S., Lessem, R., & Altman, Y. (1996). *Comparative management: A transcultural odyssey*. London: McGraw-Hill Book Company.

Gomez-Mejia, L. R. & Welbourne, T. M. (1988). Compensation strategy: An overview and future steps. *Human Resource Planning: HR*, 11, 173–189.

Granovetter, M. (1985). Economic actions and social structure: The problem of embeddedness. *American Journal of Sociology*, 91, 481–510.

Guillén, M. (1994). *Models of management: Work, authority, and organization in a comparative perspective*. Chicago: University of Chicago Press.

Haggard, S., Kim, B., & Moon, C. (1991). The transition to export-led growth in South Korea: 1954–1966. *Journal of Asian Studies*, 50, 850–873.

Hamada, T. & Sibley, W. E. (Eds.) (1994). *Anthropological perspectives on organizational culture*. Lanham, MD: University Press of America.

Hamilton, G. G., Zeile, W., & Kim, W. (1990). The network structures of East Asian economies. In S. R. Clegg & S. G. Redding (Eds.), *Capitalism in contrasting cultures* (pp. 105–130). Berlin: W. de Gruyter.

Hampden-Turner, C. & Trompenaars, A. (1993). *The seven cultures of capitalism: Value systems for creating wealth in the United States, Japan, Germany, France, Britain, Sweden, and the Netherlands*. New York: Currency Doubleday.

Hickson, D. J. & McMillan, C. J. (Eds.) (1981). *Organization and nation: The Aston Programme IV*. Hampshire, England: Gower Publishing Co.

Hill, C. W. L. (1995). National institutional structures, transaction cost economizing and competitive advantage: The case of Japan. *Organization Science*, 6, 119–131.

Hitt, M. A., Dacin, T., Tyler, B. B., & Park, D. (1997). Understanding the differences in Korean and U.S. executives' strategic orientations. *Strategic Management Journal*, 18, 159–167.

Hofstede, G. (1980). *Culture's consequences: International differences in work-related values*. Beverly Hills, CA: Sage.

Hofstede, G. (1983). National cultures in four dimensions. *International Studies in Management and Organization*, 13, 46–74.

Hofstede, G. (1991). *Cultures and organizations*. London: McGraw-Hill.

Hollinshead, G. & Leat, M. (1995). *Human resource management: An international and comparative perspective*. London: Pitman.

Hundley, G. & Jacobson, C. K. (1998). The effects of *keiretsu* on the export performance of Japanese companies: Help or hindrance? *Strategic Management Journal*, 19, 927–937.

Ito, H. (1994). Japanese human resource management from the viewpoint of incentive theory. In M. Aoki & R. Dore (Eds.), *The Japanese firm: Sources of competitive strength* (pp. 233–264). Oxford: Oxford University Press.

Ito, T. (1996). *The Japanese economy*. Cambridge, MA: The MIT Press.

Ito, K. & Rose, E. L. (1994). The genealogical structure of Japanese firms: Parent-subsidiary relationships. *Strategic Management Journal*, 15, 35–51.

Joynt, P. & Warner, M. (1996). *Managing across cultures: Issues and perspectives*. London: International Thompson Business Press.

Jürgens, U., Naumann, K., & Rupp, J. (2000). Shareholder value in an adverse environment: The German case. *Economy and Society*, 29, 54–79.

Kim, E. M. (Ed.) (1998). *The four Asian tigers: Economic development and the global political economy*. San Diego, CA: Academic Press.

Kocka, J. (1980). The rise of the modern industrial enterprise in Germany. In A. D. Chandler, Jr. & H. Daems (Eds.), *Managerial hierarchies: Comparative perspectives on the rise of the modern industrial enterprise* (pp. 77–116). Cambridge, MA: Harvard University Press.

Kogut, B. (1991). Country capabilities and the permeability of borders. *Strategic Management Journal*, 12, 33–47.

Kohn, M. L. (1987). Cross-national research as an analytical strategy. *American Sociological Review*, 52(6), 713–731.

Kroeber, A. & Kluckhohn, C. (1985). *Culture: A critical review of concepts and definitions.* New York: Random House.

Kurz, R. (1991). Federal republic of Germany. In F. Somers (Ed.), *European economies: A comparative study* (pp. 25–54). London: Pitman.

Lammers, C. J. (1978). The comparative sociology of organizations. *Annual Review of Sociology, 4,* 485–510.

Lane, C. (1992). European business system: Britain and Germany compared. In R. Whitley (Ed.), *European business systems: Firms and markets in their national contexts* (pp. 64–97). London: Sage Publications.

Lange, P. & Regini, M. (Eds.) (1989). *State, market, and social regulation: New perspectives on Italy.* Cambridge: Cambridge University Press.

Lawrence, P. (1991). The personnel function: An Anglo-German comparison. In C. Brewster & S. Tyson (Eds.), *International comparisons in human resource management* (pp. 131–144). London: Pitman Publishing.

Leminsky, G. (1980). Worker participation: The German experience. In B. Martin & E. M. Kassalow (Eds.), *Labor relations in advanced industrial societies: Issues and problems* (pp. 139–160). Washington, DC: Carnegie Endowment for International Peace.

Lewin, A. Y. (1982). Public enterprises, purposes and performance: A survey of Western European experience. In W. T. Stanbury & F. Thompson (Eds.), *Managing public enterprises* (pp. 51–78). New York: Praeger.

Lewin, A. Y., Long, C. P., & Carroll, T. N. (1999). The coevolution of new organizational forms. *Organization Science, 10,* 535–550.

Lincoln, J. R. & Kalleberg, A. L. (1990). *Culture, control, and commitment: A study of work organization and work attitudes in the United States and Japan.* Cambridge: Cambridge University Press.

Lorsch, J. W. (1996). German Corporate Governance and Management: An American's Perspective. In A. V. Werder (Ed.), *Grundsätze ordnungsmäßiger Unternehmungsführung (GoF) für die Unternehmungsleitung (GoU), Überwachung (GoÜ) und Abschlußprüfung (GoA)* (pp. 199–225). Düsseldorf: Handelsblatt.

Macey, J. R. & Miller, G. P. (1995). Corporate governance and commercial banking: A comparative examination of Germany, Japan, and the United States. *Stanford Law Review, 48,* 73–109.

Maddison, A. (1991). *Dynamic forces in capitalist development: A long-run comparative view.* Oxford: Oxford University Press.

Meyer, J. W. (1994). Rationalized environments. In W. R. Scott & J. W. Meyer (Eds.), *Institutional environments and organizations* (pp. 32–54). Thousand Oaks, CA: Sage Publications.

Miner, A. S. (1987). Idiosyncratic jobs in formalized organizations. *Administrative Science Quarterly, 32,* 327–351.

Mitchell, T. (1999). Society, economy, and the state effect. In G. Steinmetz (Ed.), *State/culture: State formation after the cultural turn* (pp. 76–97). Ithaca, NY: Cornell University.

Murtha, T. P. & Lenway, S. A. (1994). Country capabilities and the strategic state: How national political institutions affect multinational corporations' strategies. *Strategic Management Journal, 15,* 113–129.

Namiki, N. & Sethi, S. P. (1988). Japan. In R. Nath (Ed.), *Comparative management: A regional view* (pp. 55–96). Cambridge, MA: Ballinger Publishing Co.

Neal, L. (1997). On the historical development of stock markets. In H. Brezinski & M. Fritsch (Eds.), *The emergence and evolution of markets* (pp. 59–79). Cheltenham, UK: Edward Elgar.

Neary, B. (1993). *Management in the U.S. and (West) German machine tool industry: Historically rooted and socioculturally contingent.* Unpublished doctoral dissertation, Duke University, NC.

Nelson, R. R. (Ed.) (1993). *National innovation systems: A comparative analysis.* New York: Oxford University Press.

Newman, K. L. & Nollen, S. D. (1996). Culture and congruence: The fit between management practices and national culture. *Journal of International Business Studies, 27,* 753–779.

Nonaka, I. & Takeuchi, H. (1995). *The knowledge-creating company.* New York: Oxford University Press.

North, D. C. (1990). *Institutions, institutional change, and economic performance.* Cambridge, England: Cambridge University Press.

Orru, M., Hamilton, G. G., & Suzuki, M. (1989). Patterns of inter-firm control in Japanese business. *Organization Studies, 10,* 549–574.

Ozaki, R. S. (1992). *Human capitalism: The Japanese enterprise system as world model.* New York: Penguin Books.

Parsons, T. (1971). *The system of modern society.* Englewood Cliffs, NJ: Prentice Hall.

Plenert, G. J. (1990). *International management and production: Survival techniques for corporate America.* Blue Ridge Summit, PA: TBA Professional and Reference Books.

Porter, M. E. (1990). *The competitive advantage of nations.* New York: Free Press.

Powell, W. W. & DiMaggio, P. J. (Eds.) (1991). *The new institutionalism in organizational analysis.* Chicago: The University of Chicago Press.

Prowse, S. (1994). Corporate governance in an international perspective: A survey of corporate control mechanisms among large firms in the U.S., U.K., Japan, and Germany. *Financial Markets, Institutions, and Instruments, 4,* 1–63.

Putnam, R. D. (1993). *Making democracy work: Civic traditions in modern Italy.* Princeton, NJ: Princeton University Press.

Quinn, D. P. & Rivoli, P. (1991). The effects of the American- and Japanese-style employment and compensation practices on innovation. *Organization Science, 2,* 323–341.

Randlesome, C. (1994). *The business culture in Germany.* Oxford: Butterworth Heinemann.

Redding, S. G. (1997). Comparative management theory: Jungle, zoo or fossil bed? In M. Warner (Ed.), *Comparative management: Critical perspectives on business and management* (pp. 1445–1479). London: Routledge.

Redding, S. G. & Whitley, R. D. (1990). Beyond bureaucracy: Towards a comparative analysis of forms of economic resource co-ordination and control. In S. R. Clegg & S. G. Redding (Eds.), *Capitalism in contrasting cultures* (pp. 79–104). Berlin: W. de Gruyter.

Ruigrok, W. & Achatenhagen, L. (1999). Organizational culture and the transformation towards new forms of organizing. *European Journal of Work and Organizational Psychology, 8,* 521–536.

Sakano, T. & Lewin, A. Y. (1999). Impact of CEO succession in Japanese companies: A coevolutionary perspective. *Organization Science, 10,* 654–671.

Sako, M. (1994). Training, productivity, and quality control in Japanese multinational companies. In M. Aoki & R. Dore (Eds.), *The Japanese firm: Sources of competitive strength* (pp. 84–116). Oxford: Oxford University Press.

Schneider, S. C. (1989). Strategy formulation: The impact of national culture. *Organization Studies, 10,* 149–168.

Schneider, S. C. & De Meyer, A. (1991). Interpreting and responding to strategic issues: The impact of national culture. *Strategic Management Journal, 12,* 307–320.

Schwartz, S. H. (1994). Beyond individualism/collectivism: New cultural dimensions of values. In U. Kim, H. C. Triandis, C. Kagitcibasi, S. C. Choi, & G. Yoon (Eds.), *Individualism and collectivism: Theory, method, and applications* (pp. 85–119). Newbury Park, CA: Sage.

Schwartz, S. H. & Sagie, G. (2000). Value consensus and importance: A cross-national study. *Journal of Cross-Cultural Psychology, 31,* 465–497.

Scott, J. (1997). *Corporate governance and control: Beyond managerialism and Marxism corporate business and capitalist classes.* Oxford: Oxford University Press.

Shane, S. (1994). The effect of national culture on the choice between licensing and direct foreign investment. *Strategic Management Journal, 15,* 627–642.

Singh, J. V. & Lumsden, C. J. (1990). Theory and research in organizational ecology. *Annual Review of Sociology, 16,* 161–195.

Skocpol, T. (1985). Bringing the state back in: Strategies of analysis in current research. In P. B. Evans, D. Rueschemeyer, & T. Skocpol (Eds.), *Bringing the state back in* (pp. 3–37). Cambridge: Cambridge University Press.

Stanbury, W. T. & Thompson, F. (1982). *Managing public enterprises.* New York: Praeger.

Steinmetz, G. (Ed.) (1999). *State/culture: State formation after the cultural turn.* Ithaca, NY: Cornell University Press.

Stinchcombe, A. L. (1965). Social structure and organizations. In J. G. March (Ed.), *Handbook of organizations* (pp. 142–193). Chicago: Rand-McNally.

Streek, W. (1992). *Social institutions and economic performance: Studies of industrial relations in advanced capitalist economies.* London: Sage Publications.

Streek, W. (1997). German capitalism: Does it exist? Can it survive? *New Political Economy, 2,* 237–256.

Tayeb, M. (1991). Socio-political environment and management-employee relationships: An empirical study of England and India. In C. Brewster & S. Tyson (Eds.), *International comparisons in human resource management* (pp. 44–63). London: Pitman Publishings.

Thurow, L. (1992). *Head to head: The coming economic battle among Japan, Europe, and America.* New York: William Morrow and Company, Inc.

Triandis, H. C. (Ed.) (1994). *Handbook of industrial and organizational psychology* (Vol. 4). Palo Alto, CA: Consulting Psychologists Press.

Tricker, R. I. (1990). Corporate governance: A ripple on the cultural reflection. In S. R. Clegg & S. G. Redding (Eds.), *Capitalism in contrasting cultures* (pp. 187–214). Berlin: W. de Gruyter.

Trompenaars, F. (1993). *Riding the waves of culture.* London: Nicholas Brealey.

Tung, R. L. (1988). People's Republic of China. In Raghu Nath (Ed.), *Comparative management: A regional view* (pp. 139–168). Cambridge, MA: Ballinger Publishing Co.

Tushman, M. L., Anderson, P. C., & O'Reilly, C. (1997). Technology cycles, innovation streams, and ambidextrous organizations: Organization renewal through innovation streams and strategic change. In M. L. Tushman & P. Anderson (Eds.), *Managing strategic innovation and change* (pp. 3–23). New York: Oxford University Press.

Ungson, G. R., Steers, R. M., & Park, S. (1997). *Korean enterprise: The quest for globalization.* Boston, MA: Harvard Business School Press.

Ursacki, T. & Vertinsky, I. (1995). Long-term changes in Korea's international trade and investment. *Pacific Affairs, 68,* 385–409.

Walsh, J. P. & Seward, J. K. (1990). On the efficiency of internal external corporate control mechanisms. *Academy of Management Review, 15,* 421–458.

Warner, M. (1996). Culture, education and industry: Managing management studies in Japan. In P. Joynt & M. Warner (Eds.), *Managing across culture: Issues and perspectives* (pp. 258–274). London: International Thompson Business Press.

Warner, M. (1997). *Comparative management: Critical perspectives on business and management.* London: Routledge.

Weber, E. U., Hsee, C. K., & Sokolowska, J. (1998). What folklore tells us about risk and risk taking: Cross-cultural comparisons of American, German, and Chinese Proverbs. *Organizational Behavior and Human Decision Processes, 75,* 170–186.

Westney, D. E. (1994). The evolution of Japan's industrial research and development. In M. Aoki & R. Dore (Eds.), *The Japanese firm: Sources of*

competitive strength (pp. 154–177). Oxford: Oxford University Press.

Whitehill, A. M. (1990). *Japanese management: Tradition and transition.* London: Routledge.

Whitley, R. (1994). Dominant forms of economic organization in market economies. *Organization Studies, 15,* 153–182.

Whitley, R. (1996). The social construction of economic actors: Institutions and types of firms in Europe and other market economies. In R. Whitley & P. H. Kristensen (Eds.), *The changing European firm: Limits to convergence* (pp. 39–66). London: Routledge.

Whitley, R. (1999). Firms, institutions, and management control: The comparative analysis of coordination and control systems. *Accounting, Organizations, and Society, 24,* 507–524.

Wiersema, M. F. & Bird, A. (1993). Organizational demography in Japanese firms: Group heterogeneity, individual dissimilarity, and top management team turnover. *Academy of Management Journal, 36,* 996–1025.

Wilkinson, B. & Oliver, N. (1990). Japanese influences on British industrial culture. In S. R. Clegg & S. G. Redding (Eds.), *Capitalism in contrasting cultures* (pp. 333–354). Berlin: W. de Gruyter.

Wolhuter, C. C. (1997). Classification of national education systems: A multivariate approach. *Comparative Education Review, 41,* 161–178.

Wright, M. & Chiplin, B. (1999). Corporate governance and control: Beyond managerialism and Marxism. *Human Relations, 52,* 1189–1204.

12

Complexity Science Models of Organizational Change and Innovation

Kevin J. Dooley

Complexity science is a term used to describe a broad and diverse group of concepts, models, and metaphors pertaining to the systemic and dynamic properties of living systems (Gell-Mann, 1994; Holland, 1995; Jantsch, 1980; Maturana and Varela, 1992; Prigogine and Stengers, 1984). Complexity science has its roots in general systems theory but also takes into account the basic principles and characteristics of living systems, such as self-renewal, construction of order from energy, self-organization, coevolution with the environment, nonlinearity, emergence, and the idiosyncratic desires, norms, preferences, and realities of humans (Lewin, 1992; Waldrop, 1992; Anderson, 1999; Guastello, 2002). Complexity science is broad and generic enough to encompass both positivist and constructivist viewpoints (Stacey, 1999) and provides a rich background for conceptual and theoretical development for both qualitative and quantitative researchers.

A common element of all complexity science models is that they explicitly incorporate the dimension of time—thus they are particularly attractive to organizational theorists studying phenomena in-volving change, as change can be defined and studied only over time. In fact, it may be that part of the appeal of complexity science is due to the fact that few existing paradigms of organizational theory incorporate the dimension of time in any significant manner. Complexity science models tend to go beyond describing the mere progression of activities and events; rather, the generative mechanisms responsible for change are often explicitly articulated. Thus, complexity science models tend to have characteristics of both a variance theory, in that they conceptualize causal links between variables and/or constructs, and a process theory, in that they make explicit how change over time occurs. Thus, complexity science models answer both the "how" and "why" of organizational change.

Complexity science–inspired models of organizational change can be categorized into four general areas. *Complex adaptive system models* are simulation-based models where agents pursue teleological ends. Agents possess action rules (schemata) that define how they interact with the environment, including resources and other agents. Agents are often modeled

354

as being heterogonous, and they learn how to improve their fitness over time. Mechanisms within the models tend to be complicated. Complex adaptive system (CAS) models describe parts of the system (agents, objects, resources) and how they interact. The dominant disciplines are computer science and cognitive psychology (and, to a lesser extent, other social sciences). Researchers use CAS models deductively, as one must specify a model a priori and then simulate it in order to learn of the emergent properties and patterns in the system.

Computational models are simulation-based models where parts of a system coevolve over time. These parts may be agents or simply elements of the whole. Change is driven by nonteleological, local interactions between the parts. Mechanisms within the models tend to be simple. The dominant disciplines are mathematics and computer science. Like CAS models, computational models are used deductively.

Dynamical models are mathematical models that formulate how, and often why, variables that we observe in complex systems change over time. These variables may or may not represent higher-level constructs. Interactions between variables may be linear or nonlinear, discrete or continuous. The dominant disciplines are mathematics and statistics. Researchers may use dynamical models inductively, by modeling empirical data and then theorizing how such observed patterns may have come about, or they may use them deductively, in a way similar to how a computational model is used.

Self-organizing models are mathematical and conceptual models that formulate how order is created in the system from within. Self-organizing models focus on the dialectical differences that exist within the system and the role that "energy" plays in transforming structure. Emphasis is placed on how significant structural changes occur, including how order is created from randomness. The dominant theoretical perspectives are biological and thermodynamics. Researchers use self-organizing models both inductively and deductively; first emergent patterns are observed that hint at a self-organizing process, then the specific causal mechanisms behind such self-organization are hypothesized.

Thus models within these four areas describe how parts of the system, and attributes of these parts, interrelate over time. The four divisions given here are descriptive and not theoretical—in reality there are features of models that overlap across these boundaries, and in general there is no consensus on a particular typology or taxonomy that categorizes complexity science models.

Models within these four categories depict change consistent with the taxonomy posited by Van de Ven and Poole (1995). CAS models are teleological in nature and portray constructive change brought about by individual agents pursuing improvement in their individual fitness level, although fitness can also have global, aggregate components. Evolutionary mechanisms, such as a genetic algorithm, may be embedded within the logic of a CAS model, so that agents learn. Self-organizing models also formulate change as constructive, but from dialectic versus teleological perspective. Whereas CAS models depict agents as responsible for change, self-organizing models emphasize how the interconnections and interactions between parts of the system produce order and change. The teleology involved in self-organization is the system's desire to dissipate an influx of energy or information in more efficient ways. Dynamical models portray change as prescribed by the generative mechanisms within the system, focusing on single entities or variables, which may be attached to parts of the system or the system as a whole. Dynamical models are rarely teleological, but rather portray change as a life-cycle process, inevitable and prescribed by the generative mechanism. Computational models also model change as an inherent property of the system, as it relates to the interaction of multiple entities. While computational models depict evolutionary processes, most do not have a component representing selection or adaptation. Thus computational models have characteristics of both evolutionary and life-cycle paradigms.

Complexity science models can be used to describe organizational change at various levels of conceptualization: an individual person, an object (e.g., entity, resource, technology), an organizational process, a team or subunit, and the organization as a whole. In practice, many authors formulate models portraying the importance of the individual person, and their interrelationships with other individual people, but this is more a bias imposed by the research community rather than the models themselves. In reality, complexity science models, like systems theory models, are generic enough to be employed at different, and even multiple levels (although many applications are not careful concerning multi-level issues).

Before discussing these four areas of models, it is worthy to note the manner in which general systems theory, the precursor to complexity science, conceptualizes phenomena of change. Systems theory has influenced the thoughts and models of social scientists since its inception midway through the twentieth century (Jantsch, 1980). Systems theory models causal relationships between variables and/or constructs—but whereas traditional science posits a unidirectional relationship between cause and effect (i.e., motivated students tend to learn more), systems theory introduced the notion of bidirectional causality (i.e., motivated students tend to learn more, which in turn makes them more motivated). This bidirectional causality is not assumed to be instantaneous, though, so variable A affects variable B, then B affects A, and so on. The effect of B on A is termed feedback.

One type of feedback is a reinforcing loop, where variables A and B affect each other in a similar direction, and this leads to cascading processes and exponential growth in both A and B (theoretically). Thus, just as a microphone and audio speaker can positively interact to the point where feedback causes the system to "explode" to its physical limits, so too will, for example, motivation and learning interact with one another positively until the limits of performance are reached. A reinforcing loop also would imply that if motivation decreases, then learning will decrease, which will further decrease motivation, and so on. Reinforcing loops are enacted in organizations in the form of incentives, social capital, economies of scale, some elements of performance evaluation, and escalation of commitment, etc.

Feedback can also establish a balancing loop, and this is typically associated with a variable's level having a goal that it is attempting to achieve, or some type of limit. A balancing loop produces decreasing returns, and exponential decay in the associated variables. So, for example, as an automobile approaches a stop sign, the driver applies negative feedback (the brakes) to slow down the car, as it approaches its final destination. Natural limits can also act as sources of balancing loops, keeping the system within boundaries of feasibility. Balancing loops are enacted in organizations in the form of (constructive) criticism, management by exception, project management control systems, organizational policies and rules.

Organizational researchers may theorize feedback within their models, but they rarely incorporate it within models that are subjected to empirical testing, because it requires the collection of longitudinal data. Strictly speaking, a model that posits that A causes B must demonstrate that A preceded B temporally. In practice, this is rarely done. In order to demonstrate bidirectional causality between A and B, A must be observed at one particular time, B must be observed to occur at a later time, and then A again at yet a later time, thus requiring a minimum of three samples at different times.

This temporal lag between cause and effect further complicates both the formulation of systems theory models and the observation of these patterns, as the lag may be indeterminable, or may itself vary over time. For example, in models that link changes in levels of organizational investment in research to changes in the company's market share, the lag between investment and realization of successful new products must be taken into account, and this may vary across and even within particular industries, or may change due to technological and market forces.

Social scientists were quick to realize the conceptual value that systems theory offered, and its use quickly spread. In particular, interest in cybernetics was keen, as people attempted to understand how the brain worked, using the computer as a model of human thinking (Minsky, 1986). Forrester (e.g., 1961) used dynamical models he named *system dynamics* to explore the relationship between key variables in large-scale social systems such as industries, communities, and ecologies. For the most part, relationships between variables were modeled using simple linear differential equations. While the behavior of a single relationship was relatively straightforward, it was the aggregate behavior that arose from complex coupling of the variables that led to surprising and revealing results.

While researchers such as Checkland, Ackoff, and Ashby continued to develop systems theory applications in the social sciences, it was not until Deming (1986) and Senge's (1990) works that systems theory enjoyed a renaissance within organizational studies and applications. The concepts of organizational learning and total quality management introduced systems theory to a whole new generation of practitioners and scholars.

While systems theory lays an important conceptual and intellectual foundation for studying complex systems, it did not adequately deal with the unique attributes associated with living systems, whether it is a cell, a biological entity, or a social system. Causal relationships, while bidirectional and existing in multitude, were still most often formulated in simple, linear ways. Systems theory describes not how entities in a system interact but rather how variables interact, and these variables are traits or characteristics of entities within the system, or the system itself. Thus systems theory models are "top-down," in that they require the modeler to identify a priori the most significant variables and how they interrelate. Systems theory models portray "life" as something that is mechanically maintained through equilibrium-seeking processes. Models in complexity science incorporate linear and nonlinear causality; they describe both entities and variables within the system; they can be both "top-down" and "bottom-up," meaning that often behavior is specified only locally, and global behavior is observed via simulation; and finally it models "life" as a dynamical process that only exists in quasi-equilibrium states. In complexity science, equilibrium is death, because life by definition means dynamic movement.

The rest of the chapter is organized as follows. First, each of these four types of complexity science models are described as they relate to organizational change, and their application to organizational studies is discussed. An example demonstrates how each of the four types of models might be applied in conceptualizing change within an organizational system. The chapter concludes by discussing some of the future challenges facing complexity science–based studies of organizational change, as they relate to both conceptual formulation and research methodology.

Complex Adaptive System Models of Organizational Change

General Description

Organizations can be thought of as examples of a general class of complex systems called complex adaptive systems, or CAS. Organizational theorists have traditionally associated the term *complexity* with a description of the inner workings of an organization (Dooley, 2002a); for example, a firm with many specialists is considered more complex than a firm with few specialists (Khandwalla, 1977). In the case of CAS, complexity refers to the manner in which the

system behaves relative to its internal structure; its aggregate behavior is not predictable from and cannot be reduced or understood from its component parts (Holland, 1995). In a complex system, two plus two does not necessarily equal four. Many systems are complex—weather, ecologies, information networks. A complex system is considered adaptive if it can change itself using nonevolutionary (or Larmarkian) processes, on time scales much quicker than bio-evolutionary time scales. Examples of a CAS include economies, automobile traffic, social organizations, and cultures (Gell-Mann, 1994). It is worthy to note that the most formal operational definition of CAS, by Holland (1995), is simultaneously a specification for a computer simulation language (Swarm). Thus the connection between a CAS perspective and computer modeling is very strong. The component elements of a CAS are shown in figure 12.1.

The basic elements of a CAS are *agents*. Agents are semi-autonomous units that seek to maximize their fitness by evolving over time. Agents scan their *environment* (both internal and external to the system) and interpret these scans via their schemata. Agents can represent individual people or larger bodies such as teams, divisions, or whole firms.[1] *Schemata* are mental templates (within a computer model, computational templates) that define how reality is interpreted and what are appropriate responses for a given stimuli. These schemata are often evolved from smaller, more basic schema (Holland, 1995). Agents are assumed to be rationally bounded, in that they have limited and perhaps biased access to information within the system, and schemata may differ across agents due to personal idiosyncrasies in how people make decisions (March, 1994). Within an agent, multiple, contradictory schema may exist, competing via a selection-enactment-retention process (Weick, 1979).

When an observation does not match what is expected, an agent can take action in order to adapt the observation to fit an existing schema. An agent can also purposefully alter a schema in order to better fit the observation. Schemata can change through random or purposeful mutation, and/or combination with other schemata. In most CAS models, random mutations are not accepted unless they correspond to an increase in the agent's fitness. When a schema changes it generally has the effect of making the agent more robust (it can perform in light of increasing variation or variety), more reliable (it can

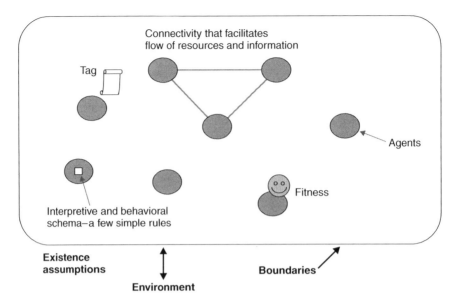

Figure 12.1 Elements of a complex adaptive system.

perform more predictably), or more capable in terms of its requisite variety (in can adapt to a wider range of conditions) (Arthur, 1994).

The *fitness* of the agent is often modeled as a complex aggregate of many factors, both local and global. Unfit agents are more likely to instigate change in their schema. Optimization of local fitness allows differentiation and novelty/diversity; global optimization of fitness enhances the CAS coherence as a system and induces long-term memory.

Schemata also determine how a given agent interacts with other agents both inside and outside of the system. Actions between agents involve the exchange of information and/or resources, occurring through lines of *connectivity*. These *flows* may be nonlinear. Information and resources can undergo multiplier effects based on the nature of connectivity in the system. Because an agent's schema includes information about other agents, an action by one agent can be considered information for other agents that are connected to it. Different types of connections exist; for example, Krackhardt and Carley (1998) define connectivity in an organizational system by a social network, a task network, and a resource network.

Agent *tags* help identify what other agents are capable of transacting with a given agent; tags also facilitate the formation of aggregates, or meta-agents.

Meta-agents help distribute and decentralize functionality, allowing diversity to thrive and specialization to occur (Holland, 1995). Agents or meta-agents also exist outside the boundaries of the CAS, and schemata also determine the rules of interaction concerning how information and resources flow externally.

A researcher using a CAS model must specify what is inside versus outside of the system, or the system's *boundary*. In some cases, boundaries may be self-evident, such as the legal boundary of a firm. In other cases, boundaries are specified according to the research questions being addressed. Because systems are decomposable, boundaries may exist and be depicted at multiple scales, leading to nested behavior. Finally, the system's reason for being is defined by *existence assumptions*. These assumptions will tend to influence how the model incorporates contributions to agent fitness that are global in nature. For example, a simulation of a corporation may use economic criteria in the agents' fitness functions, whereas a simulation of a nonprofit agency may use altruistic criteria.

How Change Occurs in a Complex Adaptive Systems

There are two types of change portrayed in CAS models. First, because agents in the CAS are constantly interacting with other agents, and adapting to or evolving with an environment, there is constant change in terms of flow of resources and information, learning by agents, and actions that agents take. CAS models portray change as something that is driven by the goals of individual agents, but the patterns that emerge are not necessarily deducible at the agent level because of the self-organizing nature of the system. Second, as a CAS model equates the organization to a particular set of elements (agents, schema, boundaries, interconnections), the deep structures of the system that portray the more quasi-permanent and stable elements of the organizational system will change as one or more of the elements of the CAS changes:

- Agents can be added or removed from the system, for example, via expansion, downsizing, and mergers and acquisitions. This is also the basic manner in which the system's boundary can be altered.
- The fitness function of an agent can be thought of as containing both extrinsic and intrinsic components, and both individual and group components. It can be altered by changing reward and incentive systems, or by changing norms and values.
- Schema can evolve over time, being strengthened or weakened, can undergo mutation, can be combined with other schemata, or can be eliminated altogether. In most CAS formulations schema change is linked to how actions and outcomes, as indicated by the fitness function, are associated. Thus if an action rule consistently improves fitness, the strength of belief in that rule will tend to increase; this attribution process (Holland, 1995) is the operational model of agent learning. Agents are assumed to be capable of single-loop, double-loop, or deutero-learning (Argyris and Schon, 1978).
- Changing a flow's pace or timing can alter the flow of information or resources between two or more agents, increasing or decreasing exchanges. For example, information technology and the Internet increase the pace of information flow, while schedules and other forms of temporal coordination alter the timing of events.
- Connections between agents can be added or removed via restructuring and redesign of the system, including changing lines of command and increasing connectivity through information technology.

- Agent tags can be changed in either a specific or symbolic fashion. For example, sales people in a growing firm may be separated into marketing and sales functions; people may be assigned titles indicating new levels of responsibility and communication.
- Changes in an organization's strategy (mission and vision) represent changes in its existence assumptions.

At a general level, a CAS model suggests means for and processes of organizational change that are not different from what already exists in the organizational literature; many of the implications that authors draw by using CAS as a framework for how organizations work can also be found in literature within general systems theory, population ecology, organizational learning, and cognitive psychology (Dooley, 1997). Novel insight comes not from the general conclusions as given above, but rather from specific conclusions based on the model at hand.

Example of a CAS Model of Organizational Change

One model that demonstrates the potential of CAS models is Axtell's (1999) computational model of the emergence of firms. Agents are individuals who self-organize into firms by considering their own fitness. First, each agent is assigned an "income-leisure" parameter that determines the amount of time it would prefer to spend at work (making income) versus at leisure (any amount of time not allocated to work effort); these assignments are made randomly so agent heterogeneity is maintained. The agent's utility, or fitness, at any given time is a multiplicative function of the amount of effort they are expending, the return on that effort at the firm level, and the amount of leisure time available. At random intervals of time an agent will consider their current position and either (a) maintain their current effort level, (b) increase or decrease their current effort level, (c) start a new firm (solo), or (d) migrate to one of two friend's firms. The amount of return that a firm gets from the aggregated efforts of its members depends on the number of members, their individual efforts, and any synergistic effects that may be included (e.g., increasing returns). Returns to the individual are equally divided among all firm participants.

Despite the number of different parameters and starting conditions that can be varied, and the fact that the simulation itself is based on some rather simplistic assumptions about human nature, the results show a great deal of validity in mimicking actual firm formation behavior. For example:

- As firms become large, an individual agent's contribution becomes miniscule compared to the whole, which produces "free riders."
- As free-riding becomes more commonplace, firm productivity decreases and those who most want "work" leave for other firms, bringing the large firm into decline.
- While "equilibrium" conditions theoretically exist that would lead to a static situation, there is sufficient dynamic instability such that these equilibrium conditions never arise.
- The history of any firm is emergent and path dependent.
- At the aggregate level, firm size, growth, and death rates mimic existing empirical evidence.

What is interesting here is not that there are free riders, or that firms die and emerge in a dynamic fashion, or even that real growth rates can be mimicked. Rather, the fundamental point is that all of these conclusions, found elsewhere in the organizational literature, emerge from a model with nothing more than semi-autonomous agents who seek to self-ishly improve a simple fitness function. As more of these kinds of simulations are done, theories that emphasize local interactions leading to global, emergent patterns will become more prevalent.

Computational Models of Organizational Change

General Description

Computational models are similar to CAS models in that they depict parts of the system (agents or objects) that interact with one another through a set of rules. Insights from the models are gained from simulation. In contrast to CAS models, most computational models are not teleological, and more often than not the rules that dictate local interactions are simple. Unlike CAS models, where there is a relatively agreed-upon framework and architecture for what

models should have in terms of components, different computational models formulate the causal system differently, and so two major models used by organizational researchers will be reviewed: cellular automata and the rugged landscape model. Other types of computational models (e.g., neural networks, genetic algorithms) are feasible, but have gotten less attention from organizational researchers.

Cellular Automata Models of Change

Cellular automata (CA) models are the most basic form of a complex adaptive system (Wolfram, 2002), and thus are a good medium in which to study the phenomena of emergence. Consider a one-dimensional CA, where a "cell" represents an agent, and where each agent may be considered in a "state." In the simplest arrangement, the state is considered binary and can be represented visually by two numbers (0, 1) or colors (white, black). The CA is finite in size—that is, it has a fixed number of cells (agents). Each cell evolves its state in a discrete manner, such that the state of cell "j" at time t, state (j, t) is determined by the state of cell "j" at time $t - 1$, state $(j, t - 1)$, and the state of some neighboring cells at time $t - 1$, for example, state $(j - 1, t - 1)$ and state $(j + 1, t - 1)$. The cells are lined up in a specific and fixed spatial order. In order to visualize change in the states over time, the combined state vector is plotted down the screen, thus becoming a two-dimensional object. Each column of the graphical object represents the evolution of a cell over time, and each row represents the combined states of all cells at a particular time.

Consider a 5-cell CA; we will assume that the cells at the left and right end "wrap-around" and consider their neighbor at the other end to be connected to them. We'll denote the states by (0, 1), and start off with a random initial configuration.

$$0 \quad 1 \quad 0 \quad 1 \quad 1$$

Suppose we use the following set of rules:

- If the sum of yourself and left and right neighbors is less than two, change to a 1.
- If the sum of yourself and left and right neighbors is two or greater, change to a 0.

These rules can be embodied into a decision table:

Self-state	Left neighbor	Right neighbor	New state
0	0	0	1
0	1	0	1
0	0	1	1
0	1	1	0
1	0	0	1
1	1	0	0
1	0	1	0
1	1	1	0

If we consider the first three columns to be in "standard order" (or in general, as long as one is consistent with a patterning system for these columns), then the rule can be called "11101000," or in its decimal equivalent, rule 232. Given the initial condition above, several iterations of the CA look like this:

0	1	0	1	1
0	1	0	0	0
1	1	1	1	1
0	0	0	0	0
1	1	1	1	1
0	0	0	0	0
1	1	1	1	1
0	0	0	0	0
1	1	1	1	1

One can see that the CA settles into a cyclical pattern with period length 2. In fact, all CAs, assuming that they are completely deterministic, will eventually settle into a repetitive cycle of length 1 or greater. This pattern is referred to as the attractor in mathematics, and the particular type of attractor that is evoked here is referred to as a limit cycle (in the special case of a period length of 1, this is referred to as a fixed-point attractor). In this particular example, no matter which initial pattern is chosen, they all lead to the same attractor as the computational model is iterated forward indefinitely. The set of initial conditions that converge to a given attractor is called the *basin of attraction*. In the case of CA rule 232, the basin of attraction for this 2-period limit cycle attractor encompasses all the possible configurations of 0s and 1s within each cell (i.e. the entire state space). Therefore regardless of the initial con-

dition, the final state of behavior is deterministic. This does not need to be true; in many CAs, different initial conditions will lead to different attractors even given the same set of rules. In this sense some CAs show sensitivity to initial conditions, and some do not.

The patterns of behavior, or attractors that emerge from CA models, are emergent (as in CAS and self-organizing models) in that they are not deducible from examination of the starting point or the rule set. CA models, like other computational models, are used to answer questions like "If systems behaved this way at a local level, what would be the global patterns that would emerge?"

For example, one of the more cited CA studies is Schelling's (1978) examination of racial segregation in metropolitan neighborhoods. Schelling's CA portrayed two agent types, black and white, and required that each agent move to a cell where a minority (not a majority) of agents around it were of the same color. Thus, an agent would remain in a cell if 3 or more of its 8 closest neighbors were of the same color; otherwise it would attempt to move to a cell that fulfilled that condition. The results show that while any individual agent is not "prejudiced," the resulting clustering of agents is highly bipolar, showing completely segregated neighborhoods.

One CA model that has gotten a lot of attention in both the physical and social sciences is Bak's (1996) sandpile model. In organizational theory, it is common to assume that if we observe a change of small magnitude that it must stem from causes that are also small in magnitude; if we observe change of a catastrophic magnitude, then it must stem from causes that are also catastrophic. While this may be the case, it also may not. In complex systems, the magnitudes of causes and effects may be not be related—big changes may have no impact, and small changes may have enormous impact. This counterintuitive behavior can cause erroneous learning and attribution to occur. It can also be leveraged, as it may be possible to induce systemic change through simple, local actions.

Bak's sandpile model suggests that when the system is in a state of self-organized criticality, effects can ripple through a system, and a small change in one element of the system may lead to systemic change. Self-organized criticality takes place when elements of the system are interconnected in such a manner that a path exists (however long) between any two elements of the system. In such a state, the magnitude of impact of small changes will probabilistically follow an inverse power law—small changes usually lead to small effects, but they can sometimes lead to catastrophic effects.

Bak (1996) describes an "organizational sandpile" in which information flows, one piece at a time, into a business office. When workers accumulate information beyond a critical threshold, they generate an action that subsequently serves as a piece of information for other workers they are connected to. If workers are connected such that the overall system is critically self-organized, then avalanches of activities— the number of activities generated due to a single piece of information flowing into the system—occur in various sizes. Most of these avalanches are small in size, but sometimes a single piece of information may generate a flurry of activity through a cascading of critical thresholds. These processes tend to be antipersistent or mean reverting, in that moderately sized or catastrophic avalanches tend not to occur back to back, but rather are distributed over time.

From an organizational standpoint, this model conceptualizes connectivity—through information technology and communication via social networks embedding friendship, proximity, resource relationships, and task relationships—as critical to organizational change. From a practitioner standpoint, the model is encouraging and frightening at the same time. Small changes (e.g., those induced by management) can lead to significant changes in system behavior, but conversely small errors or perturbations outside the "control" of management may also lead to significant change.

Despite the importance of connectivity to change, organizations should not follow the simplistic tendency recommendation, "Everyone should be connected to everyone." While this ensures self-organized criticality, it is at a great cost. Not only does massive connectivity cost, but also it leads to information overload and extremely high coordination costs. Worse yet, it provides little benefit; critical connectivity can actually be achieved with (typically) only a few connections between each agent in the system (Kauffman, 1995).

Whether or not a state of self-organized criticality is desirable or not is situational. In the case of information or innovation diffusion, such connectivity is desirable. It ensures that if an idea is good enough, it has the potential to spread throughout the system. In the case of error propagation, such connectivity can be lethal. It means that any small error in one part of the system has the potential to spread and produce errors throughout the system. A classic example of this is the spread of computer viruses aimed at attacking a person's mailing list contained in an e-mail application.

Self-organized criticality refers to potentially large-scale change in the outcomes of a system with no corresponding change in the generative mechanisms behind the outcomes. For example, the size of meteorites that hit the earth follows a pattern of self-organized criticality—large, disastrous meteors are generated from the same mechanisms as small rocks that appear as shooting stars in our sky. Large-scale change may also stem from a basic reorganization of the system's elements, and this is discussed in the next section concerning rugged landscape models.

CA models have not been used extensively by organizational researchers (an exception is in the area of technology diffusion described in Leydesdorff and Van Den Besselaar, 1994), as those that are friendly to the notion of using simulation are more drawn to CAS models, since they enable explicit modeling of an agent's schema, whereas CA models do not model agents in as sophisticated a manner. But one of the basic findings of CA models—that simple, local rules of interaction can lead to complex patterns of behavior—has spawned much interest and discussion around the topic of "simple rules" (Sull and Eisenhardt, 2001). For example, the Institute of Medicine's 2001 report on the state of quality in health care in the United States suggested that the current state of the system is due to the "simple rules" that govern health care transactions, and that changing this rule set (essentially relating to the values of the system) will change the emergent patterns of behavior. For example, they advocate moving from "patient records are secret" to "patient records are transparent." While there is little debate in complexity science that simple rules can generate complex behavior, there is still debate as to whether all complex behavior we see is due to simple rules.

The Rugged Landscape Model of Change

Systems are consistently looking for new ways of operating and organizing, so as to improve their fitness, however defined. These searches can be simple or complex, depending on how options and alternatives arrange themselves. Often the changes encompass more than one critical variable in the system. When a system changes a set of critical variables, it may be understood to be changing its configuration. To the extent that a single best configuration or strategy exists, purposeful organizational change becomes a simple teleological process. If multiple solutions exist that are attractive, then search becomes more difficult. These solutions exist on a landscape, and Kauffman's work (1995) provides a scientific base to understand the basic nature of these searches.

In the world of landscapes, the position on the landscape represents a configuration or form that defines the elements of the system, and the topography relates to the fitness of that configuration. The managerial task is to examine and explore different configurations so as to improve fitness. The natural of the search depends on the nature of the landscape.

Kauffman defines the landscape using two parameters: n, the number of elements within the system (the dimensionality of the configuration), and k, which relates to the interconnectedness within the system. We shall confine our current discussion to the k parameter. When k is low relative to n, the system has a smooth landscape with a single peak, as shown in 12.2.[2] When k is 0, it means that optimizing the individual components of the system can optimize the fitness of the system; no interactions need to be taken into account. A university is an example— making each department better can make the overall university better. An improvement in bachelor's level education within the (e.g.) the chemistry department does not necessarily require coordination with the university's sociology department. Systems with a k of 0 are considered modular.

As k increases, fitness of the system depends not only on the individual components, but also on their interactions and synergies. For example, consider a health care organization. If one changes the responsibilities of nursing, one must also change the tasks of technicians and doctors. One cannot add a new service without also altering insurance coverage. When k is an intermediate value, the landscape is rugged with several local peaks; when k is large (up to $n - 1$), the landscape can turn jagged. The value of k can also be thought of as relating to the type of coupling present in the system (Weick, 1979). A value of 0 corresponds to no coupling; intermediate values of k correspond to loose coupling, while high values of k correspond to tight coupling. Systems with a high k value are considered *integral*.

The process of search is one that is path dependent; organizational members learn where to search

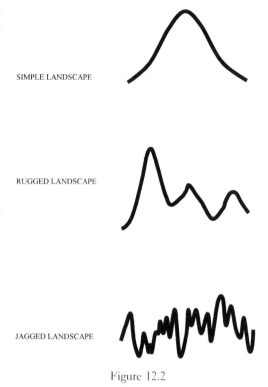

SIMPLE LANDSCAPE

RUGGED LANDSCAPE

JAGGED LANDSCAPE

Figure 12.2

next by carefully examining where they have been in the past. The utility of such an approach depends on the nature of the landscape. If k is 0, then neighboring points in the design space (configurations that are close to one another) are highly correlated, and one can learn which direction to head for improved fitness. When k is intermediate (as small as 3 or 4), correlation between neighboring configurations becomes weaker; in the extreme, a large value of k leads to a random landscape, in which learning is of little or no use in the search process.

In smooth landscapes, change via search tends to occur incrementally, through *trial-and-error learning*. The challenge is to determine which factors in the system configuration make a difference, and to determine the direction and magnitude of change that optimizes fitness. Traditional quality improvement methods focused on incremental, daily change are an example of this type of search process.

In a rugged landscape, improvement is more difficult. People tend to be myopic in terms of their knowledge about potential configurations; they tend to assume that the current configuration is the only feasible one, and that optimization is just a matter of fine-tuning the existing system. This may lead to sub-optimization, as a search finds itself atop a local maximum, with no sense that other configurations exist that may in fact provide even better fitness. In this situation, change is very dependent on the initial starting condition, as it is likely that a search will end at the optimal point closest to the start. To avoid this, multiple searches should occur simultaneously. Parallel searching enables *learning by creating alternatives*. Many organizations employ this type of search within their innovation processes, pursuing multiple alternatives at once. This divergent activity is pruned only as specific alternatives are deemed to have no potential.

In a jagged landscape, many different configurations will render about the same level of fitness. Because neighboring conditions are relatively un-correlated, search strategies that rely on historical information are rendered useless. Such situations are likely to lead to either an overly conservative or aggressive stance toward change. Some managers may seek change for change's sake, as they scramble across the landscape looking for better fitness, while other managers may be more comfortable staying put, as they cannot discern any rational means to improve and learn. When organizational writers use the word *chaos* in the vernacular sense, a jagged landscape may be their implied context (Dooley and Van de Ven, 1999). In such environments, *learning by mistake* and *learning by copying* may be dominant processes. Innovation searches are known to benefit from serendipity, and benchmarking and organizational acquisitions are examples of the vicarious learning process embedded in copying.

The type of change strategy that is appropriate depends on the nature of the landscape. If organizational actors have an incorrect view of the landscape, though, erroneous learning is likely. Imagine a manager searching on a jagged landscape with a mental model that the landscape he or she is operating on is smooth. Changes and experiments are likely to yield results that appear irrational and inconsistent. Errors in diagnosis and attribution are likely to ensue. The manager may believe that he or she chose the wrong variables to change or changed them too much or too little, or that implementation went awry.

These situations may be commonplace in systems. *Single-variable thinking* tends to be a human trait (March, 1994). Managers tend to believe that landscapes are simple, and their challenge is to find the couple of variables that make a difference. In a rug-ged or jagged landscape, only holistic thinking will likely lead to determination of an appropriate change strategy. When a system is conscious that a complex landscape may exist, it may attempt to centralize the change process as a means to deal with contingencies that cut across different areas of the larger system. For example, reengineering projects often involve systemic, large-scale change. While such change is advocated to occur from the "bottom-up," involving the workers closest to the tasks in the redesign of the system, in reality it often occurs "top-down," as managers and consultants take over the change process (Jaffe and Scott, 1998). There is a perception that only a top-down approach can consider all of the complex interactions that exist.

The change process may be simplified by making the landscape simpler. One way of doing this is via *modularization*. If system components are designed to operate independently, then each component can be optimized without regard to its impact on others. Modular design is becoming commonplace in products (Meyer and Lenhnerd, 1997), and there appears no reason why it could not extend to larger systems such as multidivisional organizations or supply networks. In fact, the divisions and profit centers can be seen as examples of modular design. Another way in which the landscape can be simplified is via *patching* (Kauffman, 1995; Eisenhardt and Brown, 2000). Patching involves purposeful loose coupling between pairs of elements; these local adjustments aggregate at the system level in a self-organized, emergent fashion.

Dynamical Models of Organizational Change

General Description

As Heraclitus said, you can never put your foot into the same river. At a microscopic level, the exact position of every water molecule is constantly changing, and their exact aggregate structure is never identical at different points in time. The structure of the river, though, as defined by its three-dimensional boundaries, demonstrates resiliency over time. The same is true of the human body. While millions of cells in our body die and are replaced daily, we are still recognizable because our structure remains roughly the same (Maturana and Varela, 1992).

Systems and their elements change constantly, if you look closely enough. It is in fact this constant dance that makes the system alive—if nothing changed and everything was at equilibrium, the system would be dead, quite literally (Dooley, 1997). Life entails constant interplay between elements of the system. These life-giving processes, or generative mechanisms, drive the routine behavior of the system—and identifying and understanding these generative mechanisms is often the key to understanding the system at its most basic level. For example, many financial processes of the firm are driven by a temporal process of entrainment that requires the sequence and timing of actions to synchronize with state and federal taxation requirements. Likewise, the inventory levels of a firm may be driven by seasonal variations in the quality and quantity of raw material. At a microlevel, variations in the output of a process may be random, at any given time being affected by innumerable physical and operational factors.

Dynamical models portray this constant change and are used in three ways. Some organizational researchers collect empirical data and then use statistical methods to see what type of dynamics are present (Poole, Van de Ven, Dooley, and Holmes, 2000). These dynamics then suggest something about the nature of the causal system. This is an inductive approach. Other researchers use quantitative, dynamical models to simulate how change occurs in organizational variables. Finally, some researchers use the qualitative characteristics of dynamical patterns, especially chaos, to theorize about the nature of organizational change.

Empirical Modeling

There are four types of patterns that can be empirically observed through statistical modeling of observed organizational variables: periodicity, chaos, white noise, and colored noise. These four patterns indicate four different, basic generative mechanisms, defined by two variables: their dimensionality and the nature of interdependence. *Dimensionality* refers to the number of variables driving behavior. For example, periodic (i.e., seasonal) processes may be low-dimensional, as they are driven by a few factors related to the environment (weather), while sales processes may be high-dimensional, as they are driven by the decisions of many independent agents (customers). These variables may behave *independently*,

where the aggregate effect is the sum of the individual effects, or there may be significant interactions between them, representing contingencies.

Low-dimensional causal systems yield periodic and chaotic dynamics, while high-dimensional causal systems yield white and pink noise dynamics. Periodic and white noise dynamics stem from systems where causal factors act independently, or in a linear fashion, while chaotic and pink noise systems stem from systems where causal factors act interdependently, in a nonlinear fashion (Dooley and Van de Ven, 1999).

White noise[3] is what is typically referred to as pure randomness, and it is generated via a high-dimensional process (Peitgen, Jurgens, and Saupe, 1992). The law of errors (Ruhla, 1992) also implies that the "many variables" affecting behavior are doing so in an independent fashion. If the observed behavior corresponds to collective social action, this implies that individuals are acting in a parallel manner, perhaps uncoordinated with one another. White noise processes progress with no memory of past behavior, so the system does not determine the future from the past—they are disconnected.

Pink noise is much the same as white noise, except that it is a sort of constrained randomness, whereby interactions between the factors/individuals constrain the system away from pure white noise (Schroeder, 1991). These interactions between factors may stem from the presence of feedback loops and/or constraints within the system. These constraints and/or feedback loops are local rather than global, as the presence of global feedback and/or constraint would tend to greatly reduce the dimensionality of the system, and thus not be indicative of a pink noise process. Pink noise processes have been found to be rather ubiquitous, showing up in social, economic, biologic, physiologic, geologic, and astronomical phenomena. The sandpile model discussed in the section on computational models is an example of a generative mechanism that exhibits pink noise dynamics.

Chaotic processes[4] are low-dimensional,[5] and nonlinear interactions exist between the factors/variables responsible for driving behavior. Low dimensionality may stem from the scope of the behavior in question, or it may imply that other mechanisms are reducing the dimensionality of the causal system via global feedback and/or constraints, because naturally a social system containing many agents will be (by definition) high-dimensional, unless something is actively constraining the potential freedom and variety of possible behaviors. These mechanisms can be thought of as representing either control of individuals, and/or cooperation between the individuals. Control and cooperation may be managerial (Simon, 1957), adaptive (March, 1994), institutional (Scott, 1995), or self-induced (Dooley, 1997).

Periodic behavior is also low-dimensional, where causal variables interact either not at all, or in a simple linear fashion. While such a system could arise naturally, it is also possible that interactions are linear (or absent) because the system was designed to be so. For example, the temporal regularity of required organizational action will entrain many processes to be periodic.

In summary, white noise processes consist of many significant factors acting in an independent fashion, and these processes demonstrate a lack of path dependency. Pink noise processes consist of many independent factors being constrained in some fashion by local feedback loops. Chaotic processes consist of a few significant factors acting in an interdependent fashion, at a global level. Such processes demonstrate path dependency and are representative of control and/or cooperation. Periodic processes consist of a few significant factors acting in an independent or simple linear fashion. These processes also indicate significant levels of control and/or cooperation.

Simulating Dynamical Models

Because periodic and chaotic dynamical models are low dimensional (they contain a few number of variables), researchers can pose specific models and simulate them to see the temporal behavior of organizational variables. For example, system dynamics models (Sterman, 2000) depict cause and effect between organizational variables using first-order differential equations and then simulate systems where variables are interrelated in complex webs of cause and effect. For example, one of the links in a system dynamics model might suggest that as the rate of R&D investment increases, so does the rate of income from licensing fees. System dynamics models indicate how rates of change in variables change, rather than how the actual level of the variable itself changes. These models begin to look more like the fundamental models of physical science, which work with rates rather than levels (McKelvey, 1997). While

system dynamic models can be linear or nonlinear in nature, they are most often linear, which leads to observed dynamics that are periodic and linear. Dynamical models that have the potential to generate chaos can also be found in some organizational studies (Feichtinger and Kopel, 1993), but these studies are more rare.

The Qualitative Characteristics of Dynamical Models

While simulation of potentially chaotic systems is not commonplace, many organizational researchers have taken the qualitative attributes of chaos and used this to theorize about organizational change. One of the most common metaphors used is "the butterfly effect," which states that small changes in the system can have large impact. This is a theme that is resonant and constant across all different complexity science models, but the ability to visualize this "sensitivity to initial conditions" brought an undue amount of attention to chaos in particular, above and beyond other complexity science phenomena. Most attention was paid to strategic planning—if chaos is present in real life, then sensitivity to initial conditions precludes prediction of the future, ever, regardless of how much information is at hand and how accurate the modeling effort is. The viability of strategic planning processes was particularly challenged (Stacey, 1992).

Many organizational researchers have misunderstood the importance of sensitivity to initial conditions. As mentioned previously, the patterns that arise in dynamical systems are referred to as attractors (Guastello, 1995). An attractor is a steady-state phenomenon; it represents the recurrent patterns of behavior or states of the system as it progresses into the future. This pattern, however, is not immediately realized. A period of time exists as the system moves from its "initial state" to its attractor. The behavior during this period of time is referred to as a transient. The amazing thing about transients is that they tend to end up at the same place—the attractor—for a wide variety of initial states. An attractor's *basin of attraction* is the set of initial states that converge toward it.

A chaotic system is sensitive to arbitrarily small changes in its initial conditions, with respect to its exact path into the future. This is significant in that we have believed until recently that deterministic systems were insensitive to such small perturbations.

But note that this sensitivity is with respect only to the exact state (or level) of the variable in question, its exact path into the future. Typically, basins of attraction tend to be large relative to their corresponding attractor; that is, a large number of initial conditions lead to the same general pattern of behavior, or attractor. Thus the system's attractor, or pattern, is not sensitive to changes in initial condition. Thus chaotic systems are sensitive in specific path, but not general overall pattern. So organizational processes that are predictive in nature may not be highly sensitive to chaos if they are qualitative in nature (e.g., strategic planning), but may be if they are quantitative in nature (e.g., demand forecasting).

Another way in which a dynamical system can change is if the parameters defining the system change. For example, consider the logistic equation that relates a variable x at some future time $t+1$ as a function of a parameter k and the value of the variable x at time t:

$$x(t+1) = k \cdot x(t) \cdot \{1 - x(t)\}$$

As k is increased from 1.0 to 4.0, the attractor changes. Between 1.0 and 3.0, the attractor of the system is a single point. For values of k between 3.0 and 3.449, the attractor is periodic, with a cycle length of 2. Above 3.449, the system bifurcates; a cyclical attractor still exists, but now has a cycle length of 4. This continues on as the value of the parameter k is increased, increasing to cycle lengths of 8, 16, 32, etc. At the Feigenbaum number of 3.569, the attractor changes from periodic to chaotic (Peitgen et al., 1992); at a value of k greater than four, the system becomes unstable and does not have a finite attractor.

In this example, shifting the critical parameter of k has a profound impact on system behavior. From an organizational standpoint, the question then becomes, What is the critical parameter that, if changed, may shift the system from one attractor to another?

Consider the example of highway traffic (Nagel and Paczuski, 1995). The patterns that emerge from the traffic system are strongly dependent on a single critical parameter, the density of traffic (the number of cars on the road at a given time). At low densities, the system operates in a high-dimensional mode, and cars travel independently of one another, at random intervals. As density increases, platoons of cars—a string of cars all going the same speed, relatively close

to one another in space—begins to form and system dimensionality is reduced. Past a critical level of density, cars begin to slow down and speed up in predictable waves that travel across space and time, the extreme version of which is stop-and-go traffic. As density increases to its maximum, dimensionality is reduced to a minimum and no cars move at all.

In organizational systems, such critical parameters may also exist. One example might be the level of connectivity between individuals, teams, and functions within the company (Burt, 1992; Rogers, 1995). It is likely that as the level of connectivity reaches certain threshold values, behavior of the system will qualitatively change (Kauffman, 1995). For example, at low levels of connectivity, information may spread slowly and in an ad hoc fashion, leading to communication patterns that were local, uncoordinated, and disjointed, perhaps mimicking a random process. At very high levels of connectivity, organizational members may be overwhelmed with information processing needs, and communication patterns may be constrained, mimicking a low dimensional process.

Self-Organizing Models of Organizational Change

General Description

A special type of change occurs when the critical parameter that changes is the level of energy within the system. Far-from-equilibrium models of change portray the system as self-organizing, renewing itself through reorganization (Goldstein, 1994). This reorganization occurs in an emergent fashion as internal and external forces push the system to a state of far-from-equilibrium. At a far-from-equilibrium state, the system's current organization is pushed to its maximum capacity for processing and dissipating energy. When it is pushed beyond this boundary, the system recognizes that its current structure is not capable of handling the excess energy, and its components reorganize to a different configuration that is more capable of dissipating the energy in an efficient manner. The transition of water from solid to liquid to gas portrays these state changes. At a far-from-equilibrium state, small fluctuations may be responsible for pushing the system to another attractive point of behavior, at which point convergent forces once again dominate and bind the system to its new attractor

(Prigogine and Stengers, 1984). In essence, change via far-from-equilibrium is a special case of the change process discussed in the previous section, whereby changing the initial state condition or a parameter within the system induces qualitatively new behavior.

Goldstein (1998) states that self-organization is a "radical reorganization of the structure of a system; the spontaneous emergence of novel patterns and configurations; the amplification and incorporation of random events; the discovery of creative alternatives for functioning; and the arising of new coherence and coordination amongst the parts of the system." The environment does not change the system, and the system does not unilaterally change the environment; rather, the environment triggers internal mechanisms that are the source for transformation (Maturana and Varela, 1992).

How Change Occurs in Self-Organizing Systems

Self-organizing models state the condition for qualitative change, rather than the exact nature of how change occurs. In general, these models state that change occurs when the system is far from equilibrium. Organizational researchers in turn have hypothesized about how a social system can be brought, or find itself at a far-from-equilibrium state.

For example, crises are well known to trigger individual or organization change. Nonaka (1988) advocates purposeful creation of crises as a means to keep the organization flexible and constantly renewed. Total quality management and other actions that open the boundaries between a firm and its customers may also be seen as a means to enable far-from-equilibrium conditions to arise. Goldstein (1994) suggests several different means by which to facilitate a system toward far-from-equilibrium:

- Increase the connectivity of the system to its environment, as the increase in information (energy) will push the system off of equilibrium.
- Perform difference questioning (a method used in psychotherapy), where an individual's assumption base is challenged.
- Challenge individuals' assumptions in other ways through visualization of the system and other creative thinking techniques.
- Identify the "self-fulfilling prophecies" within the system that act as an attractor and break the

connections that maintain the recurrent pattern of behavior.

Olson and Eoyang (2001) present a general model of self-organization in social systems; in order for self-organization to occur, there needs to be a container (a boundary that defines what is inside and what is outside of the system, and that constrains interaction), differences that distinguish agents or elements within the system, and transforming exchanges. For example, in a project team, the norms of the group emerge in a self-organized fashion because of (a) boundaries that define the team as a real entity within the organizational system, creating "us and them," (b) differences that exist between team members, such as functional specialty or personality, and (c) exchanges (i.e., discourse) that move the cognitive states of the agents from one position to another. Olson and Eoyang thus posit that organizational change can be induced by changing containers, focusing on different differences, or changing the nature of exchange.

Example of a Self-Organizing Model of Organizational Change

Lichtenstein (2000) presents a model of self-organized change in the context of entrepreneurial activities. He challenges the standard convention that in social systems information is akin to energy and instead equates energy directly with the level of actual organizational activity. His model is composed of three stages (and is thus a life-cycle model). First, increased resources generate increased organizing. In this phase small increases in resources will be readily adapted to, but the organization will resist major change. As the gap between required and actual performance begins to strain because the original configuration of the system becomes suboptimal for handling a qualitatively different level of energy, tension develops and the system is pushed to the threshold of change. It is at this far-from-equilibrium state that a small change or perturbation to the organization—the departure or arrival of an individual, a comment made by someone, a performance measure that slightly slips—can induce significant changes in organizing. The third stage brings about the emergence of a new configuration, which is path dependent and yet novel, has increased capacity, and often possesses greater complexity (via interconnectedness between elements of the system) than the original configuration.

Conceptualizing Change

A single system can demonstrate how change may be conceptualized from these four different modeling perspectives. Consider the project management of a software development effort. The work of the project is accomplished by a team of software engineers, who report to a project manager. The team exists within the engineering function of an organization. We shall assume that the project has started and we are viewing this team (our system) in terms of what pattern of behavior is observed over time, and how it might change. The particular issue at hand is how the team collectively solves problems that arise in the coding of the software.

A researcher using a CAS model would build a simulation of the team with software engineers as agents. These agents would be have a goal (i.e., to minimize problems with the product while expending the least energy), and a schema to interpret the environment and other agents and to produce action. The schema may be "if-then" rules in the form of a genetic algorithm that tells the agents which solutions to try, and agents may be able to see a corresponding representation of the problem at hand. So within the computer, these agents are attempting to "recognize" the problem and then apply a solution that fits the problem. Individual agents could be constrained in how much of the problem they see, or how accurately they recognize the problem, and thus interconnections between agents could be used to assimilate communication and coordination. Agents would probably also be programmed to learn, over time, how to respond to problems more effectively by giving parts of their schema "credit" according to the quality of their attempted solutions. Some typical research questions that could be investigated by the model would include:

- What level of connectivity provides enough collaboration and collective learning and yet does not swamp the agents with communication tasks?
- How do agents learn to generalize so they can solve problems they have not seen before?
- Is it better to have many agents having the same deep skills (ability to recognize and solve one type of problem), have agents with different deep skills, or have agents with broad skills?

A researcher using a computational model might focus on the cascading of errors that occur when one problem is solved, but the change incurs other errors. A network model of the software code could be built, where each node represents a variable within the software and the connections between the nodes represent connections within the algorithms embedded in the software. For example, if the code were a spreadsheet, the nodes could represent cells in the spreadsheet with connections indicating cross-referencing between the cells. The researcher could then induce different magnitudes of change in different nodes and examine how those changes cascaded across the entire system.

A researcher might also examine the problem solving of the team from the perspective of Kauffman's landscape models. By examining the nature of the software and modeling it as a genomic configuration, the researcher estimates the number of genes and their average connectivity, using Kauffman's simulation results to examine how long it would take to solve all of the code's problems, whether the software should be fixed in incremental or holistic steps, and how often the team would stop at a solution that was suboptimal.

A researcher using dynamical models could take one of two approaches. First, he or she could collect empirical time series data from the actual team and analyze them using a variety of statistical methods, in order to determine whether periodic, chaotic, random, or pink noise patterns were present. Variables that might be observed could include number of errors found, and/or fixed, per day; amount of time between error corrections, number of e-mails between team members per day; or the number of lines of code written by the team per day. Such diagnosis might reveal periodic patterns of entrainment between the team and other "clocks and calendars" defining the organization and its environments, or indicative of self-organized routines, chaotic patterns demonstrating adherence to general patterns with novelty moment-to-moment, or random or pink noise patterns indicating the open nature of their system and the multitude of causes impacting the observed variables.

Second, the dynamical modeler may build a set of equations depicting the dynamics of the team and then simulate it to see what patterns emerge. The first step would be to identify key variables: number of defects discovered, number of defects remaining to be found, problem-solving capabilities, information load, resources, and so on. The next step would be to propose causal connections between these variables, typically in the form of differential equations, and then simulate the system as a whole. What might be found, for example, is that when the rate of new defects reaches a certain level, it overloads the team beyond its capacity to keep up with new problems and they shortchange normal problem solving methods, leading to inadequate solutions and yet more load.

A researcher using a self-organizing model to study change in the team would look for significant, qualitative changes in the way the team was organizing, and then look for the increased tension and the trigger that brought about that transformation. He or she would also examine the norms and routines of the team to see how they constrain the team from moving to a different pattern of behavior.

On the other hand, the project manager of the team, desiring to bring about changes in the team's behavior, might envision leverage points differently depending on what model the manager hand in mind. Viewing the system in a traditional non-complexity manner, the manager would likely ascertain the group's behavior to individual motivation and/or skill, and/or the resources and processes the team is working with, and suggest changes in process and/or structure, or seek to give team members incentives and disincentives to push to the desired behavior. If the manager viewed the team as a CAS, he or she would focus on the mental models of the software engineers, and the simple rules that led their interaction. If the manager viewed the team as computational, he or she might focus on the interconnectedness of the engineers, and components of the problem. If the manager viewed the team as chaotic, he or she might look for small changes to make that would have a large effect. Finally, if the manager viewed the team as self-organizing, he or she may seek ways to bring the team "far from equilibrium" in order to induce self-change.

What, then, do complexity science models have in common, in terms of how they conceptualize change? First, all models are dynamic—time is the most significant variable in all of the different models. Second, they are empirical. Either data are observed from a real system, or a system is simulated and data analyzed. Patterns in these data become the fodder for theorizing. Third, they generate behavioral patterns

that are emergent, inherently not deducible from the component parts. Fourth, they are practically useful only with the aid of a computer, to either simulate the system and/or detect patterns from observed data. Fifth, either explicitly within their component behaviors or implicitly through the coupling of components, the models depict behavior that is nonlinear, where changes in causes are not necessarily proportional to the corresponding changes in effects. Finally, these models depict change as having both divergent and convergent components (Van de Ven, Polley, Garud, and Venkataraman, 1999).

Future Challenges

Despite its apparent ability to generalize many of the more specific characteristics of models of organizational change, complexity science is still lacking in one important regard—it does not have theory or models that explicitly incorporate the most human of exchanges in a complex adaptive organization, namely, discourse. Without discourse, organizational systems would not exist, or at least they would not be very interesting. Discourse in the form of both conversation and text is the lifeblood of social systems (Boden, 1997). It is through discourse that organizational members coordinate their intentions, goals, and actions, but it is also through discourse that organizational members construct reality, define what is important and what is not, create alternatives, and create order amid confusion, ambiguity, uncertainty, and equivocality (Weick, 1995).

Simulations of complex adaptive systems treat discourse as a matter of message passing. While this may be adequate to model how agents coordinate with one another to perform unambiguous tasks, it is certainly not adequate to capture the richness of actual human discourse. Stacey (1999) recognized this and suggests that the application of CAS to human organizations is inappropriate, that instead we should develop a model of "complex responsive processes." In such a model, *memes* (elemental bits of ideas, culture, norms, etc.) take the place of humans as agents.

While this is a step in the right direction, there is a key problem—memes do not have agency. A meme may have a life of its own, but without a "human carrier" it cannot exist and persist. If one takes away the agency in a CAS, then one is left with a fairly static and boring system that can change only via

Lamarkian-type evolution. Clearly a more attractive answer is to develop a model of CAS that incorporates discourse as something that flows between agents. As such, discourse would be indicative of knowledge, perceptions, beliefs, values, intentions, and identity. These characteristics can be thought of as belonging to a single person, but it is primarily through discourse that they are enacted and made observable.

A basic premise of many theories and models of change in social systems is that if you change what you say, you can change what you do and what you believe in. This is perhaps the most basic strategy for change within individuals or groups of people, and it is a phenomenon that is still not captured adequately by complexity science. In order to incorporate discourse into a model, it must be explicitly represented in a way that is amenable to computation. Corman, Kuhn, McPhee, and Dooley (2002) created "centering resonance analysis" as a means to represent texts as networks. Discourse can then be modeled as the evolution of textual networks, which occurs as agents exchange texts and evolve new ones based on rules of recombination, mutation, and cloning (Dooley, Corman, McPhee, and Kuhn, 2003).

Even the explicit incorporation of discourse into complexity science models might not be enough. Researchers generally agree that the complexity observed in existing complexity science models, while novel and insightful, does not match the complexity we see in real living organisms and systems. It may be that a different form of mathematics, and thus causal reasoning, will be necessary to see what we're missing.

A final challenge that exists is disciplinary: in order for further discoveries to be made and new models to be developed, a critical mass of social scientists and organizational researchers must emerge. This is not simple, as these concepts are difficult to understand at first, and many require significant mathematical prowess to understand deeply. The typical methods that organizational researchers use for building and testing theory are for the most part inadequate at capturing complexity, as they do not easily enable the modeling of mutual causality, feedback, and nonlinearity.

The organizational research community first paid attention to models of self-organization, primarily because their employment required no mathematical skills per se, but rather was used metaphorically. CAS, computational, and certain dynamic models require expertise to develop and analyze computer-based simulation models. The presence of software packages like Stella and NetLogo make simulation more readily available to organizational researchers, but the methodological rigor of these studies is questionable (Dooley, 2002b). Conversely, inductive-base dynamical modeling requires significant statistical skills, and software tools are not readily available.

Perhaps most significantly, the concepts of complexity science sometimes call into question the validity of existing paradigms within the discipline of organizational theory and behavior. Thus adoption and diffusion of these models depends on their ability to provide superior explanatory power and to yield elegant and insightful theoretical conceptualizations.

Notes

1. Unless otherwise stated, agents represent individual people in this chapter.

2. These figures depict only a single variable landscape; in reality, the landscape is n-dimensional, where n is the number of elements in the systems that contribute to fitness. One can view the images as a cross-section of a higher dimensional landscape.

3. Technical descriptions of these phenomena can be found in Peitgen et al. (1992), Poole et al. (2000), and West and Deering (1995).

4. Many authors use the term *chaos* in many different ways; the definition used here refers to the mathematical rather than vernacular use of the term.

5. High-dimensional chaos is possible, but for all practical purposes high-dimensional chaos may be treated as white noise.

References

Anderson, P. (1999). Complexity theory and organization science. *Organization Science*, 10, 216–232.

Argyris, C. & Schon, D. (1978). *Organizational learning: A theory of action perspective*. Reading, MA: Addison-Wesley.

Arthur, W. B. (1994). On the evolution of complexity. In G. A. Cowen, D. Pines, & D. Meltzer (Eds.), *Complexity: Metaphors, models, and reality*. New York: Addison-Wesley.

Axtell, R. (1999). *The emergence of firms in a population of agents*. Santa Fe Institute, paper no. 99-03-019.

Bak, P. (1996). *How nature works*. New York: Springer-Verlag.

Boden, D. (1997). Temporal frames: Time and talk in organizations. *Time and Society*, 6, 5–33.

Burt, R. S. (1992). *Structural holes: The social structure of competition*. Cambridge, MA: Harvard University Press.

Corman, S., Kuhn, T., McPhee, R., & Dooley, K. (2002). Studying complex discursive systems: Centering resonance analysis of organizational communication. *Human Communication Research, 28*, 157–206.

Deming, W. E. (1986). *Out of the crisis*. Cambridge, MA: MIT-CAES.

Dooley, K. (1997). A complex adaptive systems model of organization change. *Nonlinear Dynamics, Psychology, and Life Sciences, 1*, 69–97.

Dooley, K. (2002a). Organizational complexity. In M. Warner (Ed.), *International encyclopedia of business and management* (pp. 5013–5022). London: Thompson Learning.

Dooley, K. (2002b). Simulation research methods. In J. Joel Baum (Ed.), *Companion to organizations* (pp. 829–848). London: Blackwell.

Dooley, K. & Van de Ven, A. (1999). Explaining complex organizational dynamics. *Organization Science, 10*, 358–372.

Dooley, K., Corman, S., McPhee, R., & Kuhn, T. (2003). Modeling high-resolution broadband discourse in complex adaptive systems. *Nonlinear Dynamics, Psychology, and Life Sciences, 7*, 61–86.

Eisenhardt, K. & Brown, S. (2000, February). Patching: Restitching business portfolios in dynamic markets. *Harvard Business Review*.

Feichtinger, G. & Kopel, M. (1993). Chaos in nonlinear dynamical systems exemplified by an R&D model. *European Journal of Operations Research, 68*, 145–159.

Forrester, J. (1961). *Industrial dynamics*. Cambridge, MA: Productivity Press.

Gell-Mann, M. (1994). *The quark and the jaguar*. New York: Freeman & Co.

Goldstein, J. (1994). *The unshackled organization*. Portland, OR: Productivity Press.

Goldstein, J. (1998). Glossary. In B. Zimmerman, C. Lindberg, & P. Plsek (Eds.), *Edgeware* (p. 270). Irving, TX: VHA.

Guastello, S. (1995). *Chaos, catastrophe, and human affairs*. Mahwah, NJ: Erlbaum.

Guastello, S. (2002). *Managing emergent phenomena*. Mahwah, NJ: Erlbaum.

Holland, J. H. (1995). *Hidden order*. Reading, MA: Addison-Wesley.

Institute of Medicine (2001). *Crossing the quality chasm*. Washington: National Academy of Sciences.

Jaffe, D. & Scott, C. (1998). Reengineering in practice: Where are the people? Where is the learning? *Journal of Applied Behavioral Science, 34*, 250–267.

Jantsch, E. (1980). *The self-organizing universe*. Oxford: Pergamon Press.

Kauffman, S. (1995). *At home in the universe*. Oxford: Oxford University Press.

Khandwalla, P. (1977). *The design of organizations*. New York: Harcourt Brace Jovanovich.

Krackhardt, D. & Carley, K. (1998). A PCANS model of structure in organizations. In *Proceedings of the 1998 international symposium on command andcontrol research and technology*, June, Monterrey, CA.

Lewin, R. (1992). *Complexity: Life at the edge of chaos*. New York: Macmillan.

Leydesdorff, L. & Van den Besselaar, O. (Eds.) (1994). *Evolutionary economics and chaos theory*. New York: St. Martin's Press.

Lichtenstein, B. (2000). Self-organized transitions: A pattern amid the chaos of transformative change. *Academy of Management Executive, 14*, 128–142.

March, J. G. (1994). *A primer on decision-making*. New York: Free Press.

Maturana, H. & Varela, F. (1992). *The tree of knowledge*. Boston: Shambhala.

McKelvey, B. (1997). Quasi-natural organization science. *Organization Science, 8*, 351–380.

Meyer, M. & Lehnerd, A. (1997). *The power of product platforms*. New York: Free Press.

Minsky, M. (1986). *Society of mind*. New York: Simon & Schuster.

Nagel, K. & Paczuski, M. (1995). Emergent traffic jams. *Physical Review E, 51*, 2909–2918.

Nonaka, I. (1988). Creating organizational order out of chaos: Self-renewal in Japanese firms. *California Management Review, 30*, 57–73.

Olson, E. & Eoyang. G. (2001). *Facilitating organizational change: Lessons from complexity science*. New York: John Wiley and Sons.

Peitgen, H.-O., Jurgens, H., & Saupe, D. (1992). *Chaos and fractals: New frontiers of science*. New York: Springer-Verlag.

Poole, M., Van de Ven, A., Dooley, K., & Holmes, M. (2000). *Organizational change and innovation processes: Theory and methods for research*. New York: Oxford Press.

Prigogine, I. & Stengers, I. (1984). *Order out of chaos*. New York: Bantam Books.

Rogers, E. (1995). *The diffusion of innovations*. New York: Free Press.

Ruhla, C. (1992). *The physics of chance*. Oxford: Oxford University Press.

Schelling, T. (1978). *Micromotives and macrobehavior*. New York: W. W. Norton and Company.

Schroeder, M. (1991). *Fractals, chaos, power laws*. New York: Freeman.

Scott, W. R. (1995). *Institutions and organizations.* Thousand Oaks, CA: Sage.

Senge, P. (1990). *The fifth discipline.* New York: Doubleday.

Simon, H. (1957). *Administrative behavior.* New York: MacMillan.

Stacey, R. (1992). *Managing the unknowable.* San Franciso: Jossey-Bass.

Stacey, R. (1999). *Strategic management and organizational dynamics.* London: Prentice-Hall.

Sterman, J. (2000). *Business dynamics: Systems thinking and modeling for a complex world.* New York: Irwin.

Sull, D. & Eisenhardt, K. (2001, January). Strategy as simple rules. *Harvard Business Review.*

Van de Ven, A. H. & Poole, M. S. (1995). Explaining development and change in organizations. *Academy of Management Review, 20,* 510–540.

Van de Ven, A. H., Polley, D., Garud, R., & Venkataraman, S. (1999). *The innovation journey.* New York: Oxford University Press.

Waldrop, M. M. (1992). *Complexity: The emerging science at the edge of chaos.* New York: Simon and Schuster.

Weick, K. (1979). *The social psychology of organization.* New York: Random House.

West, B. & Deering, B. (1995). *The lure of modern science.* Singapore: World Scientific.

Wolfram, S. (2002). *A new kind of science.* Champaign, IL: Wolfram Press.

13

Theories of Organizational Change and Innovation Processes

Marshall Scott Poole & Andrew H. Van de Ven

The jacket of this book shows a man peeping through the shell of the stars and planets to discern the glorious order behind their complex movements. What he sees is not a simple clockwork, but a dazzling manifold of spirits and mechanisms that realize the will of these spirits. Sometimes the order beneath complexity—while more illuminating than the surface—is itself complex and difficult to understand. Our challenge is to sort out the images in this illumination, to discern the shadows and gradations that give it form.

This handbook highlights an amazing variety of approaches to explaining organizational change and development, including stage models, evolutionary processes, interacting archetypes, dialectical tensions and contradictions, environmental jolts, institutional analysis, multilevel systems models, and complexity theory. In several cases two or more of these generative mechanisms are combined. Theories and models are cast at several different levels of analysis and some crosslevels. But even these complicated formulations sometimes seem to oversimplify and invite the development of even more complex theories. How are we to make sense of this multiplicity

of theoretical possibilities? The goal of this chapter is to provide a general framework for addressing this question by extending our earlier typology of change theories (Van de Ven and Poole, 1995; Poole and Van de Ven, 1989/2001).

Instead of attempting to stipulate one theory as the best theory of change or to derive a single broad integrative theory of change, we believe it more productive to consider a range of theories and models that can be applied to understanding change and innovation. As Popper (1962) argued, science is most likely to advance when a variety of theories and perspectives are in play. In some cases these will be competing alternatives, as Popper envisioned, while in others they will be compatible and even complementary.

Explanations of change processes in organizations must often span more than one level of analysis, involve multiple actors or perspectives, and incorporate dynamic generative mechanisms. They must also take into account characteristics of organizational change such as its path dependence, the powerful influence that a single critical event often has on the direction and impacts of change, and the role of human agency in molding change according to plans or implicit models. Hence, theories of organizational change and innovation tend to be complex, often combining several different generative mechanisms. The challenge in developing such theories is that most approaches to building theories and most social scientific methods are designed for simplification and parsimony. We must grant that simple ideas are often powerful and useful. However, an emphasis on simplicity tends to foster satisfaction with incomplete understanding and a sort of resigned acceptance of partial theories that may be pleasing to students and practitioners, yet fail to capture important aspects of change.

The chapters of this handbook attempt to move past an oversimplified, insufficient picture of organizational change and innovation. They conceptualize complex phenomena such as the inherent tensions in planned change efforts, the coevolution of organizational populations and communities, the complicated process of individual change that organizations require as they change, institutional change, and change in complex systems with varying levels of interdependence. They challenge us to increase the complexity of our thinking. If the resulting theories or research agendas seem complicated and in some cases unwieldy, then we would suggest that it is because we have become habituated to simplicity.

The fields that social science takes as models— physics, biology, chemistry, engineering—have long recognized that the relatively simple models of Newton, Lavoisier, and Darwin overlay complexities that must be theorized if science is to accurately reflect the workings of the world. Indeed, the field that we believe most apt as a model for organizational research, biology, is presently engaged in perhaps the greatest explosion of "complexification," as theory and research on genetic and biochemical bases of biology and behavior continue to develop at a breathless pace. We believe it is incumbent on scholars to also acknowledge and address the complexity of organizational change and innovation.

While fields like biology and physics have developed robust approaches to complex phenomena, this has just begun in organizational studies (and in the social sciences in general). This trend is illustrated by discussions of complexity theory (Anderson, 1999; Dooley, 2002; Olson and Eoyang, 2001; Poole, Van de Ven, Dooley, and Holmes, 2000), system dynamics (Sterman, 2000), and evolutionary dynamics (Baum

and McKelvey, 1999), and earlier it was developed by followers of systems theory (Katz and Kahn, 1978; Miller, 1978). It is also evident in the chapters of this handbook.

In previous papers (Van de Ven and Poole, 1995; Poole and Van de Ven, 1989/2001) we presented a foundation for theorizing about complex processes of organizational change and innovation. We identified four distinct process theories: life-cycle, teleology, dialectic, and evolution. Each of these theories relies on a different generative mechanism, or motor, that drives the change process. Complex change processes are generated by the interaction of more than one of these process theories. Indeed, very few applied theories of change, development, or innovation are built around a single ideal-type theory as defined in Van de Ven and Poole (1995). Most involve two or more theories operating together, at different levels, or during different time periods. In our earlier papers we ventured some suggestions on how motors of different types might fit together in complex process theories. In this chapter we attempt to extend our framework by specifying more completely how composite theories of change can be built by aggregating the interactions of change motors that may operate at different organizational levels, temporal intervals, and degrees of interdependence. We believe the resulting framework encompasses the manifold explanations of change offered in this volume.

The next section provides a background summary of our initial framework that was advanced in Van de Ven and Poole (1995) and Poole and Van de Ven (1989/2001) and discusses variations of each ideal type theory. In section three we turn to the unfinished business in our previous versions and examine interactions among the change theories. We discuss how motors at different levels may interact, the forms interactions among motors may take, and temporal parameters that govern interactions among motors. We then break down two theories from this book, representing them in terms of the simpler theories in the framework. This analysis also suggests aspects of the two theories that might be developed further.

One premise that we should make clear at the outset is that organizational change and innovation are best captured by process theories (see also chapter 1 of this volume). Mohr (1982) distinguished process theories, which focus on explaining how changes unfold over time via the path of events they follow, from variance theories, which focus on explanations in terms of causal relations among variables. Mohr's original conceptualization can be broadened by recognizing that a more general concept—a theoretical narrative—underlies process explanations (Abbott, 1990, 1992). This narrative incorporates final and formal causation, in addition to the efficient causation emphasized by variance theories. In a detailed analysis of the process approach as applied to organizational change and innovation, Poole et al. (2000) noted several advantages of process theory: (1) it gives a deep understanding of how change comes about by describing the generative mechanism that drives the process; (2) it can account for path dependence and the role of critical events in change and innovation; and (3) it can incorporate the role of human agency in change without reducing it to causal terms.

An Expanded Typology of Theories of Change and Innovation

Figure 13.1 illustrates the four ideal type theories defined by Van de Ven and Poole (1995). As the cells of this figure illustrate, each theory views the process

of development as unfolding in a fundamentally different progression of change events, and as governed by a different generative mechanism or motor. As table 13.1 outlines, the theories can also be distinguished in terms of: (1) whether the end state of the process can be predicted from the outset, (2) if the path of development is predetermined, (3) if the process is convergent or divergent, and (4) if time is based on events or cycles. Variations of each of the basic theories will also be discussed.

Life-Cycle Process Theory (Regulated Change)

A life-cycle model depicts the process of change in an entity as progressing through a necessary sequence of stages or phases. The specific content of these stages or phases is prescribed and regulated by an institutional, natural, or logical program prefigured at the beginning of the cycle.

A life-cycle motor drives change through realizing a form or pattern that is either immanent in the developing entity or imposed on it by external institutions. Examples of life-cycle theories include Bales's

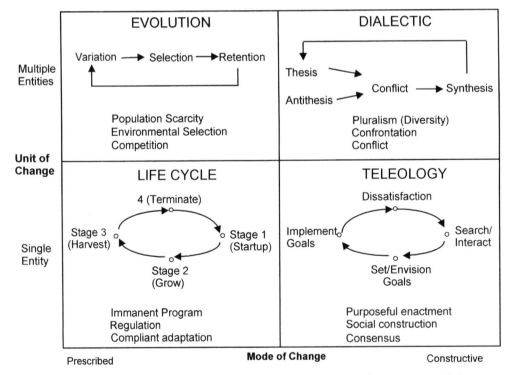

Figure 13.1 Typology of theories of change and innovation. Note: Arrows on lines represent likely sequences among events, not causation between events. *Source*: Van de Ven and Poole (1995).

Table 13.1 Comparison of four ideal type theories of organizational change

Characteristic	Theory			
	Life-Cycle	Teleological	Dialectical	VSR
Generative mechanism	regulated	planned	conflict	competition
Process of change	set sequence of stages; full sequence has initiation, growth, decline, termination stages	unit perceives problem or opportunity, sets goals, acts to achieve goals, monitors outcomes	unit changes through coping with or due to effects of conflicts tensions, or contradictions	unit changes through random or planned variation, which are then selected by environmental pressures; effective variations are retained in the unit
Is the end state of the change process defined at the outset?	yes; final point in sequence	yes; by the goal	no; end state emerges from process	no; end state emerges from process
Is the path of development predetermined?	yes	no	no	no
Change process	convergent	divergent	divergent	convergent
Concept of time	cyclical	event	event	cyclical
Variants of basic theory	logical; natural; institutional	intentional; sensemaking	Hegelian; paradoxical	Darwinian/Lamarkian/ Mendelian/Gould

(Bales and Strodtbeck, 1951) model of group problem solving, Cameron and Whetten's (1983) organizational life cycle, and Greiner's (1972) model of organizational growth. The goal and end point of the change process is defined from the start for a life cycle through a natural or logical developmental progression or through institutionally prescribed rules or regulations. In Bales's model, the stages of problem solving are logically required, while Tushman and Moore (1982) argue that stage transitions are driven by changes in industry structure following the product life cycle. The developmental path of the life cycle is deterministic; there are one or a few paths that the developing unit can follow, generally defined in terms of a set of stages of development.

Change in a life-cycle theory tends to be morphogenic, involving the progression from one stage to the next as the unit develops. While there may be continuous development within stages in a life-cycle theory, transitions from stage to stage involve a qualitative change in the unit and sometimes in the nature of the developmental process itself. As the name implies, time for a life-cycle theory is cyclic: life-cycle models are comprised of repeating milestones that take the unit from inception to demise or fulfillment.

Once the end of the cycle has been attained, the process is set to commence anew, with either the same or a different entity.

A life cycle requires convergence in the developing unit. There may be conflict or divergence within stages, and conflict may also trigger transitions between stages, but the unit as a whole undergoes the changes associated with the life cycle and the ultimate result of a life cycle is a completed unit. For example, in Greiner's (1972) model of organizational growth, crises arise within each stage that trigger responses which move the organization to the next stage. Early growth through creativity, for instance, results in a crisis that requires the emergence of a strong leader with a vision for the organization; when this leader emerges, the organization enters a stage of growth through direction. This progression occurs through crisis, but the organization as an entity is undergoing change.

There are three variations of life-cycle theory, depending on whether the generative mechanism is regulated by natural, logical, or institutional requirements. Sequences driven by natural or logical requirements exert a stronger determinism on the developing unit than do those driven by institutional norms or rules. Natural and logical life cycles exert strong influence on the process, because later stages in the sequence depend on and are defined in terms of accomplishments in earlier stages. In some cases later stages in these two variants literally cannot occur without the completion of earlier stages. For example, later stages in a person's life cannot occur without earlier ones—we cannot have the onset of young adulthood without having gone through the physical, mental, and psychological changes of adolescence. The reinstitutionalization stage of the institutional change model presented by Hinings, Greenwood, Reay, and Suddaby in this book cannot occur unless the deinstitutionalization stage has occurred. Deinstitutionalization is logically prior to reinstitutionalization. In contrast, an institutional life cycle is defined by socially constructed rules and norms (see Van de Ven and Hargrave, chapter 9), which ultimately depend on the authority or power of some social institution external to the process. For example, in the United States the approval process for new medicines must conform to a regulatory procedure set up by the Food and Drug Administration. This process is designed to be logical and incremental, but steps may be changed as the law and administrative procedures change, and it is even possible that in exceptional cases administrators may waive steps or requirements. As a result, institutional life cycles are less stringent in shaping organizational change processes.

Natural life and logical life cycles are adapted to different phenomena. Logical life cycles are found in processes governing intangibles such as the development of ideas, decisions, and cultures or changes in language and symbols in an organization. Natural life cycles are more pertinent for tangible phenomena that are grounded in space and time, such as the life cycle of organizations (which are grounded in their facilities, industries, markets, and personnel) or the growth of infrastructure. In the case of natural life cycles, current structure and function form the foundation for later structure and function. In the case of logical life cycles, the form or purpose of the idea or symbolic construction defines the trajectory of changes.

Teleological Process Theory (Intentional Change)

A teleological process views development as a cycle of goal formulation, implementation, evaluation, and modification of actions or goals based on what was learned or intended by the entity. This sequence emerges through the purposeful enactment or social construction of an envisioned end state among individuals within the entity.

Examples of teleological change theories can be found in the theories of epigenesis (Etzioni, 1963), adaptive learning (March and Olsen, 1976), and most models of strategic planning and decision-making (Chakravarthy and Lorange, 1991; Mintzberg, Raisinghani, and Theoret, 1976; Nutt, 1984). In a teleological theory of change, setting a goal in response to a perceived problem or opportunity puts the process in motion. The unit is assumed to be purposeful and adaptive; by itself or in interaction with others, it constructs an envisioned end state, takes action to reach it, and monitors its progress. Thus, teleological theories view development as a repetitive sequence of goal formulation, implementation, evaluation, and modification of goals based on what was learned or intended by the unit.

The theory can operate in a single unit or among a group of cooperating units who are sufficiently likeminded to act as a single collective unit. Because teleological processes are goal driven, the developmental path followed by the unit is not predetermined, but is generated by activities necessary to achieve the goal. Since there are many ways to meet any given goal, multiple paths are possible and there is no present sequence of stages or steps. While a number of teleological theories define steps or stages, there are multiple paths through these steps, and the path is determined by exigencies that arise during the process as problems to be solved by the developing unit.

In Mintzberg et al.'s (1976) model of strategic decision making, for example, management must recognize problems or opportunities, develop a diagnosis of the situation, come up with a solution, satisfy stakeholders, and gain authorization. Ten distinct activities contribute to producing the five prerequisites, and decision makers engage in many different sequences and combinations of these activities, depending on internal and external exigencies. Nor is there a particular order in which the prerequisites are addressed. In one instance a diagnosis will guide solution generation and choice, while in another a solution option may prove so persuasive that the decision makers redefine the problem and diagnosis to fit it. The process is oriented toward achieving the prerequisites of a good decision "by hook or crook" and without a necessary sequence of activities.

Teleological theories presuppose event-based time. Mintzberg et al.'s model provides a good illustration. The unit's purpose and strategy are enacted in a series of events whose significance stems from their contribution to the overall pattern that emerges during the activities. Finally, teleological theories, like life-cycle theories, emphasize convergence. For change to occur, the unit must be guided by a unifying goal that lends coherence to its activities. When the unit is comprised of multiple entities, they must agree to a goal and collective action for a teleological motor to hold.

In the teleological family, processes with intentional planning and post-hoc rationalization can be distinguished. Proactive processes seem to be the most natural model for teleology for most U.S. social scientists, in view of the common emphasis on the classical conception of rationality in the economic and decision making traditions. However, while processes may unfold in an anticipated manner, sometimes reason operates after the fact (March, 1994). In such cases, agents rearrange the process as they make sense of what is happening (Weick, 1995). As the process unfolds, their understanding of it changes and they act according to their emerging sense of the situation; their actions form the basis for future interpretations that in turn reestablish the grounds for action. In the case of such sense-making processes, the "plan" emerges post hoc, refashioned according to formal patterns or intentions. Mintzberg has labeled this "emergent strategy." For example, Scottish knitware manufacturers who employed labor intensive handwork rather than highly capitalized factories gradually articulated a strategy that focused on "selling premium quality expensive garments through specialist distribution channels to a limited number of high income consumers" (Porac, Thomas, and Baden-Fuller, 1989, p. 409). The strategy was not consciously planned but emerged as manufacturers struggled to find a market niche in the face of fierce competition. However, the strategy has the hallmarks of intention and purpose once it emerges, and it shapes subsequent activity as through it were carefully set out from the beginning.

Dialectical Process Theory (Conflictual Change)

In dialectical models of development, conflicts emerge between entities espousing an opposing thesis and antithesis that collide to produce a synthesis, which in time becomes the thesis for the next cycle of a dialectical progression. Confrontation and conflict between opposing entities generate this dialectical cycle.

Change emerges from a dialectical motor through efforts to deal with contradictions, conflicts, or tensions within or around the unit. Exemplary dialectical theories of change include Marx's (1954) theory of economic development and its many variants, Smith and Berg's (1987) theory of paradoxes in group life, and Sztompka's (1993) theory of social change. The tensions and oppositions that Seo, Putnam, and Bartunek (chapter 4 of this volume) discuss in planned theories of change also trigger dialectical processes of change.

In dialectical theories, unlike life-cycle theories, the goal or endpoint of a change process is not clear at the beginning but emerges from the dialectical process. In some cases change is driven by the conflict or contradiction itself. For example, in Marx's theory, each new economic era emerges due to the conflict between thesis and antithesis. Capitalism emerged due to the contradiction between feudal economic organization and the growing forces of production, driven by scientific discoveries such as the steam engine and clock. The nature and structure of capitalist economic organization retained shadows of feudalism (a hierarchy of power, for one thing, but this time those at the top were capitalists and not hereditary nobility), but also wholly new characteristics (concentration of workers in factories and cities). In other cases, change results from the attempts of the unit to resolve the conflict or tension and mitigate its negative effects. Smith and Berg (1987) posit that groups sometime deal with the tension between individual identity and the desire to be part of a collective by emphasizing one pole over the other. One group might overemphasize loyalty and conformity, while another might put up with less cohesiveness and focus on allowing members to express their individualism. How the group deals with the tension sets the course of change in the group.

The developmental path of dialectically driven change is not predetermined. Units react to and cope with conflicts, contradictions, and tensions in many different ways, and the resulting path will vary greatly from case to case. While basic moments of the dialectical process can be distinguished at a conceptual level—for example, thesis, antithesis, synthesis—often they are intertwined and can be sorted out only at the end of the change process. A group confronting the individualism-collectivism tension may immediately converge on a coping strategy (e.g., emphasize one pole over the other) or it may shuttle from one strategy to another in an attempt to deal with the inevitable negative consequences of any specific coping mechanism. Though facing the same dialectical tension, the paths of the two groups will differ considerably, and there is literally no way to project ahead of time the shape or form of the developmental path.

Premised as they are on conflict, contradiction, and tension, dialectical theories emphasize divergence. Difference and the conflicts and struggles it spawns is at the heart of dialectical explanations of change. Dialectical theories, like teleological theories, incorporate an event-based conception of time. The dialectic is driven by tensions and contradictions, whose occurrence at irregular intervals mark the significant points in the process.

Two variants of dialectical change theory can be distinguished: (1) the Hegelian conflict-based process of thesis, antithesis, and synthesis and (2) a Bakhtinian process of tension-based dialectics.

Conflict dialectics operate through the emergence of an antithesis in response to a thesis and the resolution of the ensuing conflict in a synthesis. While a new cycle may begin within the achieved synthesis, the synthesis represents a temporary resolution of the conflict or contradiction. For example, the conflict between the interests of workers and those of management in a corporation in financial difficulty might be conceptualized in the following terms: the worker's position emerges as an antithesis to the typical managerially controlled firm (thesis) and a common resolution is for the workers to buy out management, hence becoming their own management (synthesis). The synthesis is comprised of elements from both thesis and antithesis and represents a stable point in the change process (at least temporarily). The movement through the Hegelian dialectic is often resisted by the unit; it may try to ignore, suppress, or counteract the antithesis, and movement often occurs only after a considerable period of conflict. An important part of the change and innovation "story" for the Hegelian dialectic is the resistance and conflict that accompanies the movement through the phases, for they may set up dynamics that create the next dialectical process.

A prominent alternative to the Hegelian dialectic is the tension dialectic (Bakhtin, 1981; Werner and

Baxter, 1994), which proposes that rather than developing through a thesis-antithesis-synthesis pattern, the dialectic plays itself out in a never-ending series of tensions between dualisms such as integration-differentiation. Each side of the dualism requires the other to exist, and there is a constant interplay between the two. Opposing terms mutually imply each other, exist through their opposition, and always remain at work as potential sources of change. As the chapter by Seo, Putnam, and Bartunek discusses, multiple tensions exist simultaneously; such as pressures for integration-differentiation, internal focus–external focus, and interdependence-independence. Change is shaped by how the unit deals with the dialectic and the problems, challenges, and conflicts it spawns. Baxter and Montgomery (Werner and Baxter, 1994) define seven possible responses to tensions and contradictions, including: (a) denial—ignoring the tension; (b) spiraling inversion—attending to one side of the tension, then to the other, then to the first again, and so on; (c) segmentation—using different parts or aspects of the unit to relate to the two poles of the tension; (d) balance, which attempts to engage both poles but reduce the pressure from each; (e) integration, which actively engages with both poles; (f) recalibration—reframing the situation so that the poles are no longer in opposition; and (g) reaffirmation—acknowledging both poles and actively incorporating both into the unit.

Evolutionary Process Theory (Competitive Change)

An evolutionary model of development consists of a repetitive sequence of variation, selection, and retention events among entities in a designated population. This evolutionary cycle is generated by competition for scarce environmental resources between entities inhabiting a population.

The evolutionary motor drives change through the core process of variation-selection-retention (VSR). In this familiar explanation, variations in existing unit characteristics occur, and those that enable the unit to compete for scarce resources in the environment are selected for survival. Surviving units spawn others like them and retain the "blueprint" for the competitive survival in the population. The VSR explanation operates at the level of the individual unit or organism and is the micro-level process by which populations of a species evolve and eventually prosper or are extinguished. Examples of theories with VSR components are Weick's (1979) theory of organizing, Aldrich's (1979, 1999) theory of organizational ecology, and Usher's (1954) cumulative synthesis model of strategic invention. While biology provided the original idea for evolution, groups, organizations, and societies are clearly different from organisms, and special assumptions have to be made about social evolution (see Baum and Rao, this volume; Baum and McKelvey, 1999). Evolutionary theorists tend to be indifferent to the source of variation; it may be produced by "blind" random or purposive events (Campbell, 1974). Selection may be driven by external environmental forces, but it may also be exercised through actor's choices. Retention may be accomplished through naturally evolved mechanisms, but it may also be carried out in specially constructed structures such as databases created for knowledge management.

In evolutionary theory, the occurrence of variations during competitive selection, and retention cannot be projected ahead of time, because of shifting competitive pressures for scarce resources in the environment. Hence, the unit's path for an evolutionary motor is weakly predetermined: one or more cycles of variation-selection-retention will occur, but the number of cycles and the specific activity paths through these cycles are not determinate. Evolutionary theory is divergent in that it emphasizes variation as the source of change. To survive the evolutionary process, variations must render the unit a better fit both internally and within its current environment, enacting a break with prior forms. Finally, evolutionary theory incorporates a cyclical view of time whose metric is defined by the three stages, successively reiterating as the entities evolve.

Alternative theories of social evolution can be distinguished in terms of how traits are inherited and the unit of analysis.[1] These variations reflect the differing perspectives of their pioneering scholars: Darwin, Lamarck, Mendel, and Gould. Organizational scholars who adopt a Darwinian view of evolution (e.g., Hannan and Freeman, 1977, 1989; McKelvey, 1982) argue that traits are inherited through intergenerational processes, whereas those who follow a Lamarckian view (e.g., Burgelman, 1991; Singh and Lumsden, 1990) argue that traits can also be acquired within a generation through learning and imitation. Darwinian organizational evolutionists argue that variations or novel organizational forms are deter-

mined and imprinted at birth and do not change throughout the duration of an organization's life, due to organizational inertia. In contrast, those who adopt a Lamarckian perspective argue that organizations learn and acquire novel variations at different times throughout their life span. Today, most organizational scholars have adopted the Lamarckian view on the acquisition of traits.[2]

Much of the research by population ecologists has used organizational birth and death rates as proxy measures of an organizational generation and examined the proposition that organizational death rates should decline monotonically with age after a brief period of growth in organizational density (see reviews in Baum, 1996, and Hannan, Carroll, Dundon, and Torres, 1995). Organizational births, often measured as the entrance of newly incorporated firms into a population, are assumed to be the carriers of either retained ancestral forms or newly selected organizational variations. Organizational deaths, often measured by legal firm dissolutions—including organizational mergers, acquisitions, and name changes—are assumed to be the carriers of organizational forms selected out by the environment that are becoming extinct.

Measuring the birth and death rates of an organizational form provides useful information about the diffusion of the form in an organizational population, but it does not capture *how* that organizational form emerged and evolved historically across generations. Organizational scholars who adopt a Mendelian genetics perspective of evolution point out that new forms of organizations are often the hybrid products of diverse ancestral forms of organizational arrangements (McKelvey, 1982; Baum and Singh, 1994; Van de Ven and Grazman, 2000). They argue that new generations of organizational forms are often (but not always) produced by events that couple or recombine preexisting organizational resources, competencies, and arrangements either to create a new organizational form or to extend an ancestral form.

The ancestral resources that are recombined to create these new generations can exist either within or outside of the subject organization. Internal organizational growth occurs when ancestral forms are situated within organizations. Commonplace examples are internal investments or recombinations of existing units, resources, or competencies that create or renovate an organization's programs, products, services, or routines. External growth occurs by combining resources and components from different organizations through, for example, organizational mergers, acquisitions, strategic affiliations, and joint ventures. Since the ancestral forms that are crossed to produce new forms are often nested in complex networks of interdependent hierarchies within and between organizations, their recombinations often generate new hybrid forms of organization. Study of these alternative ways to recombine ancestral organizational forms to create new ones requires tracing the genealogical lineage of organizational arrangements from their ancestral forms to the present. A *genealogy* is a record of descent or lineage of a group from its ancestors. As McKelvey (1982) suggested, in comparison to studying organizational birth and death rates, a genealogical study may better capture how organizational forms are created, modified, and reproduced through the coupling, union, or interaction of their progenitors in a population.

Another factor that distinguishes evolutionary theories is level of analysis. Gould and Eldridge (1977), Arnold and Fristrup (1982), and Gould (1989) point out that classical Darwinism locates the sorting of evolutionary change at the level of the unitary organism. This sorting is natural selection operating through the differential births and deaths of individual organisms, as exemplified by many population ecology studies of organizational birth and death rates. Gould's punctuated equilibrium model adds a hierarchical dimension to evolutionary theory by distinguishing *sorting* (the growth or decline of organisms of a given species) from *speciation* (the process by which new species or groups are formed). This multilevel view of evolution will be important as we explore inter-level relationships among change motors later in this chapter.

Practical Implications

While the typology was designed primarily as an aid to theory development, it also has a practical side. In particular, it suggests implementation errors that may occur in change processes for each of the motors. Teleological processes of planned change are subject to individual cognitive biases (Kahneman, Slovic, and Tversky, 1982)—errors in critical thinking and decision making (Nutt, 2002), escalating commitments to failing courses of action (Ross and Staw, 1986), and groupthink (Janis, 1989). Dialec-

tical processes of change often fail due to dysfunctional methods of conflict resolution and negotiation (Bazerman, 1985). The chapters by Hinings, Greenwood, Reay, and Suddaby and by Seo, Putnam, and Bartunek discussed how regulated changes in institutional life-cycle models are often resisted, resulting in sabotage of or mere compliance with mandates, rather than internalizing them. Finally, the chapter by Baum and Rao points out that evolutionary processes of variation, selection, and retention work only under conditions of competition for scarce resources; they break down when resources are munificent and competition is low. To study these implementation errors it is useful to build on the distinction between theories of change and theories of changing (Bennis, 1966, discussed in chapter 4 of this volume). Our four theories of change attempt to answer the question of how and why change occurs. Theories of changing focus on implementation questions, that is, how a change process is implemented and guided in constructive directions.

Utility of the Framework

This framework has several useful functions. First, it describes process theories in relatively simple, abstract terms, offering a way to untangle complicated theories of development into component motors. The four ideal type motors serve as theoretical primitives, and the complexities of the developmental process can be analyzed as interplays among these primitives.

Second, the four basic theories can be used as standards to evaluate the form, completeness, and tightness of specific developmental theories. When theories are developed for a specific context, such as new product innovation, they are tailored to the phenomenon. However, theories built from the ground up sometimes have missing components not suggested by study of a particular phenomenon, but which are necessary for a well-formed, complete explanation. For example, a surprising number of phasic theories of development do not clearly specify what motivates or causes transitions from one phase to another. However, the description of the life-cycle motor indicates that this is a vital component of this generative mechanism, and would suggest that this must be specified for a particular phase theory to be complete. The four motors delineate the necessary parts of an adequate explanation, providing standards for constructing and evaluating theories of change and development.

Third, the framework supports inductive research by spelling out the characteristics of the four motors and the conditions under which they are likely to operate. Rather than relying on preconceptions of which theory is best, researchers can apply tests for the four motors in order to see which fit the complex phenomenon being examined. This helps to prevent the self-fulfilling prophecies that may occur when we expect a certain number of stages of development or a certain process; it is too easy to find evidence in complex processes for whatever we expect, and ignore other motors (Poole, 1981).

Finally, the framework offers insights into the relationships among diverse explanations of organizational change and development. As this book shows, a wide variety of theories have been advanced, many borrowed from disciplines such as biology and human development. The diversity of theories and concepts borrowed from different disciplines has often encouraged compartmentalization of perspectives that do not enrich each other and produce isolated lines of research (Gioia and Pitre, 1990). Any single theoretical perspective invariably offers only a partial account of a complex phenomenon. As discussed in the next section, it is the interplay between different perspectives that helps researchers gain a more comprehensive understanding. The typology can be used to uncover similarities in seemingly different theories and to highlight the "differences that make a difference" in explanations. This makes it possible to discern commonality among a broad range of specific theories that might otherwise be overlooked.

Complex Theories of Organizational Change and Innovation

Most observed processes of organizational change, development, and innovation are more complicated than the ideal types. One reason for this is that organizational change and innovation unfold across space and time, as discussed in chapter 1. As a result, more than one motor may come into play in any particular case. Organizational development and change are influenced by diverse units and actors, both inside and outside the organization. Their spatial dispersion means that different influences may be acting simultaneously on different parts of the organization, each

imparting its own particular momentum to the change process. For example, in a study of product development effort, Van de Ven and Garud (1993) found that a teleological process explained the course of development in the firm's R&D lab. In the regulatory affairs department, which focused on FDA approval of the product, a life-cycle model corresponding to the steps in the approval process governed activity. These two different motors interacted as product development progressed. As the product progressed, yet another motor was operating in the larger field of the health care industry, an evolutionary process. The firm's pioneering product design was initially supported by the researchers, but evidence mounted that led most researchers and clinicians to switch allegiance to a competing firm's design, thus "selecting out" the product. Motors may also vary in strength as a process unfolds. As time passes, there is opportunity for different motors to come into play, especially given the spatial dispersion of influences. As the product studied by Van de Van and Garud matured, the life-cycle motor governing regulatory approval became dominant, overshadowing the teleological process and entraining it to the stepwise approval process. The resulting observed process is multilayered and complex, and to adequately capture it a theory must incorporate more than one motor.

Organizational change and innovation processes are also complex due to the inherent incompleteness of any single motor. Each of the motors pictured in figure 13.1 has one or more components that are determined exogenous to the model. For example, in the evolutionary model variations are assumed to arise randomly, but the process that gives rise to variation is left unspecified. In the dialectical model, the origin of thesis and antithesis is not accounted for, nor is the source of dissatisfaction in the teleological model, and the processes that launch start-up and conclude termination in the life-cycle model. The exogenous inputs to each model can be found in other models. For instance, the selection process in the evolutionary model can terminate the life cycle, and the implementation step in the teleological cycle can trigger the start-up step in the life cycle and the antithesis in the dialectic. The synthesis in the dialectic could be the source of variation in the evolutionary cycle. There are other possibilities whereby other models may complement the incompleteness of any single model of change.

Granting the likelihood that many theories of change and innovation will incorporate more than one motor, we will now consider the types of interactions among the motors. Throughout the subsequent discussion we will draw on and try to put into perspective the theories and ideas advanced in previous chapters.

Building Composite Theories by Combining Motors

A good composite theory of change or innovation specifies clearly and completely where the different motors fit—the spatial and temporal spheres within which they operate and the nature and degree of influence they have on each other. Three key aspects can be distinguished. First, we address different types of interlevel relationships. Organizations are multilevel phenomena, and theories of organizational change or innovation must consider how processes at different levels affect each other. The most common assumption is hierarchical relationships in which higher levels encapsulate and set the parameters for lower level processes. However, this is only one of three types of interlevel relationships that we will discuss. Second, we discuss the form relationships among motors may take, both across and within levels. While positive and negative linear relationships are the most common, recent work on complexity theory and nonlinear systems theory suggests that other more complex relationships may often hold. Finally, we consider the time scales at which different motors operate and how motors with different time scales relate to one another.

We should note that the motors in a composite theory may be of either the same or different types. A common approach in recent ecological models of organizational change is to describe the change process in terms of nested evolutionary motors (e.g., Van de Ven and Grazman, 1999). In such models the same logic applies at different levels of analysis, and relationships among motors are often depicted as one process feeding a similar process at a higher level and one process shaping a similar process at a lower level. However, things can be more complicated than this. Van de Ven and Poole (1995) discuss several examples of theories that incorporate different types of motors, some at different levels of analysis and others operating on the same level. The issue in this case is how motors operating under different generative

mechanisms mesh together. As the following discussion illustrates, this too can occur in many different ways.

Relationships among Motors at Different Levels

Most studies of organizational change have focused on a single level of analysis. However, most organizational units are situated in a multilevel system—individuals within departments within organizations within industries or communities within nation-states or cultures. In some cases the units are nested within a hierarchy such that they are interdependent, and so also is change in a unit at a given level dependent on changes in units at higher and lower levels. In other cases different levels operate more independently, but still influence each other. While a multilevel model of change has been acknowledged as useful in *describing* organizational life, it has yet to be widely incorporated into *explanations* of organizational change. As a result, we know relatively little about how or why change processes in one level facilitate or constrain change at other levels of a hierarchy or series.

Meyer, Goes, and Brooks (1993) provide an insightful account of how their research design, reflecting good contemporary theory, was unable to adequately measure or explain the hyperturbulent changes experienced by hospital organizations and the industry during the 1980s in the San Francisco Bay Area. They concluded that "the most pressing need was to develop a broader framework for thinking about organizational change; . . . [one that examines] the *mode* of change [our four motors of change] and the level at which it occurs (organization or industry)" (p. 71). In terms of social evolutionary theory, Baum and Singh (1994) and Miner (1994) have also called for an expansion of the theory to include study of the processes of variation, selection, and retention between different levels of organizational entities.

If organizational change is a multilevel phenomenon, and motors are likely to operate on different levels of analysis, then what types of cross-level relationships might there be? We can distinguish *nested*, *entangled*, and *aggregated* motors.

Motors are *nested* when a lower-order motor is tightly linked with the higher-order motor, serving functions at the lower level that connect directly with the operation of the higher-level motor. For example, a life-cycle or teleological motor may describe the actions of individuals that participate in the VSR process in an evolutionary motor. In this case, the lower-level motor models the actors that go to make up the evolutionary process in a way that is compatible with the higher-level process. However, the functions performed by a nested motor need not be positive or supportive; they merely need to help drive the higher-level motor. Greiner's (1972) model of organizational development posits a life cycle of creativity, direction, delegation, coordination, and collaboration. Each of these stages culminates in a different dialectical crisis (of leadership, autonomy, control, red tape, and "?"), which propels the organization into the next stage of growth. These crises are produced by struggles among individuals who are attempting to deal with organizational problems. The conflict process undermines the stage by precipitating a crisis that advances the process.

In the nested hierarchical structure of individuals within organizations within populations or industries, the organization itself represents but a single level of analysis, both encompassing and encompassed by other levels. Organizations are viewed as evolving systems nested in other coevolving systems at higher (e.g., industry or population) and nesting lower (e.g., work groups or individual managers) levels of analysis, as described by Baum and Rao in chapter 8. At the higher, community level of analysis, Astley (1985) described how multiple populations of organizations also go through their own variation, selection, and retention processes as they coevolve with lower-level organizational and management changes, as well as more macro technological and social developments, as illustrated in Schumpeterian cycles of creative destruction. The development of an explanatory role for hierarchical structure in evolutionary theory represents a vibrant vein of research in evolutionary biology (see, for example Arnold and Fristrup, 1982; Buss, 1987; Gould, 1982; Gould and Eldridge, 1977).

This multilevel view of evolution is important for understanding how selection and adaptation can occur at multiple levels. At any focal level, selection focuses on the evolutionary process of choosing or shifting between new branches (i.e., variations or speciations), while adaptation is the class of heritable characters that have a positive influence on the fitness of an entity within a constraining situation—that is, on extending the persistence of a branch that is chosen. So selection assumes branching in a lineage, while adaptation assumes fitting or adjusting within a

selected branch. Arnold and Fristrup (1982) go on to argue that branching and persistence are the essential components of fitness at all levels. Branching indicates variation or speciation rates, while persistence indicates the fitness (or extinction rates) of entities in selected branches.

While hierarchical relationships are attractive because of their order and elegance, other types of cross-level relationships also occur. Motors are *entangled* when lower and higher order motors influence each other but are not tightly linked into a single, coherent process. In this case the motors operate independently to some degree. In contrast to nested motors, which have tight coupling, entangled motors are moderately or loosely coupled. As a result, the motors run their own courses and interact with each other, but are not "in synch" to the extent nested motors are. For example, a teleological model of a planned change in an organization may be premised on development of a common mission shared by individuals (Bryson, 1988). However, these same individuals develop along their own life course and may experience the tension between inclusion and independence as the organization attempts to get them to hew to the common mission (Putnam and Stohl, 1996). These tensions may lead some individuals to choose to "opt out" of the organization by devoting their energy to other parts of their lives. In this case, individual-level processes may undermine organizational-level processes or they may promote them, depending on how the individual processes intersect with the stages of the life cycle (Moreland and Levine, 1988). In turn, the organizational life cycle affects individuals' lives because it is one, though not the only, factor in their worlds. The two processes—individual and organizational—have their own integrity, and each influences the other.

There is "slippage" in the relationships of entangled motors. The influence of a motor at one level on a motor at a different level is mediated by the process through which the motors engage each other. The nature of this process filters interlevel impacts and affects the strength and manner of influence. Depending on the process, interlevel influence may be strong or weak and may also change over time. As the examples illustrate, hierarchical relationships typically involve tight couplings whereby the interlock of motors is clear. In biological models, the genetic material offers a common boundary object on which the process can operate from several levels. In organizational versions of evolutionary theory, the analogue of genetic material has been difficult to identify, but Van de Ven and Grazman (1999) suggest that organizational form (defined in terms of dimensions such as mission, authority structure, technology, and market) is the basic stuff of organizational evolution (see also Baum and Rao in this volume). They posit that aspects of forms are borrowed, recombined, and created in the process of organizational evolution, resulting in a genealogy of organizational forms. Entangled motors do not have this common ground of operation. Instead, it is necessary to specify a process independent of the motors themselves that connects the entangled motors.

To continue the example of individual participation in organizational change efforts, the individual and organizational levels are connected by the process that governs the degree of investment individuals have in the higher-level entity. Individuals are members of many higher-order units—families, voluntary associations, friendship networks, and the focal organization—and because they have limited attention and energy to devote to these units, individuals must make choices about where they will invest their time and energy (Putnam and Stohl, 1996). Factors that affect this allocation process include the motivation the higher-level unit offers compared to other units, the individual's needs, and whether a transformational leader has emerged in the organization. The connecting process affects the nature and strength of interlevel influence. For example, a strong leader with a clear vision for change may galvanize individual energy around the change and draw it away from other units, resulting in a convergence of individuals around the change effort. This would show up as a strong interlevel influence. The nature and strength of influence may also change over time as the connecting process changes. If the leader is discredited, we would expect the strength of the connection to wane as individuals reallocate their energy to other agendas. This would show up as a decline in interlevel influence or perhaps even as a disconnect between levels.

It is more difficult to theorize entangled motors than hierarchies or the aggregated motors we will discuss next. Moreland and Levine's (1988) model of individual socialization into groups provides a good example. They offer a convincing picture of how individuals are shaped by groups and in turn influence the group. However, Moreland and Levine con-

fine themselves to the case of single members and do not devote much attention to membership configurations or interactions among members. The complexity that this would add to the Moreland-Levine theory is daunting and it is often difficult to even conceive of how such connections could be modeled. However, that something is difficult does not mean it is impossible, and we hope that future theorists will turn their attention to questions such as this. Entangled motors are probably much more common than the existing literature would suggest. Their very difficulty may have discouraged researchers from conceptualizing them or encouraged them to force fit them into the hierarchical mold.

Aggregated motors, the third type, represent the case where a process on a higher level emerges from or is constituted by an aggregation of lower-level processes. In this case, a higher-level process is constituted by a collective of interdependent lower-level processes. Collective action models, in which rational action by a group of individuals leads to a change in a social structure or collectivity, are a well-developed example of aggregated motors (Coleman, 1990). Whereas nested motors are tightly coupled and entangled motors are moderately coupled; in aggregated motors the higher-level process is strongly dependent on the lower-level motors. However, rather than a linkage or coupling, the higher-level process literally is the combination of the lower-level motors. The different forms of combination determine different types of higher-order processes.

Theories of social action by Arrow (1970) and Coleman (1973, 1986, 1990) offer one view of how aggregation could occur. Basically, their approach assumes individuals can act but organizations cannot. It attempts to specify models by which individual actions can combine to create collective outcomes at the organizational level. These system-level outcomes may, in turn, impose constraints on individual (Coleman, 1986, p. 1312). Coleman (1990) argues that a fully specified macro-micro system must consist of three types of propositions indicated in table 13.2: (1) a proposition indicating how the higher level influences the lower level, which consists of an independent variable characterizing society and a dependent variable characterizing the individual; (2) a proposition indicating how one characteristic of the lower level influences another characteristic on the same level, in which both independent and dependent variables characterize the individual; and (3) a

Table 13.2 A chain of three linked propositions showing how macrolevel effects result from microlevel mediation.

Proposition Type	Examples
1. Macrolevel cause to microlevel effect	Improved social conditions cause lower class individuals to realize that their lives could get better and this heightens their frustration at current conditions
2. Microlevel cause to microlevel effect	Frustration of lower class individuals causes them to behave aggressively toward upper class individuals
3. Microlevel effects aggregate to lead to macrolevel effect	Aggressive behavior by individuals drives revolution in the society

proposition indicating how the lower level influences the higher level, which consists of an independent variable characterizing the individual and a dependent variable characterizing society. This third proposition, which marks the micro-macro transition, is not a simple effect of a *single* individual on society, but rather is a combined or aggregate effect of multiple individuals that is shaped by the nature of interdependence among them. The first proposition, which marks the macro-micro transition, also hinges on the nature of interdependence among individuals. Coleman conceives of these two components as "the rules of the game, rules which transmit consequences of an individual's action to other individuals and rules which derive macro-level outcomes from combinations of individuals' actions" (Coleman, 1990, p. 19).

Coleman (1990) discusses a number of forms of interdependence among individual interests, which lead to different types of social organizations. He gives three examples of such organizations in his 1986 article: A *pure market* is a configuration in which there are "independent actors, each with differing private interests and goals and each with resources that can aid others' realization of interests. The actions that purposive actors will engage in when this configuration of interests and resources exists is social exchange, and when a number of these exchange processes are interdependent, we describe the whole set as a market institution" (Coleman, 1986, p. 1324). A *hierarchy* is a set of relations "in which one actor's actions are carried out under the control of another and advance the other's interests." The associated institution is the formal organization or authority structure (pp. 1324–1325). A *federation* (our term) is a set of independent actors linked by common interests. They are connected by a constitution embodying a set of norms regarding rights and obligations (Coleman, 1986, p. 1326).

Each type of interdependence and associated organizational scheme has different formats for combining individual interests and actions into collective action and macrostructural outcomes.

While individuals are assumed to be the prime movers behind any organizational activity, Coleman's approach allows for several different kinds of macro-level actors (Coleman, 1990, pp. 12–13). In some cases, the macro level is most appropriately conceived as the behavior of a system of actors whose actions are interdependent. In other cases, the system is sufficiently coherent that its behavior can be regarded as the behavior of a "supraindividual" actor, such as an organization. And in still other cases,

no unitary actor emerges at the macro level, but there are well-defined properties or concepts characterizing that level. The determination of price in an economic market is an example which illustrates this case well. The micro-level actors are the individual traders and the price of each good gives the exchange rate ... for that good when there is equilibrium, that is, when no additional trades will take place beyond those already arranged. The relative prices of two goods as a concept characterizing the market as a whole ... is an abstraction made possible by the fact that market competition compresses the various exchange rates for the same pair of goods among different trading partners toward a single rate, as each trader attempts to get the best exchange possible for the good or goods that the trader holds. (p. 13)

Aggregated motors enable researchers to directly address the issue of how macro-level phenomena such as organizations or communities are constituted. Both nested and entangled motors presume the existence of the two levels without questioning how one or both come into being.

Forms of Relationships among Motors

Regardless of what level relationships are on, we can distinguish several different forms that they may take. In our earlier paper (Van de Ven and Poole, 1995; for a summary see chapter 1), we discussed how combinations of the motors create, in effect, hybrid change theories capable of capturing the complexity of change and innovation processes. The simplest type of combination is to determine which of the generating mechanisms underlying the four ideal types are in operation in the organizational change process. By specifying the presence (operation) or absence (non operation) of the four motors in a given situation, we can define an array of sixteen logically possible explanations of organizational change and development. This array, shown in table 13.3, is analogous to examining the simple main and interaction effects of each of the four motors on alternative applied theories in the management literature.

The first four alternatives represent the "main effects" of the generating mechanisms, "single-motor theories" that apply to cases when only one of the four generating mechanisms or change motors is in operation. The remaining twelve alternatives represent "interaction effects" of the interdependent operation of two or more of the four generative mechanisms. Alternatives 5 through 10 represent cases when only two of the four change motors are in operation. Alternatives 11 through 14 are "tri-motor theories," when three of the four change motors operate interdependently. Alternative 15 is the most complex situation, when all of the four generating mechanisms operate interdependently in a given situation. Examples of several of these motors and examples are discussed in Van de Ven and Poole (1995), Poole et al. (2000), and chapter 1.

These sixteen logical combinations represent *direct* relationships among the four motors, where one or more motors immediately influences another. For example, in Greiner's organizational development model, the maturation of a given stage of development fosters the emergence of crises. For sake of clarity, a direct relationship should be defined as unidirectional. Recursive relationships among motors are comprised of two direct relationships, one from

Table 13.3 Logically possible theories of organizational change and development

	Interplays Among Generating Mechanisms			
	Imminent Program	Purposeful Enactment	Conflict & Synthesis	Competitive Selection
1. Life-cycle	yes	no	no	no
2. Teleology	no	yes	no	no
3. Dialectics	no	no	yes	no
4. Evolution	no	no	no	yes
Dual-motor theories				
5. Design hierarchy theory (Clark, 1985)	yes	yes	no	no
6. Group conflict (Simmel, 1908; Coser, 1958)	no	yes	yes	no
7. Community and population ecologies (Astley, 1985)	no	no	yes	yes
8. Adaptation-selection models (Aldrich, 1979)	yes	no	no	yes
9. Org. growth and crisis stages (Greiner, 1972)	yes	no	yes	no
10. Org. punctuated equilibrium (Tushman and Romanelli, 1985)	no	yes	no	yes
Tri-motor theories				
11. Partisan mutual adjustment (Lindblom, 1965)	yes	yes	yes	no
12. ?	no	yes	yes	yes
13. ?	yes	no	yes	yes
14. Social psychology of organizing (Weick, 1979)	yes	yes	no	yes
Quad-motor theories				
15. Human development progressions (Riegel, 1976)	yes	yes	yes	yes
16. ?—Garbage can (Cohen, March, and Olsen, 1972)	no	no	no	no

Source: Adapted from Van de Ven and Poole (1995).

motor A to motor B and a second from motor B to motor A. Continuing our example of Greiner's model, the crises fostered by the maturing stage advance the organization to its next stage of development. Hence there is a recursive influence of stages on crises and crises on stages.

In addition to these direct relationships, there may also be *indirect* relationships between motors when there is another process that mediates the relationship between them. In some cases, motors are linked not by the direct action of one on another, but because they operate in the same context or environment and therefore are subject to the same external influences or because they are linked by the action of a third process. Motors operating in the same context are coordinated by external forces and so may act in concert. The life cycles of organizations operating in a poor economy, for example, will be shaped by negative economic events and hence will exhibit similar patterns. Motors linked by a third process may influence each other, but that influence is filtered, dampened, or sometimes even amplified by the intervening process.

The types of direct relationships are well known and include *reinforcing* (positive), *dampening* (negative), and *complex* (nonlinear). Direct relationships are fairly straightforward when considered individually, but they become less easy to fathom when three or more motors are linked in a system. In such a case, even if all have reinforcing relationships, the cumulative impact may be nonlinear. Chapter 12 discusses several different approaches to modeling nonlinear relationships among motors. Multiple interlinked motors may also give rise to indirect relationships in which one motor mediates the effect of another. This type of relationship has been widely discussed in the literature on causal modeling as indirect effects (Bollen, 1989).

Motors that operate across levels also add complexity, because the same motor may have different types of direct relationships on different levels, for example, a positive effect at one level and a negative effect at another. Organization and management strategy scholars have tended to draw attention to the harmony of functional alignment between organizational levels, but we cannot expect all units to have similar effects at all levels in the hierarchy. For example, a selfish or opportunistic top manager may select strategies and clone successors that extend the persistence of his or her leadership regime, at the expense of decreasing the fitness of the structural form of the encompassing organization. So also, overspecialization of organizational units increases short-term advantages of selected units at the aggregate organizational or industry disadvantage of limiting variations for adaptation and innovation.

In addition to mediated causal relationships, there are also two other notable types of indirect relationships among motors. *Entrainment* occurs when motors at the same or different levels operate independently but come into coordination due to an external pacing factor (see chapter 3). In one common example, teleological motors of individual group members become entrained in terms of their pace of work and orientation to time by working on a common task with a characteristic pace. In this case, the task is the external pacing factor; other common pacing factors for individuals are diurnal cycles and pheromones, while for organizations, the calendar and government mandates are examples of pacing factors.

A *cyclical* relationship among motors occurs when two or more motors alternate in their impact on the change process. This alternation is choreographed by a factor or process that determines the relative weight given to the motors as a function of time. For example, in the sociological theory of morphogenesis (Buckley, 1967), action and structure alternately dominate social processes in a cycle: initially active processes undermine current social structures and then commence to build up new ones, but at a certain point the new structures become constraints on action and a period of structural inertia ensues until new actions can undermine structures and start the cycle anew. In this case, the cycle between the predominance of action and structure respectively is governed by an evolutionary process that determines the rate at which possible changes are introduced and accepted by the system (a VSR motor). This process determines the rate of the cycle and its regularity, as well as the particular direction in which the social system develops. An effective system would have relatively short cycles with fairly equal action and structure phases, which would enable it to respond effectively to changes in its external environment. A less regular system might on the one hand exhibit longer phases of structural dominance, indicative of a system resistant to change, or on the other, longer phases of action dominance, indicative of disorganization and anomie. The pace and regularity of the evolutionary process is influenced by the balance between the openness of the social system to change and the degree of stability of relationships and institutions in the social system. Buckley notes, "a sociocultural system with high adaptive potential, or integration as we might call it, requires some optimum level of both stability and flexibility" (1967, p. 206). He discusses several elements of complex adaptive systems that promote a good balance of stability and flexibility, including maintenance of an optimal level of tension for change, yet satisfaction of individual needs; a full communication network that provides adequate linkage of system components and feedback; a self-reflective selection system; and effective mechanisms for retention.

Terms commonly used in theories of change and innovation such as "influences," "causes," "generates," or "leads to" seem to be fairly specific. However, as this section indicates, much ambiguity remains as to the form of relationship they refer to. The various forms discussed in this section, both direct and indirect, offer a "vocabulary" for theory building that focuses on the verbs in our theories in addition to the nouns—constructs—that are often the main concern. The models discussed by Dooley in chapter 12 offer a still more precise means of specifying theories of change and development, when our thinking gets to that level of sophistication.

Temporal Relationships among Motors

The interplay of motors depends also on issues of timing. Motors may operate with quite different temporal cadences, and the relationships among cadences shape interactions among motors.

Poole et al. (2000) argued that the generality of a process explanation depended on its versatility, "the degree to which it can encompass a broad domain of developmental patterns without modification of its essential character" (p. 43). For a versatile model, the same change process applies to different cases, regardless of timing; for example, a group's development may take a few days or it may take years, yet the group may work through the same stages (Lacoursiere, 1980). Hence, the most general process theories are developed without reference to actual timing. However, in composite theories timing must be considered, because it determines how motors interact. At least four temporal characteristics of change and innovation processes can be distinguished.

First, processes may vary in terms of their *temporal velocity*, how quickly the change process progresses. The same organizational life cycle, for example, may be completed in two months or two years. The first case clearly speeds the development process much more than the second. Processes may also vary in terms of *duration*, how long a process takes, controlling for velocity. Two life cycles with the same velocity of moving through their phases differ in duration if one is composed of three phases and the other of eight. Third, processes may vary in terms of their *acceleration*, whether and the degree to which their velocity changes. Some processes may accelerate or decelerate as they progress, while others maintain a constant pace. Finally, processes may differ in their *temporal orientation*, the degree to which past, present, and/or future influence the process. Usually temporal orientation is due to the focus of human agents in the change and innovation process, as they often highlight the past or future as they act. For example, organizations making strategy may be driven primarily by past defeats or victories, or alternatively by visions of future gains or threats. In each case the change process takes on a different coloration.

When motors with different temporal properties interact, the intersection of these properties should be taken into account in specifying relationships among them. However, these relationships are often complex, and we have not been able to work out reliable rules for inducing them a priori. For instance, it is often the case that higher-level processes have longer duration and slower velocity than lower-level processes. In a nested hierarchy, we would expect to see a greater number of changes to occur in lower-level units because changes at these lower levels are less complex, smaller in magnitude, and entail a shorter time scale to complete. Since time scales associated with these changes are far shorter for subunits than for higher-level units on average, the rate of adaptation and evolution at micro-levels tends to exceed that at macro-levels (Arnold and Fristrup, 1982). However, there are also cases that run in the opposite direction. An individual's life cycle, for example, is usually longer and develops at a slower pace than a work group's life cycle, though the individual is nested within the group. Composite theories are best developed in response to the exigencies of specific cases rather than according to general rules.

Some Examples

To illustrate the application of the concepts developed in this review, we will consider a couple of the more ambitious theories in this volume, Baum and Rao's multilevel theory of population and community coevolution and Hatch's theory of organizational culture change.

Figures 8.1 and 8.2 in chapter 8 diagram the relationships in Baum and Rao's theory. They are reproduced here for reference. They adopt a *Lamarckian* evolutionary stance that assumes that in addition to random variation, organizations and their members learn and engage in planned entrepreneurial activity that generates within-generation variations in response to contextual demands. The variations are selected during interactions within the ecological hierarchy and retained within the genealogical hierarchy.

Cross-level influence runs downward in the ecological hierarchy, with each level nested in the one above (job, work group, organization, population, community). Changes in the higher-level concepts that occur through various forms of competition and through community disruptions influence lower-level concepts directly. The closing of a factory, for instance, immediately eliminates its work groups, but it does not necessarily change the population of like organizations materially. Since levels are nested, there are also indirect relationships between levels mediated by intervening levels. Influence may also jump a level in the hierarchy in the Baum and Rao model. It is unclear how this occurs based on their description; the changes seem to be nested as well: change in the community affects an organization directly.

However, as the arrows in figures 13.2 and 13.3 indicate, cross-level relationships in the genealogical hierarchy run both upward and downward in the

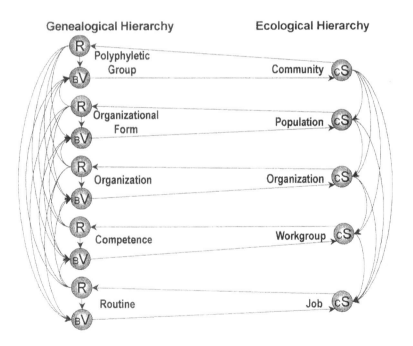

BV = **(Blind) Variation**

CS = **(Competitive) Selection**

R = **Retention**

Figure 13.2 Multilevel VSR.

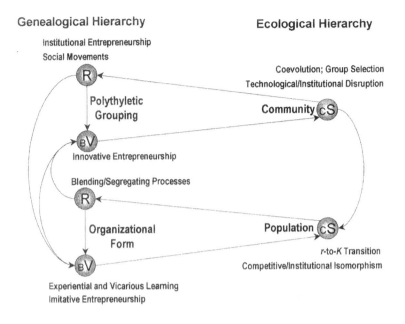

BV = **(Blind) Variation**

CS = **(Competitive) Selection**

R = **Retention**

Figure 13.3 Micro-macro evolutionary interactions.

hierarchy. Upward influences in genealogical hierarchies come through the influence of retention on variation. Downward influence comes through the influence of variations at one level on those at another and through the influence of higher-level retention on lower-level variation. Just as with the ecological hierarchy, downward relationships are nested in that change in higher-level elements constrains lower-level elements. There are both direct relationships and relationships that are mediated downward.

Baum and Rao's analysis is somewhat ambiguous on the nature of the upward relationships in the genealogical hierarchy. In some cases this may be aggregate, in that a change in enough units at the lower level will translate into a change on the higher level. However, an entangled relationship seems more consistent with Baum and Rao's description:

The lower-level VSR process produces a variation that happens to be successful. This "seed" is taken into the higher-level VSR process to be eliminated or to prosper, depending on the particular dynamics of the higher-level process and the associated community selection process. While the process at each level can be described as VSR, the specific means by which this occurs differs from level to level, thereby suggesting that the VSR motor is not wholly synchronized and well coupled across levels. Hence, the different VSR processes are better regarded as entangled with respect to upward change.

In terms of temporal properties of the change process, velocity and duration tend to increase as one moves down the hierarchy. Groups generally change more rapidly than organizations do, and organizations more rapidly than populations or communities. The Baum and Rao model makes no reference to the possibility of acceleration, and it would be interesting to consider pacers for evolutionary processes. In recent years, some biologists have argued that human intervention is speeding up biological evolution. There may well be factors—human or not—that change the pace of population and community evolution. Finally, temporal orientation is also not given much attention in this model. For the most part, evolutionary theory is present oriented, but the fact that organizations learn and their members may consciously plan changes also implies that a future orientation may also exist.

Overall, Baum and Rao's model is fairly well specified in terms of relationships and temporal properties, but our analysis suggests some points that might be clarified. The model advances a large set of constructs, and interactions among them are quite complex, so it is not surprising that additional detail is required.

Hatch advances a four-process model that explains both stability and change in culture. As shown in figure 13.4, she focuses on the relationships among four elements of culture: values, assumptions, interpretations, and symbols (three of these were originally defined by Schein, 1992). The relationship between values and assumptions is termed *manifestation*, whereby deep assumptions are connected with values and changes in values can alter deeper assumptions. Manifestation constitutes expectations of "how things should be" in a culture. Through the realization relationship, values influence the creation of artifacts, and artifacts may reshape values (as the American flag has reshaped the meaning of patriotism in the United States over the years). This makes values real to the members of the culture by moving them into objects that the members encounter regularly. In symbolization, artifacts become symbols and symbols influence the form of artifacts. Symbolization involves active meaning creation by members of the culture. And in interpretation, symbols are read in terms of basic assumptions and basic assumptions in turn may be slowly reshaped by symbols. Through these four processes, values, assumptions, symbols, and meanings are constantly adjusted and culture is stabilized or changed.

By moving the focus away from the terms themselves and onto the relationships among them, Hatch created a dynamic theory of culture change. She describes the dynamics in terms of two interconnected "wheels" of the four processes, one moving forward from assumptions to values to artifacts to symbols and finally returning to assumptions (the prospective wheel) and the other moving backward from symbols to artifacts to values to assumptions and finally symbols (the retrospective wheel). "A truly dynamic appreciation of culture is found in the counteraction of the two wheels" (Hatch, 1993, p. 686). Hatch's model can be captured with a dialectical motor in which the two wheels and the terms within them are caught in tensions that require constant adjustments. These tensions are in part represented by the poles of objectivity and subjectivity and of proactive and reflexive modes of action, as Hatch discusses. There are also more complex tensions involved, such as the tension between a symbol, which tends to achieve a life of its own, and the interpretive processes that are always seeking to "rein in" the symbol by assigning a limited meaning to it.

A teleological motor operates on the micro-level in Hatch's model as well, because members of the

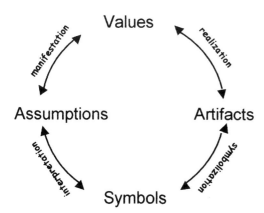

Figure 13.4 Hatch's model of cultural dynamics.

culture carry out the operations that constitute the processes. Both proactive and retrospective agencies are included in Hatch's view, represented by the two wheels. The link between the microlevel teleological motor and the macrolevel dialectic is not specified at present. It seems most likely that the motors and the component processes within them operate in entangled mode: due to the impact a single creative or influential individual may have on the four processes, aggregation does not seem to be a viable mechanism. The form of relationship is cyclic, as constituted by the wheels. The nature of the cycle also needs to be described in more detail; Hatch does not discuss the particulars of how the wheels operate as a whole, focusing instead on relationships between pairs of the parts. With the cyclic form comes a view of time as cyclic, but beyond this issues of velocity, acceleration, or orientation are not discussed. Certainly the social construction of time within the culture will in part set temporal parameters such as velocity. This implies that the dominant cultural view of time discussed in chapter 1 is most appropriate for Hatch's theory.

These examples illustrate how our framework can be employed to analyze and understand complex theories of change and innovation. This not only allows us to understand the theory better, but also suggests aspects that could be added to make the theory more complete.

As with all exercises in interpretation, alternative readings can be offered. For example, the long tradition of evolutionary theories of culture described in chapter 7 suggests that the wheels of Hatch's theory might be interpreted as operating through VSR processes rather than dialectical tensions. Our view is that the dialectic better captures the interactions of the four processes, which are in constant tension, than the VSR cycle, which presumes atomic components in competition. A life-cycle motor has obvious applications to the cycles in Hatch's model as well. Our view is that the dialectic offers an explanation of how and why cultures remain stable or change, whereas a stage theory would only describe movement through the cycles. To explain movement through the phases in a manner consistent with Hatch's discussion of her model requires a generative mechanism built on tension and systemic adjustment. A stagewise developmental process based on immanent programs in the culture is not as consistent with Hatch's description. These brief comments, however, are not sufficient to establish which com-

bination of motors best represents Hatch's model. A lengthier discussion and debate would be required.

Translating theories into the well-specified terms of this framework enables us to think through how the relationships in a theory operate. It may also divulge gaps in the theory and may surface contradictions that have inadvertently been incorporated. Notwithstanding, there is little doubt that this framework itself is incomplete. Applying it to the analysis of other theories will assist in further development.

Summary

Developing specific explanations of change or innovation in terms of composite theories means working out the relationships among motors across levels and time scales. And it is not just at the level of theory that relationships should be specified. Empirical research, too, should be aimed at identifying relationships among models and at testing hypothesized relationships. In recent years considerable progress has been made in research on multilevel relationships (Klein and Koslowski, 2000). Temporal issues have also received increasing attention, though how to approach issues of timing and temporal relationships is less clear (see chapter 1). Applying these insights and methods to change and innovation processes will raise a whole set of questions for future research to address and should lead to further advances.

We will conclude this section by raising an even more complicated possibility: Relationships among motors themselves may also change over time. In this case, we would need to have a theory of change in the change processes, as discussed by Hernes (1976). This may be the ultimate goal of dynamic theories of organizations.

Conclusion

We began this chapter with a hymn to complexity. We believe it is crucial that our theories rise to the challenge of organizational change and innovation processes. This means that we must meet complexity head on, acknowledging it and building commensurate theories. Complexity theory offers one way to do this in its view of phenomena as comprised of multiple interacting agents. The framework advanced in this chapter offers a similar view, but in this case the agents are simple theories of change that interact to produce complex patterns of change and innovation. Our theories are rather more complex than the agents of complexity theory, which typically are fairly simple programs that execute a few operations. The motors also interact with one another in a more complex fashion than the simple agents of complexity theory. However, just as unexpected results may emerge from agent-based models, so the interaction of multiple motors can produce complexities commonly found in change and innovation processes.

In concluding, let us return to our scholar peeping through the shell of stars and planets to discern the glorious order behind their complex movements. His challenge is to appreciate this order, which at times seems confusing and perhaps even threatening. A natural human tendency is to project oneself onto this backdrop, to assume that our "clear and discrete ideas" offer adequate understanding and that ultimately everything can be reduced to a few simple and powerful concepts and models. It is, however, becoming more and more evident that simple blinding insights are simply that—blinding. To appreciate the subtle complexities of change and innovation processes, we need to bring subtle tools to bear and avoid force-fitting our simple theories onto them. This means somehow achieving a degree of comfort with complicated theories. We offer this framework as one lens for discerning order in chaos.

But it would also be a mistake to complicate our thinking simply for the sake of complexity. There is a deceptive joy in finding connections and weaving webs of thought that ultimately tangle us and collapse of their own weight. Within the search for the sources of complexity there must also be an impulse toward the fundamental, toward simplicity. It is through the dialectic between simplification and complexification that our understanding of change and innovation processes will ultimately advance.

Notes

1. Van de Ven and Poole (1995) point out that another distinction often made between social evolutionary theories is whether change proceeds gradually and incrementally or rapidly and abruptly. Social Darwinian theorists emphasize a continuous and gradual process of evolution. In *The Origin of Species*, Darwin (1936, p. 361) wrote, "as natural selection acts solely by accumulating slight, successive, favourable variations, it can

produce no great or sudden modifications; it can act only by short and slow steps." Other evolutionists posit a saltational theory of evolution, such as punctuated equilibrium (Gould and Eldridge, 1977; Arnold and Fristrup, 1982), which Gersick (1991) introduced to the management literature. Whether evolutionary change proceeds at gradual versus saltational rates is an empirical matter, for the rate of change does not fundamentally alter the theory of evolution—at least as it has been adopted thus far by organization and management scholars.

2. This sidesteps (but does not solve) a central problem confronting research on organizational evolution. McKelvey (1982) points out that to date no adequate way has been found to operationally identify an organizational generation and a vehicle for transmitting or inheriting traits from one generation to the next. Traditionally, evolution focused on intergenerational processes of inheritance, while development dealt with intragenerational processes of growth and change within the life span of an entity. The Lamarckian view that heritable traits can be acquired within generations collapses this distinction between evolution and development. While this shifts the problem from intergenerational inheritance to intragenerational development, it does not eliminate the problem of understanding how organizational traits or competencies are developmentally acquired within a generation or transmitted and ascend from one generation to the next.

References

Abbott, A. (1990). Conceptions of time and events in social science methods: Causal and narrative approaches. *Historical Methods*, 23, 140–150.

Abbott, A. (1992). From causes to events: Notes on narrative positivism. *Sociological Methods and Research*, 20, 428–455.

Aldrich, H. E. (1979). *Organizations and environments.* Englewood Cliffs, NJ: Prentice-Hall.

Aldrich, H. E. (1999). *Organizations evolving.* London: Sage.

Anderson, P. (1999). Complexity theory and organization science. *Organization Science*, 10, 216–232.

Arnold, A. J. & Fristrup, K. (1982). The theory of evolution by natural selection: A hierarchical expansion. *Paleobiology*, 8(2), 113–129.

Arrow, K. (1970). *Social choice and individual values* (2nd ed.). New Haven, CT: Yale University Press.

Astley, W. G. (1985). The two ecologies: Population and community perspectives on organizational evolution. *Administrative Science Quarterly*, 30, 224–241.

Bakhtin, M. M. (1981). *The dialogic imagination: Four essays by M. M. Bakhtin* (C. Emerson & M. Holquist, Trans.). Austin, TX: University of Texas Press.

Bales, R. F. & Strodtbeck, F. L. (1951). Phases in group problem solving. *Journal of Abnormal and Social Psychology, 46,* 485–495.

Baum, J. A. C. (1996). Organizational ecology. In S. Clegg, C. Hardy, & W. Nord (Eds.), *Handbook of organization studies* (pp. 77–114). London: Sage.

Baum, J. A. C. & McKelvey, B. (Eds.) (1999). *Variations in organization science: In honor of Donald T. Campbell.* Thousand Oaks, CA: Sage.

Baum, J. A. C. & Singh, J. V. (1994). Organizational hierarchies and evolutionary processes: Some reflections on a theory of organizational evolution. In J. A. C. Baum & J. V. Singh (Eds.), *Evolutionary dynamics of organizations.* New York: Oxford University Press.

Bazerman, M. H. (1985). Norms of distributive justice in interest arbitration. *Industrial and Labor Relations Review, 38,* 558–570.

Bennis, W. G. (1966). *Changing organizations.* New York: McGraw-Hill.

Bollen, K. A. (1989). *Structural equations with latent variables.* New York: Wiley.

Bryson, J. M. (1988). *Strategic planning for public and nonprofit organizations: A guide to strengthening and sustaining organizational achievement.* San Francisco: Jossey-Bass.

Buckley, W. (1967). *Sociology and modern systems theory.* Englewood Cliffs, NJ: Prentice-Hall.

Burgelman, R. A. (1991). Interorganizational ecology of strategy making and organizational adaptation: Theory and field research. *Organization Science, 2*(3), 239–262.

Buss, L. W. (1987). *The evolution of individuality.* Princeton, NJ: Princeton University Press.

Cameron, K. & Whetten, D. (1983). Models of the organizational life cycle: Applications to higher education. *Review of Higher Education, 6,* 269–299.

Campbell, D. (1974). Evolutionary epistemology. In P. A. Schilpp (Ed.), *The philosophy of Karl Popper* (pp. 413–463). Lasalle, IL: Open Court Press.

Chakravarthy, B. S. & Lorange, P. (1991). *Managing the strategy process.* Englewood Cliffs, NJ: Prentice-Hall.

Coleman, J. S. (1973). *The mathematics of collective action.* Chicago: Aldine.

Coleman, J. S. (1986). Social theory, social research and a theory of action. *American Journal of Sociology, 16,* 1309–1335.

Coleman, J. S. (1990). *Foundations of social theory.* Cambridge, MA: Harvard University Press.

Darwin, C. (1936). *The origin of species.* New York: Modern Library.

Dooley, K. (2002). Organizational complexity. In M. Warner (Ed.), *International encyclopedia of business and management* (pp. 5013–5022). London: Thompson Learning.

Etzioni, A. (1963). The epigenesis of political communities at the international level. *American Journal of Sociology, 68,* 407–421.

Gersick, C. J. (1991). Revolutionary change theories: A multilevel exploration of the punctuated equilibrium paradigm. *Academy of Management Review, 16,* 10–36.

Gioia, D. A. & Pitre, E. (1990). Multiparadigm perspectives in theory building. *Academy of Management Review, 15,* 584–602.

Gould, S. J. (1982). Darwinism and the expansion of evolutionary theory. *Science, 216,* 380–387.

Gould, S. J. (1989). Punctuated equilibrium in fact and theory. *Journal of Social and Biological Structures, 12,* 117–136.

Gould, S. J. & Eldridge, N. (1977). Punctuated equilibria: The tempo and model of evolution reconsidered. *Paleobiology, 3,* 115–151.

Greiner, L. (1972). Evolution and revolution as organizations grow. *Harvard Business Review, 50,* 165–174.

Hannan, M. T. & Freeman, J. (1977). The population ecology of organizations. *American Journal of Sociology, 82,* 929–964.

Hannan, M. T. & Freeman, J. (1989). *Organizational ecology.* Cambridge, MA: Harvard University Press.

Hannan, M. T., Carroll, G. R., Dundon, E. A., & Torres, J. C. (1995). Organizational evolution in a multinational context: Entries of automobile manufacturers in Belgium, Britain, France, Germany, and Italy. *American Sociological Review, 60,* 509–528.

Hatch, M. J. (1993). The dynamics of organizational culture. *Academy of Management Review, 18,* 657–693.

Hernes, G. (1976). Structural change in social processes. *American Journal of Sociology, 82,* 513–545.

Janis, I. L. (1989). *Crucial decisions.* New York: Free Press.

Kahneman, D., Slovic, P., & Tversky, A. (1982). *Judgment under uncertainty: Heuristics and biases.* Cambridge: Cambrige University Press.

Katz, D. & Kahn, R. (1978). *The social psychology of organizations,* 2nd ed. New York: Wiley.

Klein, K. J. & Koslowski, S. W. J. (2000). *Multilevel theory, research, and methods in organizations: Foundations, extensions, and new directions.* San Francisco: Jossey-Bass.

Lacoursiere, R. B. (1980). *The life cycle of groups: Group developmental stage theory.* New York: Human Sciences Press.

March, J. G. (1994). *A primer on decision making.* New York: Free Press.

March, J. G. & Olsen, J. (1976). *Ambiguity and choice in organizations.* Bergen: Universitetsforlagen.

Marx, K. (1954). *Capital.* Moscow: Progress Publishers.

McKelvey, B. (1982). *Organizational systematics.* Los Angeles: University of California Press.

Meyer, A. G., Goes, J. B., & Brooks, G. G. (1993). Organizational reacting to hyperturbulence. In G. P. Huber & W. Glick (Eds.), *Organizational change and redesign.* New York: Oxford University Press.

Miller, J. G. (1978). *Living systems.* New York: McGraw-Hill.

Miner, A. S. (1994). Seeking adaptive advantage: Evolutionary theory and managerial action. In J. A. C. Baum & J. V. Singh (Eds.), *Evolutionary dynamics of organizations* (pp. 76–93). New York: Oxford.

Mintzberg, H., Raisinghani, D., & Theoret, A. (1976). The structure of "unstructured" decision processes. *Administrative Science Quarterly, 21,* 246–275.

Mohr, L. (1982). *Explaining organizational behavior.* San Francisco: Jossey-Bass.

Moreland, R. L. & Levine, J. M. (1988). Group dynamics over time: Development and socialization in small groups. In J. M. McGrath (Ed.), *The social psychology of time* (pp. 151–181). Thousand Oaks, CA: Sage.

Nutt, P. C. (1984). Types of organizational decision processes. *Administrative Science Quarterly, 29,* 414–450.

Nutt, P. C. (2002). *Why decisions fail: Avoiding the blunders and traps that lead to debacles.* San Francisco: Berrett-Koehler.

Olson, E. & Eoyang, G. (2001). *Facilitating organizational change: Lessons from complexity science.* New York: John Wiley and Sons.

Poole, M. S. (1981). Decision development in small groups I: A test of two models. *Communication Monographs, 48,* 1–24.

Poole, M. S. & Van de Ven, A. H. (1989/2001). Toward a general theory of innovation. In A. H. Van de Ven, H. Angle, & M. S. Poole (Eds.), *Research in the management of innovation* (pp. 637–662). Cambridge, MA: Ballinger.

Poole, M. S., Van de Ven, A. H., Dooley, K., & Holmes, M. E. (2000). *Organizational change and innovation processes: Theory and methods for research.* New York: Oxford University Press.

Popper, K. (1962). *Conjectures and refutations.* New York: Harper.

Porac, J. F., Thomas, H., & Baden-Fuller, C. (1989). Competitive groups as cognitive communities: The case of Scottish knitwear manufacturers. *Journal of Management Studies, 26,* 397–416.

Putnam, L. L. & Stohl, C. (1996). Bona fide groups: An alternative perspective for communication and small group decision making. In R. Y. Hirokawa & M. S. Poole (Eds.), *Communication and group decision making* (2nd ed., pp. 147–178). Thousand Oaks, CA: Sage.

Ross, J. & Staw, B. (1986). Expo 86: An escalation prototype. *Administrative Science Quarterly, 31,* 274–297.

Schein, E. (1992). *Organizational culture and leadership* (2nd ed.). San Francisco: Jossey-Bass.

Singh, J. V. & Lumsden, C. J. (1990). Theory and research in organizational ecology. *Annual Review of Sociology, 16,* 161–195.

Smith, K. K. & Berg, D. N. (1987). *Paradoxes of group life.* San Francisco: Jossey-Bass.

Sterman, J. (2000). *Business dynamics: Systems thinking and modeling for a complex world.* New York: Irwin.

Sztompka, P. (1993). *The sociology of social change.* Oxford: Blackwell.

Tushman, M. & Moore, W. L. (Eds.) (1982). *Readings in the management of innovation.* Boston: Pitman Press.

Usher, A. P. (1954). *A history of mechanical inventions.* Cambridge, MA: Harvard University Press.

Van de Ven, A. H. & Garud, R. (1993). Innovation and industry development: The case of cochlear implants. In R. Rosenbloom (Ed.), *Research on technological innovation, management, and policy* (Vol. 5, pp. 1–46). Greenwich, CT: JAI Press.

Van de Ven, A. H. & Grazman, D. N. (1999). Evolution in a nested hierarchy: A genealogy of Twin Cities health care organizations, 1853–1995. In J. A. C. Baum & B. McKelvey (Eds.), *Variations in organizational science: In honor of Donald T. Campbell* (pp. 185–212). Thousand Oaks, CA: Sage.

Van de Ven, A. H. & Poole, M. S. (1995). Explaining development and change in organizations. *Academy of Management Review, 20,* 510–540.

Weick, K. (1979). *The social psychology of organizing* (2nd ed.). Reading, MA: Addison-Wesley.

Weick, K. (1995). *Sensemaking in organizations.* Thousand Oaks, CA: Sage.

Werner, C. M. & Baxter, L. A. (1994). Temporal qualities of relationships: organismic, transactional, and dialectical views. In M. Knapp & G. R. Miller (Eds.), *Handbook of interpersonal communication* (2nd ed., pp. 323–379). Thousand Oaks, CA: Sage.

Author Index

Aaker, 123, 156
Abbey, 41
Abbott, 11, 242, 262, 288, 312, 376
Abernathy, 5, 118, 229, 241–242
Abolafia, 337
Abraham, 170
Abrahamson, 277, 290, 297, 316
Abzug, 164
Ackerman, 36
Adizes, 168
Adler, 324, 334
Agrawal, 112
Aharoni, 329
Aiken, 178
Ainamo, 337–338
Ajzen, 33
Albach, 333, 345–346
Alban, 85–89
Albert, 23, 318
Alchian, 125
Aldrich, 137, 139, 168, 177, 213–214, 216, 220–221, 224, 227, 232–233, 235–240, 242–246, 251, 273, 284–285, 290–291, 297, 317, 381
Alexander, 135, 308
Alford, 164–165, 179, 237, 242, 244–245

Alinsky, 267, 289, 296–297
Allen, 170, 328, 334
Allmendinger, 65
Allport, 170
Altman, 343
Amabile, 41
Amazeen, 52
Amburgey, 137, 139, 155, 226
Amel, 123
Amit, 113
Ancona, 21, 51, 57, 59, 65
Anderson, 119, 149, 170, 224, 229, 241, 282, 285, 290–291, 297, 302, 311, 345, 354, 375
Andrews, 132
Angle, 178, 297
Annett, 41
Aoki, 155, 332, 344
Argote, 57, 65, 116, 177–178, 223
Argyres, 126–127
Argyris, 19, 78–79, 84, 92–93, 114–115, 164, 177–178, 359
Armenakis, 45
Arnold, 382, 385, 390, 395
Arrow, x, 51–54, 65, 68, 386
Arthur, 245, 296, 358
Ashby, 170, 356
Ashford, 37, 41
Ashforth, 36, 37

Ashkenas, 163
Astley, 138–139, 162, 232–234, 240, 242, 288, 297, 385
Athanassiou, 156
Athos, 190
Audia, 234
Auster, 139
Austin, 73, 95, 173
Axelrod, 170
Ayres, 298

Backoff, 74, 86
Baden-Fuller, 379
Badie, 324, 326–327, 329
Baer, 336
Bak, 361–362
Bakhtin, 101, 380
Balakrishnan, 125
Baldwin, 62
Bales, 13, 59–60, 62, 168, 376
Bamforth, 80, 172
Banaszak-Holl, 236
Bandura, 230
Barfield, 326
Barkema, 21
Barker, 316
Barlett, 336
Barley, 13, 266, 268, 294, 297, 305
Barnard, 166

Subject Index

absorptive capacity, 115–117, 131, 143, 149, 178
acculturation, 37–38, 192, 196, 198–199, 207
  selective borrowing, 196, 198
Ackerman & Humphrey's schema on individual
    difference
  affective, 27, 34, 36, 38, 41, 43, 46
  cognitive, x, 11, 27, 33–34, 36, 38, 43, 45–46, 54,
    56–57, 88, 92, 108, 114, 126, 163–166, 170,
    174, 177, 181, 239, 242, 244–246, 259, 261,
    268–269, 273–274, 280, 283, 295–296, 315,
    355, 359, 368, 382
  conative, 34, 36, 38, 41–42, 46
acquiescence, 267
action phase model, 61
action theory/action research, x, 50–52, 55, 67, 74,
    79, 82–86, 93, 96
  action inquiry, 79
  action science, 79
  cooperative inquiry, 79
  participatory (action) research, 79
action rules, 16, 354
action-structure paradox, 162, 294
  methodological paradox, 162
  theoretical paradox, 162
activity, x, xii, 5, 6, 13, 19, 22–24, 54, 56, 59–61, 88,
    118, 131, 137, 161, 165, 171, 173, 174, 180,
    197, 198, 203, 206, 216, 222–223, 231–234,
    239, 241, 246, 264, 273, 280–283, 286, 291,
    306, 317, 326, 338, 362, 364, 368, 379, 381,
    383, 387, 391

goal choice, 60, 61
policy choice, 60
actor, 32, 61, 162, 177, 261, 263, 267, 277, 283,
    288–289, 291, 293, 312, 381, 387
adaptation, x, 6, 51–52, 55, 59, 65–67, 86, 93, 108,
    109, 113–120, 124–127, 129, 131, 134, 136,
    137, 140–141, 143–144, 146–149, 161,
    163, 176, 179, 180, 192, 217, 230, 232, 250,
    262, 268, 273, 276–277, 280, 292, 293,
    324, 331, 333, 345–346, 355, 385,
    389–390
  directed adaptation, 66
  choice, 4–5, 9, 15, 17, 19, 24–25, 53, 60–61,
    66, 74, 75, 77, 97, 100–101, 109, 119–21,
    123, 125–126, 128, 132, 134, 136, 141,
    144, 147, 162, 174, 177, 193, 197, 205,
    245, 265–267, 275–277, 285, 289,
    316, 378
  information processing, 54–55, 66, 108, 115,
    119, 141, 261, 367
  planning, ix, xi, 4, 40, 57, 58, 60, 61, 66, 83, 85,
    87, 88, 91, 120, 216, 272, 310, 313, 329
  self-regulation, 66
  undirected adaptation, 66
  selection, x, xi, 7, 24, 43, 55, 57, 66, 76, 84,
    85, 89, 91, 95, 97–100, 108–109, 117,
    119, 121, 124–126, 129, 130–131, 137,
    138–141, 143, 146, 147–149, 162, 196,
    197, 212–214, 216–219, 221–229,
    232–237, 239–241, 244, 248–251, 263,

Printed in the USA/Agawam, MA
February 25, 2015

609402.004